Word 2016 Complete

Student Edition

30 Bird Media
510 Clinton Square
Rochester NY 14604
www.30Bird.com

Word 2016 Complete

Student Edition

CEO, 30 Bird Media: Adam A. Wilcox

Series designed by: Clifford J. Coryea, Donald P. Tremblay, and Adam A Wilcox

Managing Editor: Donald P. Tremblay

Instructional Design Lead: Clifford J. Coryea

Copyeditor: Robert S. Kulik

Keytester: Kurt J. Specht

Visit www.30bird.com for more information.

Trademarks

Some of the product names and company names used in this book have been used for identification purposes only and may be trademarks or registered trademarks of their respective manufacturers and sellers.

Disclaimer

We reserve the right to revise this publication without notice.

WORD2016-A1-R10-SCB

Table of Contents

Introduction

Welcome to Word 2016 Complete. This course provides everything you need to go from the basics to using some of the most powerful features of Microsoft Word 2016: how to create, format, and set up a document; add graphics and tables; use character and paragraph styles; use footnotes and tables of contents; share documents various ways and in many formats; use document management tools; handle references and indexing; perform mail merges; and create simple macros and forms. This course maps to the objectives of the Microsoft Office Specialist and Expert exams for Word 2016. Objective coverage is marked throughout the course, and you can download an objectives map from http://www.30bird.com.

You will benefit most from this course if you want to accomplish both basic and advanced workplace tasks in Word 2016. If you intend to take a Microsoft Office Specialist or Expert exam for Word, this course will fully prepare you for any of the exams.

The course assumes you know how to use a computer, and that you're familiar with Microsoft Windows. It does not assume that you've used a different version of Word or another word processing program before.

After you complete this course, you will know how to:

Create and save documents, cut and paste text, and use different document views

- Format characters and paragraphs; use styles, Quick Styles, and themes; and create bulleted and numbered lists
- Set up page layout, set tab stops, use headers and footers, and apply templates
- Insert, format, and lay out pictures
- Insert and format tables
- Insert and format shapes and text boxes, and insert and format SmartArt diagrams
- Create custom themes, use building blocks and section breaks, and apply page backgrounds
- Insert footnotes and endnotes, insert a table of contents, and apply hyperlinks
- Edit a document for spelling and grammar, navigate a large document, and use master documents and subdocuments
- Save documents in various sharable formats, add and manage comments, and protect a document from unwanted changes
- Use advanced formatting features such as text formatting, custom styles, embedded objects and charts, building blocks, and linked content
- Manage documents by configuring Word documents, creating or modifying templates, and tracking and reviewing document changes

- Use references within documents by creating bookmarks, cross-references, and indexes, and citing external sources to create a bibliography or table of authorities
- Define or import data sources to create a mail merge for use with form letters, envelopes, or labels
- Record and manage simple macros, and create forms using content controls and legacy form fields

Course setup

To complete this course, each student and instructor will need to have a computer running Word 2016. Setup instructions and activities are written assuming Windows 10; however, with slight modification the course will work using Windows XP Service Pack 3, Windows Vista Service Pack 1, Windows 7 or Windows 8.x.

Hardware requirements for Windows 10 course setup include:

- 1 GHz or faster processor (32- or 64-bit)
- 1 GB (32-bit) or 2 GB (64-bit) RAM
- 25 GB total hard drive space (50 GB or more recommended)
- DirectX 10 (or later) video card or integrated graphics, with a minimum of 128 MB of graphics memory
- Monitor with 1280x800 or higher resolution
- Wi-Fi or Ethernet adapter

Software requirements include:

- Windows 10 (or alternative, as above)
- Microsoft Word 2016 or any Microsoft Office 2016 edition
- The Word 2016 Level 1 data files and PowerPoint slides, available at http://www.30bird.com
- An email application and a working email account for a single exercise in one chapter on attaching a workbook to an email (which can instead be skipped or demonstrated by the instructor)

Network requirements include:

- An Internet connection to use online templates and images (which can be skipped or demonstrated by the instructor)

Because the exercises in this course include viewing and changing some Word defaults, it's recommended to begin with a fresh installation of the software. But this is certainly not necessary. Just be aware that if you are not using a fresh installation, some exercises might work slightly differently, and some screens might look slightly different.

Note: Opening downloaded files in Office applications can result in the document being displayed in Protected View. This can be overridden by clicking **Enable Editing** at the top of the document window.

1. Install Windows 10, including all recommended updates and service packs. Use a different computer and user name for each student.
2. Install Microsoft Word 2016 or Office 2016, using all defaults during installation.
3. Update Word or Office using Windows Update.
4. Copy the Word 2016 Level 1 data files to the Documents folder.

Chapter 1: Fundamentals

You will learn how to:

- Get around the Word interface
- Create and save a new document
- View documents in different ways

Module A: Getting around

First thing you'll need to do is start Word. Once you're in, at the top of the screen you'll see a set of tools called the *ribbon*. You'll use commands and buttons on the ribbon and elsewhere to create documents.

You will learn:

- The layout of the Word interface and the ribbon
- About Backstage view
- How to open and close documents

The Word interface

The most prominent feature of the Word 2016 interface is the ribbon. Other features include the Quick Access toolbar, rulers, and the status bar.

The Word 2016 interface

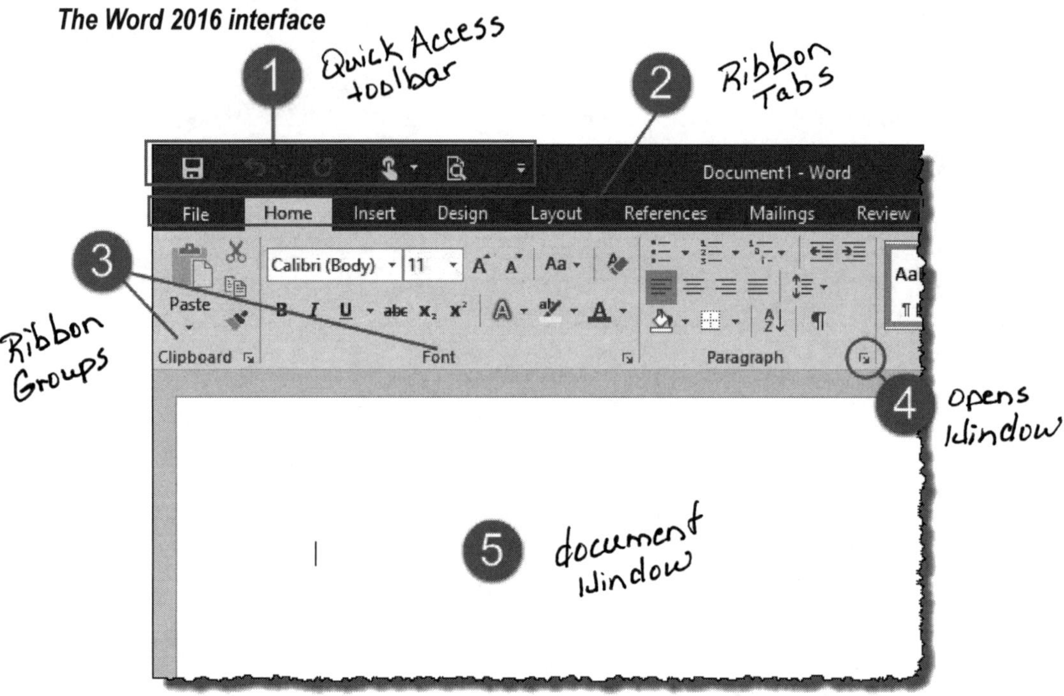

1 The *Quick Access toolbar* holds a few of the commands that you use most.

2 The ribbon *tabs* divide ribbon commands into general categories. Some tabs appear only in certain contexts. For instance, if the cursor is in a table, then table Design and Layout tabs will appear.

3 Ribbon *groups* further divide commands on a tab into logical groupings, like Font and Paragraph. You can hide the groups by clicking (the Collapse the Ribbon button) on the right end of the ribbon. The groups are hidden until you click a tab, and remain hidden again until you return to the document.

4 Some ribbon groups have a button in the lower-right corner that opens a window with more options.

5 The *document window* is where you create your documents.

Along the bottom of the Word window you'll see the *status bar*, which shows information such as page number and word count, and the current document view and zoom percentage.

The Word status bar

Starting Microsoft Word 2016

You can start Word from the Start menu, or you can add icons to the desktop or the taskbar. In Windows 10, use of the Start menu is greatly simplified.

1. Move your mouse pointer to the lower-left corner of the screen to display the Windows Start icon.
2. Click **Start**.

   To display the All apps menu.
3. Scroll down to see the Word 2016 icon.
4. Click **Word 2016**.

   The Word startup window opens. Any recent files you've opened appear on the left, and there are tiles for different types of documents you can open on the right.
5. Click **Blank document**.

   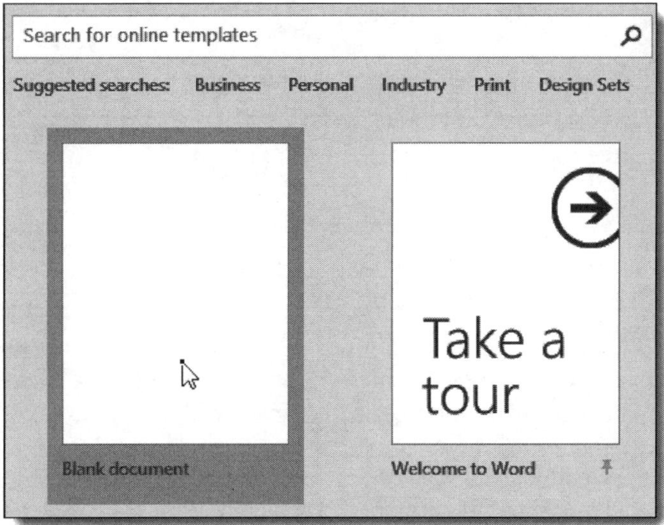

   The Word window opens to a blank document.

If you want to pin the Word icon to the taskbar, right-click the icon, and click **Pin this program to taskbar**.

Backstage view

Most ribbon tabs have a set of related tools and commands. The File tab, though, opens Backstage view. This view gives you access to saving and printing, document information and protection, program options, and more.

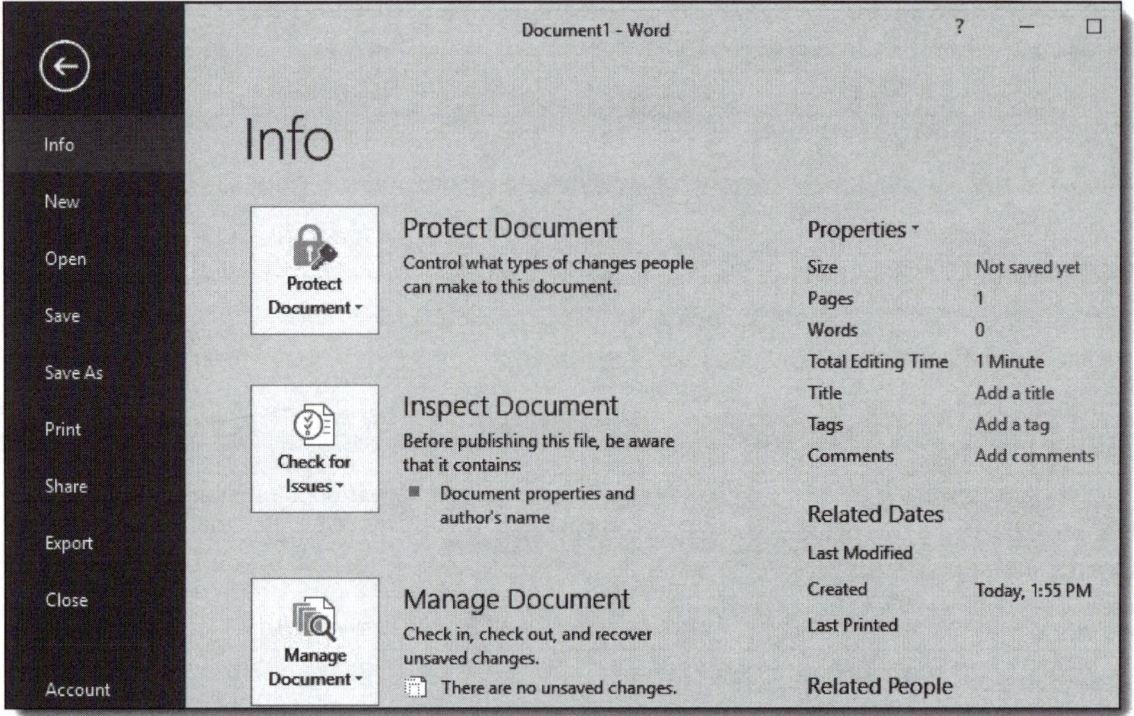

To return to your document, click the arrow at the top left.

Opening a document

When you start Word, a startup screen gives you the choice of opening a recent document, a blank document, an existing document, or one based on a template. Once you've opened a blank document, if you leave it blank and then open another document, the blank document automatically closes without being saved.

Note: Opening downloaded files in Office applications can result in the document being displayed in Protected view. To be able to make and save changes to a document in Protected view, click **Enable Editing** at the top of the document window.

Exam Objective: MOS Word Core 1.1.1

1. On the File tab, click **Open**.

   You will see various options for locations on the left, and a list of recently opened documents (if any) on the right.

2. Either click a file to open it, or click a location to display the **Open** window.
3. Navigate to the document you want to open, select it, and click **Open**.

   You can instead double-click the file.

After you've opened documents, they will appear in the Recent section of Backstage view. You can re-open files from there without browsing for them. If you open a document when you already have another document open, it opens in a new window. One exception is if you open a document when you first start Word; in that case, the new document replaces the blank document that opens with Word.

Closing documents

Each document in Word opens in its own window. There are several ways to close documents. If you haven't yet saved the document you're trying to close, you'll be asked if you want to do so.

- On the File tab, click **Close**.

  If more than one document is open, that particular document closes; any other document(s) remains open. If it is the only Word document open, the blank Word window remains open.

- Click the close button ✕ in the upper-right corner.

  If this is the only Word document open, Word closes as well.

- To close one of multiple open documents, right-click the Word taskbar icon, hover over the document, and click its close button.
- To close all open documents, right-click the Word taskbar icon, and click **Close all windows**.

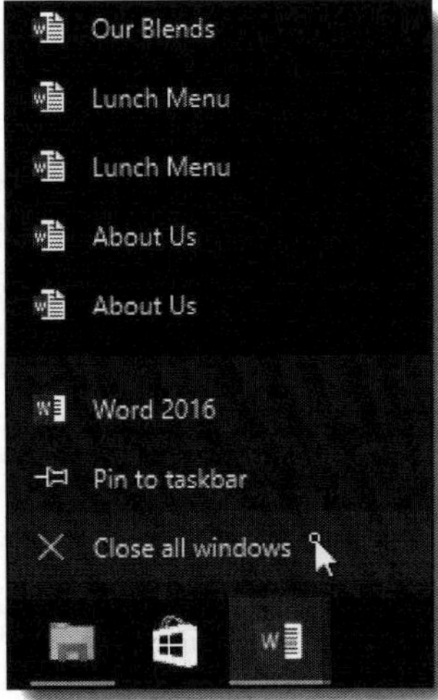

Depending on your graphics settings, you might see thumbnail pictures instead of document names.

Whichever way you choose to close a document, you'll be prompted to save any unsaved changes.

Customizing the Quick Access toolbar

You can easily add commands to or remove them from the Quick Access toolbar to better suit the way you like to work.

Exam Objective: MOS Word Core 1.4.3

1. Click the Customize Quick Access Toolbar button.

   On the right of the Quick Access toolbar.

   To display the Customize Quick Access Toolbar menu.

   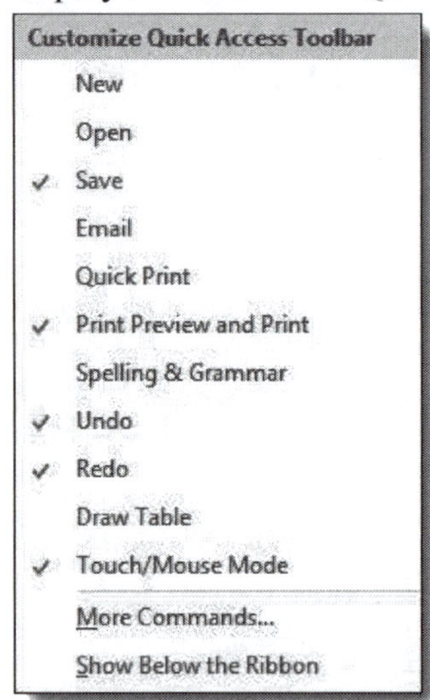

2. Click a command in the menu to show or hide it.

   The commands that are shown on the toolbar will have a checkmark.

3. To add other commands, click **More Commands**.

   The Customize the Quick Access Toolbar screen appears in the **Word Options** window. Here, you can choose any command in Word to add to the Quick Access toolbar.

4. Click **OK** to accept your changes and close the window.

Exercise: Getting around Word

Exam Objective: MOS Word Core 1.1.1

Do This	How & Why
1. Click **Start > All apps > Word 2016**.	To start Microsoft Word 2016. You will see the startup screen.
2. In the startup screen, click **Blank document**.	The Word window opens to a blank document with the Home tab active. If you see an area on the left of the screen that is called "Navigation," close it by clicking its Close button (the "x"). Navigation

Do This	How & Why
3. Observe the commands on the Home tab.	These are mostly commands for formatting text and paragraphs. The Clipboard group helps you to move text around.
4. Open the Font window.	
a) In the Font group, in the lower-right, click the Font button.	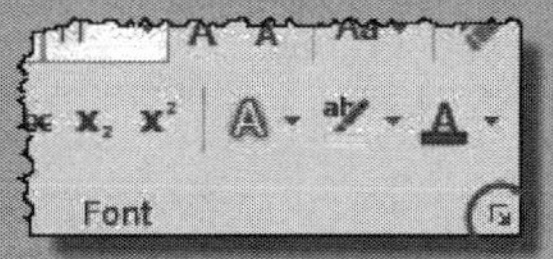 To open the Font window.
b) Observe the font options.	There are many options for formatting text.
c) Click the **Advanced** tab.	These options allow fine control over formatting, such as character spacing.
d) Close the Font window.	Click the **Close** button or click **Cancel**.
5. On the Ribbon's View tab, in the Show group, check **Ruler**.	Click its box to check it. 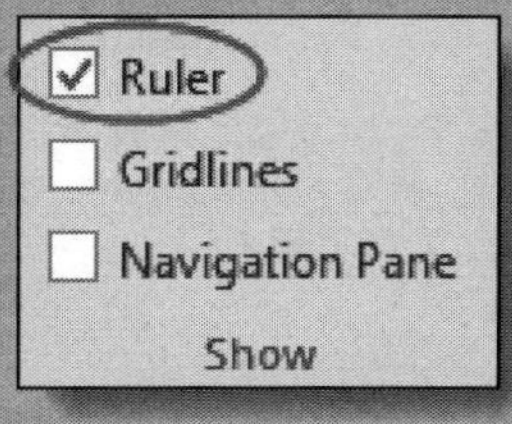 To show the ruler, which shows you where margins and tab stops are located for the current paragraph. 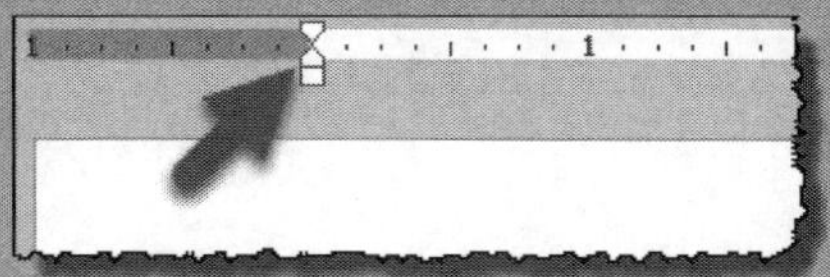
6. Click the **File** tab.	To display Backstage view.
7. Open `About Us` from the current chapter's data folder.	
a) On the File tab, click **Open**.	
b) Under Open, click **Browse** to display the **Open** window.	
c) Navigate to the current chapter's data folder.	Follow your instructor's directions.
d) Select **About Us**, and click **Open**.	To open a document with information about Java Tucana, a fictional chain of cafés.
8. On the File tab, click **Close**.	To close the document. Word remains open, but there is no document open.

Assessment: Getting around

1. Which toolbar holds a few common commands and can be customized? Choose the single best answer.
   - Ribbon
   - Group
   - 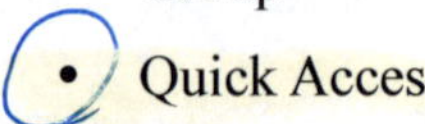 Quick Access
   - Ruler
2. Which view gives you access to saving and printing, document information and protection, and other options?
   - Outline
   -  Backstage
   - Info
   - Options

Module B: Creating documents

Creating a document in Word is as simple as starting the program and beginning to type. Much of what you'll do, besides typing, involves cutting and pasting text, and the very important ability to undo an action.

You will learn how to:

- Create a new blank document
- Cut, copy, and paste text
- Undo actions
- Save a document

Creating a new blank document

When you start Word, the startup screen gives you the options to open a new, blank document. You can also do so after Word is open.

Exam Objective: MOS Word Core 1.1.1

1. On the File tab, click **New**.
2. Click **Blank document**.
   A new, blank document opens in a new Word window.
3. Enter text in the document window by typing.
   There are many ways to enter and manipulate text, and you'll be learning about them shortly.

Entering symbols

Sometimes, you will want to enter text that isn't readily available on the keyboard, such as a foreign character (like the French accent aigu over the e, é) or a copyright symbol (©). Word has a gallery of such symbols.

1. Place the insertion point where you want the symbol.
2. On the Insert tab, in the Symbols group, click **Symbol**.
   The Symbol gallery appears, giving you a choice of common or recently-used symbols.

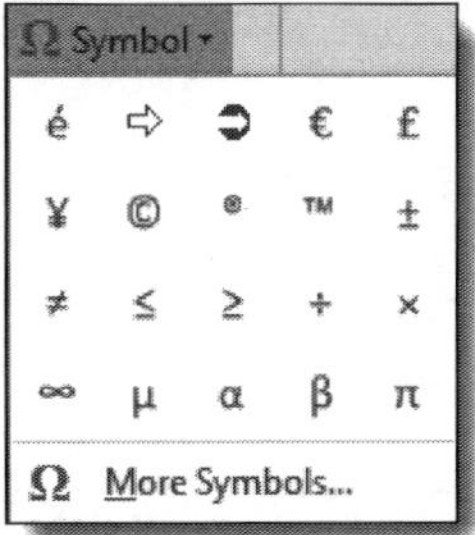

3. Click the symbol you want to place it at the cursor.
   If the symbol you want is not in the gallery, click More Symbols to open the Symbols window, where you can choose from a large variety of symbols.

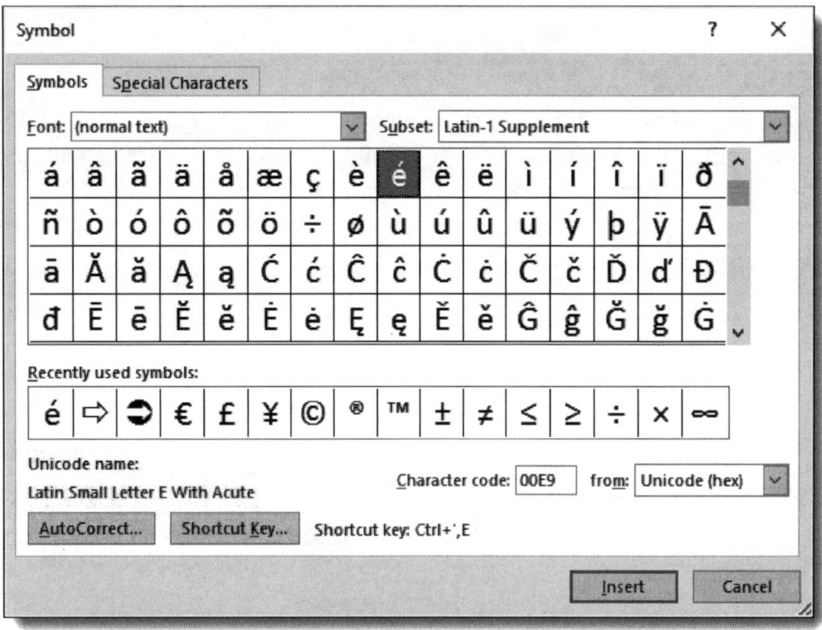

Saving a document

There are several ways to save an open document.

- Click (the Save button) in the Quick Access toolbar.
- Use the **Ctrl+S** keyboard shortcut.
- On the File tab, click **Save** or **Save As**.
- When you close Word, you're prompted to save any unsaved documents that are open.

Regardless of which method you use, the first time you save a document, you'll see the **Save As** window, which prompts you for a name and location for the file, and offers access to other options. After that, the Save command updates the file with no further prompting.

If you want to change the name or location of a previously saved file, on the File tab, click **Save As > Browse**.

Note: If saving to a location other than your computer—for example, to OneDrive—you would instead click **OneDrive**.

The Save As window

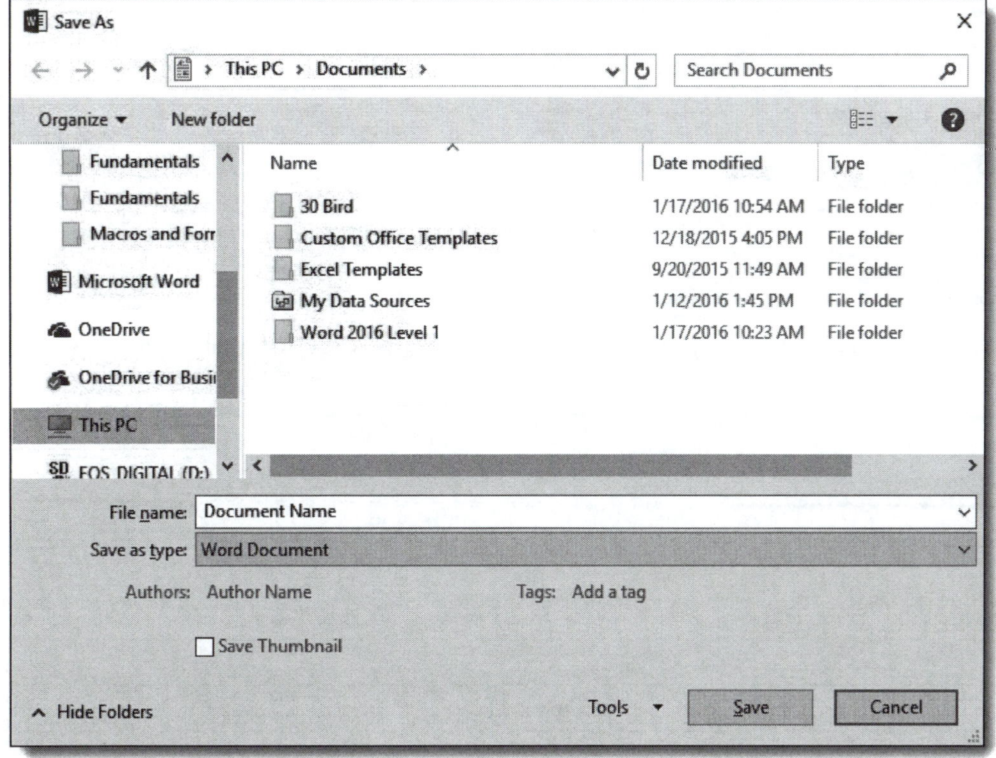

Managing draft versions

If you experience a software crash or a power outage while you're working, there's a chance you won't lose all your work. You might be able to recover some or all of what you were working on, even if you hadn't saved your work. Word keeps temporary copies of open files, and deletes them when you save a document or close it without saving. Unfortunately, this feature does not keep track of previous versions of a document once you save changes or close it without saving.

Exam Objective: MOS Word Expert 1.1.3

If Word shuts down suddenly, however, the draft version remains on your hard disk. Often, the Document Recovery pane will be open when you restart Word, and you can recover the document from there.

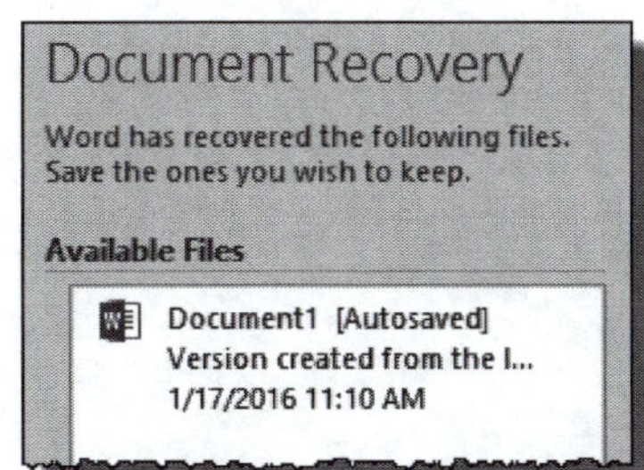

If the Document Recovery pane does not open, or you want to search for earlier unsaved draft versions, you can use the Manage Versions button in Backstage view.

- To recover a draft version, on the File tab, click **Info**, then click **Manage Documents** > **Recover Unsaved Documents**. Select the document you want, and click **Open**.

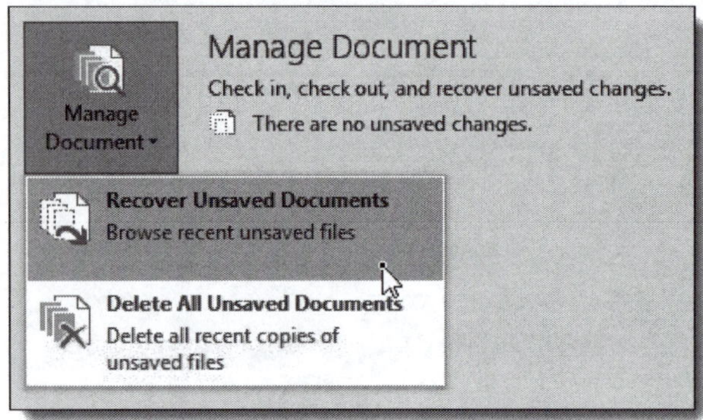

- If you are sure you don't need the unsaved files, click **Manage Documents > Delete All Unsaved Documents**.

Exercise: Creating a new document

Word is open with no documents open.

Exam Objective: MOS Word Core 1.1.1, 2.1.2

Do This	How & Why
1. Start a new, blank document:	
a) On the File tab, click **New**.	
b) Click **Blank document**.	
2. Observe the title bar.	It shows a generic document name. Document1 - Word
3. Enter some of the following information: • Your occupation • Your name • Your address • Your phone number • Your email address	Press **Enter** after each line. If you don't want to use your own information, make up something.
4. Save the document:	The document is saved and you return to the document window.
a) In Backstage view, click **Save**.	"Backstage view" is what you see when you click the File tab. Because this document has never been saved, the **Save As** window opens.
b) Click Browse, then navigate to the current chapter's data folder.	Follow your instructor's directions.
c) In the File name box, type `Contact Info`.	

Do This	How & Why
d) Click **Save**.	
5. Observe the title bar.	It shows the file name you entered.
6. Change the occupation text.	
a) Drag over the text.	Editor Johnny Lightning To select it. You will briefly see a gallery of formatting options when you select the text. You'll learn about that soon. For now, move the mouse slightly and the gallery will disappear.
b) Type a different occupation.	The text you type replaces the selected text. If you had just placed the cursor somewhere, what you typed would have been inserted.
7. Click [Save button].	On the Quick Access toolbar. You can also you the keyboard shortcut, **Ctrl+S**. To save your change to the document. When you click the Save button, the file is saved in the same location and with the same name. To change the name or location, you would click Save As in Backstage view.
8. At the end of the document, press **Enter** to create a new paragraph.	You will enter a symbol here. Not all of the text you will need is readily available on the keyboard.
9. On the Insert tab, click Symbol.	To display the symbol gallery. Common and recently-used symbols appear here. As you work more with Word, you'll almost always find the symbols you use most here.
10. Click ©.	To insert the copyright symbol in the document. If you don't see the copyright symbol, try another.
11. Click **Symbol**, then click **More Symbols**.	To display the Symbol window. Here, you can choose from a huge variety of symbols in many fonts.
12. Click **Cancel**.	
13. Close the document.	Try clicking the Close box on the far right of the title bar. Sign in Share Close Find Word prompts you to save your changes. When you attempt to close a document without having saved your most recent changes, you will see this.
14. Click **Don't Save**.	To close the document without saving changes.

Manipulating text

The most basic way to get information into your documents is to type it. But you will also want to move text after entering it, or copy it to a second location. In order to do that, you'll need to know how to select text (which is also important for formatting). There are many techniques for moving and copying text, and a great variety of selection techniques that use the mouse, the keyboard, or both. You should familiarize yourself with as many of these techniques as possible in order to be an efficient, productive user of Word.

Moving the cursor

Selecting text

There are many ways to select text so that you can then format, copy, or delete it.

- Double-click a word to select it.
- Triple-click in a paragraph to select it.
- Drag over text to select multiple words or paragraphs.
- Hold down Shift and use the arrow keys to extend the selection from the current cursor position.
  You can also use the **Home**, **End**, **Page Up**, and **Page Down** keys.
- Click or drag in the left margin to select lines.
- Press **Ctrl+A** to select all text in a document.

Exercise: Moving the cursor and selecting text

Do This	How & Why
1. Open `About Us` and save it as `About Us Selecting`.	You'll use this document to experiment with techniques for moving the cursor and selecting text.
2. Use the arrow keys to move the cursor.	The most basic keyboard technique for moving the cursor (or the "insertion point") is to press the arrow keys. Left and right move one character at a time, up and down one line at a time. This is efficient when you're moving to a location that is close to the current location.
3. Press **Ctrl+Home**.	This will always bring you to the top of the document.
4. While holding **Ctrl**, press the right arrow key a few times.	Each time will move the cursor one word to the right. Holding Ctrl while pressing left arrow, similarly, moves one word to the left. Ctrl plus the up or down arrow keys moves the cursor a paragraph at a time.
5. Place the cursor in the first full paragraph, then press **End**.	To move to the end of the current line.
6. What does pressing **Home** do?	By itself, pressing **Home** takes you to the beginning of the current line. You've already seen that pressing **Ctrl+Home** will take you to the beginning of the document. **Ctrl+End** move to the end of the document.

Do This	How & Why
7. Click at the beginning of the document.	To move the cursor there. You can always place the cursor by clicking where you want it.
8. Drag over "About Java Tucana".	To select it. You can always select text by dragging.
9. While holding **Shift**, click at the end of the first full paragraph.	To extend the selection to include everything from the current selection through the point at which you clicked. This can be useful for selecting larger areas of text.
10. Try using **Shift** with the other selection techniques.	Shift with an arrow key extends the selection by one character or one line. Using Ctrl+Shift with an arrow key extends the selection one word or one paragraph at a time. You should practice these techniques and become familiar with them. Staying on the keyboard can really increase your productivity.
11. Double-click a word.	To select it.
12. Triple-click within a paragraph.	To select the entire paragraph. This can be very handy. As you can see, there are many ways to select text and to move the cursor. You should try a variety of techniques to see which work best for you in different situations.

Cutting and copying text

Deleting text removes the text without saving it. Cutting text removes the text but keeps a copy of it in a special location called *the clipboard* for further use. Copying text leaves the text in place *and* saves a copy to the clipboard. After you've placed text on the clipboard, you can use Paste commands to put it elsewhere.

Exam Objective: MOS Word Core 2.1.2

- To delete selected text, press **Delete** or **Backspace** on the keyboard.

  Pressing either of these keys with no text selected will delete one character at a time at the location of the cursor: **Delete** removes the character immediately to the *right*; **Backspace** deletes the character immediately to the *left*.
- There are three ways to cut selected text:
  - Press **Ctrl+X** on the keyboard.
  - Right-click the selected text, and click **Cut**.
  - On the Home tab, click Cut.
- Similarly, there are three ways to copy selected text:
  - Press **Ctrl+C** on the keyboard.
  - Right-click the selected text, and click **Copy**.
  - On the Home tab, click Copy.

Pasting text

There are several methods and options for pasting text from the clipboard.

Exam Objective: MOS Word Core 2.1.2

- Right-click where you want to paste, and click one of these paste options:
  - **Keep source formatting**: Pastes clipboard contents with only its original formatting intact.
  - **Merge formatting**: Pasted contents are applied with a blend of original and destination formats.
  - **Keep text only** (adopt destination formatting): Retains the original text but with destination formats applied.
- On the Home tab, click **Paste**.

  This uses the current default paste options. Click the drop-down arrow under the button for more options.

- Press **Ctrl+V** on the keyboard.

  This uses the current default paste option.
- Another way to cut and paste in one move is to drag selected text to its new location.

Using Undo

You can undo almost any number of actions while you have a document open. However, once you close and reopen a document, the Undo stack for that document is cleared. There are two common ways to undo actions.

- Press **Ctrl+Z**.

  To undo the most recent action. Hold down **Ctrl** and press **Z** multiple times to step back through and undo multiple actions.
- Click (the Undo button).

  To undo the most recent action. Click it multiple times to step back through actions. You can also use the drop-down list to select an action. All actions since the one you've selected are undone.

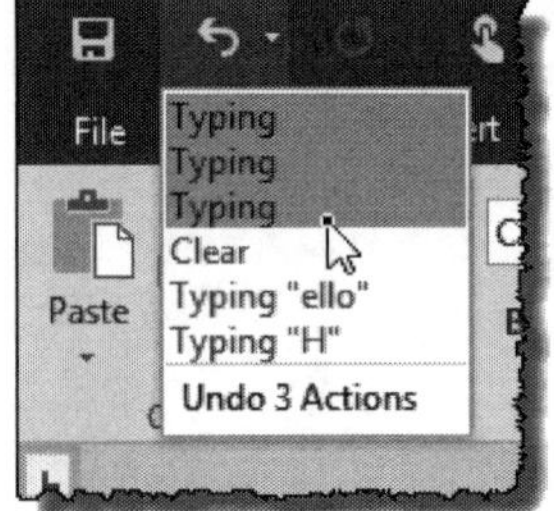

Exercise: Moving and copying text

About Us Selecting should be open at the beginning of this exercise.

Do This	How & Why
1. Move the Java Tucana Coffee and Tea section above the Java Tucana Services section.	
a) Select the entire Java Tucana Coffee and Tea section.	You can drag over it, or try another method, such as clicking at the beginning of the heading, then Shift-clicking at the end of the document.
b) Click Cut.	In the Clipboard group on the left of the Home tab. To remove the selected text from the document and place it in a temporary location called the clipboard.
c) Click before the Java Tucana Services heading.	Here. Java·Tucana·Services¶ Office·coffee·service¶ We'll·supply·your·office·with·early
d) Click **Paste**.	The Paste button is the Clipboard group on the Home tab. Paste The cut text now appears before the other text. Moving text like this is a four step process: select the text to move, cut it, select the location to paste it, then paste it. There are faster ways, though, in many situations.
2. Undo the paste.	Click the Undo button on the Quick Access toolbar.
3. Click again.	To undo the cut. The undo button keeps track of many of your last actions. You'll now use a different method to move the text.
4. Move the text by using the mouse.	
a) Select the entire Java Tucana Coffee and Tea section.	
Continued...	

Do This	How & Why
b) Drag the selected text before the Java Tucana Coffee and Tea heading.	As you drag, there is a box attached to the pointer, and the insertion point shows where the text will appear.
5. Save the document.	Click the Save button on the Quick Access toolbar.
6. Copy the heading "Java Tucana's Blends" and the list of blends.	
a) Select the paragraphs.	
b) Press **Ctrl+C**.	To copy the selection to the clipboard. Notice that the selected text is not removed when you copy it (unlike when you cut it). You could also have clicked the Copy button in the Clipboard group of the home tab.
c) Place the cursor at the beginning of the Java Tucana Services heading.	You will paste the copied text here.
d) Press **Ctrl+V**.	To paste the text here. You could also have clicked the Paste button.
7. Edit the text as shown.	You'll need to delete the teas from the first list, edit the second heading, and delete the two coffee blends from the second list.
8. Save the document.	Click the Save button, or press **Ctrl+S**.
9. Do you know how to copy text using the mouse?	You can do this by holding down **Ctrl** while dragging selected text. If your instructor says you have time, experiment with copying using the mouse.
10. Close the document.	You do not need to save any changes.

Assessment: Creating documents

1. If you click Save in a document you haven't saved before, the Save As window opens instead. True or false?

   ✓ • True.
   • False.

2. What is the keyboard shortcut for selecting everything in a document?

   ✓ • Ctrl+A
   • Ctrl+E
   • Ctrl+S
   • Alt+E

3. What is the keyboard shortcut to paste text?

   • Ctrl+P
   • Alt+P
   • Alt+V
   ✓ • Ctrl+V

Module C: Document views

Word offers several ways to view a document, and the ability to zoom in and out. You can also switch between multiple documents or view them side by side.

You will learn:

- About different document views
- How to split a document window
- How to view and switch between multiple open documents
- How to use Zoom features

Document views

There are five document views. You select which to use, either on the status bar or on the View tab.

Exam Objective: MOS Word Core 1.4.1

Document views on the View tab

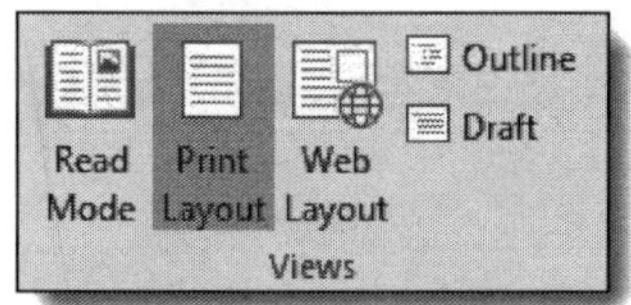

Read Mode	Maximizes area for reading and commenting. Provides tools to research, translate, highlight, and comment.
Print Layout	Shows how the document will look printed on the page.
Web Layout	Shows what the document will look like saved as a web page.
Outline	Shows the document in outline form and provides outline tools.
Draft	Used mainly for editing content. Headers, footers, and print layout are not visible.

Besides different document views, Word allows you to split the document window, to view two documents side by side, to switch between any number of open documents, and to zoom in and out while viewing a document.

Splitting a document window

You can split the document window so you can see and edit different parts of the same document.

Exam Objective: MOS Word Core 1.4.4

1. On the View tab, in the Window group, click **Split**.

   The document window splits into two windows, each with its own scroll bars. You can edit in either window. The Split command changes to "Remove Split."
2. To resize the windows, drag the dividing bar up or down.
3. To remove the split: on the View tab, in the Windows Group, click **Remove Split**; or just double-click the bar dividing the windows.

Viewing documents side by side

You can view two documents side by side, and if you want, synchronize scrolling between them. You need to have at least two documents open to use this feature.

1. On the View tab, in the Window group, click **View Side by Side**.
2. If more than two documents are open, select the other document you want to view, and click **OK**.

   The two documents appear side by side, taking up the whole screen. By default, synchronized scrolling is enabled. That is, when you scroll in one window, the other scrolls also.
3. To toggle synchronized scrolling, on the View tab, click the **Synchronized Scrolling** button.
4. If the windows get moved or misaligned, click **Reset Window Position** to return them to full-screen, side-by-side view.

Switching between open documents

If you have more than one Word document open, there are at least four ways you can switch between them.

- Click any part of the window to which you want to switch, if it's visible.
- Click or hover over the Word icon on the taskbar. When a list of open documents appears, click the document you want.

  Depending on the graphics options you've set, this is either a list of document titles or thumbnails of each window, with titles.
- Hold down **Alt** and press **Tab** repeatedly until you select the document you want, then release **Alt**.

  Doing so flips through all open programs, not just Word documents. Exactly what this looks like varies, depending on your graphics settings.

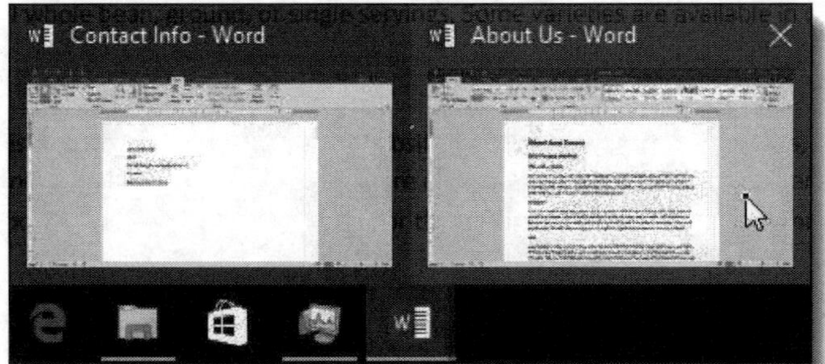

- On the View tab, in the Window group, click **Switch Windows**, and select the document you'd like.

Selecting Zoom options

There are three options for using the Zoom feature.

Exam Objective: MOS Word Core 1.4.2

- Press and hold down the **Ctrl** key, and roll the mouse wheel forward or backward to zoom in and out, effectively enlarging and reducing the document elements, respectively.
- Use the Zoom control at the right end of the status bar. Click the plus or minus buttons, or drag the slider.

- Use the commands in the Zoom group on the View tab.

Exercise: Changing document views

Exam Objective: MOS Word Core 1.4.1, 1.4.2, 1.4.4

Do This	How & Why
1. Open the documents `About Us`, `Our Services`, and `Our Blends`.	From the `Fundamentals` folder. **Note:** Opening downloaded files in Office applications can result in the documents being displayed in Protected view. This can be overridden by clicking **Enable Editing** at the top of the document window.
2. Observe the Word icon in the taskbar.	It shows several documents open.
3. Point to the Word icon.	Depending on your graphics settings, you'll see a list of file names or thumbnail images of open files.
4. Click one of the open files.	One that isn't currently active in Word. To switch to that file.
5. Switch to `About Us`.	If necessary.
6. On the View tab, click **Split**.	To split the window. You can now scroll separately in each window, viewing different parts of the same document at the same time.
7. Remove the split using one of these methods: • On the View tab, click **Remove Split**. • Double-click the split line.	
8. Try different Zoom features: • Hold down the **Ctrl** key, and scroll the mouse wheel. • On the right of the status bar, use the slider. • On the View tab, use the Zoom group options.	

Do This	How & Why
9. On the View tab, in the Zoom group, click **100%**.	
10. On the View tab, click **View Side by Side**.	
11. Select one of the other documents, and click **OK**.	The documents each take up half of the screen.
12. Try scrolling in one of the documents.	Notice that both documents scroll. By default, when you view documents side-by-side, their scrolling is synchronized. You can turn this off by clicking the Synchronous Scrolling option on the View tab.
13. Close all open documents.	
14. Close Word.	

Assessment: Document views

1. If you click View Side by Side with more than two documents open, what happens?
   - You have to choose which other document to view.
   - ✓ Documents are arranged in columns.
   - Nothing happens.
   - You can't; the option is grayed out.
2. Which of these actions will cause the document to zoom in?
   - Ctrl+I
   - Alt+Z
   - Ctrl+Up Arrow
   - ✓ Ctrl+Mouse wheel forward

Summary: Fundamentals

You should now know:

- About the Word interface, Backstage view, and opening and closing documents
- How to create blank documents; save, cut, and paste text; and undo actions
- How to change the view of a document, split the document window, view documents side by side, zoom in and out, and switch between open documents

Synthesis: Fundamentals

In this synthesis exercise, you'll start Word, open two documents, and experiment with various view options.

1. Start Word.
2. Open `Lunch Menu` and `About Us`.
   From the `Fundamentals` folder.
3. View the documents side by side.
4. Split the document window in the About Us document.
5. Zoom in and out on the menu.
   Try different methods: keyboard, status bar, and Zoom group.
6. Save `Lunch Menu` as `Lunch Menu Edited`.
7. In the menu, make the Surf and Surf item first under the Lunch Menu heading.
8. Save the menu and then close it.
9. Try different document views for About Us.
10. Close the document.
    Leave Word open.

Chapter 2: Formatting

You will learn:

- How to format characters
- How to format paragraphs
- About Quick Styles, style sets, and themes
- How to create bulleted and numbered lists

Module A: Formatting characters

It's important to understand the difference between character and paragraph attributes. You can avoid some confusion and frustration by knowing when and how to apply each. The simplest type of formatting is character formatting, things like making a word bold or italic, increasing its size, or changing its font.

You will learn:

- How to format characters
- How to use Format Painter

Formatting characters

Word allows you to change many visual attributes of the text. Most of these attributes you might never need to change. There are a few attributes, though, that you'll probably adjust quite often.

Font Also called font face or typeface, this is the actual shape of the characters. Examples include Arial, Helvetica, and Times New Roman.

Font size The height, in points, of the largest capital characters. Width is adjusted accordingly. Microsoft Office applications use the American-British point system, which defines a point as 1/72 of an inch (.351 mm).

Font style The term *style* is used in different ways in Word. In this case, it refers the whether or not the font is bold, italic, underline, or any combination of these.

Font color You can choose from many defined colors, or make a color by entering specific color and brightness values. Plus, you can adjust underline and highlight color independently of font color.

Effects These include strikethrough, superscript, and subscript. Not to be confused with *text effects*, which are graphic effects such as 3-D and drop shadows.

Applying character attributes

After you select the text you want to format, there are a number of ways to apply individual character attributes.

Exam Objective: MOS Word Core 2.2.1, 2.2.5

- Use the commands on the Home tab, in the Font group. Hover the mouse pointer over a command to see its description.

  You can apply many attributes, such as text effects, text highlight color, and font color.

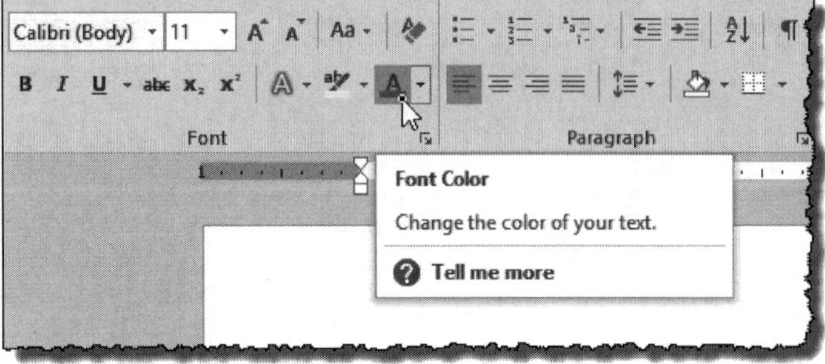

- Click the expansion arrow in the lower-right corner of the Font group to open the **Font** window.
- Right-click selected text, and click **Font** from the shortcut menu.
- Right-click selected text, and use the mini toolbar that appears above the selection.

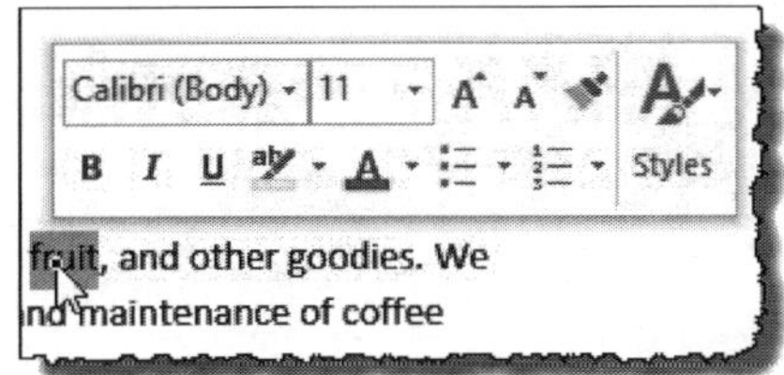

- Use keyboard shortcuts for font styles: **Crtl+B** for bold, **Ctrl+I** for italic, and **Ctrl+U** for underline.

Using Format Painter

You can use Format Painter to copy text formatting from one place and apply it to text in another.

Exam Objective: MOS Word Core 2.2.2

1. Select the text with the formatting you want to copy.

   If you want to copy the paragraph style as well, select the entire paragraph, including the paragraph mark at the end.
2. On the Home tab, in the Clipboard group, click **Format Painter**.

   To format multiple items, double-click **Format Painter**. This keeps it active for multiple selections.

   The mouse pointer shows a paintbrush when it is over text.
3. Drag the pointer over text you want to format.

   If you are formatting one item, the text is formatted and the pointer returns to normal.
4. If you are formatting multiple items, once you're finished, press **Esc** or click **Format Painter** again to stop formatting.

You can also use format painter to copy some graphic formatting, such as the border, fill color, and 3-D format of a shape.

Exercise: Formatting characters

Exam Objective: MOS Word Core 2.2.1, 2.2.2, 2.2.5

Do This	How & Why
1. Open `Coffee-text`. Save it as `Coffee-text-formatted`.	The document is in the current chapter's folder, and you should save it there as well.
2. Select the first line.	The heading Java Tucana Coffee.
3. On the Home tab, in the Font group, select **Arial**.	Click the drop-down arrow next to the Font box.
4. From the Font Size list, select **16**.	
5. Press **Ctrl+B**, and then press **Ctrl+I**.	To make the heading bold and italic. You could also use the Bold and Italic buttons in the Font group.
Continued...	

Do This	How & Why
6. Highlight the text "Tucana Roast," in the second full paragraph.	
a) Select the text.	
b) In the mini toolbar, click the Text Highlight Color arrow, then click a color you like.	The highlighting appears over the text.
7. Select the "Java Tucana Coffee" heading.	You'll copy it's formatting to another heading.
8. In the Clipboard group, click the **Format Painter** button.	The pointer changes to a paintbrush when it is over text.
9. Select the heading Our Blends.	It takes on the formatting of the first heading, and the pointer returns to normal.
10. In the first paragraph under Our Blends, italicize "Bourbon Santos."	Select it and click *I*.
11. Double-click **Format Painter**.	Be sure that "Bourbon Santos" is still selected. Double-clicking enables Format Painter to be used for multiple selections.
12. In the same paragraph, select "Coban." In the next paragraph, select "Bogota," and then select "Tarrazu."	Note that you can select a whole word by double-clicking it. These are all now italic.
13. Press **Esc**.	To deactivate Format Painter.
14. Save and then close the document.	

The document with formatted text

Java Tucana Coffee

Coffee has been cultivated in South America since the 1700's. Most of the plants are of the Arabica variety, but regional differences in climate, elevation, and soil mean a wide range of flavor, body, and acidity. Java Tucana carries the best South American coffees our buyers can find. We also produce our own blends of coffee.

Our Blends

Tucana Roast, our signature blend, combines Brazilian *Bourbon Santos* with Guatemalan *Coban*. The result is a coffee that is remarkably rich and fragrant yet clean, sweet, and snappy. It's the perfect cup for after a meal or as an afternoon refresher.

Phoenix Roast can help you rise from the ashes of a late night or a long meeting. A blend of Columbian *Bogota* and Costa Rican *Tarrazu*, this cup is full-bodied, fragrant, and complex, but never bitter. Its rich flavor and clean finish make it the perfect coffee for the first cup of the day.

Assessment: Formatting characters

1. Helvetica and Arial are examples of what? Choose the single best answer.
    - Font size
    - ✓ Font face
    - Font effects
    - Font style
2. Which of the following are examples of character formatting? Select all correct answers.
    - ✓ Font size
    - Line spacing
    - Alignment
    - ✓ Font style

Module B: Formatting paragraphs

Paragraph formatting applies to everything in a paragraph: where it appears on the page, its alignment, indents, tabs, spacing, and much more.

You will learn how to:

- Apply paragraph attributes such as alignment and spacing
- Control indenting for paragraphs
- Control tab settings for paragraphs

Paragraph attributes

In Word, a paragraph is any number of words, even just one (or none at all), ending with (or consisting of) a paragraph mark. To see the paragraph mark and other hidden characters, click the **Show/Hide** button on the Home tab in the Paragraph group.

You can consider the paragraph's attributes to be attached to its paragraph mark. The attributes most commonly changed are alignment, indentation, and spacing.

Alignment	The paragraph can be justified right, center, left, or full.
Outline level	The level of the paragraph in a bulleted or numbered list.
Indentation	You can indent the left and/or right edge of the paragraph. You can also indent the first line only, or create a hanging indent (all lines except the first).
Spacing	Spacing before and after a paragraph, as well as the line spacing within it.
Color and border	You can put a line border around a paragraph and change its background color. If the color is dark, the text color is automatically white in contrast to it.

Applying paragraph attributes

To change attributes of several paragraphs, they should be selected, including the paragraph mark at the end of the selection. To change the attributes of a single paragraph, though, the cursor just needs to be placed anywhere in the paragraph; the entire paragraph does not have to be selected.

Exam Objective: MOS Word Core 2.2.3

- Use the options available on the Home tab, in the Paragraph group.
  Hover the pointer over a command to see its description.

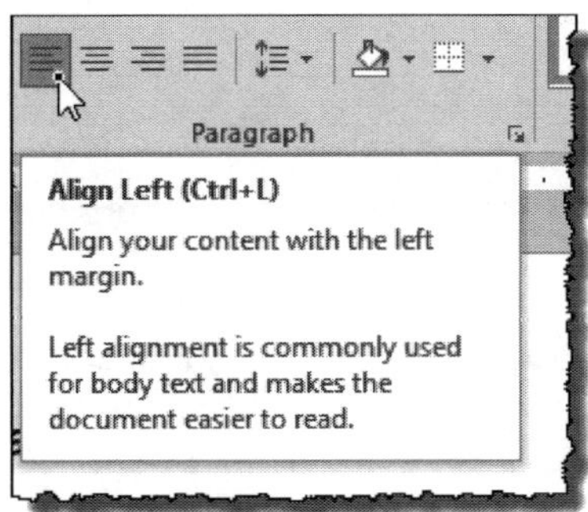

- To open the **Paragraph** window, click the Paragraph Settings button in the lower-right of the Paragraph ribbon group.
  You can instead right-click the selected paragraph(s) and click **Paragraph**.

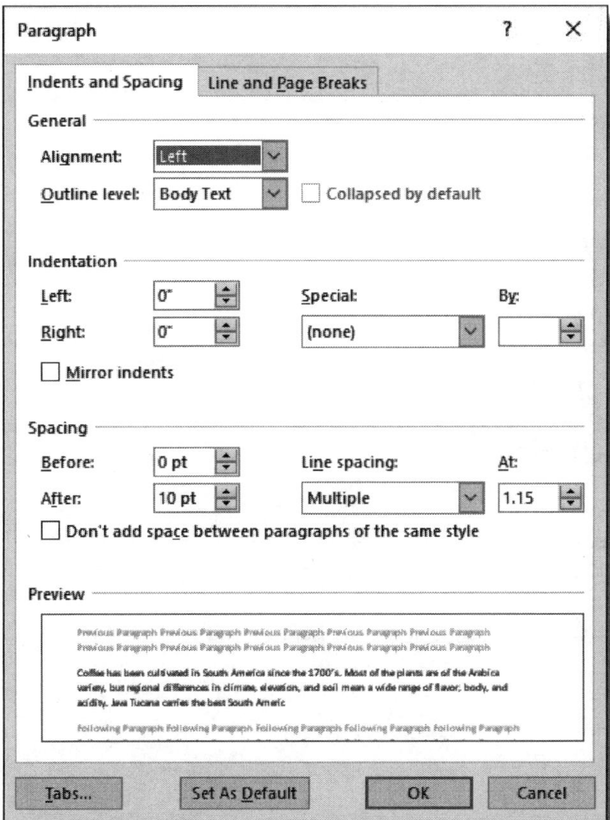

- Indents and tabs can also be set by clicking and dragging markers directly on the ruler. Hover the mouse pointer over a marker to see its description.

Setting line spacing

You can change the spacing before and after paragraphs and between lines in a paragraph.

After you select the paragraphs you want to format, either use the **Line and Paragraph Spacing** button, or open the **Paragraph** window.

1. On the Home tab, in the Paragraph group, click the **Line and Paragraph Spacing** button, and select an option.

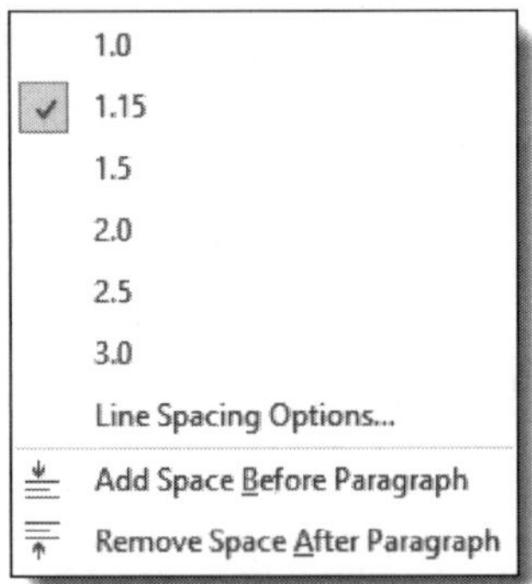

2. If you need more spacing options, click **Line Spacing Options**.

   To open the **Paragraph** window, which you can also do from the lower-right corner of the Paragraph group.

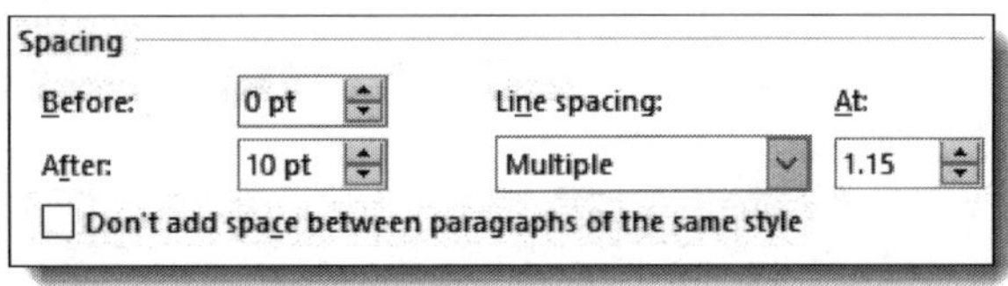

3. Set the spacing options, and click **OK**.

   The Add Space Before Paragraph and Add Space After Paragraph options set spacing above and below entire paragraphs, respectively. You can also choose not to add space between paragraphs of the same style.

Exercise: Controlling alignment and spacing

Exam Objective: MOS Word Core 2.2.3

Do This	How & Why
1. Open `Coffee-paragraphs` and save it as `Coffee-paragraphs-formatted`.	This is similar to the document you applied character formatting to.
2. Place the cursor in the first full paragraph.	Click anywhere in the paragraph beginning, "Coffee has been cultivated..."

Do This	How & Why
3. In the Paragraph Group, click [line spacing button].	To display the Line and Paragraph Spacing menu. Here, you change the space between paragraphs, or choose commands to open the Paragraph window where you will have finer control. ¶ Normal 1.0 1.15 1.5 2.0 2.5 3.0 Line Spacing Options... Add Space Before Paragraph Remove Space After Paragraph
4. Click **1.5**.	To change the space between lines of the current paragraph to 1.5 lines. When you change line spacing, it applies to all lines in the selected paragraph.
5. In the Paragraph group, observe the alignment buttons.	The Align Left button is highlighted, because the paragraph is aligned along the left margin (as paragraphs are by default).
6. Click [center button].	To center-align the paragraph.
7. Right-align the paragraph.	Click [right-align button]. Alignment along the right margin is unusual but sometimes useful.
8. Justify the paragraph.	Click [justify button]. This is how we want the paragraph, with both margins aligned, like in a newspaper.
9. Apply the same formatting to the other two descriptive paragraphs.	
a) Double-click **Format Painter**.	
b) Click once in each of the other paragraphs.	There's no need to select them.
c) Press **Esc**.	To turn off the Format Painter.
10. Update the document and compare it to the results below.	

After you've completed the exercise, the document should look like the following figure:

Java Tucana Coffee

Coffee has been cultivated in South America since the 1700's. Most of the plants are of the Arabica variety, but regional differences in climate, elevation, and soil mean a wide range of flavor, body, and acidity. Java Tucana carries the best South American coffees our buyers can find. We also produce our own blends of coffee.

Our Blends

Tucana Roast, our signature blend, combines Brazilian *Bourbon Santos* with Guatemalan *Coban*. The result is a coffee that is remarkably rich and fragrant yet clean, sweet, and snappy. It's the perfect cup for after a meal or as an afternoon refresher.

Phoenix Roast can help you rise from the ashes of a late night or a long meeting. A blend of Colombian *Bogota* and Costa Rican *Tarrazu*, this cup is full-bodied, fragrant, and complex, but never bitter. Its rich flavor and clean finish make it the perfect coffee for the first cup of the day.

Setting indents

You can apply an indent or hanging indent to the first line of a paragraph, or indent the entire left and/or right edge of the paragraph.

After you select the paragraphs you want to format, there are two places to set indents: the ruler and the Paragraph window. The latter provides more precision.

- On the ruler, drag the First Line Indent, Left Indent, and Right Indent markers to where you want them on the ruler. Hover the mouse pointer over the marker to see its description.

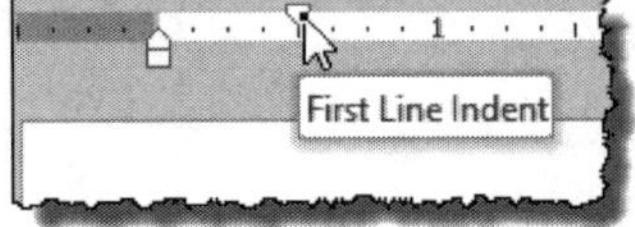

- On the Home tab, in the Paragraph group, open the **Paragraph** window. Set the options in the Indentation sections. The Special drop-down list provides options for first line and hanging indents. When you are done, click **OK**.

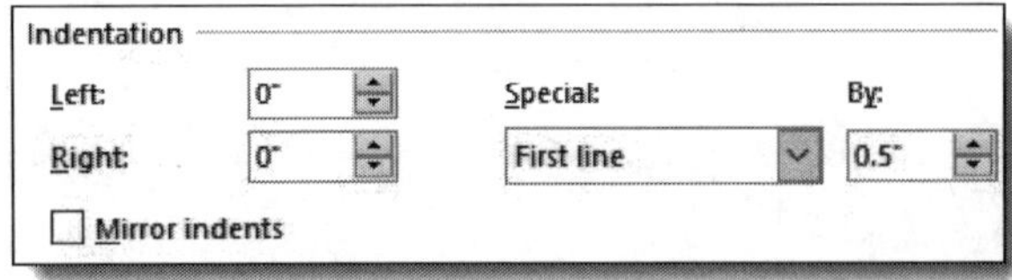

Exercise: Controlling indentation of paragraphs

Coffee-paragraphs-formatted should be open.

Exam Objective: MOS Word Core 2.2.3

Do This	How & Why
1. Click within the first full paragraph.	The one that begins "Coffee has been cultivated...". You will change experiment with the indenting of the paragraph.

Do This	How & Why
2. On the ruler, drag the Left Indent box to the half-inch mark.	The Left Indent box is the bottom, square one of the three indent icons. 
3. Point to each of the triangular indent icons.	To view their screen tips. The top triangle is the First Line Indent marker. Use this to control where the first line of a paragraph begins. The right triangle is the Hanging Indent marker, which controls where all the lines after the first begin. 
4. Drag the Hanging Indent icon back to the zero mark.	To make all the lines after the first align with the left margin. The paragraph should look like this. Notice that the First Line Indent icon is at the half-inch mark on the ruler. 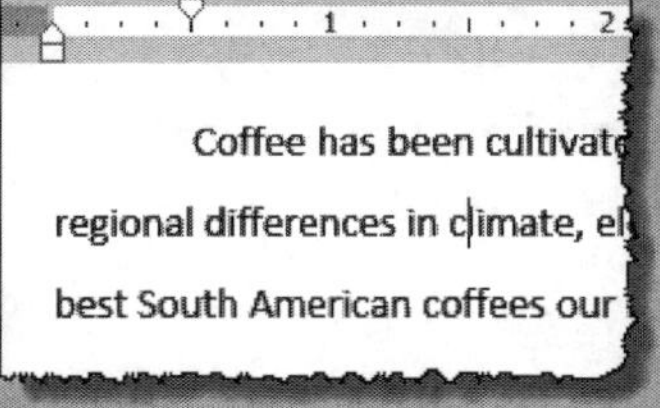
5. With the cursor in the same paragraph, click the Paragraph Settings button.	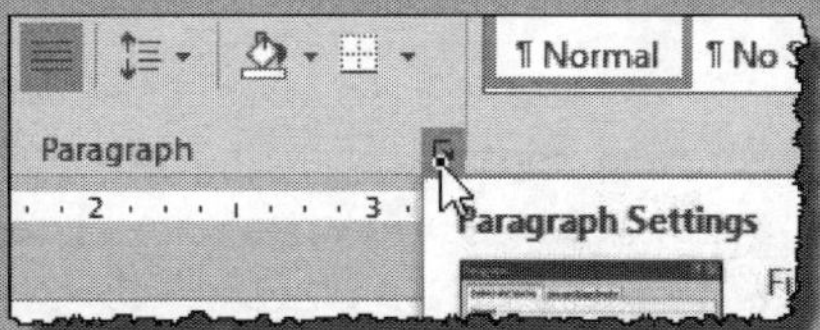 To open the Paragraph window to the Indents and Spacing tab.
6. Observe the Indentation settings.	They reflect the indents you set on the ruler. There is no left or right indent, but the first line is .5 inches to the right.
7. Set left and right indents for the paragraph at 0.5 inches.	Change the values in the Left and Right boxes to 0.5, then click **OK**. The paragraph is indented a half inch from both sides. 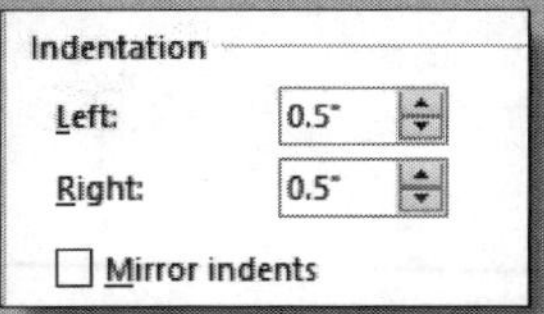
8. Copy the formatting of the paragraph to the other two under "Our Blends".	Select the paragraph, click the Format Painter, and then drag over the other two paragraphs.
9. Save and then close the document.	An example follows.

The document with indented paragraphs

Java Tucana Coffee

Coffee has been cultivated in South America since the 1700's. Most of the plants are of the Arabica variety, but regional differences in climate, elevation, and soil mean a wide range of flavor, body, and acidity. Java Tucana carries the best South American coffees our buyers can find. We also produce our own blends of coffee.

Our Blends

Tucana Roast, our signature blend, combines Brazilian Bourbon Santos with Guatemalan Coban. The result is a coffee that is remarkably rich and fragrant yet clean, sweet, and snappy. It's the perfect cup for after a meal or as an afternoon refresher.

Phoenix Roast can help you rise from the ashes of a late night or a long meeting. A blend of Colombian Bogota and Costa Rican Tarrazu, this cup is full-bodied, fragrant, and complex, but never bitter. Its rich flavor and clean finish make it the perfect coffee for the first cup of the day.

Tabs

Tab stops are the locations to which the cursor skips when you press the **Tab** key on your keyboard. To see tab stops in a document, the ruler has to be showing. If necessary, check **Ruler** in the Show group on the View tab.

Ruler with custom tab stops

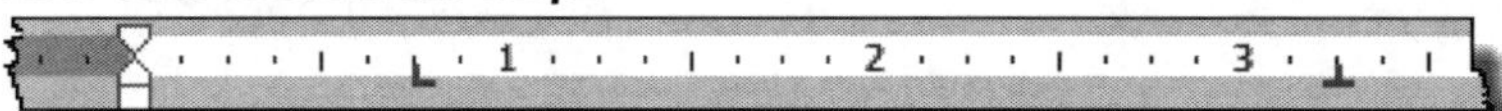

By default, there are tab stops every half inch. You can change the distance between default tabs. You can also add custom tab stops with different alignments and leaders. These will appear as bold marks directly on the ruler, with different marks for different types of tab stops.

Tab stops can be set and cleared using the ruler or the **Tabs** window. The latter provides better precision and more options. When you set a custom tab stop, the default tab stops to the left of it are cleared.

Note that added tab stops are paragraph attributes, and they behave like other paragraph attributes. For instance, if you create new tab stops and then press Enter, the new paragraph will inherit the same stops. However, if you create tab stops in one paragraph and then move to a different existing paragraph, those stops will no longer apply. To add tab stops to multiple existing paragraphs, you need to select them all first.

Tab stop types

Whether you set tab stops from the ruler or in the **Tabs** window, you have five types to choose from.

Tab types in Word

Ruler icon	Name	Description
L	Left tab	Text is left-aligned to the stop.
⊥	Center tab	Text is center-aligned to the stop.
┘	Right tab	Text is right-aligned to the stop.
⊥.	Decimal tab	The decimal point is aligned to the stop. Usually used for a column of numbers.
I	Bar tab	Draws a vertical bar at the stop position. Text entered at this tab stop is left-aligned.

Setting tabs on the ruler

The simplest way to add tab stops is to use the ruler. If the ruler isn't showing, you need to click the **View Ruler** button in the upper-right corner of the document window.

1. Select the paragraph(s) to which you want to apply tab stops.
2. To the left of the top ruler, click the tab icon.

   Multiple times, if necessary, to step through the tab types. Note that you also step through indent icons.

   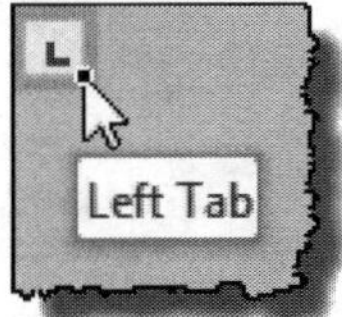

3. Click the ruler where you want the tab stops.

   New tab markers are added to the ruler. The default tab stops are cleared from the left margin up to your custom tab stops.
4. To move a stop you've already set, drag it left or right.

Exercise: Understanding types of tab stops

Do This	How & Why
1. Open Coffee-tabs and save it as Coffee-tabs-formatted.	This document contains information about Java Tucana's coffees. You will format the lists of information using tab stops and tabs.
2. Click ¶.	To show paragraph and other symbols in the document. When working with tabs, it's often useful to show symbols. These symbols will not print, but can help you to better control formatting.
3. Select all the paragraphs under "Coffees by Region".	When setting tab stops, it's very important to first select all the paragraphs to which you want to apply the same settings. If you do them one at a time, you will almost certainly get inconsistent results.
4. Observe the left tab icon.	It looks like the letter "L". By clicking the ruler, you will create a left-aligned tab stop. 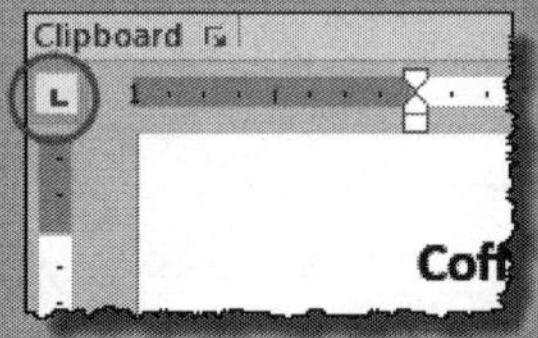
5. Click at the 2-inch mark on the ruler.	To place a left tab stop for the selected paragraphs. But the text doesn't move. Creating tabs is a two-step process: you must set the tab stops and enter tab characters. The order in which you do these two steps doesn't actually matter. 
6. Click right before the word "Region" and press **Tab**.	To insert a tab character between "Type" and "Region", which will act as the headings for the rest of the information. The word is now left-aligned at the two-inch mark on the ruler. Note that with symbols showing, you can see the tab character. 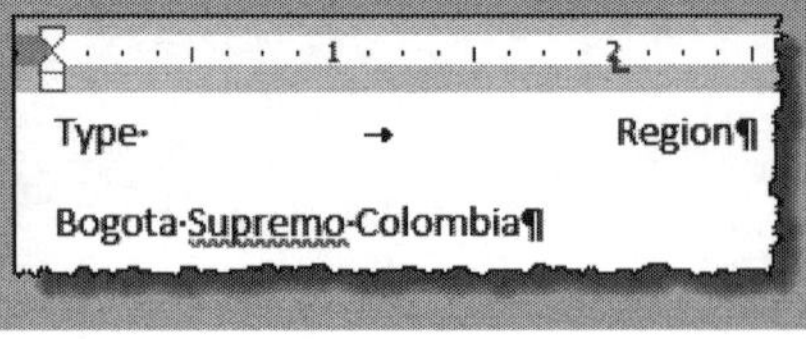

Do This	How & Why
7. Insert the rest of the tab characters as shown.	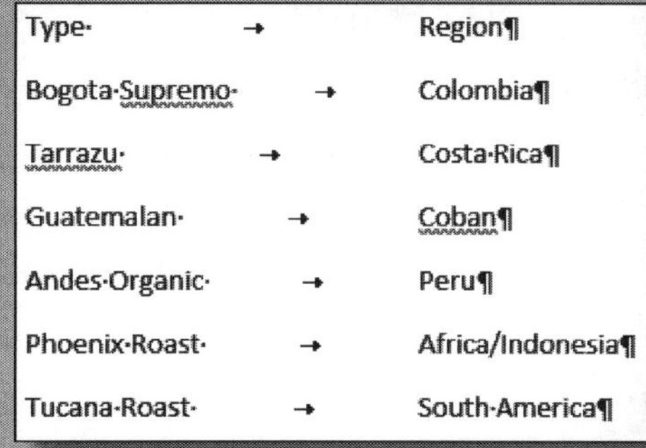
8. Replace the left tab stop with a right tab stop.	
a) Select all the paragraphs containing tabs.	
b) Drag the left tab stop off the ruler.	
c) Click the tab icon twice to activate the Right Tab icon.	
d) Click at the 2-inch mark on the ruler.	Because the tab characters are already in the paragraphs, you immediately see the result. Placing a right-aligned tab stop at 2 inches makes the text kind of crowded. 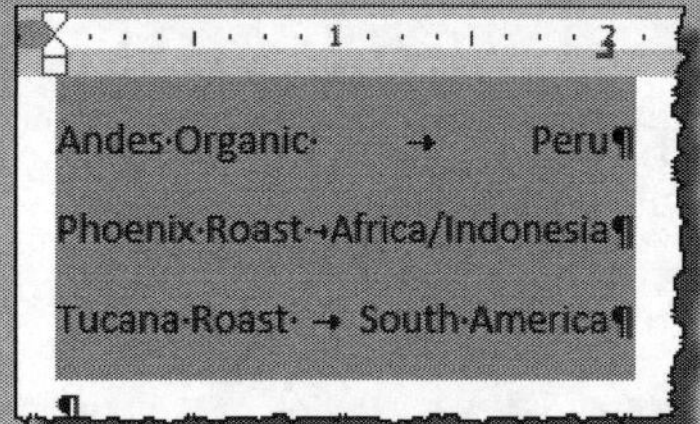
9. Move the right tab stop to the 3-inch mark.	
a) Verify that the paragraphs are all still selected.	Always important to maintain consistency.
b) Drag the right tab stop to the 3-inch mark.	Notice that as you drag, a dotted line appears in the document showing you where the text will align when you release the mouse. 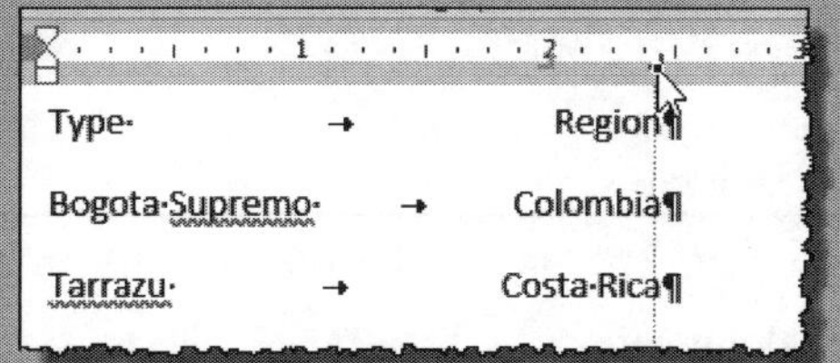
10. Save the document.	An example follows.

The region information formatted using tabs

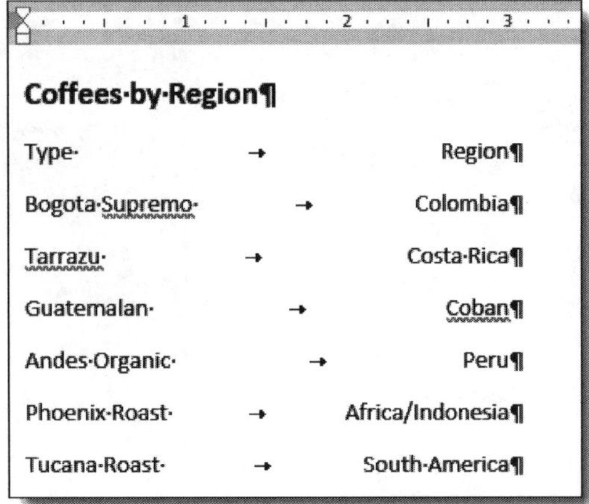

Setting tabs in the Tabs window

If you need more tab options than you get by setting tab stops on the ruler, you can use the **Tabs** window.

1. On the Home tab, in the Paragraph group, open the **Paragraph** window.
2. Click **Tabs**.

   The **Tabs** window opens.

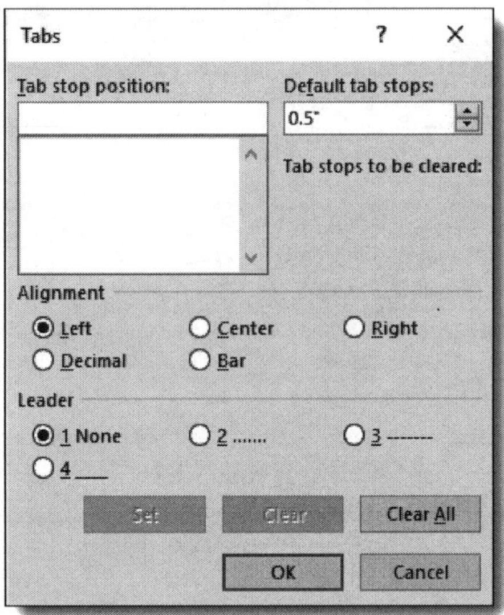

3. Set the options for each tab stop.
   a) Set the position in inches.
   b) Select the alignment and leader type.
   c) Click **Set**.
   d) Repeat for each tab stop you want to set.
4. You can also use the **Tabs** window to change the default tab stops for the current document.
5. When you are done, click **OK**.

Tab leaders

A *tab leader* is a repeating character that leads up to a tab stop, such as the row of periods that often appears between headings and page numbers in a table of contents. By default, tabs are set without leaders, but you can select from several leader types when you set tab stops in the **Tabs** window.

Tab stop with leader

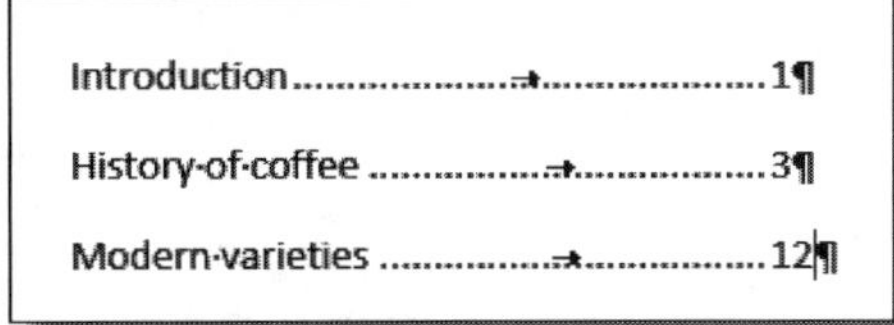

Clearing tab stops

You can clear tab stops by dragging them downward off the ruler. You can also clear all or individual tab stops from selected paragraphs by using the **Tabs** window.

1. On the Home tab, in the Paragraph group, open the **Paragraph** window.
2. Click **Tabs**.
   The **Tabs** window opens.
3. To clear an individual stop, select it from the list, and click **Clear**.
4. To clear all stops at once, click **Clear All**.
5. Click **OK**.

Exercise: Using the Tabs window to set tab stops

Coffee-tabs-formatted is open.

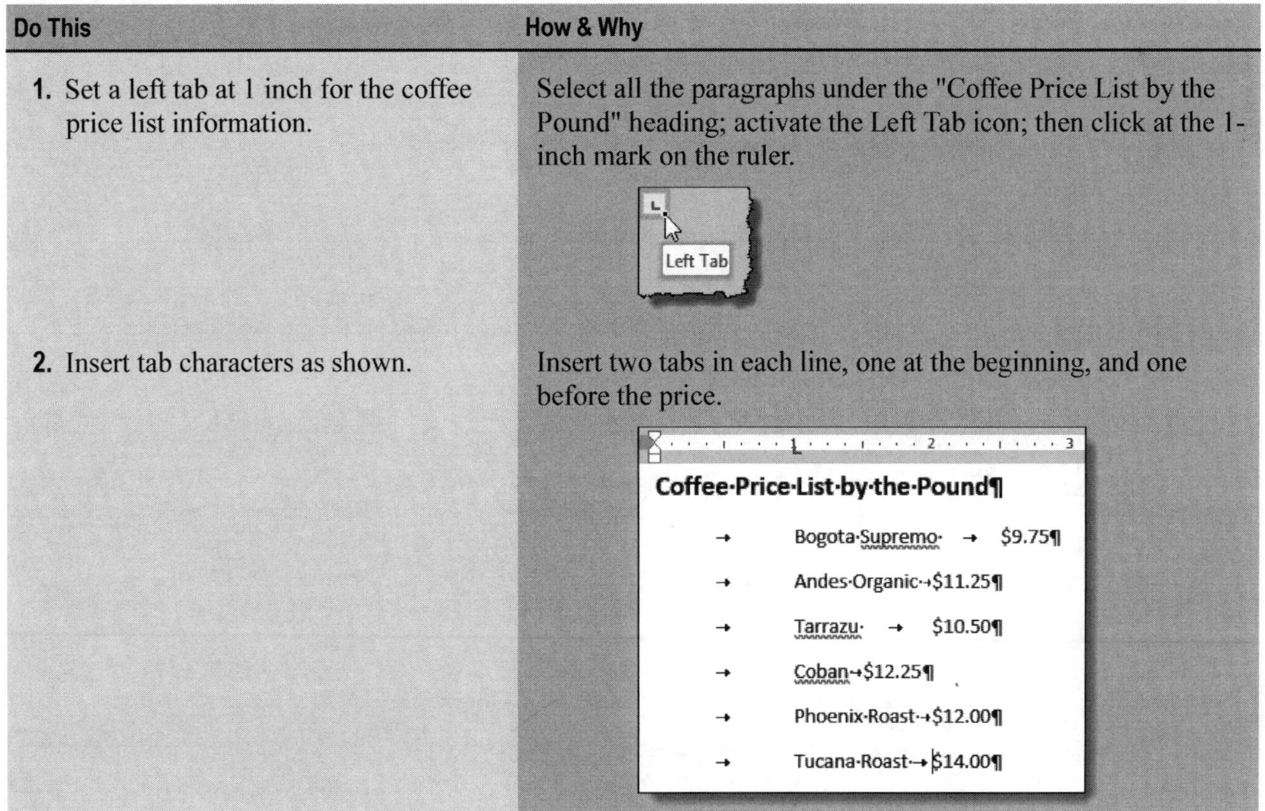

Do This	How & Why
1. Set a left tab at 1 inch for the coffee price list information.	Select all the paragraphs under the "Coffee Price List by the Pound" heading; activate the Left Tab icon; then click at the 1-inch mark on the ruler.
2. Insert tab characters as shown.	Insert two tabs in each line, one at the beginning, and one before the price.

Do This	How & Why
3. Select all the price list paragraphs, right-click, and click **Paragraph**.	To open the **Paragraph** window.
4. Click **Tabs**.	To display the **Tabs** window.
5. Add a decimal tab stop with a dot leader: a) In the position box, enter **3**. b) Under Alignment, click **Decimal**. c) Under Leader, click **2**. d) Click **Set**, and then click **OK**.	A new stop is added at 3 inches, and you can see the results on the paragraphs because of the tab stops you entered.
6. Observe the price list paragraphs.	The prices are now aligned on their decimal points, and there is a dot leader between the coffees and their associated prices.
7. Save and close the document.	

The coffee price list using dot-leader tab stops

Coffee·Price·List·by·the·Pound¶

→ Bogota·Supremo· ....→.........$9.75¶

→ Andes·Organic·.........→.........$11.25¶

→ Tarrazu·...............→...............$10.50¶

→ Coban·................→................$12.25¶

→ Phoenix·Roast ....→..........$12.00¶

→ Tucana·Roast..........→...........$14.00¶

Assessment: Formatting paragraphs

1. Indenting is a paragraph attribute. True or false?
   - ✓ True
   - False
2. What is it called when the first line of a paragraph is not indented, but the rest of the paragraph is indented?
   - Reverse indent
   - Inverse indent
   - ✓ Hanging indent
   - Outdent
3. What style can apply character and paragraph attributes at once?
   - ✓ Linked style
   - Combo style
   - Dual style
   - Charagraph style
4. Which tab-stop type aligns a decimal point to the stop?
   - Number stop
   - Column stop
   - Ledger stop
   - ✓ Decimal stop
5. What is the string of repeated characters called that leads up to a tab stop?
   - ✓ Tab leader
   - Tab line
   - Tab score
   - Tab tracer
6. The Tabs window provides more precision and more options than setting tabs on the ruler. True or false?
   - ✓ True
   - False
7. You can clear an individual tab stop by dragging it down off the ruler.
   - ✓ True
   - False

Module C: Quick Styles

Quick Styles provide styles for headings, emphasis, and body text. Unlike defined character or paragraph styles, Quick Styles change depending on the style set and theme that is applied.

You will learn:

- About Quick Styles, style sets, and themes
- How to apply Quick Styles
- How to use style sets and themes
- How to clear formatting

Character and paragraph styles

A set of text attributes taken together is called a *style*. Styles can be saved and then applied to text in order to change several attributes at once. Styles can also be copied using the Format Painter and applied to other text.

Exam Objective: MOS Word Core 2.1.2

Character style refers to a set of character attributes. *Paragraph style* is a collection of paragraph attributes. A *linked style* can change both character and paragraph attributes at once.

Quick Styles and themes

Quick Styles are sets of styles that are meant to go together for both function and formatting. Functionally, if you use Quick Style titles and headings, Word can create a collapsible outline in the navigation pane. You can then also change the look of all the text at once by changing the theme.

The difference between styles and themes is not immediately obvious, and there is some overlap in functionality.

- You change the style from the Styles group on the Home tab. Changing a style set changes the font, color scheme, and effects, including the alignment of some elements.
- You change the theme from the Design tab. Changing the theme changes font and color scheme, but not the effects or alignment.
- The Theme button provides options for changing the font and color scheme individually.

Using Quick Styles

Using Quick Styles allows you to take advantage of Word's theme and style features, as well as use document outlines.

Exam Objective: MOS Word Core 1.3.3, 2.2.6

1. Select the text you want to format.

   For title and headings, be careful to select all of the text to be formatted, including the paragraph mark. Other styles, such as Strong or Intense, can be used on individual words.

2. On the Home tab, from the Styles gallery, select the style you want.

   The gallery reflects the currently selected style set. You can use the arrow keys at the right end of the gallery to scroll through or open the gallery. If you point to a style, you will see a preview of how it will affect the selected text.

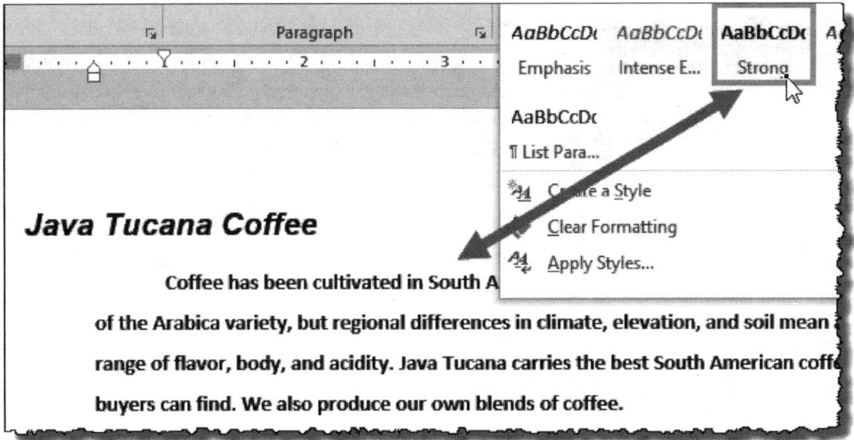

3. Repeat Steps 1 and 2 for other text.
   You can use **Format Painter** to format multiple headings and other text.

Changing styles, themes, and other attributes

You can use Quick Styles to format headings and body elements, but you can quickly change the look of an entire document by changing the style set or theme. You can also quickly change other attributes, such as color, font, and paragraph spacing.

Exam Objective: MOS Word Core 1.3.2, 1.3.3

- To change the style set, on the Design tab, select a style set in the Document Formatting group.
  Changing the style set changes all the styles in your document in a single step.

- To change the theme, click the **Themes** button in the Design tab's Document Formatting group.

You can then select a theme from the gallery. After you've applied a theme, you can hover over theme options to see a preview. Themes control the colors, fonts, and other effects of the current style set.

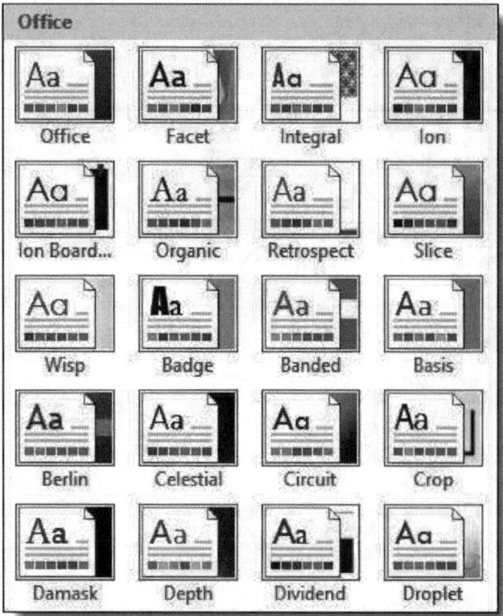

- You can further customize a theme (and thereby change the styles it governs) but using the Design tab's galleries for Colors, Fonts, Paragraph Spacing, and Effects.

  Note that the Effects button is for shapes and has no effect on text.

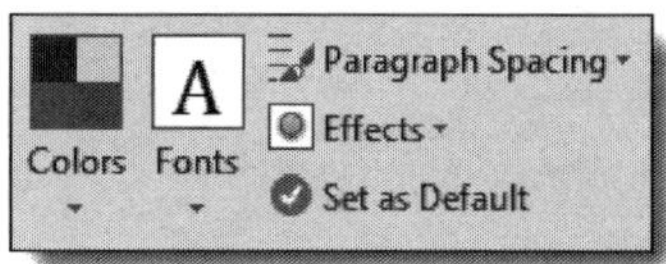

Clearing formatting

Sometimes you want to clear all previous formatting and start over with all text in the Normal, default style, which is Calibri, 11 points in Word 2016.

Exam Objective: MOS Word Core 2.2.4

1. Select the text you want to return to default formatting.
   You can press **Ctrl+A** to select the whole document.
2. On the Home tab, click .
   In the Font group.

All formatting is removed, and text is returned to the Normal style.

Exercise: Using Quick Styles

Exam Objective: MOS Word Core 1.3.2, 1.3.4, 2.2.4, 2.2.6

Do This	How & Why
1. Open `JT-Coffee`, and save it as `JT-Coffee-QS`.	From the `Formatting text` folder. The document is manually formatted with character attributes.

Do This	How & Why
2. Clear formatting in the document.	
a) Press **Ctrl+A**.	To select all the text in the document.
b) Click 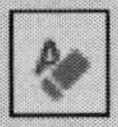 [button].	The Clear All Formatting button is in the Font group on the Home tab.
3. Select the first line.	"Java Tucana Coffee."
4. On the Home tab, in the Styles gallery, click **Title**.	To apply the Title Quick Style to the text. It is now formatted as Cambria, 26 pt, and has a line beneath the paragraph.
5. Apply the Heading 1 style to "Single-region South American coffees."	Select the line, and click **Heading 1** in the Styles gallery.
6. Apply Heading 1 to "Java Tucana's blends."	Use the Style gallery or Format Painter. This paragraph is about halfway through the document.
7. Apply Heading 2 to the coffee variety and blend headings.	Apply Heading 2 to Brazilian Bourbon Santos, then double-click the Format Painter to apply the style to the other variety and blend names. When you finish using the Format Painter, press **Esc**. The result should look like this example. 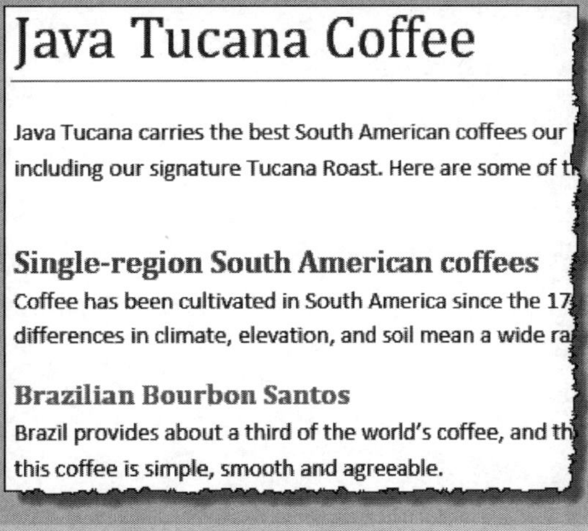
8. On the Design tab, select a different Style set.	Use the gallery in the Document Formatting group. Style Sets change all of the styles you are currently using.
9. On the Design tab, click **Themes**.	To open a list of themes.
10. Point to different themes.	A theme preview is applied immediately to the page as you point to each.
11. Click **Badge**.	The document is changed, and the Document Formatting gallery reflects the look of the current theme.
12. Save and close the file.	An example follows.

The document with Casual style and Badge theme

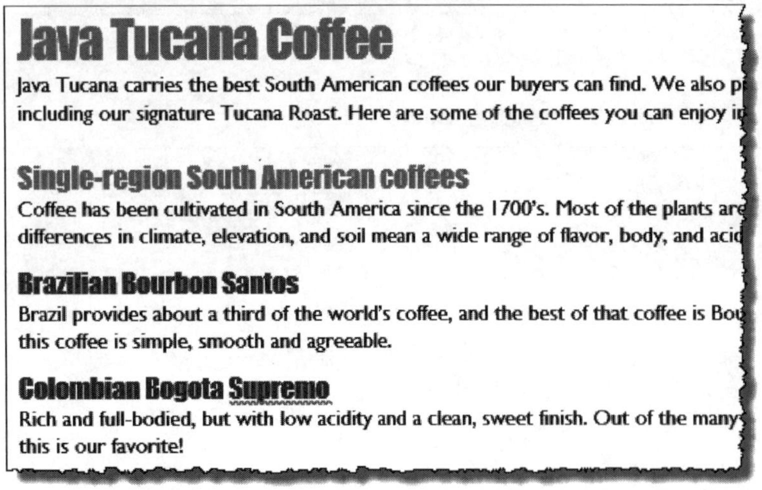

Java Tucana Coffee

Java Tucana carries the best South American coffees our buyers can find. We also p
including our signature Tucana Roast. Here are some of the coffees you can enjoy i

Single-region South American coffees

Coffee has been cultivated in South America since the 1700's. Most of the plants ar
differences in climate, elevation, and soil mean a wide range of flavor, body, and aci

Brazilian Bourbon Santos

Brazil provides about a third of the world's coffee, and the best of that coffee is Bo
this coffee is simple, smooth and agreeable.

Colombian Bogota Supremo

Rich and full-bodied, but with low acidity and a clean, sweet finish. Out of the many
this is our favorite!

Assessment: Quick Styles

1. Both themes and styles can change which two attributes?
   - Font face/color
   - Font effects
   - Paragraph spacing
   - Heading colors
   - Paragraph alignment
2. The Document Formatting group allows you to change themes, colors, fonts, and paragraph spacing individually. True or false?
   - True
   - False

Module D: Making lists

Bulleted and numbered lists are types of paragraph formatting in which a bullet or number is applied to the beginning of each paragraph.

You will learn how to:

- Start a new bulleted or numbered list
- Promote or demote list items
- Use symbols as bullets
- Use pictures as bullets

Creating lists

You can create a bulleted or numbered list with AutoFormat or with ribbon commands.

Exam Objective: MOS Word Core 3.1.1

- To start a new bulleted list with AutoFormat, type `*` and press **Space** or **Tab**.
- To start a new numbered list with AutoFormat, enter `1.` and press **Space** or **Tab**.
- To start a new list using the ribbon, click one of the list buttons in the Paragraph group on the Home tab.

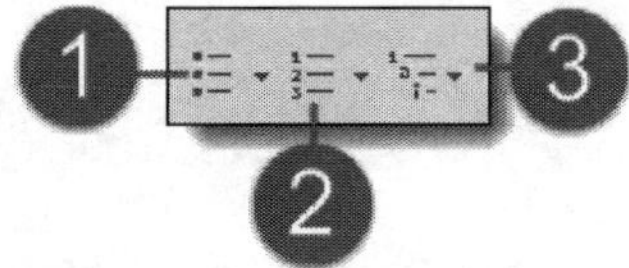

1. *Bullets* apply a character such as a dot at the beginning of each list item.
2. *Numbering* applies sequential numbers or letters to the items in the list.
3. A *Multilevel List* has an outline structure for the items.

- When you press **Enter** at the end of a list item, one of three things will happen:
  - If the current item is not empty, and new line will start with a bullet or number at the same level.
  - If the current item is empty and at the highest list level, the list will end and the paragraph will go back to a normal style.
  - If the current item is empty and not at the highest list level, it will be promoted.
- To apply bullets or numbering to existing paragraphs, select the paragraphs first, and then click the button for the type of list you want.

Exercise: Making a list

Exam Objective: MOS Word Core 3.3.1, 3.3.4

Do This	How & Why
1. Open `French Press`, and save it as `French Press lists`.	From the current chapter's folder.
2. Select the five lines under the heading.	Don't select the heading.
3. On the Home tab, click .	The Numbering button is in the Paragraph group. The steps are numbered.
4. Press the right arrow key.	To move the cursor to the end of the last line.
5. Press **Enter**.	A new step starts.
6. Enter `Depress the plunger`.	
7. Add `Pour` as the final step.	Press **Enter** and type the text.
8. Press **Enter** three times.	The first time adds a new step, the second removes the number, and the third adds a blank line.
9. Type `Notes` and press **Enter**.	
10. Type `*` and then press the space bar.	A bullet list starts.
11. Create the following list items: • Heat water to 90-95C • Use course, dust-free grinds • Steep 2-3 minutes for small pots	
12. Press **Enter** twice.	To end the list. Compare your document to the one below.
13. Save and close the document.	

Using a French press

1. Heat water, but don't boil it
2. Grind coffee coarsely
3. Pour grinds into press
4. Pour water into press
5. Put lid on press and wait 4-5 minutes
6. Depress the plunger
7. Pour

Notes

- Heat water to 90-95C
- Use coarse, dust-free grinds
- Steep 2-3 minutes for small pots

List formatting

You can control the formatting of lists in a variety of ways.

- Promote and demote list items
- Change numbering formats
- Control where the numbering begins in a numbered list
- Change bullet formats
- Use other symbols as bullets
- Use pictures as bullets

Promoting and demoting list items

You can change the list level of an item from the ribbon or from the keyboard.

Exam Objective: MOS Word Core 3.3.4

- To promote or demote list items using the ribbon, select the items, and on the Home tab, in the Paragraph group, click the **Increase Indent** button or the **Decrease Indent** button.

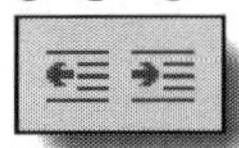

- To demote (increase indent) a list item from the keyboard, place the cursor at the beginning of the line, and press **Tab**.
- To promote (decrease indent) an item from the keyboard, place the cursor at the beginning of the line, and press **Shift+Tab**. If the line contains no text, you can instead press **Enter**.
- To demote or promote multiple list items, select the items, and press **Tab** or **Shift+Tab**, respectively.

Using symbols as bullets

You can use a symbol, letter, or number from any installed font as a bullet. The Symbol and Wingdings font families are good resources for bullet symbols.

Exam Objective: MOS Word Core 3.3.2, 3.3.3

1. On the Home tab, in the Paragraph group, click the drop-down arrow on the Bullets button.

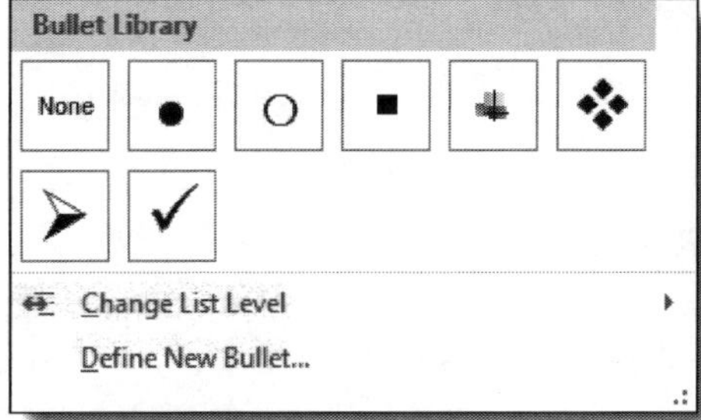

You'll see the Bullet Library, and might also see recently used bullets and document bullets, if you've used this feature before. You can click any of the symbols in the library to immediately apply it to the current level of the list.

2. Click **Define New Bullet**.

The **Define New Bullet** window opens. Here, you can define new bullet characters from any available font.

3. Click **Symbol**.

   The **Symbol** window opens.

4. Choose the symbol you want to use.

   a) Select a different font, if necessary.

   b) Select the symbol or letter, or enter the character code, if you know it.

   c) Click **OK**.

5. Click **OK**.

   You return to the document with the new bullet in place.

After you use a symbol once, it is automatically added to the bullet library.
You can repeat this process at different levels in the list hierarchy to change the symbol for all items at that level.

Using pictures as bullets

You can also use a picture file from the hard disk or from Office.com as a bullet symbol.

1. Click the drop-down arrow on the Bullets button, then click **Define New Bullet**.

   The **Define New Bullet** window opens.

2. Click **Picture**.

   The **Insert Pictures** window appears, giving you several choices for sources.

3. Select a picture source.

   - From a file: Click Browse next to this option to pick a file on your computer.
   - From SharePoint: If you are connected to a SharePoint server, you can use this option to select pictures from SharePoint.
   - Bing Image Search: Use the Bing search engine to find pictures online.

4. Select a picture and click **Insert**.

5. Click **OK** twice.

   To close both the **Picture Bullet** and the **Define New Bullet** windows.

   You return to the document with the new bullet in place.

After you use a picture once, it is added to the bullet library. You can repeat this process at different levels in the list to change the bullets for all items at that level.

Exercise: Formatting a list

Exam Objective: MOS Word Core 3.3.2, 3.3.3, 3.3.4

Do This	How & Why
1. Open `JT-Coffee-Service`, and save it as `JT-Coffee-Service-bullets`.	In the `Formatting text` folder.
2. Select the lines *between* Java Tucana Services and Java Tucana Coffee and Tea.	Do not select these headings.
3. Click [Bullets button].	The Bullets button is in the Paragraph group on the Home tab. The select paragraphs are now formatted as bullets.
4. In the list, select the three lines *between* "Cafés" and "Office coffee service."	
5. Click [Increase Indent button].	One the Home tab, in the Paragraph group. The selected paragraphs are indented one level to the right, or *demoted.*
6. Select the items *between* "Office coffee service" and "Wholesale."	
7. Press **Tab**.	This is another way to increase the indent.
8. Increase the indent for the three items under Wholesale.	
9. Click on the item Wholesale.	To place the cursor there. You don't need to select it.
10. Change the symbol for bullets at this level:	
a) Click the drop-down arrow next to the Bullets button, and click **Define New Bullet**.	
b) Click **Symbol**.	
c) Select a Font.	Wingdings are good sources for bullets.
d) Select the character you want to use, and click **OK** twice.	All bullets at this level are changed.
11. Change the symbol for the bullets at the indented level.	Put the cursor in any item at this level, and change the symbol.
12. Use **Format Painter** to apply these bullets to items under Java Tucana Coffee and Tea.	The top level should be applied to "Single-region South American Coffees" and to "Java Tucana's blends." Everything else should be at the second level.
13. Save and close the document.	An example follows.

Your document should look something like the following figure, with whatever symbols you chose.

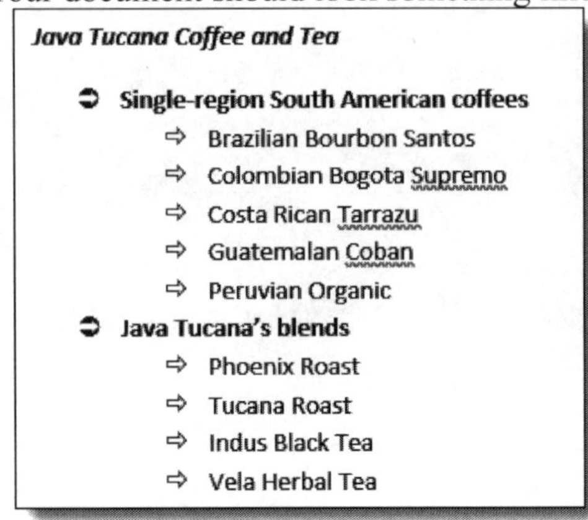

Changing numbering format in lists

You can easily change the format of the numbers in numbered list by using the Numbering Library gallery.

Exam Objective: MOS Word Core 3.3.2

1. Select a paragraph at the level of the list you want to change.
2. Click the Numbering dropdown arrow, then select a format from the gallery.

   There are numbered and lettered options to choose from. To create a new number format, click **Define New Number Format**.

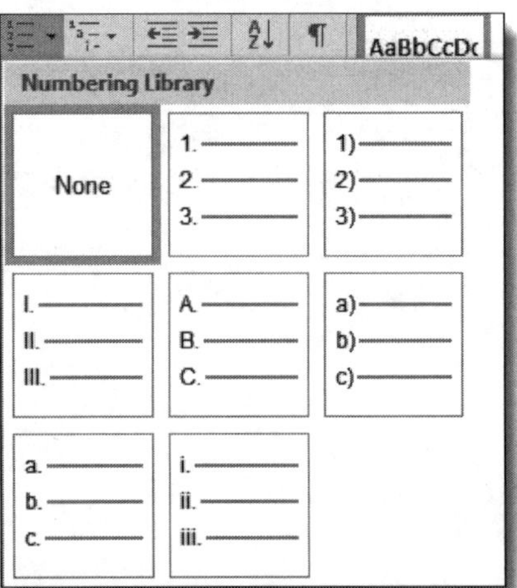

Controlling list numbering

You might sometimes find that a numbered list is continuing numbering from a previous list when you'd prefer that it start over. Or, you might have a list that you *do* want to continue from a previous one. You also might want a list to start from a particular number or letter. Here are some ways to control list numbering.

Exam Objective: MOS Word Core 3.3.5, 3.3.6

- To cause a list to continue the numbering of the previous list, right-click one of the numbers in the list you want to change, and then click **Continue Numbering**.

- To start list numbering over from "1" (or "A" or "i," depending on your format), right-click a number and then click **Restart at 1**.
- To start list numbering from a specific number, right-click a number, and then click **Set Numbering Value**.

  You can then use the **Set Numbering Value** window to control whether this is a new list or a continuation, and what the starting value will be (by using the "Set value to" control).

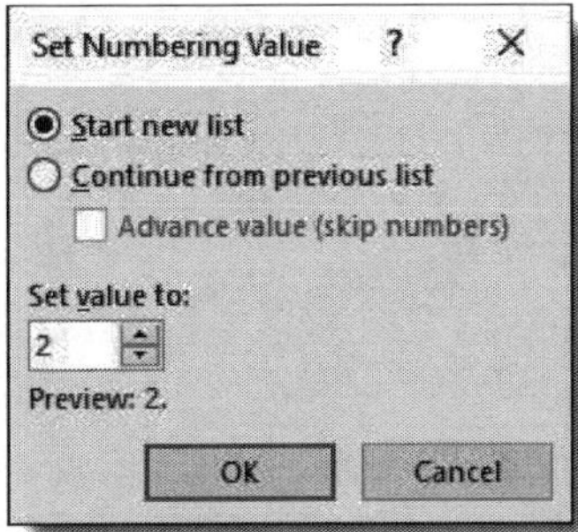

Exercise: Formatting numbered lists

Exam Objective: MOS Word Core 3.3.5

Do This	How & Why
1. Open `Café Latté` and save it as `Café Latté Numbered`.	This document contains a simple recipe for café latté. You will format it in a couple of ways to experiment with numbered lists.
2. Select all the paragraphs after "Prepare the milk".	
3. Click [numbered list button].	To create a numbered list. This is ok, but we actually want "Prepare the latté" to be a heading, not part of the list.
4. Select **Prepare the latté**, then click [numbered list button].	The text is no longer part of the list, but the list before it continues the numbering of the previous list. 1. Warm milk over medium heat. 2. Whisk the milk to a froth. *Prepare the latté* 3. Make a half cup of espresso for each cup. 4. Pour milk, but not foam, into each cup. 5. Spoon foam onto the top of each cup.
Continued...	

Do This	How & Why
5. Right-click within step 3, then click **Restart at 1**.	Adjust List Indents... Restart at 1 Continue Numbering Set Numbering Value... Now the second list starts at 1. Sometimes, you will need to correct lists in this manner. If a list restarts numbering, but you want to continue the numbering from a previous list, right-click the step and click **Continue Numbering**.
6. Undo all the numbering you just did.	Click Undo several times. Now, you'll look at formatting options for a multilevel list.
7. Select all the paragraphs after the main heading, "Making Café Latté".	
8. Format the selected paragraphs as a numbered list.	Click .
9. Promote the steps under "Prepare the milk" and "Prepare the latté".	Select the steps, then click . The document should look like this. *1. Prepare the milk* a. Warm milk over medium heat. b. Whisk the milk to a froth. *2. Prepare the latté* a. Make a half cup of espresso for each cup. b. Pour milk, but not foam, into each cup. c. Spoon foam onto the top of each cup.
10. Observe the multilevel list options.	Select all the steps in the list, then click . There are
11. Press **Esc** to close the gallery.	
12. Save and then close the document	

About·Java·Tucana¶

Java·Tucana·Services¶

Office·coffee·service¶

We'll·supply·your·office·with·early·morning·deliveries·of·coffee,·tea,·bagels,·fruit,·and·other·goodies.·We·have·whole·bean,·ground,·and·single·serving·options.·We·also·offer·rental·and·maintenance·of·coffee·brewing·systems.·If·you·have·a·problem·with·any·of·our·equipment,·in·most·cases·we'll·repair·or·replace·it·the·same·day.·Call·or·email·for·details·and·a·cost·estimate.¶

Wholesale¶

If·you·own·a·coffee·shop,·deli,·restaurants,·or·any·commercial·enterprise·that·can·sell·coffee,·then·you·can·sell·Java·Tucana·coffee!·We·sell·to·vendors·at·wholesale·prices,·and·our·coffee·will·bring·you·more·business.·We·have·our·own·coffee·and·tea·blends,·as·well·as·selections·of·South·American·coffees·and·popular·teas.·We·sell·whole·bean,·ground,·or·single·servings.·Some·varieties·are·available·in·decaf.¶

Cafés¶

Java·Tucana·has·cafés·in·many·major·cities.·See·our·website·for·locations,·hours,·and·menus,·and·more.·While·we·distribute·our·coffee·and·tea·nationally,·we·are·committed·to·local·trade·whenever·possible.·Our·cafés·seek·out·local·bakers,·grocers,·and·farmers·for·the·pastries,·bread,·and·produce·that·we·serve,·so·you·know·you're·eating·fresh,·local·food.¶

Java·Tucana·Coffee¶

Java·Tucana·carries·the·best·South·American·coffees·our·buyers·can·find.·We·also·produce·our·own·blends·of·coffee,·including·our·signature·Tucana·Roast.·Here·are·some·of·the·coffees·you·can·enjoy·in·our·cafés·or·at·home:¶

Single-region·South·American·coffees·¶
- Brazilian·Bourbon·Santos¶
- Colombian·Bogota·Supremo¶
- Costa·Rican·Tarrazu¶
- Guatemalan·Coban¶
- Peruvian·Organic¶

Java·Tucana's·blends¶
- Phoenix·Roast¶
- Tucana·Roast¶

Assessment: Making lists

1. Which character do you type at the beginning of a line, followed by Space or Tab, to start a new bulleted list?

   - Period (.)
   - Asterisk (*)
   - Plus sign (+)
   - Hyphen (-)

2. You can use any character from any installed font as a bullet. True or false?

   - True
   - False

3. Which of the following are methods you can use to increase the indent level of (demote) a selected list item? Choose all correct responses.

   - Press Alt+Space
   - Press Tab
   - Press Alt+Tab
   - Click Increase Indent on the Home tab
   - Press Space

Summary: Formatting text

You should now know how to:

- Format characters by using the ribbon, and copy formatting using Format Painter
- Change paragraph attributes such as indents and line spacing, control indents, and set and use various kinds of tab stops
- Understand the different between character and paragraph styles, use Quick Styles to quickly format your documents, control the appearance of styles by using themes, and clear formatting
- Create bulleted and numbered lists, promote or demote items in a list, and control numbering format and bullet characters

Synthesis: Formatting text

1. Open `About Us` and save it as `About Us formatted`.
2. Format the following using Quick Styles:
   - The first line with **Title**
   - Java Tucana Services and Java Tucana Coffee with **Heading 1**
   - Headings under Java Tucana Services with **Heading 2**
3. Indent the entire service paragraphs by one-half inch.
4. Format the lists of coffees with bullets:
   - The top-level bullets should be "Single-region South American coffees" and "Java Tucana's blends."
   - Specific coffee names should be indented one level.

   Compare your document to the figure following the exercise.
5. Change the symbols used in both levels of the bulleted list.
6. Change any combination of styles, themes, colors, fonts, and spacing to achieve a look you like.
7. Save and close the document.

The document after step 3

Chapter 3: Document setup

You will learn how to:

- Change page layout settings, use columns, and control section breaks
- Check document spelling and grammar, and use AutoCorrect
- Print documents, and add and control headers and footers
- Base new documents on templates

Module A: Page layout

There are a number of ways to adjust page layout so that each new page looks the way you want at the start. The most commonly used of these options is setting the margin widths.

You will learn how to:

- Change margins
- Adjust pagination setting and add page breaks
- Change the way Word hyphenates
- Format text in columns
- Insert section breaks

Page layout

Most page layout settings can be managed on the Page Layout tab, and most of what you'll use is in the Page Setup group and window. Here you can set margins and orientation, set options for multiple pages (such as having facing pages mirror each other), select paper, and set options for sections, headers, and footers.

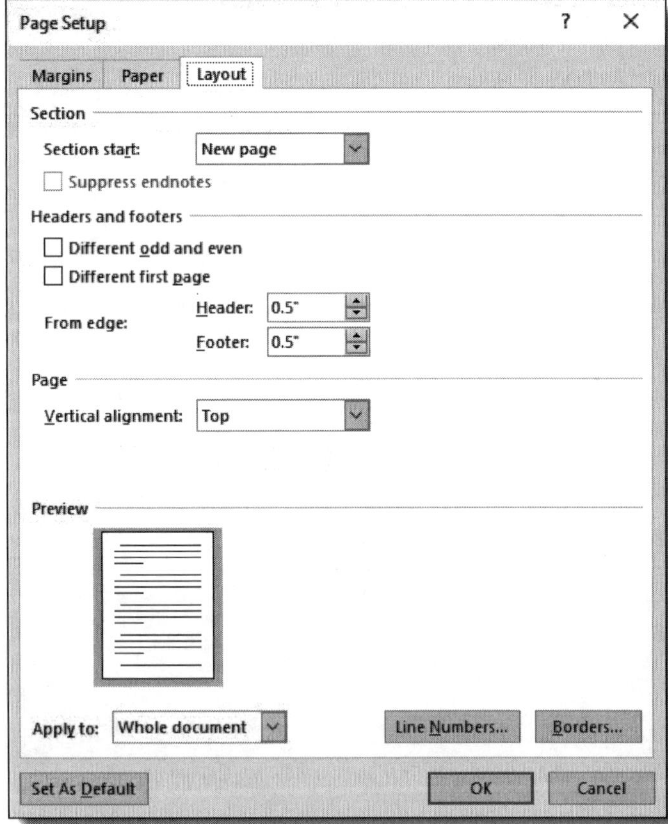

Other options can be set in the **Paragraph** window, which is available from both the Home and the Page Layout tabs.

Setting margins

You can select from a number of predefined margin widths, or you can define custom margins.

Exam Objective: MOS Word Core 1.3.1

1. On the Page Layout tab, click **Margins**.

   A gallery of predefined margins opens.

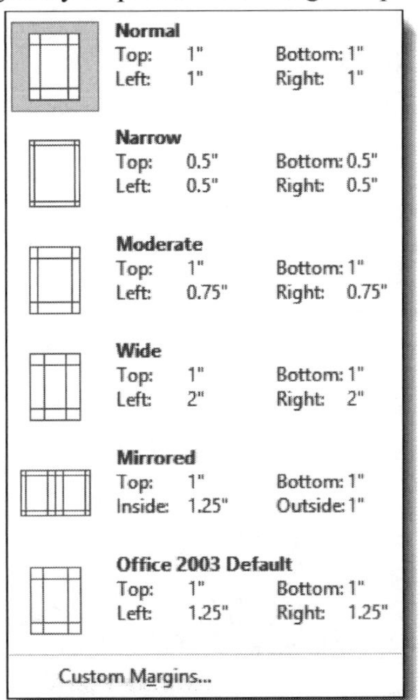

2. Select the margin layout you want.
3. If none of the predefined margins meets your needs, create your own:
   a) At the bottom of the margins gallery, click **Custom Margins**.

      The **Page Setup** window opens, with the Margins tab active.

   b) Enter values for the top, bottom, left, and right margins.

      To make your custom margins the default for all new documents, click **Set As Default**.

   c) Click **OK**.

The margins are adjusted for the document.

Adding breaks and non-breaking spaces

You can force line breaks without starting a new paragraph. You can also force page breaks or insert blank pages into a document. To see these normally hidden characters, click ¶ (the Show/Hide button) on the Home tab. Often, showing paragraph and space symbols can be very helpful in understanding exactly what is happening in your document.

Exam Objective: MOS Word Core 1.4.6, 2.3.2

- To add a line break without starting a new paragraph, press **Shift+Enter**.

  If hidden characters are shown, the line break character looks like an Enter or Return symbol.

  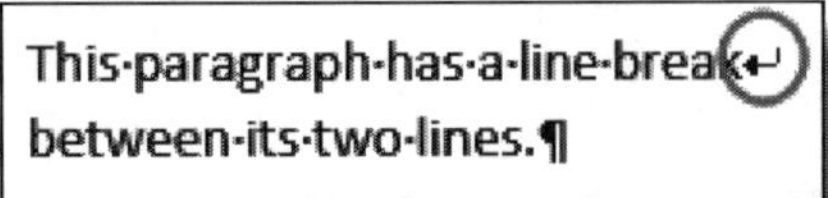

- To add a non-breaking space between words, press **Ctrl+Shift+Space**.

  This keeps words together and prevents a line break between them.

  If hidden characters are shown, the non-breaking space looks like a small circle at the top of the space, like this:

- To add a page break, press **Ctrl+Enter**; or on the Insert tab, click **Page Break**.

  If hidden characters are shown, you'll see a dotted line and the words Page Break:

  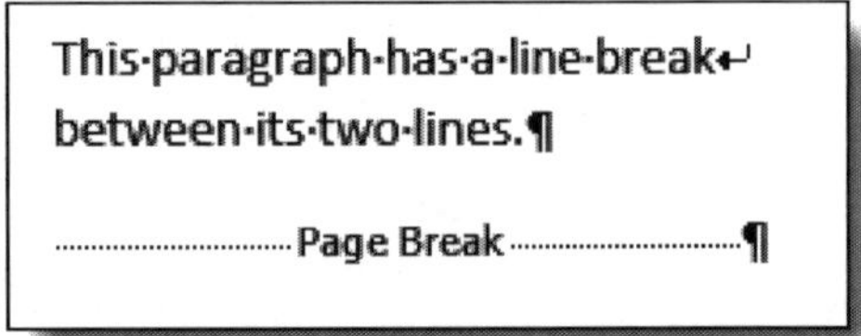

- To add a blank page, add two consecutive page breaks, or click **Blank Page** on the Insert tab.
- Like any other characters, you can remove line breaks, non-breaking spaces, and page breaks by deleting them.

Using hyphenation

By default, Word does not use hyphenation. If a word is too long to fit at the end of a line of text, it is automatically bumped down, or "wrapped," to the next line. You can add hyphenation manually or automatically.

Exam Objective: MOS Word Expert 2.1.3

1. On the Page Layout tab, click **Hyphenation**.

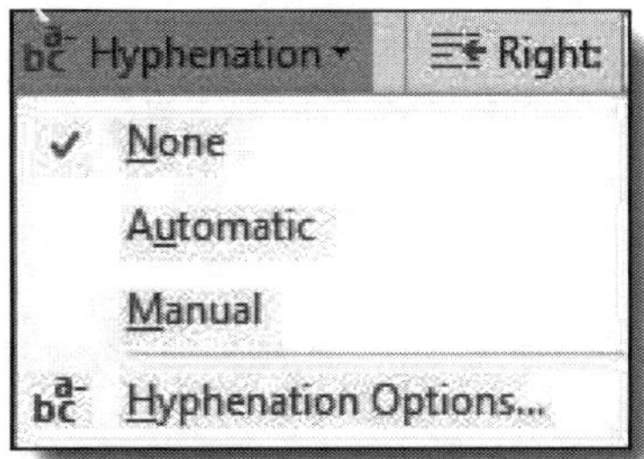

2. Click one of these options:
   - **Automatic** automatically hyphenates words that can be split.
   - **Manual** steps through the document and suggest words to be hyphenated. You accept, reject, or edit the suggestions.

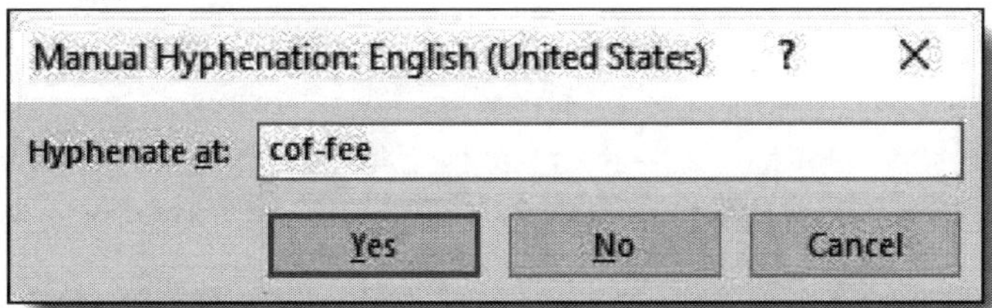

   - **Hyphenation Options** opens the **Hyphenation** window, where you can set automatic or manual hyphenation. You can also specify a maximum number of lines in a row in which a hyphen may appear, and a minimum distance from the edge that words should be hyphenated. Words that start closer to the edge than this are bumped to the next line, even if they could be hyphenated.

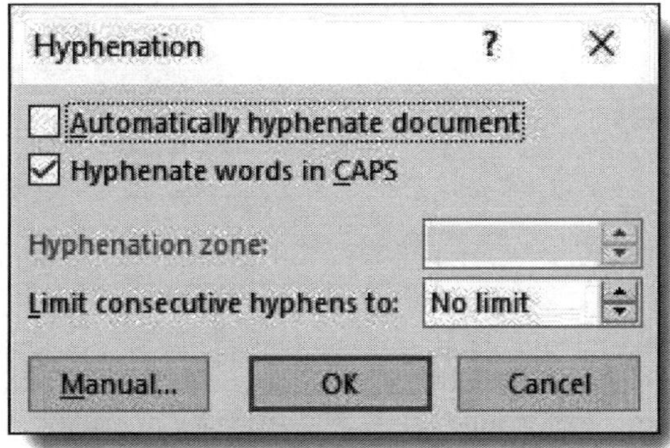

Showing line numbers

Sometimes, it's useful to show line numbers in a document, such as when proofing documents or when using them for legal purposes.

Exam Objective: MOS Word Core 2.1.3

1. On the Layout tab, in the Page Setup group, click **Line Numbers**.

   To display the Line Numbers menu.

   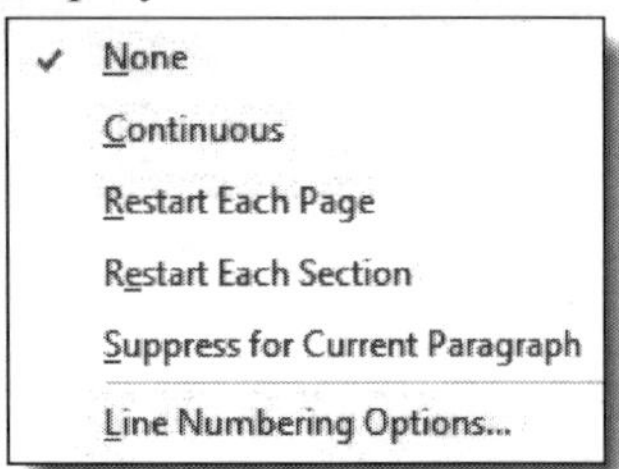

2. Click an option.

   You can have line numbers run continuously throughout the document, restart on each page, or restart for each section.

3. For more control, click **Line Numbering Options**.

Pagination

When the first line or last line of a paragraph is left alone on a page, it can be hard to read and looks bad. Word allows you some control over what happens when paragraphs cross page breaks. To use these options, select the paragraphs you want to adjust, open the **Paragraph** window, and click the **Line and Page Breaks** tab.

Exam Objective: MOS Word Expert 2.1.5

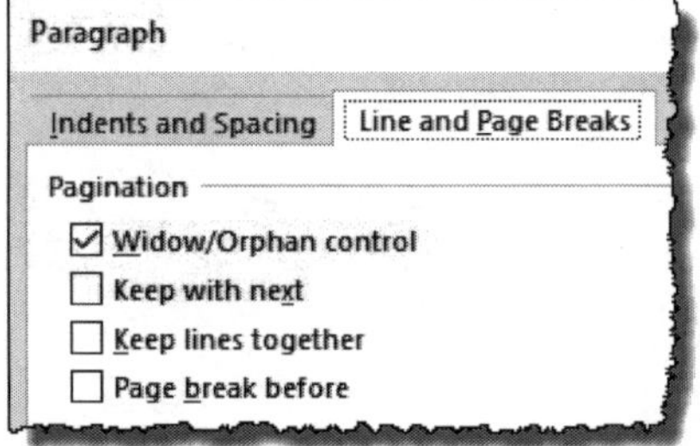

Here are the options you have under Pagination:

Window/Orphan control	Prevents first or last lines of the selected paragraph(s) from being left alone on a page. If the last line of a paragraph is by itself at the top of a page, Word pushes the second-to-last line down with it. If the first line of a paragraph is alone at the bottom of a page, Word pushes it down so the paragraph begins on the next page.
Keep with next	Keeps the selected paragraph on the same page as the next paragraph. This is useful for headings that should stay with the text that follows.
Keep lines together	Keeps all of the selected paragraphs on the same page.
Page break before	Inserts a page break before the selected paragraph.

Widow/Orphan control is enabled by default and applies to the whole document, but you can change settings for individual paragraphs.

Exercise: Changing basic page layout

Exam Objective: MOS Word Core 2.1.3 and Expert 2.3.2

Do This	How & Why
1. Open `About JT`, and save it as `About JT Layout`.	From the current chapter's data folder.
2. Show symbols in the document.	If necessary. Click ¶. It's useful to show symbols when doing any kind of document layout work.
3. Place the cursor at the start of the Java Tucana Coffees heading.	You will insert a page break so that this heading begins on a new page. JAVA·TUCANA·COFFEES¶ Java·Tucana·carries·the·best·South·American·coffees·our·buyers·ca coffee,·including·our·signature·Tucana·Roast.·Here·are·some·of·the
4. Hold down **Ctrl** and press **Enter**.	To insert a hard page break and force the heading onto the next page. The text now flows onto a third page.
5. Observe the hard page break symbol.	It is at the bottom of the previous page. Anything you type or enter after this symbol will go on the next page. To delete a hard page break, you simply delete this symbol. That's one reason why showing symbols is useful; without them, it can be difficult to tell exactly where the hard page break is. ....Page Break............¶
6. On the Layout tab, click **Margins > Moderate**.	This makes the side margins a little narrower, allowing all the text to fit on two pages.
7. On the Page Layout tab, click **Hyphenation > Automatic**.	Several words in the document are now split across lines with hyphens.
8. Turn "Set hyphenation" back to **None**.	Hyphenation doesn't generally look good, and should only be used if saving every character of space is critical.
9. Save and close the document.	

Columns

You can format your document into two or more columns. Though the default values will often suffice, Word gives you control over the width of each column and the space between columns. As with other formatting options, columns can be applied to the whole document or only to the sections you want. Even without creating section breaks, you can specify that columns are applied only to selected text or only from the cursor location onward.

Creating simple column layouts

To use default setting and quickly format a document in columns, here's what you do.

Exam Objective: MOS Word Core 2.3.1

1. Select the location where you want to have columns, or select the text that you want to format in columns.
2. On the Layout tab, click **Columns**.

   A gallery appears with several possible options.

   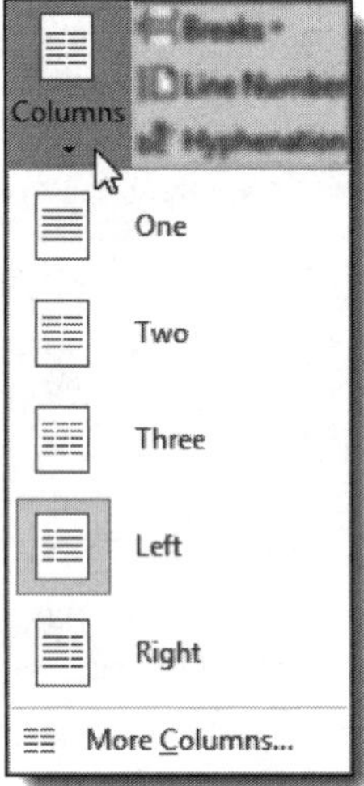

3. Click an option.
   - Click **One**, **Two**, or **Three** to create that many columns.
   - Clicking **Left** or **Right** will format the text in two columns with the left or right column bigger than the other.
   - For more control, click **More Columns** to display the **Columns** window. Here, you can choose the number of columns, set their width and the space between them, and add lines between them. You can also choose to apply the columns to the whole document, to selected text, or from the cursor location onward. The minimum width for a column is half an inch, so the number of columns you can fit on a page depends on the width of the page, the column spacing, and the margins.

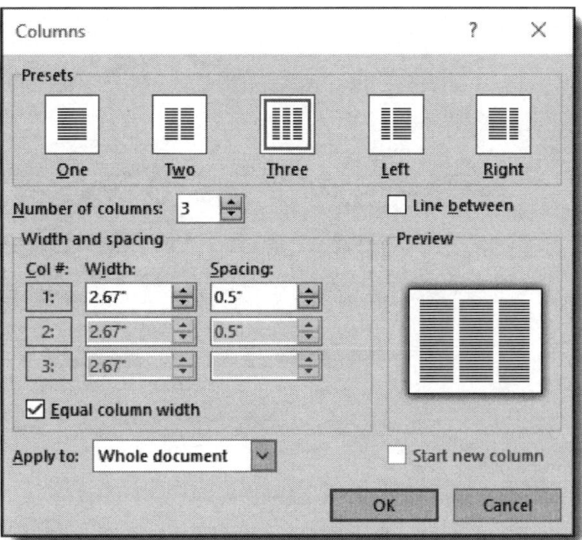

Inserting column breaks

To insert a column break, place the insertion point where you want it, then, on the Layout tab, click **Breaks**, then click **Column**.

Exercise: Using columns

Exam Objective: MOS Word Core 2.3.1

Do This	How & Why
1. Open `Services` and save it as `Services Columns`.	This document describes Java Tucana services. The cursor should be at the top of the page.
2. Verify that symbols are showing in the document.	Click the Show/Hide button if necessary.
3. On the Layout tab. click **Columns** > **Two**.	The document is split into two columns. When you choose a column setting when the cursor is in flashing, the setting will apply to the entire section of the document. This document has just one section. You'll learn more about sections soon.
4. Place the cursor just before "South American Coffees."	Before the "S" but on the same line.
5. On the Layout tab, click **Breaks** > **Column**.	To force the text into the next column.
6. Undo the first two steps.	Press **Ctrl+Z** twice to return to the document as it was when you opened it.
Continued...	

Do This	How & Why
7. Select the first three paragraphs and headings under Java Tucana Services.	Don't select the main heading.
8. Click **Columns > Three**.	The selection is split across three columns. Because these paragraphs are the same size, the headings ended up at the top of the columns. If they don't you can add column breaks to adjust the heading locations. See the example following the exercise.
9. Click **Columns > More Columns** and observe the options.	You can adjust the number of columns, column and spacing widths, and other options.
10. Click **Cancel**.	To close the window.
11. Put the South American coffees and their descriptions into two columns.	
a) Select the coffees and their descriptions.	Do not select the "South American Coffees" heading or the paragraph that follows it.
b) Click **Columns > Two**.	On the Layout tab. The coffees appear in two columns, but most of the text is in the first column.
12. Insert a column break before Costa Rican Tarrazu.	
a) Click before "Costa Rican Tarrazu".	
b) Click **Breaks > Column**.	The columns of coffee are better balanced this way.
13. Save but do not close the document.	

Formatting the Java Tucana South American Coffees section in two columns

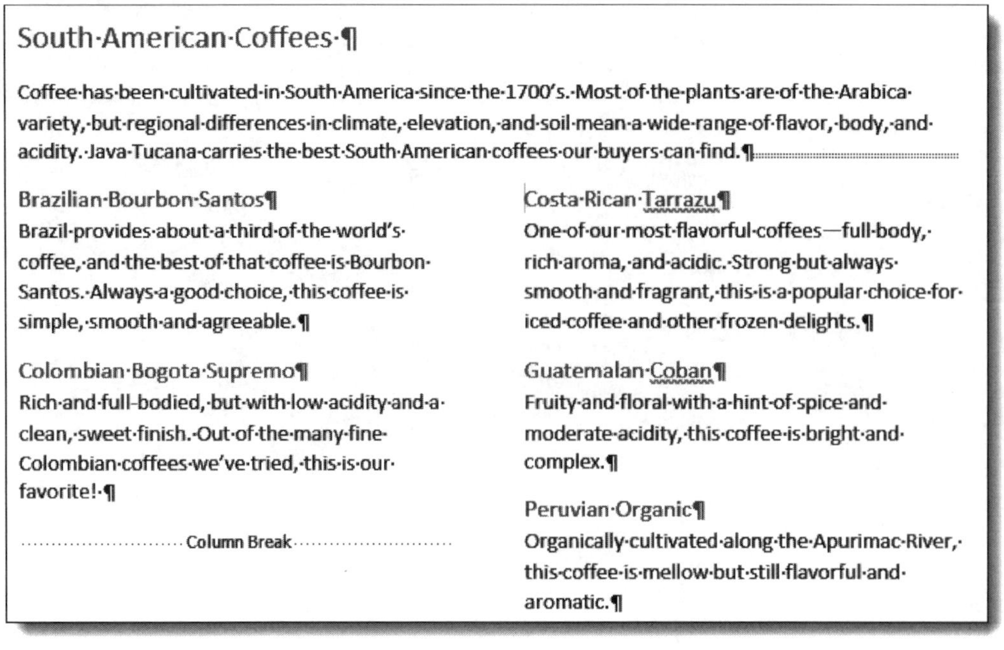

South·American·Coffees·¶

Coffee·has·been·cultivated·in·South·America·since·the·1700's.·Most·of·the·plants·are·of·the·Arabica· variety,·but·regional·differences·in·climate,·elevation,·and·soil·mean·a·wide·range·of·flavor,·body,·and· acidity.·Java·Tucana·carries·the·best·South·American·coffees·our·buyers·can·find.¶

Brazilian·Bourbon·Santos¶
Brazil·provides·about·a·third·of·the·world's· coffee,·and·the·best·of·that·coffee·is·Bourbon· Santos.·Always·a·good·choice,·this·coffee·is· simple,·smooth·and·agreeable.¶

Colombian·Bogota·Supremo¶
Rich·and·full-bodied,·but·with·low·acidity·and·a· clean,·sweet·finish.·Out·of·the·many·fine· Colombian·coffees·we've·tried,·this·is·our· favorite!·¶

Column Break

Costa·Rican·Tarrazu¶
One·of·our·most·flavorful·coffees—full·body,· rich·aroma,·and·acidic.·Strong·but·always· smooth·and·fragrant,·this·is·a·popular·choice·for· iced·coffee·and·other·frozen·delights.¶

Guatemalan·Coban¶
Fruity·and·floral·with·a·hint·of·spice·and· moderate·acidity,·this·coffee·is·bright·and· complex.¶

Peruvian·Organic¶
Organically·cultivated·along·the·Apurimac·River,· this·coffee·is·mellow·but·still·flavorful·and· aromatic.¶

Sections

Understanding *sections* is very important to working effectively in Word. Many types of document setup—such as column layouts, margins, and headers and footers—are specific to a section of the document. A new document has only one sections, but you can insert section breaks when you want different document setup in different parts of the document. Some things you do—such as creating columns on only part of a document—automatically create sections.

Working with sections

When you want to create a new document setup of some kind in the same document, you will need to insert a section break. You can also specify that the status bar show the section number you are in.

Here are some ways to work with sections.

- Click ¶ to show symbols when working with multiple sections. This helps you to see exactly where the breaks are.
- To insert a section break, on the Layout tab, click Breaks, then click an option under Section Breaks.

  Next Page will start a new section on the next page, while Continuous will start a new section right where you are. The other two options allow you to have facing-page setups like in most books.

  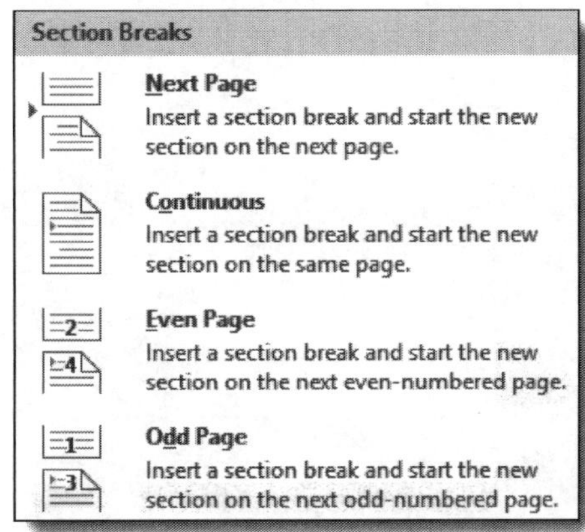

- To show the section number on the Status bar, right-click it and then click **Section**.

Exercise: Observing how sections work

Services Columns should be open.

Do This	How & Why
1. Verify that symbols are showing.	You should see paragraph marks, spaces, and other symbols in the document. If you don't, click the Show/Hide button on the Home tab. Symbols are very useful when working with sections and breaks.
2. Observe the section breaks in the document.	There is one after the first heading. This is because that heading is in a part of the document that has a single column, while the next section of the document has three columns.
3. Where are the other section breaks in the document?	There is one after the services columns, then one more before the columns of coffee descriptions.
4. Right-click the Status bar, then click **Sections**.	To show section numbers on the status bar.
5. Click in the **South American Coffees** heading.	You can see that this is Section 3 by looking at the Status bar.
6. Go to the end of the document.	Press **Ctrl+End**. This is Section 4.
7. Click **Breaks > Continuous**.	On the Layout tab. There is now a fifth section, which is set up in two columns. When you use a continuous section break, the new section inherits the layout of the previous one.
8. Undo the section break, and insert a next page section break.	
a) Click .	To remove the section break.
b) Click **Breaks > Next Page**.	Now, the new section begins on a new page. But it still inherits layout settings from the previous section, such as being in two columns.
9. Click **Columns > One**.	To specify that section 5 have just a single column.
10. Save and close the document.	

Assessment: Page layout

1. Which of the following key combinations will insert a page break?
   - Shift+Enter
   - Ctrl+Enter
   - Ctrl+P
   - Shift+Enter
2. By default, Word will not hyphenate long words over a line break. True or false?
   - True
   - False
3. What setting prevents first and last lines of a paragraph from being left alone on a page?
   - Changeling control
   - Line item control
   - Abandoned line control
   - Widow/Orphan control
4. What is the minimum width for a column in Word?
   - .25 inches
   - .5 inches
   - .75 inches
   - 1 inch
5. Section numbers appear on the Status bar by default. True or false?
   - True
   - False

Module B: Proofing documents

You will learn how to:

- Proof a document by checking its spelling and grammar.
- Use AutoCorrect and add AutoCorrect entries

Automatic spell checking

Word checks spelling and grammar continually and automatically by default. When it finds a possible error, Word underlines the word or phrase with a wavy line in either of two colors:

- Red indicates the word is misspelled or is not in the current dictionary.
- Blue indicates grammatical and typographic errors, such as two spaces between words. It also indicates a contextual spelling error—that the word is spelled correctly but is possibly not the word you meant. Examples would be using "your" when you meant "you're" or "it's" when you meant "its." Word's proofing options can also be set to check for issues such as sentence fragments, subject-verb disagreement, or run-on sentences; however, these options are not selected by default.

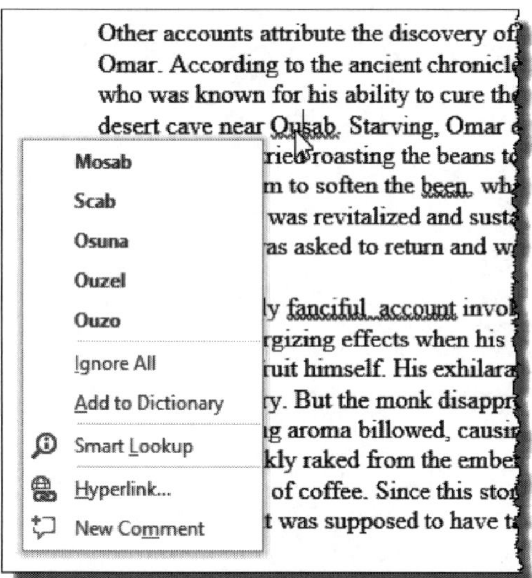

To address these issues, right-click the underlined text, and click the appropriate option. Word may suggest one or more terms, though it doesn't always have a suggested correction.

Sometimes, a proper name or an uncommon word will be flagged as a misspelling. In this case, you can choose to ignore all instances of the word in the document, or you can select and add the word to the dictionary, so that it is not flagged in the future. If you choose Ignore or Ignore All, and the underline will be removed.

Using the Spelling and Grammar panes

Although Word continually checks spelling and grammar on the fly, you might want to check an entire document at once, for instance, if you are editing or reviewing someone else's document.

1. On the Review tab, click **Spelling & Grammar**.
   The **Spelling** pane or **Grammar** pane opens, depending on the type of the first error found, if there is one.

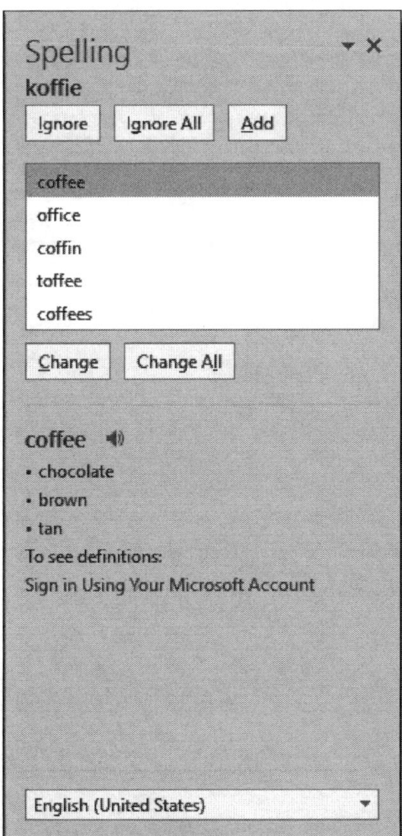

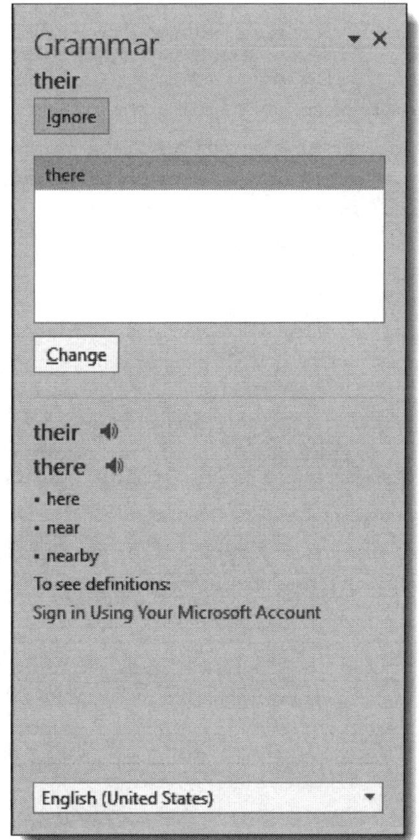

2. Take one of several actions:
   - Click **Ignore** to remove the underlining and move to the next issue.
   - Click **Ignore All** to remove the underlining from and ignore all instances of the term.
   - Click **Add** so that Word considers the term correct, even in other documents.
   - Select a suggestion, or edit in the window, and click **Change** or **Change All**.

   The **Options** button opens the Proofing options for Word, where you can change spelling and grammar settings.

Proofing options

To open proofing options, on the File tab, click **Options**, then click the **Proofing** category in the left pane.

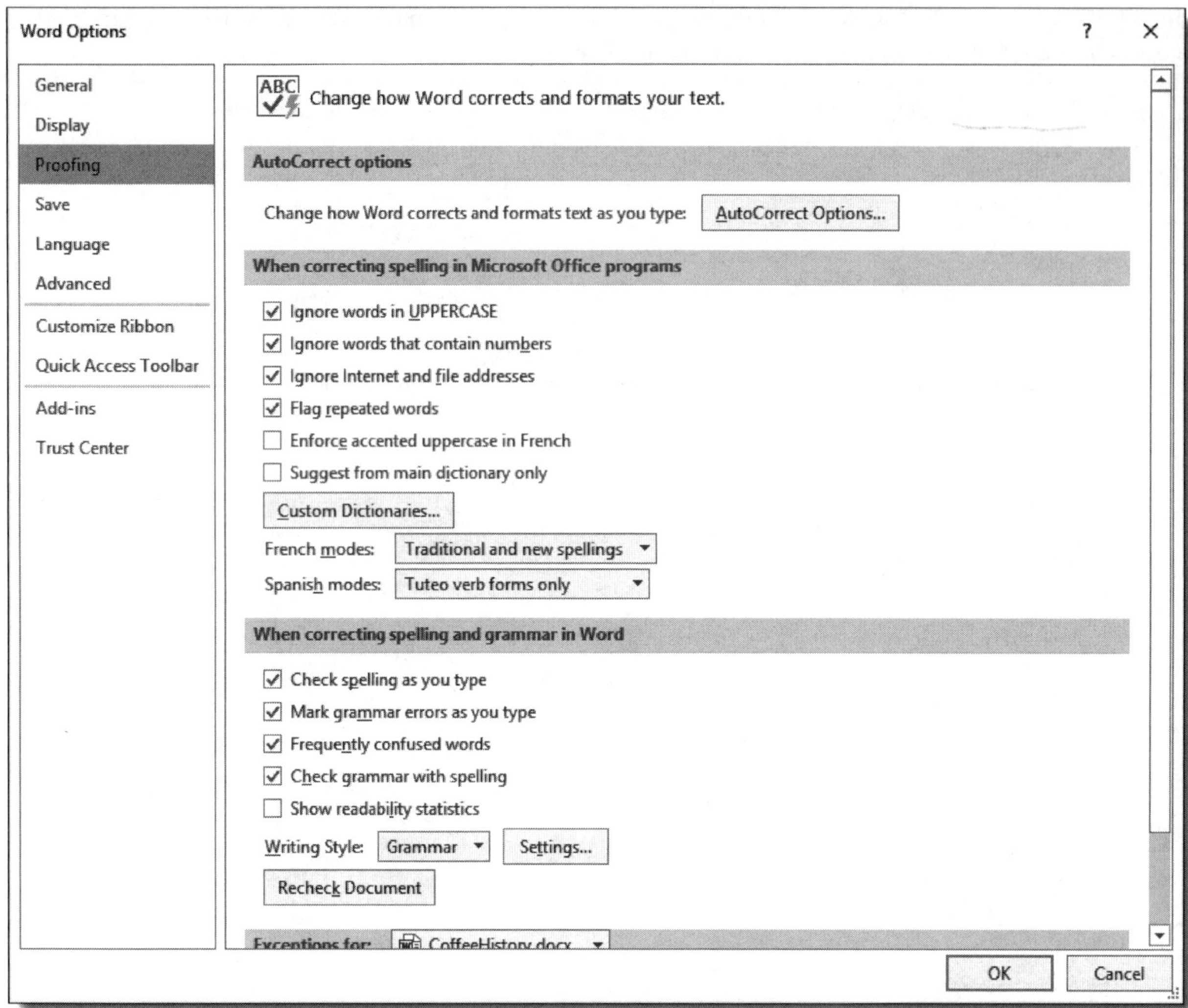

There are check boxes for many spelling and grammar options, as well as buttons to open AutoCorrect options, custom dictionaries, and grammar settings.

To change the language Word uses to proof a document, click **Language** on the Review tab.

Grammar settings

To open Grammar Settings from the Proofing options, click the **Settings** button.

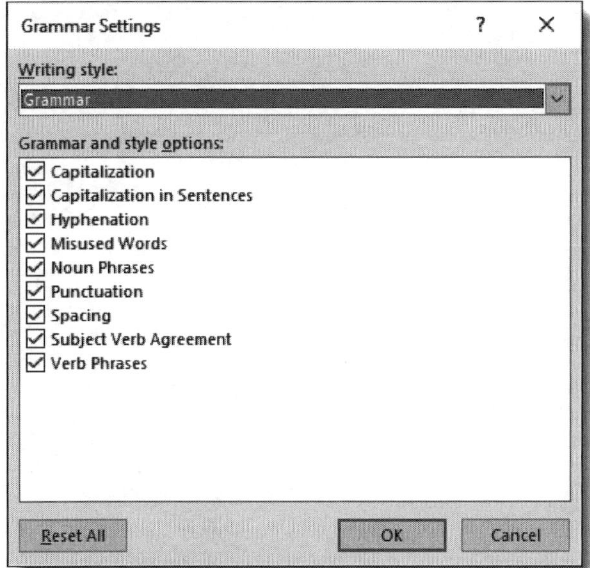

The **Grammar Settings** window provides options for both grammar and punctuation. By default, Word checks only for grammar issues such as proper capitalization, sentence fragments, and subject-verb agreement, among others.

Exercise: Proofing a document

Do This	How & Why
1. Open `Coffee in the Americas`, and save it as `Coffee in the Americas-ed`.	
2. Scan the document for errors.	You should see underlines in red and blue, indicating errors of spelling, and grammar and word choice, respectively.
3. At the end of the first full paragraph, right-click the word "their" underlined in blue.	A context menu provides another spelling option for this word ("there"). You can simply click on the suggested word to replace the error.
4. On the Review tab, click **Spelling & Grammar**.	To open the **Grammar** pane. It contains the two spellings, "their" and "there", and their definitions. The suggested replacement word, "there", is selected in the box.

Do This	How & Why
5. Click **Change**.	In the Grammar pane. The word is replaced in the sentence to correct it. The pane now shows the next issue that it found, and is now called the Spelling pane.
6. Observe the first spelling issue.	The Spelling pane shows that "Réunion" might be misspelled. But this is actually the name of an island and is correct.
7. Click **Ignore**.	To ignore the word and move to the next, "arabica", which needs to be capitalize.
8. Click **Change**.	To correct the error.
9. Continue to proof the document: a) Review each flagged item. b) If there is an error, select the right suggestion, and click **Change**. c) If the word is correct but unrecognized, click **Ignore**.	
10. When the spelling and grammar check is complete, click **OK**.	
11. Save and close the document.	

AutoCorrect

The term AutoCorrect is a bit of a misnomer: In many cases, AutoCorrect replaces a combination of common characters with characters or symbols that are not on a typical keyboard. For instance, the characters `(c)` are replaced by the copyright symbol.

Exam Objective: MOS Word Core 2.1.3

To open the **AutoCorrect** window, in Backstage view, click **Options**, then click **Proofing**, and finally click the **AutoCorrect Options** button.

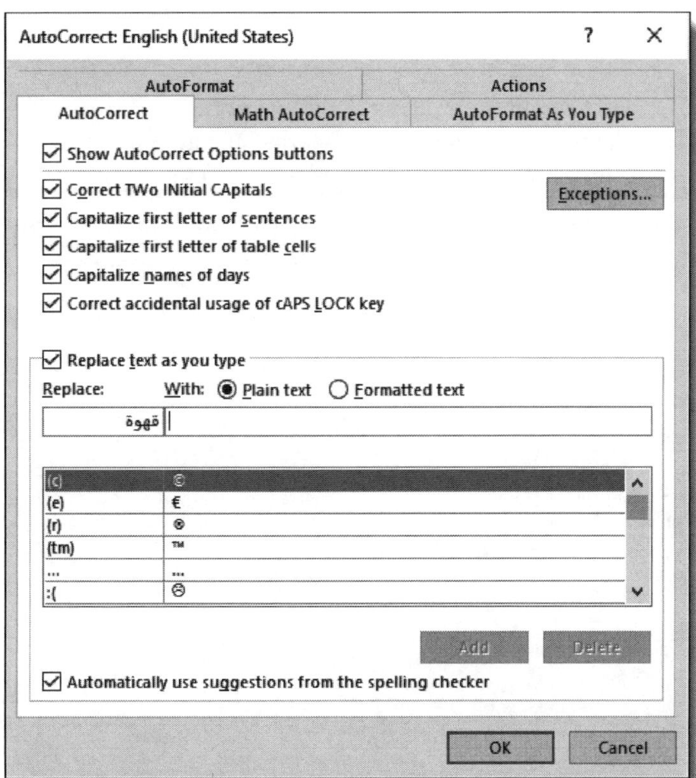

AutoCorrect capitalizes the first letter of a sentence. It also corrects instances of two capital letters starting the first word of a sentence, assuming this to be a mistake, such as "THe." You might want to add or remove exceptions for these rules, for instance, if there is a term you use that starts with two capital letters, or an abbreviation that ends in a period. Many abbreviations and the term "IDs" are already included in the exceptions.

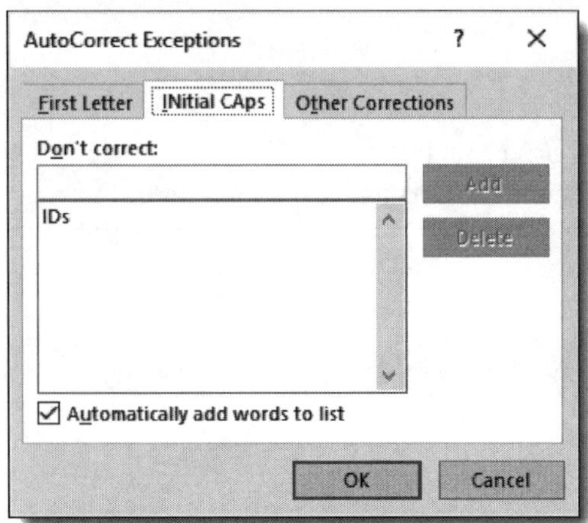

The **AutoCorrect** window also has tabs for AutoFormat and AutoFormat As You Type options. These options include such things as replacing straight quotation marks with angled quotation marks, and automatically starting numbered and bulleted lists when you begin a line with a number or asterisk, respectively.

The Math Autocorrect tab is specifically for mathematical symbols and formulas. The Actions tab allows you to add options to the right-click menu for text in a format that Word recognizes. For instance, if you right-click a date or phone number, you can access your calendar or contacts.

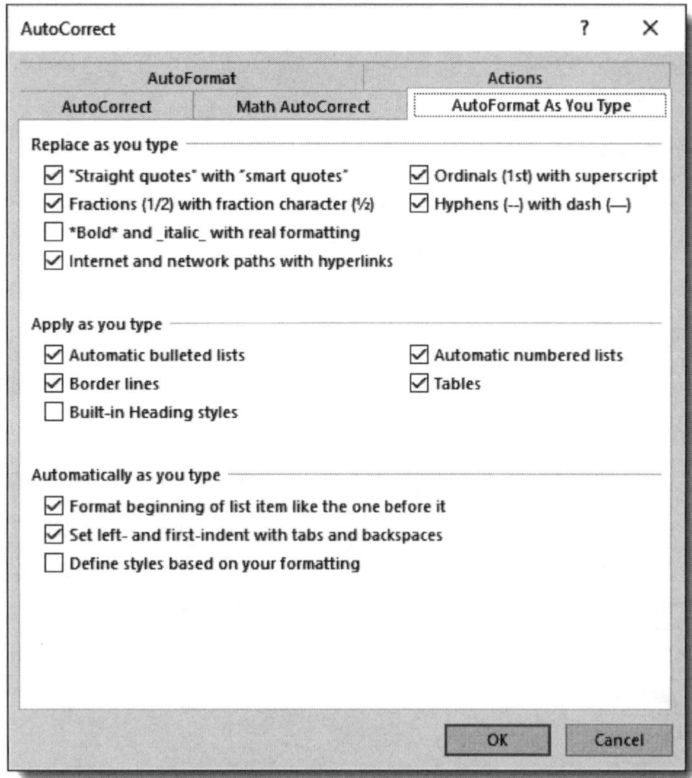

Although AutoFormat and AutoCorrect features are normally useful, there are situations in which the automatic replacements are an unwelcome nuisance, in which case you can turn off the corrections you don't want.

Creating an AutoCorrect entry

If you have text you type often, such as your full name, your company's address, or a descriptive product paragraph, you can create an AutoText entry to quickly enter that text when you type an abbreviation.

1. Display the AutoCorrect Options window.

2. Under Replace text as you type, enter the abbreviation you want to use under Replace, and the text to replace it with under With.
3. Click **Add**.

The entry will be added to the AutoCorrect feature. If you type the abbreviation and then press **Enter** or the spacebar, AutoCorrect will enter the full text for you.

Exercise: Using AutoCorrect

Do This	How & Why
1. Open a new, blank document.	You'll use this to experiment with AutoCorrect.
2. Type `the` and press **Enter**.	Be sure not to capitalize it. As soon as you press Enter, Word capitalizes "The". This is an example of Word's AutoCorrect feature, which will automatically fix many types of spelling and grammar mistakes you might make. But what if you had *wanted* "the" to be uncapitalized?
3. Click  .	To undo the automatic "correction". When you don't like what AutoCorrect does, just click Undo.
4. Type `teh`, then a space.	Word changes what you typed to "the". When you type a common misspelling like this one, then press either the spacebar or Enter, Word will often correct it. You can also add your own common misspellings, or use AutoCorrect to create typing shortcuts.
5. Create an AutoCorrect shortcut for "Java Tucana".	
a) In Backstage view, click **Options**, then click **Proofing**.	To display Word's proofing options.
b) Click **AutoCorrect Options**.	To display the AutoCorrect window. Here, you can control the rules AutoCorrect uses and manage the AutoCorrect "Replace text as you type" entries.
c) In the Replace box, type `JT`.	You will use this abbreviation for the company name, "Java Tucana".
d) In the With box, type `Java Tucana`.	
e) Click **Add**.	To create the AutoCorrect entry.
f) Click **OK** twice.	To return to the document.
6. Type `JT`, then press the spacebar.	AutoCorrect replaces "JT" with "Java Tucana". This is useful for text you type often.
7. Close the document without saving it.	

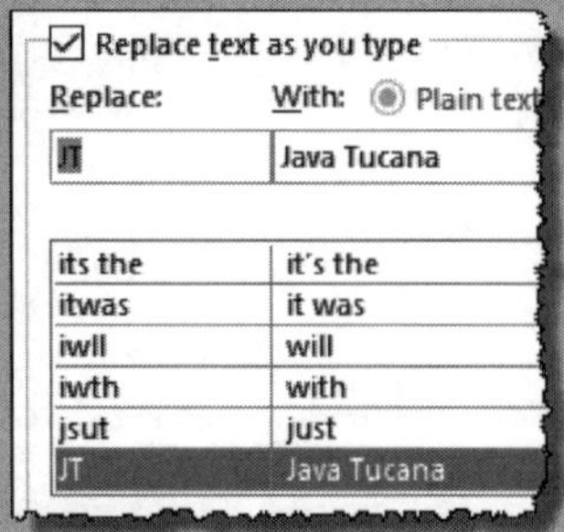

Assessment: Proofing documents

1. Word always suggests at least one option for an incorrect word or phrase. True or false?
   - True
   - False
2. Which option do you choose when you want Word to remember a spelling, even for future documents?
   - Change All
   - Ignore All
   - Add or Add to Dictionary
   - AutoCorrect
3. What is the feature that can automatically replace a combination of common characters with other characters or symbols not typically found on your keyboard?
   - AutoChar
   - AutoReplace
   - AutoFormat
   - AutoCorrect
4. What feature is responsible for starting a new numbered list when you start a line with a number?
   - AutoFormat
   - AutoCorrect
   - AutoList
   - AutoNumber

Module C: Printing, headers, and footers

Although you will probably share many documents electronically, you will also sometimes need to print documents. For any document longer than three or four pages, it's useful to have headers or footers to show the current page number, document and chapter titles, creation date, and other information.

You will learn how to:

- Print a document and control print settings
- Add and edit headers and footers
- Use different first page or odd and even page headers and footers

Printing

While a lot of document sharing is now done digitally, sometimes you might need to print a document. To see the print options, click Print on the File tab.

Exam Objective: MOS Word Core 1.5.3

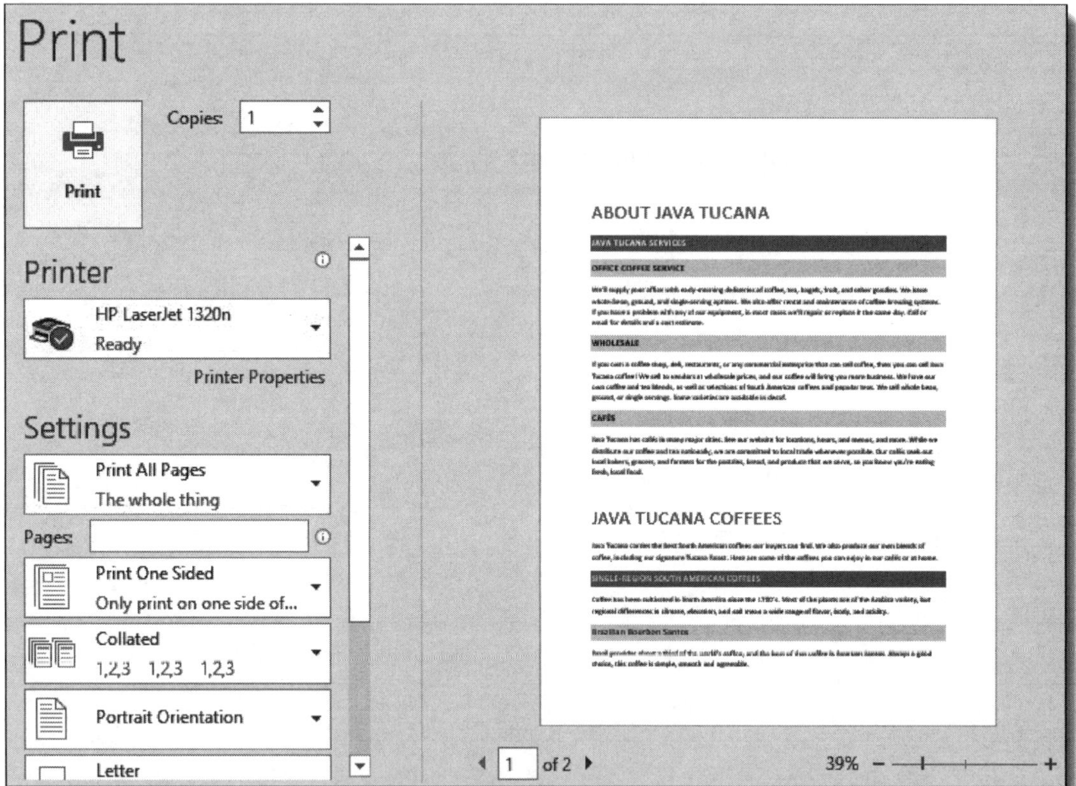

Microsoft automatically installs a software document writer, even if you don't have a physical printer, so the print function will always be available. Depending on what other hardware and software you have installed, you might be able to print to multiple printers, or directly to PDF or graphics files.

The print preview shows you what the output will look like. You can flip through the pages and zoom in an out.

Modifying print settings

There are many option on the left of the Print screen.

Exam Objective: MOS Word Core 1.5.1

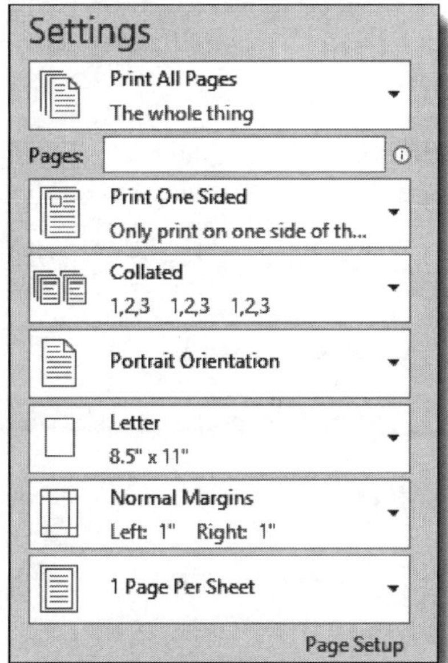

1. Click **File > Print**.

   The Print screen appears, giving you many options for modifying print settings.
2. Select the options you want.
   - Print all pages, the current one, a selection, or a range of pages.
   - Some printers can print on both sides of the page automatically. If your printer has this feature, the option will be available. Otherwise, you can choose to print on both sides of the page by manually flipping the output and feeding it back into the printer.
   - Some printers give you collation options.
   - Orientation controls whether the document will print tall (*portrait*) or wide (*landscape*).
   - Paper size.
   - Margins.
   - Page per sheet.

Exercise: Exploring printing options

Exam Objective: MOS Word Core 1.5.1, 1.5.3

Do This	How & Why
1. Open `JT Info` and save it as `JT Info Printing`.	The document contains information about Java Tucana.
2. Click **File > Print**.	The print screen appears in Backstage view. A preview appears on the right, and a gallery of print settings options on the left.
3. Click the preview, then press **Page Down**.	In this way, you can move through the pages of the preview to see what the document will look like when you print it.
4. Click the dropdown arrow next to Print All Pages.	You can print all pages, a selection, the current page, or document information.
5. Click the orientation dropdown arrow.	You can print the document portrait (tall) or landscape (wide).
6. Observe the other print settings.	The options available will depend on your current printer.
7. Return to the document.	Press **Esc** or click the return arrow.

Headers and footers

The header and footer put the same content on each page, though there are options to make the first page different, and to make even and odd pages different.

Exam Objective: MOS Word Core 1.3.4

To add or edit content in the header/footer area, you have to open it for editing. Header and footer areas always open together; that is, you won't open only one or the other for editing. There are three ways to open the header/footer for editing:

- Double-click the header or footer area on any page.
- Right-click the header or footer area, and click **Edit Header** or **Edit Footer**. They both open, regardless of which you choose.
- Use one of the header or footer options on the Insert tab.

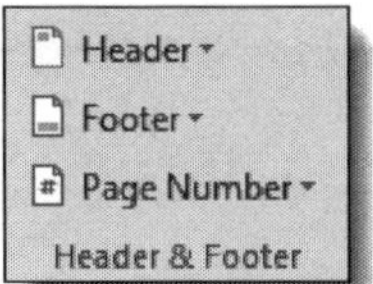

When the header and footer area is open, you see a Header & Footer Tools/Design context tab. You can do a lot right from here.

Think of the header and footer areas as small documents. When the header/footer area is open, the functions on other tabs are still available, so most of the things you can do in the main body, you can also do in the header and footer. Here are some things you can do with headers and footers:

- Add text, pictures, tables, and other elements.
- Insert fields to display page numbers, the current date and time, and other information.

- Format header content using the font and paragraph tools on the Home tab, as you would any text. This includes character formatting, lists, alignment, and indenting.
- When the header and footer are open, use the ruler to set margins, indents, and tab stops that are different than those in the main document.
- Control the position of the header and footer user tools in the Position group of the Header & Footer Tools Design tab.

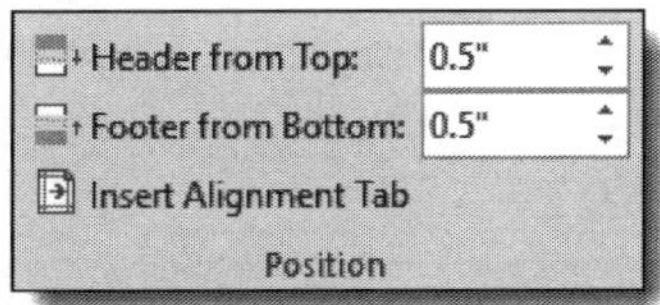

- Make the headers and footers different on the first page, and different on even and odd pages. Select the check boxes on the Header & Footer Tools tab, and edit the different headers accordingly.

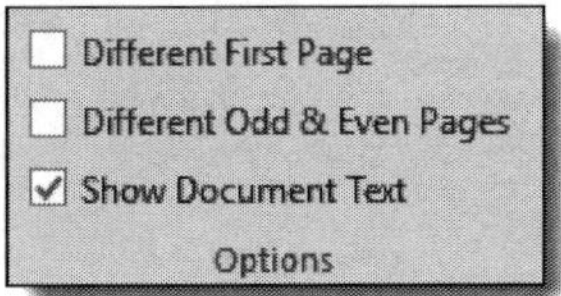

- Click the **Header** or **Footer** button in the Header & Footer group to choose from a gallery of complete built-in headers and footers, which have sets of elements in different styles. You can also save your own headers and footers to the galleries.

To remove a header or footer you don't want, click **Header > Remove Header** or **Footer > Remove Footer**.

Adding page numbers

Adding a page number field to the header, footer, or side margins ensures that each page automatically has the right page number. You can choose from many locations and styles, and you can format these numbers as you would any text.

Exam Objective: MOS Word Core 1.3.5

1. Double-click in the header or footer area of any page.
   To activate the Header & Footer Tools Design context tab.
2. Click **Page Number**, and then click the general location where you want the page numbers.
   To open the page number gallery for that location.

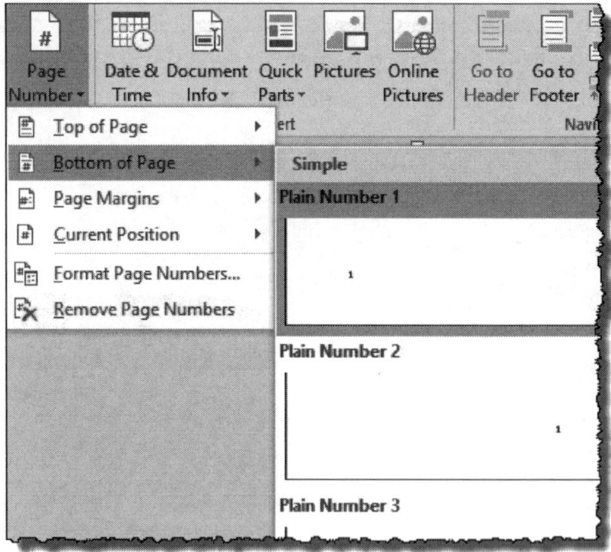

3. Select the number style you want.

   Scroll down the gallery.

   The number is added where you specified, in the style you selected. You can repeat the process to add page numbers in more than one place, if you want.

4. To remove page numbers, click **Page Number > Remove Page Numbers**.

Formatting page numbers

In addition to the locations and styles you can choose from, you can format page numbers in a couple other ways. With the header/footer sections active for editing, format page numbers as follows:

- Click **Page Number > Format Page Numbers**.

  This opens the **Page Number Format** window, where you can change the format from numbers to letters or Roman numerals. You can also include chapter numbers or change the starting page number.

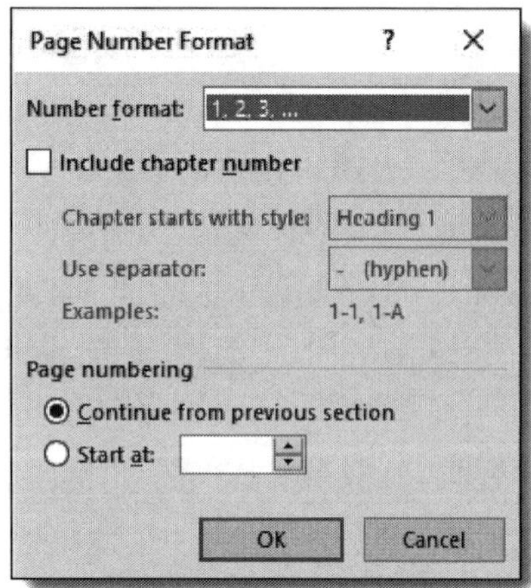

- You can select the page number text on any page and use the formatting options available on the Home tab, such as font face, size, color, style, and text effects.

  Formatting you apply to any page number is applied to all page numbers in the same header or footer location.

Adding the date and time

You can add the current date and time to the header or footer.

1. Double-click in the header or footer area of any page.
   To edit these areas and activate the Header & Footer Tools tab.
2. Click **Date & Time**.

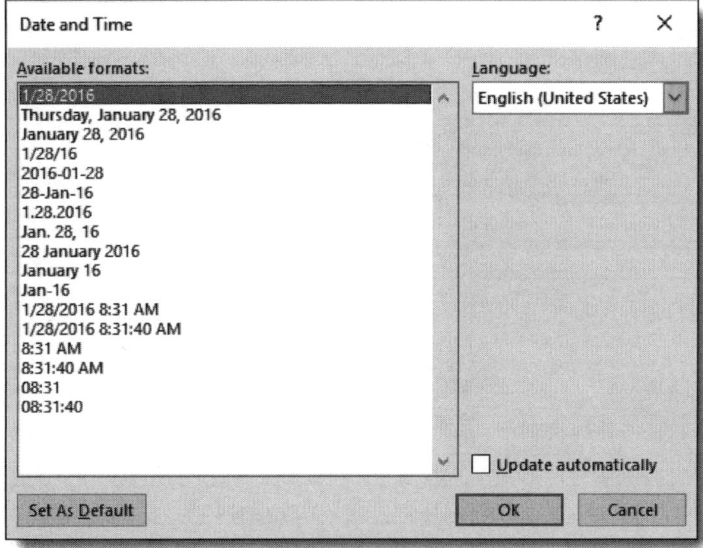

3. In the **Date and Time** window, select the format you want.
4. Check or clear the **Update automatically** check box.
   If you don't use this option, the date will be static text. If you do, Word will keep changing the date to the current date when you save the document. To update the date while the document is open, click it and then click **Update**.

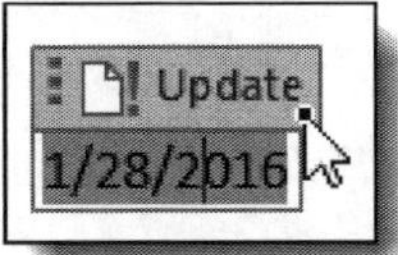

5. Click **OK**.
   The current date and/or time appears.
6. Format the date and time text.
   You can format all or part of the date and time by selecting the date and time text on any page and using the format options on the Home tab, such as font face, size, color, style, text effects, and alignment. Formatting you apply to the date and time on any page will be applied to the date and time on every page.

Using built-in headers and footers

Word comes with several built-in headers and footers. These have different elements and styles. You can use these as-is or start with one and edit it. After you create a header that you like, you can save it as a custom built-in header for future use.

1. Double-click in the header or footer area you want to edit.
   To open the areas for editing and display the Headers & Footers Tools tab.
2. Click **Header** or **Footer**.
3. Scroll down the Built-in gallery and select the header or footer you want.

   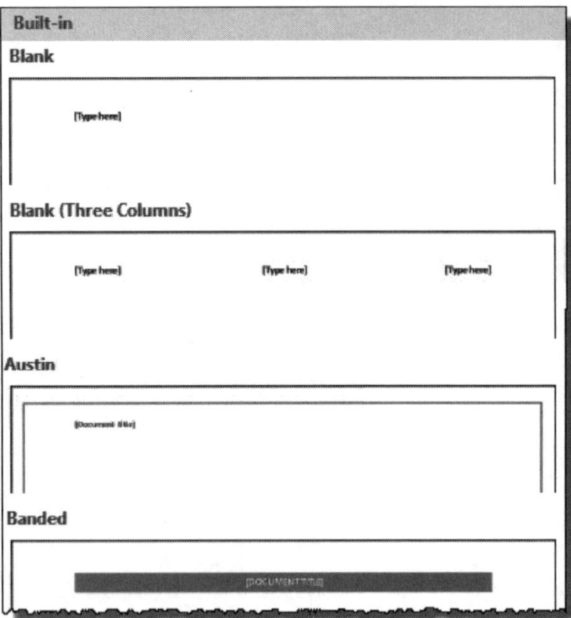

   The header or footer is inserted. You can edit this if you want.
4. You can save a header or footer you created or edited for later reuse:
   a) With the cursor in the header or footer, press **Ctrl+A** to select all.
   b) On the Header and Footer Tools tab, click **Header > Save Selection to Header Gallery** or **Footer > Save Selection to Footer Gallery**.
      The **Create New Building Block** window opens.
   c) Enter a name, and click **OK**.
      The header or footer now appears in the corresponding built-in gallery.

Exercise: Adding headers and footers

JT Info Printing is open.

Exam Objective: MOS Word Core 1.3.4, 1.3.5

Do This	How & Why
1. Observe the Header option on the Insert tab.	Click Header to view the gallery. Word has many build-in headers that you can insert simply by clicking an option here.
2. Double-click at the top of the page, in the header area.	The header area is activated, and the rest of the document is faded. The Header & Footer Tools become available. You'll add a page number and some text to the header area.
3. On the Header & Foot Tools Design tab, click **Page Number > Top of Page > Plain Number 2**.	A page number is place in the middle of the header.
4. Just before the page number, type `About Java Tucana `.	Include a space at the end.
5. Select all the text in the header.	About Java Tucana 1
6. On the Home tab, change the font to Arial, 12-pt.	You can format header text as you would any other text.
7. On the Header & Footer Tools Design tab, click **Close Header and Footer**.	The header is closed and the main document is active. You could also have double-clicked in the document area.
8. Scroll down and observe the numbers.	They change on each page.
9. Add the date to the footer.	Double-click the footer; then, on the Design tab, click **Date & Time**; click a format of your choosing and click **OK**; and then close the footer area.
10. Save the document.	

Different first or odd and even page headers and footers

Often you won't need a header on the first page of a document (because you have the title there already). And if you're publishing a document in a book format, you'll probably want different alignment of the headers and footers on the odd and even pages. Use the settings in the Header and Footer Tools Design tab's Options group to specify these settings. Then, you can create a separate header and footer for the first page, odd pages, and even pages.

Also note that headers and footers are specific to sections. If you need to have the headers change once you get to the beginning of a new chapter, for example, you can create a new section, then create all new headers and footers for it.

Exercise: Using different headings for the first page or for odd and even pages

JT Info Printing is open.

Do This	How & Why
1. Observe the header on the first page.	It's not really necessary. Usually, a first page has a title, and we already *know* it's the first page.
2. Activate the Header and Footer areas.	Double-click them, if necessary.
3. In the Options group, click **Different First Page**.	Now the header is identified as the First Page Header, and is blank. Of course, the first page footer is now blank as well, and you might want to enter the date there. 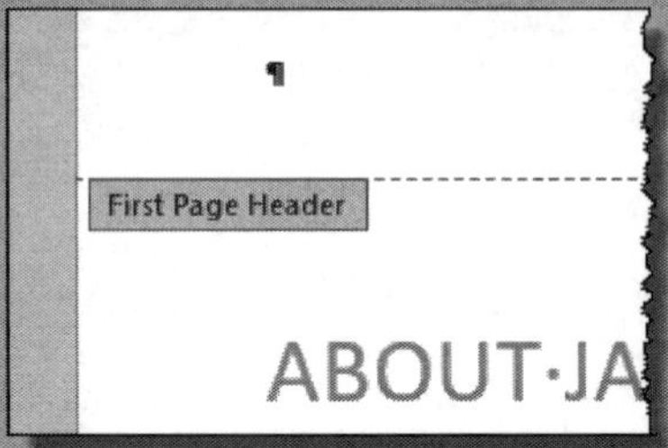
4. Click **Different Odd & Even Pages**.	In the Options group of the Header & Footer Tools Design tab. Now you can create different odd and even pages, to make the document look good when printed as a booklet or book.
5. Insert an even page header for the even pages.	
a) Click in the Even Page Header box.	You'll need to scroll down to the second page.
b) On the Insert tab, click **Header**.	To display the gallery of header options.
c) Click **Motion (Even Page)**.	To insert this header entry. Notice that it is left-aligned (even pages are on the left in a book). 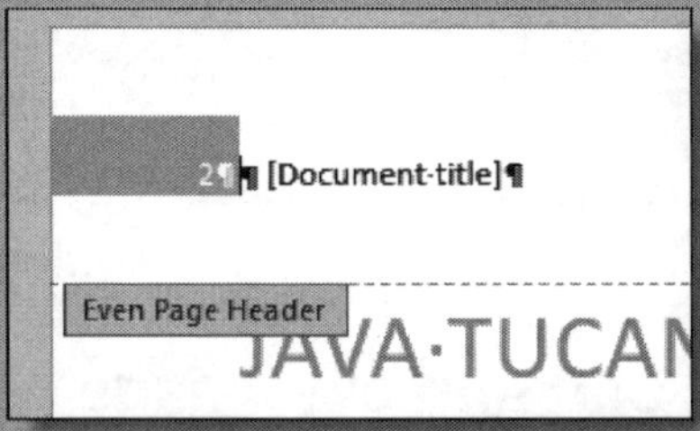
6. Insert the Motion (Odd Page) header for odd pages.	Click in the Odd Page Header box on page 3, then, on the Insert tab, click **Header** and then click **Motion (Odd Page)**.
7. Preview the printed document.	You'll see that the headers on pages 2 and 3 are aligned oppositely, which looks good. You'll also notice that the date footer is appearing only on odd pages. You'd want to fix that before actually printing.
8. Save and close the document.	An example follows.

The previewed document showing different odd and even headers

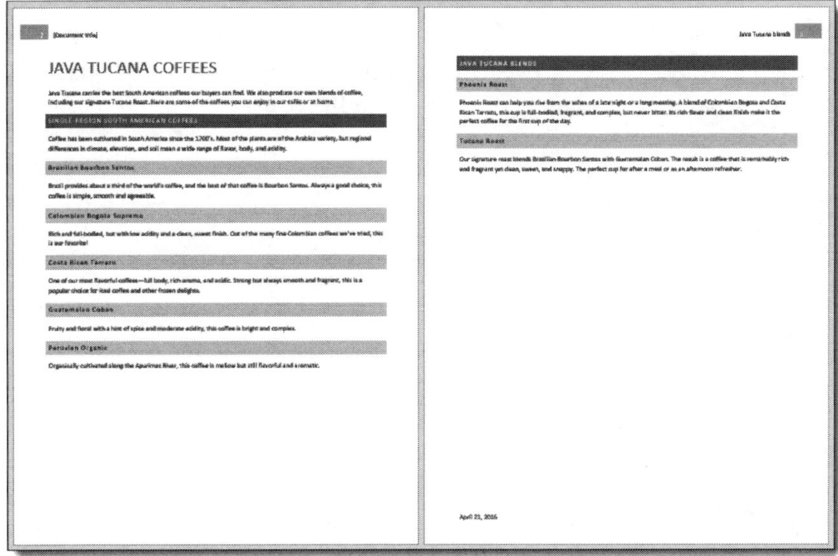

Assessment: Headers and footers

1. Which of the following techniques will open the header and footer areas for editing? Choose the single correct answer.
    - Press Ctrl+H
    - Press Ctrl+Alt+H
    - Double-click the header area
    - Press Ctrl+Alt+F
2. Page number fields automatically update as you add or delete pages. True or false?
    - True
    - False
3. By default, a header will not print on the first page of a document.
    - True
    - False

Module D: Templates

There is a staggering number of Word templates available for everything from mailing labels to memos to menus. The biggest challenge is not finding what you need, but choosing from the possibilities.

You will learn how to:

- Find, download, and apply a template from the web
- Apply a local template file

Templates

Templates provide the default formatting and layout for a new document. A template can have a specific purpose, such as a resume or an invoice, or it can be more general-purpose. Every document uses a template. The template that opens by default in Word is called the Normal template. It has 1-inch margins and uses 11-point Calibri as the default font for body text. It uses various other fonts for headings.

There are many templates for many purposes available in Word and online. The figure shows a few of the templates from Office.com, and gives you suggestions for searches. These can be accessed when you create a new document.

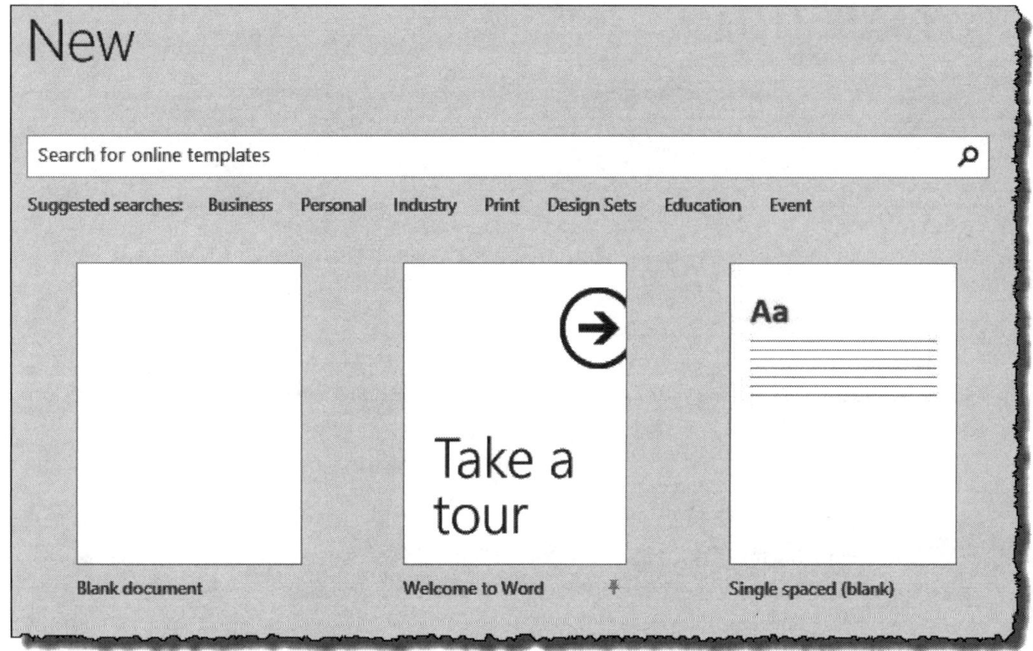

Template file names for Word have a .dot or .dotx extension. Templates that you create or download outside of Word and store on the local hard disk can be opened directly from Word or Windows explorer. When you store then in the default templates folder, you can access them from the New screen in Backstage view.

Applying templates from the web

The **New** command of the File tab provides access to templates. In addition to any templates you may have stored locally, there are many available from Office.com that you can access through searches.

Exam Objective: MOS Word Core 1.1.2

1. On the File tab, click **New**.

   You will see some templates from which you can choose, along with a search box and links for suggested searches. If you have saved your own templates, you will see a link for accessing those.
2. Click a suggested search.

   The Business category has many useful templates.

   You will see a list of found templates, and a list of sub-categories on the right.
3. Browse to locate a sub-category of templates that fits your requirements.

   Here, you see a list of available Business Plan templates. There are literally thousands of templates available online.

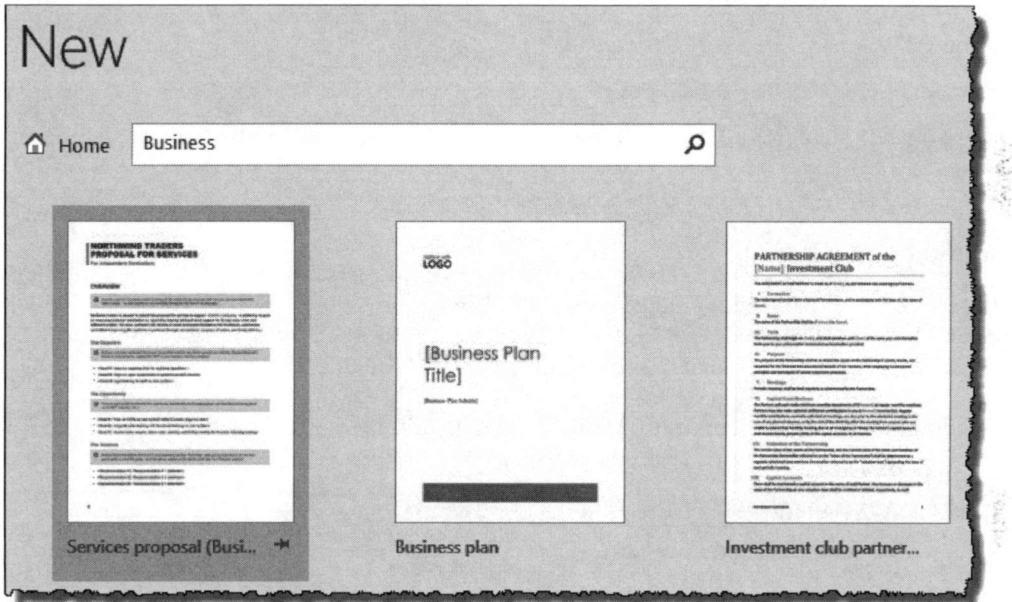

4. Select a template that you think might work.

   A preview is shown. You can click the arrow to the right of the preview to see previews of the next templates.

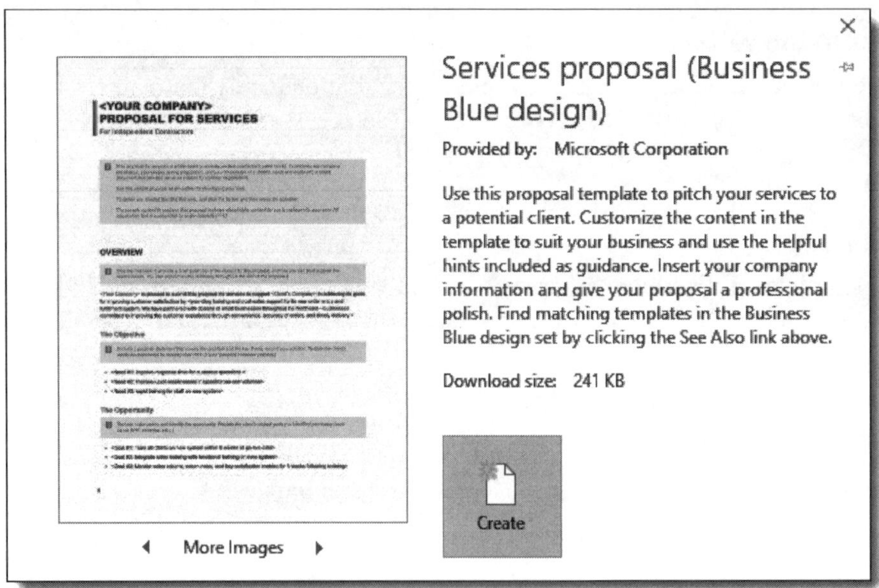

5. Click **Create**.

   A new document opens using the template.

Once you download a template, it will be available in your list of templates on the New screen.

Saving a document as a templates

In additional to basing documents on templates you find online, you can also create your own templates. Then, you can use them as the starting point for documents in the future. The templates you create will appear in the Personal category if you save them in the default templates folder.

1. Create a document with the elements and formatting you want in your template.
2. Click **File** > **Save As**.

   To open the Save As window.
3. In the "Save as type" list, click **Word Template**.

   Word will automatically change the active folder to Custom Office Templates. Unless you have a strong reason to do otherwise, you should save your templates here, because then they will appear on the New screen under the Personal category.
4. Enter a name for the template and click **Save**.

You will then be able to create new documents based on your template. Click **File** > **New**, click **Personal**, then click the template you want.

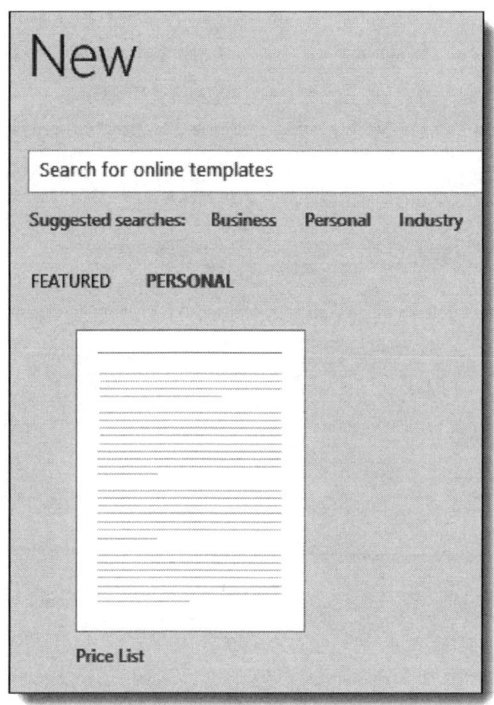

Exercise: Using templates

You need an Internet connection to complete some of these steps as written. You can still work with the local template file without an Internet connection.

Exam Objective: MOS Word Core 1.1.2

Do This	How & Why
1. Click **File > New**.	To display the New screen in Backstage view. You see a list of Featured templates, and a search box.
2. Next to Suggested Searches, click **Business**.	You see a list of online templates you could download and use, along with a list of sub-categories on the right. Category Business 252 Small Business 206 Industry 85 Design Sets 59 Finance - Accounting 44
3. Click **Finance - Accounting**.	To view available templates.
4. Observer the previews of some of the available templates.	Click one to view the preview, then use the arrow to scroll through others.
5. Return to the document.	Press **Esc** to close the preview.

Do This	How & Why
6. Open `Menu`.	This document is a starting point for future Java Tucana menus. You will save it as a template.
7. Save the document as a template.	
a) Click **File > Save As**, then click **Browse**.	To open the **Save As** window.
b) In the "Save as type" list, click **Word Template**.	Notice that when you select the template file type, Word switches to the Custom Office Templates folder.
c) Click **Save**, then close the document.	
8. Create a new document based on your menu template.	
a) Click **File > New**.	There is now a Personal category in the New screen.
b) Click **Personal**, then click the **Menu** template.	A new document opens based on the template. Note that the document name (in the title bar) is not "Menu," but "Document" with a number.
9. Close the document without saving it.	

Assessment: Templates

1. Every Word document is based on a template. True or false?
   - True
   - False
2. What is the name of the template that opens when you first start Word? Choose the one correct answer.
   - Default
   - Basic
   - Blank
   - Normal
3. Which of the following are file extensions used for Word templates? Choose all the correct answers.
   - .dot
   - .wtm
   - .dotx
   - .wtmx

Summary: Document setup

You should now know how to:

- Change page layout options such as margins, page and line breaks, and hyphenation; create and control columns layouts; and insert new sections and show section numbers
- Use automatic spell checking or the Grammar and Spelling panes to proof documents, use AutoCorrect, and create an AutoCorrect entry
- Print documents, control print settings, add headers and footers, insert page numbers and dates in headers and footers, and use different first page or even and odd page headers and footers
- Use online templates, and create your own templates based on documents

Synthesis: Document setup

In this synthesis exercise, you will create a small baked goods menu, change layout settings, and add a header and a footer.

1. Open `Full Menu` and save it as `Full Menu Setup`.
2. Set the margins to moderate.
3. Use page breaks to put the Sandwiches and Soups of the Day sections on new pages.
4. For the Baked Goods items, set a right tab stop at 7 inches with a dot leader.
   It should look like this.

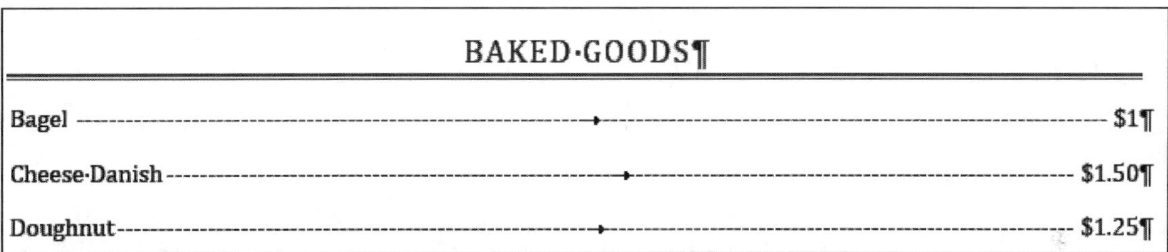

5. Format the Sandwiches items in two columns.
6. For the Sandwiches items, add a right tab stop at 3.25 inches with a dot leader.
7. Add a column break before "Tucana Banana".
   It should now look like this.

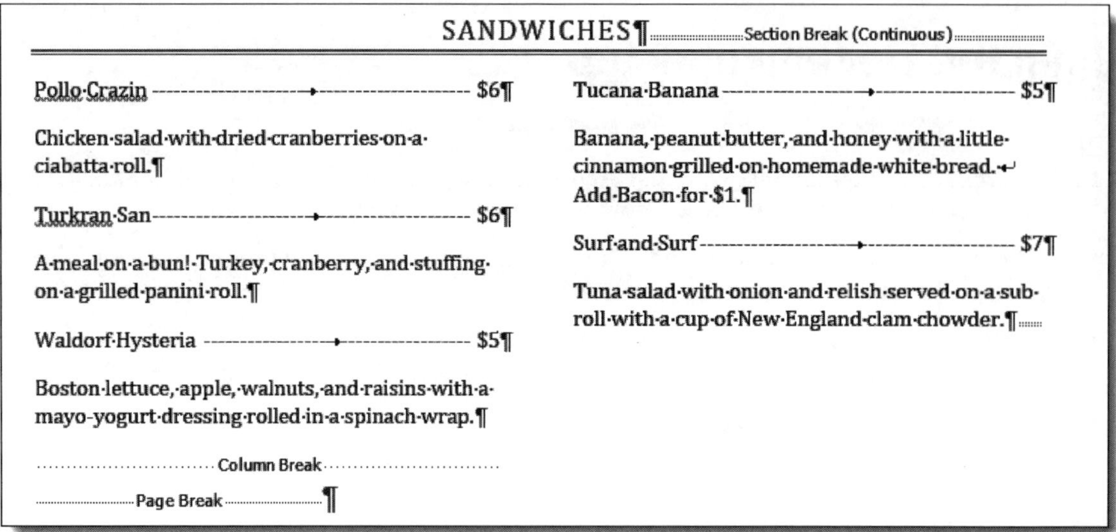

8. Format the Soups of the Day items the same as the Baked Goods.
   Try using the Format Painter.
9. Add a footer that looks like the following image.
   Hint: You can use the footer's default tab stops to right align the page numbers.

10. Add a Header that says `Java Tucana`, in Title style.
11. Make the first page have no header or footer.
12. Print preview the document.
13. Save and close the document.

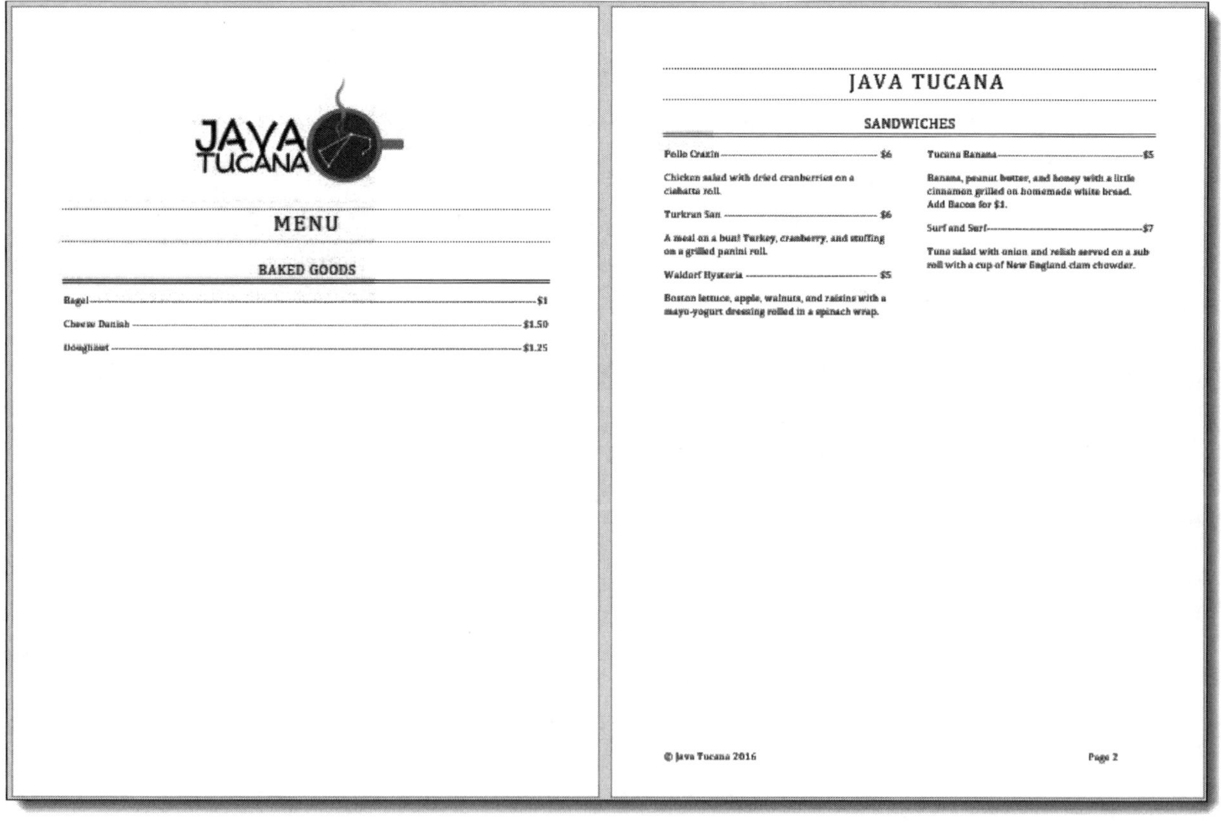

Chapter 4: Graphics

You will learn how to:

- Insert pictures
- Change picture layout
- Format pictures

Module A: Inserting pictures

There are several ways to insert pictures into a Word document, including pasting, opening a graphics file, and taking a screenshot.

You will learn how to:

- Insert graphics from files or the clipboard
- Insert screenshots
- Insert pictures from the web

Pictures in Word

There are several types of graphic elements you can add to Word documents. The term "picture" generally refers to graphics added from a file or the clipboard. Other graphics elements in Word include shapes, text boxes, SmartArt, WordArt, and charts.

Although pictures downloaded from the web and screen shots are inserted differently than most pictures, they are really graphics files, and once they are in a document, you format them as you would any other picture. One way to know if an object in Word is a picture is to select it. When a picture is selected, the Pictures Tools Format tab appears on the ribbon. The exact appearance of the tab you see might be different depending on your screen size.

Inserting pictures

To insert a picture quickly, you can copy it from another source and paste it at the cursor, just as you would copy and paste text. You can also insert a picture from a file. Word recognizes many picture file formats.

Exam Objective: MOS Word Core 5.1.2

1. Put the cursor where you want the picture.
   You can move and resize the picture later.
2. On the Insert tab, in the Illustrations group, click **Pictures**.
   The **Insert Picture** window opens.
3. If you want, select a file format from the file types list.
   If you need to narrow the search. By default, the window shows all supported graphics files.

4. Select the file you want, and then click **Insert**.

   The window closes, and the picture is inserted into the document.

Inserting screen shots

Word allows you to insert a picture of an open window or part of your computer screen. Windows have to be open (not minimized) to be available for a screen shot.

Exam Objective: MOS Word Core 5.1.3

1. Place the insertion point where you want the screenshot to appear.
2. On the Insert tab, click **Screenshot**.
   - To capture and place a shot of an open window, select it in the Screenshot gallery. You cannot take a screenshot of the Word window you are working in, but you can capture other open Word windows.

     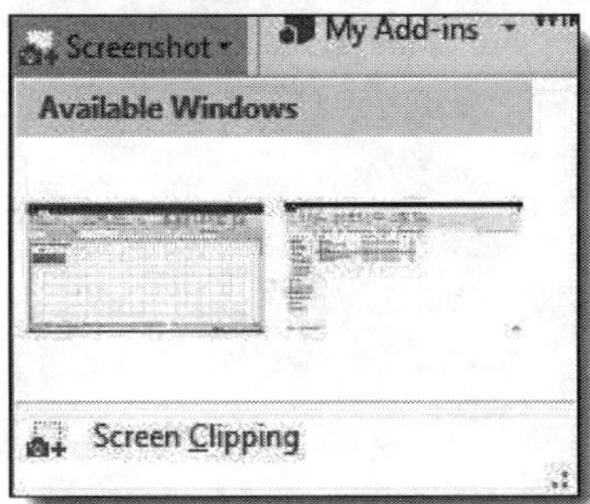

   - To select a section of your screen to capture, click **Screen Clipping**, then drag over the area of the screen you want to capture. Again, the current Word window is not visible for capture.

With either method, the screenshot is inserted at the point of the cursor.

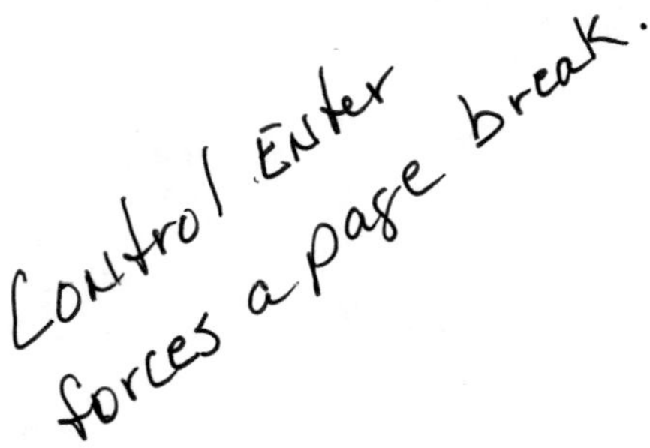

Exercise: Inserting a picture

Exam Objective: MOS Word Core 5.1.2, 5.1.3

Do This	How & Why
1. Start a new blank document, and save it as `Pics`.	Save it in the current chapter's data folder.
2. In Windows, click **Start**, type `paint`, and then press **Enter**.	To open the Paint program.
3. In Paint, open the image file `Table`.	From the current chapter's data folder.
4. Copy and paste the picture from Paint to Word:	
a) In Paint, on the Home tab, click **Select > Select All**.	
b) Press **Ctrl+C**	
c) Switch back to Pics, and press **Ctrl+V**.	To paste the image into Word. This is one way to get graphics into a document: simply copy and paste them.
5. Press **Enter**.	To put the cursor below the image.
6. On the Insert tab, click **Pictures**.	The **Insert Picture** window opens.
7. In the data folder, select the file `CoffeeCup`, and then click **Insert**.	You could instead double-click the file. The picture is placed in the document.
8. Press the right arrow key, and then press **Enter**.	To place the cursor below the image.
9. On the Insert tab, click **Screenshot**.	You'll see thumbnail images of all open windows except that of the active document.
10. Click the thumbnail for the **Paint** window.	A screenshot of the Paint window is inserted, scaled to fit in the document.
11. Close Paint, and save and close Pics.	

Inserting pictures from the web

There is an online pictures browser built into Word. You can search for and insert pictures and graphics, and save them locally for future use.

1. On the Insert tab, in the Illustrations group, click **Online Pictures**.
   To open the **Insert Pictures** window. Note that you need to be connected to the Internet to search for online pictures.

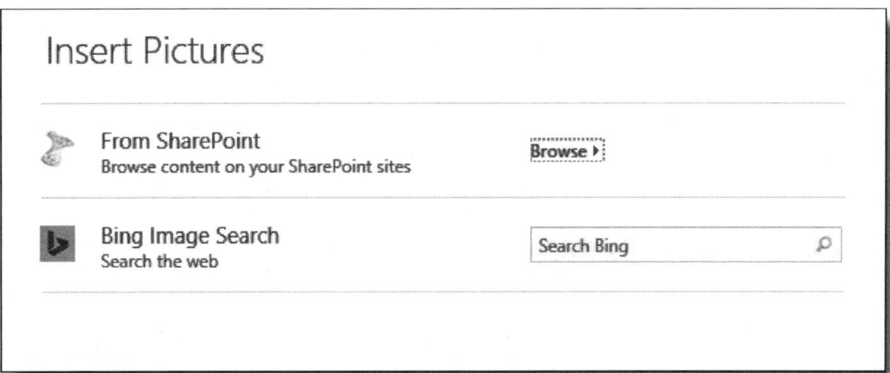

2. In the Bing Image Search box, type one or more search terms, and press **Enter**.
   To display your search results. By default, Bing shows you only images licensed under Creative Commons, meaning that you should be able to use them without any concern about rights.

3. Scroll through the images, click the one you want, then click **Insert**.
   It is downloaded and inserted into your document at the location of the cursor.

Exercise: Working with online images

An Internet connection is needed to search for images online.

Do This	How & Why
1. Open a new blank document, and save it as `Web Pic`.	
2. On the Insert tab, click **Online Pictures**.	The **Insert Pictures** window opens.
3. In the Bing Image Search box, type `coffee cup`, and then press **Enter**.	
4. In the search results, click any image you want.	To see information about the picture.
5. Click **Insert**.	It is inserted in the document.
6. Save and close the Web Pic document.	

Assessment: Inserting pictures

1. Which one of these is stored in a graphics file like other pictures?
   - Online pictures
   - Shapes
   - WordArt
   - SmartArt
2. A program window must be open (not minimized) to be captured by the Word Screenshot command. True or false?
   - True
   - False

Module B: Formatting pictures

When you want to do more than adjust a picture's size and place on the page, Word offers a number of formatting options to adjust color and contrast, apply artistic effects, and apply other visual effects, such as shadows, reflections, and soft edges.

You will learn how to:

- Make picture adjustments
- Apply artistic effects and picture styles
- Compress pictures in a document

Picture adjustments

You can adjust several visual features of a selected picture using the tools in the Adjust group on the Picture Tools Format tab. Any of these tools that has a gallery shows you small previews, and pointing to an option shows you a live preview in the document.

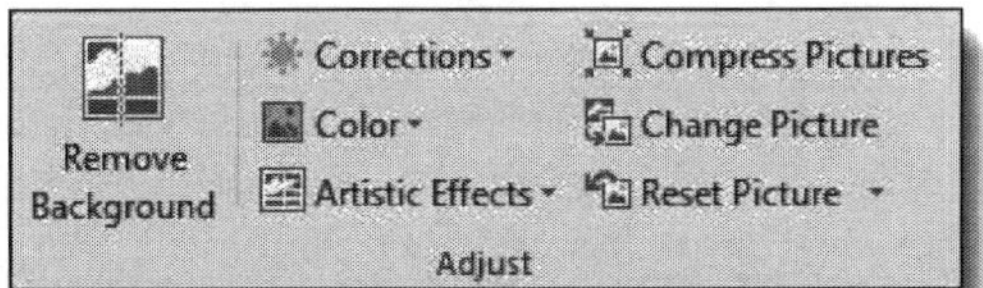

Exam Objective: MOS Word Core 5.2.3

Remove Background If the picture background is a smooth color with little variation (like a white background), this tool can replace it with a transparent area. You will be able to see text and the document background through the transparency, and text can be wrapped around the remaining image. The figure shows an image before and after removing the background.

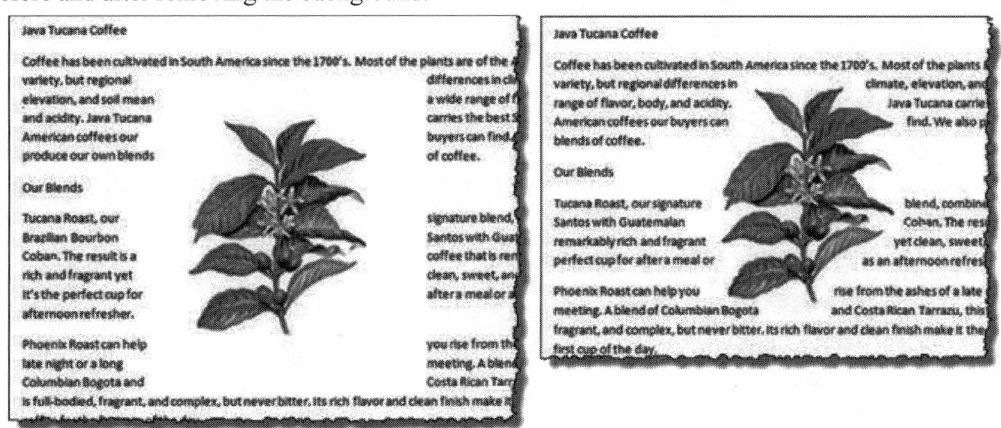

Corrections Sharpen or soften image edges, and adjust contrast and brightness.

Color Change color saturation and tone, or recolor the image.

Artistic Effects These effects might make the picture look like a painting or a drawing, or make it blurry or granular, or look as though it's behind frosted glass.

Compress Pictures This reduces the size of the picture data stored in the document, so that the overall document size is smaller.

Change Picture Allows you to select a different image to go in the same place as the selected image.

Reset Picture Removes adjustments and effects, and returns the image to its original state.

Applying effects

Artistic Effects is a tool that can alter a picture in a number of ways. For instance, it can make a picture look as if it's painted, drawn with a pencil, or being seen through frosted glass. Picture effects add to the outline or presentation of a picture as a whole, for example a beveled or drop-shadow look.

Exam Objective: MOS Word Core 5.2.1, 5.2.2

1. Select the picture you want to modify.
   The Picture Tools Format tab appears.
2. On the Picture Tools Format tab, do one of the following.
   - In the Adjust group, click **Artistic Effects** to open the Artistic Effects gallery showing small previews. You can point to effects to see a live preview in the document. After you apply an artistic effect, you can change how it works by clicking **Artistic Effects** > **Artistic Effects**.

     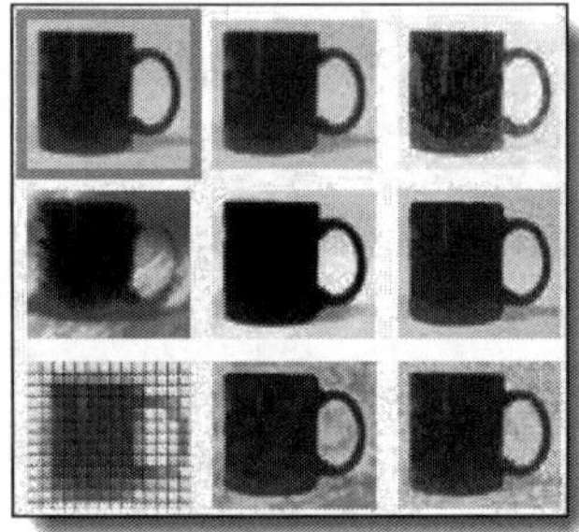

   - In the Picture Styles group, click **Picture Effects**, then one of the choices for an effect type to see a gallery of options. This figure shows some of the shadow options.

     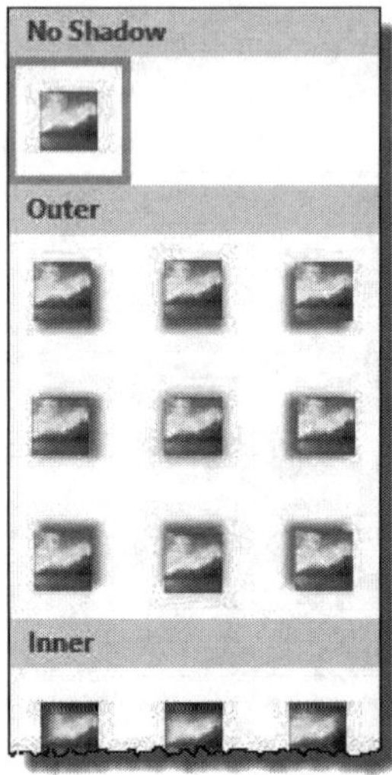

3. Click the effect you want to apply.
   The gallery closes, and the effect is applied.

Compressing pictures

When you insert a picture from the clipboard or a file, it is imported into the document at its full size and resolution. Its visible size is automatically reduced if the picture is too large for the document, but all the picture data are still there—even after you shrink or crop the picture. This can increase document file size considerably.

If smaller pictures and/or lower resolution are adequate for your project, and you are sure you won't need to undo any shrinking or cropping, then you can compress pictures to reduce your document's file size.

1. Select a picture.
   Any picture, unless you want to compress an individual picture, in which case, select that one.
2. On the Picture Tools Format tab, in the Adjust group, click **Compress Pictures**.
3. Select the compression options and output resolution.
   If you want to compress all pictures in the document, be sure to clear the **Apply only to this picture** check box.
4. Click **OK**.
5. Save to document.
   The reduced file size displays in Windows Explorer.

Note: Once the document is saved and closed, the original picture information is lost and compression cannot be undone. You would have to re-insert the picture to return it to its original size and resolution.

Picture styles

A picture style is a set of picture effects applied at the same time. These effects do not change image values such as contrast, brightness, color, or artistic effects. Instead, picture styles affect and enhance the picture's presentation, including borders, drop shadows, reflections, beveling, and 3-D rotation.

Exam Objective: MOS Word Core 5.2.5

You can experiment with these effects using the commands in the Picture Styles group on the Picture Tools Format tab.

To change individual effects, use the **Picture Border** and **Picture Effects** tools. As with other galleries, these show you small previews; pointing to a specific choice shows you a live preview in the document.

To apply picture styles to a selected picture, in the Picture Styles gallery, click the style. The figure here shows a picture with some effects applied; the picture on the right has a brown border, shadow, bevel, and 3-D rotation.

The Picture Layout command allows you to couple the picture with other graphical elements, such as shapes and text boxes.

The Format Picture pane

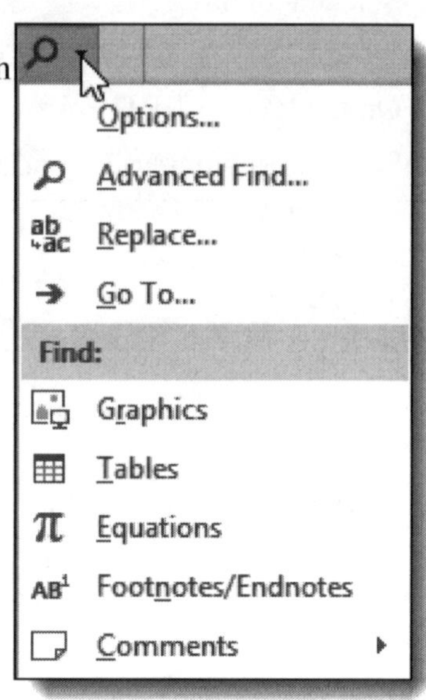

You might never need more than a few ribbon commands to format pictures in Word, but for more options and precision, you can use the Format Picture pane. To open it, right-click a picture, and click **Format Picture**. Here, various formatting options are in grouped categories.

Exam Objective: MOS Word Core 5.2.4, 5.2.8

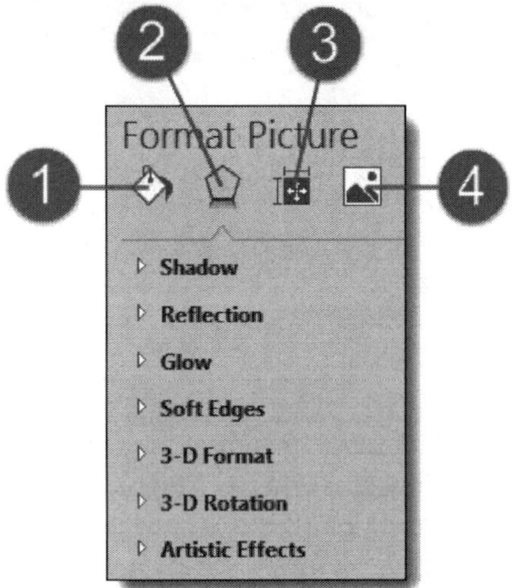

1. *Fill & Line* options control the appearance of colors inside and along the border of the picture.
2. *Effects* options control various effects.
3. *Layout and Properties* is for settings such as alignment and alternative text. To add alternative text to a graphic, which is important for accessibility, click this category, expand the Alt Text group, and enter a title and description of the graphic.
4. *Picture* settings allow you to control corrections, color, and cropping.

Many of the commands on the Picture Tools Format tab are also in the Format Picture pane. Here, you can precisely adjust settings for applied effects. You can also get to this window via the **Options** command at the bottom of most effects galleries.

Exercise: Formatting a picture

Exam Objective: MOS Word Core 5.2.1, 5.2.2, 5.2.5, 5.2.8

Do This	How & Why
1. Open `Logo`, and save it as `Logo Formatted`.	The document contains a graphic of the Java Tucana logo.
2. Select the picture.	
3. On the Format tab, click **Corrections**, and under Brightness and Contrast, select the setting two options below the current (center) one.	To increase contrast 40%.

Do This	How & Why
4. On the Format tab, click **Artistic Effects**, and click **Cement**.	To apply a textured effect.
5. Point to different options in the Picture Styles gallery.	To see the live preview.
6. Experiment with picture effects like Shadow, Reflection, and 3-D Rotation.	In the Picture Style group, click **Picture Effects**, then try several of the galleries. If you want, you can click **Reset Picture** at any time to remove all effects and start over.
7. Add alternative text to the logo.	
a) Right-click the picture, then click **Format Picture**.	To display the Format Picture pane.
b) Click the Layout and Properties button.	To view layout and properties settings.
c) Add `JT Logo` as the Alt Text title.	Expand the Alt Text category, then type in the Title box.
d) Close the Format Picture pane.	Click its close button.
8. When you find an overall design you like, save and close the document.	

Assessment: Formatting pictures

1. If you crop a picture and then save and close the document, you can still recover the whole picture when you open the document again. True or false?
   - True
   - False
2. Which command removes effects and adjustments and returns a picture to its original state?
   - Remove Formatting
   - Reset Picture
   - Change Picture
   - No Style

Module C: Picture layout

Rarely do you insert a picture in Word and leave it as it is. In most cases, you want at least to adjust the image size and location, and the way text wraps around it.

You will learn how to:

- Adjust a picture's size and position
- Specify the way in which text wraps around a picture
- Add captions to pictures

Picture layout and formatting

When you select a picture in Word, the Picture Formatting tab becomes available. Many of the picture layout and formatting commands you need are on this tab. In general, layout refers to the way a picture is situated in the context of a document: its size, its place on the page, the way text wraps around it, and its caption. Formatting refers to adjusting a picture's visual qualities. These include adjustments in color and contrast, artistic effects, and special effects such as blur, shadow, framing, and 3-D rotation.

Manually changing size and position

By default, when you insert a picture in a Word document, it's treated as a character. That is, the picture appears at the cursor location, and text is wrapped around or pushed below it, as in this figure:

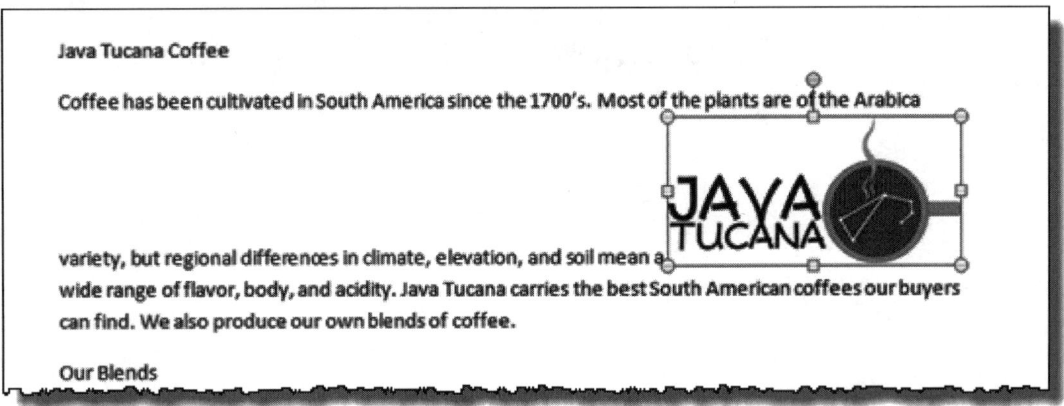

When you select a picture, a box appears around it with small circles and squares called *handles*. When you point to a handle, the cursor changes to reflect its function. You can use the handles to adjust the shape, size, and position of a selected picture.

Exam Objective: MOS Word Core 5.2.4, 5.2.6, 5.2.7

- Drag a corner handle in or out to adjust the picture's size. This ensures that the ratio of height to width doesn't change.
- Drag the side handles in or out to change the width or height individually. This modifies the picture's shape from its original aspect ratio.
- Drag the top handle (the green circle) around to freely rotate the picture.
- Point inside the frame and drag the picture to a new location. It can be placed only where a character can, unless you change the Wrap Text setting. Then, you can drag it anywhere on the page.
- To crop a picture (cut off part of it), on the Picture Tools Format tab, click **Crop**. This will add cropping handles that you can drag to where you want.

Wrapping text around pictures

Exam Objective: MOS Word Core 5.2.6

After inserting a picture, you can change the way text flows around it. You can do this with the **Position** and **Wrap Text** commands on the Picture Tools tab, which appear only when a picture is selected. If a picture has transparent areas, wrapped text can flow into it. You can also place the picture behind or in front of the text, without changing its normal flow.

- Use the **Position** command to both place the picture on the page and wrap the text around it.

  Point to an option to see a live preview in your document.

  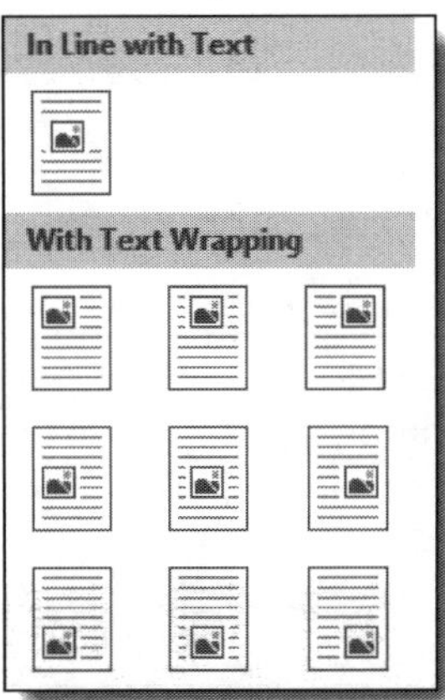

- Use the **Wrap Text** command to change only the way the text flows around the picture, but not the picture's position on the page.

  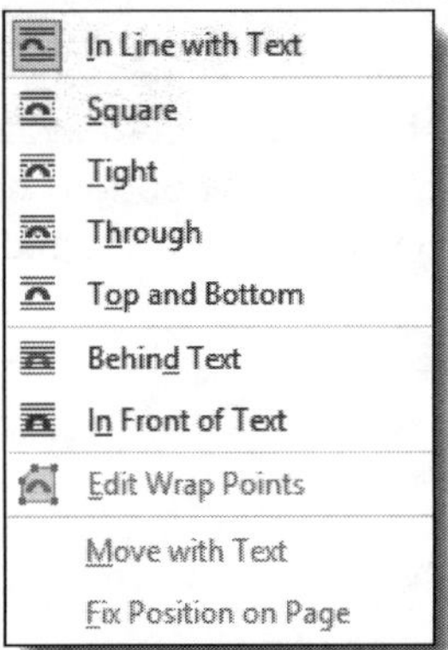

This command is also available from the shortcut menu when you right-click a picture. Once you change the style of text wrapping, you can drag the picture around to different positions. Before doing so, a picture is like a big character, and can be placed only in paragraphs.

- Another way to affect image position and text wrapping is through the Layout Options gallery.

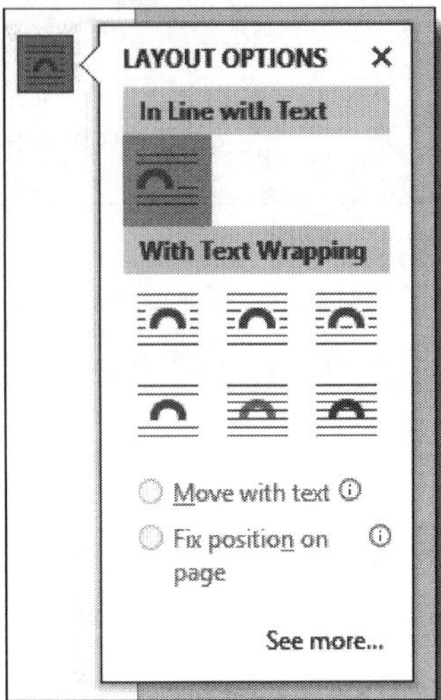

The Layout Options button appears to the right of a selected image. The Layout Options gallery contains some of the same layout and text-wrapping options as the Position and Wrap Text galleries. However, it's important to note that you can't preview the effects of selecting options by hovering over them in the Layout Options gallery.

The Layout window

Exam Objective: MOS Word Core 5.2.7

You might never need more than a picture's handles and a few ribbon commands to arrange pictures in Word, but if you need more precision, you can use the **Layout** window. To open it, right-click a picture, and click **Size and Position**. If you choose a Text Wrapping option other than "In line with text," the options on the Position tab become available, giving you precise control over horizontal and vertical alignment, and the position of the graphic.

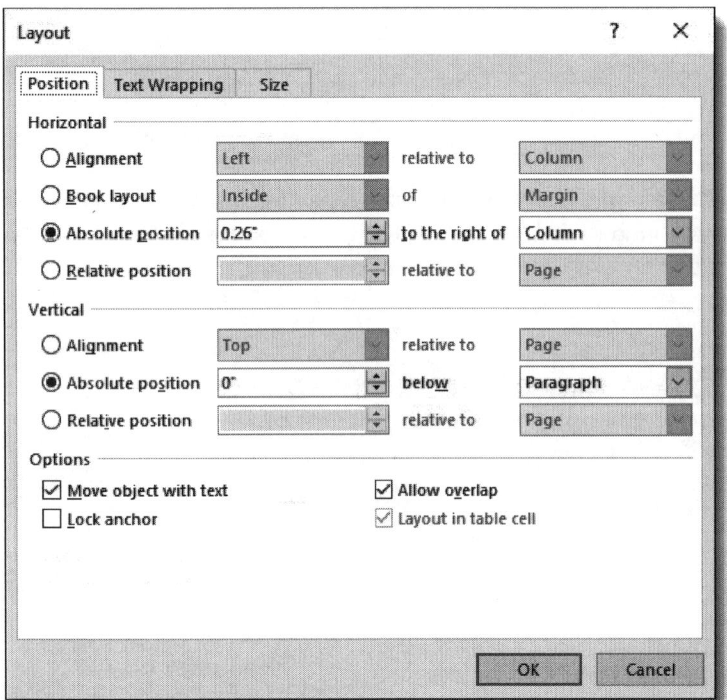

Adding captions to pictures

Adding a caption to a picture inserts a line of text and an automatic number in the Caption style. Captions are added the same way for most graphical objects, including pictures, shapes, WordArt, SmartArt, and clip art.

Exam Objective: MOS Word Expert 3.2.2

1. Right-click the picture, and click **Insert Caption**.

   To open the Caption window.

   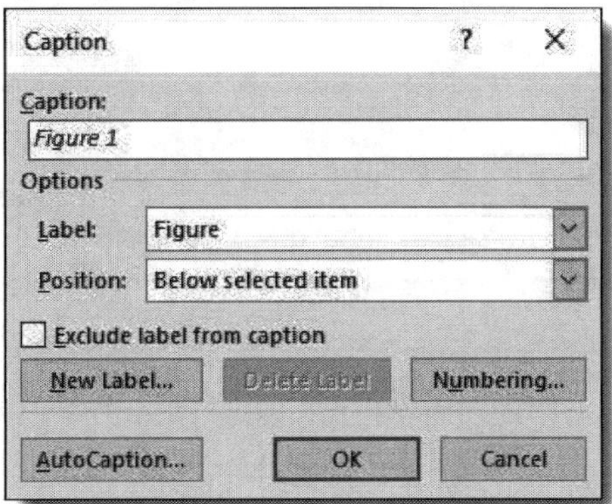

2. You can leave the default label as-is, or set any caption options you want:
   - Add a caption to the label.
   - Change the label to **Equation**, **Figure**, or **Table**.
   - Position the caption above or below the picture.
   - Exclude the label (the number will remain).
   - Create a new label to add to the list.
   - Change the numbering style.
3. Click **OK**.

   The caption is added above or below the picture.

Note that the caption is not functionally tied to the picture, and can be either moved or deleted individually. If you change the order of captions, you'll have to update fields for the numbers to display in order again. To do this, press **Ctrl+A** to select all text, and then press **F9**.

Exercise: Changing picture layout

Exam Objective: MOS Word Core 5.2.3, 5.2.4, 5.2.7

Do This	How & Why
1. Open `Blue Brew`, and save it as `New Blue Brew`.	In the current chapter's data folder.
2. Click the picture to select it.	Handles appear around the picture to indicate that it is selected.
3. Drag any corner handle to the center of the image.	To shrink it.
4. Remove the background from the image. a) On the Format tab, click **Remove Background**. b) Drag out the border in the pink area to show the whole cup. c) Click **Keep Changes**.	
5. Right-click the image, and click **Wrap Text > Tight**.	
6. Drag the image to the lower left of the text.	Adjust it until you like the results. It should look something like the image below.
7. Save and close the document.	

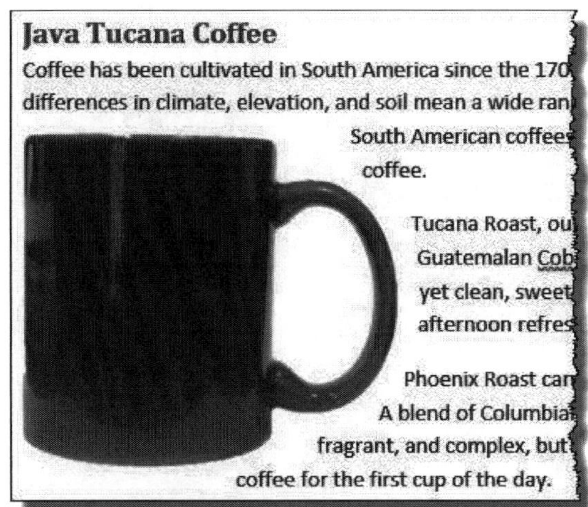

Assessment: Picture layout

1. Which method will preserve aspect ratio when you resize a picture?
   - Hold down Shift when you resize it.
   - Right-click and drag the side handles.
   - Drag a corner handle.
   - Check Lock Aspect Ratio on the Format tab.
2. To be able to drag a picture around more freely, change its Text Wrap setting to anything other than In Line with Text. True or false?
   - True
   - False
3. A picture caption is grouped with the picture, so if you move one, the other will move. True or false?
   - True
   - False

Summary: Graphics

You should now know how to:

- Insert pictures, screenshots, and online images in your documents
- Adjust picture settings, add effects, apply picture styles, compress pictures, and use the Format Picture pane to control various aspects of pictures and to add alternative text
- Change picture size and position, wrap text around graphics, and add captions to them

Synthesis: Graphics

1. Open `JT Services`, and save it as `JT Services Pic`.
2. Insert the picture `JT-Logo`.
3. Reduce the picture to about a quarter of its original size, maintaining its aspect ratio.
4. Change the Text Wrap setting to **Square**.
5. Drag the logo to the upper-right so it is to the right of the first two headings.
6. Using options on the format tab, apply any effect you want to the logo.
   You might need to readjust its position, depending on what effects you apply.
7. Insert the picture `CoffeeTime`.
8. Change the Text Wrap to **Tight**, and drag the picture to the location shown in the figure.
9. Remove the background, so the text wraps more closely to the image.
10. When the document looks good to you, save and close it.

Your document should look something like this after this exercise.

The document with graphics inserted and formatted

Java Tucana Services

Cafés

Java Tucana has cafés in many major cities. See our website for locations, hours, and menus, and more. While we distribute our coffee and tea nationally, we are committed to local trade whenever possible. Our cafés seek out local bakers, grocers, and farmers for the pastries, bread, and produce that we serve, so you know you're eating fresh, local food.

Office coffee service

We'll supply your office with early-morning deliveries of coffee, tea, bagels, fruit, and other goodies. We have whole-bean, ground, and single-serving options. We also offer rental and maintenance of coffee brewing systems. If you have a problem with any of our equipment, in most cases we'll repair or replace it the same day. Call or email for details and a cost estimate.

Wholesale

We offer our products to coffee shops, delis, restaurants, and other vendors at wholesale prices. We have our own coffee and tea blends, as well as selections of South American coffees and popular teas.

Chapter 5: Tables

You will learn how to:

- Insert tables in a document
- Format tables

Module A: Creating tables

Tables in Word can be used for a number of things, including lists of data, calendars, checklists, and layout structure. Anything you put in your documents can also go in a table, such as text, numbers, shapes and pictures, and even another table. You can create a simple blank table, draw a table, convert a selection of text into a table, or make use of one of the built-in tables that come with Word.

You will learn how to:

- Insert a table
- Use the Draw Table tool
- Insert Quick Tables
- Convert text into a table

Tables

Tables are rows and columns of information. Each juncture of a row and column is called a *cell*, and this is where data are stored.

Tables can have header rows and/or header columns to describe the information, as shown in the figure. This table of information about the Greek alphabet is included with Word as a Quick Table.

Letter name	Uppercase	Lowercase	Letter name	Uppercase	Lowercase
Alpha	Α	α	Nu	Ν	ν
Beta	Β	β	Xi	Ξ	ξ
Gamma	Γ	γ	Omicron	Ο	ο
Delta	Δ	δ	Pi	Π	π
Epsilon	Ε	ε	Rho	Ρ	ρ
Zeta	Ζ	ζ	Sigma	Σ	σ
Eta	Η	η	Tau	Τ	τ
Theta	Θ	θ	Upsilon	Υ	υ
Iota	Ι	ι	Phi	Φ	φ
Kappa	Κ	κ	Chi	Χ	χ
Lambda	Λ	λ	Psi	Ψ	ψ
Mu	Μ	μ	Omega	Ω	ω

In this example, there is an external border, but no visible internal borders, so the data looks like a tabular list. There are many options for setting borders in rows, columns, and cells. Borders refer to lines that are visible on screen and that will print. If you want to see the grid lines (or not) while you are working on a table with no borders, you can click **View Gridlines** on the Layout tab. This makes the same example look like this:

Letter name	Uppercase	Lowercase
Alpha	Α	α
Beta	Β	β
Gamma	Γ	γ
Delta	Δ	δ
Epsilon	Ε	ε
Zeta	Ζ	ζ

Gridlines are visible while you are working, but they don't print.

Inserting simple tables

There are two ways to insert a simple, blank table.

Exam Objective: MOS Word Core 3.1.3

- On the Insert tab, click **Table**, then click on the grid.
  To insert a table with corresponding dimensions. Rows will be one line high and columns will be evenly spaced. The table will take up the width of the page. Formatting can be adjusted after the table is in place.

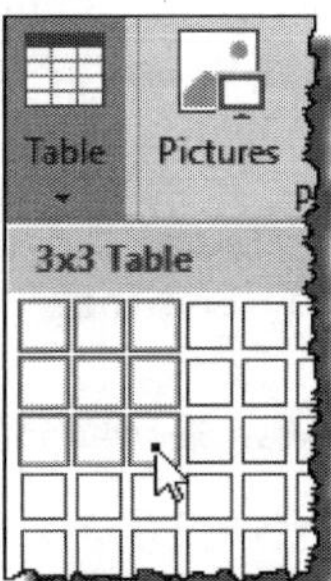

- Click **Table > Insert Table**.
  To open the **Insert Table** window. Here, you can specify the number of rows and columns, and set column width and AutoFit behavior. Click **OK** to insert the table.

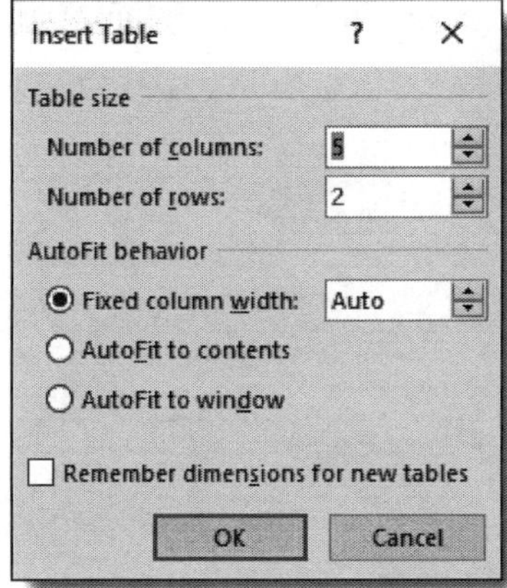

Drawing tables

Drawing a table allows you a little more control and is suitable for tables with irregular dimensions.

1. On the Insert tab, click **Tables > Draw Table**.
   The pointer looks like a pencil, and the Table Tools Design tab is available.
2. Drag to draw lines and boxes.
   - Drag straight across or up and down to draw lines.
   - Drag diagonally to draw a box. You can draw individual cells or draw bigger boxes and draw lines within it.

     Continued...

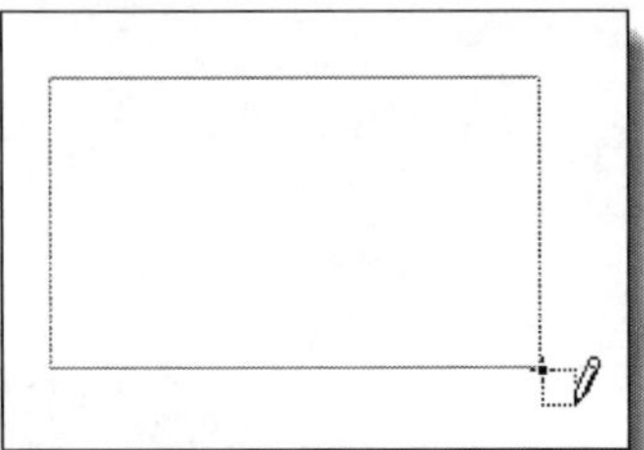

- Drawn tables don't have to be regular or symmetrical.
- To remove a line you don't want, click **Eraser** on the Table Tools Design tab. The pointer changes into an eraser. Click on lines to remove them, or drag over areas to remove areas of a table or the whole table.

3. To exit the tool, press **Esc** or click anywhere outside the table.

   You can use the table drawing and erasing tools on any existing tables, not just on those that were drawn in the first place.

Using tables for layout

We often think of tables as containers for lists of data, such as employee information or sales data, but tables in Word can also be used to control page layout. For example, if you want to create a one-page company newsletter, you could create a table that takes up the whole page, and then use cells to contain text and graphics. This way, paragraphs and pictures stay in place and are not easily shifted by other things moving on the page.

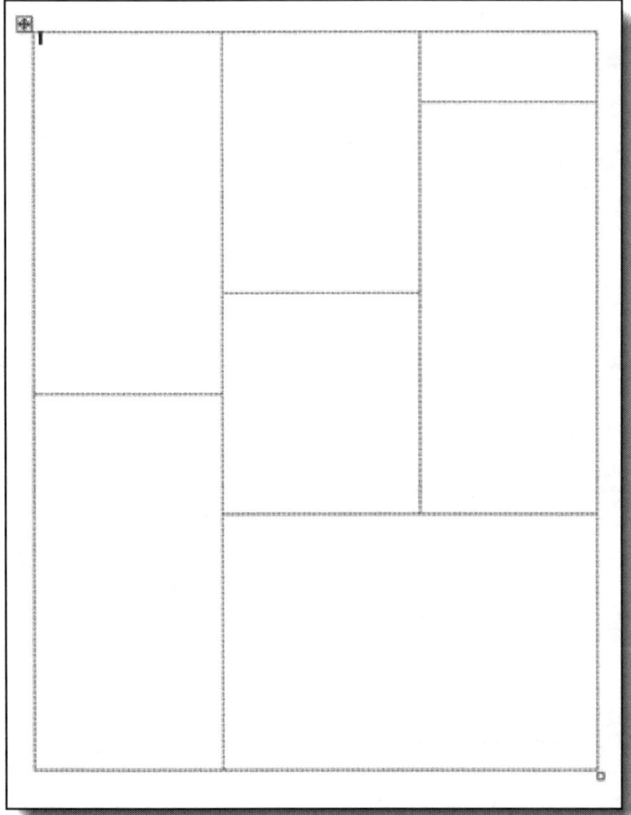

The table drawing tool is especially useful for drawing irregular tables like the one in the figure, which could be used to control page layout. Word has many options for manipulating a table once it is in place. For instance, you can insert, remove, and resize rows and columns; merge and split cells; define a header row; and sort table content.

Quick Tables

Quick Tables are already formatted and in some cases populated with sample data. For instance, calendar Quick Tables have a month name and dates entered, so you can get some idea of how it might look. After inserting one of these, you can delete the data and enter the month and dates you need.

On the Insert tab, click **Table > Quick Tables** to display the Quick Tables gallery, then choose the one you want.

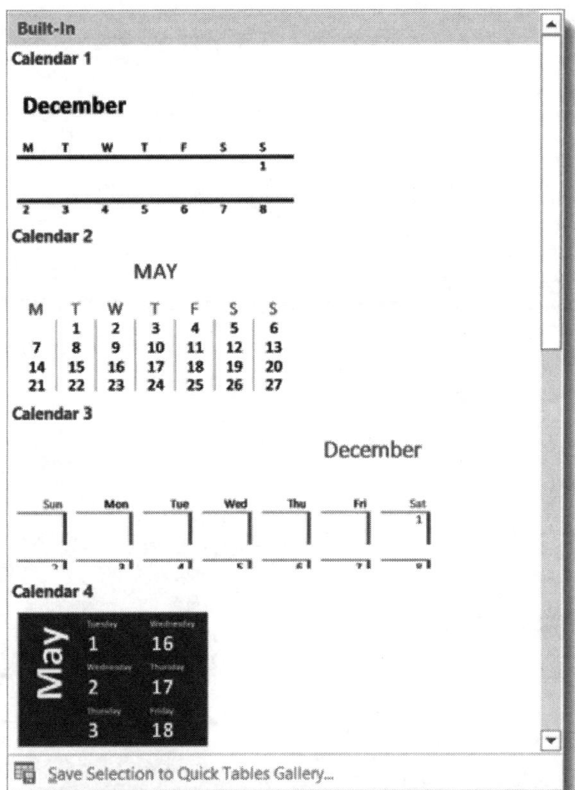

One of the most useful features of Quick Tables is the ability to add your own tables to the gallery. After you create and format your own table, click **Save Selection to Quick Tables Gallery** (at the bottom of the gallery). Your table is then available in the gallery.

Exercise: Creating tables

Exam Objective: MOS Word Core 3.1.3

Do This	How & Why
1. Start a new, blank document in Word.	
2. On the Insert tab, click **Table**.	To display the Insert Table grid.
3. Click the 4x6 location on the grid.	To insert a table that's four columns by six rows.
4. On the Table Tools Layout tab, click **Draw Table**.	
5. Experiment with the Draw Table tool: • Drag to draw a large box. • Draw lines inside the box for columns and rows. • Try irregular rows or cells that don't span the whole table.	
6. Experiment with the **Eraser** tool: • Click on a single line to remove it. • Drag over areas to remove several lines.	
7. Use the **Eraser** tool to remove all of the tables on the page.	You should now be back to a blank page.
8. On the Insert tab, click **Table** > **Insert Table**.	To open the **Insert Table** window.
9. Set the table options: a) Set columns to `4` and rows to `6`. b) Select **Fixed column width** and set it to `1"`. c) Click **OK**.	The table is added with 1-inch columns. The cursor is in the first cell.
10. On the Table Tools Layout tab, click **Delete** > **Delete Table**.	You are back to a blank page.

Do This	How & Why
11. On the Insert tab, click **Table > Quick Tables.**	To open the built-in tables gallery.
12. Click the table of your choice.	To add it to the document.
13. Close the document without saving.	Leave Word open.

Converting text to table

You might decide that existing content would look better or be better organized in a table.

Exam Objective: MOS Word Core 3.1.1, 3.1.2

1. Select the text you want to put in a table.
2. On the Insert tab, click **Table > Convert Text to Table.**

   To open the **Convert Text to Table** window.

   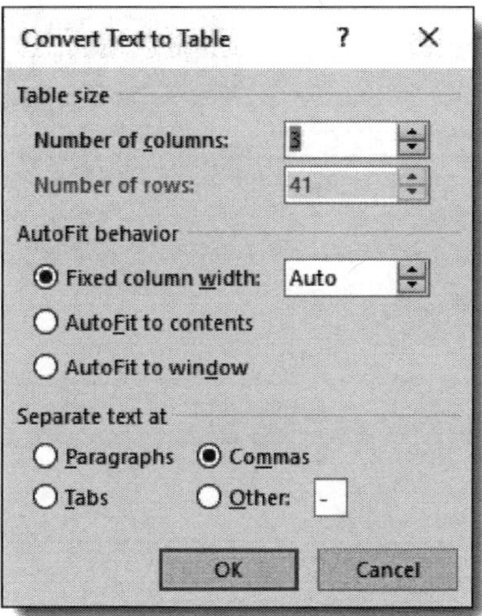

3. Set options, if necessary.
   - Word guesses an appropriate table size according to the text selected. You can change it, but choices are limited by what's selected.
   - Word also guesses the *delimiter* that separates units of data to go into different cells.
4. Click **OK**.

   The table is inserted and the selected text moved into it. You can adjust and edit this table just as you would any other.

To reverse the process and convert a table to text, select the table, then click **Convert to Text** on the Table Tools Layout tab.

Exercise: Converting a list into a table

Exam Objective: MOS Word Core 3.1.1

Do This	How & Why
1. Open `Coffee List` and save it as `Coffee Table`.	In the current chapter's data folder. This document contains a list of coffee origins and types. The two pieces of information are separated by a tab character.
2. Select the tabular list.	
3. On the Insert tab, click **Table** > **Convert Text to Table**.	The **Convert Text to Table** window opens.
4. Select **AutoFit to Contents**.	Notice that Tabs is selected under "Separate text at." Word recognized the tab characters in the selected text.
5. Click **OK**.	The table is created with columns that are just wide enough to contain the contents.
6. Save and close the file.	

Assessment: Creating tables

1. Gridlines show you where table borders are, but they do not print. True or false?
   - True
   - False
2. Which tool is best for creating a table with irregular rows, columns, and cells?
   - Insert Table window
   - Draw Table tool
   - Quick Tables
   - Insert Table grid
3. The table eraser tool can only be used on tables created with the table drawing tool. True or false?
   - True
   - False

Module B: Formatting tables

Once a table is in place, you can format it in many ways. You can resize the whole table or individual rows and columns. You can apply background shading and borders in different colors. You can also define headers for each column and sort the table on column data.

You will learn how to:

- Resize tables
- Add, remove, and move rows and columns
- Define a header row
- Sort a table

Table formatting

When you select all or part of a table, or when the cursor is in a table, these Table Tools tabs appear: Design and Layout. The Design tab allows you to add shading and borders and apply table styles. It also has the table drawing tools. The Layout tab provides commands to manipulate rows, columns, and cells, as well as data alignment and sorting.

Exam Objective: MOS Word Core 3.1.4

The Table Styles section on the Table Tools Design tab allows you to pick a pre-defined table format from a gallery. Styles include borders, shading, and header highlighting.

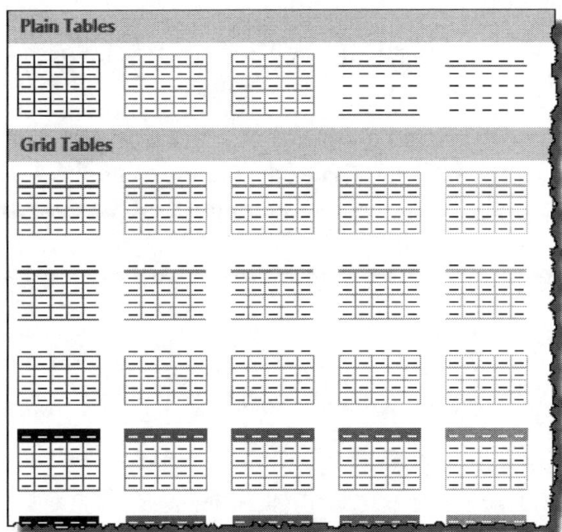

You can also set borders and shading individually for parts of a table by using those buttons on the Table Tools Design tab. For instance, you could select a cell or range of cells and apply a thick border around them for emphasis.

Resizing tables

There are a number of ways to manually or automatically control and change the size of rows, columns, and tables.

Exam Objective: MOS Word Core 3.2.3, 3.2.4, 3.2.5

- On the Table Tools Layout tab, click **AutoFit**, and then click an option.
- To change the size of rows or columns, drag the borders to where you want them.

  Where you can drag a border might be restricted by what you've selected, cell content, page size, and table settings. When you drag a column border in selected rows, the column width changes only in the selected rows. Thus, you can also select a single row and drag the border of one of its cells to change its margins.

Colombia	Colombian
Ethiopia	Harar
Ethiopia	Sidamo
Hawaii	Kona

- To merge multiple cells into one, select two or more adjacent cells, right click them, and then click **Merge**.
- To split a cell, right-click in it, and click **Split Cells**. Set the number of rows and columns into which to split them, then click **OK**.
- To split a table in two, click within the row you want to be first in the split table, then click **Split Table** on the Table Tools Layout tab.
- To distribute rows or columns evenly, select all or a range of rows and/or columns, right-click, and click **Distribute Rows Evenly** or **Distribute Columns Evenly**.
- To specify row and column size, set the values on the Row and Column tabs of the **Table Properties** window.
- To specify cell/column margins, first display the ruler, if necessary (on the View tab, click **Ruler**); click in the cell/column you wish to adjust; and on the ruler, drag the left- and right-edge column handles for that cell/column to reduce or enlarge its width. Or, on the Table Tools Layout tab, in the Cell Size group, click in the Table Column Width box, and specify the size numerically.

Manipulating rows and columns

Although there are many commands on the Table Tools tabs, most of what you want to do can be done from the menu that opens when you right-click a table.

- For some operations, you need to select a column, row, cell, or range of cells first:
  - To select a column, point above it, and click when you see a heavy down arrow.

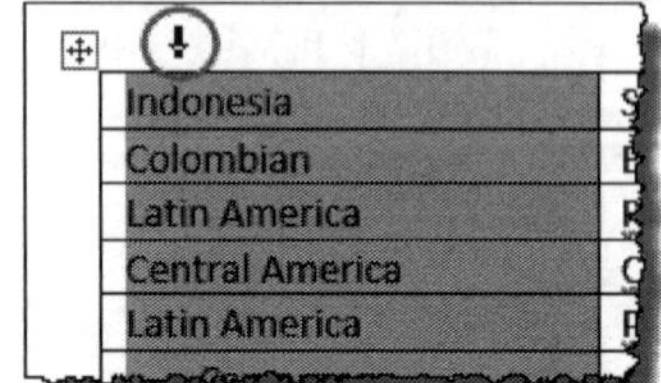

  - To select a row, click in the margin to the left of it.
  - To select a cell, triple-click in it.
  - To select a range of cells, drag over them the way you would to select text.
- There are a couple of ways to add a new row or columns.

- Right-click the existing row or column where you want to add another, then click **Insert**, and click the option you want. You can instead use the insert options on the Layout tab. If you right-click on a value in a cell, you might get a different menu.
- Select a row, then point in the margin just above or below the selected row and click the plus sign that appears. The same mouse-based method works for columns.

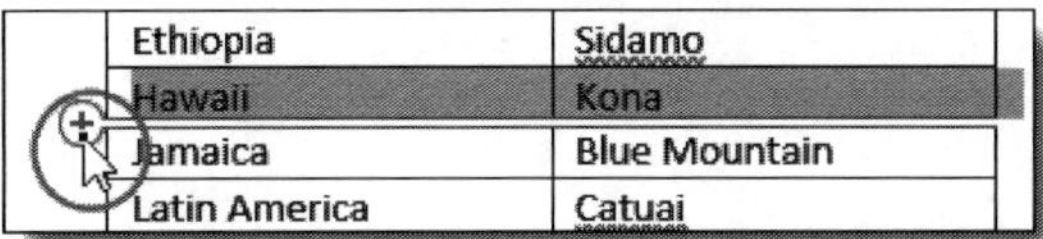

- To move rows or columns, select the row or column you want to move, then drag it to the location you want.

  Be careful about where you actually release the mouse button.
- To delete rows or columns, select the row(s) or column(s) you want to delete, right-click the selected item(s), and then click **Delete Rows** or **Delete Columns**.

  Pressing the **Delete** key just deletes the data, leaving the cells empty.

Defining a header row

If you have column headings in the first row of a table, and that table might be split across two or more pages, you might want to repeat the header at the top of each new page.

Exam Objective: MOS Word Core 3.2.6

1. Click in any cell in the first row.

   You can define only the first row as a header row.
2. On the Table Tools Layout tab, click **Repeat Header Rows**.

   You can also do this from the Row tab in the **Table Properties** window.

   This defines the first row as a header row, and repeats that row if the table is split across two or more pages.

Specifying a table title

You can specify a table title and description in the **Table Properties** window. Doing so provides a text representation of the table (or other object), known as *Alt Text*. This can be helpful as a clarifying description of the table and its contents. It's also helpful to those with visual disabilities.

1. With the table selected, click **Properties**.

   On the Table Tools Layout tab, in the Table group.

   The **Table Properties** window opens.
2. Display the Alt Text tab.
3. Specify a table title.

   In the Title box. You can also describe the table in the Description box.

   Continued...

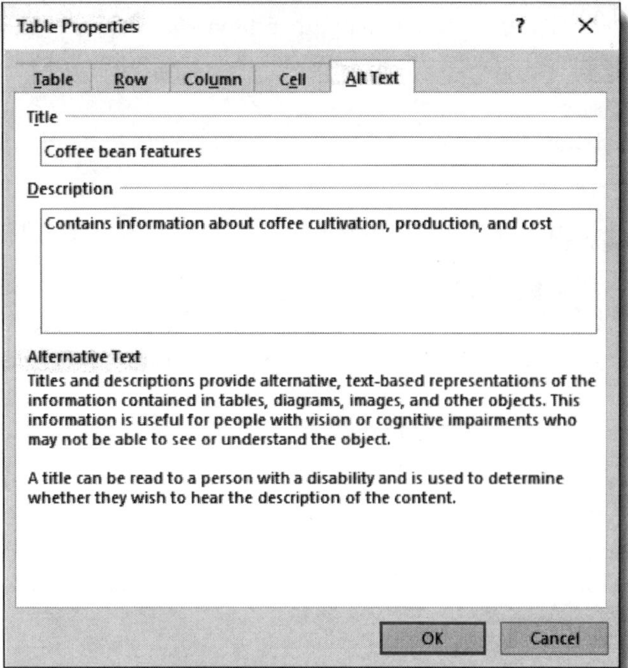

4. Click **OK**.

Sorting table content

You can sort a table on one or more columns. If there is a header row defined, the column names appear in the sort options. If not, columns are designated as Column 1, Column 2, and so on.

Exam Objective: MOS Word Core 3.2.1

1. Click in any cell.

   To put the cursor in the table and make the table tools available. You can also select a column, or a range of rows, if you plan to sort only that column or range.

2. On the Table Tools Layout tab, click **Sort**.

   To open the **Sort** window.

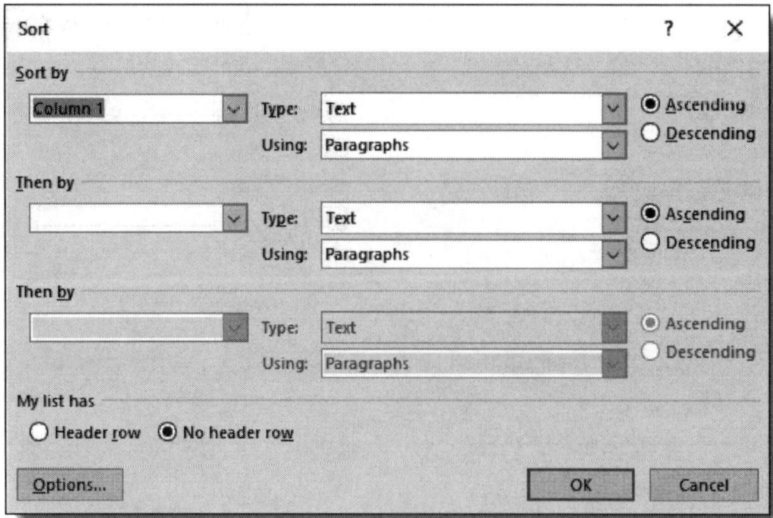

3. Set the sorting options, if necessary:

- Select a column to sort on. If you have defined a header row, you see column headers in the list. Otherwise, columns are numbered.
- You can select a second column to sort on, if you want. For instance, in a table of names, you might sort by last name, and then by first name.
- If your first row is headers, be sure to select **Header row**, so that these values don't get sorted in with the data.
- The **Options** button opens the **Sort Option** window, providing a few more settings, such as language, and whether to sort the selected column only.

4. Click **OK**.

   The table is sorted by the information in the column(s) you selected. By default, the data in each row stays together. For instance, if you sort employee records by last name, the employee first name and contact information stays with the last name. Sometimes you might want to sort only the selected column, and you can choose that option in the **Sort Options** window.

Exercise: Formatting and sorting a table

Exam Objective: MOS Word Core 3.2.1, 3.2.4, 3.2.6

Do This	How & Why
1. Open `Region Table`, and save it as `Region-Variety Table`.	
2. Drag the border between the two columns to the left.	Indonesia / Suma; Colombian / Bogot; Latin America / Pacas; Central America / Catur To make just the first column narrower.
3. Double-click the border between the columns.	To "best fit" the first column, making it just wide enough to fit the longest text it contains.
4. On the Layout tab, click **AutoFit** > **AutoFit Contents**.	To fit the all the data better.
5. Select the bottom two rows.	The micro formatting toolbar is displayed.
6. Click **Delete** > **Delete Rows**.	Insert; Delete; Delete Cells...; Delete Columns; Delete Rows; Delete Table
7. Select the top row. On the micro formatting toolbar, click **Insert** > **Insert Above**.	

Do This	How & Why
8. In the top row, enter the values `Region` and `Variety`.	Region / Variety; Indonesia / Sumatra; Colombian / Bogota Supremo; Latin America / Pacas; Central America / Caturra
9. With the cursor in the first row, on the Table Tools Layout tab, in the Data group, click **Repeat Header Rows**.	To define it as a header row.
10. Also in the Data group, click **Sort**.	The **Sort** window opens, with Region in the "Sort by" field.
11. In the "Then by" list, click **Variety**.	Sort by: Region, Type: Text, Using: Paragraphs; Then by: Variety, Type: Text, Using: Paragraphs
12. Click **OK**.	The table is sorted first by region, then by variety name. If you look at the Latin American varieties, this will be clear.
13. Save and close the file.	

Assessment: Formatting tables

1. By default, sorting a table on a column will sort only that column, leaving data in the other columns in place. True or False?
   - True
   - False
2. To delete a column, select it and press Delete. True or false?
   - True
   - False
3. Besides the Insert Table window, where can you find AutoFit options for a table?
   - Design tab
   - Table Tools Layout tab
   - Right-click menu
   - Table Properties

Summary: Tables

You should now know how to:

- Insert simple tables and quick tables, draw tables, and convert text into a table
- Format a table by resizing, manipulate rows and columns, define a header row, and sort table data

Synthesis: Tables

In this synthesis exercise, you'll open a document with a list of customer information, convert it to a table, manipulate its data, and format it using a style.

1. Open `Customer List`, and save it as `Customer Table`.
2. Convert that tabular list to a table.
   AutoFit the contents. Don't include the title.
3. Add a header row with the values `Customer`, `Rep`, and `Region`.
4. Define the first row as a header row.
5. Move the first column to make it the last column.
   Select the column, and drag it right.
6. Sort the table by **Rep**.
7. On the Design tab, apply a table style of your choosing.
   You might want to clear the **First Column** check box in the Table Style Option group.

The result should look something like the figure below, depending on which style you picked.

The customer list turned into a formatted table

Java Tucana Customer List

Rep	Region	Customer
Blackwell	International	The Grand
Daniels	US	BlazerFire
Daniels	US	CrossCountry Airways
Franklin	Eurozone	Central
Franklin	Eurozone	Imagenie
Franklin	Eurozone	YourWay Airline
Hernandez	Eurozone	Earth Farm
Hernandez	Eurozone	Gleeson Associates
Hernandez	Eurozone	Red Rock Mountain Tours

Chapter 6: Shapes, WordArt, and SmartArt

You will learn how to:

- Insert shapes and use WordArt
- Insert and format SmartArt

Module A: Shapes and text

You can add different shapes to your Word document, combine several shapes to make more complex shapes, and edit and format shapes after they are inserted.

You will learn how to:

- Insert a shape
- Modify shape borders
- Apply shape styles
- Add text to shapes and apply WordArt

Inserting shapes

Unlike a picture or clip art, a shape does not go in as a character. By default, it's drawn on top of any exiting text.

Exam Objective: MOS Word Core 5.1.1

1. On the Insert tab, click **Shapes**.
   To open the shapes gallery.
2. Select the shape you want to create.
   The gallery closes, and the pointer resembles a large plus sign.

3. Drag on the document where you want the shape to be.
   To keep the original aspect ratio, hold **Shift** while you drag.
   The shape is drawn on the document.
4. To move the shape, point to an edge, but *not* on a handle, and drag it where you want.

Once the shape is in place, you can edit its size, shape, and location in many ways. Use the **Position** and **Wrap Text** commands to change the way the shape interacts with surrounding text.

Modifying shape borders

There are a number of ways to modify the path of a shape's border after you've inserted it. First, select the shape, if necessary, by clicking it. Then, click the Drawing Tools Format tab.

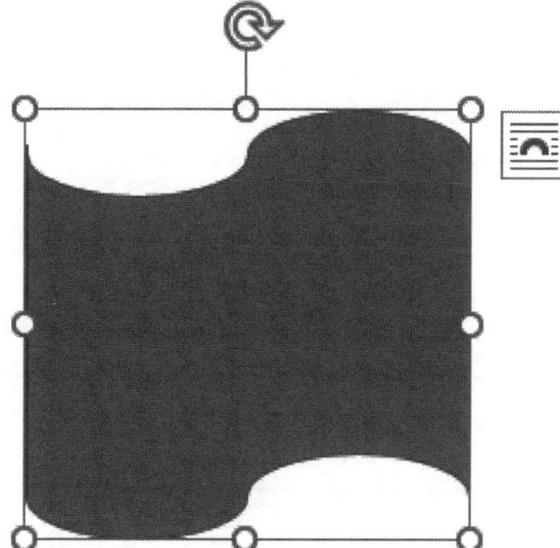

- To resize the shape, drag the corner or edge handles. To preserve the aspect ratio, hold down **Shift** while dragging a corner handle.
- To rotate the shape, drag the rotation handle around. It's the circular arrow.
- Some shapes also have yellow handles to resize certain parts of the shape.
- On the Drawing Tools Format tab, in the Insert Shapes group, click **Edit Shape > Change Shape** to select a different shape from the gallery.

  The new shape will replace the old in the same bounding box; that is, at the same location, size, and rotation.
- In the Insert Shapes group, click **Edit Shape > End Points**.

  Black square handles appear along the path of the border. The more complicated the path, the more handles there are.

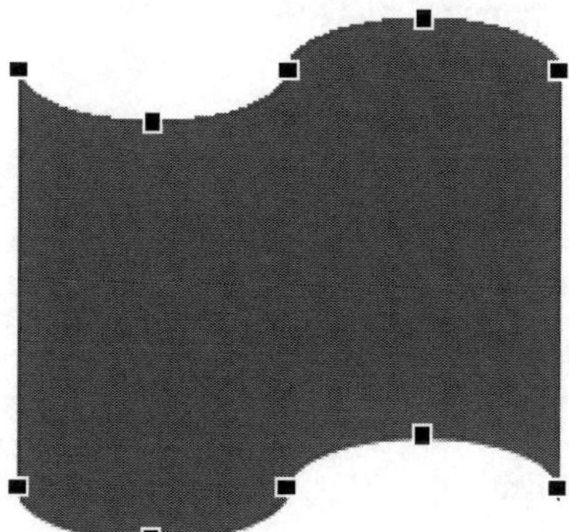

- Drag the endpoint handles to change the shape.
- Drag any point on the border to create a new point and change the shape.
- When you click (or drag) a point, two lines with white handles appear on either side. Drag these to control the shape of the curve on that side of the point.

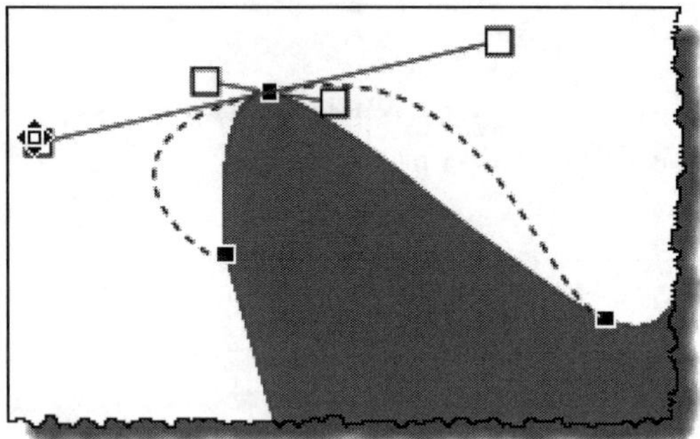

- Right-click a point to see a menu of other options for adding, removing, and changing points, as well as the micro formatting toolbar.

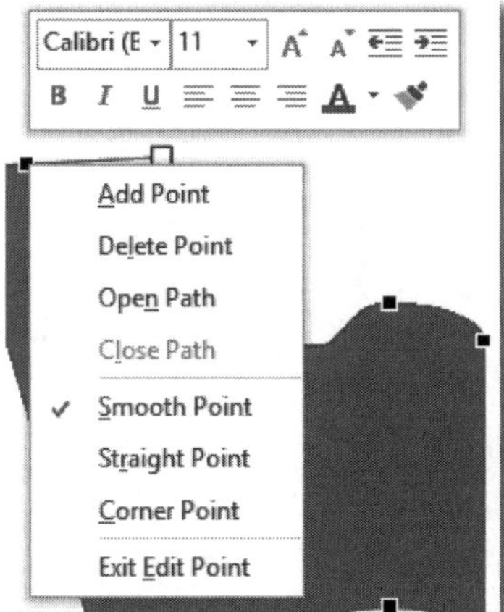

The best way to learn about adjusting points and curves is to experiment.

Shape styles

After you insert a shape, you can apply various styles to it by using the options in the Shape Styles group on the Drawing Tools Format tab. This tab becomes available when a shape is selected.

A shape's style is the combination of three general attributes:

- *Shape Fill* is the color and gradient of the fill. You can also use a picture or texture image as fill.
- *Shape Outline* is the color, thickness, and dash pattern of the border.
- *Shape Effects* are special effects like shadow, bevel, and 3-D rotation.

You can choose from the shape styles gallery to apply several of these attributes at once, or you can apply your own combination. The figure shows the same shape, a rounded rectangle, with the default formatting (left) and with a different color and effects applied: reflection, bevel, shadow, and 3-D rotation. You can also use the format painter to copy a shape's style and apply it to another shape.

The menu commands will suffice for much of what you want to do, but if you need more precise control over shape effects, right-click a shape and click **Format Shape**. You can also use the dialog box launcher in the Shape Styles group. This opens the Format Shape pane, in which you can, for example, expand the Fill and/or Line options to set angles of rotation, transparency of reflections, and the details of beveled and reflective shapes. You can leave the Format Shape pane open as you select different shapes.

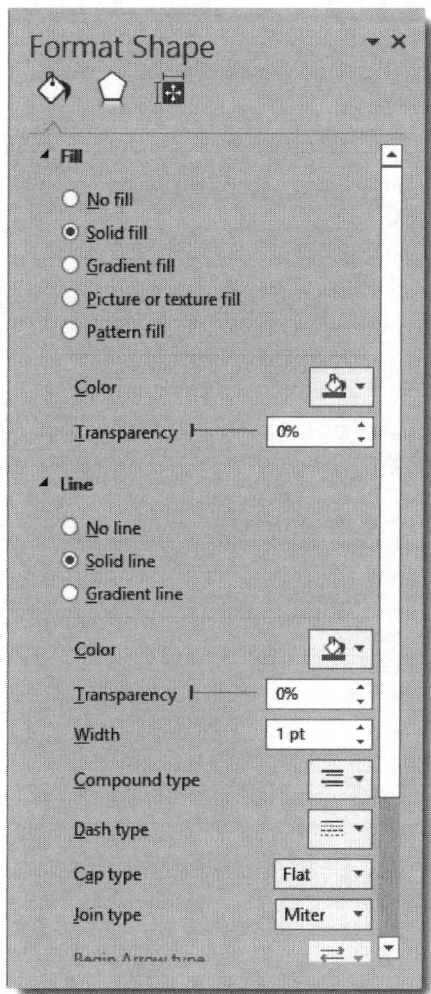

Exercise: Inserting a shape

Do This	How & Why
1. Start a new, blank document, and save it as `Shapes`.	
2. On the Insert tab, click **Shapes** and select a rectangle shape with rounded or clipped corners.	Pick any rectangle except a simple one. The pointer changes into a large plus sign.
3. Drag a rectangle that's about 2 in x 4 in (5cm x 10 cm).	
4. Experiment with dragging different handles and edges. • Corner handles adjust size while maintaining aspect ratio. • Side handles change size and aspect ratio. • Yellow handles, when present, change characteristics of curves and angles. • The round, white handle freely rotates the shape.	
5. On the Format tab, experiment with various shape effects.	Try changing the shadow, reflection, bevel, and rotation, and whatever else you want.
6. Experiment with other shapes and effects, as time allows.	If time allows. Right-click a shape, and click **Format Shape**. Experiment with the options in this pane.
7. Save and close the document.	

Text on shapes

To place text on a shape, select the shape and start typing.

If at first you don't like the way it looks, don't worry about it; you can adjust it. For one thing, you can select text on a shape and then use font and paragraph options on the Home tab, just as you would with any text.

Also, when text on a shape is selected, the Drawing Tools Format tab appears, which contains the WordArt Styles and Text groups.

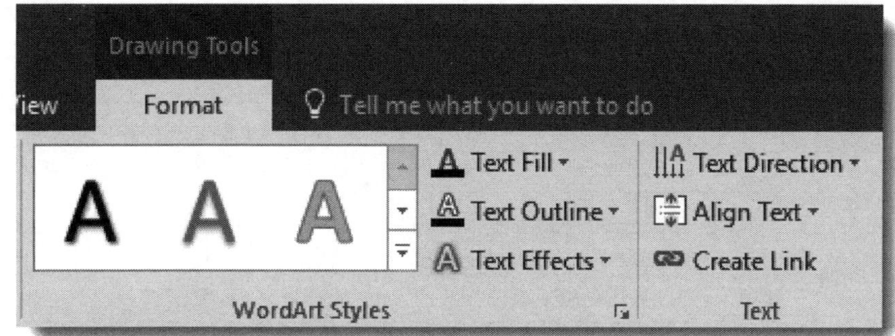

- The **Text Direction** command allows you to make the text run vertically, so that it runs up or down the page. This is useful, for instance, for having a section title along the edge of the page.

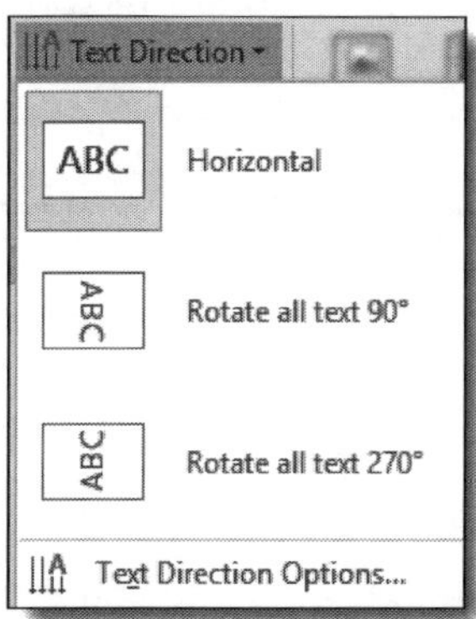

- The **Align Text** command aligns the text within the shape—top, middle, or bottom. For other text alignment options, use the paragraph group on the Home tab.
- The **Create Link** command allows you to link text boxes, so that text can run from one text box to another. This is not to be confused with creating hyperlinks.

Inserting text boxes

It is helpful to remember that there is no difference in Word between a shape and a text box. A text box is a shape with text on it. Some text boxes have the text in a container, but the box is still a shape.

Exam Objective: MOS Word Core 5.1.4

There are several ways to insert a text box.

- In the Insert tab, click **Shapes**, then click the text box icon in the shapes gallery.
  It's under Basic Shapes.

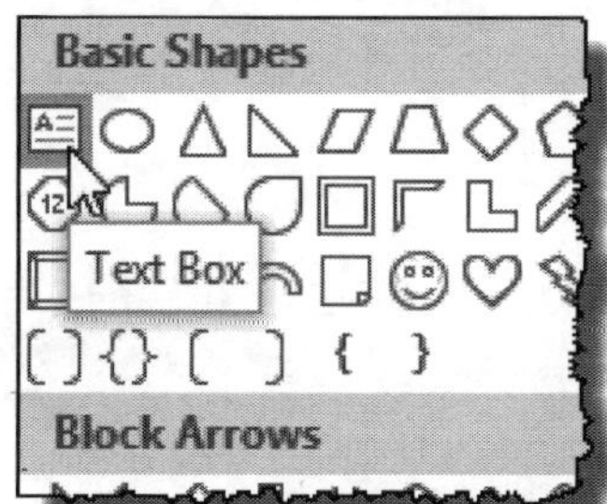

- Select any shape, and enter text.
- On the Insert tab, click **WordArt**, and then select a style.
  This creates a text box with formatted text.

- On the Insert tab, click **Text Box**, and then select a text box from the gallery.
  It contains text boxes that have been formatted and positioned for various purposes.
- On the Drawing Tools Format tab, in the Insert Shapes group, click the down arrow to the right of the shapes gallery, and then select a text-box shape.

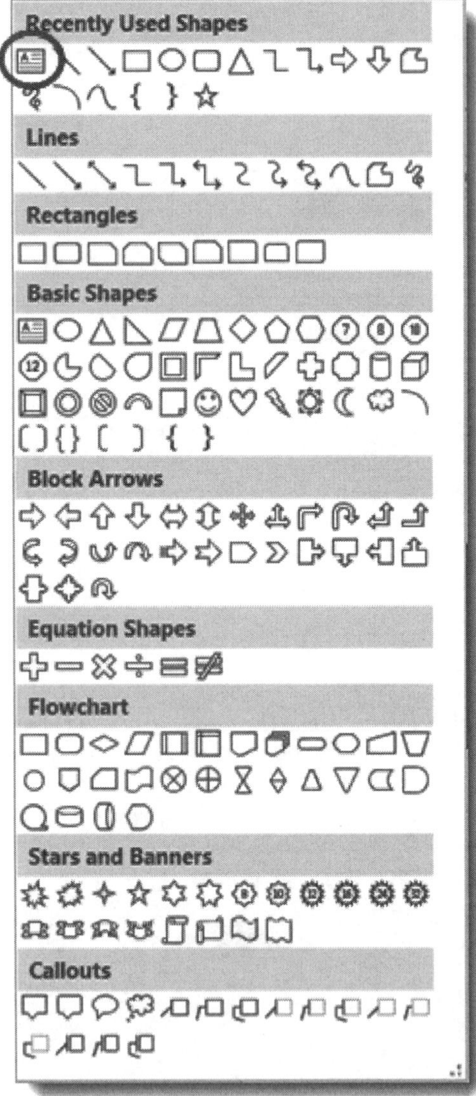

If you want to save the style for a text box that you've created, select the text box, then, on the Insert tab, click **Text Box > Save Selection to Text Box Gallery**.

WordArt

Exam Objective: MOS Word Core 2.2.10

Text both inside and outside text boxes can be formatted with the font and paragraph options on the Home tab. You can change things like font face, size, color, spacing, and alignment. You can even apply some font effects such as glow and reflection to either text type.

But only text in a text box can receive the full WordArt treatment, which includes 3-D rotation, following a path, and warping. In fact, to change text to WordArt, just apply a WordArt style to text in the document body; the text is then pulled out and put in a text box.

WordArt essentially treats text characters like a set of shapes, and WordArt styles are much like shape styles, with many of the same options. The WordArt group is on the Drawing Tools Format tab, which appears when a shape or text box is selected.

- *Text Fill* is the color and gradient of the text. The gradient is applied across all the text in the box, not each letter.
- *Text Outline* is the color, weight, and dash pattern of the character outlines.
- *Text Effects* include many of the options available for shapes, such as shadow, reflection, glow, bevel, and 3-D rotation. In addition, WordArt has options to transform the text to follow a path or to be warped, as in the figure below.

If you are going to apply both WordArt styles to the text and shape styles to the text box, you'll need to experiment with how the effects work together. For instance, if you reflect the text box, you won't need to reflect the text, because it will already be reflected. Some combinations of text box and text formatting will give you unpleasant results.

Note that you can't use a 3-D rotation for the text that is different than that of the text box. Whichever option you set last applies to both.

Exercise: Using WordArt

Do This	How & Why
1. Start a new, blank document, and save it as `Textbox`.	
2. On the Insert tab, click **Text Box > Draw Text Box**.	
3. Drag a rectangle on the document.	A simple rectangle is drawn with a cursor in it.
4. Type your full name.	Or anything else you want.
5. Increase the font size:	
a) Select all of the text, or select the shape by clicking its border.	
b) On the Home tab, change the font size to `36`.	
c) Resize the shape to fit the text, if necessary.	
d) Switch back to the Format tab.	
6. In the WordArt Styles group, experiment with Text Effects.	Experiment especially with Transform effects, which apply only to text. Transformed text also has yellow handles which you use to change the transform effect. Also experiment with gradients, under Text Fill.
7. Experiment with other text boxes, as time allows.	See how the Shapes Styles and WordArt Styles interact.
8. Save and close the document.	

Assessment: Shapes and text

1. A text box is a shape with text on it. True or false?
   - True
   - False
2. How can you access the Drawing Tools Format tab?
   - Select a shape.
   - Right-click a shape, and click Format Shape.
   - Press Ctrl+F.
3. Which two ways can you open the Format Shape pane to have precise control over shape effects?
   - Right-click a shape, and click Format Shape.
   - Click the lower-right corner of the Shape Styles group.
   - Double-click a shape.
   - Right-click a shape, and click More Layout Options.

Module B: SmartArt

SmartArt is a set of professionally designed diagrams made up of shapes and text.

You will learn:

- How to insert and format SmartArt

About SmartArt

Exam Objective: MOS Word Core 5.3.1, 5.3.2, 5.3.3

You add a SmartArt diagram from the Insert tab. The SmartArt gallery is organized by design and purpose. The shapes in SmartArt can hold text, pictures, or both.

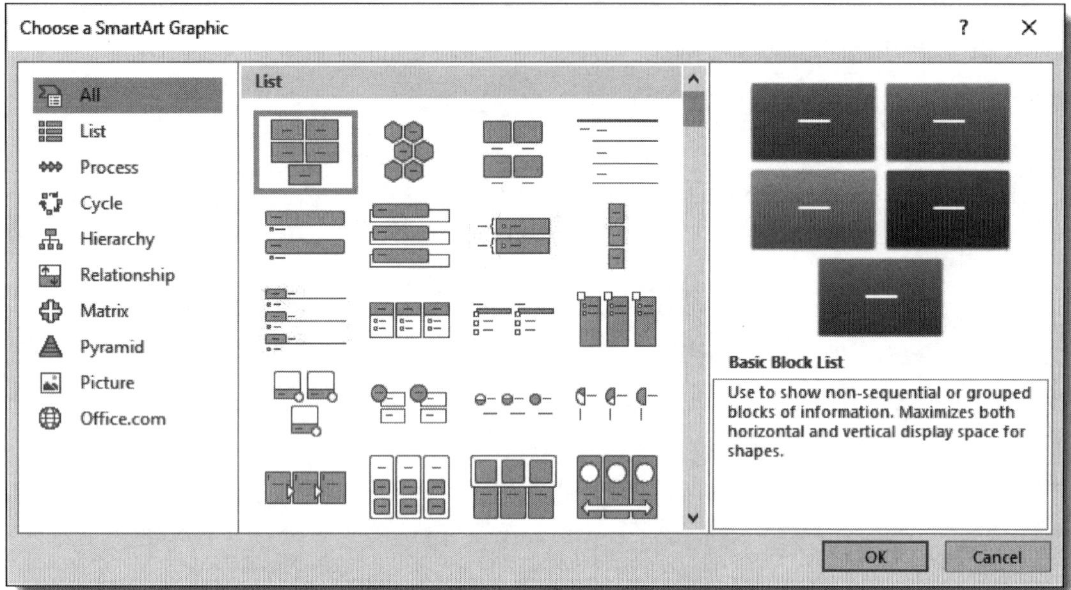

The parts of a SmartArt diagram are inserted into you document in a container that can be moved and resized. When you resize the container, the diagram is resized accordingly.

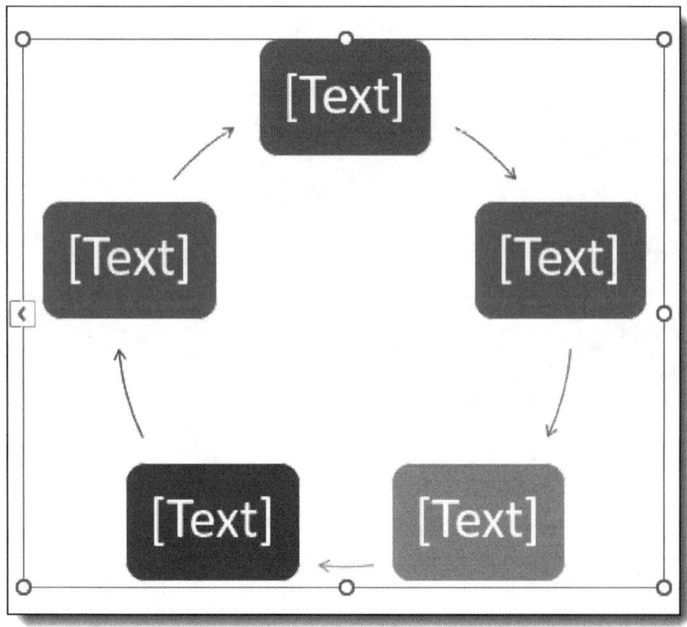

When SmartArt is selected in a document, two related tabs become available: Design and Format. The Design tab has options for the overall layout and color of the diagram. The Format tab has options for shape and WordArt formatting, and is very similar to the Drawing Tools Format tab.

SmartArt formatting

Exam Objective: MOS Word Core 5.3.1, 5.3.2, 5.3.3

You can add text directly to the shapes in a SmartArt diagram, or you can click the expand button on the left edge of the container to open the text pane.

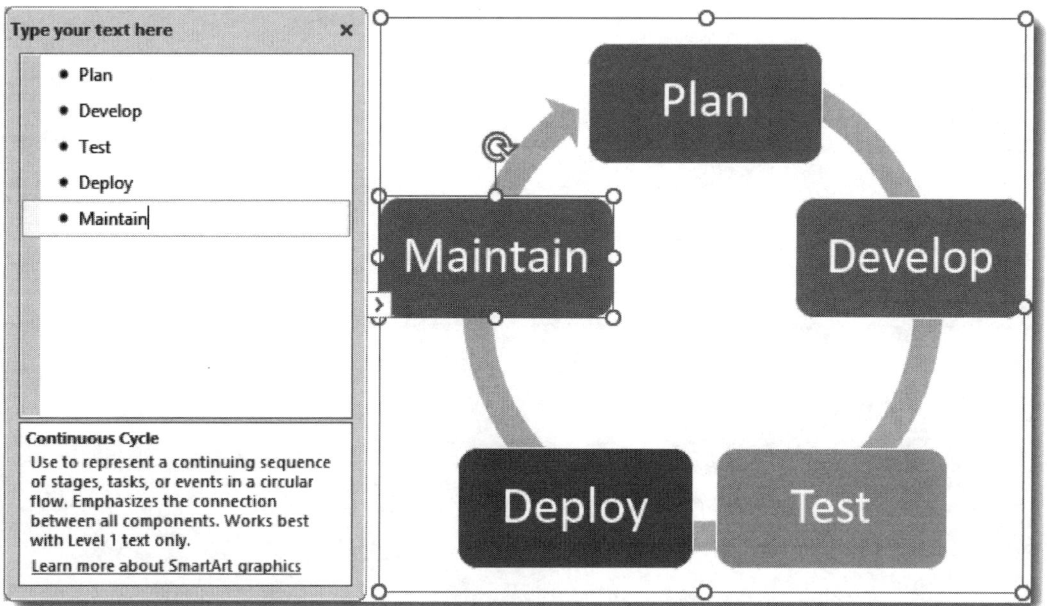

The text pane allows you to indent items, which makes them sub-items of the list item above, and puts them in the same shape.

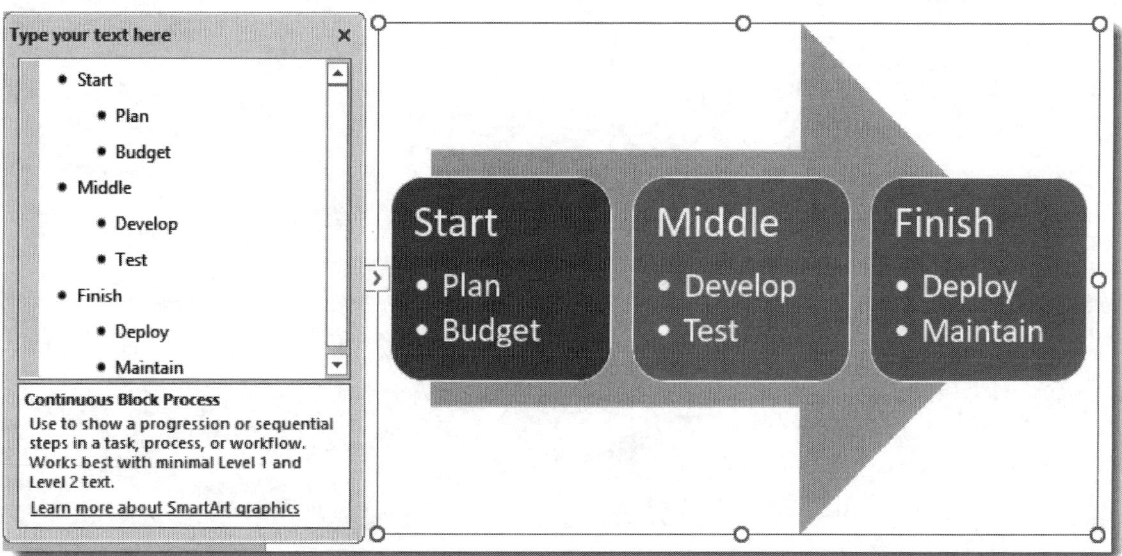

Using the Design tab, you can change the layout and colors of the diagram. The Format tab lets you format the shapes and text using shape styles and WordArt styles. You format shapes in SmartArt just as you would standalone shapes. If you select a single shape in the diagram and then apply shape styles or WordArt styles, the effects are applied only to the selected shape. If you have the whole diagram selected, the shape and WordArt formatting is applied to all parts of the diagram.

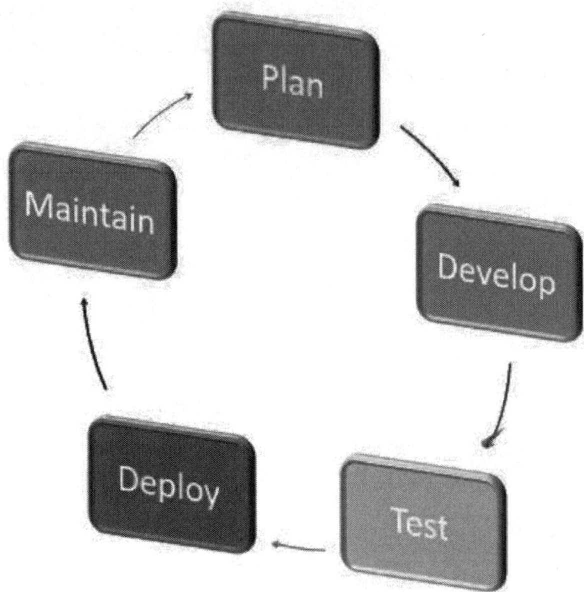

To remove all effects and return to the default formatting, click **Reset Graphic**. This doesn't remove any shapes or text you've added.

Exercise: Inserting SmartArt

Do This	How & Why
1. Start a new blank document, and save it as `SmartArt`.	
2. On the Insert tab, click **SmartArt**.	The Choose a SmartArt Graphic window opens.
3. Look through the graphics for various categories.	
4. In the Cycle category, select **Radial Cycle**, and click **OK**.	The cycle graphic is inserted into a container with the default color.
5. On the SmartArt Design tab, in the Create Graphic group, click **Add Shape**.	To add a circle to the cycle.
6. On the left edge of the graphic container, click the expand button.	

Do This	How & Why
7. Enter the following text in the six bullets: • Development Cycle • Research • Design • Code • Test • Deploy	
8. Close the text entry box.	
9. On the Design tab, click **Change Colors**, and click the first choice under Colorful.	
10. Drag the bottom center of the frame down.	To make the diagram bigger.
11. On the Design tab, in the SmartArt Styles group, select a style of your choosing from the gallery.	You diagram should look something like the figure, depending on which style you chose.
12. Save and close the document.	

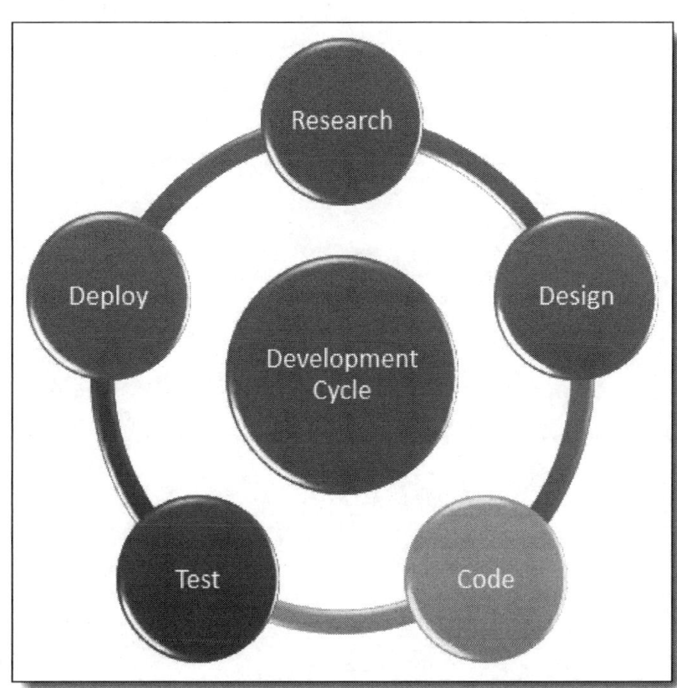

Assessment: SmartArt

1. Clicking Reset Graphic returns a graphic to its original state, immediately after you've inserted it. True or false?
   - True
   - False
2. You can apply different styles to individual shapes in a SmartArt diagram. True or false?
   - True
   - False

Summary: Shapes, WordArt, and SmartArt

You should now know how to:

- Insert shapes, change shape borders and styles, add text to shapes, and apply WordArt
- Insert and format SmartArt

Synthesis: Shapes, WordArt, and SmartArt

1. Start a new, blank document, and save it as `FoodArt`.
2. Insert the SmartArt Bending Picture Caption List.
   It's in the Picture category.

   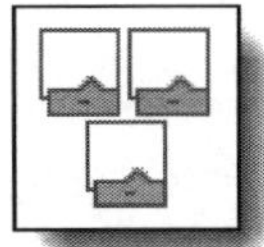

3. Resize the frame, so that there are two shapes over one shape and the graphic is a little larger.
   Drag the bottom down.
4. Add the following text in the text pane:
   - `Specialty Drinks`
   - `Baked Goods`
   - `Sandwiches`
5. Change the color to **Colored Fill - Accent 2**.
   Click **Change Colors**, and click the second orange option.
6. Change the bevel to **Riblet**.
   Use Shape Effects on the Format tab. Ensure that the frame is selected but not any individual shapes.
7. Add a picture to the first shape:
   a) Click the image icon in the center of the first shape.
   b) Click **Browse**.
   c) Select the picture file `Drinks`.
   d) Click **Insert**.
8. Add the pictures `Baked` and `Sandwich` to the other two shapes.
9. De-select the SmartArt frame.
   Your graphic should look something like the figure on the next page.
10. Save and close the file.

Specialty Drinks
Baked Goods
Sandwiches

Chapter 7: Managing documents

You will learn how to:

- Divide a document using sections
- Insert Quick Parts
- Customize document themes
- Format page backgrounds

Module A: Custom themes

Word comes with a variety of themes you can apply to your documents, but if none of them fits your needs, you can customize one and even save it as a new theme of your own.

You will learn how to:

- Set individual theme elements
- Create new theme fonts and colors
- Save or load themes

Theme elements

A theme consists of three elements, as shown in the Document Formatting group on the Design tab.

Exam Objective: MOS Word Core 4.2.3 and Expert 1.3.2

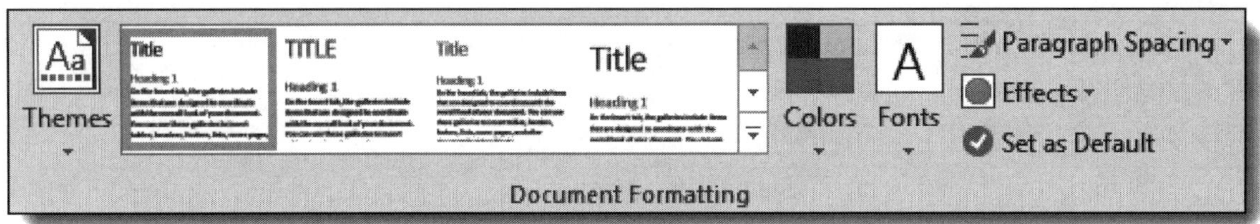

Colors A theme has twelve colors. Ten are those you see in the Theme Colors section of the color menus throughout Word. These include lighter and darker variants: one *Light Text/Background*, two *Dark Text/Background*, and six *Accents*. The last two are *Hyperlink* and *Followed Hyperlink*.

Fonts A theme has two fonts: a heading font and a body font. They can be the same or different.

Effects Theme effects apply only to graphical elements like shapes, charts, and SmartArt graphics. Beyond that, they're visible only if you format those shapes with theme effects. Although effects are less frequently visible than colors and fonts, they still can make a vivid difference in a document's graphics.

Different theme effects applied to the same shape.

By clicking any of the three galleries, you can set that element independently. By default, each gallery contains an entry for each installed theme. For example, you can use the colors of the *Civic* theme, the fonts of *Black Tie*, and the effects of *Slipstream*.

Remember, when you change a theme or its elements, any formatting that uses colors, fonts, or effects that aren't part of the theme remain unchanged.

- Colors change only if they are from the Theme Colors list. Standard Colors and Custom Colors do not change.
- Fonts change only if they are selected from the Theme Fonts list, either by styles or by manual formatting.
- Shape effects are a little less obvious. They mostly apply to shape styles that contain "Effect" in the name, but this isn't universal. For instance, whether a chart style uses theme effects isn't obvious from its name.

Creating theme colors

Exam Objective: MOS Word Expert 4.2.1

If none of the existing themes has the colors you want, you can create a new set in the Create New Theme Colors window.

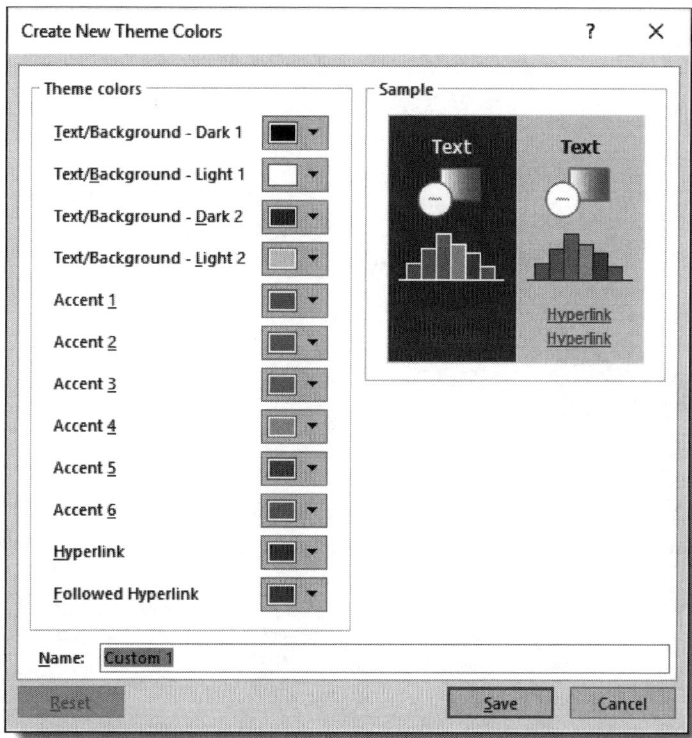

1. Click **Colors** > **Customize Colors.**
2. Set each theme color.
   If the color you want isn't listed, click **More Colors** to open the Colors window.

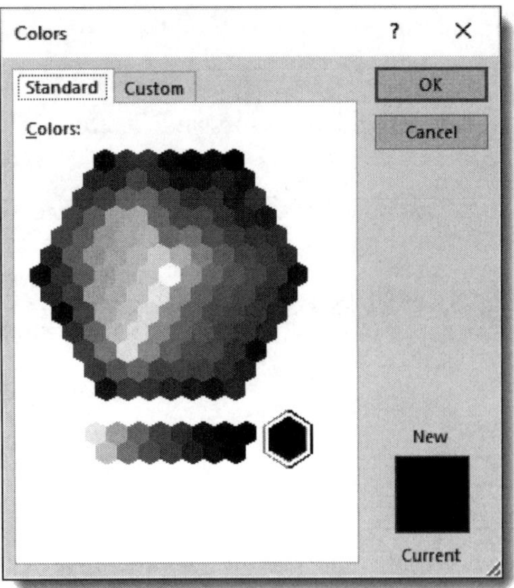

3. Type a name for the new theme color set.
4. Click **Save**.

Creating theme fonts

Exam Objective: MOS Word Expert 4.2.2

You can choose new theme fonts from the Create New Theme Fonts window.

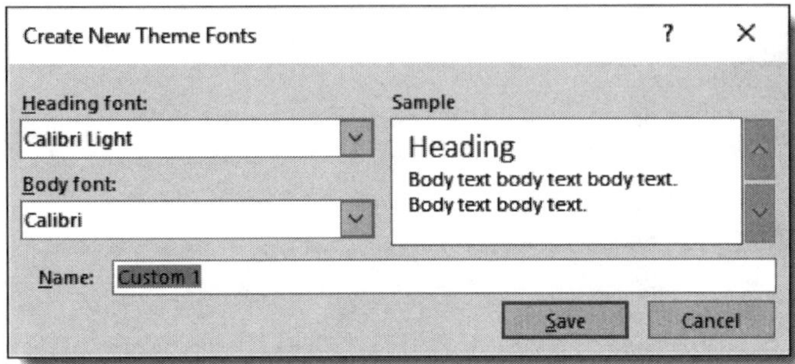

1. Click **Fonts > Customize Fonts**.
   To open the Create New Theme Fonts window.
2. Choose a heading font and body font.
3. Type a name for the theme.
4. Click **Save**.

Managing custom themes and style sets

Exam Objective: MOS Word Core 1.3.3

Word groups themes into Style Sets, which provide a convenient way to format your documents' elements at one go. You can save, load, or reset themes by using the commands at the bottom of the Themes and Style Sets galleries.

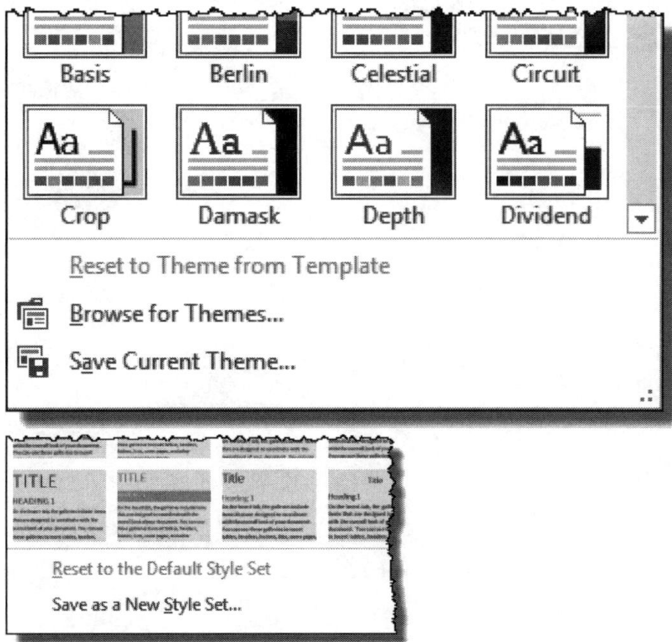

Exam Objective: MOS Word Expert 4.2.3, 4.2.4

The Themes gallery contains commands specific to the themes themselves.

- Click **Themes > Save Current Theme** to save your current customizations for other documents.
  Themes by default are stored in the `Templates\Document Themes` folder.
- Click **Browse for Themes** to load a new theme file from elsewhere on your computer.
- Click **Reset to Theme from Template** to return to the theme specified in the document template.
- At the right of the Style Sets gallery, click the down arrow to open the gallery. Click **Reset to the Default Style Set** to return to default settings.
- Click **Save as a New Style Set** to create a new style set using the themes you've applied.

Exercise: Creating a custom theme

In this exercise, you'll apply customized theme elements to a document, and then save them as a new theme.

Exam Objective: MOS Word Core 4.2.3 and Expert 1.3.2

Do This	How & Why
1. Open `Sales chart` and save it as `Regional sales chart.`	The file already includes theme colors, fonts, and effects in the chart. **Note:** Opening downloaded files in Office applications can result in the document being displayed in Protected mode. This can be overridden by clicking **Enable Editing** at the top of the document window.
2. Customize the theme.	First, you'll change each element of the theme independently.
a) On the Design tab, in the Document Formatting group, click **Colors**.	Colors To open the gallery. There's a set of colors for each built-in theme.
b) Point to different color sets in the gallery.	The chart columns change to preview each set, as do the title text and the line beneath it.
c) Click **Slipstream**.	To set the colors.
d) Click **Fonts**.	A Fonts Each set of fonts shows the name of each font in its own typeface.
e) Click **Arial Black**.	You can preview others first, if you like. It changes all the fonts in the document: the title, the following paragraph, and the chart labels.
f) Click **Effects > Glossy**.	The outlines and shading on the chart columns are more distinct, to make up for the more subdued color scheme.
3. Create a new set of theme colors.	You'll alter the accent colors to make them stand out more clearly.
a) Click **Colors > Customize Colors**.	To open the Create New Theme Colors window.

Do This	How & Why
b) Click the color menu next to **Accent 2**.	To see some available colors.
c) Click **More Colors**.	To open the Colors window. You'll pick a new one.
d) Click a light orange color, as shown.	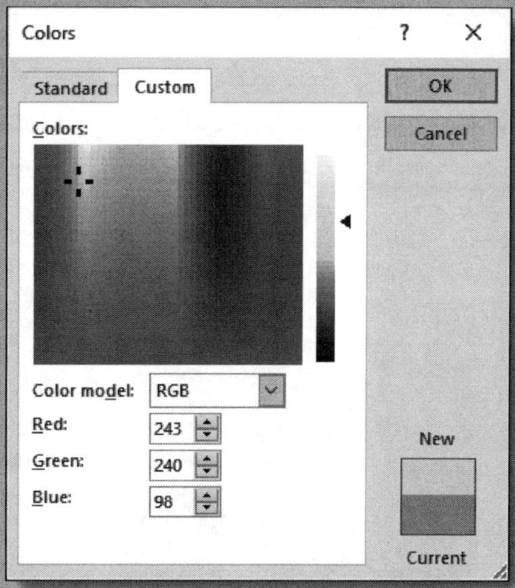
e) Click **OK**.	To return to the Create New Theme Colors window. Accent 2 is now the color you selected.
f) In the Name field, type `Tucana`.	
g) Click **Save**.	To apply the colors to the chart, and save them as a new theme color.
h) Click **Colors**.	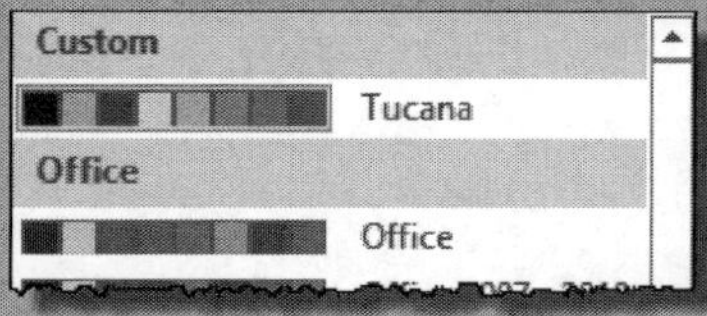 The Tucana color scheme now appears in the gallery.
i) Close the gallery.	
4. Save the customized theme.	You'll want to apply this theme to future sales reports, so you need to save it.
a) Click **Themes > Save Current Theme**.	You'll need to scroll to the bottom of the gallery. The Save Current Theme window opens. The Document Themes folder is selected.

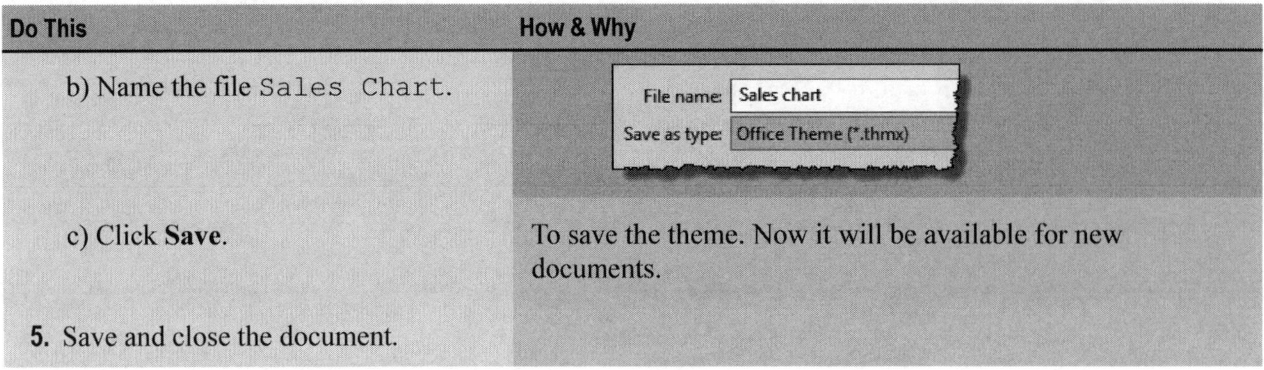

Do This	How & Why
b) Name the file `Sales Chart`.	File name: Sales chart Save as type: Office Theme (*.thmx)
c) Click **Save**.	To save the theme. Now it will be available for new documents.
5. Save and close the document.	

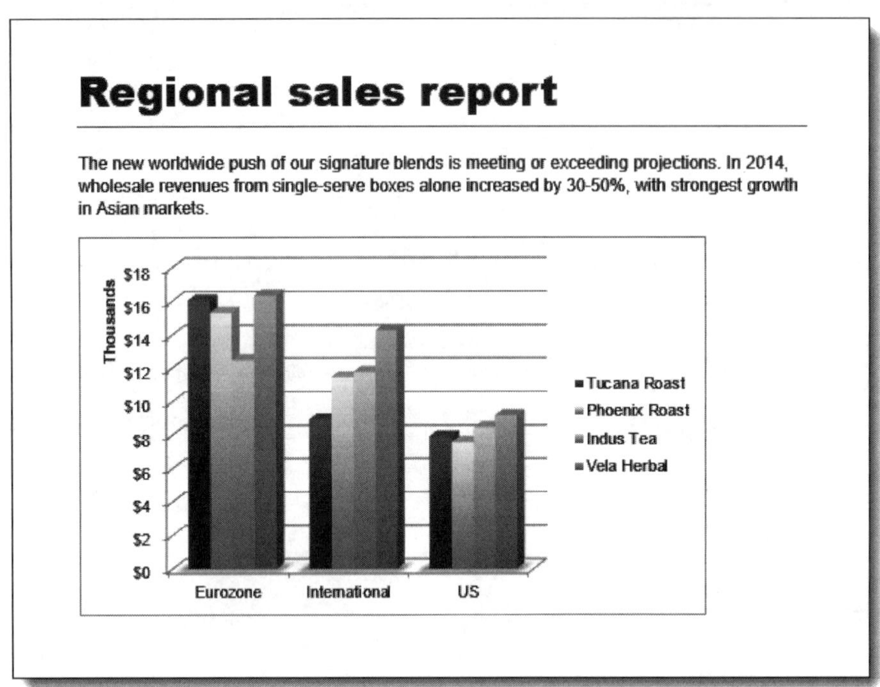

Regional sales report

The new worldwide push of our signature blends is meeting or exceeding projections. In 2014, wholesale revenues from single-serve boxes alone increased by 30-50%, with strongest growth in Asian markets.

Assessment: Custom themes

Checking knowledge about theme customization.

1. What elements of a theme can you customize independently? Choose all that apply.
   - Colors
   - Effects
   - Fonts
   - Shapes
   - Styles
2. How many fonts can be defined in a theme? Choose the best answer.
   - 1
   - 2
   - 3
   - 4
3. When you change theme effects, doing so affects any graphical elements that use shape styles. True or false?
   - True
   - False
4. A Style Set can contain only a single theme. True or false?
   - True
   - False

Module B: Building blocks

Word includes a number of pre-formatted pieces of content, called building blocks, which you can insert into your documents. These include headers and footers, text boxes, cover pages, watermarks, and more.

You will learn:

- About building blocks
- How to insert building blocks
- How to insert Quick Parts

About building blocks

Exam Objective: MOS Word Core 4.2.3

Most building blocks have a combination of formatting and graphics, as well as placeholder fields into which you can type your own text. You've probably used building blocks before when adding built-in headers and footers; others work mostly the same way. Building blocks don't generally do anything you can't do with manual formatting, but they make it quicker and easier to place and format content in your documents. Additionally, the built-in building blocks of different types have a number of matching formats. For example, you can use Puzzle footers, Puzzle sidebars, and a Puzzle cover page to give the whole document a consistent graphical style.

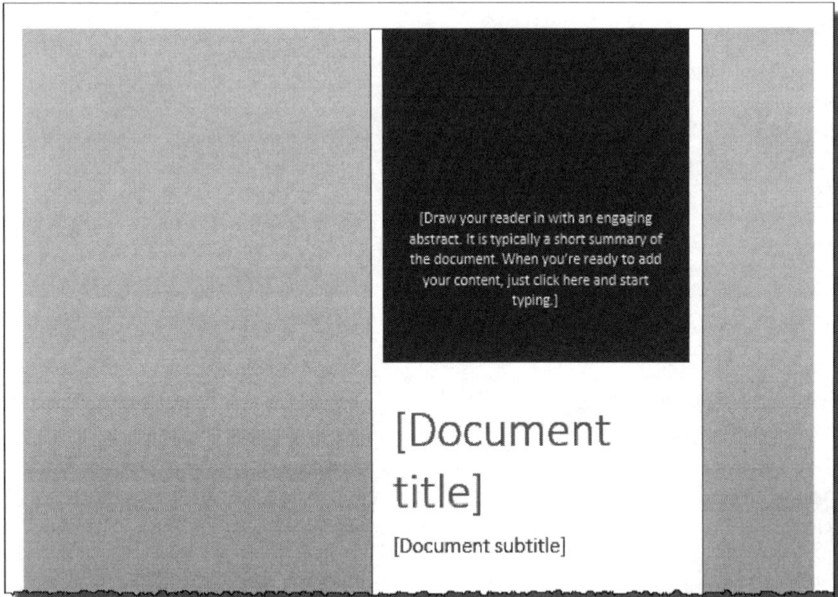

Inserting building blocks

Exam Objective: MOS Word Core 4.2.3

When you insert a building block, it is placed in an appropriate location for its type. For example, a header is placed at the top of every page, while a text box is inserted onto the current page, and you can move it if you like. Some building blocks are simply placed at the insertion point.

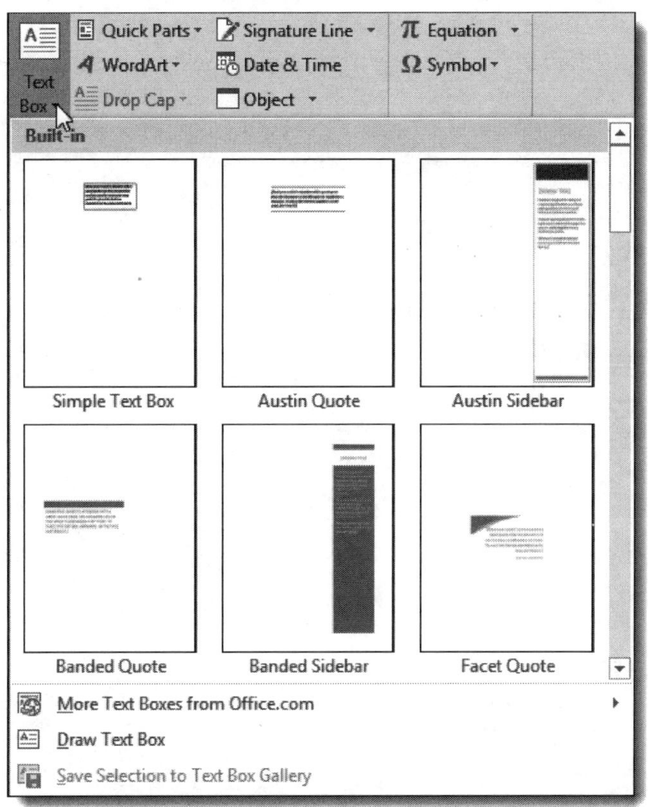

You can insert most building blocks by opening the gallery and clicking a selection, but some are a little more complex or are located inside other menus.

- The Insert tab contains most of the building-block galleries.
  - Click **Cover Page**, **Header**, **Footer**, or **Text Box** to open their respective galleries.
  - To view the Quick Tables gallery, click **Table > Quick Tables**.
  - To view the AutoText gallery, click **Quick Parts > AutoText**.
  - There are four Page Number galleries, grouped by where the number is located on the page: *Top of Page*, *Bottom of Page*, *Page Margins*, and *Current Position*. The first two appear in the header and footer areas, and replace any headers or footers you already have.
  - The Text Box gallery contains both quotes and sidebars. *Quotes* are small boxes meant to hold quotes or summaries from the main document, while *sidebars* are larger boxes meant to be placed on page edges and hold standalone supplements to the main document content. You can still move or use either however you like.
  - To open the Equations gallery, you must click the down arrow on the right of (or below) the ribbon command. Otherwise, you'll just insert a blank equation field.

    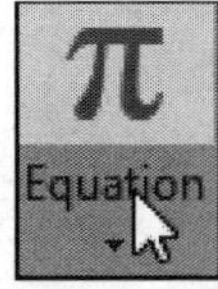

- On the Design tab, click **Watermark** to open the watermark gallery.
- On the References tab, click **Table of Contents** or **Bibliography** to open its respective gallery.

Exercise: Inserting building blocks

In this exercise, you'll add built-in building blocks to a document.

Do This	How & Why
1. Open `Coffee houses`, and save it as `Building blocks`.	
2. Add page numbers to the document.	
a) On the Insert tab, click **Page Number**.	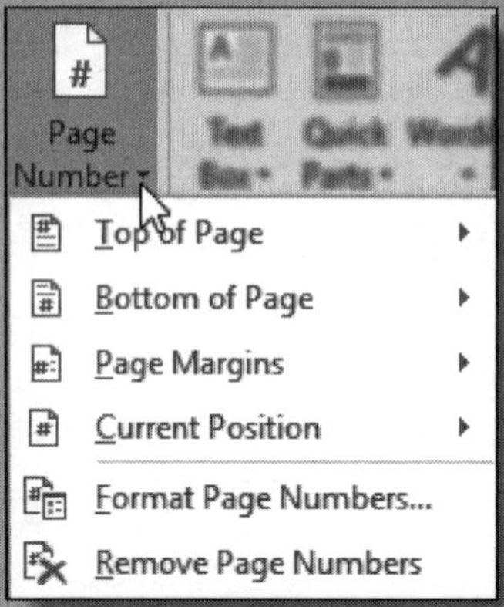 You can add page numbers in different areas of the page. Each has its own gallery.
b) Click **Bottom of Page**.	The gallery has several categories, each with its own set of page number styles.
c) Click **Thick Line**.	It's around the middle of the list. The page number is inserted under a thick line at the bottom of the page and the footer text is active.
d) Click **Close Header and Footer**.	On the Header & Footer Tools Design tab. You could also just double-click the main body text. Like a normal footer, it's applied to the entire document.
3. Add a quote box.	Instead of directly quoting, you'll add a brief summary of the first section.
a) On the first page, place the insertion point at the beginning of the fourth paragraph.	Beginning with "Another account."
b) On the Insert tab, click **Text Box > Austin Quote**.	A pull-quote-style formatted text box is inserted, along with placeholder text explaining how to use it.
c) In the text box, type `"The history of coffee houses, ere the invention of clubs, was that of the manners, the morals and the politics of a people."`	You can cut and paste from the second paragraph.

Do This	How & Why
4. Insert a cover page.	You'll use the Austin cover page, to match the text boxes.
a) On the Insert tab, in the Pages group, click **Cover Page > Austin**.	The cover page is inserted at the beginning of the document. It has placeholder fields for Abstract, Title, Subtitle, and Author.
b) In the Title field, type `The Coffee Houses of Old London`.	
c) In the Subtitle field, type `From All About Coffee`.	
d) Select the text box containing the Author field.	It shows the Author field from the document's properties. It's not what you want here.
e) Press **Delete**.	
f) In the Abstract field, type `From William H. Ukers' All About Coffee, 1922. All content is public domain.`	
5. Save and close the document.	

Assessment: Building Blocks

1. You can best add page numbers using the Header or Footer galleries. True or false?
    - True
    - False
2. Which ribbon tab has most of the building block galleries? Choose the best answer.
    - Home
    - Insert
    - Design
    - References
3. Before inserting a building block, you always need to place the insertion point where you want it to go. For example, before adding a header building block, you should edit the header. True or false?
    - True
    - False

Module C: Section breaks

Normally, page layout options such as margins, columns, and page numbers affect the whole document. Very often, that's just how you want it, but when you need to, you can instead break your document into sections, and change page layout for each section independently.

You will learn:

- About section breaks
- How to change layout options for individual sections
- How to change page numbers for individual sections
- How to use headers and footers in multi-section documents

About section breaks

Exam Objective: MOS Word Core 2.3.2, 2.3.3

When you break a document into sections, each section can have its own layout options. Not all layout features can be applied section by section, but many can. These include:

- Paper size
- Page orientation
- Margins
- Columns
- Headers and Footers
- Page and line numbering

A section break can be continuous (the next section begins on the same page) or can include a page break. A section break isn't obvious when printing—only its effects are. When you display formatting symbols, a section break appears as a double dotted line labeled "Section Break (Type)."

Two section breaks in a document, one Next Page and one Continuous.

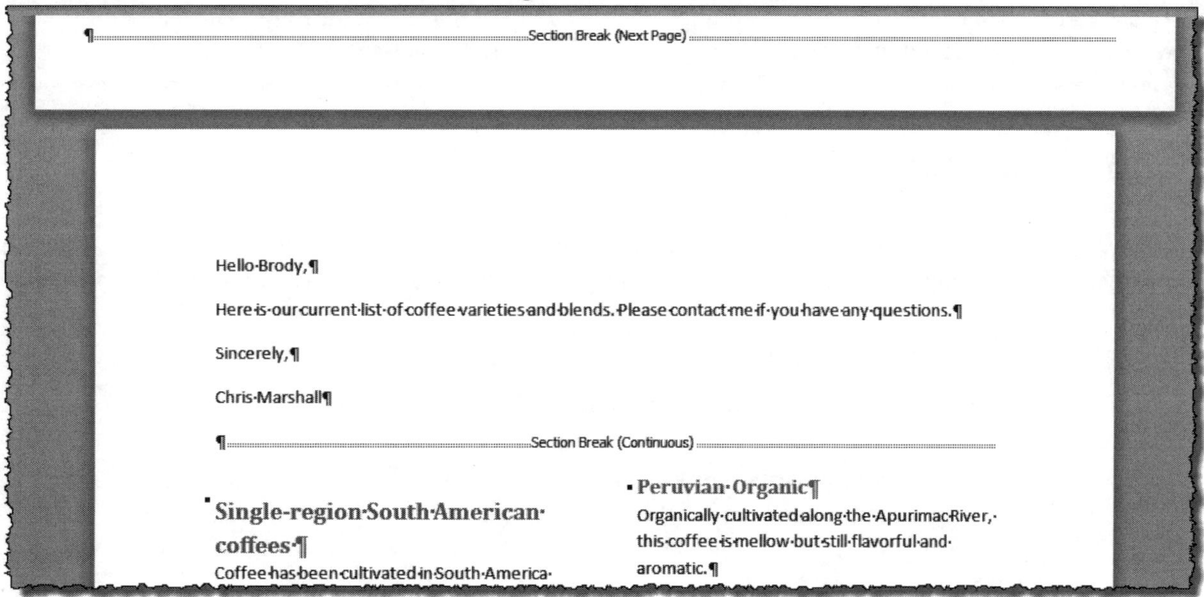

Inserting section breaks

To insert section breaks, click **Breaks** on the Page Layout tab and pick a type. Which type you should choose depends on what you plan to do with the new section.

Exam Objective: MOS Word Core 2.3.2

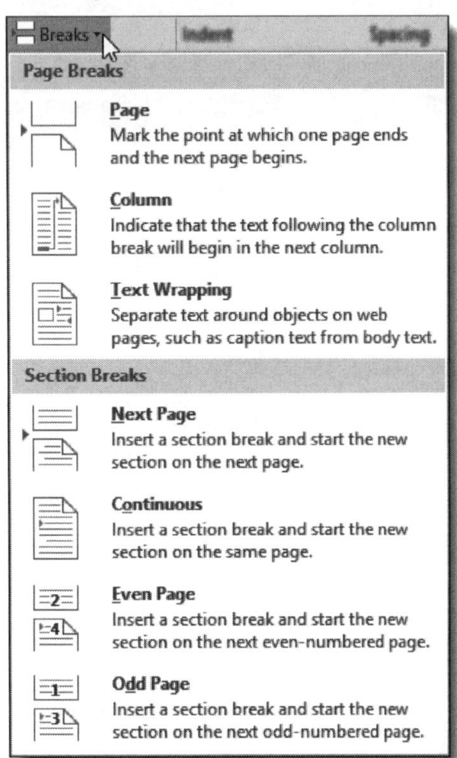

- To begin the new section on the next page, click **Breaks** > **Next Page**. This is best when you want to change something like page numbers, headers and footers, or page orientation.
- To start a new section on the same page, click **Breaks** > **Continuous**. This is best if you want to change something like columns or margins without otherwise disrupting the flow of the text.
- To start a new section on the next even-numbered page—inserting a new blank page, if necessary—click **Breaks** > **Even Page**.
- To start a new section on the next odd-numbered page, click **Breaks** > **Odd Page**. This is useful if you want each chapter of a document to begin on an odd-numbered (right-side) page.

Formatting document sections

Once you've inserted section breaks, most layout changes affect only the current section by default. If you want to apply the same change to more than one section, you can apply it individually to each. Depending on the type of change, you might be able to apply it to multiple sections at once, or even to the entire document.

Exam Objective: MOS Word Core 2.3.3

- When formatting symbols are displayed, you can cut, paste, or delete a section break as you would any other content.

  Note: Word stores all formatting information for a section in the section break at its end. This means that if you delete a section break, the formatting of the *previous* section will be removed. It also means that if you move or copy a section break, its properties will apply to the section above its new location.

- To apply any compatible formatting to a single section, click within the section, and apply the formatting as you would to a normal document.
- You can apply changes in margins, paper size, or page orientation to multiple sections from the appropriate tab of the **Page Setup** window. To open it, click the launcher button in the Page Setup group.

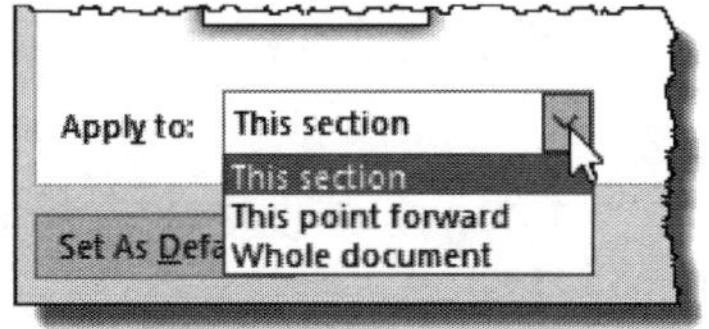

  - Choose **This Section** to apply only to the current section.
  - Choose **Whole document** to apply to all sections in the document.
  - Choose **This point forward** to apply to the current section and all following sections.
- To change a section break from one type to another, click in the following section and open the Page Setup window. Choose an option from the Section Start list on the Layout tab.

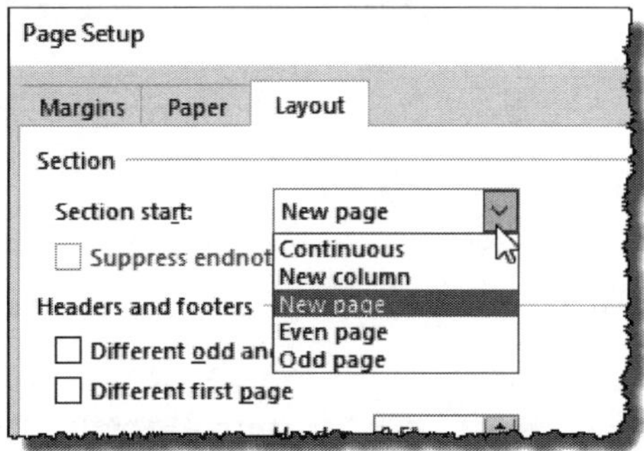

- In addition to changing page number formats for each section, you can also have a section's page numbers begin wherever you like. This is useful if you want each chapter of a document to have its own formatting. In the Insert tab's Header & Footer group, click **Page Number > Format Page Numbers**, and then select the desired options in the Page Number Format window.

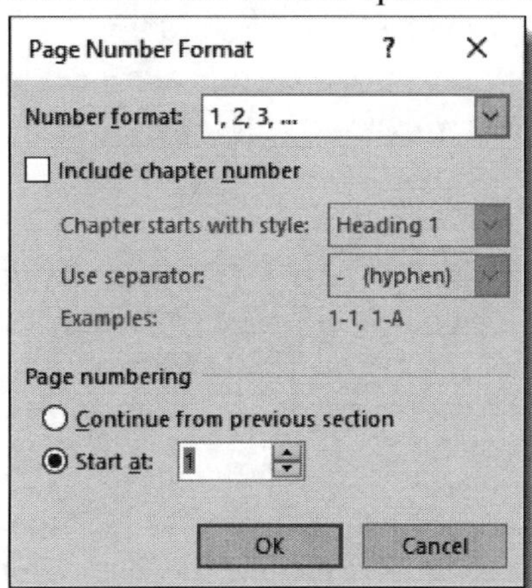

- A section break is often used as to signal a major division in a document. Thus, each section often has its own heading or title, signaling an important demarcation point to the reader. When working with section breaks, it's important to remember that any added section title should be placed *after* the break, not before it. This ensures that the title appears at the beginning of the new section.
- Each section can be formatted in significantly different ways. For example, a section could be formatted entirely in a multi-column format by using the **Page Layout > Columns** command.

Linked headers and footers

When you apply a header or footer to a document with multiple sections, it appears to apply to the whole document. This isn't because you can't apply it to one section at a time, but instead because by default each header and footer is linked to that of the previous section, and it to the one before that, back to the beginning of the document. Don't confuse this with other kinds of "linking" in Word: it simply means that all the linked headers or footers are identical, and changing one changes all of them.

You can tell if a header or footer is linked just by looking at it while it's selected: On the left side, it shows the section number, and if it's linked, the right side displays the label "Same as Previous."

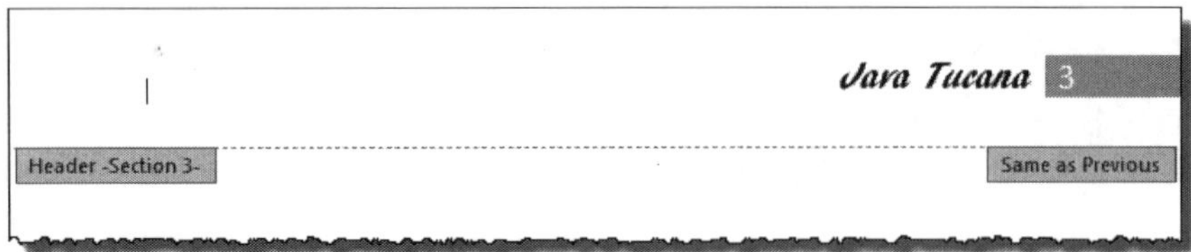

You can also look at the Header & Footer Tools Design tab, in the Navigation group. If the section is linked, the Link to Previous button is highlighted.

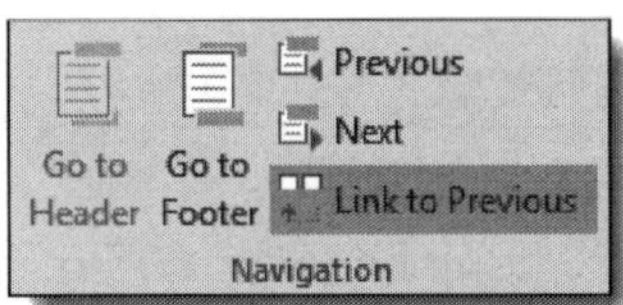

Because headers and footers are linked by default, it's easy to use one set through the entire document, no matter how many sections you make.

Managing section headers and footers

Linking and unlinking section headers or footers is simple in itself, but it can be confusing and frustrating if you don't keep in mind how the process works. The most important thing to remember is that links are always between the current section's header or footer and that of the previous section. If you're just going to unlink them all and set them individually, that's not a problem, but if you want to have an identical header in some sections but not others, you'll have to think carefully about the order in which you edit them.

Exam Objective: MOS Word Core 2.3.3

For example, if you want sections 1 and 3 to have one header and section 2 to have a different one, you'll have to break the link for both section 2 and the one for section 3. It might be quickest for you to set the header for 1 and 3, then break the links, and finally change the header for 2.

For another example, imagine that you have a document with nine sections, and you break the header link between section 4 and section 3. This now means you have two headers, each for a different series of sections. If you were to change the header for section 2, it would affect sections 1–3, while if you changed the header for section 7, it would change sections 4–9. When you change a header for one section, always keep in mind what other sections might be changed.

If the current header or footer is unlinked, and you link it again, you're prompted to confirm the link. This is because it deletes the current section's header or footer, along with that of any following sections, and replaces it with the previous one. If you've spent a lot of time carefully formatting the current header or footer, this can cost you work.

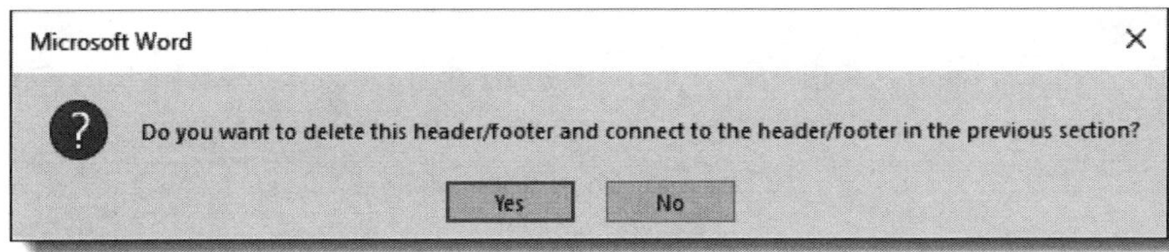

Finally, remember that headers and footers are linked or unlinked independently. Even if you use a different header for each section, you can have a linked footer for the whole document, and vice-versa.

1. Double-click the header or footer you want to edit.
2. On the Design tab, in the Navigation group, use the **Previous** and **Next** buttons to find the section you want to link or unlink.
3. Click **Link to Previous** to link or unlink the current section's header/footer.

Exercise: Using section breaks

Demonstrating use of section breaks.

In this exercise, you'll use section breaks to format individual parts of a document.

Exam Objective: MOS Word Core 2.3.2, 2.3.3

Do This	How & Why
1. Open `Coffee houses`, and save it as `Coffee house sections`.	
2. Display formatting marks, if necessary.	On the Home tab, click ¶ or press **Ctrl+***.
3. Insert section breaks.	You want to have each first-level heading begin a new section, on a new page.
a) Place the insertion point right before "The First London Coffee House."	At the beginning of the line.
b) On the Layout tab, click **Breaks** > **Next Page**.	of the manners, the morals and the politics of a people." And so the London coffee houses of the seventeenth and eighteenth c indeed the history of the manners and customs of the English pe period.¶ Section Break (Next Page) The new section now starts on page 2.
c) Navigate to page 6.	The next Heading 1 text is "Strange coffee mixtures."
d) Insert a new section break before the heading.	Place the insertion point, then click **Breaks** > **Next Page**. The heading now begins the next page.
e) Insert Next Page section breaks for the remaining first-level headings.	First-level headings are in green text. You'll find them on pages 10, 12, and 13 as you move forward.
4. Change the column settings for one part of the document.	

Do This	How & Why
a) Place the insertion point at the beginning of the poem on page 3.	You'll format these verses to appear in two columns on the page.
b) Click **Columns > Two**.	The change applies to the whole section. That isn't what you want.
c) Press **Ctrl+Z**.	To undo the change. You'll make the poem its own section.
d) Click **Breaks > Continuous**.	a zealous partisan addressed wn Head and half his Body in don":¶ Section Break (Continuous) To insert a section break without a page break.
e) Insert a continuous section break at the end of the poem.	Place the insertion point at the beginning of the second paragraph on page 4, then insert the break.
f) Place the insertion point in the poem, and click **Columns > Two**.	St. Michael's Alley, next the first Coffee-Tent in London":¶ Section Break (Continuous) Were not the fountain of my Tears Each day exhausted by the steam Of your Coffee, no doubt appears But they would swell to such a stream As could admit of no restriction To see, poor Pasqua, thy Affliction. What! Pasqua, you at first did broach This Nectar for the publick Good, Must you call Kitt down from the Coach To drive a Trade he understood No more than you did then your creed, Or he doth now to write or read? Pull Courage, Pasqua, fear no Harms From the besieging Foe; Make good your Ground, stand to your Arms, Hold out this summer, and then tho' He'll storm, he'll not prevail—your Face Shall give the Coffee Pot the chace.¶ Eventually Pasqua Rosée disappeared, some say to open a coffee house on the Continent, in Holland or Germany. Bowman, having married Alderman Hodges's This time the formatting applies only to the poem itself.
5. Add a header and footer to the document.	
a) On the Insert tab, click **Header > Austin**.	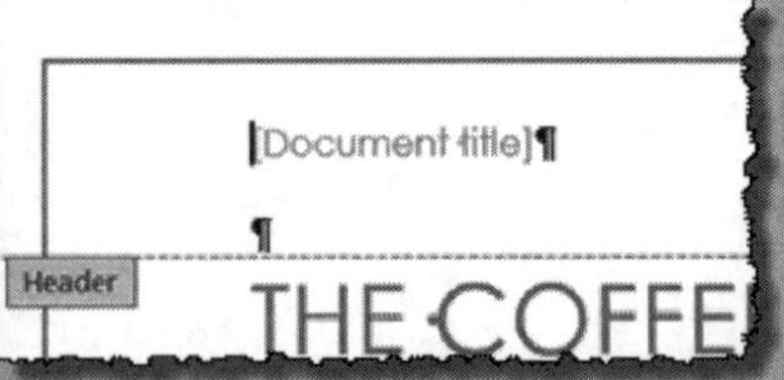 This header has a field for the document title.
b) In the title field, type `The Coffee Houses of Old London`.	
c) Insert the Austin footer.	On the Insert tab, click **Footer > Austin**. This footer just has a page number, so you don't need to edit anything.
d) On the Design tab, click **Close Header & Footer**.	Or double-click the document body.

Do This	How & Why
6. Scroll through the document.	Because headers and footers are linked, the same set was applied to all sections of the document.
7. Remove the header from the first section.	If you just removed it directly, it would affect the entire document.

a) Double-click the header.

The section number you see depends on how far down you scrolled.

The section number is shown on the left. The right shows that it's linked to the previous section.

Do This	How & Why
b) On the Design tab, in the Navigation group, click **Previous**.	Previous To move to the previous section. It's also linked.
c) Navigate to Section 2.	Keep clicking **Previous** until it displays Section 2.
d) Click **Link to Previous**.	Link to Previous To deselect it. The "Same as Previous" marker vanishes.
e) Navigate to Section 1's header.	Removing the link didn't change the header, but now you can edit it without affecting the other sections. You'll remove the title text but keep the border.
f) Delete the Title field.	Select the whole field, and press **Delete**. You might have to click in the text to make the frame appear.
8. Scroll to the bottom of page 2.	Section 2's Footer is still linked, but that's how you want it.
9. Click **Close Header & Footer**.	The title still appears in the header starting on page 2. Page 1 shows only the page number at the bottom.
10. Save and close the document.	

Assessment: Section breaks

1. You want a full-page graphic in the middle of your document to print in landscape format. What's the best thing to do before changing the page orientation?
    - Insert a Next Page section break before the graphic.
    - Insert a Next Page section break after the graphic.
    - Insert Next Page section breaks before and after the graphic.
    - Insert Continuous section breaks before and after the graphic.
2. There are two sections in your document: the first has two columns, and the second has one column. If you delete the section break between them, what happens? Choose the best answer.
    - The whole document will have one column.
    - The whole document will have two columns.
    - It depends whether it was a New Page or Continuous break.
3. You can change margins, paper size, or page orientation for multiple sections at a time. True or false?
    - True
    - False
4. After creating 8 sections in a document, you unlink section 4's footer and then edit it. What parts of the document are changed?
    - The headers and footers for sections 1–4.
    - The headers and footers for sections 4–8.
    - The footers for sections 1–4.
    - The footers for sections 4–8.
    - Only section 4's footer.

Module D: Page backgrounds

In addition to placing content on the pages of your document, you can also place it on the *page background*, as though your document were printed on colored or patterned paper. You can thus format the pages of your documents with watermarks, colors, textures, or borders.

You will learn how to:

- Apply watermarks
- Set background colors and patterns
- Set page borders

About page backgrounds

There are three types of page background options. All three are found on the Design tab in the Page Background group, but each has a distinct function, and Word handles each in a different way.

Exam Objective: MOS Word Core 1.3.6

Watermark An image or text, usually transparent, centered on the page. Watermarks are generally functional, showing where the document comes from or how it's meant to be used. For example, you might insert your company logo as a watermark, or you might place a "CONFIDENTIAL" watermark on a document you don't want freely distributed.

Page Color A background across the entire page, usually just to enhance the document's appearance. It can be a solid color, as the name implies, but can also be a gradient, texture, or picture of your choice.

Page borders A border placed around the entire page, just like one around a paragraph or table cell. It can simply be a line, or one of a variety of built-in artistic effects.

You can add any combination of page backgrounds you want, but only one of each type.

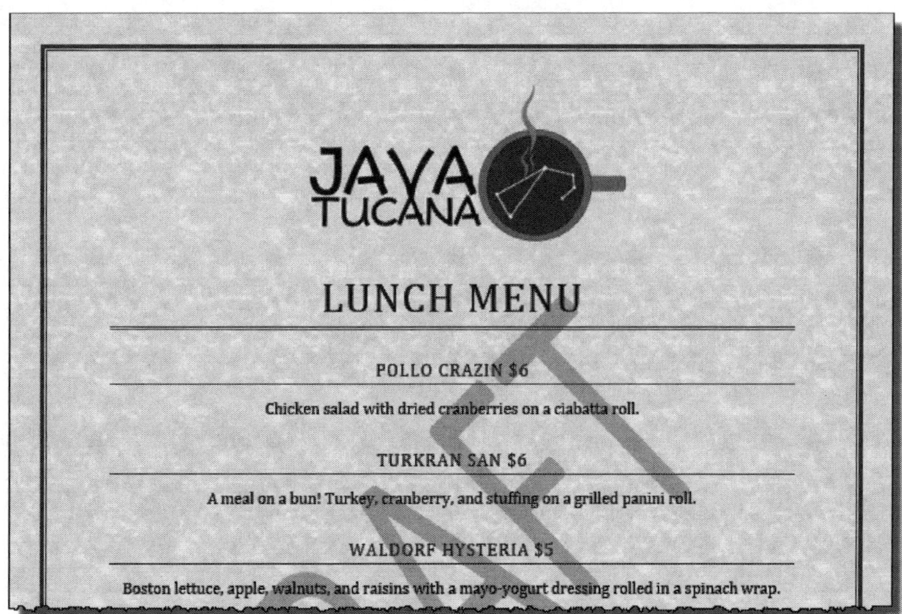

Creating custom watermarks

The Watermark gallery contains several predefined options that you can insert as you would any other building block, but you can also create a custom watermark.

Exam Objective: MOS Word Core 1.3.6

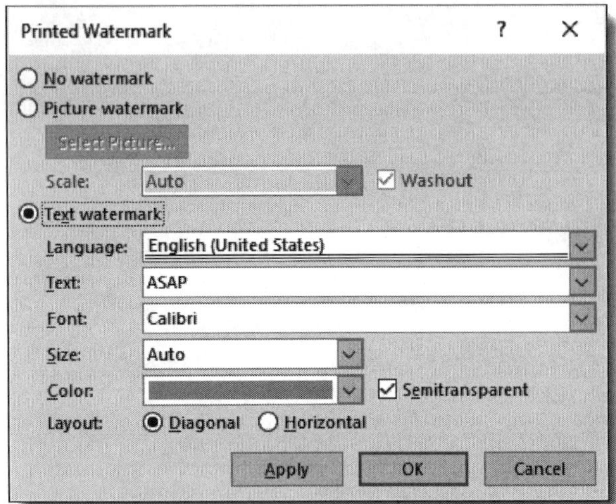

1. On the Design tab, click **Watermark > Custom Watermark** to open the Printed Watermark window.
2. Click **Picture Watermark** or **Text watermark**.
3. Set watermark options.
   - For a picture watermark, click **Select Picture** to choose an image file from your computer.
   - For a text watermark, choose one of the text options, or type your own. You can also choose the language, font, and color, and whether to place the watermark horizontally or diagonally on the page.
   - By default, watermarks are automatically sized to fit the page. To override this setting, choose an option from the Scale or Size field, depending on the watermark type.
   - By default, watermarks are transparent, so that they don't make the document text hard to read. To override this, clear **Washout** or **Semitransparent**, as available.
4. Click **OK**.

Setting page colors and fills

Setting a solid page color is like coloring any other element: click **Page Color**, and choose the color you want. Click **Fill Effects** to set more advanced options from the Fill Effects window. The available options vary for each type of effect.

Exam Objective: MOS Word Core 1.3.6

- Gradient effects cover the page in a smooth color transition.
  - The gradient can contain two colors of your choice, one color plus a grayscale value, or a set of predefined colors.
  - You can choose the direction of the gradient by clicking one value from the Shading styles list, and one from the Variants list.

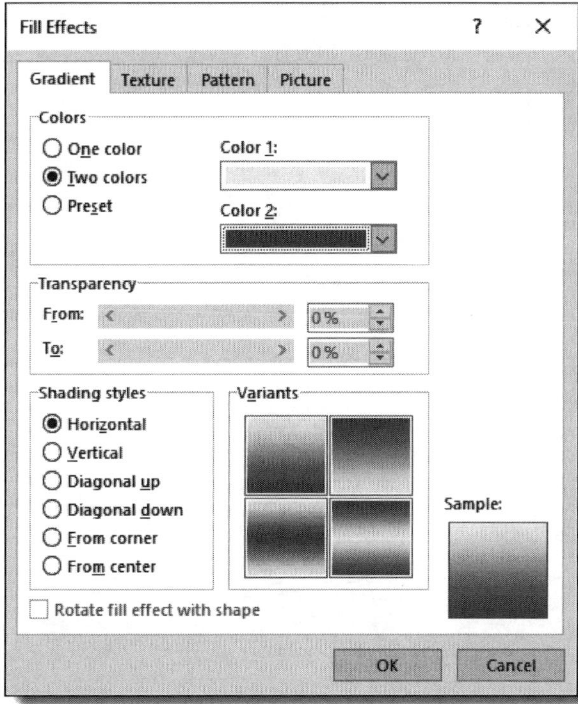

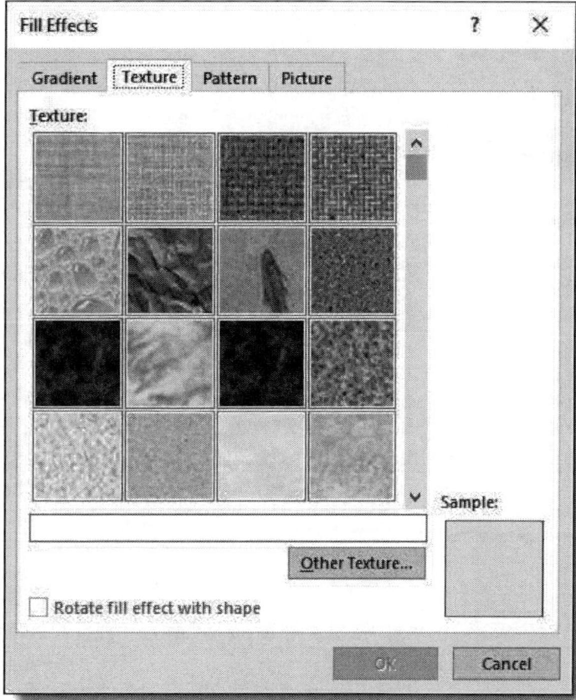

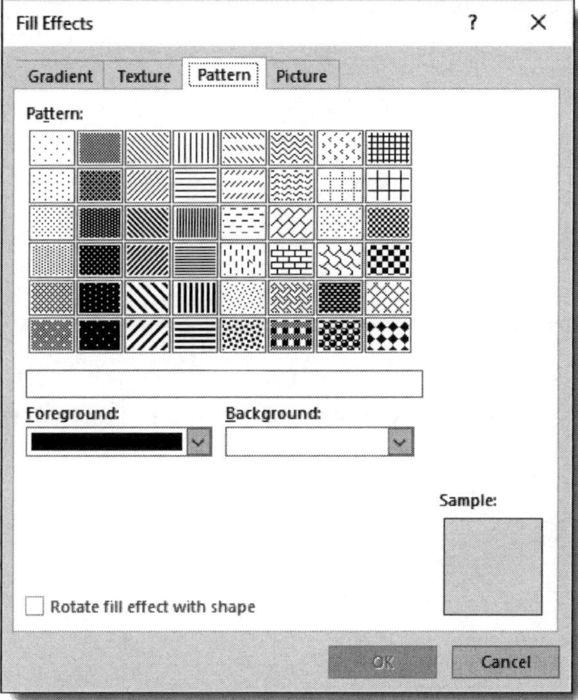

- Texture effects smoothly tile a small image over the whole page. You can choose a predefined texture or insert an image of your own.
- Pattern effects tile a simple graphical pattern over the page. You can select only from predefined patterns, but you can set the foreground and background colors for each.
- Picture effects place an image file of your choice across the page. Pictures tile like textures, but are intended more for a single, large image across the page.

Page colors and fills are generally intended to add graphical interest to a digital document. On paper, they can waste ink or make the document hard to read, so by default Word won't print them. To change this setting, check **Print background colors and images** in the Display section of the Word Options window.

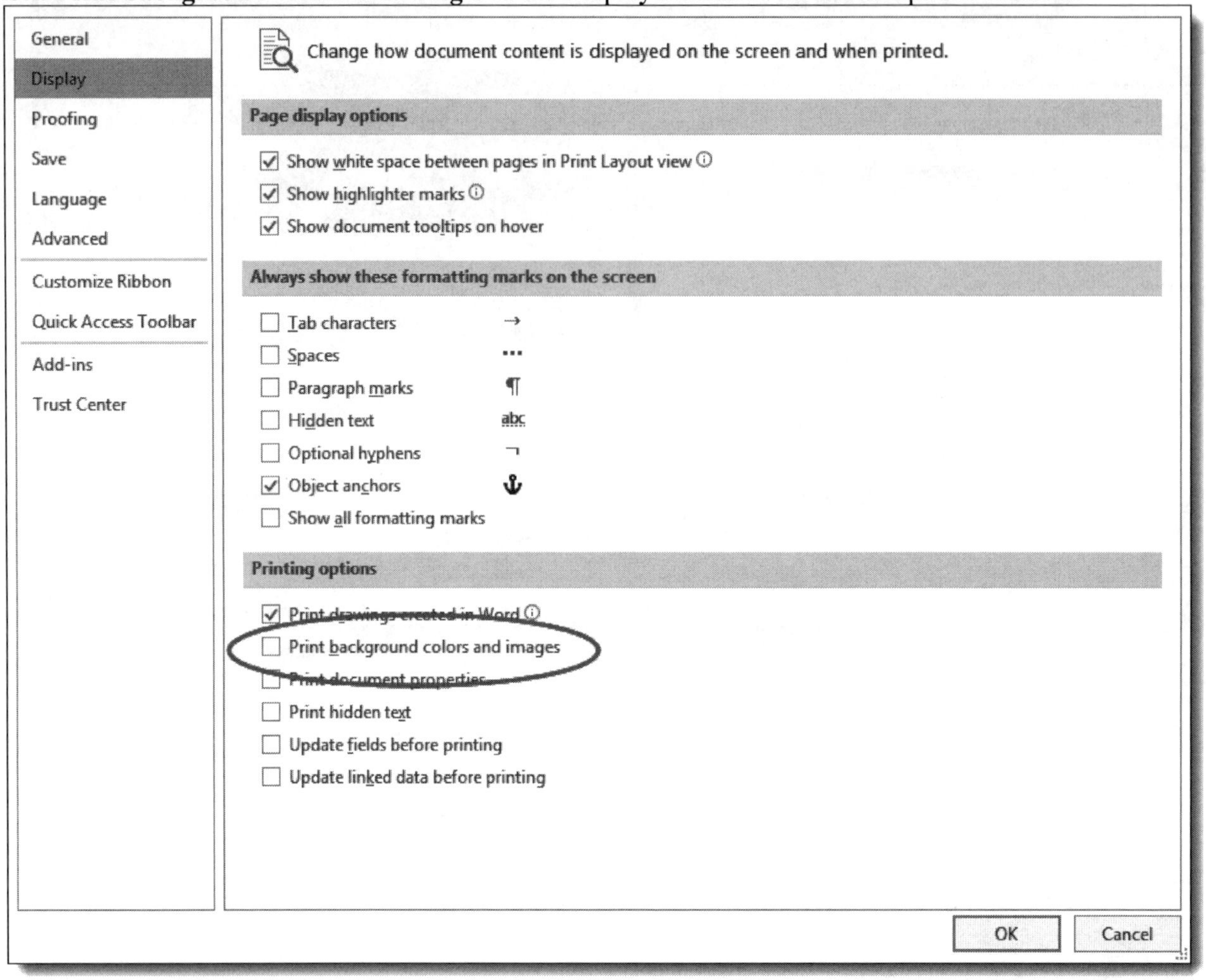

General
Display
Proofing
Save
Language
Advanced
Customize Ribbon
Quick Access Toolbar
Add-ins
Trust Center

Change how document content is displayed on the screen and when printed.

Page display options

Show white space between pages in Print Layout view
Show highlighter marks
Show document tooltips on hover

Always show these formatting marks on the screen

Tab characters →
Spaces ···
Paragraph marks ¶
Hidden text abc
Optional hyphens ¬
Object anchors
Show all formatting marks

Printing options

Print drawings created in Word
Print background colors and images
Print document properties
Print hidden text
Update fields before printing
Update linked data before printing

OK
Cancel

Setting page borders

You can define a page border from the Design tab, in the Page Background group, by clicking **Page Borders**, then setting options in the Borders and Shading window.

Exam Objective: MOS Word Core 1.3.6

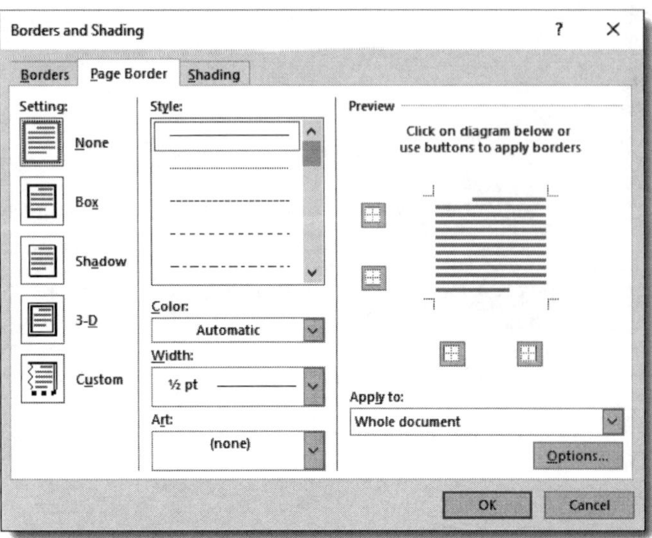

If you've set other borders in Word, you can set page borders, as they aren't much different. There are multiple kinds of options you can configure, but not all combinations are compatible.

- Choose the overall effect of the border from the Setting section. It can be a simple box, a box with a drop shadow, a 3-D effect, or a custom design.
- Click the buttons in the Preview section to display or remove individual sides of the border. This changes the Setting option to **Custom**, if it isn't already.
- Choose either a line style from the Style list, or a clip-art border from the Art list.
  - The Width field affects the thickness of both line and art borders. In general, clip-art borders should be thicker.
  - You can set a color for any line border, and for some—but not all—image borders.
- Choose what pages you want the border to appear on from the "Apply to" list. You can apply a border to the whole document, the current section, the first page, or everything but the first page.
- Click **Options** to choose position and display options in the Border and Shading Options window.

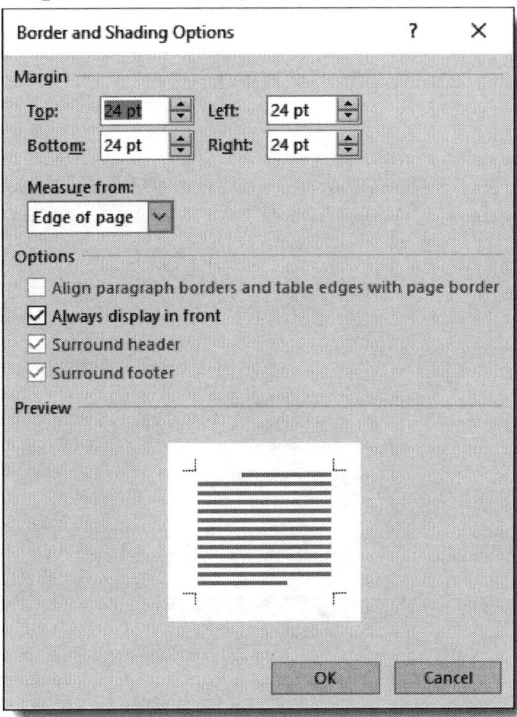

Page backgrounds and sections

When you use page backgrounds in documents with multiple sections, you might notice inconsistent behavior. This is because each of the three types of page background interacts differently with sections.

- As you just saw, page borders can be applied to the current section or the whole document from the Borders and Shading window.
- Any page color option applies to the entire document, regardless of whether you use sections or not. If you want to color just part of a document, you need to use another method, such as a shape placed behind the text.
- Watermarks function a little less intuitively in Word. Watermarks are tied to the document header and share the same linking structure. By default, this means it applies to the whole document, but if you want to watermark individual sections, you first need to unlink their headers.

Exercise: Setting a page background

In this exercise, you'll set a page color, page border, and watermark on a document.

Exam Objective: MOS Word Core 1.3.6

Do This	How & Why
1. Open `Lunch Menu`, and save it as `Lunch Menu background`.	
2. Add a page background.	The print menu in the café uses colored, textured paper, so you want the digital version to look similar.
a) On the Design tab, click **Page Color > Fill Effects**.	To open the Fill Effects window.
b) Click the **Texture** tab.	It shows a selection of image textures. You'll use one of these.
c) Click the **Parchment** texture, as shown.	
d) Click **OK**.	The background is applied to the page.
3. Add a page border.	
a) Click **Page Borders**.	The Borders and Shading window opens, with the Page Border tab active.

Do This	How & Why
b) Click the border style shown.	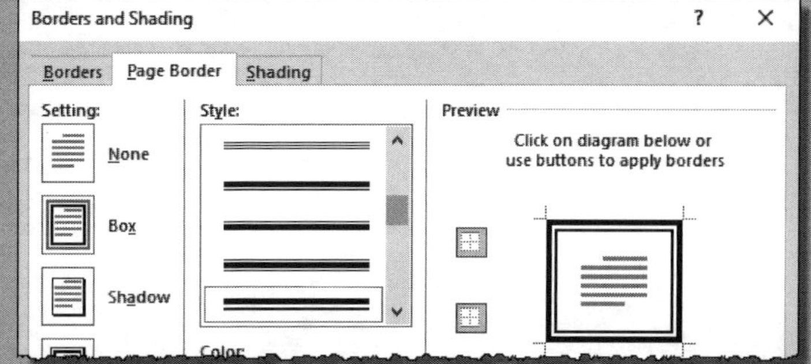 It's about halfway down the list. Notice that it's reflected in the preview, and the Box setting is automatically selected as well.
c) In the Color list, click **Red, Accent 2, Darker 25%**.	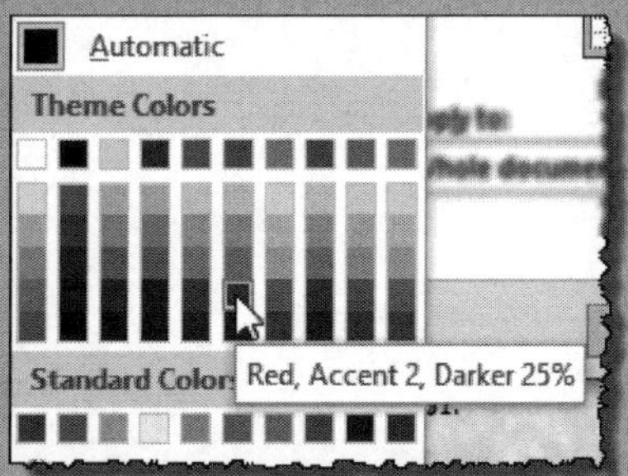
d) Click **OK**.	The border appears around the whole page.
4. Add a watermark.	This is still just a draft version, so you don't want any potential customers to think the menu and prices are final.
a) Click **Watermark > Draft 1**.	Scroll down to the Disclaimers section of the menu. A building-block watermark appears. It doesn't show up very well against the current page color, so you'll customize it.
b) Click **Watermark > Custom Watermark**.	To open the Printed Watermark window. Text Watermark is already selected, with the current settings.
c) From the Color list, click **Red, Accent 2**.	You'll leave the other settings the same.
d) Click **OK**.	The new color makes it stand out more, and because it's semitransparent, even similarly colored text is easy to read over it.
5. Save and close the document.	See the example on the next page.

Time & language
Speech, region, date

JAVA
TUCANA
LUNCH MENU
POLLO CRAZIN $6
Chicken salad with dried cranberries on a ciabatta roll.
TURKRAN SAN $6
A meal on a bun! Turkey, cranberry, and stuffing on a grilled panini roll.
WALDORF HYSTERIA $5
Boston lettuce, apple, walnuts, and raisins with a mayo-yogurt dressing rolled in a spinach wrap.

Assessment: Page backgrounds

1. You can apply multiple watermarks to a single page. True or false?
   - True
   - False
2. What fill effect would you use to cover the page in a smooth color transition? Choose the best response.
   - Gradient
   - Pattern
   - Picture
   - Texture
3. If you like, you can create a page border that appears only on the left and right of the page. True or false?
   - True
   - False
4. How can you apply a watermark to a single section?
   - Choose "This Section" from the "Apply to" list when you create it.
   - Make sure the section's header is unlinked from the other sections.
   - You can apply a watermark only to the entire document.

Summary: Managing documents

You should now know how to:

- Create custom themes by separately choosing fonts, themes, and effects
- Quickly insert pre-formatted document content using building blocks
- Vary page layout throughout a document by separating it into sections
- Apply page backgrounds behind the text of a document

Synthesis: Managing documents

Bringing together your knowledge of document management.

In this exercise, you'll format a large document with page layout and reusable content tools.

1. Open **Coffee houses**, and save it as `Coffee houses synthesis`.

   Note: Because you'll be doing similar work, you might want to start with `Coffee House Sections` instead.
2. Improve the document's layout on a section-by-section basis.
   - Each page after the first should have a header corresponding to a first-level heading.
   - All quoted poetry should be displayed either in two columns or using wider margins, depending on which fits better.
3. Customize the document's appearance to make it more visually appealing.
   - Create a custom theme using a mix of colors, fonts, and effects.
   - Insert a cover page, header and footer, text boxes, and other building blocks. Coordinate your choices with your theme decision.
   - Choose a page color and border to match the rest of your customizations.
4. Save and close the document.

Chapter 8: Styles

You will learn how to:

- Create and modify character styles for applying combinations of formatting to characters, words, and phrases.
- Create and modify paragraph styles for applying formatting to paragraphs as a whole

Module A: Character styles

You will learn how to:

- Use advanced character formatting attributes.
- Create and modify character styles.
- Use paste options to copy only certain attributes of text.

Advanced character formatting

Most common font controls are located on the ribbon, but you can access the rest from the Font window. In addition to providing the same controls found in the Font group, the Font window gives you additional control over font attributes, effects, character spacing, and advanced features used in OpenType fonts.

Exam Objective: MOS Word Core 2.1.1

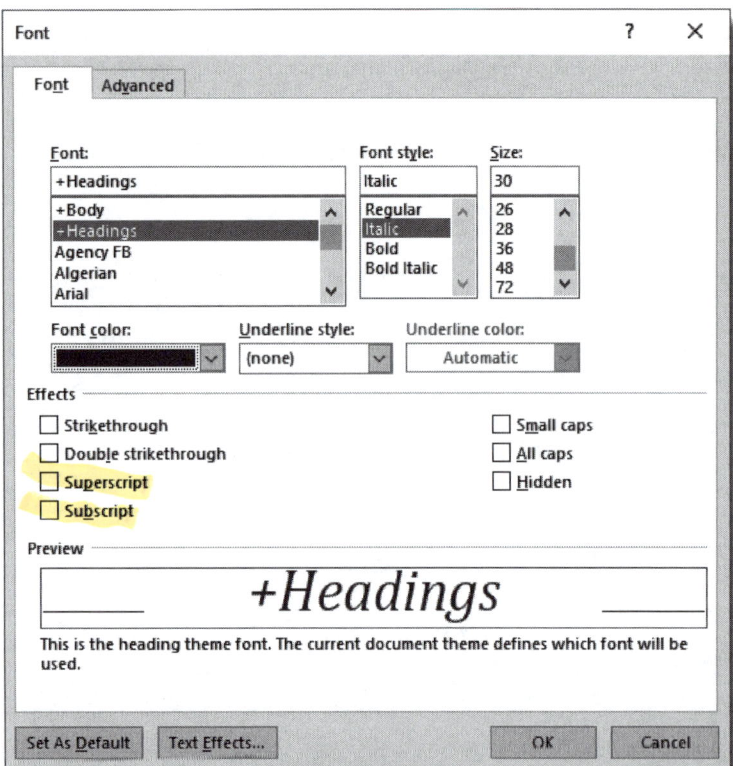

At the bottom of the window, a preview shows the result of the selected attributes.

Setting font attributes

Exam Objective: MOS Word Core 4.3.4 and Expert 2.2.1

To open the Font window, click the **Launcher** button in the Font group. Most of the controls correspond or add directly to those on the ribbon, but there are other useful ones.

- The +Body and +Headings fonts correspond to the Theme fonts on the ribbon, and change whenever the document's theme does. Other fonts override theme settings.

- Clicking **Text Effects** at the bottom of the window opens the Format Text Effects window, which provides more detailed settings than the Text Effects menu on the ribbon.
- The Character Spacing section on the Advanced tab lets you stretch or compress text horizontally, adjust its spacing, and shift its vertical position.
- If you're using newer OpenType fonts, the OpenType Features section lets you set options for ligatures, number spacing, number forms, and stylistic sets.

Using nonbreaking spaces

One very useful special symbol is the *nonbreaking space*. Sometimes, you want a two- or several-word phrase to stay together on line, without breaking across an automatic line break. This might be true for a product name, for example. There are a couple of ways to insert a non-breaking space.

- On the Insert tab, click **Symbol** > **More Symbols**. Click the Special Characters tab, click **Nonbreaking space**, and then click **Insert**.
- Hold **Ctrl+Shift**, and press the spacebar.

  If you have symbols showing in your document, the nonbreaking space will look slightly different than a normal space.

1 Normal space.

2 Nonbreaking space.

Exercise: Applying advanced character attributes

In this exercise, you'll apply character attributes using the Font window.

Do This	How & Why
1. Open `JT-Coffee` and save it as `JT-Coffee-formatting`.	In the data location for the chapter. **Note:** Opening downloaded files in Office applications can result in the document's being displayed in Protected View. This can be overridden by clicking **Enable Editing** at the top of the document window.
2. In the Phoenix Roast section, select "Columbian Bogota."	You'll format coffee names inside paragraph text so they stand out.
3. Set font attributes for the text.	
a) In the Font group, click ⧉	You can instead press **Ctrl+D**. The Font window opens.

Do This	How & Why
b) From the Font color list, choose the following color.	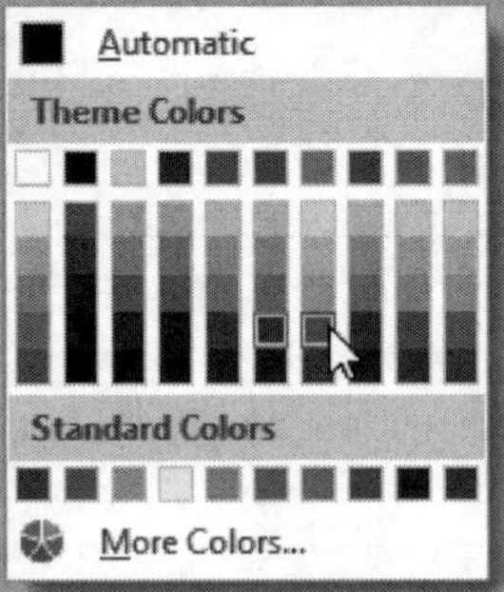 **Olive Green, Accent 3, Darker 25%**.
c) From the Underline style list, choose the first line option.	
d) From the Underline color list, choose **Orange, Accent 6**.	The top color in the last column. 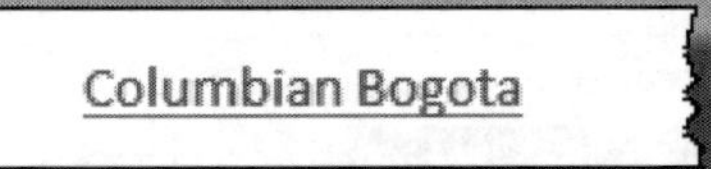 The results are displayed in the Preview section, so it doesn't matter whether you can see the page.
4. Adjust the character spacing.	Switch to the Advanced tab.
a) From the Spacing list, select **Condensed**.	Under Character Spacing. In the preview, the letters grow closer together.
b) From the Scale list, select **150%**.	The letters are stretched out horizontally. You'll reduce the effect a bit.
c) In the scale list, type `120%`	You can enter your own values as well as select them.
d) Press **Tab**.	The text is now only a little wider than before, but with broader letters. 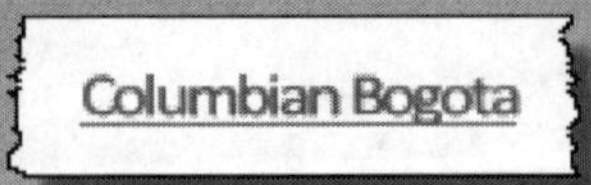
5. Click **OK**.	The formatting is now applied to the text.
6. How could you format the other coffee names the same way?	Doing it all manually would be slow. You could do it fairly quickly by using the Format Painter. But you're going to see a better way: using a character style.
7. Observe the Costa Rican Tarrazu product name.	It breaks across a line break. You will use nonbreaking spaces to prevent this.

Do This	How & Why
8. Insert nonbreaking spaces in the Costa Rican Tarrazu product name.	
a) Select the space between "Costa" and "Rican".	
b) While holding **Ctrl+Shift**, press the spacebar.	To insert a non-breaking space in the product name. Now, the first two words stay together, moving to the next line in the document.
c) Insert a non-breaking space between "Rican" and "Tarrazu".	Select the space between he words, hold **Ctrl+Shift**, then press the spacebar.
9. Save the file.	Do not close it.

Custom styles

For a novice user, it's easy to see the Styles gallery as a convenient box of pre-defined formatting options, and font and paragraph controls as something to use when there isn't a style with the right look. When you're making simple documents, this approach is fine, but the real strength of styles is how you can modify them throughout the entire document, or create entirely new ones for formats you use often.

For example, by default the Strong style looks exactly like bold text, so you might wonder why you need the style at all. But suppose that later on you decide you want to make all the bold text red or set it in a different font. If you were to use the Strong style, you could change it all at once by modifying the style, but if you were simply to use the Bold button, you would have to select and reformat every occurrence of bold text all over again throughout the document.

There are three types of styles: character, paragraph, and linked. Which you use depends on what you want to do with them.

Exam Objective: MOS Word Expert 2.2.1, 2.2.2

- *Character styles* contain only font formatting elements, not paragraph formatting elements. This means you can apply them to any amount of text, from a single character to an entire message.
- *Paragraph styles* can contain both font formatting elements and paragraph formatting elements. You can apply a paragraph style only to entire paragraphs, not to part of one.
- *Linked styles* can also contain both font and paragraph formatting elements, but can behave as either character or paragraph styles, depending on how you apply them. If you apply a linked style to an entire paragraph, it has the effect of a paragraph style, but if you apply it to part of a paragraph, only its character elements are applied.

Using a custom character style to format text

Tucana Roast

Our signature roast blends Brazilian Bourbon Santos with Guatemalan Coban. The re
is remarkably rich and fragrant yet clean, sweet, and snappy. The perfect cup for aft

Creating character styles by example

Exam Objective: MOS Word Expert 2.2.1

You can create new styles from either the Styles gallery or the Styles pane. In either case, the style is initially based on whatever text you have selected, so you might want to start by formatting or selecting text to match somewhat the style you want to make. The simplest way to create a style is by example; you just format the text as you want the style, then define a name for it.

1. Format text for which you want to create a style and select it.

   You don't have to do this, but it gives you a head start on defining the style.

2. In the bottom-right of the Styles group, click the Styles button.

   This is the Styles button.

   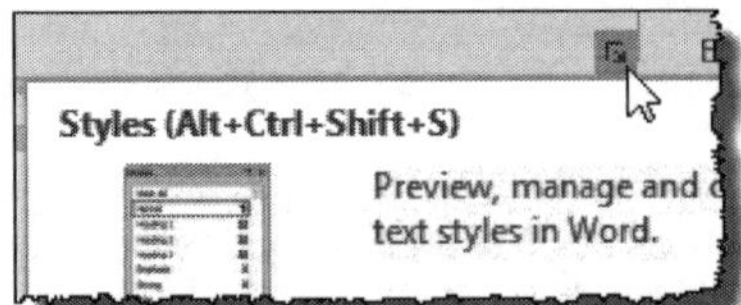

   The Styles pane appears on the right side of the window. You can use to the Style to create, apply, and modify styles.

   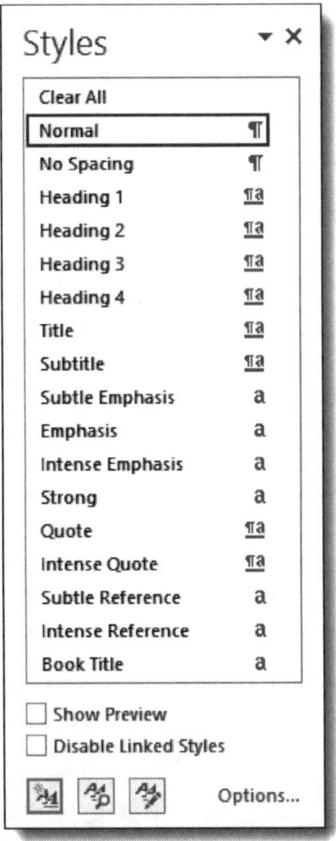

3. Click .

   The New Style button displays the Create New Style from Formatting window.

4. Type a name for your style.

   When you create a style in this way, it will be a linked style by default. You will need to modify the style to make it a character style.

5. Click **Modify**.

   To display the full Create New Style from Formatting window.

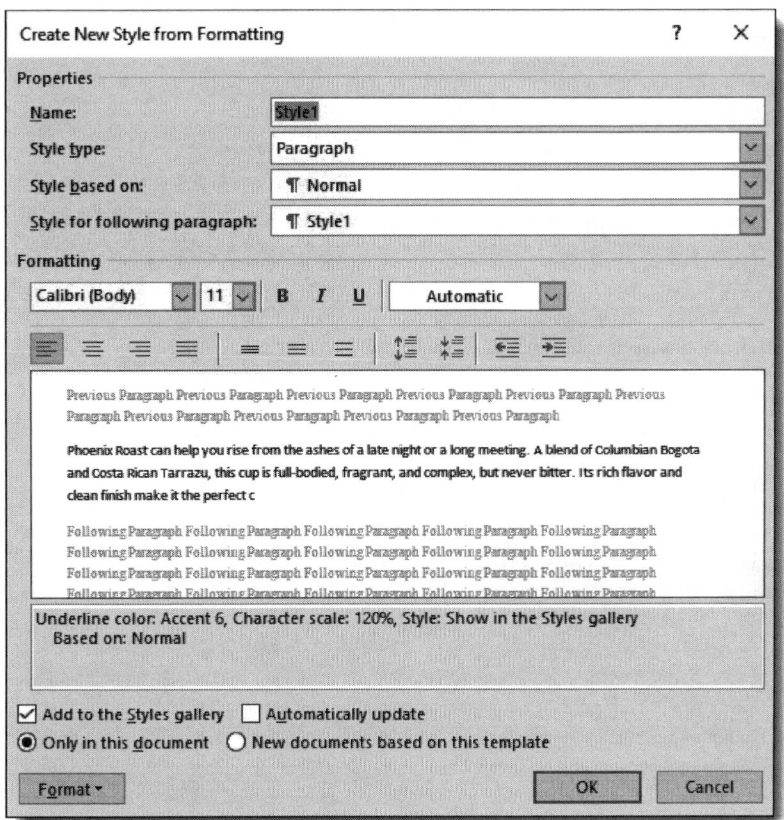

6. In the Name box, enter a name for the style.
7. In the Style Type list, click **Character**.

   This will make this a character style rather than a Paragraph style.
8. Click **OK**.

Defining a new character style

If you want to definite or modify style attributes while you create a style, you'll want to use the full Create New Style from Formatting window.

1. Format text for which you want to create a style and select it.
2. Display the Create New Style from Formatting window.

   In the Styles pane, click the New Style button.
3. Set the properties for the style.

   These include the name, the type, and what the style is based on.
4. Define formatting for the style.
   - Use the formatting toolbar in the window to apply simple formatting like font, bold, and italic.

   - Click the **Format** button, then an option to display deeper formatting options.

5. Click **OK**.

After creating a character style, you can easily apply to selected text by clicking the style name either in the Style gallery or in the Styles pane.

Exercise: Creating and applying character styles

For this exercise, you need to have `JT-Coffee-formatting` open, and to have completed the **Applying advanced character attributes** exercise. You'll create a character style for coffee names, then apply that style to other text in the document.

Exam Objective: MOS Word Expert 2.2.1

Do This	How & Why
1. Observe the coffee names within the document's paragraphs.	Only one ("Columbian Bogota") is formatted. You would like to create a character style so you can format all the similar text in the same way.
2. Select **Columbian Bogota**.	The formatted text under the Phoenix Roast heading.
3. Open the Styles pane.	Click the launcher button in the Styles group. Styles (Alt+Ctrl+Shift+S) Preview, manage and text styles in Word. The Styles pane appears to the right of the document. You can use the Styles pane to create, apply, and modify styles in your documents.
4. In the Styles pane, click [New Style button].	The New Style button. The Create New Style from Formatting window opens.
5. In the Name box, enter `Product Name`.	To create a name for the new style you are are creating. This name will appear in both the Style gallery and Style pane.
6. Define this as a character style.	
a) Observe the Style type box.	The default type of style is Paragraph, but you want this to be a Character style.
b) In the Style type list, click **Character**.	

7. Observe the style's definition.

Below the sample box. It shows all the formatting that has been applied to the style on which your style is based.

Underline, Underline color: Accent 6, Font color: Accent 3, Condensed by 1 pt, Character scale: 120%, Style: Show in the Styles gallery, Priority: 2
Based on: Default Paragraph Font

Do This	How & Why
8. Observe the formatting options. • The toolbar in the window gives you quick access to simple formatting such as the font, its size, and bold or italic. • Click the **Format** button to display a menu of options you can click to display other formatting windows.	
9. Click **OK**.	To create the style, which now appears in the list in the Styles pane.
10. Apply the Product name style to other coffee names in the body text. a) In the same paragraph, select "Costa Rican Tarrazu."	
b) Click **Product Name**.	You can click it in the Styles pane or Styles gallery. Notice that there is a small "a" to the right of the style name in the Styles pane. This, as opposed to the paragraph symbol (¶) indicates that this is a character style. The text is now formatted to match the style.
c) Apply the Product name style to other coffees named as blend ingredients.	Brazilian Bourbon Santos and Guatemalan Coban in the Tucana Roast paragraph. You don't need to apply it when a coffee is referenced in its own description.
11. Save the file.	

Character styles applied to the document

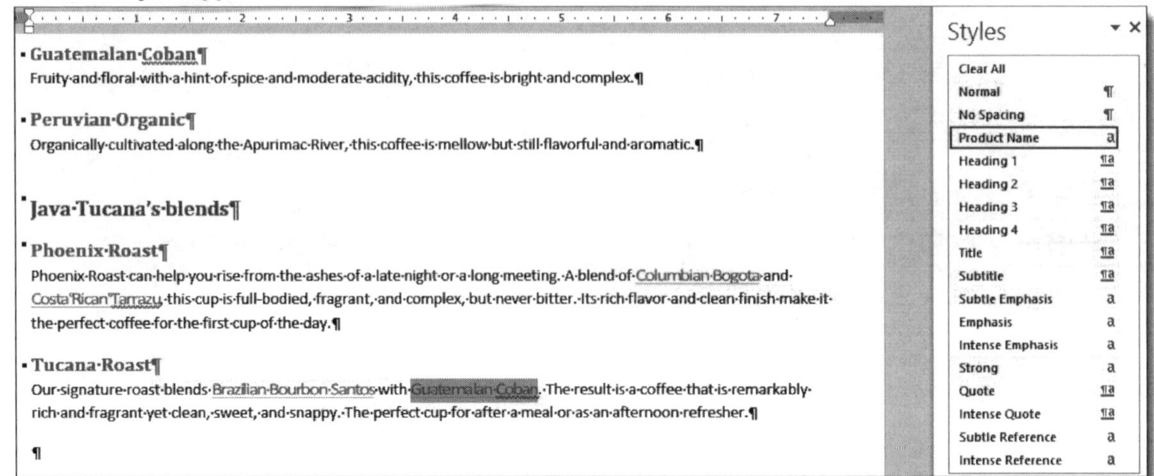

Modifying styles

When you modify an existing style, it automatically updates any text using that style. You can update a style to match selected text, such as some you've manually formatted already. You can also modify it in the Modify Style window, which is almost exactly like the full Create New Style from Formatting window.

Exam Objective: MOS Word Expert 2.2.2

- To update a style that's based on existing text, such as some you've manually modified, right-click the style name, and click **Update <Name> to Match Selection**.
- To freely update a style in the Modify Style window, right-click the style name in either the gallery or the Styles pane, and click **Modify**.

Clearing character formatting

Sometimes it's useful to get rid of all the character formatting on text and start over from the underlying paragraph-level formatting. You can do this quickly by selecting the formatted text, and then pressing **Ctrl+Spacebar**.

Exercise: Modifying a character style

Modify text formatting, update a style to reflect the change.

JT-Coffee-formatting is open and the preceding exercises have been completed.

Exam Objective: MOS Word Expert 2.2.2

Do This	How & Why
1. Observe the coffee names in the Java Tucana blend descriptions.	They are all formatted using the Product Name style.
2. Change the font color for "Columbian Bogota".	
a) Select "Columbian Bogota".	In the Phoenix Roast description paragraph.
b) Change the font color.	Use the Font Color gallery in the Font group on the Home tab. You can change it to any color you like. The text changes color, but the other product names do not. You changed the formatting, but not the style.
3. Change the Product Name style to reflect the new color.	

Do This	How & Why
a) Select "Columbian Bogota" again.	
b) In the Styles pane, display the menu for the Product Names style.	Click the arrow to the right of the style. 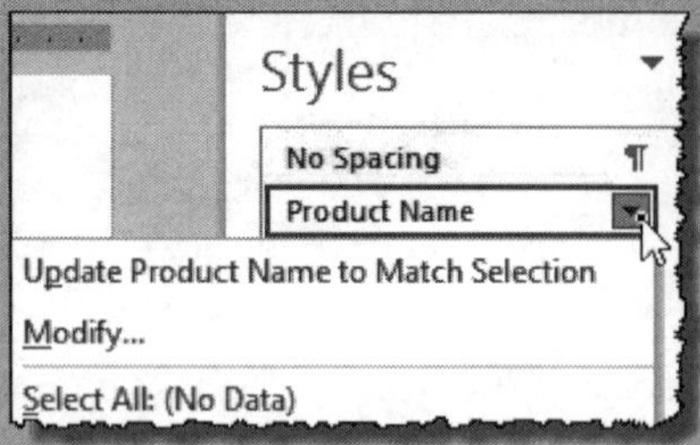
c) Click **Update Product Name to Match Selection**.	Now, all the product names formatted using the style reflect the change. This is the true power of using style: consistent formatting, and fast changes across an entire document.
4. In the Product Name style's menu, click **Modify**.	To display the Modify Style window. This is another method of modifying a style. Here, you can make changes just as if you were defining a new style.
5. Click **Cancel**.	To close the Modify Style window.
6. Remove the character formatting from "Columbian Bogota".	
a) Select the text.	
b) Press **Ctrl+Spacebar**.	This is a quick way to remove all character formatting from selected text.
7. Return the character formatting to "Columbian Bogota".	You can use the Undo button or reapply the style.
8. Save and close the file.	

Paste options

When you paste content from another location, document, or application, you can use Word's paste options to control exactly how the content is formatted. For example, when you paste content from an Outlook message or just a document with different formatting, you might want to preserve the font of the original document, or you might want to keep only the text, with formatting from the destination document.

Exactly what options are available depends on the type of content you're pasting and what application you've copied it from. In general, you have more options (and potential success) pasting content from other Office applications, but you can paste from a web browser or nearly any other application that lets you select content.

Exam Objective: MOS Word Expert 2.1.6

Paste options from another Word document

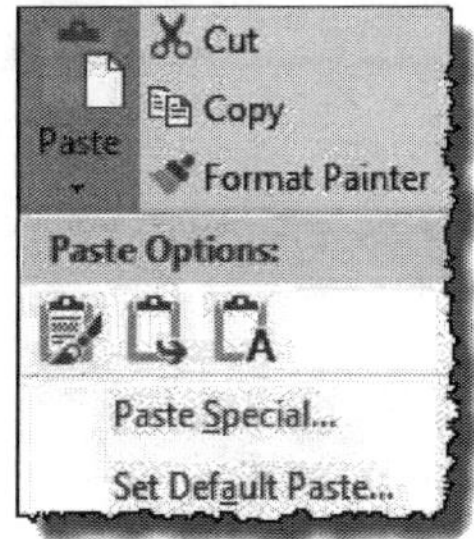

Some paste options you might use include:

Icon	Name	Description
	Use Destination Theme	Pastes the content and styles, but shows the styles using the theme defined for the document. This makes the pasted content match anything already in the document.
	Keep Source Formatting	Pastes the content in Normal style, but with manual formatting from the source document or web page. This preserves the original look as closely as possible, but it's all direct formatting instead of style-based.
	Merge Formatting	Keeps some formatting elements from the source document, while incorporating it with the style in use at the insertion point. For example, this preserves bold text but not necessarily the font or paragraph options.
	Keep Text Only	Pastes only the text itself, without the original formatting. This is often the safest choice when you want to control the formatting in the destination document.
	Paste Special	Opens the Paste Special window, with additional pasting options.
	Set Default Paste	Opens the Word Options window, with settings for the default behavior of the Paste button.

You can point to each option to see a live preview of the results, so you don't need to experiment blindly. Additionally, immediately after you paste content, a clipboard icon appears next to it. Clicking it, or pressing **Ctrl**, opens the Paste Options menu again, in case you've made a mistake.

Paste special

You can choose **Paste Special** from the paste list to view more options.

The Paste Special window, when pasting from an Excel document

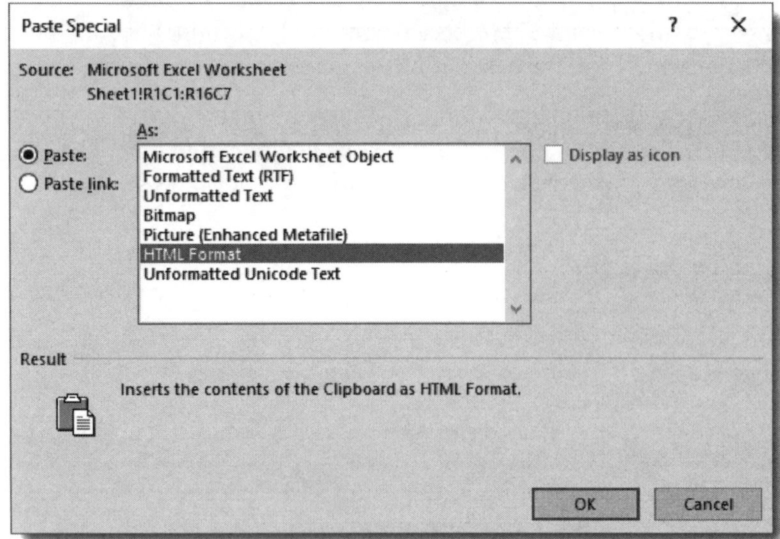

Although the included options vary, depending on what you're pasting, common options include:

- *Microsoft [Office Application] Object*: Place a movable object that's displayed in Word but can be opened and edited in its own application.
- *Formatted text (RTF)*: Preserve formatting using Microsoft's Rich Text Format.
- *HTML format*: Preserve formatting using HTML.
- *Unformatted text*: Paste only the text, without formatting.
- *Unformatted Unicode text*: Like unformatted text, but preserving the larger character set of Unicode fonts.
- *Picture ([Format]):* Paste the content as a graphic, preserving the appearance of the original content. Note that you can't select or edit text once it's been turned into a picture.
- *Bitmap*: Paste the content as an uncompressed graphic. This perfectly preserves the appearance of the copied content, but it can make a very large file size, so it usually isn't ideal.

Additionally, when pasting from another document, you can choose the **Paste Link** option. Although this looks the same as standard pasting, pasting as a link means you can update the source document; the changes are then reflected in the message content.

Exercise: Pasting content

In this exercise, you'll test paste options both from Word documents and external applications.

Exam Objective: MOS Word Expert 2.1.6

Do This	How & Why
1. Create a new document and save it as `Pasted content.`	You'll practice pasting content into a blank document.
2. Copy some text from another Word document.	
a) Open `About Us.`	
b) Copy all the text on the first page.	From the title down to "local food."
3. Paste the text into the blank document.	
a) In `Pasted content`, click the lower half of the **Paste** button.	Paste
b) Point to [icon].	Don't click it yet. In the Live Preview, the headings and styles are preserved, but instead of the theme colors and fonts in the original document, they use Word's default. Java Tucana Services / Office coffee service / We'll supply your office with early-morn / have whole-bean, ground, and single-se
c) Point to [icon].	The Live Preview now uses the exact formatting of the source document; however, it would all be pasted as Normal text with direct formatting.
d) Point to [icon].	This option preserves manual formatting such as bold or italic formatting from the original text, but no theme or style information.
e) Point to [icon].	This option pastes only the text itself, with all formatting discarded.
f) Click [icon].	To paste the text with the style information, but using the theme in the destination document (which is the Word default theme in this case).
4. On the Design tab preview different themes and style sets.	Use Live Preview. Because you pasted the content into the destination theme, it changes whenever existing themes or styles change.

Do This	How & Why
5. Insert a page break at the end of the document.	Press **Ctrl+Enter**.
6. Copy content from an Excel workbook.	You'll view paste options when pasting data from another application, in this case, Microsoft Excel.
a) In Excel, open `Sample budget.xlsx`.	
b) Select the entire table, including the logo at the top.	Because of the graphic, it's easiest to click **G16** first and drag up to **A1**.
c) Press **Ctrl+C**.	
7. Paste the Excel content into Word.	
a) In **Pasted content**, open the Paste Options list.	The options are different this time.
b) Point to each option in turn.	In addition to the options you have when pasting from a Word document, you can also paste as a link, either using destination styles or source formatting. You can also paste the content as a picture, but there is no Merge Formatting option.
c) Click **Paste Special**.	The Paste Special window opens. By default, HTML format is selected.
d) Click each option in turn.	There's no Live Preview, but description text appears in the Result section, telling you what to expect.
e) Select **HTML Format** and click **OK**.	The worksheet is pasted as a table, in a fair approximation of how it looked in Excel.
8. Save and close `Pasted content`.	

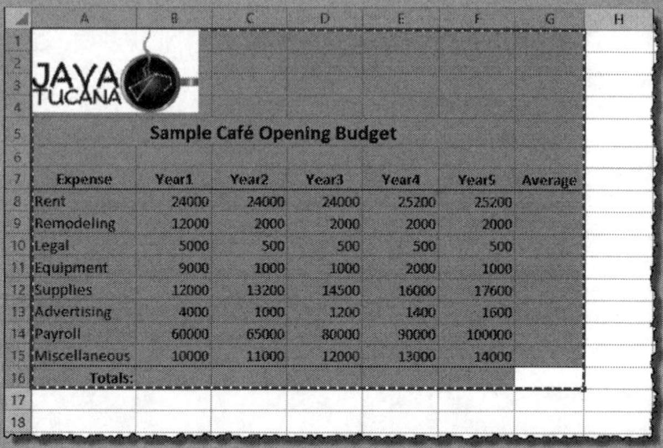

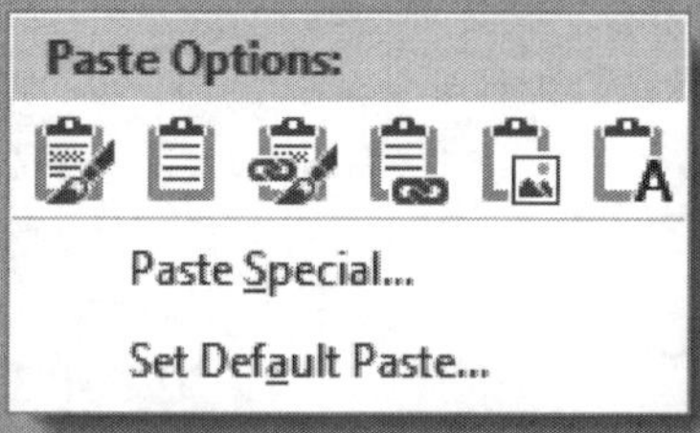

Do This	How & Why
9. Close all other files without saving.	Close Excel as well.

Assessment: Character styles

1. You're creating a document in which all employee names are colored and italicized, and you decide to do so using a style. What style type should you choose?
    - Character
    - Linked
    - Paragraph
2. Which method of creating a style gives you the most control over the formatting included with the style? Choose the one best answer.
    - Creating a style by example
    - Defining a style from scratch
3. When copying text into a document, you want to preserve its layout and font exactly, even if you decide to later change themes in the rest of the destination document. What paste option will take the least amount of work?
    - Keep source formatting
    - Keep text only
    - Merge formatting
    - Use destination styles

Module B: Paragraph styles

You will learn how to:

- Create and modify paragraph styles
- Control the relationships among paragraph styles

Defining paragraph styles

The difference between character styles and paragraph styles is that paragraph styles comprise formatting elements that apply to the paragraph as a whole, such as indents, line spacing, and tabs. Paragraphs can also include font attributes, but again, these will apply to an entire paragraph.

Exam Objective: MOS Word Core 2.2.1

You can create paragraph styles in the same ways you do character styles.

- Format a paragraph as you like, then create the style by example. To do this, place the insertion point within the formatted paragraph, display the menu for the Styles gallery, then click **Create Style**. Name the style and you're done.
- Display the Create New Style from Formatting full window. You can do this by clicking the Modify button in the window displayed by the previous technique, or by clicking the New Style button in the Styles pane. Be sure to specify that you want to create a paragraph style.

Exercise: Creating and using paragraph styles

Format a paragraph, then create a style based on that formatting and use it on other paragraphs.

Exam Objective: MOS Word Core 2.2.1

Do This	How & Why
1. Open `JT-Coffee paragraphs` and save it as `JT-Coffee paragraphs styled`.	This is similar to the document you used to create character styles. You'll format a coffee description paragraph, then create and use a style to format the other descriptions.
2. Set left and right indents for the Brazilian Bourbon Santos description paragraph.	
a) Place the insertion point within the paragraph and display the Paragraph window.	On the Home tab, click the Paragraph Settings button at the bottom of the Paragraph group.
b) Set both the left and right indents to `0.5"`.	The window should look like this. Indentation Left: 0.5" Right: 0.5"
c) Click **OK**.	To apply the indents. How would you apply these settings to all the other paragraphs? The best way is to use a style.

Do This	How & Why
3. Create a style called **Coffee Descriptions**.	
a) Place the insertion point within the indented paragraph.	
b) Click the Style gallery's dropdown arrow, then click **Create a Style**.	 To open the Create New Style from Formatting window.
c) Name the style `Coffee Descriptions`.	This is the simplest, quickest way to create a paragraph style. 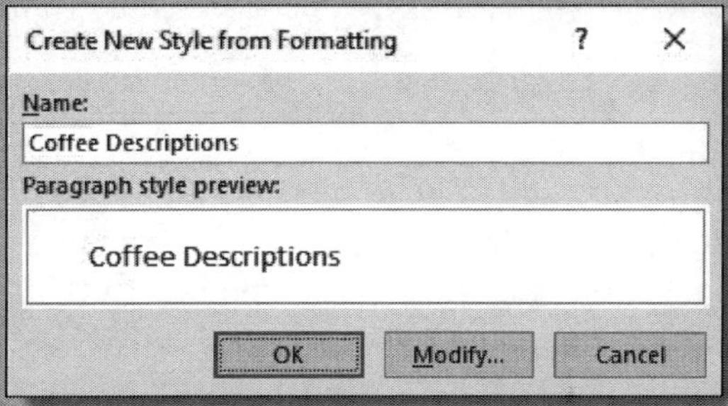
d) Click **OK**.	
4. Apply the new style to the other description paragraphs.	
a) Display the Styles pane.	Click the Styles button at the bottom right of the Styles group. You will see the new style in the list.
b) Click within the Columbian Bogota Supremo description, then click Coffee Descriptions.	In the Styles pane. The paragraph is now indented.
c) Apply the style to the rest of the descriptions.	
5. Modify the Coffee Descriptions style so that the indents are .75 inches.	
a) In the Styles pane, right-click **Coffee Descriptions**, then click **Modify**.	The Modify Style window appears, which gives you full control over the definition of the style.

Do This	How & Why
b) Click **Format**, then click **Paragraph**.	
c) Change the left and right indents to `.75"`.	Indentation Left: 0.75" Right: 0.75"
d) Click **OK** twice.	Because you modified the style, all of the paragraphs to which the style was applied now reflect the larger indentation.
6. Save the document.	Do not close it.

Relationships among paragraph styles

The relationships among paragraph styles can affect your documents in many ways. Often, you might be unaware of these relationships until you have some unintended consequence that does not, at first, make sense. There are two important types of style relationships to pay attention to.

- Basing a style on another style
- Heading levels

When you create a style, by default it will be based upon the underlying style of the paragraph where the insertion point is, or of the style you are modifying. This gives you a head start, in a sense, on the formatting, because all of the formatting of the base style will already be there for you to build upon. But it also means that if you modify one style, you will be modifying any styles that are based upon it.

This is a good thing in practice. If you create a base style for you document (like the normal style in the default Word template), and then build your styles from there, you will be able to modify the main font for the document simply by changing the font for the base style. But it can lead to sudden changes to dependent styles when you aren't aware of the relationship.

When you use Word's built-in heading styles, you are, in effect, creating a hierarchy of headings in your documents. If you plan to create an outline of your document, or a table of contents, use the numbered heading styles exclusively. That way, you'll have consistent, logical outlines and tables of contents.

Exercise: Exploring relationships among styles

Observe heading levels and the relationship between dependent styles.

`JT-Coffee paragraphs styles` is open.

Do This	How & Why
1. Observe the styles used in the headings.	
a) Click within the title.	The title uses the Title style.
b) Click within the first main heading.	"Single-region South American coffees." This heading and the other main section use the built-in Heading 1 style. This means that these paragraphs will appear at the top level of an outline of the document or of the table of contents.
c) Click within one of the coffee headings.	These headings use the Heading 2 style. Consistent use of heading level styles will result in documents that are well-organized, that look good, and that result in useful outlines and table of contents.
2. Change the color for the "Phoenix Roast" heading.	Select it, then use the Font color gallery to change the color to one you like.
3. Create a new style for the blend headings.	
a) Click within the "Phoenix Roast" heading.	You're going to create a style for the blend headings that is based on the Heading 2 style so you can observe how dependent styles are linked.
b) In the Styles pane, click the New Style button.	To display the Create New Style from Formatting window.
c) Name the style `Blend Headings`.	
d) Observe the Style based on box.	This style is based on the Heading 2 style.
e) Click **OK**.	
f) Apply the style to the other blend heading.	
4. Change the font for the Heading 2 style.	
a) In the Styles pane, right-click **Heading 2** and then click **Modify**.	
b) Select a different font and then click **OK**.	All of the single-region South American coffee headings change, but so do the blend headings. Why is that?
5. Save and then close the document.	

Assessment: Paragraph styles

1. Paragraph styles cannot be created by example. True or false?
    - True
    - False
2. Which of the following approached to creating styles in a document makes most sense? Choose the one best answer.
    - Create the lowest-level headings first and work backwards to the base style.
    - Create the base style first and build the heading styles from that.
3. All styles are associating with a heading level. True or false?
    - True
    - False

Summary: Styles

In this chapter, you learned how to:

- Use advanced character formatting, create and modify character styles, and use paste options to copy only certain attributes of selected text.
- Create and modify paragraph styles, and understand and control the relationships among those styles.

Synthesis: Styles

In this exercise, you will create character and paragraph styles to use in formatting a menu document.

1. Open `Lunch Menu` and save it as `Lunch Menu styles`.
   This document contains an unformatted menu for a Java Tucana Café.
2. Format one of the item names in a way you like ("Pollo Crazin," for example). Format just the name of the item, and not the price or the paragraph as whole.
3. Create a character style based on the item you just formatted, then apply that style to the other items in the menu.
4. Apply the Title style to "Lunch Menu."
5. Apply the Heading 1 style to "Soups of the Day".
6. Apply the Heading 2 style to the lunch item paragraphs.
7. Does the character style still show on the lunch items after you applied the character style?
8. Create a new paragraph style for the item descriptions, and apply it to the description paragraphs.
9. Modify the description style to be centered on the page.
10. Save and close the document.

The menu formatted using styles

Chapter 9: References and hyperlinks

You will learn how to:

- Create endnotes and footnotes
- Create a table of contents
- Apply a hyperlink

Module A: Reference notes

You can use footnotes and endnotes to cite sources or provide extra information.

You will learn:

- The difference between footnotes and endnotes
- How to insert notes
- How to change note options and note format

Footnotes and endnotes

Exam Objective: MOS Word Core 4.1.1, 4.1.2

Footnotes appear on every page where a note is marked, below a separator line but above the footer area. Endnotes appear at the end of the document, after a separator line.

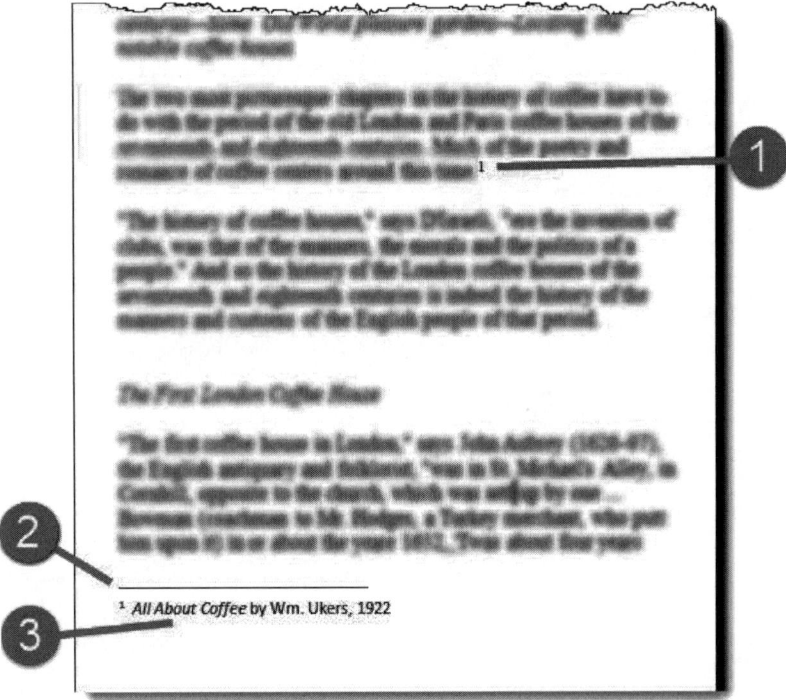

1. Reference mark
2. Separator line
3. Footnote text

After you've added a note, you can view the note text by holding the mouse pointer over the reference mark.

By default, footnotes use Arabic numerals and endnotes use roman numerals, but you can instead use letters, traditional symbols like asterisks and daggers, or define custom symbols using characters from any installed font. Numbering (or lettering) can be continuous or restart for each page or section. You can also change the text style of notes. You can convert footnotes to endnotes or vice versa, or swap all footnotes and endnotes.

Inserting notes

Both footnote and endnote features can be found in the Footnotes group on the References tab. Word automatically keeps track of the numbering or lettering of the notes.

Exam Objective: MOS Word Core 4.1.1, 4.1.2

1. Place the cursor in the text where you want the note reference.
2. Click **Insert Footnote** or **Insert Endnote**.

   The reference mark is inserted, and a note created at the bottom of the page or the end of the document. The cursor is at the start of the new note.
3. Enter the note text.

If you are adding endnotes to a large document, you can quickly return to your place in the text: just right-click the endnote number, and then click **Go to Endnote**.

Note options

Exam Objective: MOS Word Core 4.1.1, 4.1.2

You can change the presentation of notes from the Footnote and Endnote window, which you can open in a couple ways:

- Click the dialog box launcher in the Footnotes group on the References tab.
- Right-click a footnote or endnote, and click **Note Options**.

Note: If Word has flagged the note for grammar or spelling (there's a squiggly, colored underline), you won't see note options in the menu when you right-click the note. To ensure you see note-related commands, right-click the reference at the start of the note text.

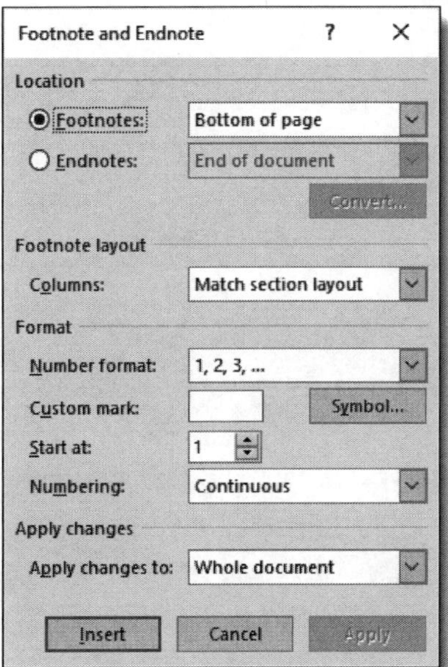

Here are some things you can do from the Footnote and Endnote window:

- Change the location of footnotes and endnotes: footnotes can be at the bottom of the page or right below the text, where the reference mark is. Endnotes can be at the end of the document or the end of each section.
- Convert all endnotes into footnotes, all footnotes into endnotes, or swap all footnotes and endnotes. To convert an individual note, right-click it, and click **Convert to Endnote** or **Convert to Footnote**.
- Select the number format. By default, footnotes use Arabic numbers and endnotes use roman numerals, but you can choose from the following: numbers, upper- and lowercase letters, upper- and lowercase roman numerals, and traditional symbols (asterisk, dagger, double dagger, section symbol).
- Select a symbol to use for the reference mark and corresponding note. If you select a symbol for one note, the next time you add a note, you're prompted to select another symbol or go back to standard marks.
- Set the starting number or letter for notes, and select whether numbering should be continuous or restart at each page or section.

Finally, you set whether any changes should be applied to the whole document or just to the current section.

Changing note format

To configure the formatting of footnote and endnote text and references, modify the styles for these elements.

Exam Objective: MOS Word Core 4.1.1, 4.1.2

1. Right-click the number at the start of the note text, and then click **Style**.

   The Style window opens with the note text selected.

   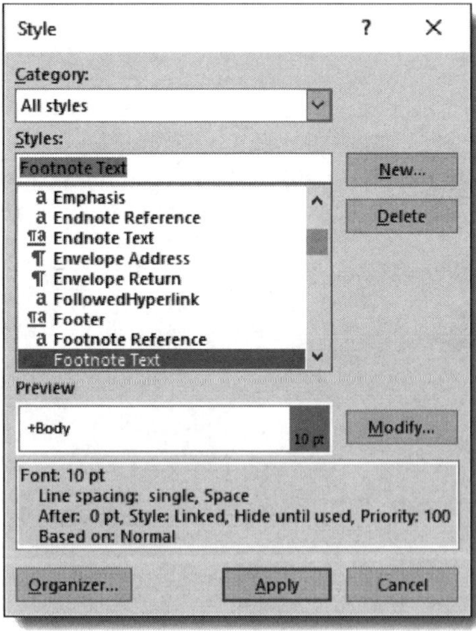

2. Select the style you want to modify.

   If necessary. You can separately modify Footnote Reference, Footnote Text, Endnote Reference, and Endnote Text.

3. Click **Modify**.

   The Modify Style window opens.

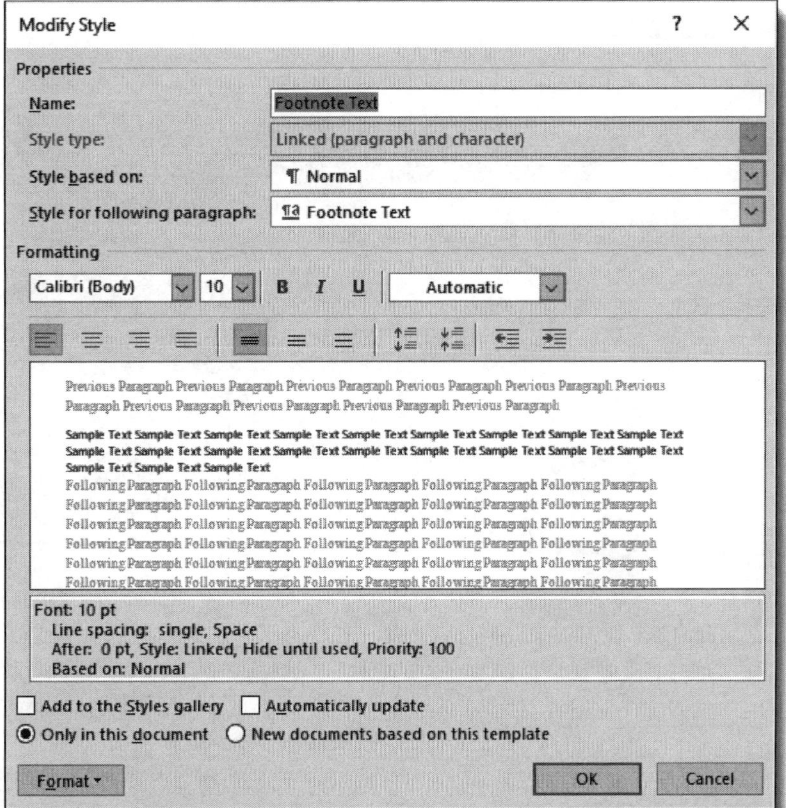

4. Change the formatting options.

   By default, "Only in this document" is selected. You can choose to apply this format to all new documents created from the current template.

5. Click **OK**.

   The formatting is applied to all instances of the style in the document.

6. Click **Apply**.

   To close the Style window.

Exercise: Inserting footnotes and endnotes

Exam Objective: MOS Word Core 4.1.1, 4.1.2

Do This	How & Why
1. Open `CoffeeHouses` and save it as `CoffeeHouses-notes`.	
2. Place the cursor at the end of the first paragraph.	After the period. You'll add a note marker here.
3. On the References tab, click **Insert Footnote**.	A marker is set, and a new note is made at the bottom of the page. The cursor is there, ready for you to type.
4. Type `Ukers, All About Coffee, p 232.`	*Don't* press Enter.
5. Place the cursor at the end of the second paragraph.	Scroll back up to it.
6. On the References tab, click **Insert Endnote**.	A note is added at the end of the document.
7. Type `Ukers, p 233.`	
8. Right-click the note letter, and click **Go to Endnote**.	You are returned to the note marker in the text.
9. Save and close the file.	

Assessment: Reference notes

1. You insert a footnote or endnote from which tab?
    - Home
    - Insert
    - References
    - Review
2. After entering an endnote, how can you return quickly to your place in the text?
    - Right-click the note text, and click Go to Endnote.
    - Right-click the note number, and click Go to Endnote.
    - Press Ctrl+G.
    - Use the Go To function.

Module B: Table of contents

The automatic table of contents function uses the heading styles in the document to build the table. If the document does not use heading styles, the table of contents can be created manually.

You will learn how to:

- Insert a table of contents
- Use the Table of Contents window
- Change table of contents styles
- Update a table of contents
- Mark image captions
- Insert a table of figures

About tables of contents

Manually assembling a table of contents from a long document can be a lot of work to compile and format, and it easily falls out of date when you edit the body of the document later. Fortunately, Word lets you insert a *table of contents* building block. Each entry in the table is a field reflecting a section of the document and its page.

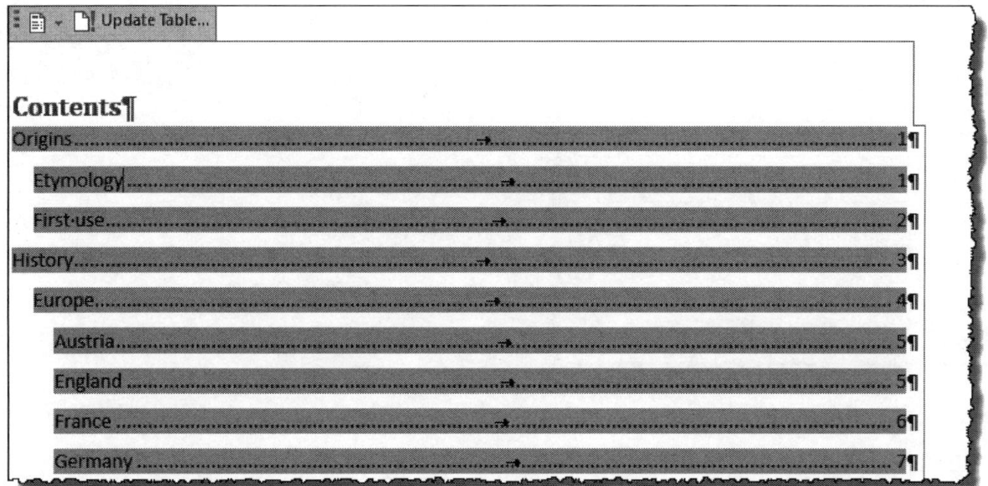

TOC building blocks can be automatic or manual. A manual table of contents is just a formatting framework you enter your own data into. An automatic TOC is more interesting, since each entry is based directly on the content of the document. By default, any text formatted as Heading 1, Heading 2, or Heading 3 appears in the TOC, arranged by level. If you want, you can also include different styles, outline levels, or even table entry fields as TOC entries. Either way, since each entry is generated based on the document, it not only includes an accurate page number, but the entry itself is a hyperlink to the content it references.

Inserting a built-in table of contents

To add a table of contents using default formats, select a built-in table of contents. Typically, you'll want to add it at or near the beginning of the document, but you can place it wherever you like.

Exam Objective: MOS Word Core 4.2.1

1. Place the cursor where you want to insert the table of contents.
   You might want to add a page break first.
2. On the References tab, click **Table of Contents**.
   To open the Table of Contents gallery.

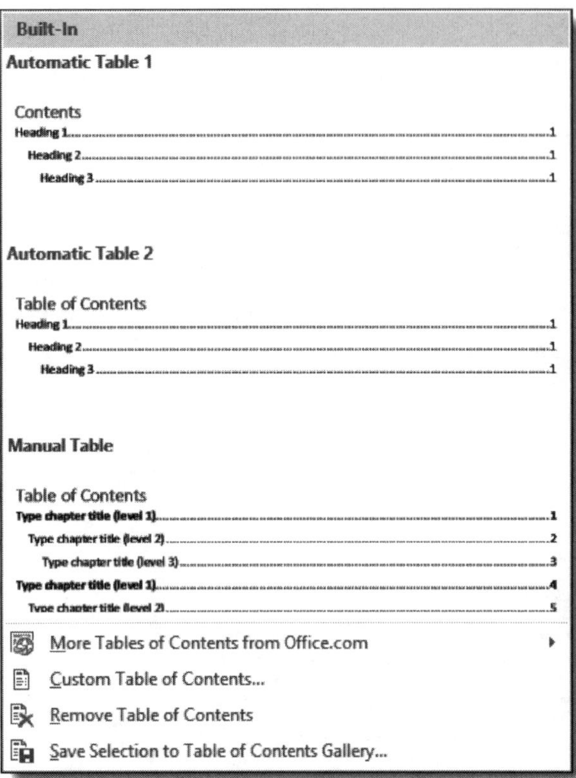

3. Click a style in the gallery.
   - By default, there are two automatic tables, but they differ only in the heading text.
   - If you choose Manual Table, you'll have to fill out the headings and page numbers yourself.

Customizing a table of contents

Exam Objective: MOS Word Core 3.2.1 and Expert 4.2.1

If one of the table of contents building blocks isn't what you want, you can use the Table of Contents window to access more options. To open it, on the References tab, click **Table of Contents > Custom Table of Contents**.

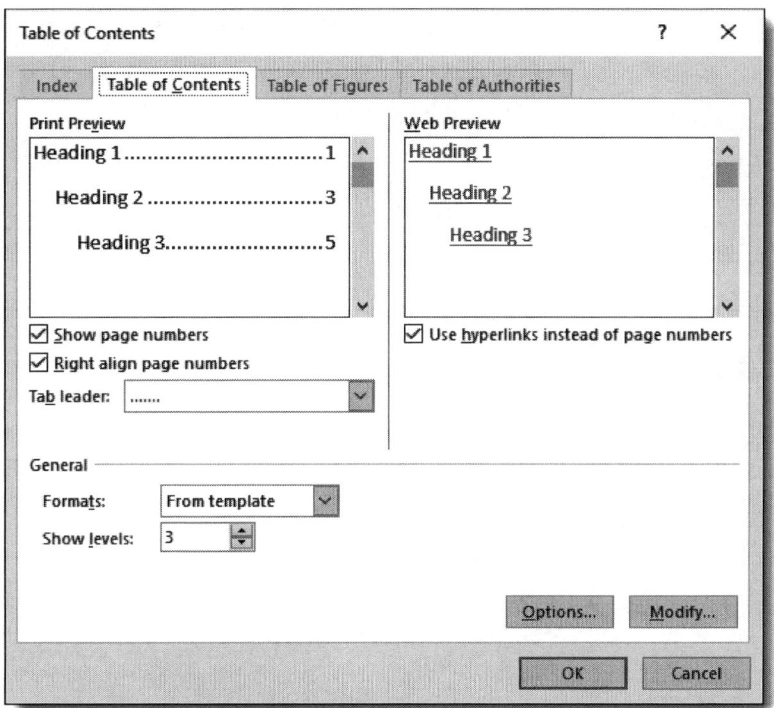

- Change overall table of contents style from the General section.
  - Use the **Formats** list to choose a general appearance.
  - Use the **Show levels** field to choose how many entry levels the table has.
- Change page display options in the Print Preview and Web Preview sections.
  - **Right align page numbers** and **Use hyperlinks instead of page numbers** (for web pages only) are only available if **Show page numbers** is checked.
  - You can only select a tab leader if **Right align page numbers** is checked.
- Click **Modify** to format the text in the table of contents itself. Each Table of Contents entry level has its own associated style, named TOC #.

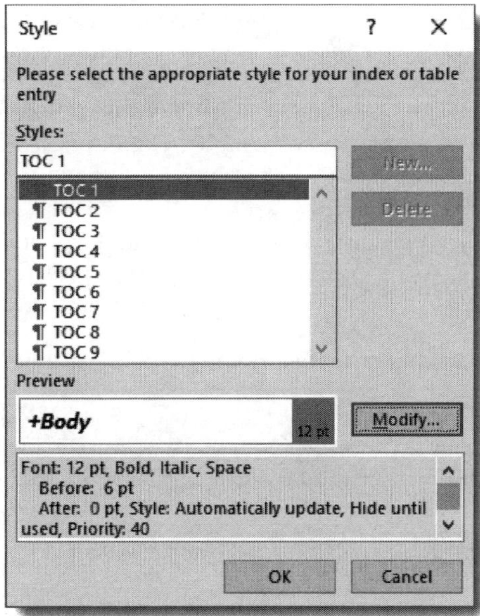

  - To modify a style, click it, then click **Modify**.

- You can only modify TOC styles if you select the **From template** format in the **Table of Contents** window.

- To select exactly what content is used to generate the table of contents, click **Options**.

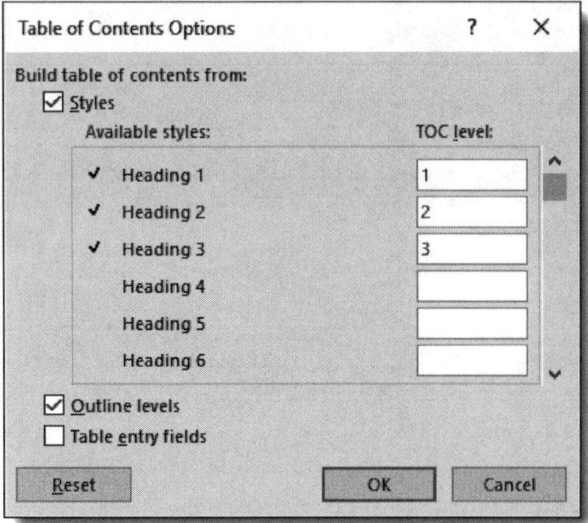

  - To base entries on particular styles in the document, check **Styles**.
  - To modify which styles are used to generate TOC entries, enter a number in the corresponding **TOC** level field.
  - Check **Outline levels** to include styles with assigned outline levels.
  - Check **Table entry fields** to include TOC entries that have been manually inserted in the document. Table entry fields are an older and usually obsolete way of creating a table of contents, but they have some uses.

- To save your settings for future use, select the entire table and click **Table of Contents** > **Save Selection to Table of Contents Gallery**.

- To remove a table of contents, click **Table of Contents** > **Delete Table of Contents**.

Planning a table of contents

It's easy to insert a table of contents, and it's not even that hard to format one, but if you're not careful you might end up with entries you don't want, or miss entries you do want. You can minimize this problem with document planning, but exactly what you need to do depends on what content your TOC automatically includes.

- If you're basing the TOC off of styles, make sure to apply styles consistently throughout the document. Unless you've assigned TOC styles differently, this means you should use numbered header styles for all text you want to appear in the TOC.
  - You'll need to use as many heading (or other) styles as you have levels in your TOC. You can use other heading styles; they just won't appear in the TOC.
  - By default, heading level and TOC level are the same, but it doesn't have to be that way. You could for example include only Heading 1 and Heading 3 in the TOC, but not Heading 2.

- Click **Add Text** in the Table of Contents group to set a paragraph to a specific TOC level. This will also change its style.

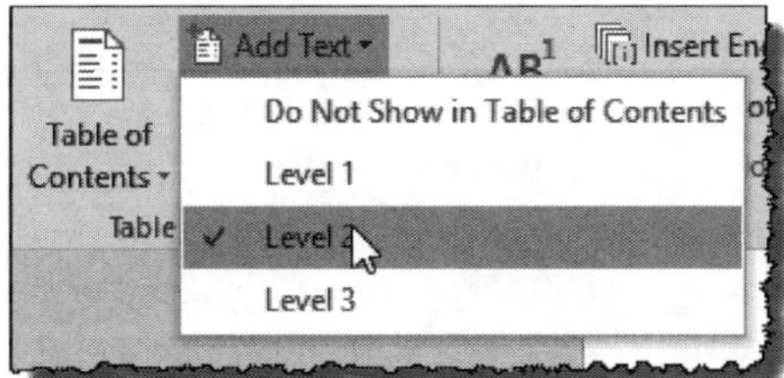

- If you're basing the TOC off of outline levels, make sure to apply outline levels consistently through the document. Remember that you can't change the outline level of a numbered heading style, though you can assign outline levels to other styles.
- If you're using table entry fields, you'll have to manually mark them in the document.
  - To mark a table entry field, place the insertion point and press **Alt+Shift+O** to open the Mark Table of Contents Entry Field window.

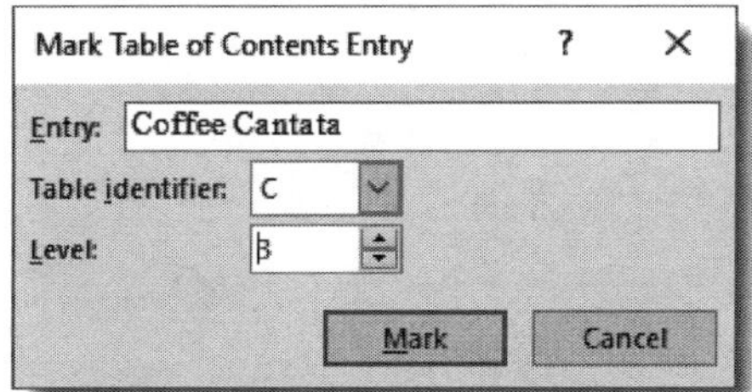

  - One good time to use table entry fields is when you want the text in the TOC to be different from the text on the page, such as for an entry name that doesn't directly appear in the document.

Modifying table of contents styles

The Table of Contents window allows you to choose from a few style sets to apply to the table, but you can also format each level individually.

Exam Objective: MOS Word Expert 3.2.1

1. On the References tab, click **Table of Contents > Custom Table of Contents**.
   The Table of Contents window opens.
2. Click **Modify**.
   This opens the Style window, which shows a preview and description of each table of contents level.
3. Select the level you want to change, and click **Modify**.
   The Modify Style window opens.

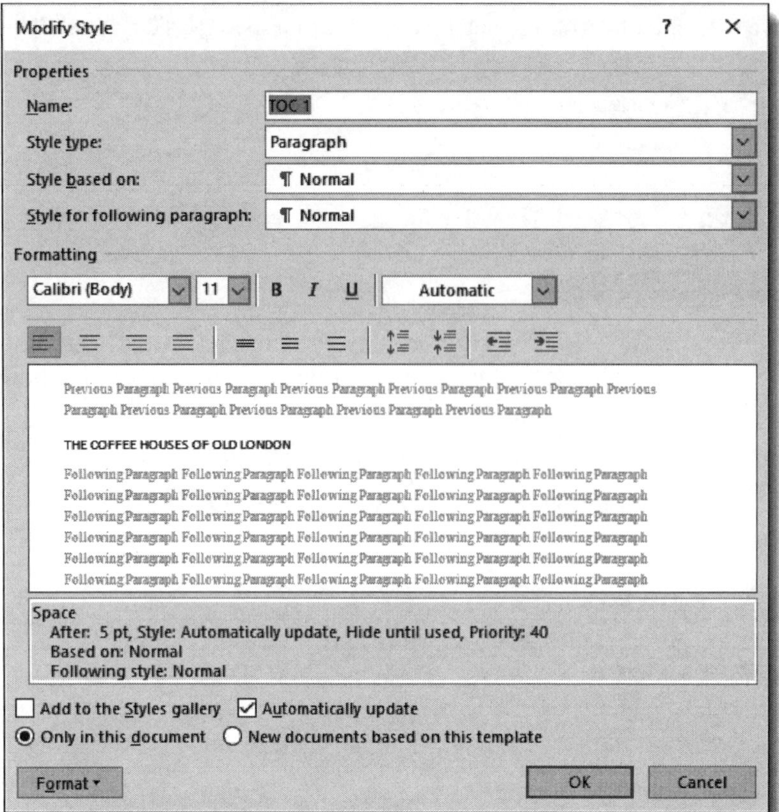

4. Make the changes you want:

   This includes formatting options and whether to apply the style to the current document only or to all new documents created from this template.

5. Click **OK** to return to the Style window, and then click **OK** again.

   You return to the Table of Contents window, where the changes are reflected in the preview.

6. Click **OK**.

   To close the window and apply the style changes.

Updating a table of contents

Exam Objective: MOS Word Core 4.2.2

If you make changes to your document that alter heading text or move headings to different pages, you can update the table of contents to reflect those changes. If headings have been moved but not changed, you can choose to update the page numbers only. If you've changed the text of the headings, choose to update the entire table.

1. Click anywhere in the table of contents.

   A tab appears at the top of the table.

   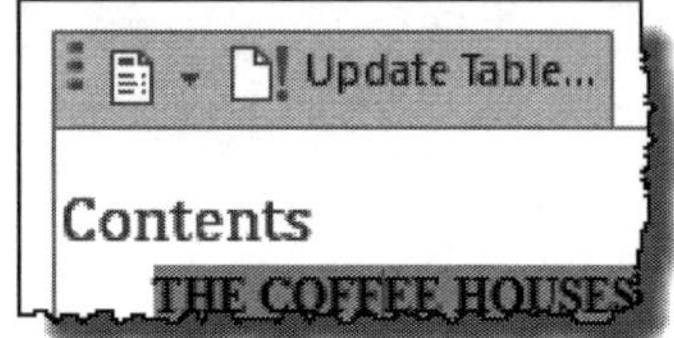

2. Click **Update Table**.

The Update Table of Contents window opens.

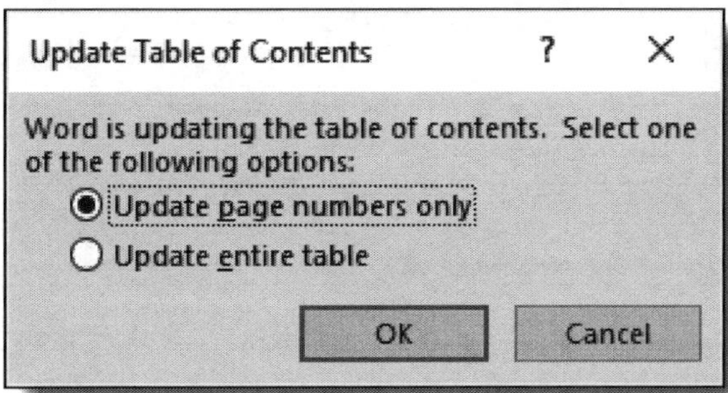

3. Select whether to update page numbers only or the entire table.
4. Click **OK**.

   The table is updated.

Exercise: Adding a table of contents

Exam Objective: MOS Word Core 4.2.1 and Expert 3.2.1

Do This	How & Why
1. Open `History` and save it as `History-toc`.	
2. Insert an automatic table of contents.	
a) Place the cursor on the blank line just below the title.	
b) In the References tab, click **Table of Contents**.	Note the automatic and manual table options. The manual table requires you to fill out the details.
c) Click **Automatic Table 1**.	The table of contents is inserted. It shows three levels of outline detail. The third level shows the Heading 3 styles for the regions under Europe and Asia.
d) Click anywhere in the table.	A tab appears at the top with options.
3. Click **Table of Contents > Remove Table of Contents**.	You'll insert a table with a custom detail level. You could also see this option from the tab on the table.
4. Insert a custom table of contents.	
a) Click **Table of Contents > Custom Table of Contents**.	The Table of Contents window opens.
b) From the Tab leader list, choose _____.	The last option.

Do This	How & Why
c) Set "Show levels" to 2.	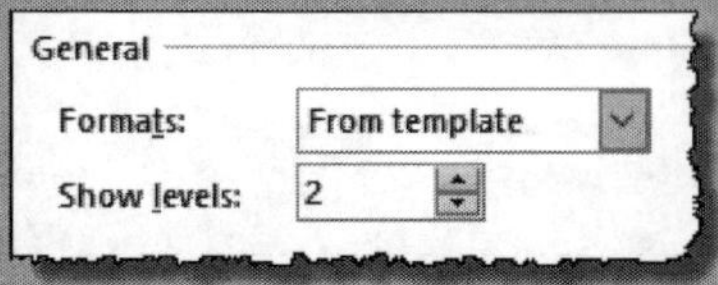 General Formats: From template Show levels: 2 Heading 3 no longer appears in the preview panes.
d) View the Formats list.	You could choose a variety of presets, but they'd reduce your other customization options.
e) Click **From template**.	To use the default.
5. Set Table of Contents options.	While you don't want Heading 3 to appear in the table, you want to show a couple of other things.
a) Click **Options**.	The Table of Contents Options window opens. By default, the table of contents is built from Heading styles and outline levels.
b) Check **Table entry fields**.	You're going to insert a manual field in the document later.
c) Next to the TOC image caption style, enter 3.	At the bottom of the styles list. 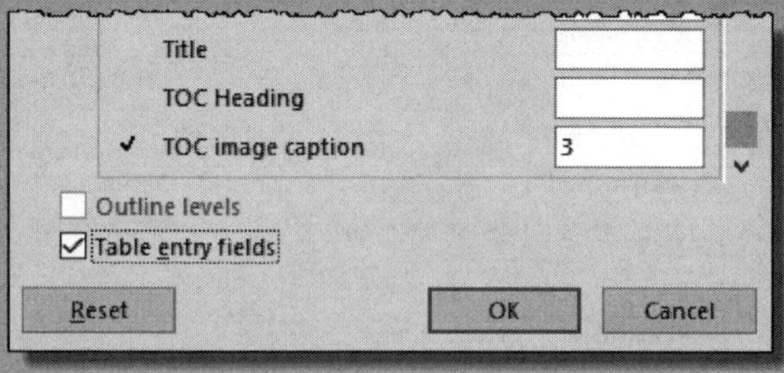 Title TOC Heading ✓ TOC image caption 3 Outline levels Table entry fields Reset OK Cancel
d) Click **OK**.	The Show levels field is no longer visible, and your changes are visible in the Preview panes. 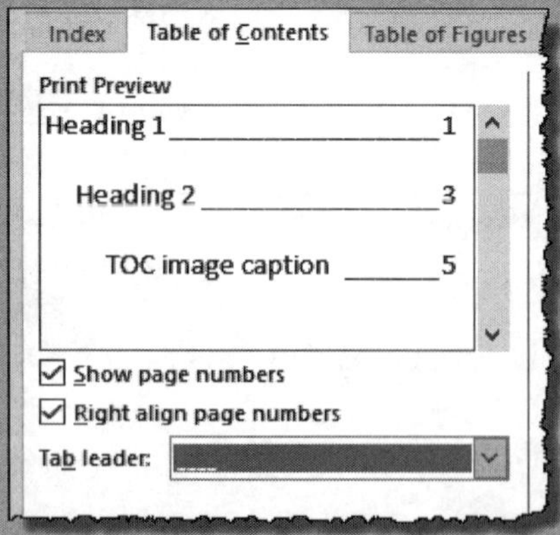 Index Table of Contents Table of Figures Print Preview Heading 1 ____ 1 Heading 2 ____ 3 TOC image caption ____ 5 Show page numbers Right align page numbers Tab leader:
6. Modify the TOC styles.	In contrast to the styles used to build the table of contents, TOC styles control how the table itself is formatted.
a) Click **Modify**.	The Style window opens. The TOC 1 style is selected.

Do This	How & Why
b) Click **Modify**.	The Modify Style window opens, exactly as though you had modified TOC 1 in the Styles list.
c) Click **B**.	To format the style as bold.
d) Click **OK**.	To close the Modify Style window.
e) Open the Modify Style window for TOC 3.	Select it and click **Modify**.
f) Apply italics to the style.	
g) Click **OK** twice.	The changes are reflected in the preview, but the Tab leader was also reset to the default. You'll keep it though.

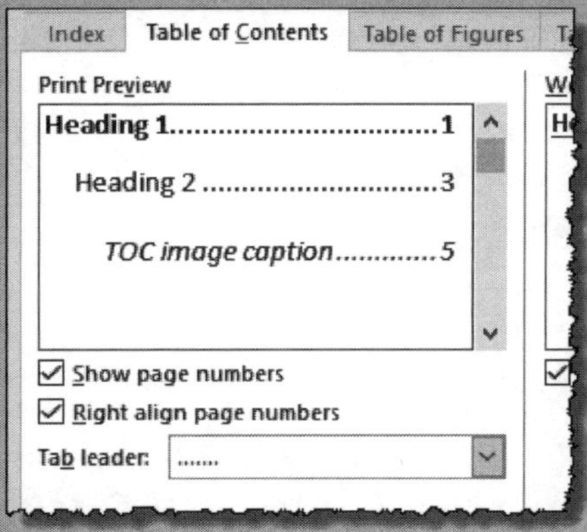

7. Click **OK**.

To insert the custom table of contents. It doesn't actually show any level 3 entries, but you'll add some.

History of coffee

Origins 2
Etymology 2
First use 2
History 3
Europe 5
Americas 9
Asia 10

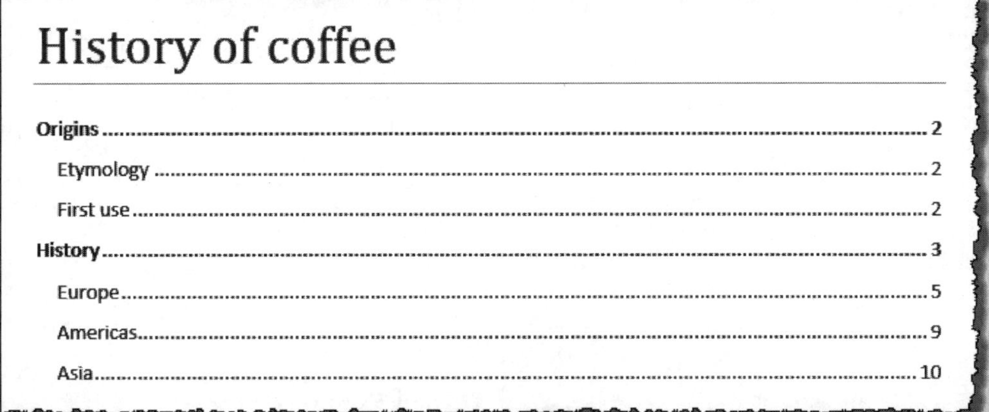

Do This	How & Why
8. Save your new TOC style to the gallery.	
a) Select the entire table of contents.	Don't select the document style.
b) Click **Table of Contents > Save Selection to Table of Contents Gallery**.	The Create New Building Block window opens.

Do This	How & Why
c) In the Name field, type `Coffee TOC`.	You'll leave the other settings as is.
d) Click **OK**.	To close the window.
e) Click **Table of Contents > Coffee TOC**.	If you don't do this, Word won't recognize your custom TOC as actually based on the building block. To apply the building block. You're asked whether to update page numbers or the whole table. For now, either will do.
f) Click **OK**.	
9. Add new entries to the table of contents.	
a) At the end of page 3, select the second image caption.	Palestinian women grinding coffee, 1905.
b) Apply the **TOC image caption** style.	Use the Styles gallery. 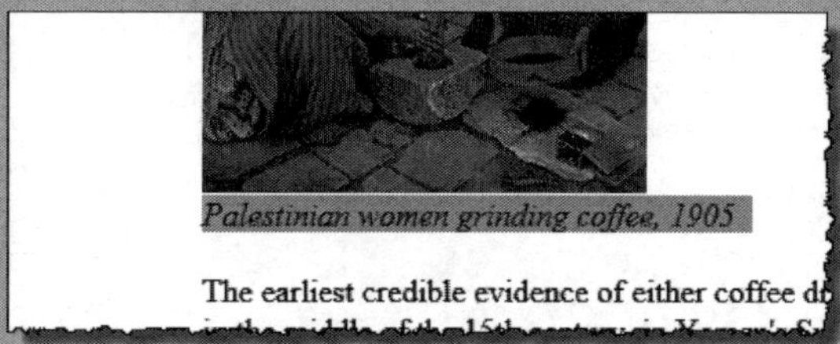 *Palestinian women grinding coffee, 1905* The earliest credible evidence of either coffee d
c) Scroll to the bottom of page 8.	You'll mark the Coffee Cantata in the TOC by adding a table entry field.
d) Click at the beginning of the first line of the quoted text.	Since you're not putting the text itself in the TOC, you can't use a style for this.
e) Press **Alt+Shift+O**.	The Mark Table of Contents Entry window opens.
f) In the Entry field, type `Coffee Cantata`.	
g) In the Level field, type `3`.	The table identifier is C since that's the default for table of contents entries. 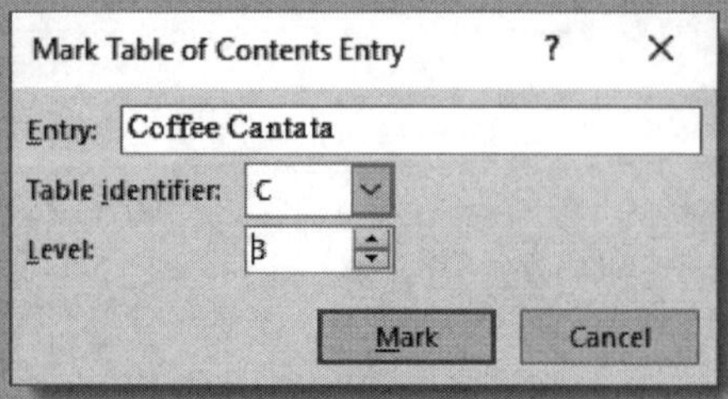 Mark Table of Contents Entry ? X Entry: Coffee Cantata Table identifier: C Level: 3 Mark Cancel
h) Click **Mark**.	The TC field is inserted. Like any field, you can only see it if formatting is shown.
i) Click **Close**.	To close the Mark Table of Contents Entry window.

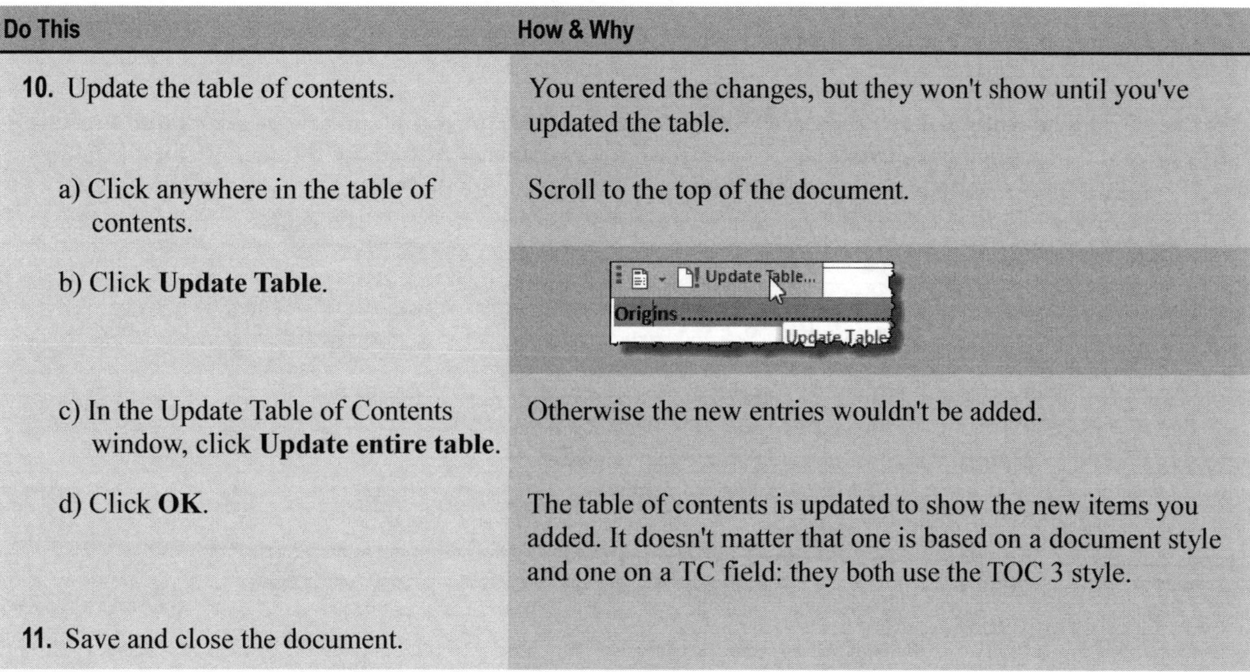

Do This	How & Why
10. Update the table of contents.	You entered the changes, but they won't show until you've updated the table.
a) Click anywhere in the table of contents.	Scroll to the top of the document.
b) Click **Update Table.**	Update Table... Origins Update Table
c) In the Update Table of Contents window, click **Update entire table**.	Otherwise the new entries wouldn't be added.
d) Click **OK**.	The table of contents is updated to show the new items you added. It doesn't matter that one is based on a document style and one on a TC field: they both use the TOC 3 style.
11. Save and close the document.	

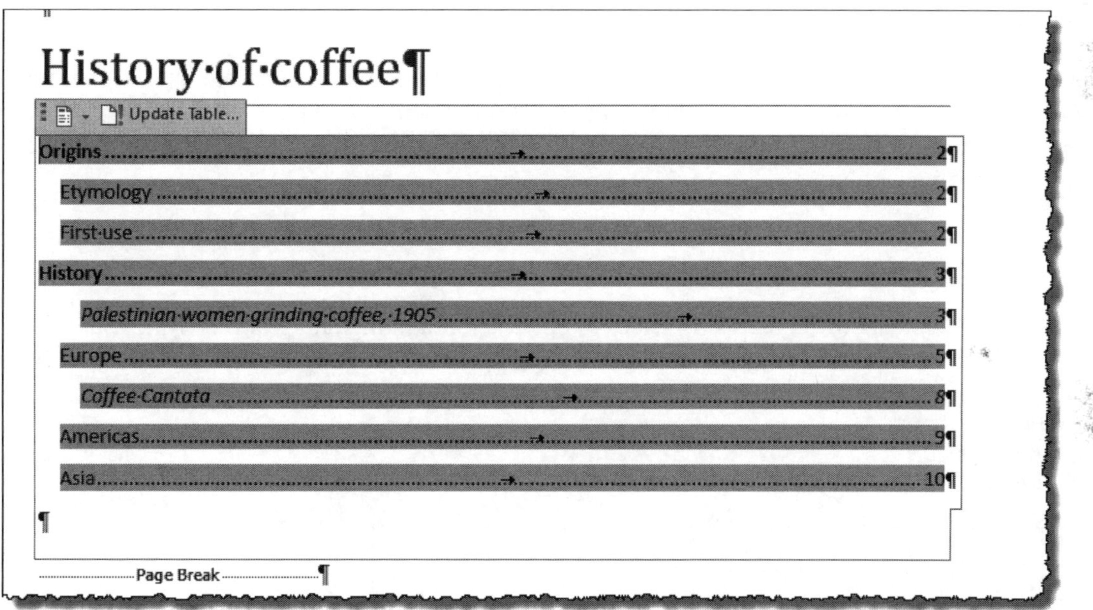

About tables of figures

You can create a table of figures, which lists all the figures in your document, as well as their captions. As with a table of contents, this is particularly useful for large documents with many figures. A table of figures appears and can be formatted very much like a table of contents, but with two major differences.

Exam Objective: MOS Word Expert 3.2.2

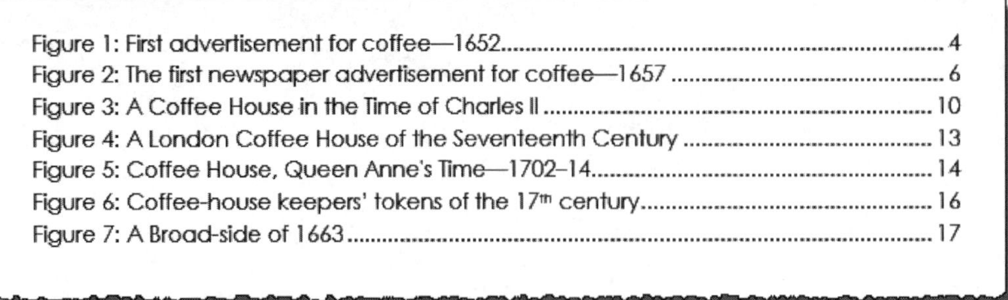

- There is only one level to a table of figures.
- By default, a table of figures isn't based on normal document content. Instead, it's based on captions you insert within the document.

To many people "Table of figures" may conjure mental images of old academic texts printed when graphics were limited and costly additions to a book, but they're pretty useful when a document has important graphical content you want readers to be able to centrally reference. It's not only suitable for pictures, but for formulas, charts, or anything similar.

- To create a table of figures, place the insertion point where you would like the table to appear. On the References tab, in the Captions group, click **Insert Table of Figures**.
- The Table of Figures window contains a variety of options for creating and working with your table. It also contains sections that preview how your table will appear both printed and published on the Web.

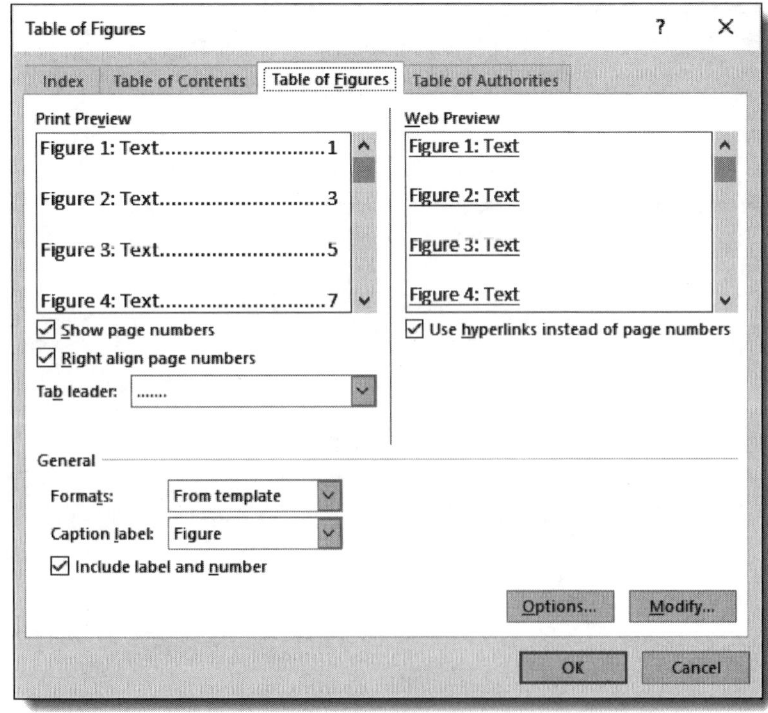

- Click **Options** to set style and field options for the creation of the overall table. Click **Modify** to open the Style window, where you can set the style for the table entries.

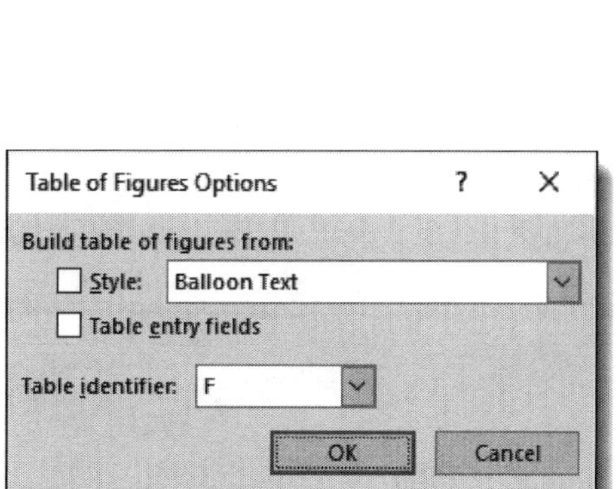

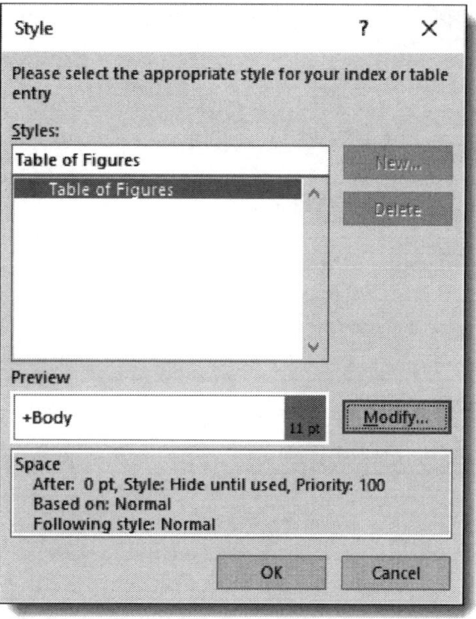

Adding captions to graphics

Adding a caption to a graphic inserts a line of text and an automatic number in the Caption style. Captions are added the same way for most graphical objects, including pictures, shapes, WordArt, SmartArt, and online pictures.

Exam Objective: MOS Word Core 3.2.1, 4.1.6, 4.1.7

To open the Caption window, either select a graphic, or place the insertion point above or below one. Then click **Insert Caption** on the References tab.

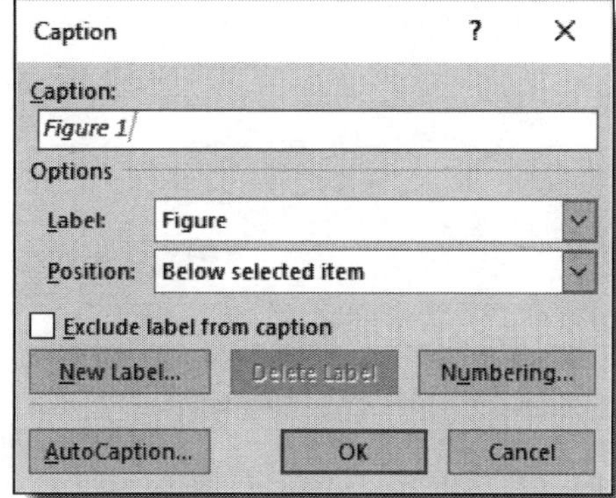

- Type the text of the caption in the Caption field.
- If you began by selecting an item, use the Position list to choose whether to place the caption above or below the graphic.
- By default, each caption has a label and a number.
  - By default, the available labels are **Figure**, **Equation**, and **Table**.
  - Labels aren't just for show: they're also important in generating a table of figures later.
  - To add a new label to the list, click **New Label**.

- Check **Exclude label from caption** to hide the label. The number will still be displayed.
- Click **Numbering** to change caption number formats.

- Click AutoCaption to configure automatic captions for inserted objects.

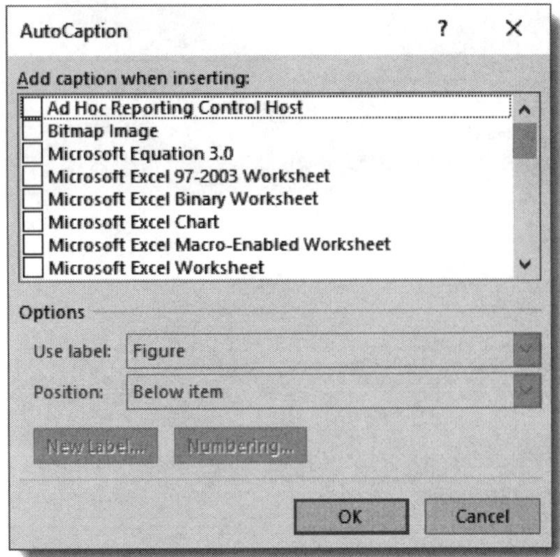

- Click **OK** when you're finished.

Note that the caption and the shape are not functionally tied, and either can be moved or deleted individually. This can be useful, but also makes it easy to do by accident. If you change the order of captions, the numbers will remain out of order until you update fields. To do this, press **Ctrl+A** to select all text, and then press **F9**.

Inserting a table of figures

Once you've inserted captions for your graphics, you can create the table of figures. To do so, click wherever you want to insert the table, then click **Insert Table of Figures**. You can then configure options in the Table of Figures window.

This table lists captions using the Figure label. It will ignore captions using other labels, but you can also create a table of equations or a table of tables from the same window. Overall, it's very similar to inserting a table of contents.

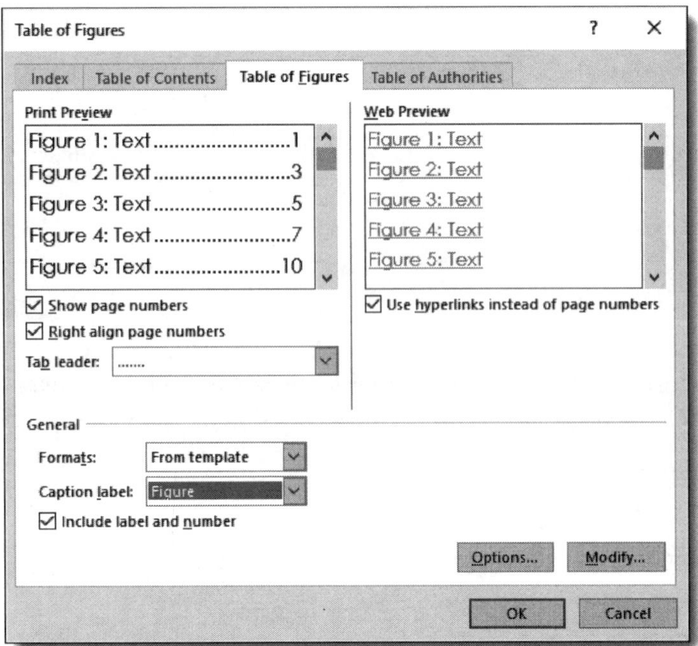

One important thing about a table of figures is that it only includes captions with one type of label. For example, a table of figures can have Figures or Equations, but not both. If you use multiple labels in a single document, each needs its own table.

- Choose the label type from the **Caption label** list.
- Change overall appearance from the General section.
  - Use the **Formats** list to choose a general appearance.
  - Clear **Include label and number** to show only the caption for each item.
- Change page display options in the Print Preview and Web Preview sections.
  - **Right align page numbers** and **Use hyperlinks instead of page numbers** (for web pages only) are only available if **Show page numbers** is checked.
  - You can only select a tab leader if **Right align page numbers** is checked.
- Click **Modify** to format the text in the table of figures itself. Unlike a table of contents, there is only one default Table of Figures style.
- Click **Options** to generate the table of figures from styles or table entry fields.

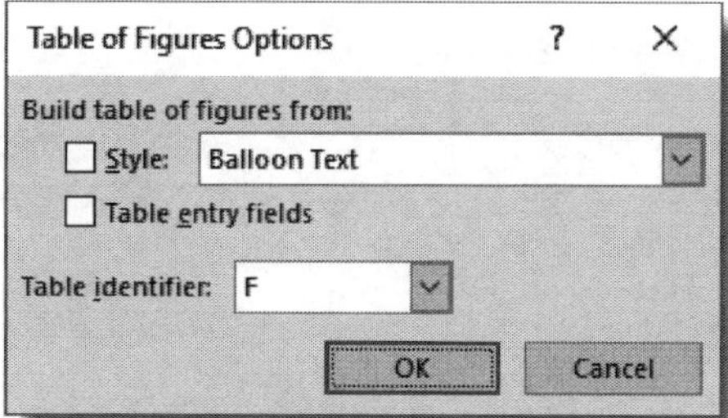

- Click **OK** when you're finished to insert the table.

You can also update a table of figures in much the same way that you can a table of contents. Click anywhere in the table, then click **Update Table** in the Captions group.

Exercise: Adding a table of figures

In this exercise you'll define captions in a document, then create a table of figures.

Do This	How & Why
1. Open `History` and save it as `History-figures`.	
2. Add a caption.	
a) Click the advertisement image at the top of page 6.	To select it. It already has a caption, but that's just ordinary text so wouldn't show up in a table.
b) On the References tab, click **Insert Caption**.	The **Caption** window opens.
c) From the Label list, select **Figure**.	If necessary.
d) From the Position list, select **Below selected item**.	If necessary.

Do This	How & Why
e) Edit the Caption field to read `Figure 1: First advertisement for coffee - 1652`.	"Figure 1" is inserted automatically.
f) Observe the window.	You could change or hide the label, or change the numbering scheme, but you'll keep the defaults. 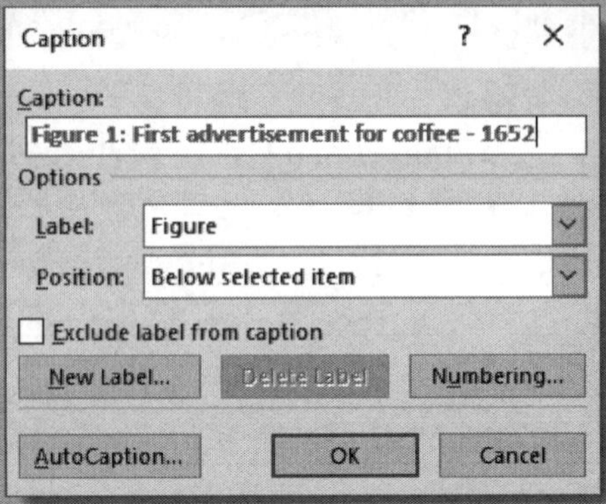 Caption ? X Caption: Figure 1: First advertisement for coffee - 1652 Options Label: Figure Position: Below selected item Exclude label from caption New Label... Delete Label Numbering... AutoCaption... OK Cancel
g) Click **OK**.	The caption is inserted. 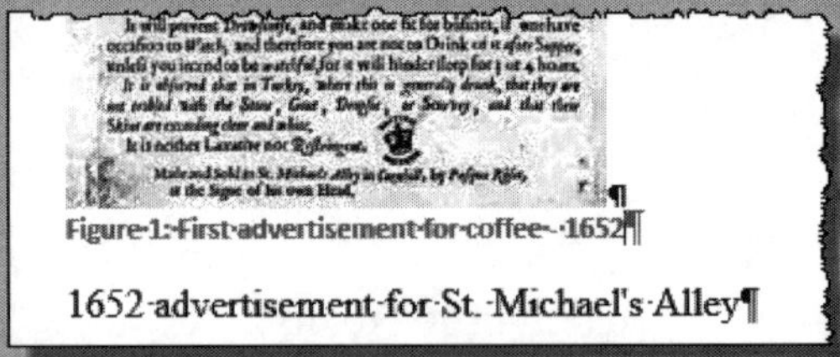 Figure·1:·First·advertisement·for·coffee·-·1652¶ 1652·advertisement·for·St.·Michael's·Alley¶
3. Delete the paragraph below the new caption.	The "1652 advertisement for St. Michael's Alley" text.
4. Insert more captions.	You'll add a couple more captions before inserting a table of figures.
a) Insert a caption for the image at the top of page 5.	Select the image, then click **Insert Caption**.
b) Name the caption `Dutch engraving of Mocha - 1692` and click **OK**.	 Figure·1:·Dutch·engraving·of·Mocha·-·1692¶
c) Delete the pre-existing caption.	Below the one you just inserted.
d) Add a caption to the image at the bottom of page 3.	Palestinian women grinding coffee. Don't forget to delete the existing caption.
5. Insert a table of figures.	
a) Place the cursor on the blank line just below the title.	

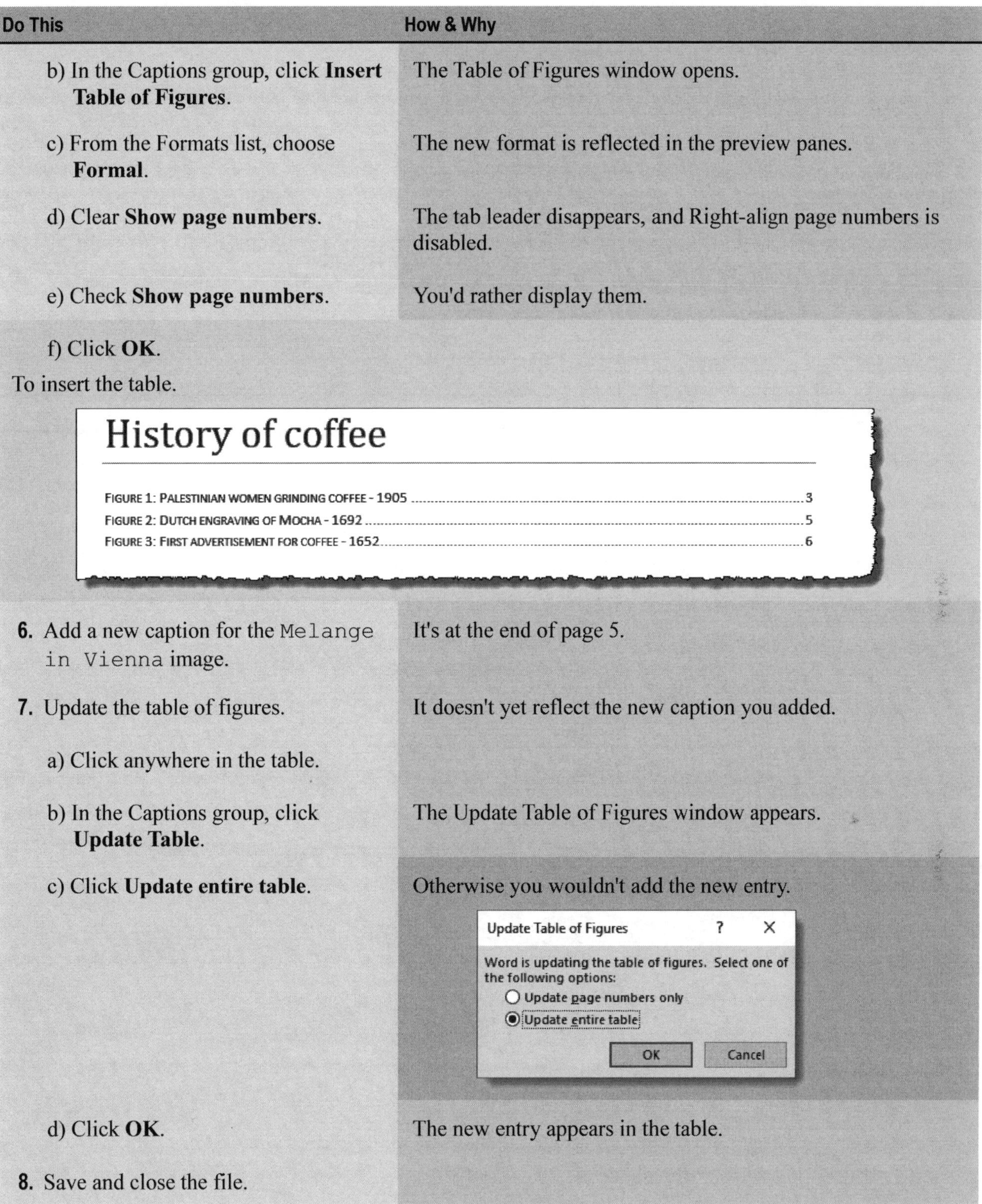

Do This	How & Why
b) In the Captions group, click **Insert Table of Figures**.	The Table of Figures window opens.
c) From the Formats list, choose **Formal**.	The new format is reflected in the preview panes.
d) Clear **Show page numbers**.	The tab leader disappears, and Right-align page numbers is disabled.
e) Check **Show page numbers**.	You'd rather display them.
f) Click **OK**.	

To insert the table.

History of coffee

Do This	How & Why
6. Add a new caption for the `Melange in Vienna` image.	It's at the end of page 5.
7. Update the table of figures.	It doesn't yet reflect the new caption you added.
a) Click anywhere in the table.	
b) In the Captions group, click **Update Table**.	The Update Table of Figures window appears.
c) Click **Update entire table**.	Otherwise you wouldn't add the new entry.
d) Click **OK**.	The new entry appears in the table.
8. Save and close the file.	

Update Table of Figures ? X
Word is updating the table of figures. Select one of the following options:
Update page numbers only
Update entire table
OK Cancel

History of coffee

Assessment: Table of contents

1. If you don't use heading styles in a document. you can fill out the table of contents manually. True or false?
    - True
    - False
2. Which option in the Table of Contents window determines what heading levels are shown?
    - Heading level
    - Formats
    - Heading depth
    - Show levels

Module C: Hyperlinks

You can apply a hyperlink to just about any object in a Word document that you can select, including text, pictures, shapes, and SmartArt.

You will learn:

- How to apply different types of hyperlinks

Applying hyperlinks

Exam Objective: MOS Word Core 1.2.2

To apply a hyperlink, right-click an object, and click **Hyperlink**. If the object already has a hyperlink, you'll see options to edit, select, open, copy, and remove the hyperlink.

If you want to apply a hyperlink to a phrase or sentence, you need to select the words first. Then, either right-click the selection and click **Hyperlink**, or on the Insert tab's Links group, click **Hyperlink**. In the Insert Hyperlink window, the display text is the same as the selected text by default, but you can change that. For instance, you could change the display text of an email address read "Email Me" instead of the actual address.

Note: If you right-click a word or phrase that has been flagged as a misspelling or grammatical error, you'll see a correction-related menu, and it won't have the hyperlink option.

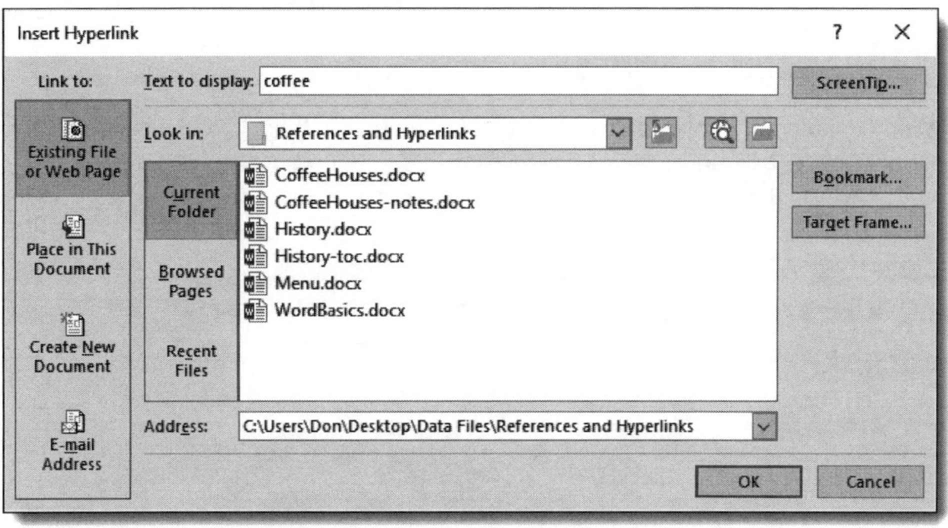

Here are the general categories of hyperlink that you can add to your document.

Hyperlinks

Type of link	Description
Existing File or Web Page	Enter the URL of a web page or the path to a file on your computer or network. You can browse for the file, and there are options to see files in the current folder, recently browsed pages, and recently opened documents. Click **Bookmark** to use a hyperlink as a bookmark for a section in the document.
Place in This Document	Choose from a list of headings in the document. Following the link jumps to that place in the document. This is the same as creating a bookmark hyperlink.
Create New Document	When the link is followed, it opens a new document in Word. You can create the document at the time you create the link, or it can be created when a user follows the link. If you don't specify a file name and location, it uses a default file name and the same location as the current document.
E-mail Address	Enter an email address and (optionally) a subject line. When the link is followed, a new message is started using the address and subject in the link. This requires the computer to have an installed email client such as Microsoft Outlook.

You can follow links in a Word document by holding down **Ctrl** and clicking the link. If you save the document as a web page, though, the link works with just a single click. Remember that links to local resources do not work on another computer unless those resources go along with the document and are in the same relative location.

Exercise: Applying a hyperlink

Exam Objective: MOS Word Core 1.2.2

Do This	How & Why
1. Open `Menu` and save it as `MenuLinks`.	
2. At the bottom of the menu, select www.javatucana.com.	D CUP OF SOUP COMBO $7 s, visit us at www.javatucana.com or emai
3. Right-click the selection, and then click **Hyperlink**.	
4. Enter the information for the hyperlink:	The URL in the document is a hyperlink.

Do This	How & Why
a) Under Link to, ensure that either Existing File or Web Page is selected.	
b) In the Address field, enter `http://www.javatucana.com`.	
c) In Text to display, enter `www.javatucana.com`.	Do this second because changing the address field will change this field.
d) Click **OK**.	
5. Create a hyperlink for the email address:	For daily specials, catering, a info@javatucana.com. The link is created. If it's not what you wanted, right-click it, and click **Edit Hyperlink**. You can hold down **Ctrl** and click the links if you want to test them, but you'll need an Internet connection and an installed mail client for both to work correctly.
a) Select the email address, right-click it, and click **Hyperlink**.	
b) Under Link to, click **E-mail Address**.	
c) Fill out the text to display, the email address, and the subject line. These can be whatever you like.	
d) Click **OK**.	
6. Save and close the document.	

Assessment: Hyperlinks

1. Hyperlinks can be applied only to text. True or false?
   - True
   - False
2. Which method(s) allow(s) you to create a hyperlink to another location in the same document?
   - Use the Place in This Document link.
   - Use Existing File or Web Page, then click Target Frame.
   - Use Existing File or Web Page, then click Bookmark.
   - Use Create New Document, then click Bookmark.
   - Use Create New Document, then click Target Frame.
3. For email addresses, the display text is always the same as the address. True or false?
   - True
   - False

Summary: References and hyperlinks

You should now know:

- The difference between footnotes and endnotes, how to insert footnotes and endnotes, and how to change note options and formatting
- How to insert a table of contents, use the Table of Contents window, change table of contents styles, and update a table of contents
- How to apply different types of hyperlinks

Synthesis: References and hyperlinks

1. Open `WordBasics` and save it as `WordBasics-ref`.
2. Place the cursor at the beginning of the document, before the title.

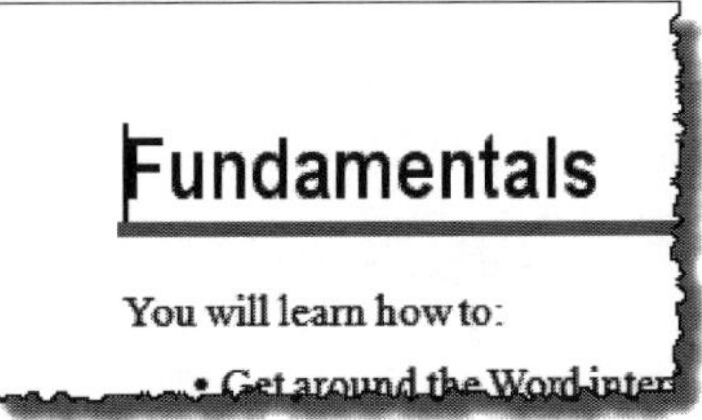

3. On the References tab, click **Table of Contents > Custom Table of Contents**.
4. Insert a table of contents with these settings:
   - Show levels: 4
   - Formats: Classic
   - Leader: Dots
5. For each of the three objectives under the title, apply a hyperlink to the corresponding module.
   In the Insert Hyperlink window, select **Place in This Document**, and then select the module from the list of headings. The first objective links to Module A, the second to B, and the third to C.
6. Add a footnote after the title. The footnote should read `From Word 2010 Level 1, copyright 2015`.
7. Save and close the document.

Chapter 10: Navigation and organization

You will learn how to:

- Navigate large documents
- Use master documents

Module A: Navigating documents

You will learn how to:

- Use the Navigation pane
- Use advanced find and replace features
- Use the Go To and Browse by features

The Navigation pane

To open the Navigation pane, press **Ctrl+F**, or click **Find** on the Home tab, or check **Navigation Pane** on the View tab. The pane opens on the left side by default, but you can drag it to another location, including outside the Word window. There are three tabs in the Navigation pane: Headings, Pages, and Results.

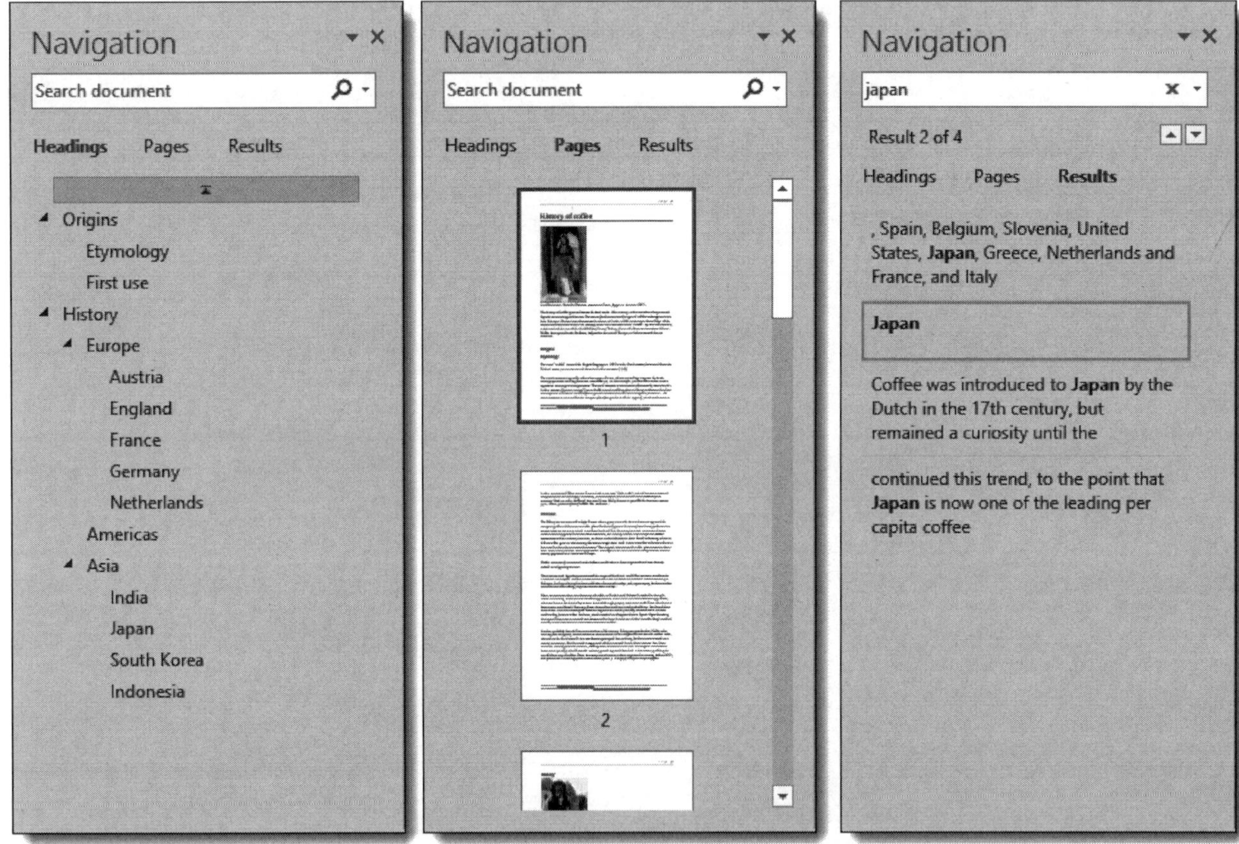

The Headings tab shows an outline of the document based on the headings styles used in it. Headings can be dragged to a new location to reorganize the document. The Pages tab shows a miniature of each page, and the Results tab shows you the context of each instance of what is entered into the search box at the top of the pane. Note that if there are too many instances of a search term in the document, the Results tab does not show them, though they are highlighted in the document.

The Find and Replace window

Exam Objective: MOS Word Core 2.1.1

The Navigation pane is adequate for many text searches, but the Find and Replace window offers a lot more control and options. To open it from the Home tab, click **Replace**, or click the arrow to the right of the Find button, and select **Advanced Find**. Both open the Find and Replace window, but to different tabs.

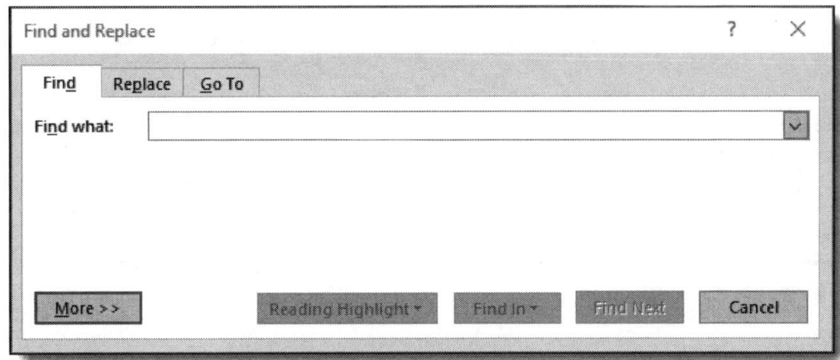

Using advanced find features

Exam Objective: MOS Word Core 2.1.1, 2.1.2 and Expert 2.1.1

When you first open the Find and Replace window, the search options are hidden. You have to click the **More>>** button to access the power of the advanced find features.

1. On the Home tab, click the arrow on the right of the Find button, and click **Advanced Find**.

   The Find and Replace window opens.

2. Click **More>>** to see more options.

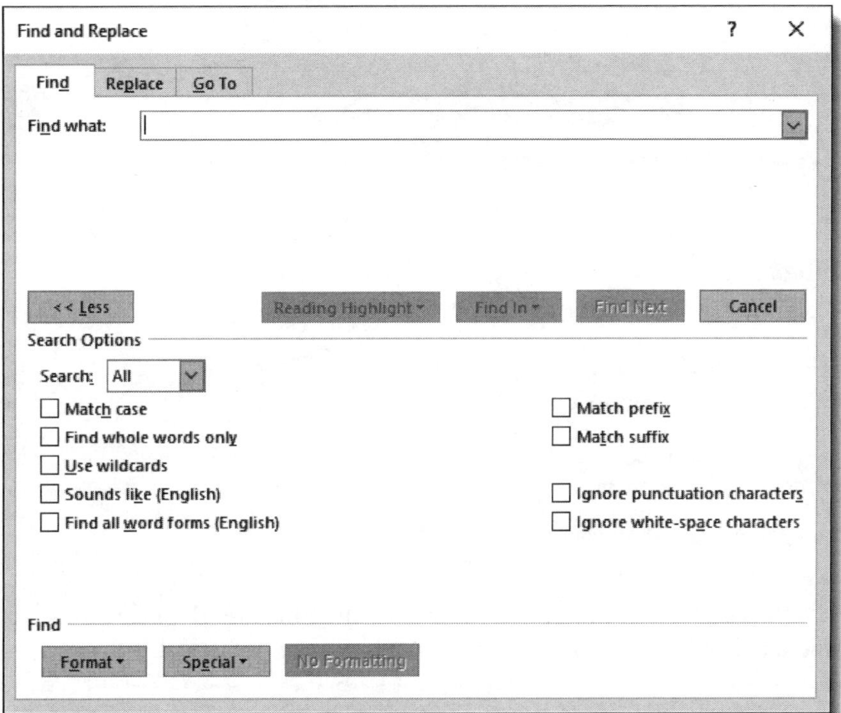

3. Enter the term you want to search for.
   Case doesn't matter unless you set that as an option.
4. If you want to highlight the terms, click **Reading Highlight**.
   You can also clear previous highlighting.
5. If you want to want to limit what text is searched, click **Find In**.
   You can limit the search to selected text, the main document, or the headers and footers.
6. Check any search options you want applied.
   Under Search Options, you can, for example, select **Match case** to search for text that appears exactly as typed.
7. To find text with specific formatting, click **Format**, and select the formatting you want.
   You can search for a formatting type without even specifying text to find. So, for instance, you can search for instances of a certain header style, regardless of the text. Or, select **Use wildcards** to find text that appears exactly as typed but that also include occurrences indicated by wildcard characters. Common *wildcards* are *?* (any single character or space; for example, typing "t?p" finds "tap," "tip," "top," "t p") and * (any string of characters; for example, "b*t" finds "bat," "bit," "burst," "broadsheet").
8. To search for special characters that are not easy to enter, such as paragraph characters or footnote marks, click **Special**, and select the character.
9. To clear previously specified formatting, click **No Formatting**.

Replacing text

The Replace tab has all the same options as the Find tab, with the exception of the highlight feature.

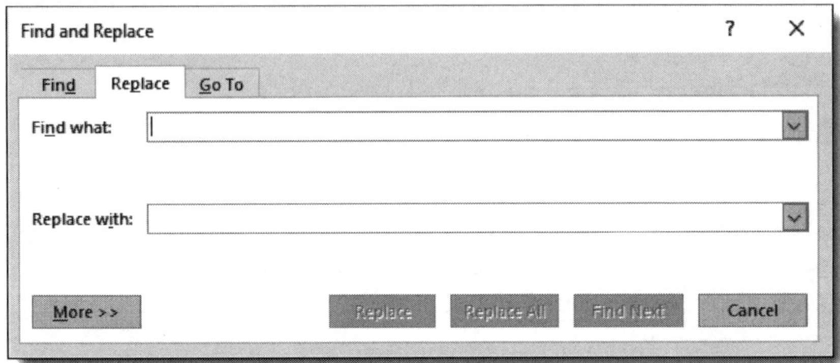

Exam Objective: MOS Word Core 2.1.1, 2.1.2 and Expert 2.1.1

1. On the Home tab, click **Replace**.
   The Find and Replace window opens to the Replace tab.
2. Enter the text you want to find and the text you want to replace it with.
3. Click **More>>** if you want to set more options.
4. Set the search options.
   These apply to the text being searched for.
5. If you want, select formatting or special characters.
   These apply to the replacement text only.
   Note: If you want to use Formatting or Special buttons in both the Find and Replace fields, you can switch between the Find and Replace tabs. The values in the fields are preserved.

Using Go To

Unlike the find feature, the Go To tab in the Find and Replace window does not search for text but for types of objects.

Exam Objective: MOS Word Core 1.2.4

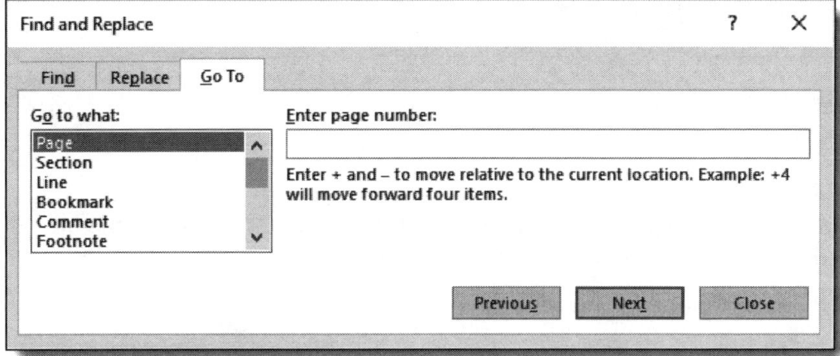

1. On the Home tab, click **Replace**.
   To open the Find and Replace window.
2. Click the **Go To** tab.
3. From the list, select the object type to search for.
4. Enter the number of the object to go to.
   This refers to the order of the objects in the document. The third graphic is number 3, but it does not need to be explicitly labeled. You can also enter + or – and a number to move relative to the current object.
5. Click **Go To**.
   This appears only if you enter a number. You don't need to enter a number to go to the next or previous object.

Finding specific document elements

You can use the Navigation pane to search for different types of document elements, such as graphics, equations, tables, footnotes/endnotes, and comments.

1. Open the Navigation pane.
   On the View tab, in the Show group, click **Navigation Pane**.
2. At the right of the Search box, click the down arrow.
   A menu appears, displaying search options and categories.
3. Under Find, click the icon of the object you want to search for.
   For example, clicking Graphics finds any graphics in a document, stopping at and selecting the one that it finds first from the initial position of the insertion point. In the Navigation pane, the results are numbered, and up and down arrows allow you to navigate through the results found.

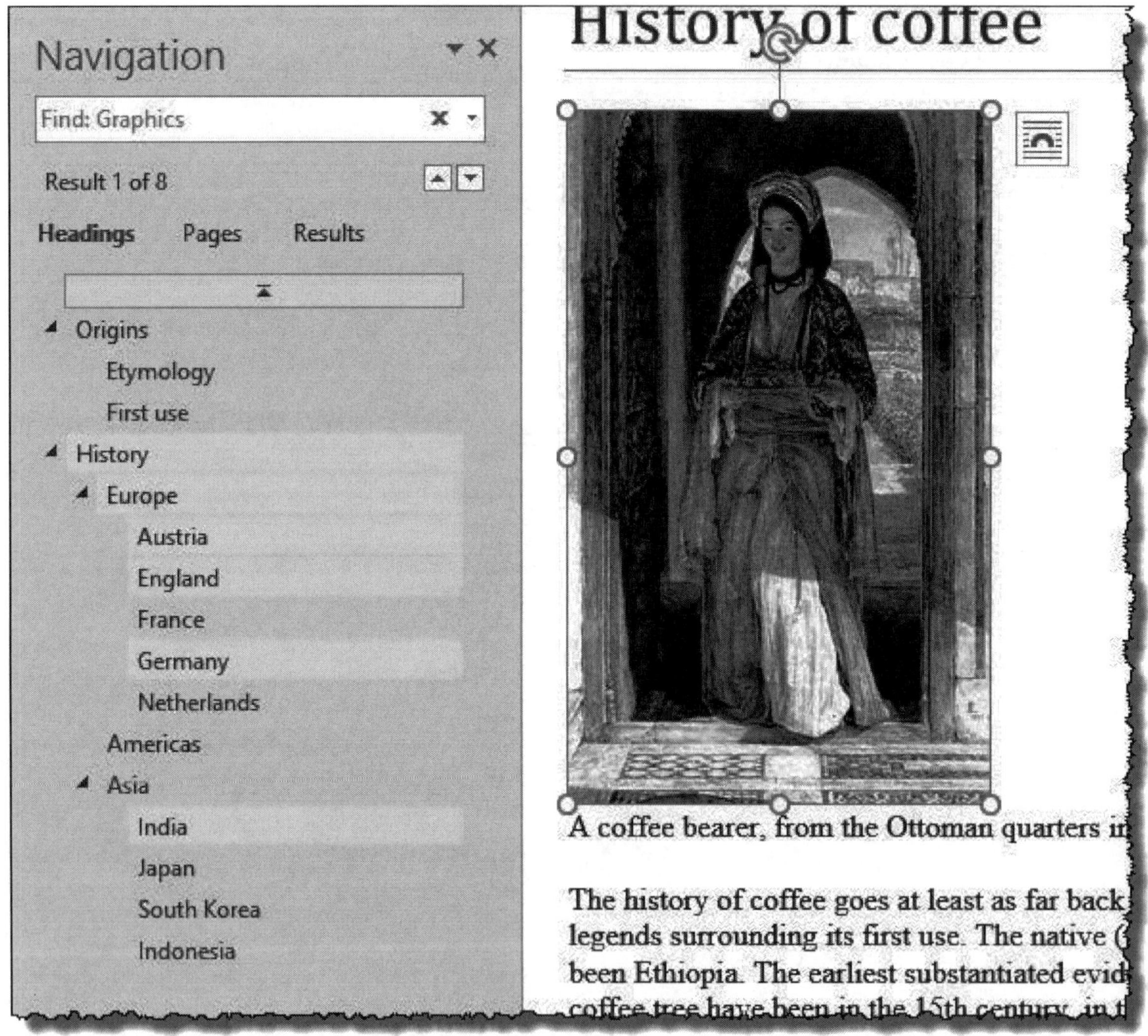

Exercise: Navigating a document

Do This	How & Why
1. Open `CoffeeHistory` and save it as `CoffeeHistory-nav`.	
2. On the Home tab, click **Find**.	To open the Navigation pane. Clear any previous search terms, if there are any.
3. In the Navigation pane, click the **Headings** tab.	It's the first one. You can see the headings in the document.
4. Click the **Pages** tab.	Scroll down to see miniatures of the pages.
5. One the Home tab, click the arrow next to Find, and click **Advanced Find**.	To open the Find and Replace window.
6. Click the **Replace** tab and then the **More>>** button.	Observe the options.
7. Click **Format**, and then **Special**.	To see the options available.
8. Replace all instances of "coffee" with "tea."	
a) In the "Find what" box, enter `coffee`.	
b) In the "Replace with" box, enter `tea`.	
c) Click **Replace All**.	A message tells you how many instances have been replaced.
d) Click **OK**, and close the Find and Replace window.	
9. Observe the document.	It is now a very inaccurate history of tea. Note that when you don't specify case, Word replaces capitalized words with the same case, as in the document title.
10. Close the document without saving.	Why would you want to save this?

Assessment: Navigating documents

1. In the Find and Replace window, which do you click to search for special characters such as footnote marks and paragraph characters?
   - Special
   - Format
   - Symbol
   - Character
2. Which features allow you to skip through instances of a specified object, such as pictures or headings?
   - Skip To
   - Go To
   - Find Object
   - Hop Along
   - Navigation pane Search box
3. Which keyboard shortcut opens the Navigation pane?
   - Alt+N
   - Ctrl+F
   - Ctrl+N
   - Alt+F

Module B: Master documents

You will learn how to:

- Insert a subdocument into a master document
- Organize your subdocuments in a logical manner

Master documents and subdocuments

If you are working on a large, multi-part document, or have multiple authors working on a project, you might want to use a master document with subdocuments. The master document is a Word file that contains references or links to subdocuments, each of which is another Word file.

There are a few important points to keep in mind when working with master documents and subdocuments.

- While you are working in the master document, it is not obvious that different parts are coming from different files, unless you are in Outline view. Otherwise, a master document behaves like any other document.
- Page numbering is continuous, and you can create a table of contents or index based on the whole document.
- Changes you make to content in the master document are saved in the subdocument that content comes from.
- You can expand and collapse the subdocuments in Outline view, and rearrange the order of the subdocuments.

Inserting subdocuments

There's nothing special about a master document; it's just a regular Word document. What makes it a master document is that is has subdocuments. You insert the subdocuments in Outline view.

1. On the View tab, click **Outline**.

   The Outlining tab opens.
2. Click **Show Document**.

   To expand options in the Master Document group.

3. Place the cursor where you want to insert the subdocument.
4. Click **Insert**.
5. Browse to the file you want to insert, select it, and click **Open**.

   You can also double-click it.

   The contents of the subdocument are added to the master document.

Note: It's important to remember that subdocuments cannot be inserted within the body text of the master document. They can be inserted only immediately below a heading.

Organizing subdocuments

There are a number of ways to manipulate subdocuments in a master document.

- To expand or collapse all subdocuments from the Outlining tab, click **Expand Subdocuments** or **Collapse Subdocuments** in the Master Document group.

  It's the same button—the text changes when the subdocuments are expanded or collapsed.

- In Outline view, you can expand and collapse headings that have a plus symbol. Double-click the symbol to expand or collapse the content under that heading.

  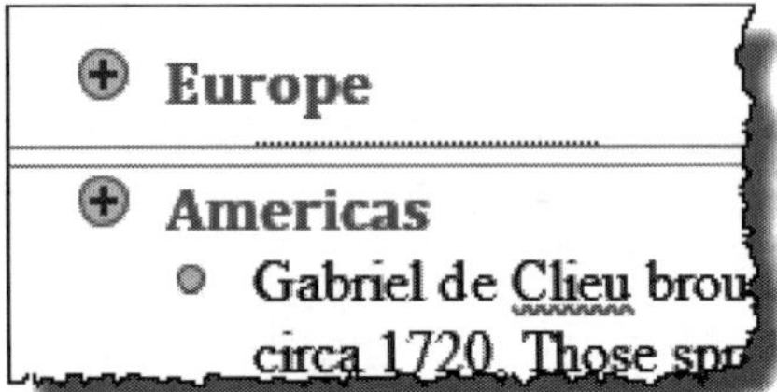

- To rearrange the order of the subdocuments, on the Outlining tab, with **Show Document** selected and the subdocuments collapsed, you can drag the page icon.

  If you get a message that the document is locked, click the lock symbol and try again.

  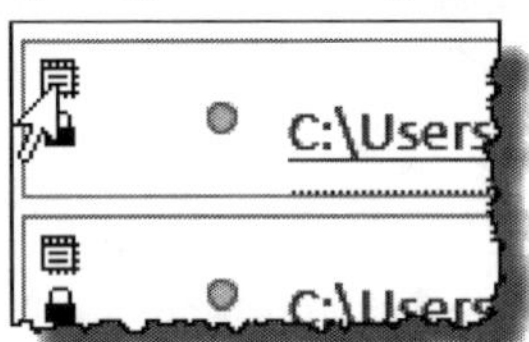

- To reorganize the document outline, expand all the subdocuments and close outline view. Then, on the Headings tab in the Navigation pane, drag headings to a new location.

  Note: If subdocuments are collapsed, the Navigation pane does not see any headings except those in the master document.

  Also note: This effectively allows you to drag content from one subdocument to another, where it is saved if you save the master.

Exercise: Inserting subdocuments

Do This	How & Why
1. Open `Europe`, observe the contents, and close it.	You'll insert this and other documents as subdocuments.
2. Open `History` and save it as `History-master`.	

Do This	How & Why
3. Put the cursor below the last line of text.	You'll insert the first subdocument here.
4. On the View tab, click **Outline**.	The Outlining tab appears.
5. On the Outlining tab, click **Show Document**.	
6. Insert the file Europe as a subdocument: a) In the Master Document group, click **Insert**. b) Navigate to the current data folder, and select **Europe**. c) Click **Open**.	The document is inserted in the outline.
7. Repeat the process to Insert `Americas` and `Asia`.	The cursor is already in the right place.
8. Scroll up the document.	You can double-click the white plus signs to collapse or expand headings.
9. Expand all sections, then on the Outlining tab, click **Close Outline View**.	It looks like a continuous document, but its various parts are still stored in separate files. Any changes made here are reflected in those individual files.
10. Press **Ctrl+F**.	To open the Navigation pane. Clear previous search terms, if necessary.
11. In the Navigation pane, on the Headings tab, drag the heading Americas below Indonesia.	This rearranges the document. Note that if you drag a heading to another subdocument, that section of text is moved from one file to the other when you save. For instance, if you dragged the England heading under Americas, that section of text is moved to the Americas file on the disk when you save the master document.
12. Save and close the document.	

Assessment: Master documents

1. When you add a subdocument to a master document, the content is copied to the master document, and you no longer need the subdocument.
   - True
   - False
2. How do you turn a document into a master document?
   - Save it as a Master Document file type.
   - On the Insert tab, check Master Document
   - On the Outlining tab, Insert a subdocument.
   - In the Navigation pane, on the Headings tab, click Add Part.

Summary: Navigation and organization

You should now know how to:

- Edit documents with automatic spelling and grammar checking, and with the Spelling and Grammar window; and set proofing, AutoCorrect, and grammar options
- Navigate a large document using the Navigations pane; and use advanced find and replace features, Go To, and the Navigation pane's Search box to find specific document elements
- Use master documents and subdocuments, and rearrange subdocuments

Synthesis: Navigation and organization

1. Open `CoffeeChem` and save it as `CoffeeChem Master`.
2. Switch to Outline view, and add the document `Green Coffee` as a subdocument, at the end.
3. Add more subdocuments, using the files `Artificial Aging`, `Damaged Coffee`, `Acids`, and `Alkaloids`.
4. Switch back to Print Layout view, and open the Navigation pane to the Headings tab.
   Some blank headings might have been added when you inserted subdocuments, and those show up in the Navigation tab.
5. In the Navigation pane, click any blank headings and press the **Delete** key.
   The Navigation pane should show no blank headings.
6. Close the Navigation pane.
7. Save and close the document.

Chapter 11: Saving and sharing documents

You will learn how to:

- Save documents in different file formats and share them with others
- Add and edit comments
- Control who can access or edit a document

Module A: Saving and sending

When you make documents, you probably plan to share them with others. If you're going to print them or save them to a shared folder for other Word users, that's simple enough, but you have many other options to save or distribute them.

You will learn:

- About Word's saving options
- How to save a document in other formats
- How to send documents via the Internet
- How to publish a document as a blog post

Document formats

Word default file format is all you need most of the time, but you can save in a number of other formats, or *file types*, used by other versions of Word or by other programs. Not all file types are interchangeable, though, and some might not support all of Word's features and formatting options. Some don't even support graphics or text formatting.

When you save a document as another file type, it's important to make sure that it's compatible with other users' software, and that it preserves any important information, including formatting, in the document. Whether you simply use **File** > **Save As** or one of these other options, you end up at the Save As window.

Exam Objective: MOS Word Core 1.5.2

The most common file types you might need are listed in Backstage view, by clicking **Export** > **Change File Type**. If you've configured Windows to show file extensions, you can tell them apart not only by their icons but by their file extensions.

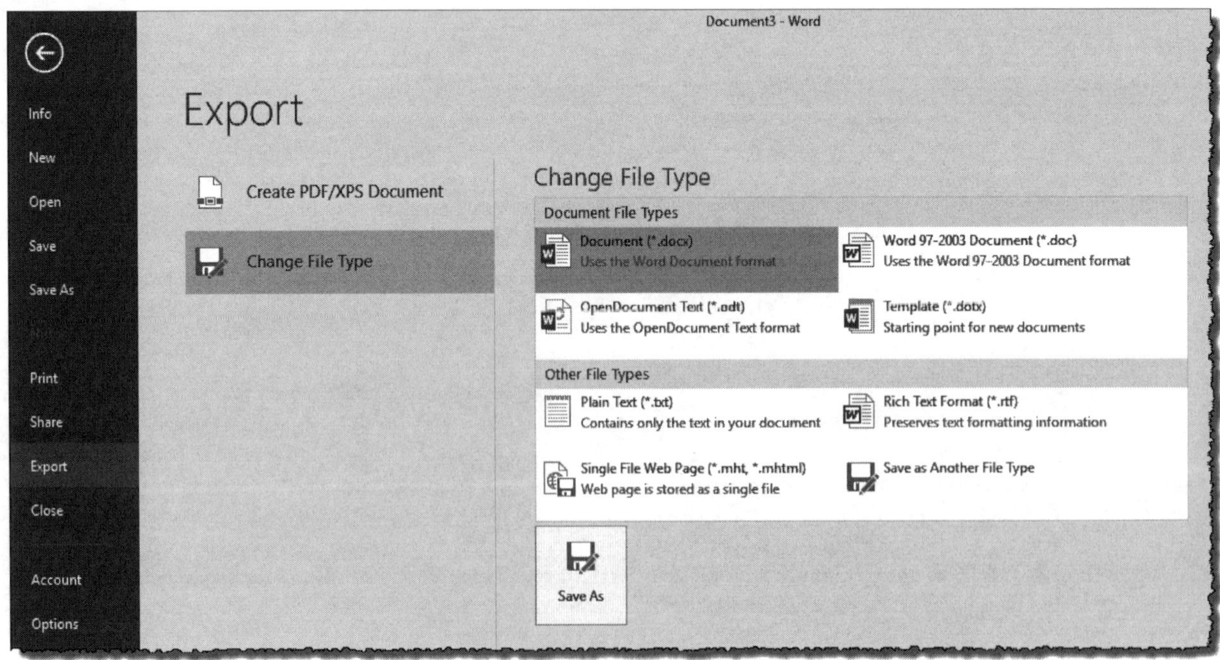

Document (.docx)	The default file format in Word 2007 and later. It supports all of Word's normal functions and is what you should use, unless you have reason not to.
Word 97-2003 Document (.doc)	The file format used by older versions of Word; .doc files are usually larger than .docx files and don't support all of Word's newer features. However, they're more compatible with older software, such as older Office versions.
OpenDocument Text (.odt)	A file format designed by the Organization for the Advancement of Structured Information Standards (OASIS) and used by many non-Microsoft office suites, including OpenOffice. It supports most Word features, but some formatting options might be lost or look different.
Template (.dotx)	The default format for templates in Word 2007 and newer. You shouldn't use this for documents, but instead to make starting points you'll later use to create documents.
Plain Text (.txt)	A simple text file, without any graphics or special formatting. It's the most compatible format, but doesn't save anything other than the text.
Rich Text Format (.rtf)	An older Microsoft format. It preserves basic text formatting information such as font sizes and typefaces, boldface, and italics, but doesn't support most of Word's more advanced features.
Single File Web Page (.mht or .mhtml)	A format meant to be opened by web browsers. Instead of having images, sounds, or other content in separate linked files like a normal web page, this format stores it all in a single easily portable file. It doesn't support all of the same features because it's meant for use by web browsers rather than word processing software.

The other option available in the Export pane is **Create PDF/XPS document**.

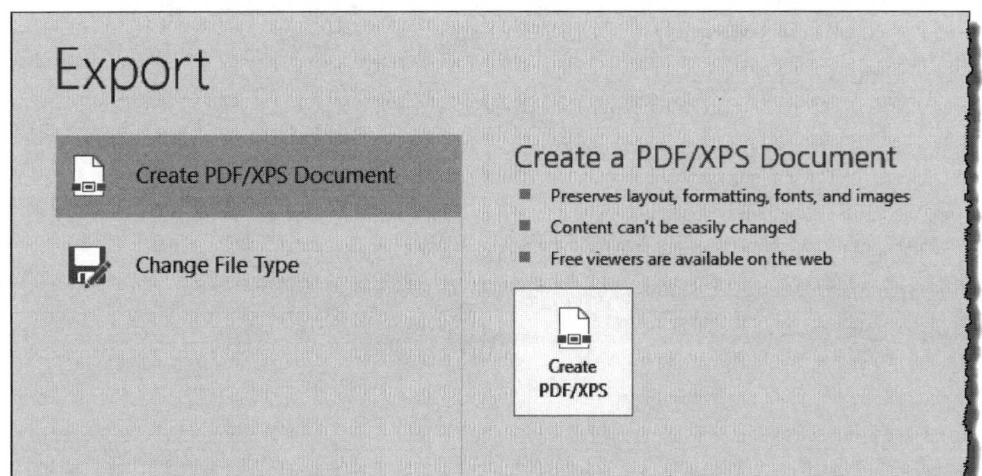

Portable Document Format (.pdf)	Developed by Adobe and broadly supported by many software vendors, PDF was designed to preserve a file's exact formatting and appearance, regardless of viewer or operating system. It is intended for distributing finalized documents, so PDF files really aren't meant to be edited after they're saved. It supports other publication features as well, such as digital signatures and DRM.
XML Paper Specification (.xps)	Microsoft's own equivalent to PDF, XPS has similar features and limitations. It's natively supported by Windows Vista and later as well as other Microsoft products, but is less widely supported by third-party manufacturers.

You can see additional file formats by clicking **Change File Type > Save as Another File Type**, or from the Save As window. These include macro-enabled documents and templates (.docm and .dotm, respectively), web pages (.htm and .html), Word XML documents (.XML), and Microsoft Works 6–9 documents (.wps).

Click **Share** in Backstage view to see options such as emailing your document or posting it to a blog.

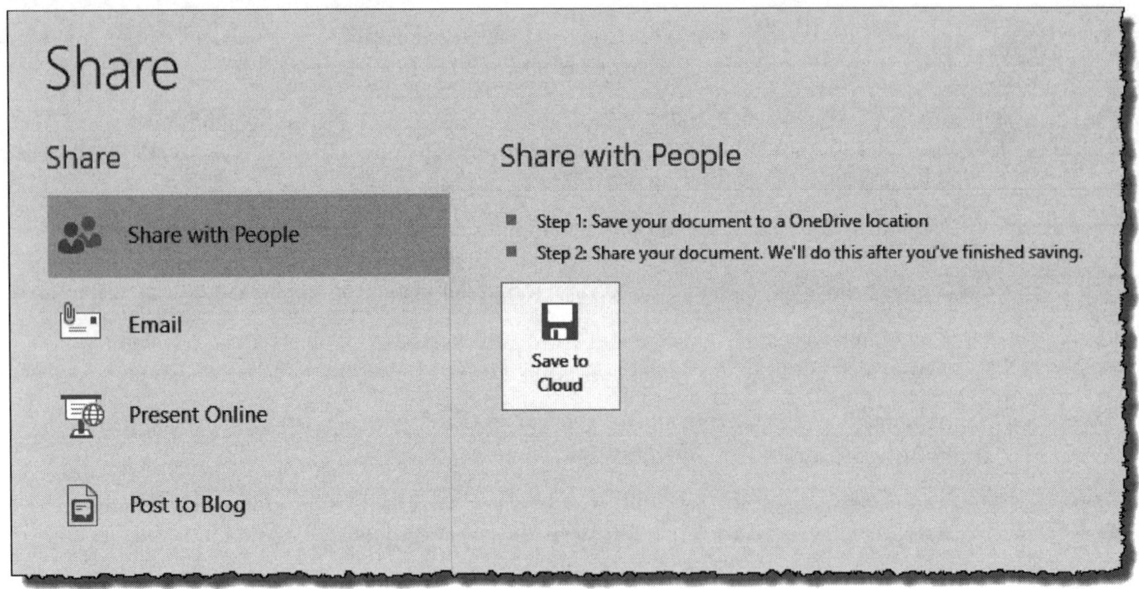

Using Save As options

Exam Objective: MOS Word Core 1.5.2

Whether you're changing a document's file type, saving a newly created file, or just saving a new copy to a different location, you need to use the Save As window. It contains options for file name and location, as well as additional properties, depending on the file type.

The Save As window, when saving a file as a web page.

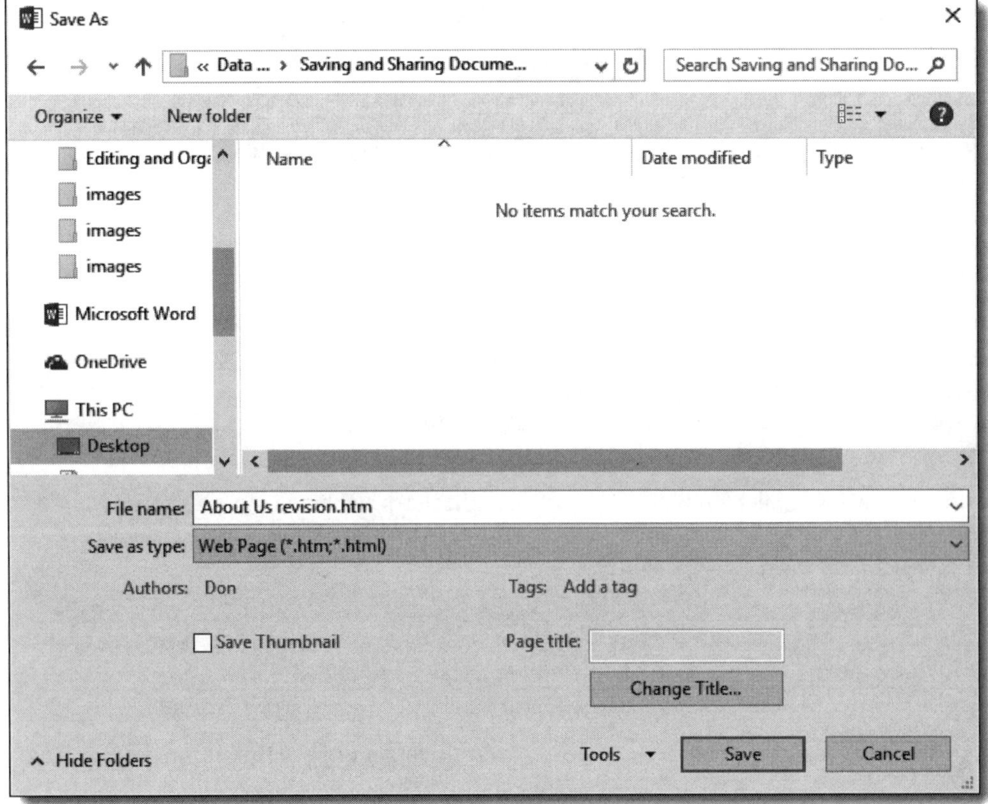

Remember that saving a document with a new name, location, or format doesn't delete the original file. It doesn't update it either. If you want to keep an updated version of the original file, be sure to save it normally before creating the new one. If you don't want to keep it at all, make sure to delete it from Windows Explorer after saving the new file.

1. Open the Save As window.
   - Press **F12**.
   - In Backstage View, click **Save As**, click the main destination location, and click **Browse**. If you select a OneDrive location, you first need to sign in to your account.
   - In Backstage View: click **Export > Change File Type**, select a file type, and click **Save As**; or click **Create PDF/XPS Document > Create PDF/XPS** to open the Publish as PDF or XPS window, another form of the Save As window.
2. Choose the file format from the "Save as type" list. If you used the Export pane, this is already chosen for you.
3. Choose the file's name and location.
   - Navigate through folders using the left pane, or type a file path into the address bar.
   - Enter the file's name, if necessary, in the File Name box.

   Your file type might influence where you want to save it. For example, templates are saved by default in the Templates folder, and you might want to make sure a web page doesn't have any spaces in its file name.
4. Set additional file properties.
   - Many of these vary by file type. For example, web pages have a page title, while PDF documents can be optimized for various publishing methods.
   - Click **Tools** to access additional options, such as file settings or graphics compression.
5. Click **Save**.

For some file types, you'll be asked to specify additional conversion details in a separate window, or you'll receive warnings about compatibility settings.

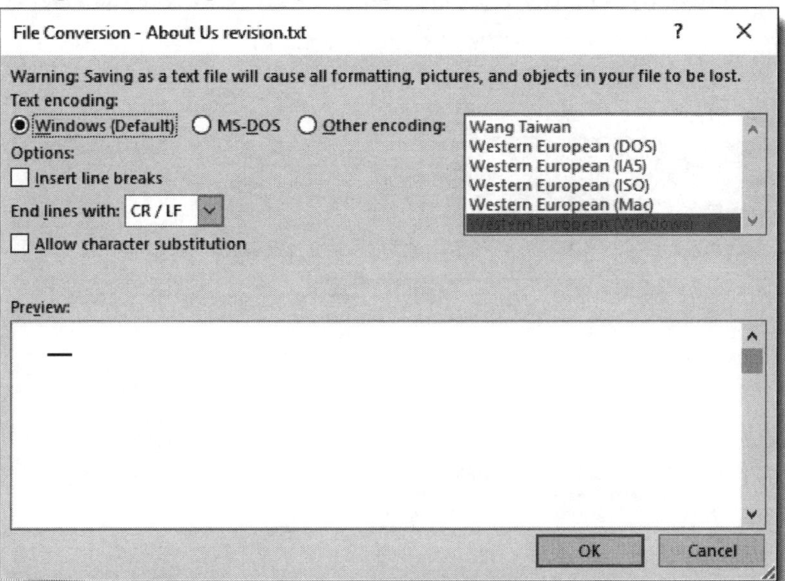

Document properties

Every Word file has various properties automatically associated with it, such as its author, size, the number of pages and words it contains, and the total time it's been edited. In addition, there are other properties that can be edited by you or by any user who has permission to do so. All such document properties as also referred to as its *metadata*.

Exam Objective: MOS Word Core 1.4.5, 1.5.4

- To view and/or edit document metadata, click **File > Info**. The metadata appears under Properties.

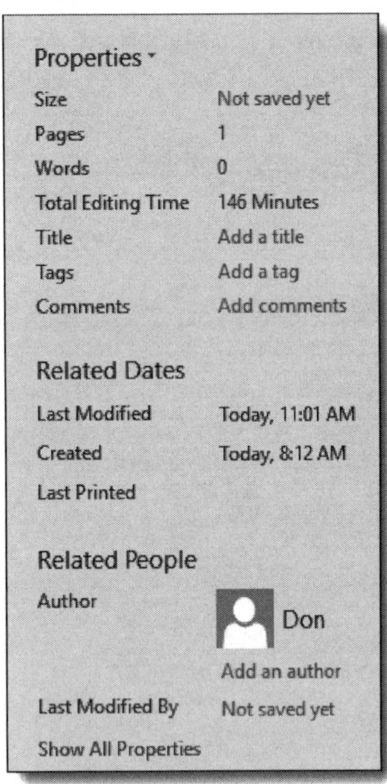

- To add or edit user-defined fields such as Title, Tags, and Comments, click in the field and type.

- To delete user-defined metadata, click in the field, and press **Backspace** or **Delete**.
- To view additional properties/metadata, click **Show All Properties**. Click **Show Fewer Properties** to return to the default setting.

Inspecting a document

When you are sharing a document, especially if you are making it public, you don't want private company or personal information to remain in the metadata. The Document Inspector tool checks for hidden properties and personal information.

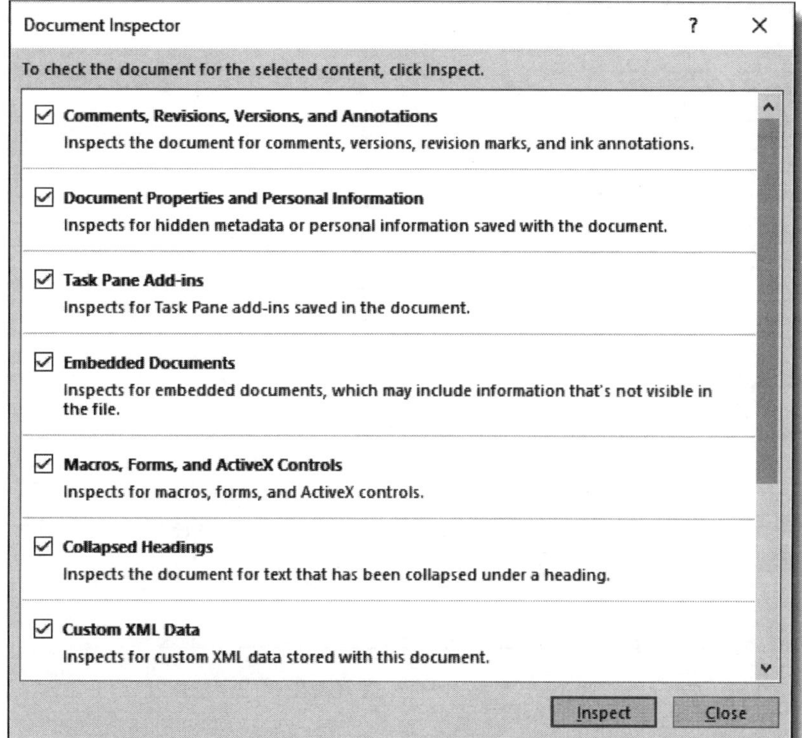

Items the Document Inspector looks for include add-ins, macros, custom XML data, personal information in the properties, and text and other objects that have been formatted to be invisible. The tool allows you to remove this information.

1. In Backstage view, click Info. Then, click **Check for Issues > Inspect Document**.
   The Document Inspector window opens.
2. Check or clear the items you want to look for.
3. Click **Inspect**.
   The inspector highlights possible issues.
4. Click **Remove All** next to any results you wish to remove.
5. Click **Close**.
   You'll still need to save the document to keep these changes.

Creating PDF and XPS documents

PDF and XPS documents are both *fixed formats*, which is to say they're meant to be read but not edited. Both can be read by an assortment of free readers, and all fonts, formatting, and images appear the same on nearly any device. The drawback is that once saved, the content can't be easily changed: think of these formats as a type of printing, even if you can create them as you would any other file type.

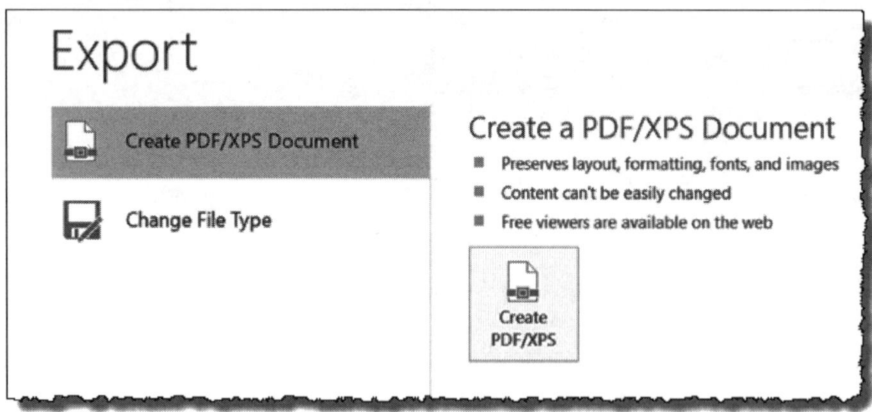

1. Open the Save As window.

   You can also open the nearly identical Publish as PDF or XPS window in Backstage view by clicking **Export > Create PDF/XPS Document > Create PDF/XPS**. The process is otherwise the same.

2. Choose saving options.

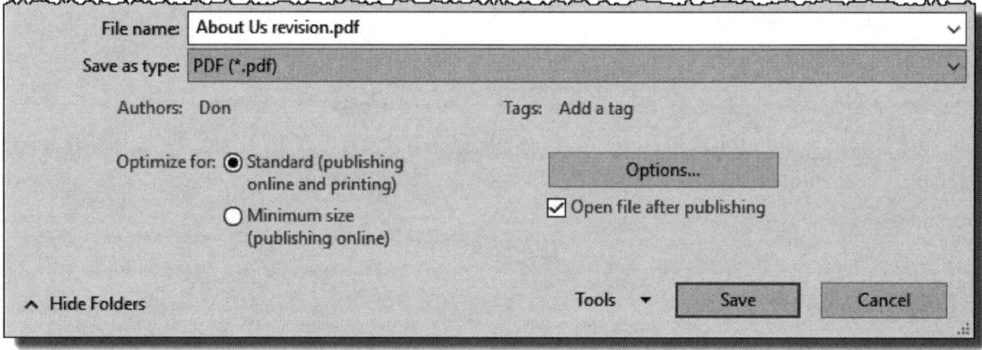

   - Choose either **PDF** or **XPS** from the "Save as type" list.
   - In the Optimize For section, click **Minimum size** to create a smaller file, and **Standard** to preserve graphical quality.
   - Check **Open file after publishing** to automatically open the document in your default PDF or XPS reader.

3. To set additional file options, click **Options**.

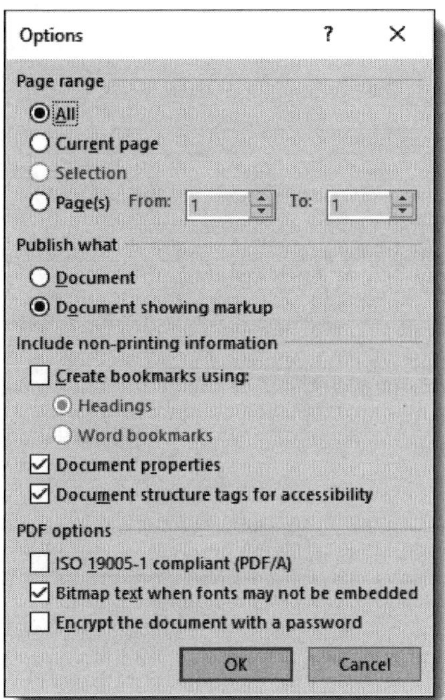

- You can publish the entire document, a page, a page range, or a selection.
- You can optionally include markup, bookmarks, document structure, and document properties.
- PDF and XPS each have additional available options.
- Click **OK** when you're done.

4. Click **Save** or **Publish**.

Importing files

Many types of files can be imported into Word, even those that are non-native to Word, such as those created using Acrobat (PDF), WordPerfect, and OpenOffice.

Exam Objective: MOS Word Core 1.1.3,1.1.4

- You can import these files by clicking **File > Open**. At the bottom of the Open window, select the extension associated with the type of file you wish to open. Then select the file, and click **Open**.

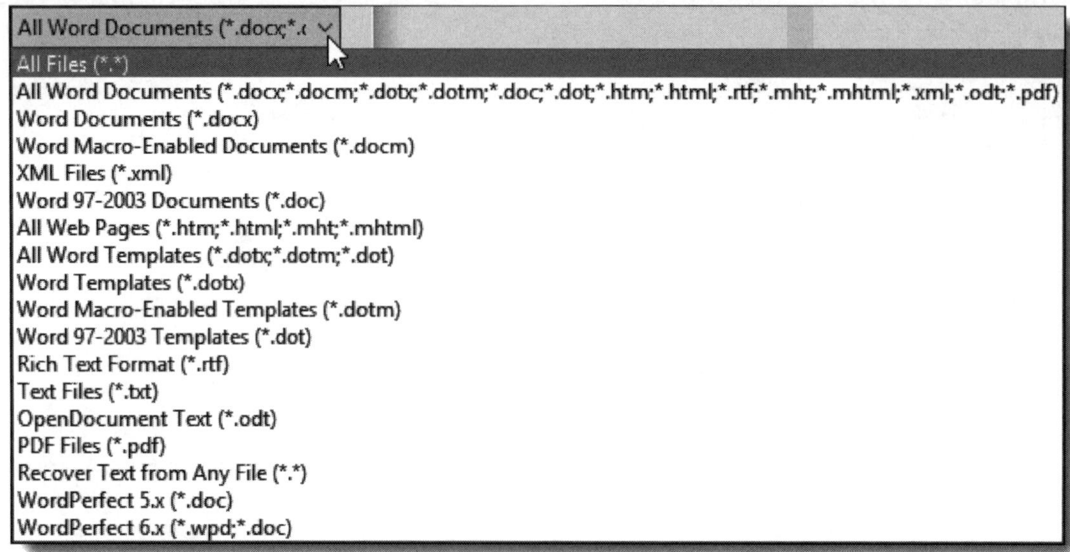

- To append documents directly to a Word document, click **Insert > Object**. In the Object window, click **Create from File**, and click **Browse**. Navigate to the file you want to insert, then click **Insert**. For certain files types, such as portable document format (PDF) files, their contents can't be edited directly in Word; you can only resize it. To edit the PDF, double-click its object to open it in the default PDF reader, then save your changes.
- To insert selected text from a file, click the arrow to the right of the Object button, and select **Text from File**. In the Insert File window, navigate to the file containing the text you wish to insert, and click **Insert**.

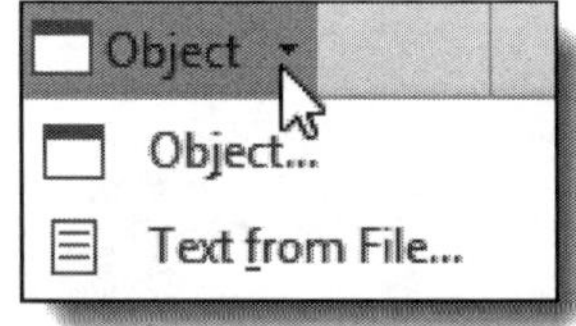

- A quick way to insert text from most types of files is to display the text in its native application, select it, and then copy and paste it into a Word document. Depending on the source of the text, you might be prompted to paste it with its formatting intact or as plain text. However, text copied from some types of files, such as PDFs, can often be pasted only as plain text.

Sending documents

You can attach Word documents to email messages from your mail client as you would any other document, but if you have a compatible mail client like Outlook, you can also send them directly from Word. If you subscribe to an Internet fax service, you can also send a document as a fax message. In addition, if you've saved the file to a shared location, you can send a link to that file. To access these options, in Backstage view, click **Share** > **Email**.

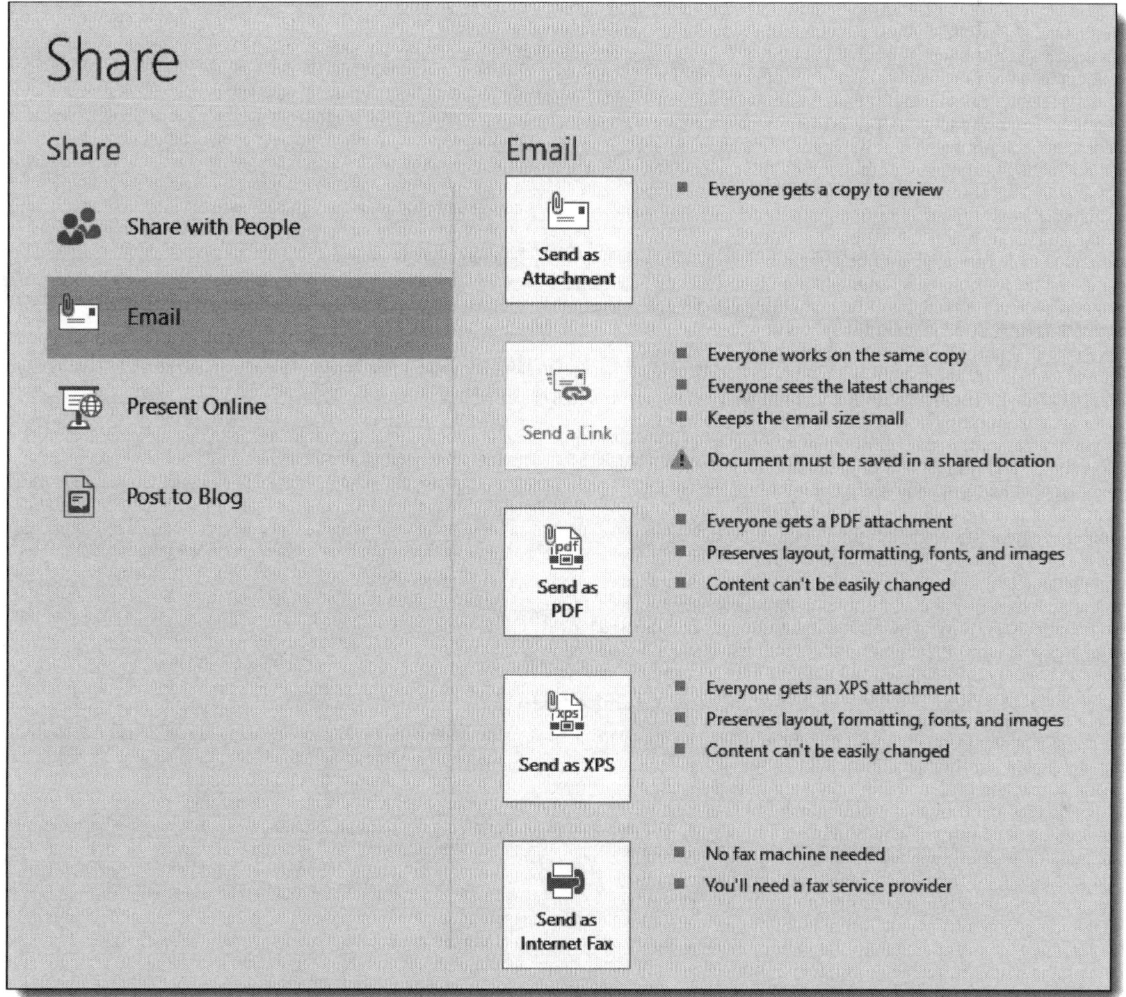

- Click **Send as Attachment** to send the document in its current state and file format.
- Click **Send a Link** to send an email with a hyperlink to the document.

  A link has some advantages over an attachment: it keeps the email size small and ensures the recipients see the original, up-to-date document. The main disadvantage is that you can send a link only if the document is first saved in a shared location the recipient can access.
- Click **Send as PDF** or **Send as XPS** to send a PDF or XPS document using the default save settings.
- Click **Send as Internet Fax** to send the document as a fax. You must be registered with a fax service provider.

Checking accessibility

Exam Objective: MOS Word Core 1.5.5

If you are going to make a document public or distribute it widely, it's good practice to check that the document is accessible to screen readers and other accessibility technology. For instance, pictures should have an alternate text property that describes the picture.

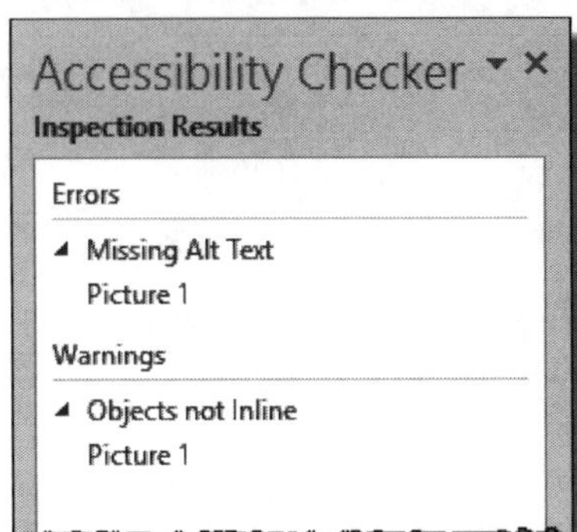

The Accessibility Checker opens as a pane on the right side of the document. It lists possible issues and offers additional information on how to fix them and why you would want to.

1. In Backstage view, in the Info category, click **Check for Issues > Check Accessibility**.

   The Accessibility Checker pane opens, showing results of the inspection.
2. Select an item to see additional information about why you would want to fix the problem and how to do it.
3. If you fix a problem with the pane open, such as adding alternate text to a picture, the results list will update automatically.
4. When you are finished, close the Accessibility Checker pane.

Saving documents to OneDrive

You can also save your documents to cloud storage using online services. If your company uses SharePoint or a OneDrive location, you can save documents to your site from Backstage view by clicking **Save As**, then clicking **OneDrive**, **Office 365 SharePoint**, or another available option. Microsoft's OneDrive service offers cloud storage to anyone with a Microsoft ID. You can create additional destinations in the Save As pane by clicking **Add a Place** and specifying a destination using a Windows SharePoint or other OneDrive location.

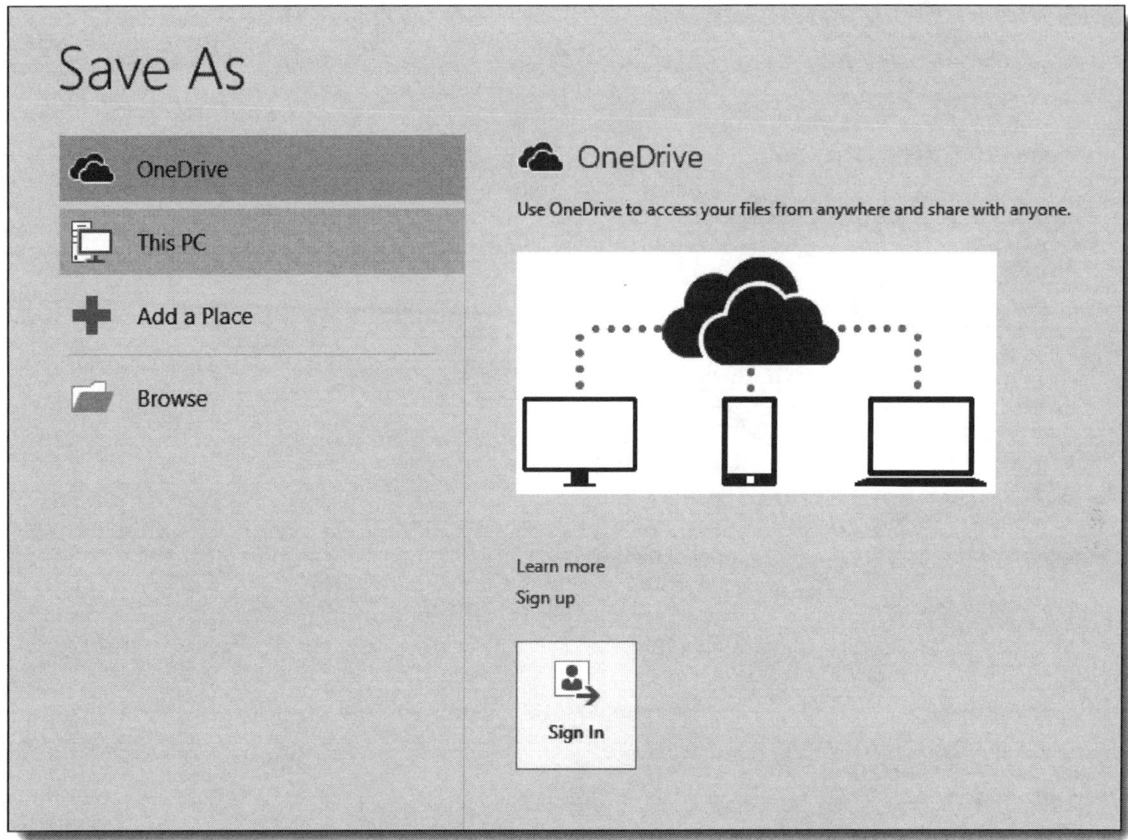

Add a Place

You can add locations to make it easier to save Office documents to the cloud.

Office 365 SharePoint

OneDrive

1. In Backstage view, click **Save As** > **OneDrive**.
2. Click **Sign In**.
3. Enter your Microsoft credentials, and click **OK**.
4. Choose a location in your OneDrive folder.

Registering blog accounts

The first time you create or publish a blog post, you're prompted to register your account in Word.

1. When prompted, click **Register Now**.
2. From the list, select your blog provider.

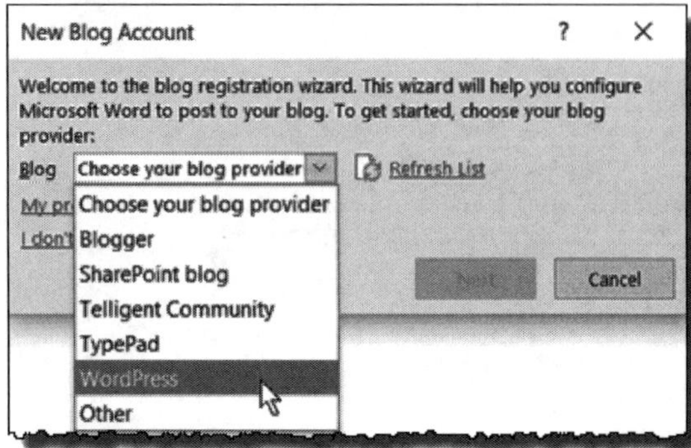

3. Click **Next**.
4. Enter information for your blog.

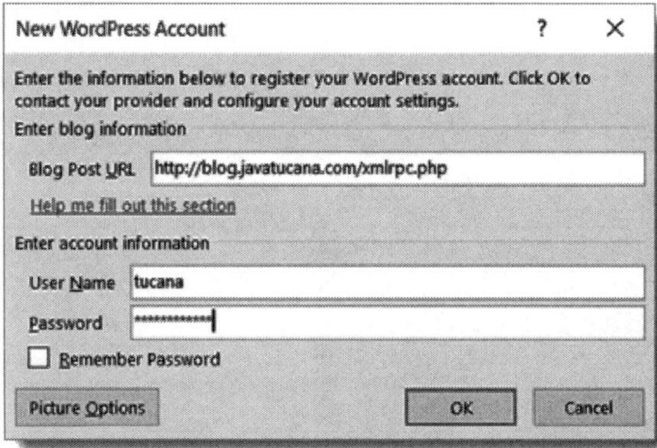

- The fields depend on the service you choose, but at the minimum require a username and password.
- Click **Picture Options** to specify how to handle images used in your blog posts.

5. Click **OK**.

Creating blog posts

You can use Word to create blog posts, but to publish them, you'll need an account with a blog service.

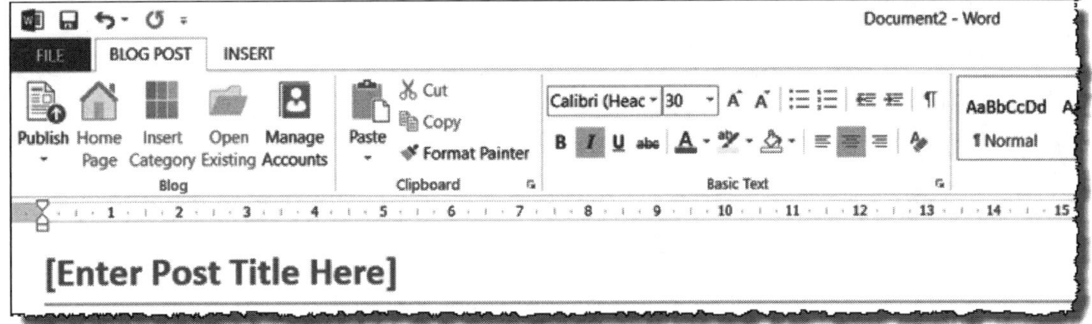

- To create a new blog post, click **New** in Backstage view, select the Blog post template, and click **Create**.
- To publish an existing document as a blog post, in Backstage view, click **Share > Post to Blog > Post to Blog**. If you haven't yet registered with a blog service, you'll be prompted to do so.
- When you're editing a blog post, you have access to the Blog Post tab of the ribbon, with formatting and publishing options.

Viewing shared documents

When you open a document someone else has sent to you, you might see a notification that Word is operating in *Compatibility Mode* or *Protected View.*

Exam Objective: MOS Word Core 1.5.6

- When you open a document in a format that doesn't support all of Word 2016's features, "Compatibility Mode" appears next to the file name at the top of the window. Word may disable any features not compatible with the document type. To leave Compatibility Mode, save the document in .docx format.

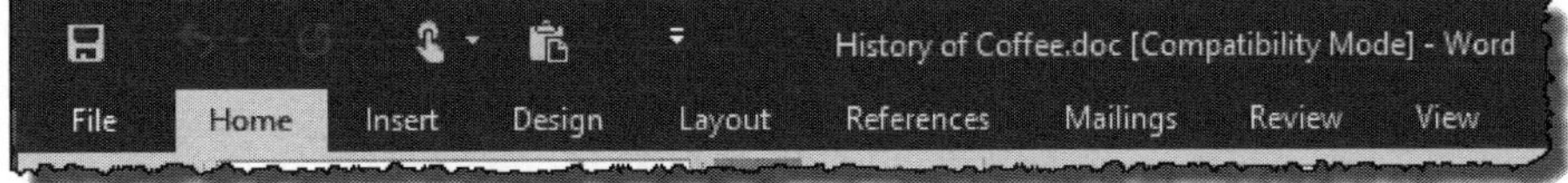

- To maintain "backward" compatibility with earlier versions of Word, so that others using those versions can open and work with your files, select the appropriate Word version in the "Save as type" list of the Save As window.
- When "Protected View" appears in the document title, it means that Word thinks your document might pose a security risk. Most ribbon commands are disabled, and although you can view or copy document content, you can't edit it. A message bar also appears, explaining the reason. If you trust the document's security, click **Enable Editing** to leave Protected view.

Note: "Protected View" doesn't necessarily mean a file is dangerous: it usually just means it came from the Internet or some other potentially unsafe location. At the same time, if you don't know and trust a file's sender, don't leave Protected View until you make sure it's safe, for example, by scanning it with an antivirus program.

Checking compatibility

If you want to save a document to an earlier Word format, you can first use the compatibility checker to see if your document uses features that are not supported in earlier versions of Word.

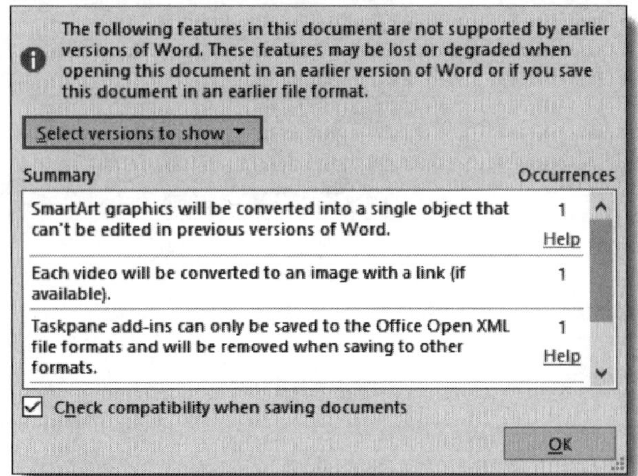

Compatibility issues include things like SmartArt and WordArt, some chart features, embedded online videos, new numbering formats and new shapes, add-ins, and several more. By default, compatibility is checked whenever you save a document to an earlier version of Word, but you can check it at any time.

1. In Backstage view, in the Info category, click **Check for Issues > Check Compatibility**.

   The Compatibility Checker window opens. Each issue is summarized with the number of occurrences in the document.

2. If you want to check compatibility with a specific Word version, you can select only that version in the "Select versions to show" list.

   By default, the document is checked against Word 97-2003, 2007, and 2010. There are no compatibility issues between Word 2013 and 2016.

3. Click **OK** to close the Compatibility Checker.

Exercise: Exploring file types

To complete this exercise, you need to have Adobe Reader installed. If you don't, and are using Windows Vista or newer, you can save as XPS instead of PDF. You'll save a document in different file types.

Do This	How & Why
1. Open `Lunch menu`.	This file is an ordinary Word document. You'll save it in other formats.
2. Save the file in OpenDocument format.	You need to make a copy of the file for someone who uses OpenOffice.
a) In Backstage view, click **Export**.	To view the available options. You want to save it as a different file type.
b) Click **Change File Type**.	

Do This	How & Why
c) In the right pane, click **OpenDocument Text**.	

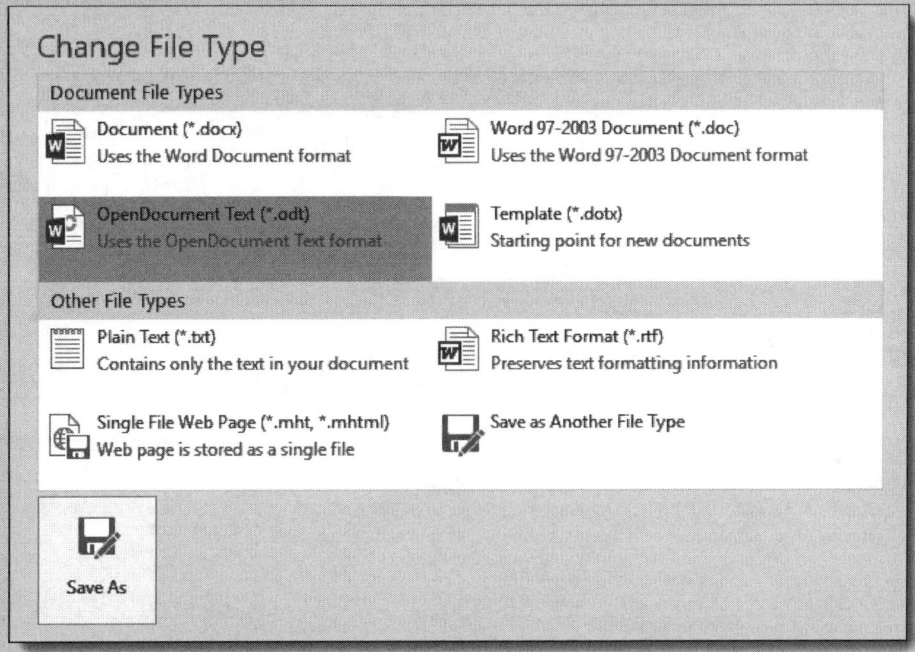

Do This	How & Why
d) Click **Save As**.	The Save As window opens. OpenDocument Text is already selected in the "Save as type" list.
e) Save the file as `Lunch menu export`.	Type the file name, and click **Save**. You are warned that the new format might not support all the features of the Word format.
f) Click **Yes**.	

To close the warning and save the document as an odt file.

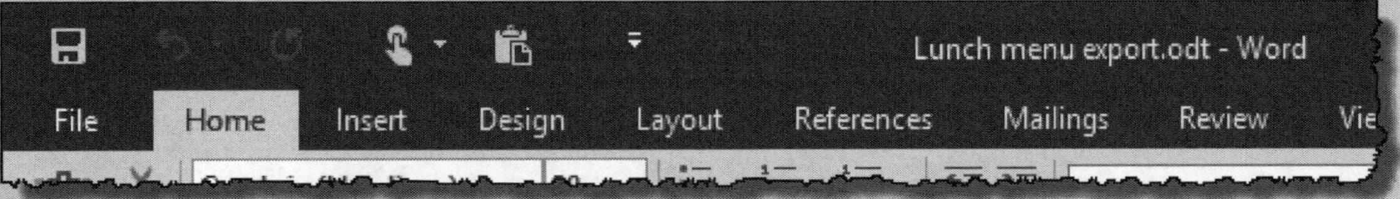

The file is now shown as OpenDocument Text (odt). Because this file doesn't use any different features, it doesn't look any different, and it can be opened by OpenOffice Writer and other programs.

Do This	How & Why
3. Save the document in PDF format.	The commercial printer making your menus prefers a fixed format to avoid any layout problems, so you'll use PDF.
a) Press **F12**.	The Save As window opens. You don't need to use Backstage view to change file types.
b) From the "Save as type" list, Choose **PDF**.	Additional options specific to PDF appear. The optimization setting is set to Standard, which is what you want.
c) Click **Options**.	The Options window opens. You'll print the whole document, and you don't need markup or bookmarks, so you'll keep these options.

Do This	How & Why
d) Click **OK**.	To close the window.
e) Check **Open File After Publishing**.	
f) Specify `Lunch menu portable` as the file name.	
g) Click **Save**.	You may need to accept the Adobe Acrobat Reader license. The PDF opens in Adobe Acrobat Reader. It looks the same, but you can't edit it.
h) Close Acrobat Reader.	**Lunch menu compatibility** is still open in Word.
4. Explore other saving options.	
a) In Backstage view, click **Share**.	You can send the document as an attachment, a link, a PDF or XPS document, or an Internet Fax.
b) Click **Invite People**, which displays the **Save To Cloud** option in the right pane.	You can log into your Microsoft account and save the document to your OneDrive folder.
c) Click **Save to SharePoint**.	To save the file to your team's SharePoint site.
d) Click **Post to Blog**. In the right pane, click **Post to Blog**.	Post to Blog The document opens in a new window as a blog post. The page color and border are no longer visible, and the Blog Post tab is active on the ribbon. Additionally, the Register a Blog Account window opens.
e) Click **Register Now**.	The New Blog Account window opens. You can connect Word to your existing blog account from here.
f) Click **Cancel**.	The New Blog Account window closes, but you're still editing the file as a blog post.
5. Close the new document window.	Don't save changes.
6. Save and close `Lunch menu export`.	

The lunch menu displayed as a blog post.

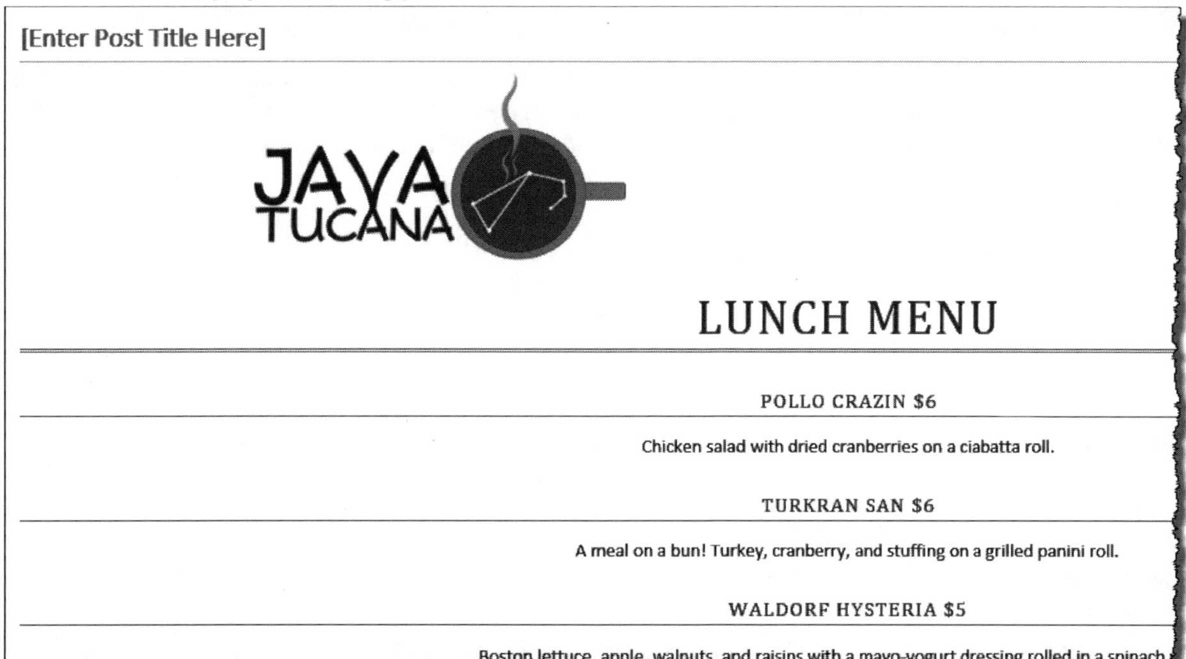

Assessment: Saving and sending

Checking knowledge about saving and sending files.

1. You need a colleague to edit a rather complex document, but his non-Microsoft word processing application can't reliably read Word's default format. What format would preserve most of your current formatting options while still being readable to the other application?
   - OpenDocument Text
   - PDF
   - Rich Text Format
   - XPS
2. XPS is natively supported by Windows Vista and later. True or false?
   - True
   - False
3. Word is really compatible only with blogs using Microsoft's Windows Live Spaces format. True or false?
   - True
   - False
4. What should you do if Word opens a document in Protected view? Choose the best response.
   - Continue as normal: Protected view lets you edit the document safely.
   - Delete or quarantine the file: Word has detected malware in it, and it's unsafe to open.
   - Disable Protected view if you trust the document's source.
   - Save the document in the default .docx format.

Module B: Comments

When you're working on a document with other people, you might want to make comments or add reminders for later. You could just add them in the text and remove them later, but they might be hard to spot or get left in by mistake. Instead, Word lets you add comments as markup, rather than as document content.

You will learn how to:

- Insert comments
- Edit comments
- Change comment display options

About comments

By default, comments appear as balloons in the document margin, but the comment text doesn't print. You can display hidden comments clicking the comment balloon, or from the Review tab by clicking **Show Comments**. When you hover over or click on a comment balloon, the document text to which it refers is also highlighted for convenience.

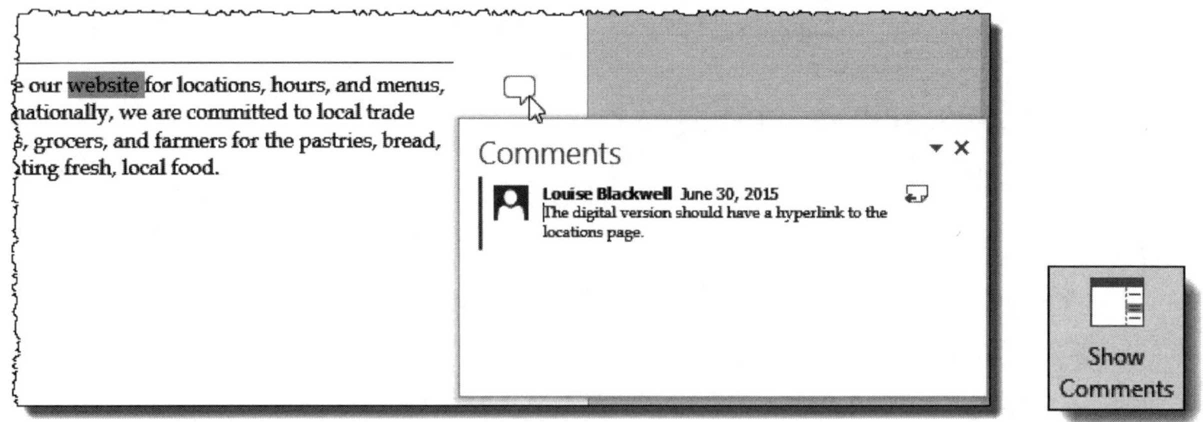

A comment is always marked with the name of the user who created it, and when a document has comments from multiple users, they're color coded. If one comment is in response to another, it will appear in the same window.

Exam Objective: MOS Word Expert 1.3.1, 1.3.2

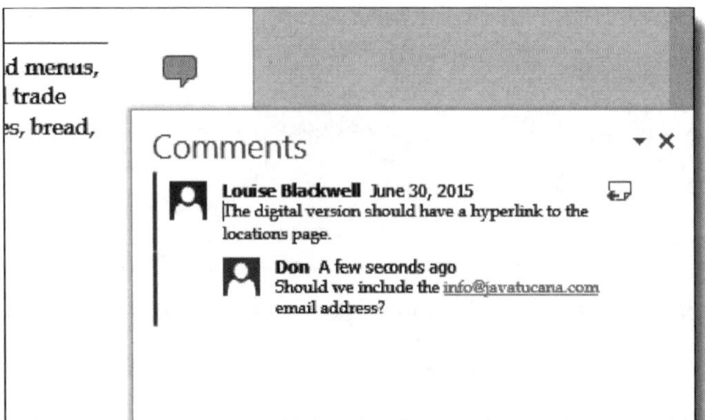

Commands for managing comments are located on the Review tab, in the Comments group. The Ink Comment options allow you to write comments by using a touch screen, the mouse, or another pointer as a pen.

Adding comments

 **Exam Objective:** MOS Word Expert 1.3.4

When you add a comment, it is attached to any content that is selected or the word nearest the cursor if no content is selected. When you're commenting on something like a sentence or graphic, this helps point it out. If you want to make a general comment about the document, you can place it wherever you like.

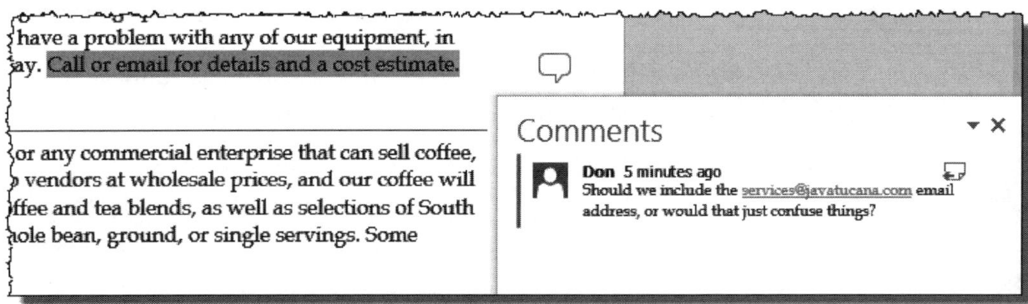

1. Place the insertion point or make a selection.
   - If you make a selection, the comment points to the whole selection.
   - If you merely place the insertion point, the comment points to the nearest word.
2. In the Comments group, click **New Comment**.
3. Write the comment.

    **Note:** Usually, you need to make comments only as plain text, but you can apply some formatting, like changing font type, and even insert images. However, you can't change text size or paragraph formatting.
4. Click outside the comment box when you're done writing it.

Managing comments

You can edit or delete existing comments. You can also navigate easily through all comments of a long document.

 **Exam Objective:** MOS Word Expert 1.3.4, 1.3.5

- To edit a comment, click anywhere in its text, and make any changes you like.
- To delete a comment, select it, and click **Delete** in the Comments group.
  - To delete all visible comments, click **Delete** > **Delete All Comments Shown**.
  - To delete all comments, click **Delete** > **Delete All Comments in Document**.
- To navigate between comments, click **Next** or **Previous**.

Displaying comments

You might not always want to display comments as balloons—or even at all—especially if you want to print a copy of the document without the comments. You can change how comments are displayed on the Review tab, in the tracking group. Most of those options are also in the **Show Markup** menu.

Exam Objective: MOS Word Expert 1.3.4, 1.3.5

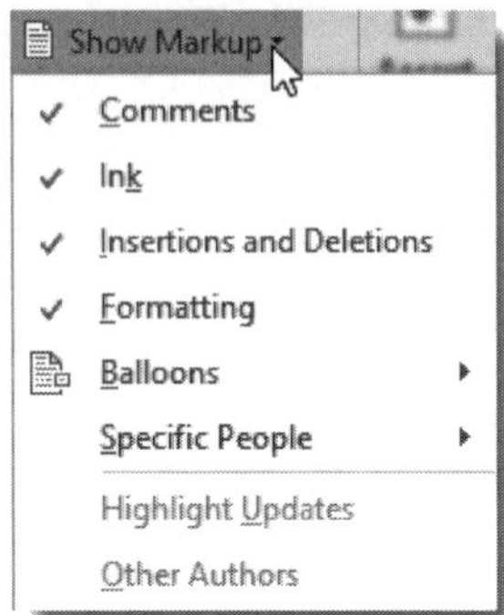

- To display or hide all comments, click **Show Markup** > **Comments**. Or, you can click **Show Comments** in the Comments group, when it's available (in other words, not dimmed).

- To display or hide comments from a specific user, click **Show Markup** > **Specific People**, and check or clear **All Reviewers** or individual users' names.

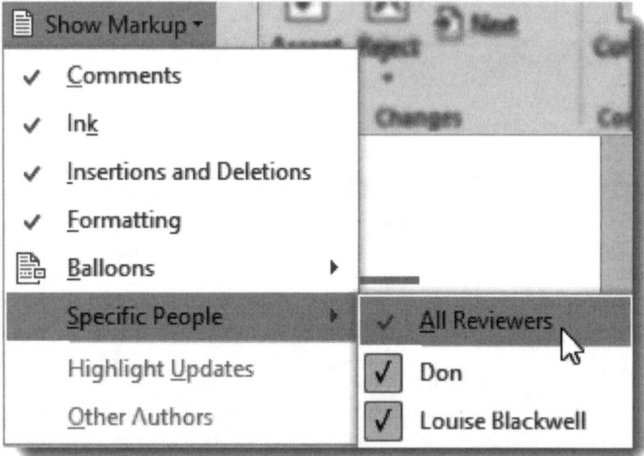

- To show comments without balloons, click **Show Markup** > **Balloons** > **Show All Revisions Inline**

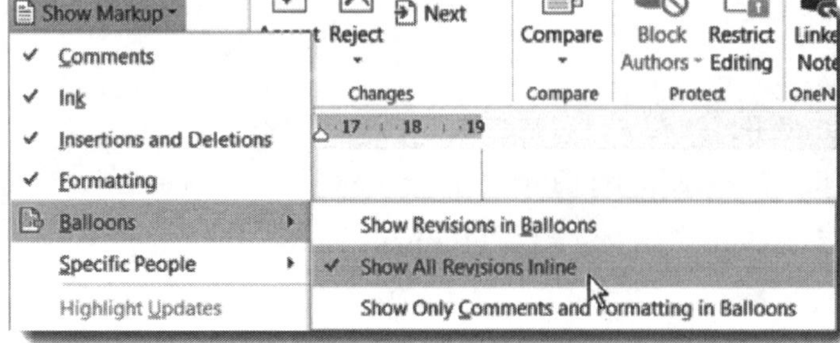

- To view further information about a comment, balloon or line, click it.

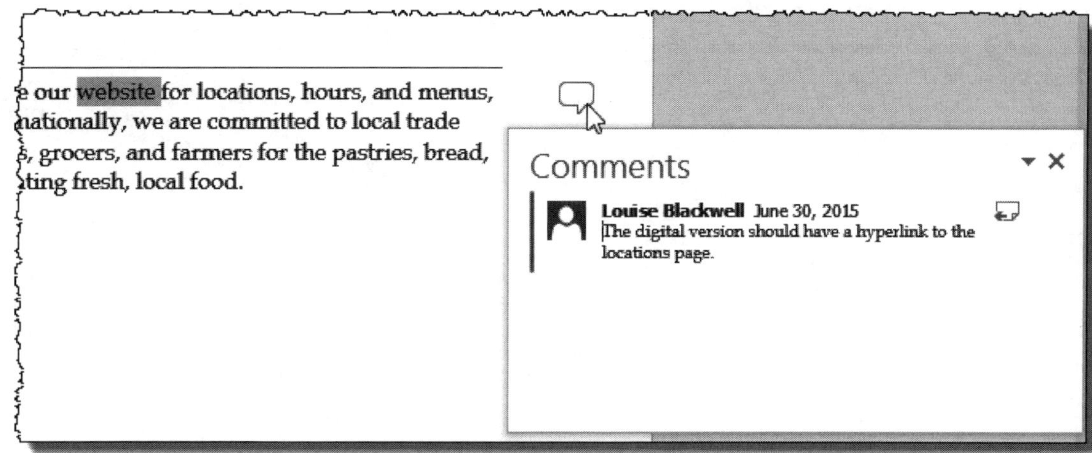

- Click **Reviewing Pane** to show all visible comments in a separate pane.

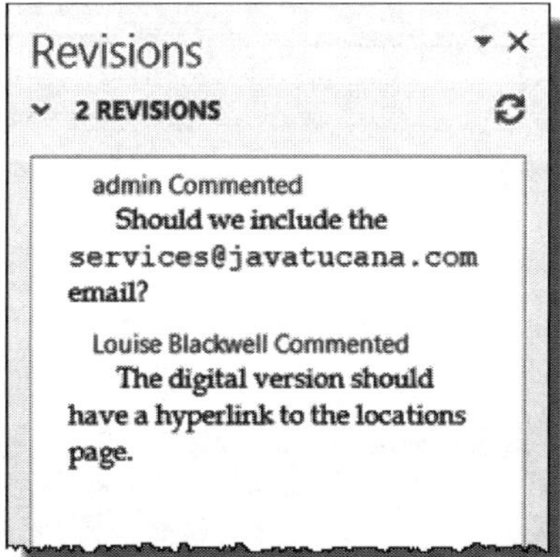

Exercise: Commenting on a document

In this exercise, you'll use comments to review a document.

Do This	How & Why
1. Open `About Us revision`, and save it as `About Us comments`.	This document already has one comment from a coworker.
2. Point to the word "website" in the document.	tea blends, as well as selections of South Louise Blackwell, 6/30/2015 7:01:00 PM commented: The digital version should have a hyperlink to the locations page. website for locations, hours, and menus, onally, we are committed to local trade To view the comment in a pop-up along with the commenter's full name and the time it was made.
3. Add comments to the document.	Instead of editing the document directly, you're just providing feedback to its author.

Do This	How & Why
a) Select the logo at the top of the document.	
b) On the Review tab, click **New Comment**.	A blank comment balloon appears in the right margin. It shows your name or initials and is a different color than the existing comment.
c) Type `Be sure to use the newest version of the logo.`	
d) Select the last sentence of the "Office coffee service" paragraph.	"Call or email for details and a cost estimate."
e) Comment `Should we include the Office coffee services email?`	Click **New Comment**, and type it.
f) Click outside the comment box.	To deselect it. The whole sentence you selected is highlighted as the target of the comment.
4. Edit your comments.	
a) Click the comment you just made.	You'll include the email address.
b) In the comment, Select "Office coffee services."	
c) Type `services@javatucana.com`.	You can edit a comment just as you would any other text.
d) In the Comments group, click **Previous**.	To move to the first comment. You've learned this is the newest logo after all, so you'll delete the comment.
e) In the comments group, click **Delete**.	 The comment is deleted.

Do This	How & Why
5. Change comment display options.	
a) In the Markup group, click **Show Markup > Balloons > Show All Revisions Inline**	The balloons in the margin vanish. Now each comment is just a colored highlight with initials and a number.
b) Point to any comment.	The comment's full content appears as a pop-up.
c) Click **Show Markup > Balloons > Show Only Comments and Formatting in Balloons**.	To return to the default view.
d) Click **Show Markup > Comments**	To hide all comments. Now you can print the document without the comments showing.
6. Save and close the document.	

Assessment: Comments

Checking knowledge about comments.

1. What can you do when editing a comment? Choose all that apply.
    - Adjust paragraph settings
    - Change character size
    - Change the font
    - Insert an image
2. If you want to print a document without showing comments, you have to delete them all. True or false?
    - True
    - False
3. To view an inline comment's full content, you need to show balloons or the Reviewing Pane. True or false?
    - True
    - False

Module C: Protecting documents

When you distribute a document, you might want to restrict who uses it or what they can do with it. Word allows you to control who can open a document, specify what kinds of changes they can make, and even make sure the document isn't changed without your knowledge.

You will learn:

- About Word's protection options
- How to mark a document as final
- How to password-protect a document
- How to restrict document editing

Document protection options

All document protection options are available in the Info section of Backstage view. Each option has a different purpose, and some can even be used together, so it's important to understand the features and limitations of each.

Exam Objective: MOS Word Expert 1.2.1, 1.2.2, 1.2.3

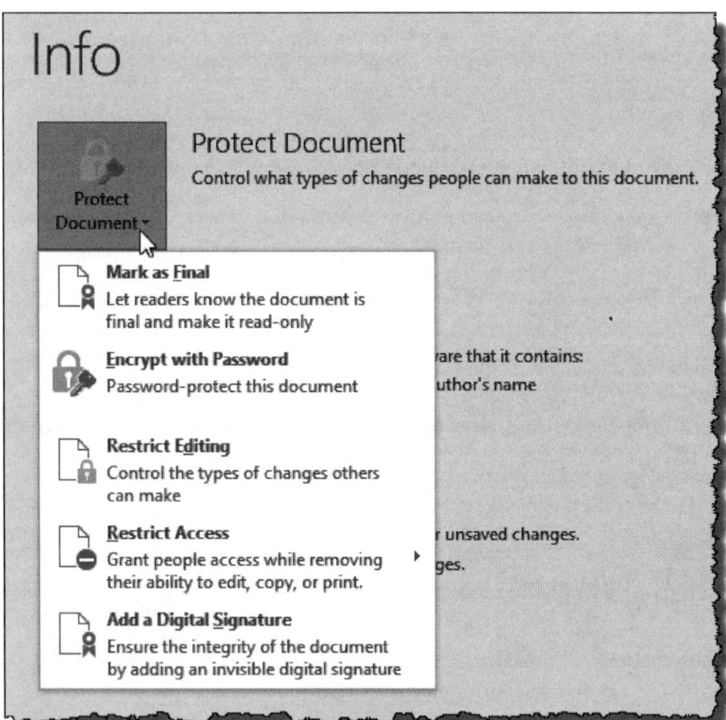

Mark as Final	Makes a document read-only and marks its status as final. This isn't a security feature: it just records your finalization of the document and keeps it from being changed by accident.
Encrypt with Password	Applies encryption to the document using a password of your choice. No one can open or read the document without the password.
Restrict Editing	Allows anyone to read the document, but controls what they can change about it. In addition to preventing all changes, you can just restrict users to using a fixed set of styles, to making tracked changes or comments, or to filling in forms.

Restrict Access	Grants access to the document using Microsoft's Information Rights Management Service. This gives you broad abilities to restrict who can open the document and what they can do with it, but you must install the free service, and you and all users must have Microsoft IDs.
Add a Digital Signature	Applies a visible or invisible cryptographic signature to the document, proving that it is from you and hasn't been altered. You can apply your own digital signature, but the full benefits of the feature require a third-party signature verification service.

Marking documents final

When you mark a document as final, Word makes it read-only and saves it as it is. When you or another user opens the document, the ribbon is minimized, all editing and proofing functions are disabled, and a Marked as Final message bar is shown at the top of the window. This doesn't actually provide any security for the document: you or anyone else can simply remove the mark and edit it again.

Exam Objective: MOS Word Expert 1.2.2

1. In the Info section of Backstage view, click **Protect Document** > **Mark as Final**.

   You are asked to confirm the change.
2. Click **OK**.

   When you first use this feature, an additional notification window appears, explaining finalized documents. You can choose not to receive this notice in the future.

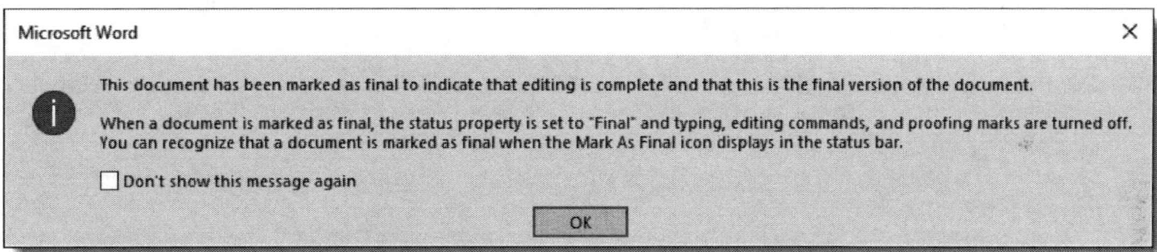

After you mark a document as final, it remains open. Because it's saved as part of the process, you can just close it without further action.

Password-encrypting documents

You encrypt a document with a password when you want to make sure unauthorized users can't read it but don't want to deal with a more involved user-based security system.

Exam Objective: MOS Word Expert 1.2.3

When you open a password-protected document, you're prompted to enter the password. If you don't, the document won't open at all. If you do, you are free to make any changes you want, including removing the password.

Note: Earlier versions of Word used weak encryption methods that could easily be defeated. The encryption used by Word 2007 and later is much improved and is suitable for protecting sensitive data when used correctly. Keep the following in mind when encrypting a document.

- Choose a password that is long and hard to guess. A simple password will never be secure, regardless of the encryption method.
- Passwords are case-sensitive, so be mindful when you create them.
- There is no password recovery feature for encrypted documents. If you forget the password for your document, there is no Word option or Microsoft service to easily retrieve your data.

1. In the Info section of Backstage view, click **Protect Document > Encrypt with Password**.

   You're prompted to create a password.

   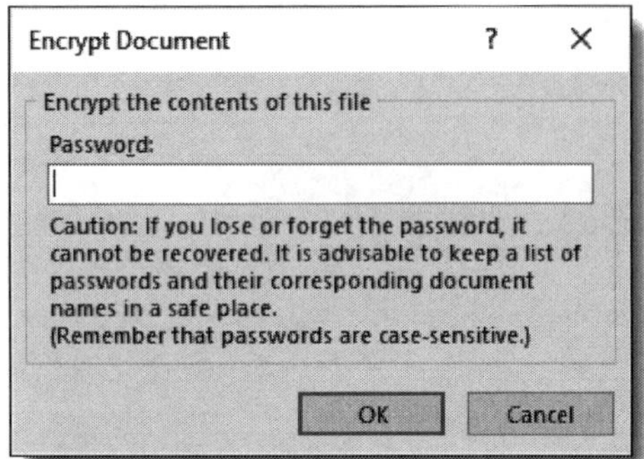

2. Enter the password you want, and click **OK**.

   To remove the password from a document that's already encrypted, delete the existing password and then click **OK**. You're prompted to re-enter the password.

3. Type the password again, then click **OK**.

Unlike finalized documents, encrypted documents aren't automatically saved, so you still need to save before closing.

Document restrictions

When you apply restrictions to a document, anyone can open and read it, but you can control what kind of changes they can make, if any. Editing protections are handled through the Restrict Formatting and Editing pane. When you apply protection to a document, the pane shows options for what you can restrict. Once protections are enabled, the pane instead shows you what changes you can make.

Exam Objective: MOS Word Expert 1.2.1

The Restrict Formatting and Editing pane before and after applying editing restrictions.

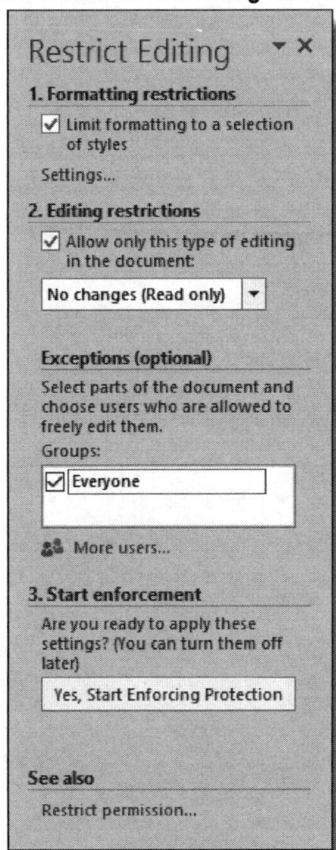

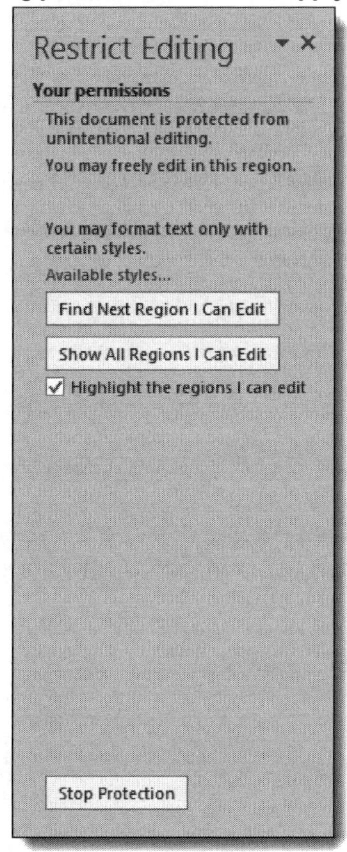

You can apply three main kinds of editing restrictions.

Formatting restrictions	Control what changes users can make to document formatting. You can prevent users from applying manual formatting, restrict the styles they can use, and even prevent them from changing the document theme or style set.
Editing restrictions	Control what changes users can make to the document's content. In addition to simply making the document read-only, you can restrict users to making only tracked changes or comments, or to filling in forms.
Exceptions	Mark areas of the document that aren't protected and can be edited freely. You can set exceptions only if you've set editing restrictions to prevent all changes, or allow comments only.

When document protection is enforced, it applies until it's removed. If you just want to keep a document from being edited by accident, you can enforce protection without authentication so anyone can turn it off. You can also require a password to remove document protection or restrict it to certain users, if you're using Information Rights Management.

Note: Don't confuse document protection with document encryption. If you're using user authentication through Windows Live IDs, the document is both protected and encrypted. If you're using passwords, they are separate. You can apply protection, encryption, or both, each with its own password.

Applying document restrictions

To apply protection to a document, you have to set restrictions, then start enforcement.

Exam Objective: MOS Word Expert 1.2.1

1. Open the Restrict Editing pane. You can do this two ways.
   - From Backstage view, click **Info > Protect Document > Restrict Editing**.
   - On the ribbon's Review tab, in the Protect group, click **Restrict Editing**.

2. Choose restrictions.
   - To set formatting restrictions, check **Limit formatting to a selection of styles**, or click **Settings** for finer control.
   - To set editing restrictions, check **Allow only this type of editing in the document**, then select an option from the list: Tracked Changes, Comments, Filling in forms, or No Changes.
   - To set an exception, select the portion of the document you want to be editable, and in the Exceptions list, check **Everyone**.
3. Click **Yes, Start Enforcing Protection**.
4. Choose enforcement options.
   - To protect the document using Information Rights Management, choose **User Authentication**.
   - To protect editing restrictions with a password, enter it in both fields.
   - To enforce restrictions without a password, leave both fields blank.
5. Click **OK**.

Editing restricted documents

When you open a protected document, you can make only whatever changes the current protection allows. The Restrict Editing pane shows further details and commands to help you.

- You can use any available commands on the ribbon; restricted commands are simply made unavailable.
- If the document is locked to allow only you to fill out form fields, you will be able to select only those fields. Otherwise, you can click in or select any part of the document, even if you can't edit it.
- By default, exceptions in the document are highlighted. To find exceptions, click **Find Next Region I Can Edit** or **Show All Regions I Can Edit**.
- Click **Stop Protection** to turn off all protection, if you have the necessary credentials.

Exercise: Using protection features

In this exercise, you'll apply various protection types to multiple documents.

Do This	How & Why
1. Open `Lunch menu` and save it as `Lunch menu protected`.	
2. Encrypt the document.	First, you'll apply password encryption to restrict who can open the menu until it's ready for circulation.
a) In Backstage view, click **Info** > **Protect Document** > **Encrypt with Password**.	The Encrypt Document window appears.
b) Type `password` and click **OK**.	 Encrypt Document ? X Encrypt the contents of this file Password: •••••••• Caution: If you lose or forget the password, it cannot be recovered. It is advisable to keep a list of passwords and their corresponding document names in a safe place. (Remember that passwords are case-sensitive.) OK Cancel For a real document, you'd want to use a stronger password. You're prompted to confirm the password.
c) Enter the `password` again.	Type `password` and click **OK**. The document now requires a password to be opened.
3. Mark the document as final.	You can apply more than one kind of protection to the same document. In this case, you just want to make sure that anyone who opens the document knows it's the final version.
a) Click **Protect Document** > **Mark as Final**.	A confirmation window appears, asking if you want to proceed.
b) Click **OK**.	An information window appears, explaining finalized documents.
c) Click **OK**.	
d) Close the document.	You aren't prompted to save changes, as finalizing the document saved it automatically.
4. Remove the document's protection.	

Do This	How & Why
a) Open `Lunch menu protected`.	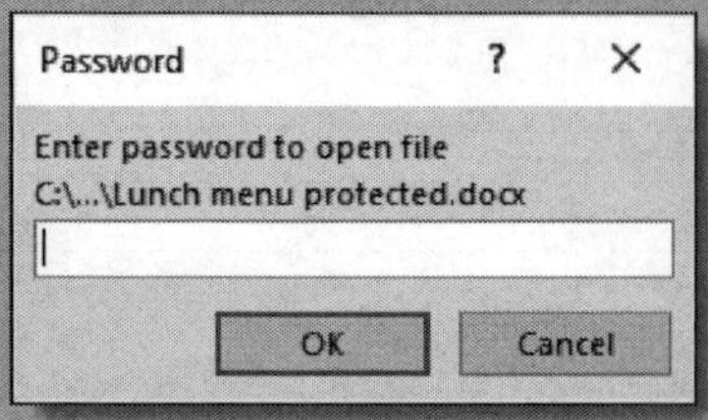 Password ? ✕ Enter password to open file C:\...\Lunch menu protected.docx OK Cancel You're prompted for a password.
b) Enter `password` and click **OK**.	You can read the document, but the ribbon is minimized, the document's title states that it's read-only, and a message bar explains that it has been marked as final.
c) Try to edit the document.	You can select document content but not modify it.
d) In the message bar, click **Edit Anyway**.	The message bar vanishes, and the ribbon is displayed.
e) In Backstage view, click **Info > Protect Document > Encrypt with Password**.	The Encrypt Document window opens. The current password is shown as dots.
f) Delete the document password, and click **OK**.	To remove the password. The document's permissions are now open.
g) Save and close the document.	
5. Open `Office services` and save it as `Office services protected`.	This document is a form.
6. Restrict editing of the document.	You'll restrict it so users can fill out the form but not make other changes.
a) On the Review tab, click **Restrict Editing**.	The Restrict Editing pane appears.
b) Check **Allow only this type of editing in the document**.	By default, No changes (Read only) is selected. That isn't what you want.
c) From the Editing restrictions list, choose **Filling in forms**.	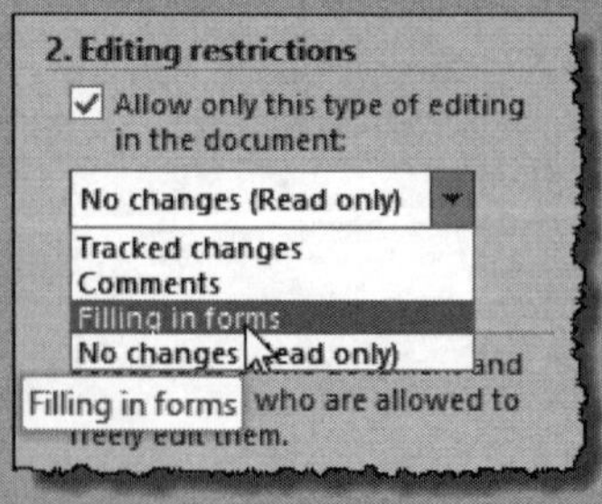 2. Editing restrictions ☑ Allow only this type of editing in the document: No changes (Read only) Tracked changes Comments Filling in forms No changes (Read only) Filling in forms who are allowed to freely edit them.
d) Click **Yes, Start Enforcing Protection**.	The Start Enforcing Protection window appears. Password is selected.

Do This	How & Why
e) In both password fields, type `12345`.	If you just wanted to protect against accidental edits, you wouldn't need to use a password.
f) Click **OK**.	Restrict Editing Your permissions This document is protected from unintentional editing. You may only fill in forms in this region.
g) Close the Restrict Editing pane.	
7. Fill out the form.	You can edit form fields, but you can't even select other parts of the document.
8. Save and close the document.	

Assessment: Protecting documents

Checking knowledge about document protection.

1. When you mark a document as final, you can specify a password needed to unlock it for editing. True or false?
   - True
   - False
2. For technical reasons, document encryption and editing restrictions don't work well together. True or false?
   - True
   - False
3. It's easy to recognize exceptions in a restricted document. True or false?
   - True
   - False
4. If you forget a document's encryption password, there's no easy way to recover it. True or false?
   - True
   - False

Summary: Saving and sharing documents

You should now know how to:

- Save documents in other file formats, publish them to fixed formats, and distribute them to others over the Internet
- Add, remove, and edit comments in a document
- Mark a document as final, encrypt its contents, or restrict how users can edit it

Synthesis: Saving and sharing documents

Bringing together your knowledge of sharing and collaboration.

In this document, you'll use saving and sharing features.

1. Open `Franchise information`, and save it as `Franchise information sharing`.
2. Apply protection to the document.
   - Encrypt the document using one password, and restrict editing using a different password.
   - Allow the document to be formatted using existing styles.
   - Don't allow users to change themes or style sets.
3. Close the document, then open it to test your settings.
4. Add comments to the document, specifying what you feel should be added or changed.
5. Save the document in multiple formats.
   - Choose at least one file format that is compatible with other word-processing software.
   - Choose at least one fixed file format.
   - If a format doesn't allow your current security restrictions or other features, discard incompatible content, as necessary.
6. Open each new file you created in Word or its own viewer. Compare its formatting and features with the original.
7. Close all open files.

Chapter 12: Advanced formatting

You will learn how to:

- Create tables and charts
- Create reusable content
- Use linked text boxes in a document

...odule A: Tables and charts

Tables don't have to be mere structural and formatting elements. Although managing complex data is best left to a spreadsheet application like Excel, you can still use formulas in tables, or use table data to create charts. You can even insert Excel worksheets as tables in your documents.

You will learn how to:

- Insert a table using Microsoft Excel data
- Insert and format charts
- Use formulas and calculations in tables

About inserting objects

When you paste text or illustrations into a document, the pasted content is treated the same as anything you might have created yourself. For example, if you paste an Excel spreadsheet into your document, you can edit its contents or use the Table Tools tabs to format it further, just as if you'd created the table yourself in Word. Sometimes this is exactly what you need, but it does limit you to using Word's editing tools for that specific content.

Exam Objective: MOS Word Expert 1.1.7

You also have the option of inserting a file as an *object*, which looks like pasted content but can be edited in the original application. This gives you access to all the editing capabilities of the source application, but it has some drawbacks. For example, you can do so only with files for applications that have Object Linking and Embedding (OLE) support, and it can result in a document file that's considerably larger than it would be from just pasting content.

There are two kinds of object: linked and embedded. They differ in where they store data and how the data is edited.

- A *linked* object points to data stored in the source file: Word stores only the file's location, and displays the linked data in the document. When you try to edit the object in Word, the source file opens in the original application. Likewise, when you (or someone else) edit the source file, the object in the Word file is updated to match it.
- An *embedded* object stores data as part of the Word document. If you double-click the object, it opens the original application inside the Word window. It doesn't matter what happens to the original file.

The decision of whether to link or embed an object depends on your needs. Linked objects make for smaller document files, as the data is stored in the source file, which others can still edit. For example, if a coworker maintains an Excel workbook on the network, you can use a linked object to create a document that always displays current data from that workbook. By contrast, embedded objects become part of the Word document itself and no longer interact with the original file. You might embed an object if you want to copy or send the document to other users, or to edit the embedded object without affecting the original file.

An embedded worksheet being edited in Excel, inside a Word window.

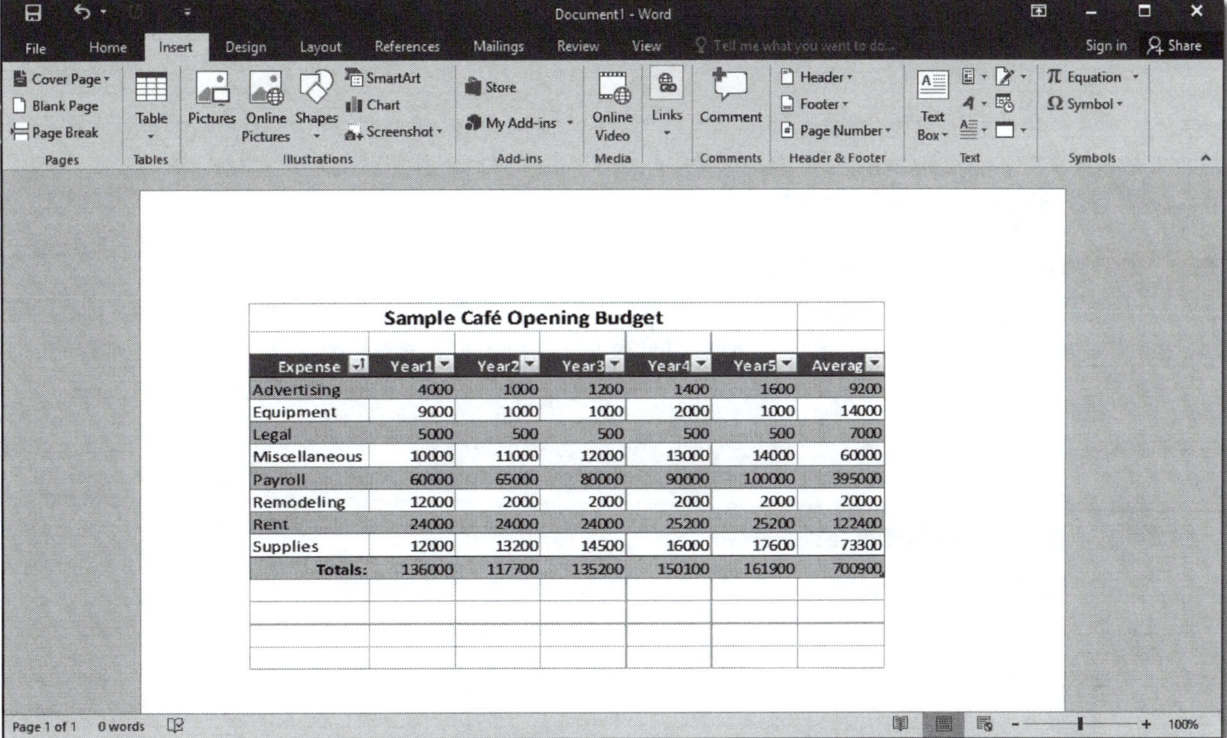

Sample Café Opening Budget						
Expense	Year1	Year2	Year3	Year4	Year5	Averag
Advertising	4000	1000	1200	1400	1600	9200
Equipment	9000	1000	1000	2000	1000	14000
Legal	5000	500	500	500	500	7000
Miscellaneous	10000	11000	12000	13000	14000	60000
Payroll	60000	65000	80000	90000	100000	395000
Remodeling	12000	2000	2000	2000	2000	20000
Rent	24000	24000	24000	25200	25200	122400
Supplies	12000	13200	14500	16000	17600	73300
Totals:	136000	117700	135200	150100	161900	700900

Linking objects

 **Exam Objective:** MOS Word Expert 1.1.7

To insert a linked object, you need to point Excel to the source file from the **Object** window.

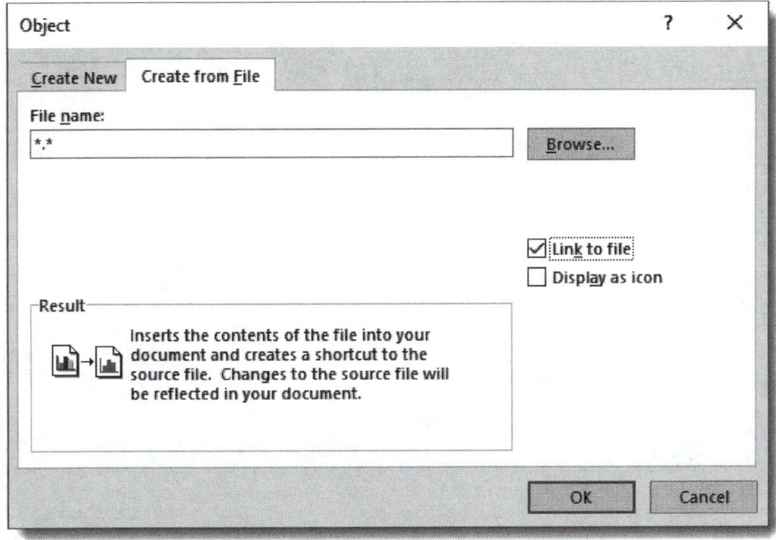

1. On the Insert tab, click Object in the Text group.
2. On the Create from File tab, click **Browse**.
3. Choose the file to which you want to link, and click **Open**.

4. Check **Link to file**.

   You can also check **Display as icon**. If you do, the file's contents don't appear in the document; only a linked icon appears.
5. Click **OK**.

Embedding objects

Exam Objective: MOS Word Expert 1.1.7

Embedding an object is almost exactly like linking to one, except that you leave **Link to file** unchecked. Additionally, you can create a new, blank, embedded object, and then edit it further in its native application.

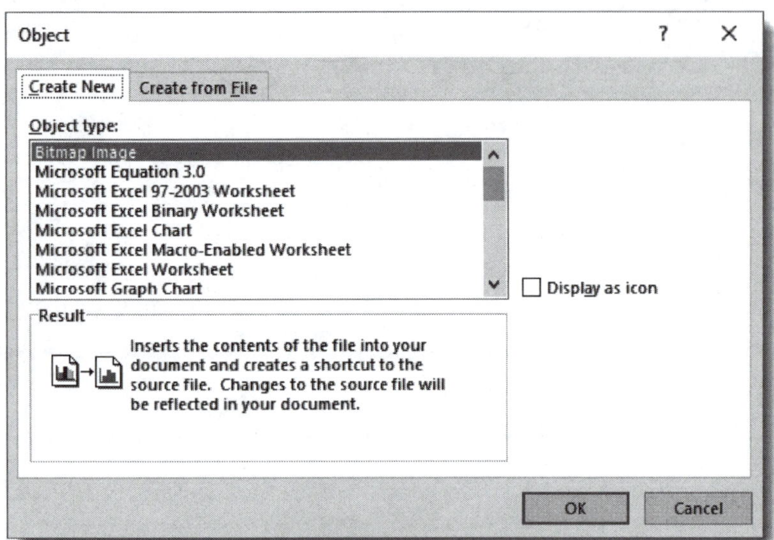

1. On the Insert tab, click Object in the Text group.
2. Choose the object to embed:
   - If you're creating a new object, select its type.
   - If you're embedding an existing file, on the Create from File tab, click **Browse**, and select the file.
3. Click **OK**.

Managing objects

Once you've linked an object, you can edit it using its source application. Depending on whether it's embedded or linked, you can also change other properties.

- To move or resize the object in Word, select it as you would an image.
- To edit the object, double-click it.
- To update a linked object, right-click it, and click **Update Link**.
- To change linking options for a linked object, right-click it, and click **Linked <Type> Object > Links**.
- To change one type of embedded object to another, right-click it, and click **<Type> Object > Convert**.

Exercise: Inserting a worksheet

For this exercise, you need to have Microsoft Excel installed. You'll embed an Excel workbook into a document.

Do This	How & Why
1. Create a new blank document.	
2. Embed `Opening budget.xlsx` as an object.	
a) On the Insert tab, click Object.	In the Text group. The **Object** window opens.
b) On the Create from File tab, click **Browse**.	A **Browse** window opens.
c) Select **Opening budget.xlsx**, and click **Insert**.	In the module data folder.
d) Click **OK**.	If you wanted to link the file instead of embed it, you can check **Link to file** first. The workbook opens in the document.
3. Click the workbook object.	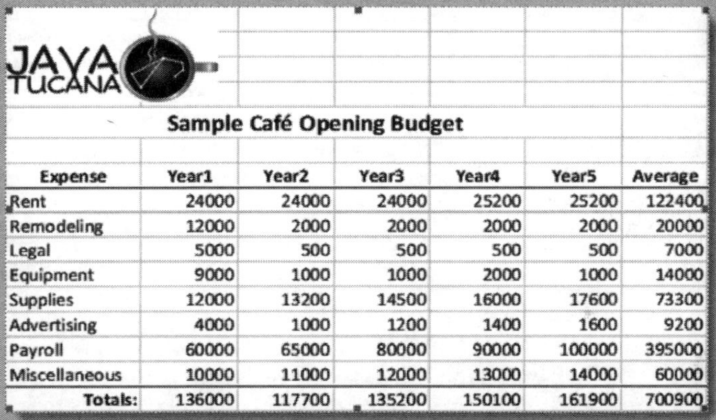 (see worksheet below) The object is selected. Resize handles appear, but you can't select anything inside it.

JAVA TUCANA

Sample Café Opening Budget

Expense	Year1	Year2	Year3	Year4	Year5	Average
Rent	24000	24000	24000	25200	25200	122400
Remodeling	12000	2000	2000	2000	2000	20000
Legal	5000	500	500	500	500	7000
Equipment	9000	1000	1000	2000	1000	14000
Supplies	12000	13200	14500	16000	17600	73300
Advertising	4000	1000	1200	1400	1600	9200
Payroll	60000	65000	80000	90000	100000	395000
Miscellaneous	10000	11000	12000	13000	14000	60000
Totals:	136000	117700	135200	150100	161900	700900

Do This	How & Why
4. Edit the object.	You'll display the workbook differently.

Do This	How & Why

a) Double-click the object.

Expense	Year1	Year2	Year3	Year4	Year5	Average
Rent	24000	24000	24000	25200	25200	122400
Remodeling	12000	2000	2000	2000	2000	20000
Legal	5000	500	500	500	500	7000
Equipment	9000	1000	1000	2000	1000	14000
Supplies	12000	13200	14500	16000	17600	73300
Advertising	4000	1000	1200	1400	1600	9200
Payroll	60000	65000	80000	90000	100000	395000
Miscellaneous	10000	11000	12000	13000	14000	60000
Totals:	136000	117700	135200	150100	161900	700900

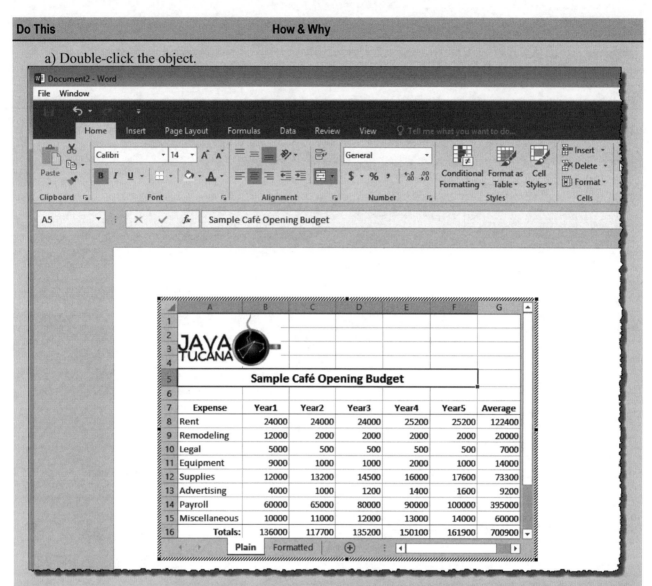

Thicker borders enclose the object. The object window itself shows the controls of an Excel workbook, and the ribbon above is replaced by Excel's ribbon.

b) Select a cell in the workbook.

You can select and edit data using any of Excel's commands.

c) At the bottom of the object, click **Formatted**.

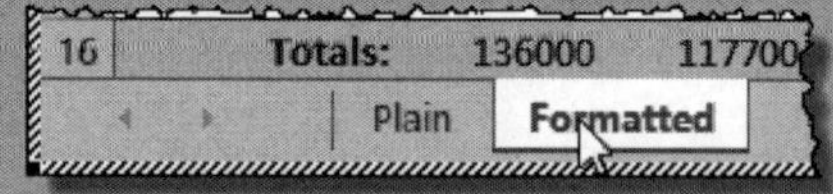

To display a different sheet in the embedded workbook. This has the same data but is formatted differently.

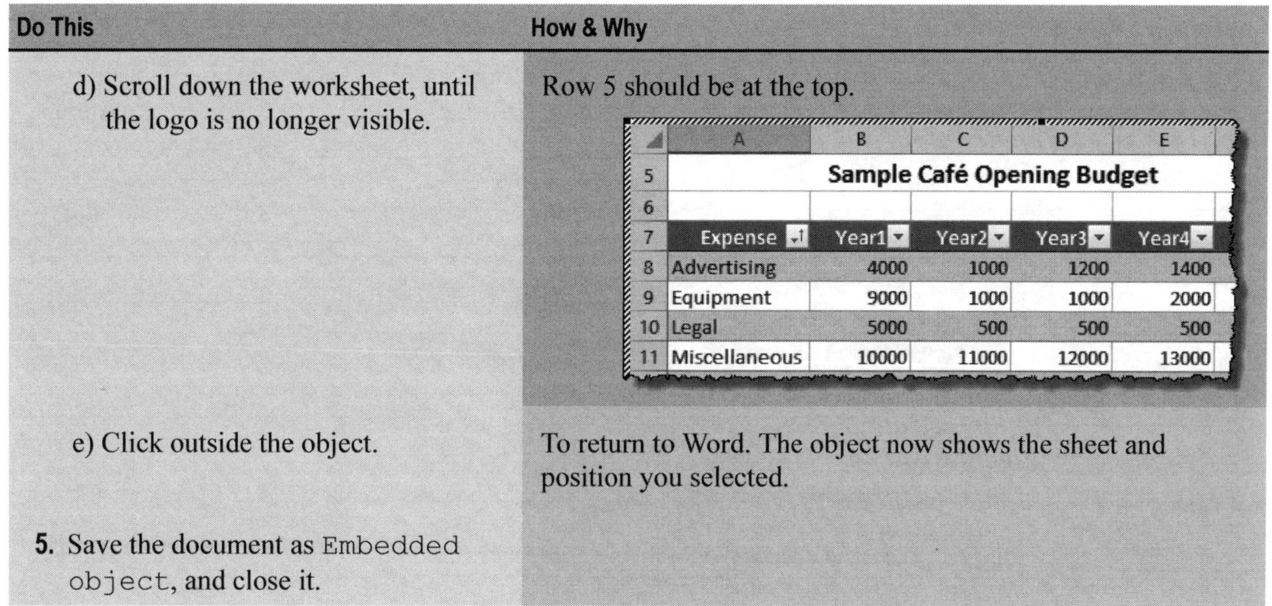

Do This	How & Why
d) Scroll down the worksheet, until the logo is no longer visible.	Row 5 should be at the top.
e) Click outside the object.	To return to Word. The object now shows the sheet and position you selected.
5. Save the document as `Embedded object`, and close it.	

	A	B	C	D	E
5	Sample Café Opening Budget				
6					
7	Expense	Year1	Year2	Year3	Year4
8	Advertising	4000	1000	1200	1400
9	Equipment	9000	1000	1000	2000
10	Legal	5000	500	500	500
11	Miscellaneous	10000	11000	12000	13000

About charts

When you insert a chart or graph into a document, it's not just a graphic. Instead, it's a graphical representation of an Excel object embedded in the document. You can edit the workbook and format the chart using all the tools included in Microsoft Excel, so there's no need to import charts from external Excel workbooks. If you don't have Excel installed, you can still create charts, but using only features included in the simpler Microsoft Graph feature included with Word.

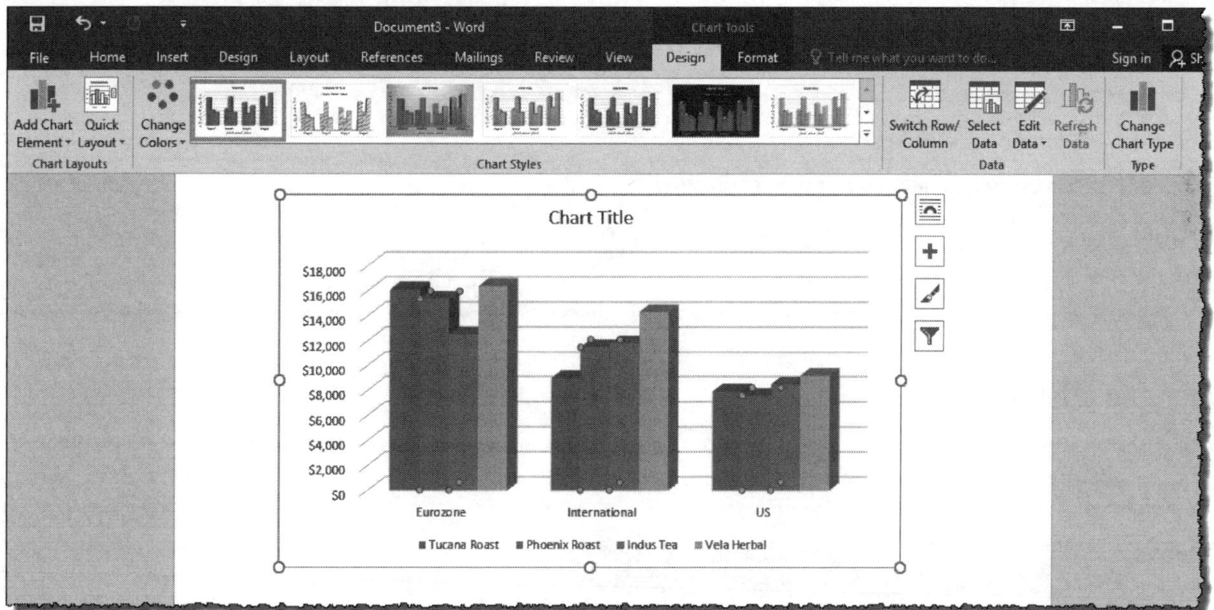

Once you've inserted a chart, you can edit its data in Excel, but the Chart Tools tabs that control its visual appearance are available on the ribbon in Word.

Inserting charts

When you insert a chart, you have to choose a chart type from the **Insert Chart** window. This creates the chart itself, as well as the underlying Excel object. The placeholder values in the Excel object are appropriate to the kind of chart you create, so although you can change the chart type later, you might need to reformat the worksheet data in doing so.

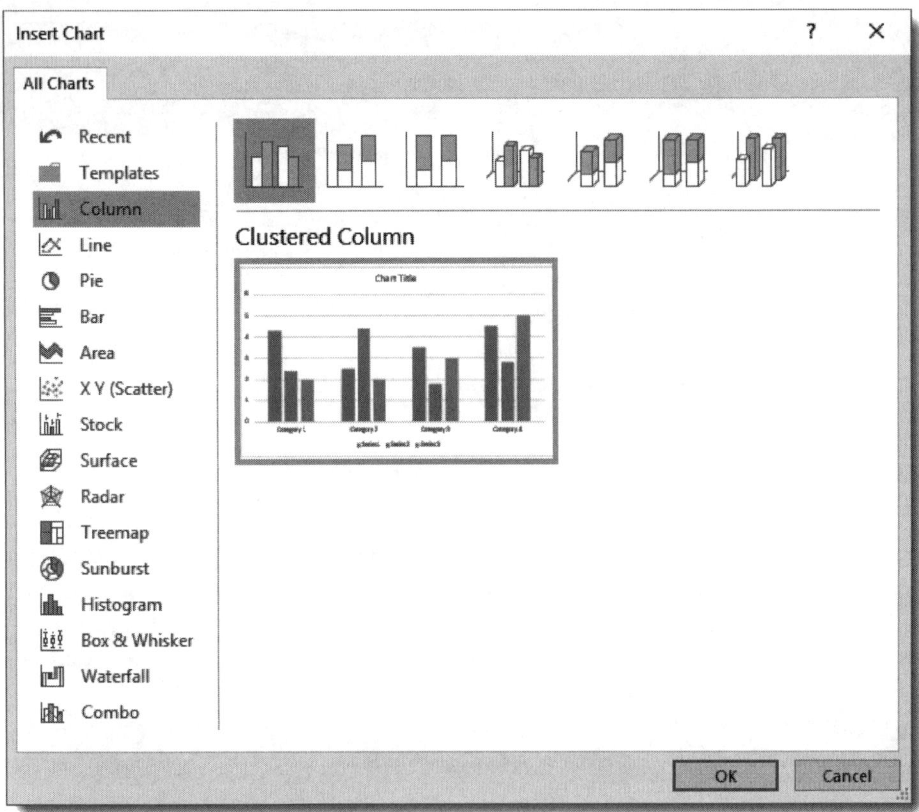

1. On the Insert tab, click **Chart**.
2. Select a chart type in the **Insert Chart** window.
3. Click **OK**.

When the chart is inserted, Excel opens with the placeholder data for you to edit.

Modifying chart data

Modifying chart data is just like editing any other Excel worksheet. You can either enter your data or paste it from another file. Excel opens automatically when you first insert a chart. To modify an existing chart, select it, and then click **Edit Data** on the Design tab.

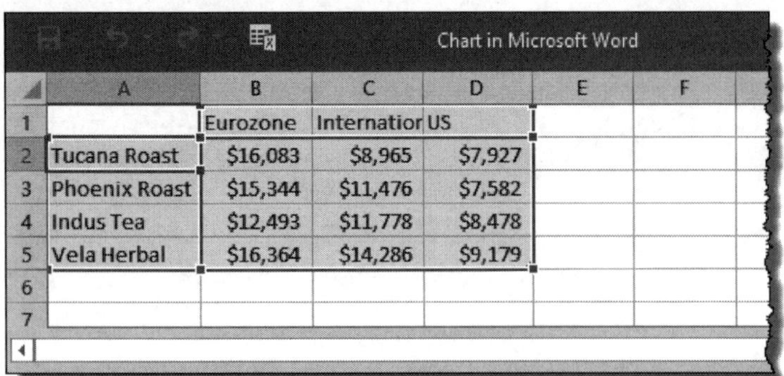

Chart in Microsoft Word

	A	B	C	D	E	F
1		Eurozone	Internatior	US		
2	Tucana Roast	$16,083	$8,965	$7,927		
3	Phoenix Roast	$15,344	$11,476	$7,582		
4	Indus Tea	$12,493	$11,778	$8,478		
5	Vela Herbal	$16,364	$14,286	$9,179		
6						
7						

- After you edit a cell, the chart automatically updates.
  You might first need to select another cell.
- The blue lines indicate the range of data represented in the chart. To change the range, drag the lower-right corner.

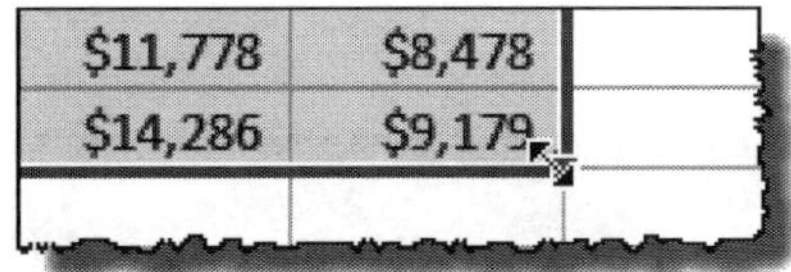

- When you're done making changes, close the workbook.
  You don't need to save your changes in Excel, only in Word.

Changing chart designs

Exam Objective: MOS Word Expert 2.1.3

When you select a chart, the Design tab appears in the ribbon's Chart Tools tab group, which provides commands for changing the data, chart type, or overall layout and style.

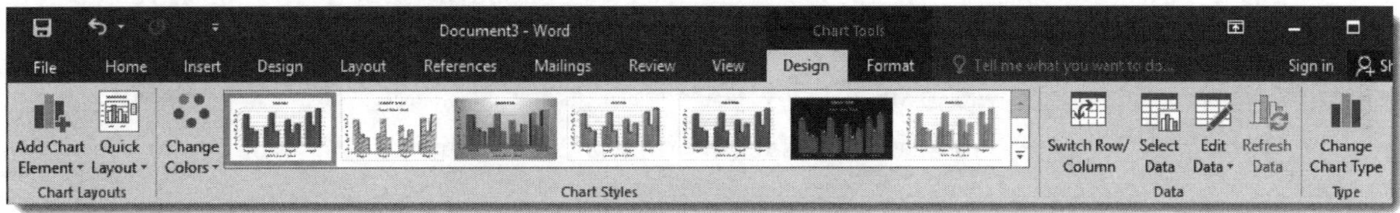

- Click **Select Data** to change the data range used by the chart.
  You can even choose a data range in another workbook you have open in Excel.
- Click **Switch Row/Column** to switch the row and column data without affecting underlying Excel data.
- Use the Chart Styles gallery to change the chart's colors and effects.
- The Chart Layouts group provides commands for adding trendlines, error bars, and other analysis indicators.
- Use the Quick Layout gallery to choose between preset chart arrangements.
- Click **Change Chart Type** to select a different chart type.
- Click **Save as Template** to save the current chart design in the Templates pane of the Change Chart Type window.
- The **Add Chart Elements** button in the Chart Layouts group has options for displaying the chart title, axes, legend, and data labels.
- The Data group provides options for manipulating chart data, such as swapping x and y axes.

Changing chart layouts

When you select a chart, the Format tab appears in the Chart Tools tab group on the ribbon. It has commands to select parts of the chart, change the display of its labels and axes, and display additional analytical markings. However, some chart layout options are located on the Design tab's Chart Layouts group.

Exam Objective: MOS Word Expert 2.1.3

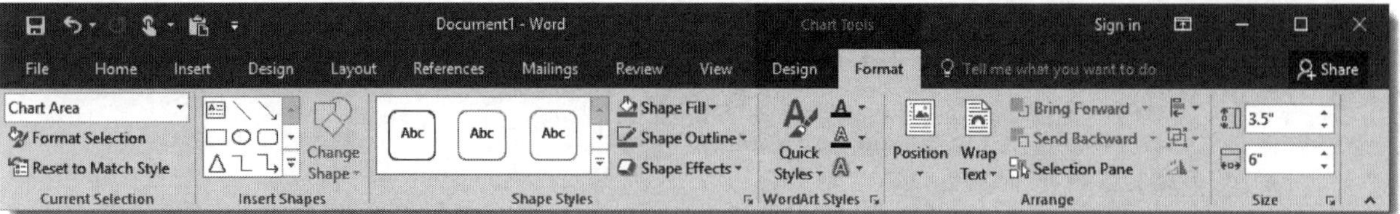

Note: The goal of any chart is the clear presentation of data. It's good to add more labels or analysis tools if they make the chart easier to read, but it's easy to display so much information that it crowds the graphic and makes it confusing rather than clearer.

- Use the Current Selection list to select a chart element. You can then click **Format Selection** or use the Format tab to change just that element.
- The Shape Styles group has options for formatting the plot area and the background of 3-D charts.
- The Insert Shapes group provides options for adding various kinds of shapes to your charts.
- The Arrange group allows you to specify how you'd like the chart to appear vis-à-vis text in a document.
- The WordArt Styles group provides options for inserting and specifying types of WordArt text in your charts.

Exercise: Creating a chart

For this exercise, you also need to have Microsoft Excel installed. You'll create and format a simple chart.

Do This	How & Why
1. Create a new blank document.	Press **Ctrl+N**.
2. Maximize the Word window.	
3. Insert a chart.	
a) On the Insert tab, click **Chart**.	The **Insert Chart** window appears.
b) Examine the available chart types.	Each category is suitable for different types of data.

Do This	How & Why
c) In the right pane, click **3-D Clustered Column**.	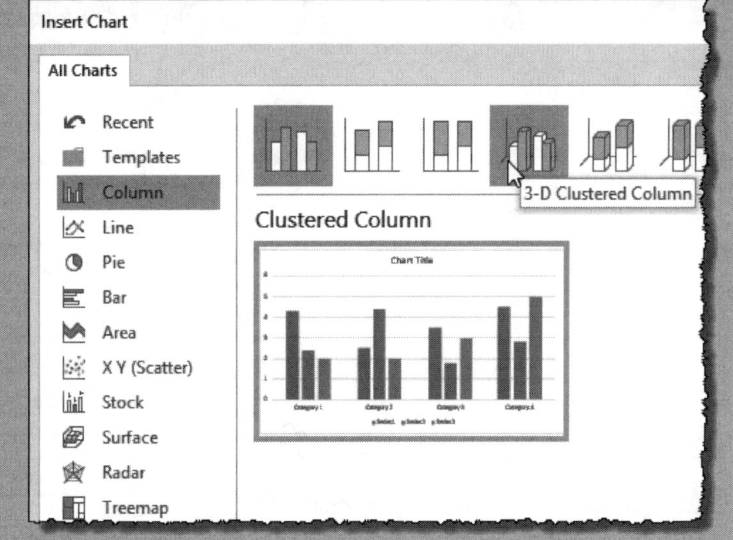

d) Click **OK**.

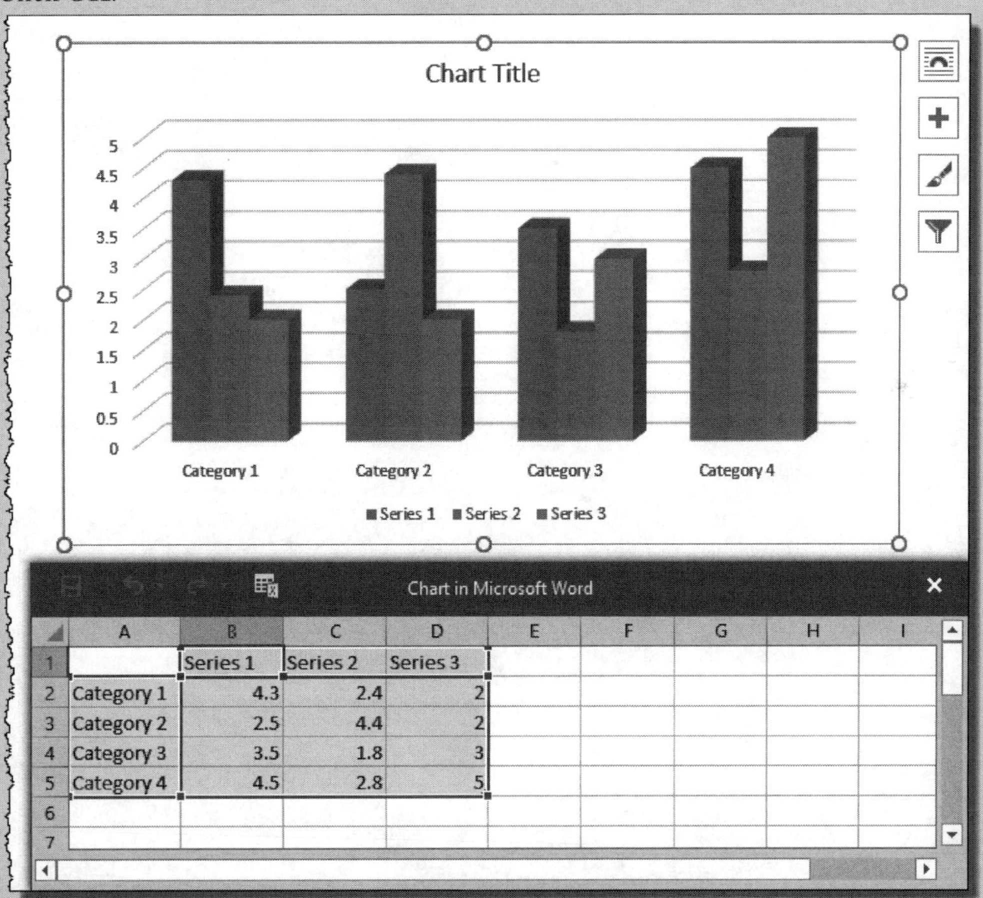

	A	B	C	D
1		Series 1	Series 2	Series 3
2	Category 1	4.3	2.4	2
3	Category 2	2.5	4.4	2
4	Category 3	3.5	1.8	3
5	Category 4	4.5	2.8	5

The chart appears in the document. Excel also appears, showing the placeholder data in a spreadsheet.

4. Modify the chart data.	You can also copy and paste the cells from `Chart data.xlsx`.

Do This	How & Why

a) In cell A2, type `Tucana Roast`, then press **Enter**.

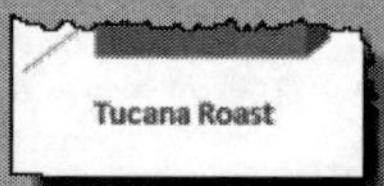

The first category on the chart is automatically updated.

b) Enter the data as shown:

	Eurozone	Internatior	US
Tucana Roast	$16,083	$8,965	$7,927
Phoenix Roast	$15,344	$11,476	$7,582
Indus Tea	$12,493	$11,778	$8,478
Vela Herbal	$16,364	$14,286	$9,179

c) In Word, on the Design tab, click **Switch Row/Column**.

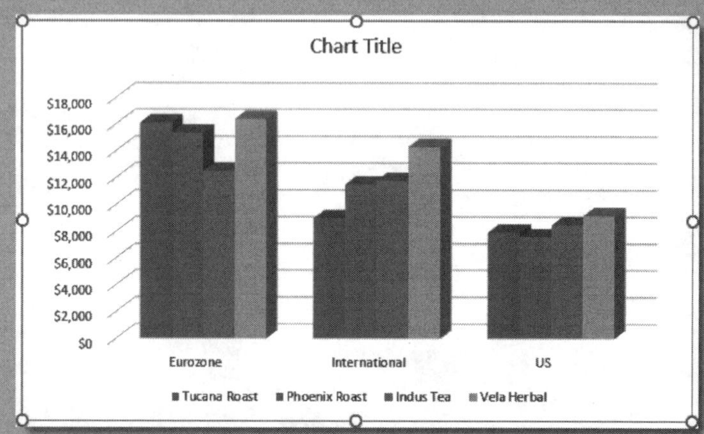

Now each zone is shown as a category, and each product as a series. The Excel data isn't changed.

d) Close Excel. — You'll do the rest of the formatting in Word.

5. Format the chart's appearance.

a) If necessary, on the Design tab, click **Add Chart Element > Chart Title > Above Chart**. — A chart title box appears above the chart, and the chart itself is resized to fit.

b) Edit the chart title to read `Sales by Region`.

c) Click **Add Chart Element > Axes > Primary Vertical Axis**. — The vertical axis labels of the chart now display sales values.

d) Right-click anywhere on the vertical axis sales values, and click **Format Axis**. — In the context menu. The Format Axis pane opens.

Do This	How & Why
e) Open the Display Units list, and click **Thousands**.	Under Axis Options. The values in the vertical axis are now displayed in thousands of dollars, and the axis label "Thousands" appears. 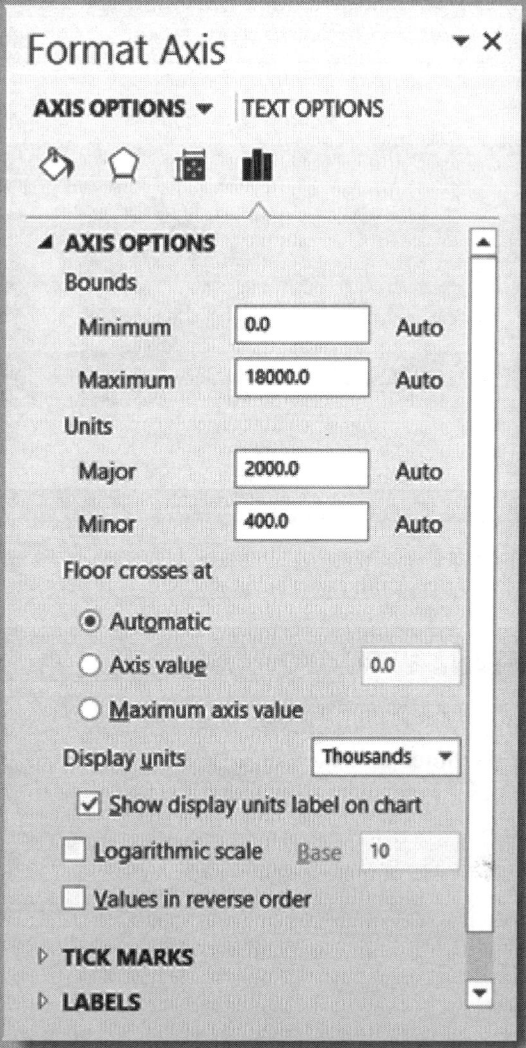
f) On the chart, click in the original vertical axis title placeholder box, and press **Delete**. Then delete the horizontal axis title placeholder.	Both these placeholders are now unnecessary.
6. Save the chart design as a template.	
a) On the Design tab, click **Save As Template**.	The **Save Chart Template** window opens.
b) Type `Sales Chart` and click **Save**.	The next time you make a chart, this design will be in the Templates section.

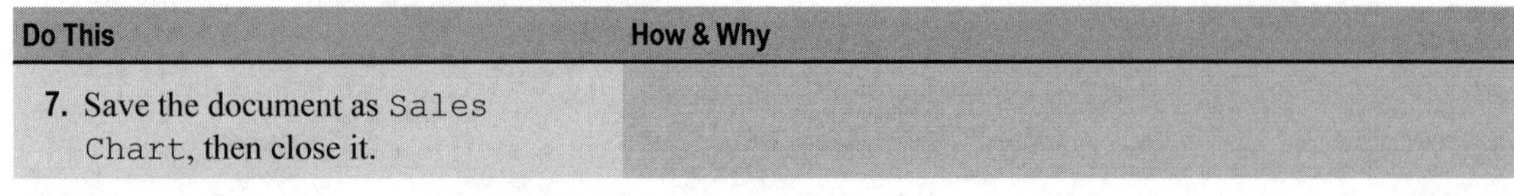

Do This	How & Why
7. Save the document as `Sales Chart`, then close it.	

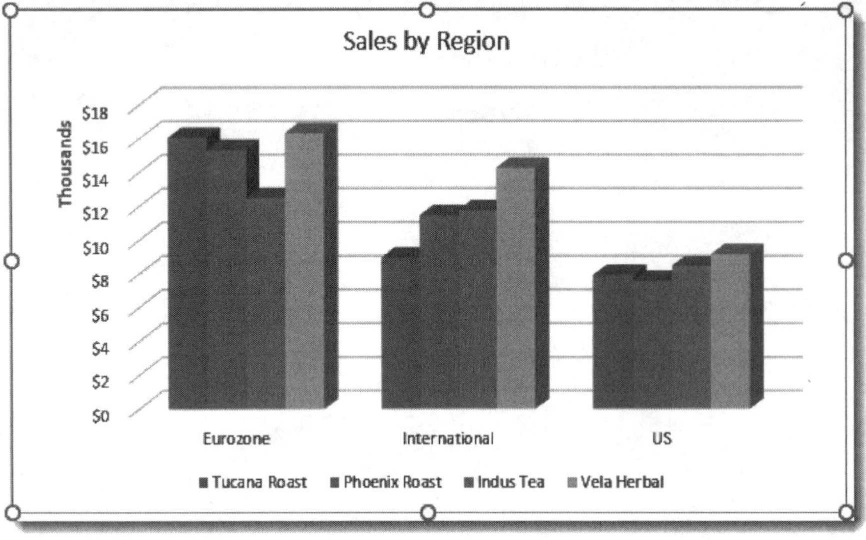

The Formula window

Tables in Word are primarily meant as a layout tool for presenting information. If you want to perform calculations on tables of data, you're better off using a spreadsheet application such as Excel. Still, if your needs are simple, you can use the **Formula** window to perform logical or mathematical operations in a table.

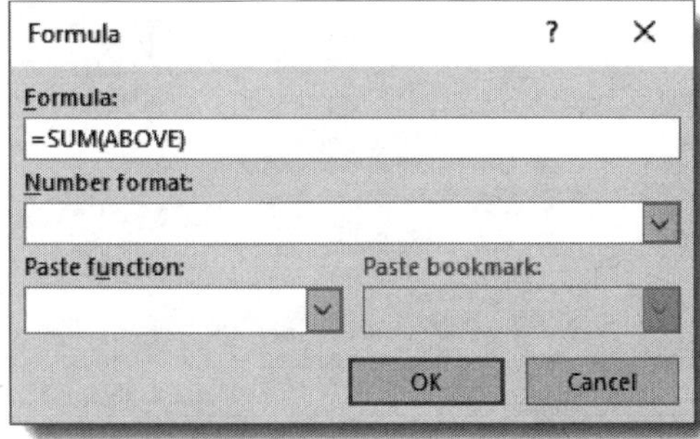

Formulas you create in Word documents are stored as field codes. They update whenever you open the document, and you can manually update them at any time.

Inserting formulas

If you're familiar with Excel formulas, Word formulas aren't difficult to construct.

- Every formula must begin with an equal sign ("=").
- Formulas themselves contain functions, and data for the functions to act upon.
- Data can be entered as values, or as references to cells or ranges in the table.

Exam Objective: MOS Word Core 3.2.5

For example, `=MAX(A1, 12)` displays the value in cell A1 or the number 12, whichever is greater.

1. On the Table Tools Layout tab, click **Formula**.
   In the Data group.

2. Enter the formula in the Formula field.
   - You can choose functions from the Paste Function list instead of typing them.
   - Depending on data already in the table, Word may automatically suggest a formula, such as a row or column sum.
3. Optionally, choose a format for the formula's results from the "Number format" list.
4. Click **OK**.

Exercise: Inserting a formula

In this exercise, you'll create formulas in a Word table.

Do This	How & Why
1. Open `Table Calculations`.	In the module data folder. This file contains a table with regional sales data for four products. You'll create regional totals from the data.
2. Save the document as `Table with totals.xlsx`.	
3. Use a formula to calculate total sales in the Eurozone region.	
a) Click inside the blank cell at the bottom of the second column.	The Table Tools tab group appears.
b) On the Layout tab, click **Formula**.	The **Formula** window opens. Because it's at the bottom of a column of data, Word already entered =SUM(ABOVE) as a formula. That's what you want, but you'll look at other options too.
c) Click the **Paste function** list.	To display a list of functions.
d) Click away from the list.	To close it again.

Do This	How & Why
e) Click **OK**,	Regional Total $60,284.00 If you click the number, you'll see that it has the gray highlighting of a field code.
4. Create totals for the International and US regions.	In each cell, click **Formula**, then click **OK**.
5. Save and close the document.	

2014 Sales:	Eurozone	International	US
Tucana Roast	$16,083	$8,965	$7,927
Phoenix Roast	$15,344	$11,476	$7,582
Indus Tea	$12,493	$11,778	$8,478
Vela Herbal	$16,364	$14,286	$9,179
Regional Total	$60,284.00	$46,505.00	$33,166.00

Assessment: Tables and charts

1. Which descriptions are true of embedded objects? Choose all that apply.
   - They can be edited in the source application.
   - They can be copied or shared without worrying about access to external files.
   - They lead to larger document file sizes than linked objects do.
   - They lead to smaller document file sizes than linked objects do.
   - They reflect any changes made to the original file.
2. What is true of linked objects? Choose all that apply.
   - They can be edited in the source application.
   - They can be copied or shared without worrying about access to external files.
   - They lead to larger Word document file sizes than embedded objects do.
   - They lead to smaller Word document file sizes than embedded objects do.
   - They reflect any changes made to the original file.
3. A Word chart is very much like an embedded Excel object. True or false?
   - True
   - False
4. If you don't have Excel installed, you can't use formulas in Word tables. True or false?
   - True
   - False

Module B: Creating building blocks

Word makes much use of building blocks, or Quick Parts. They're not only found in the Quick Parts gallery, but in other galleries throughout the application: headers, footers, tables, text boxes, and more. You're not limited to what's built in; you can create your own building blocks from content you want to reuse.

You will learn how to:

- Create building blocks
- Manage building blocks
- Save building blocks

The Building Blocks Organizer

Exam Objective: MOS Word Core 5.1.3

It's easy to use building blocks without really thinking much about them, but the more you do, the more ways you find to use them. If you've ever saved a custom header or watermark, you've created a building block that appears in its own appropriate gallery. If you keep formatting your page numbers the same way by hand, that's something you can save as a building block. If you have your company contact information saved in a document somewhere, and paste it into new documents rather than typing it out every time, you're basically working with a building block. However, you could save even more time just by saving it as a quick part.

Whether they're headers, footers, formulas, quick parts, or anything else, you can access your full list of building blocks from the Building Blocks Organizer. To do so, in the Insert tab's Text group, click **Quick Parts > Building Blocks Organizer**.

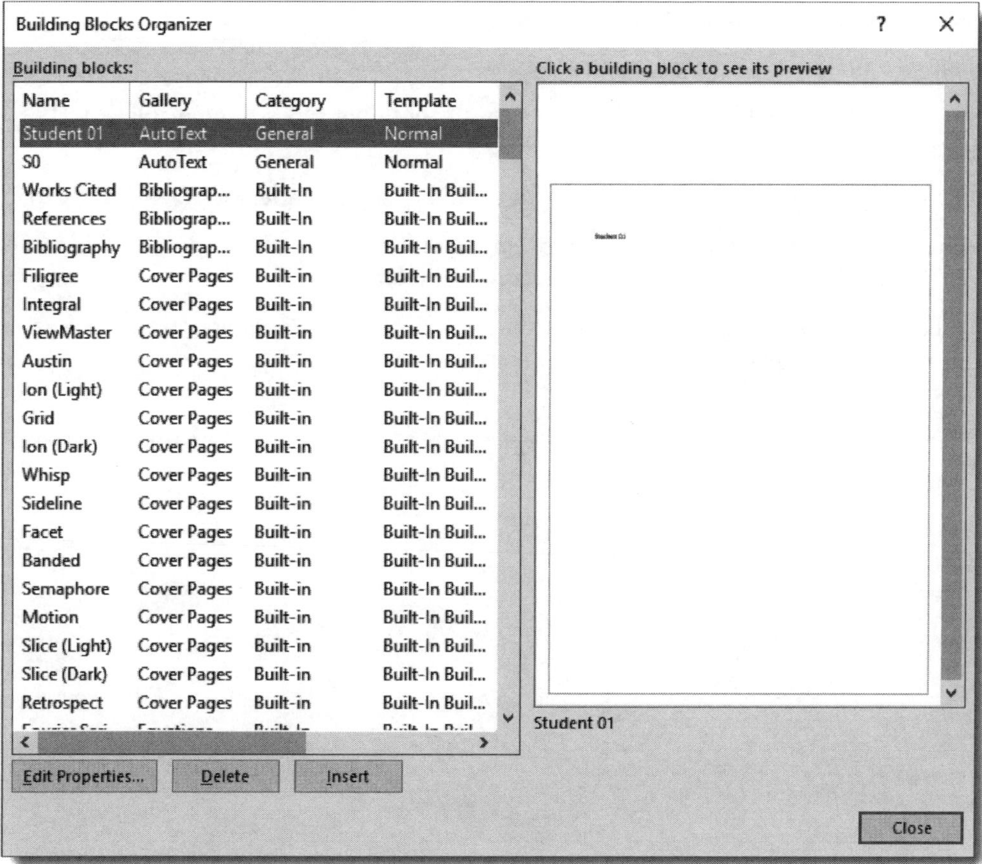

Creating building blocks

You can create any kind of building block from any selection you want, preserving both the content and its formatting. Regardless of what gallery you add the content to, you just need to open the **Create New Building Block** window.

Exam Objective: MOS Word Expert 1.1.8, 4.1.1, 4.1.3, 4.1.4

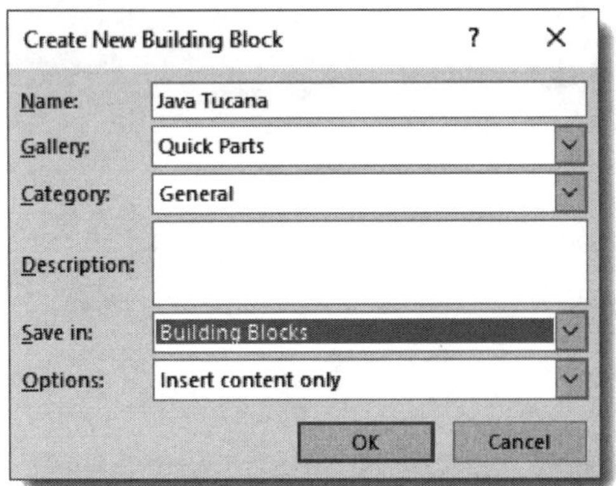

You can create a new building block in any gallery from any command that lets you open the window. Although the following steps show you how to use the Quick Parts gallery, you can likewise click **Header > Save Selection to Header Gallery**. All that would be different is the default gallery listed in the window: you can still even save it as a Quick Part.

1. Select content that's already formatted exactly as you want to save it.
2. On the Insert tab, click **Quick Parts > Save Selection to Quick Parts Gallery**.

   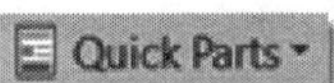

3. Type a name and description for the building block.
4. Choose how you want the building block to be saved.
   - From the **Gallery** list, choose the gallery in which you want the building block to be displayed. By default, it is Quick Parts.
   - From the **Category** list, choose from the existing categories in the chosen gallery, or create a new one.
   - From the **Save in** list, choose the template where you want the building block to be stored. This can be `Normal.dotm`, `Building Blocks.dotx`, or a custom template.
5. Choose insertion options for the building block. You can choose to have it inserted wherever you place it, in its own paragraph, or on its own page.
6. Click **OK**.

Modifying building blocks

To modify existing building block settings, click **Quick Parts > Building Blocks Organizer** on the Insert tab.

Exam Objective: MOS Word Expert 4.1.3, 4.1.4

- To change a building block's settings, select it, and choose **Edit Properties**.

  The **Modify Building Block** window is exactly like the **Create New Building Block** window. You can not only change the building block's name and description, but also its options and where it's stored.
- To delete a building block, select it, and click **Delete**.
- To edit building block contents, don't use the Building Block Organizer; instead, edit it in the document, then save it as a new building block using the same name.

  You're asked if you want to redefine the building block.

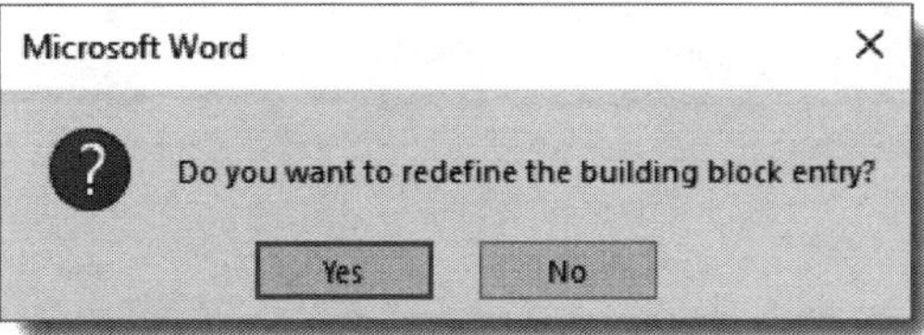

Saving building blocks

The Building Blocks template is a file, so when you change it, those changes need to be saved. Because it's not a normal file, you can't simply click the Save button; instead, you're asked whether you want to save it when you close Word.

1. Save and close all open documents.
2. Close Word.

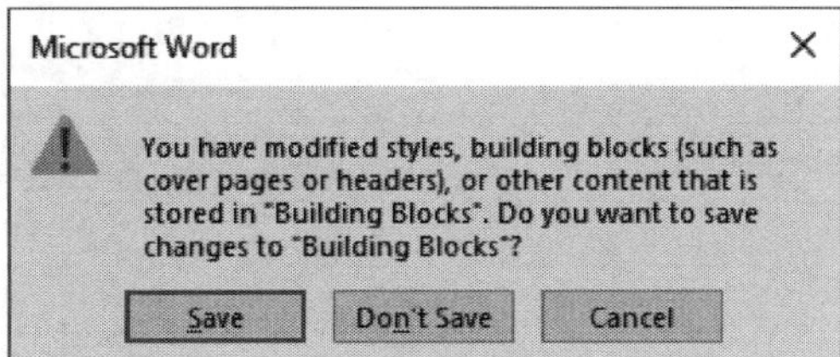

3. Click **Save**.

Exercise: Using building blocks

In this exercise, you'll create new building blocks from formatted text, then insert them into another document.

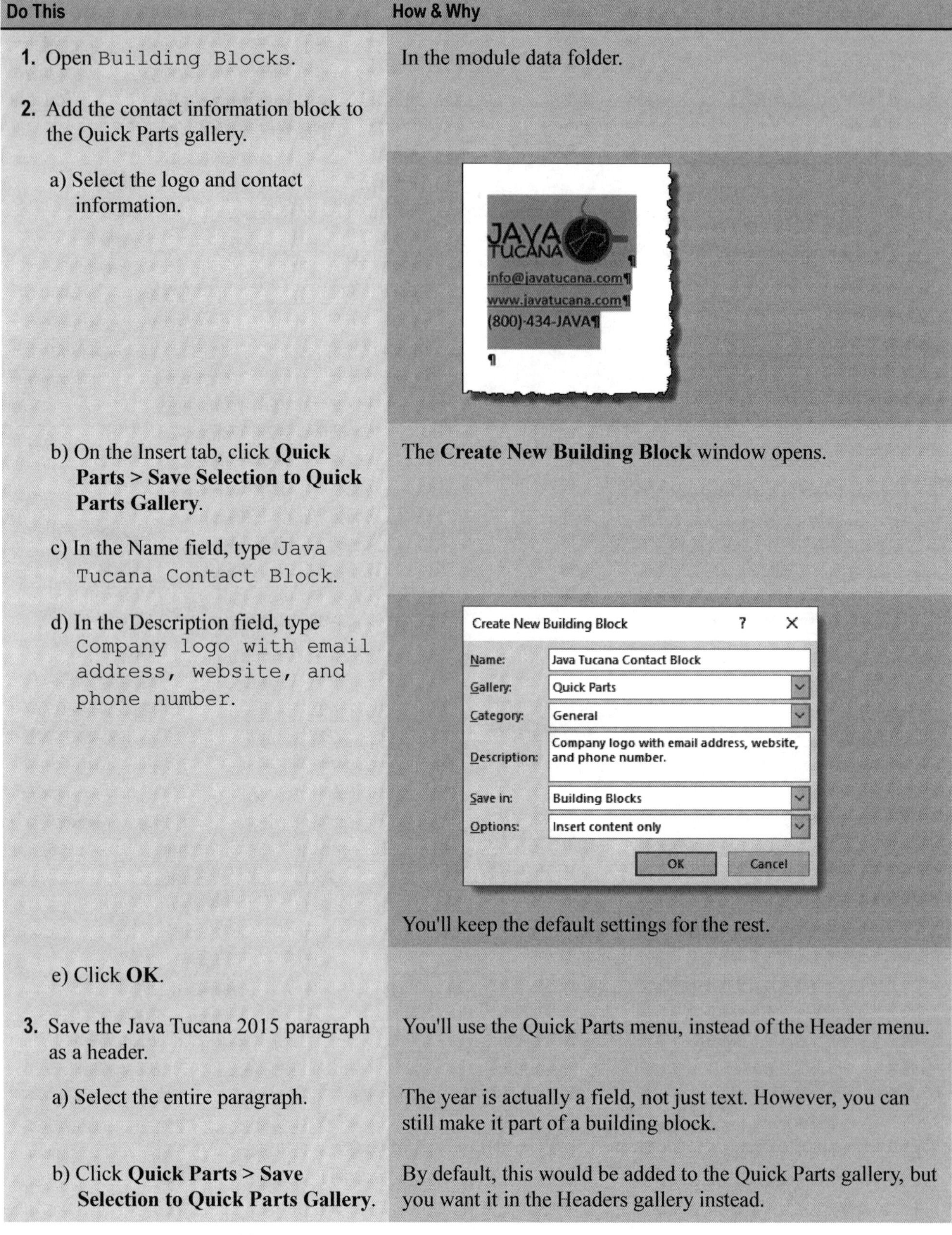

Do This	How & Why
1. Open `Building Blocks`.	In the module data folder.
2. Add the contact information block to the Quick Parts gallery.	
a) Select the logo and contact information.	JAVA TUCANA ¶ info@javatucana.com¶ www.javatucana.com¶ (800)-434-JAVA¶ ¶
b) On the Insert tab, click **Quick Parts > Save Selection to Quick Parts Gallery**.	The **Create New Building Block** window opens.
c) In the Name field, type `Java Tucana Contact Block`.	
d) In the Description field, type `Company logo with email address, website, and phone number`.	Create New Building Block ? X Name: Java Tucana Contact Block Gallery: Quick Parts Category: General Description: Company logo with email address, website, and phone number. Save in: Building Blocks Options: Insert content only OK Cancel You'll keep the default settings for the rest.
e) Click **OK**.	
3. Save the Java Tucana 2015 paragraph as a header.	You'll use the Quick Parts menu, instead of the Header menu.
a) Select the entire paragraph.	The year is actually a field, not just text. However, you can still make it part of a building block.
b) Click **Quick Parts > Save Selection to Quick Parts Gallery**.	By default, this would be added to the Quick Parts gallery, but you want it in the Headers gallery instead.

Do This	How & Why
c) From the Gallery list, select **Headers**.	Notice that the Category automatically changes, as the Headers gallery has a different set of categories.
d) From the Category list, choose **Create New Category**.	The **Create New Category** window opens. 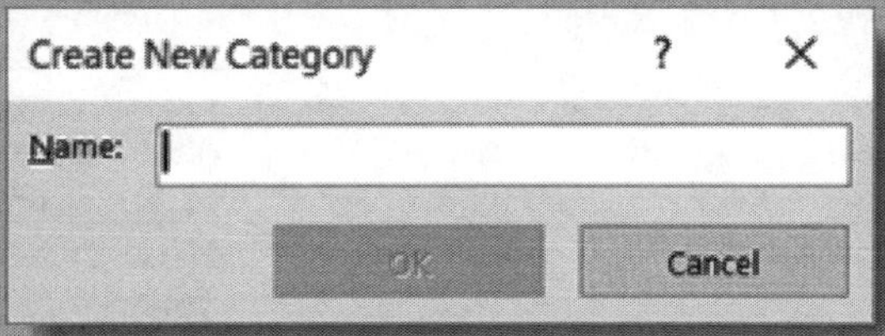 Create New Category ? X Name: OK Cancel
e) Type `Custom Headers` and click **OK**.	Custom Headers is now shown in the Category list.
f) Click **OK**.	
4. Close **Word**.	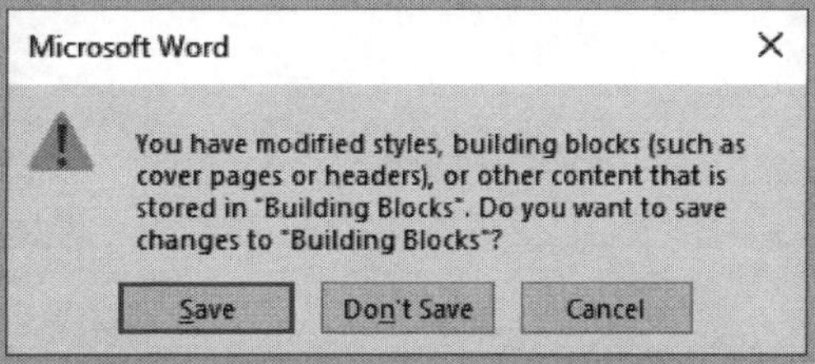 Microsoft Word X You have modified styles, building blocks (such as cover pages or headers), or other content that is stored in "Building Blocks". Do you want to save changes to "Building Blocks"? Save Don't Save Cancel Word asks whether you want to save changes to the Building Blocks template.
5. Click **Save**.	
6. Open `About Us`.	Open Word again, or just double-click the file in Windows Explorer.
7. Save the file as `About Us 2015`.	Or the current year.
8. Insert the new building blocks you've created.	
a) Place the insertion point immediately to the left of Java Tucana Services.	Just below the document title.

Do This	How & Why
b) Click **Quick Parts > Java Tucana Contact Block**.	 Because you saved the quick part in the Building Blocks template, it's now available for all documents. The contact information block is inserted just below the title. The formatting isn't changed, but because it used style colors, it's updated to match those of the current document.
c) On the Insert tab, click **Header**.	To open the Headers gallery.
d) Scroll down.	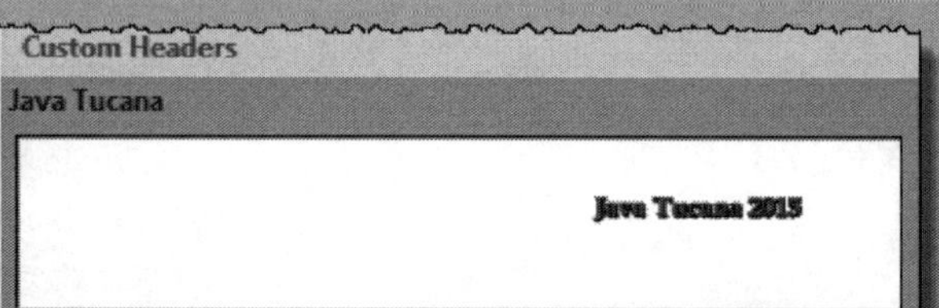 The Custom Headers category appears at the bottom of the gallery.
e) Click **Java Tucana**.	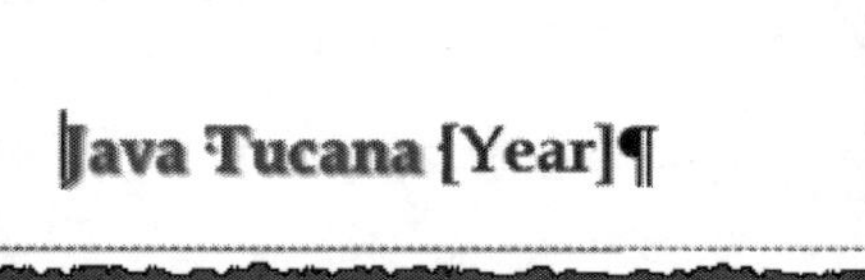 Because the building block was saved as a header, it automatically inserts itself into the document header. The formatting is preserved, but the field is blank.
9. Set the year in the header.	
a) Click **[Year]**.	To activate the field.
b) Click the arrow to the right of the field code.	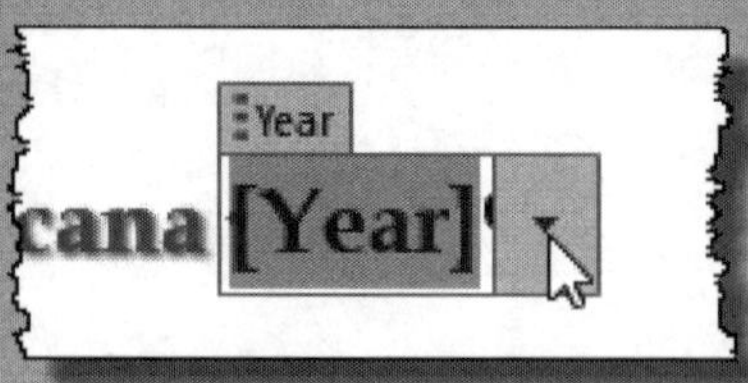 A **Date Picker** window opens.

Do This	How & Why
c) Click **Today**.	To enter the current year. 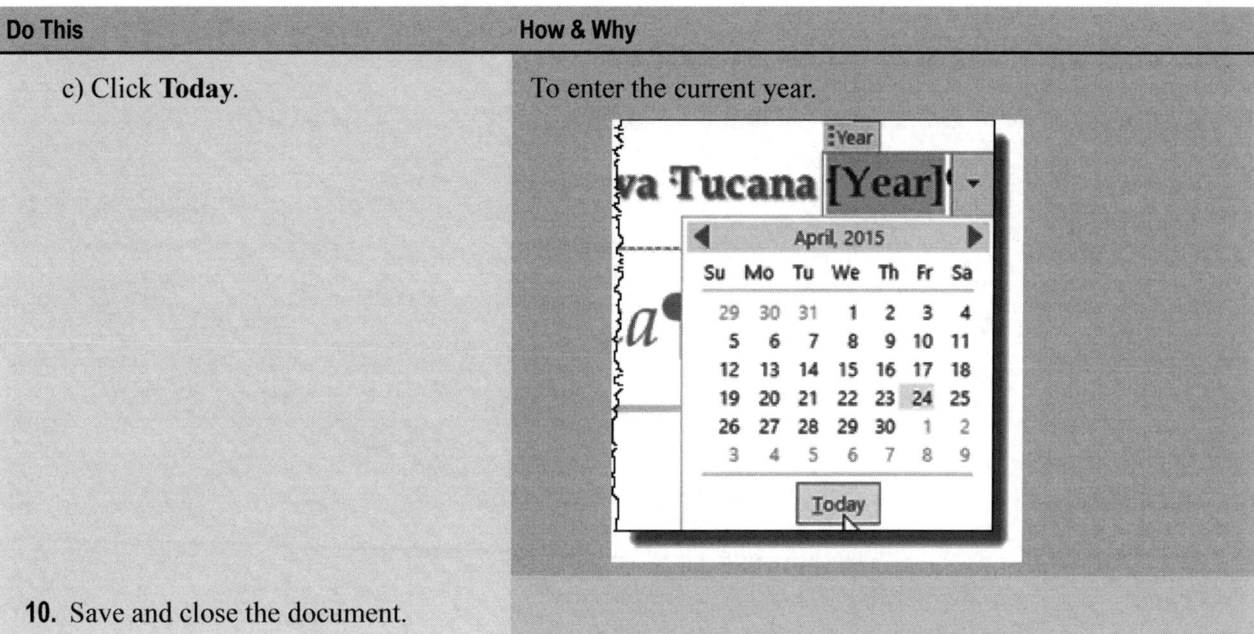
10. Save and close the document.	

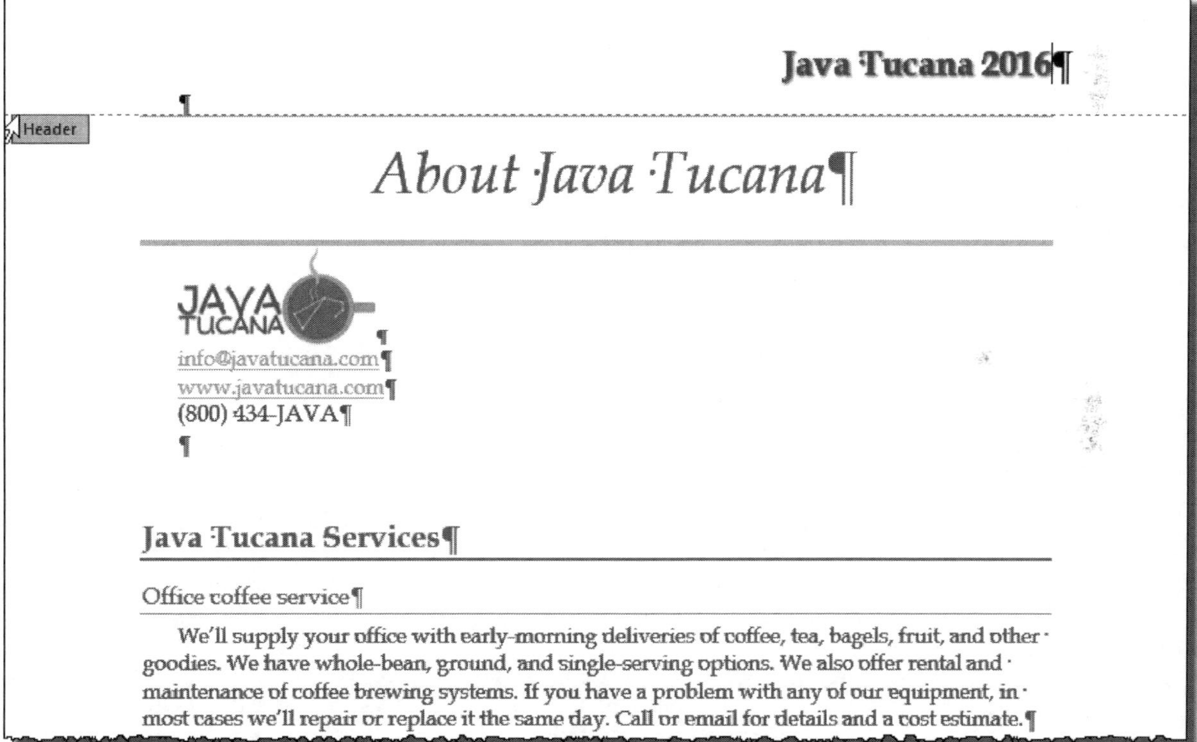

Assessment: Creating building blocks

1. What can't you do from within the Building Blocks Organizer?
    - Delete a building block.
    - Edit a building block's contents.
    - Edit a building block's properties.
    - View all your building blocks in one place.
2. The Building Blocks template is saved in the background without any user interaction. True or false?
    - True
    - False
3. It's easy to move a building block from one gallery to another. True or false?
    - True
    - False

Module C: Linking text

It's common to use text boxes as a stylized way to present a few choice words, but you can also use them as a layout element for larger amounts of text. You can even format your entire document by *linking* multiple text boxes so that text can flow smoothly from one to the next.

You will learn how to:

- Link text boxes
- Break links between text boxes

About linked text boxes

Word isn't really intended for desktop publishing, but it still has most of the features you need to make complex layouts for flyers, magazines, books, or other publications. One of these features is the concept of the *story*, or a single flow of text that passes from one layout box to another, and can be selected or edited together as one.

Text selected across multiple linked boxes

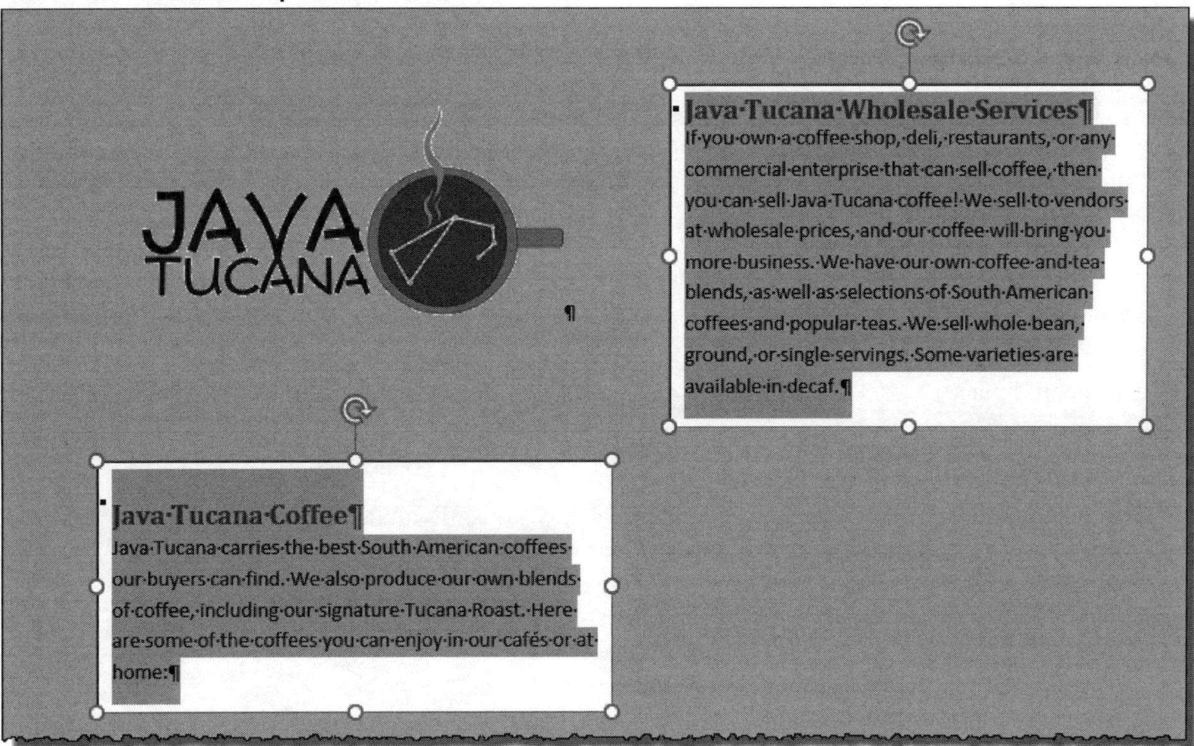

When you link text boxes together into a single story, you can type or paste text into the first of them, and when it fills up that box, it moves to the next text box, in sequence. Within the story, you can select and format text just as if it were in a single contiguous part of the document; however, the boxes are arranged on the page. The boxes themselves define how the text is placed and in what order: when you edit text, or resize the boxes, Word automatically rearranges it to fit the available space.

Linking text boxes

You can create a single story using up to 32 text boxes. The order of text boxes within one story isn't determined by their placement in the document, but only by the order in which you link them.

Exam Objective: MOS Word Expert 2.1.7

1. Select the first text box.
2. Click Create Link on the Format tab.
3. Click the next text box.

   You know when you're pointing to an appropriate place when the pointer turns into a pitcher icon.

   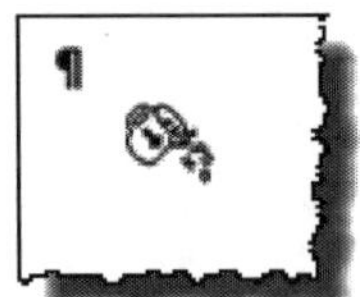

4. Repeat the process as necessary, selecting the second text box and then linking it to the third.

Breaking text box links

To break a link anywhere in a story, select the box just before the link, and click Break Link on the Format tab. When you've linked just two text boxes, this is simple; but especially for longer stories, there's more to keep in mind.

- Only the link you selected is broken. For example, if you had four boxes linked in sequence, and you broke the link between box 2 and box 3, you'd have two stories: one consisting of boxes 1 and 2, and the other of boxes 3 and 4.
- The text all remains on the side before the link: in the above example, boxes 3 and 4 would be empty, and you could place new text there.
- No text is lost when you break a link, but if there's not enough space, it doesn't all display until you add more space.
- Deleting a box in the middle of a story doesn't break any links. If you had three boxes and deleted the middle one, the text would now flow directly from the first to the third.

Exercise: Creating a story

In this exercise, you'll lay out a flyer using linked text boxes.

Do This	How & Why
1. Open `Wholesale flyer`.	From the module data folder. This document has three text boxes, with space left for placing graphics around each.
2. Save the document as `Wholesale linked`.	
3. Paste the contents of `Wholesale services` into the first text box.	
a) Open `Wholesale services`.	This document contains the text you'll place across the three text boxes.
b) Copy the entire document.	Press **Ctrl+A** to select all, then **Ctrl+C** to copy.
c) Close `Wholesale services`.	`Wholesale linked` is still open.
d) Paste the selection into the upper-right text box.	Click inside the box, then press **Ctrl+V**. 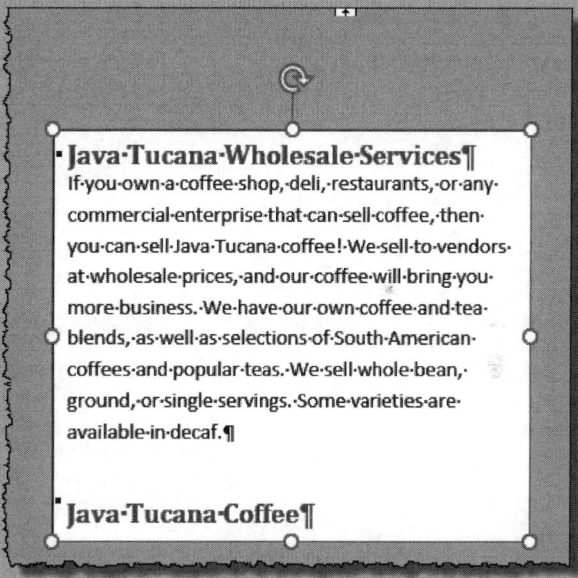
4. Link the three text boxes into a single story.	Notice that the document already contained a link between the first and third text boxes. You need to remove it to fix the link order.
a) Select the first text box again.	
b) On the Format tab, click  Break Link.	In the Text group. The text in the third box vanishes. It's still in the first box, but it's too long for it.
c) Click  Create Link.	In the same place the Break Link button was.

Do This	How & Why
d) Point to the second text box.	The pointer turns to a pitcher icon. 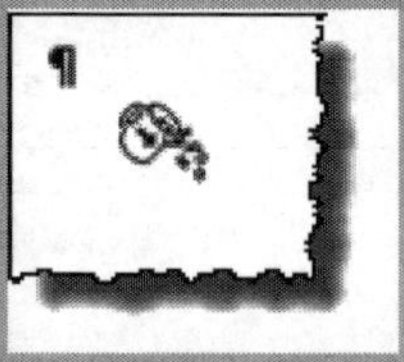 ¶
e) Click inside the middle box.	 Java·Tucana·carries·the·best·South·American·coffees·our·buyers·can·find.·We·also·produce·our·own·blends·of·coffee,·including·our·signature·Tucana·Roast.·Here·are·some·of·the·coffees·you·can·enjoy·in·our·cafés·or·at·home:¶ Single-region·South·American·coffees·¶
f) Link the second box to the third.	Select the middle box, if necessary, and click **Create Link**. Then click the last box.
5. Rearrange the text flow through the three boxes.	The story doesn't break evenly across the three boxes. You could edit the text, but in this case, you'll resize the boxes.
a) Select the top text box.	
b) Point to the lower resize handle of the box.	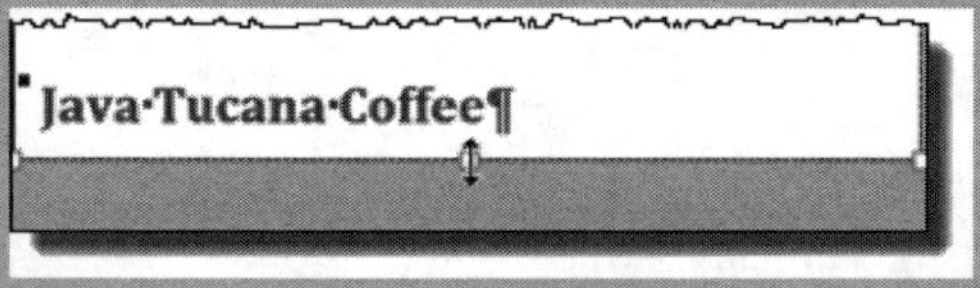 Java·Tucana·Coffee¶
c) Drag the lower edge of the text box upward.	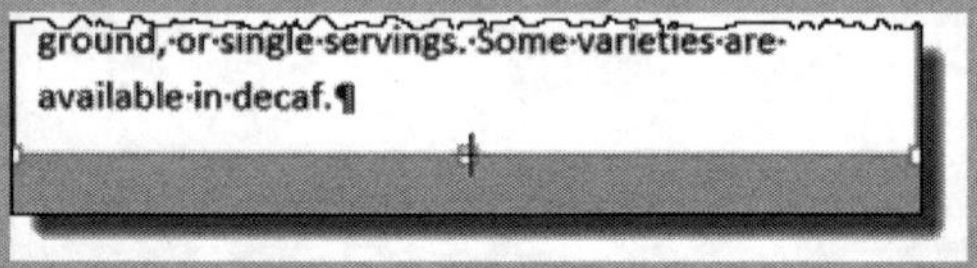 ground,·or·single·servings.·Some·varieties·are·available·in·decaf.¶ The middle box now begins with the Java Tucana Coffee header.
d) If necessary, resize the middle box to fit the entire paragraph below the header.	Select the lower resize handle and pull it downward.
e) Resize the last box to fit only the remaining text and paragraph mark below it.	
6. Save and close the document.	

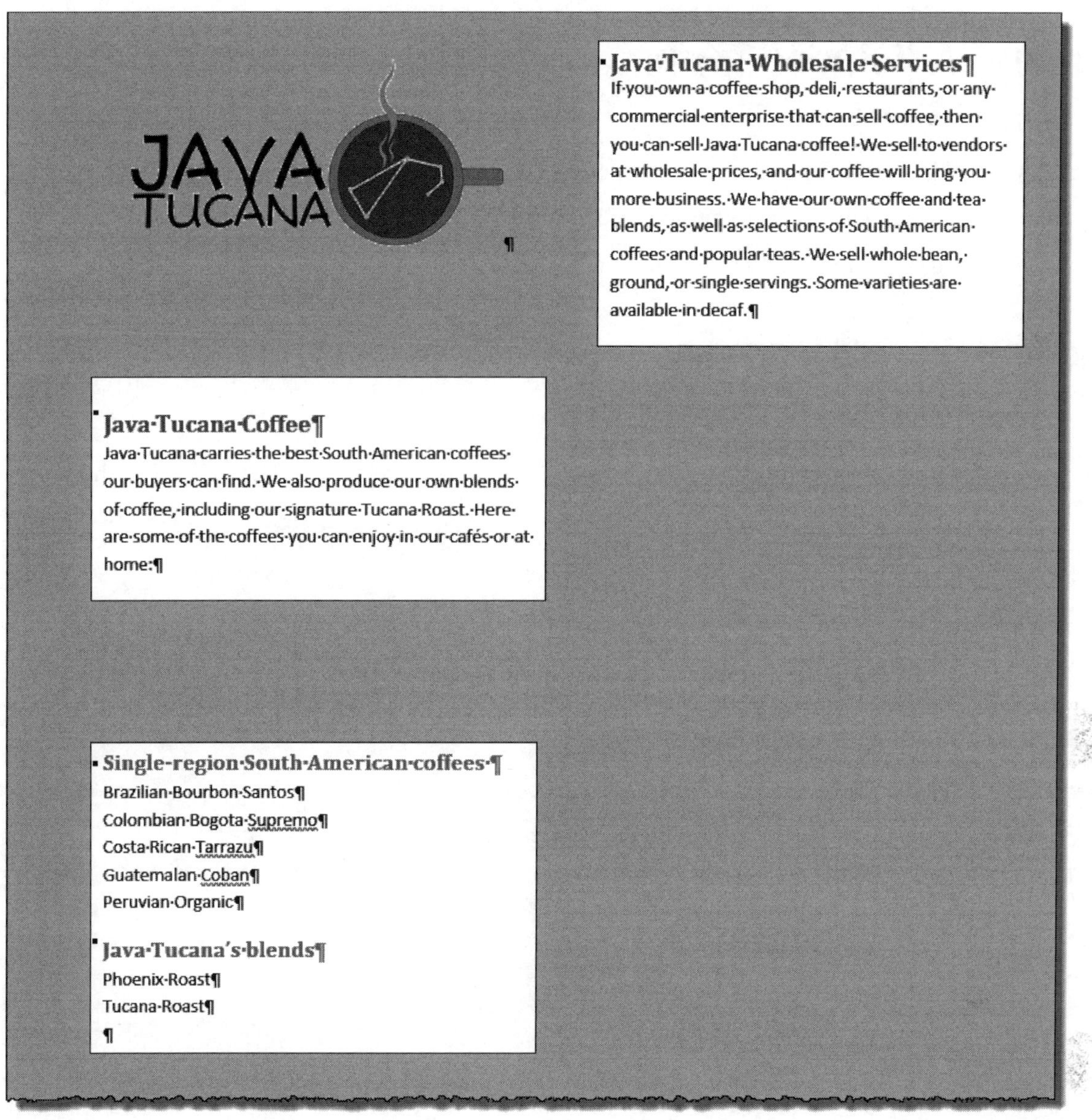

Assessment: Linking content

1. When you delete a text box in the middle of a story, it splits it into two separate stories. True or false?
   - True
   - False
2. If you unlink a text box, the text that was in it might not be displayed but won't be erased. True or false?
   - True
   - False
3. If you had a series of five linked text boxes, and broke the link between the second and third, the last three would still be linked together. True or false?
   - True
   - False

Summary: Advanced formatting

In this chapter, you learned how to:

- Insert OLE objects like Excel documents or charts into documents, and use formulas in Word tables
- Create and manage building blocks using the Building Blocks Organizer
- Lay out content by linking text boxes into a single story

Synthesis: Advanced formatting

In this exercise, you'll format a document.

1. In a new blank document, type the text `Java Tucana Franchising Information`. Choose an appealing format for the text.
2. Select the formatted text, and add it to the Headers gallery as a building block. Close the file when you're done.
3. Open `Franchise Information` and save it as `Franchise Information Synthesis`.
4. Apply custom formatting to the document, and modify the Heading 1 and Heading 2 styles to reflect your changes.
5. Apply the header you made earlier to the document.
6. Insert a chart using the data from `Sample budget.xlsx`.
7. Insert an object with a link to `Franchisee.application.pdf`. Show the link as an icon.

Chapter 13: Advanced document management

You will learn how to:

- Configure Word options
- Work with templates
- Track and review documents

Module A: Configuring Word options

You might have noticed by now that Word makes a lot of decisions for you without requiring any input. It has a default behavior for how documents are displayed, how they're saved, how to paste content or look for misspelled words, and so on. If you need to override Word's defaults on a case-by-case basis, you usually can, but if there's something you often or always want to behave differently, you should check Word's program options.

You will learn how to:

- Change default program options
- Change spelling options
- Change grammar checking options

The Word Options window

If a Word setting isn't on the ribbon or in one of the windows you can open from it, it's probably in the **Word Options** window. You can open it by clicking **Options** in Backstage view.

Exam Objective: MOS Word Expert 2.1.3

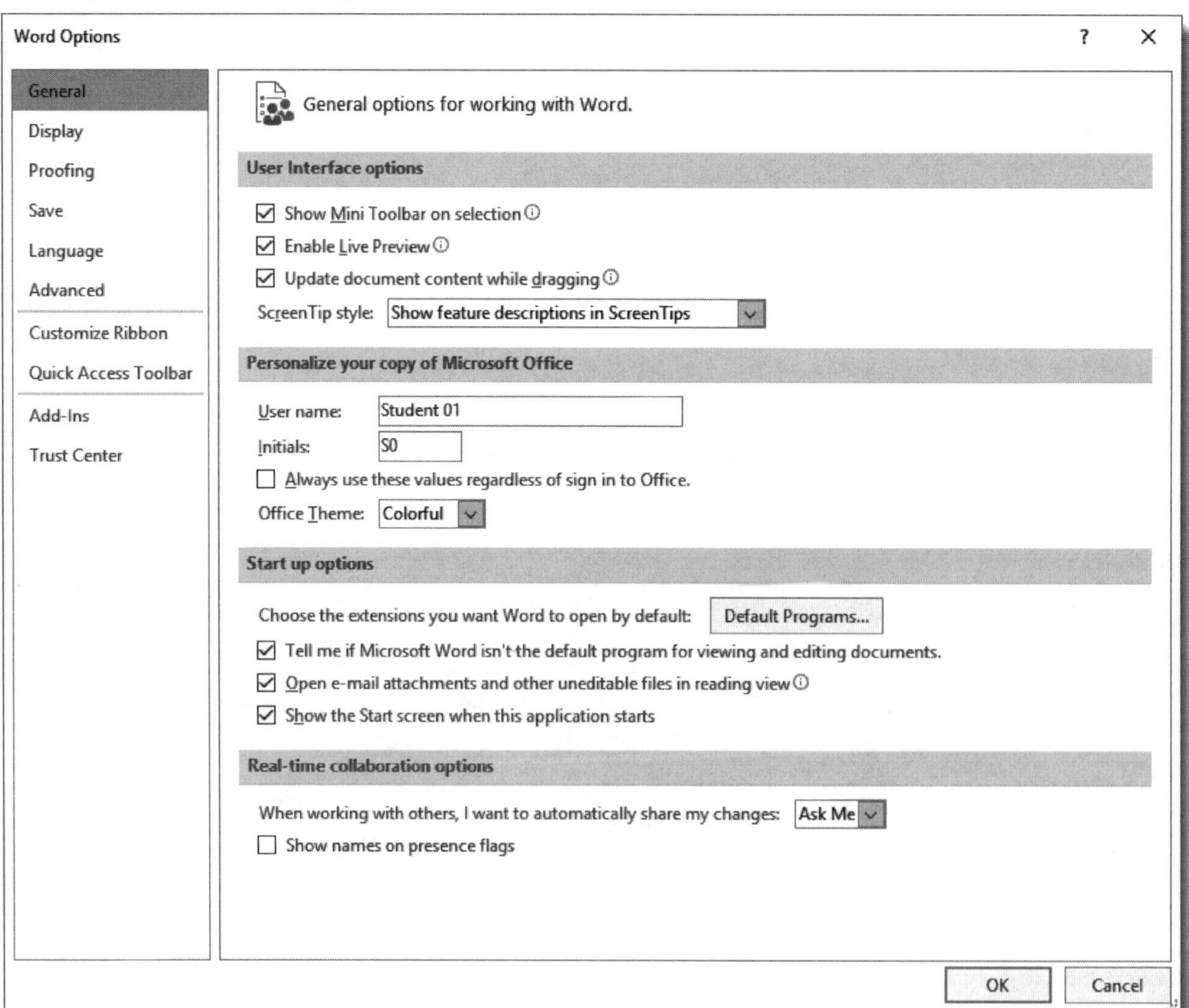

The left pane of the window displays a list of sections, while the right displays a list of options from the current section.

General	User interface and personalization options.
Display	Options for what document elements and formatting marks are shown, both on screen and when printed.
Proofing	Spelling, grammar, and AutoCorrect options, both for Word and for other Microsoft Office programs.
Save	Saving options for documents, including default formats, locations, and AutoRecover options.
Language	Language settings for the Word interface, and for document editing features such as dictionaries and grammar checking.
Advanced	Additional options for a variety of Word features. Includes sections for editing and layout options, display features, paste behavior, printing, saving, and compatibility.
Customize Ribbon	Options for changing the contents of the ribbon and displaying the order of its elements.
Quick Access Toolbar	Options for adding commands to or removing them from the Quick Access toolbar.
Add-Ins	Management options for Office add-ins used by Word.
Trust Center	Contains links to Microsoft's privacy and security documentation, and the Trust Center window, which lets you change Word's security settings.

Most settings in the **Word Options** window apply to how Word behaves in general, but some sections have document-specific options. In these cases, you can choose to apply the settings either only to the current document or to all new documents you create.

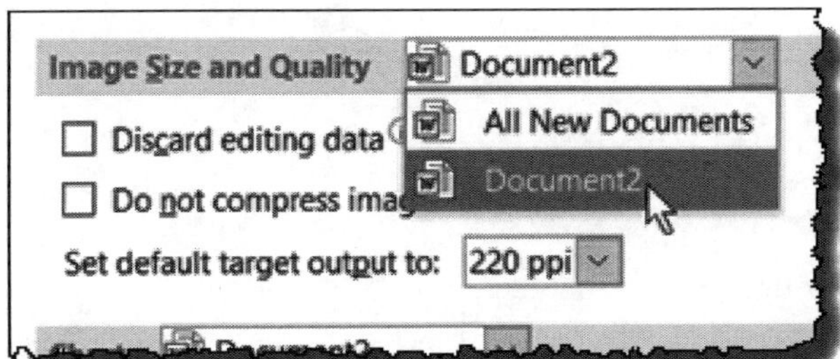

Changing proofing options

A common example of Word options you might want to change is its spelling and grammar settings, located in the Proofing section of the window. This can be important even if you don't use Word very often, as other Office programs use Word's dictionaries and spell-checking settings.

Exam Objective: MOS Word Expert 4.3.1

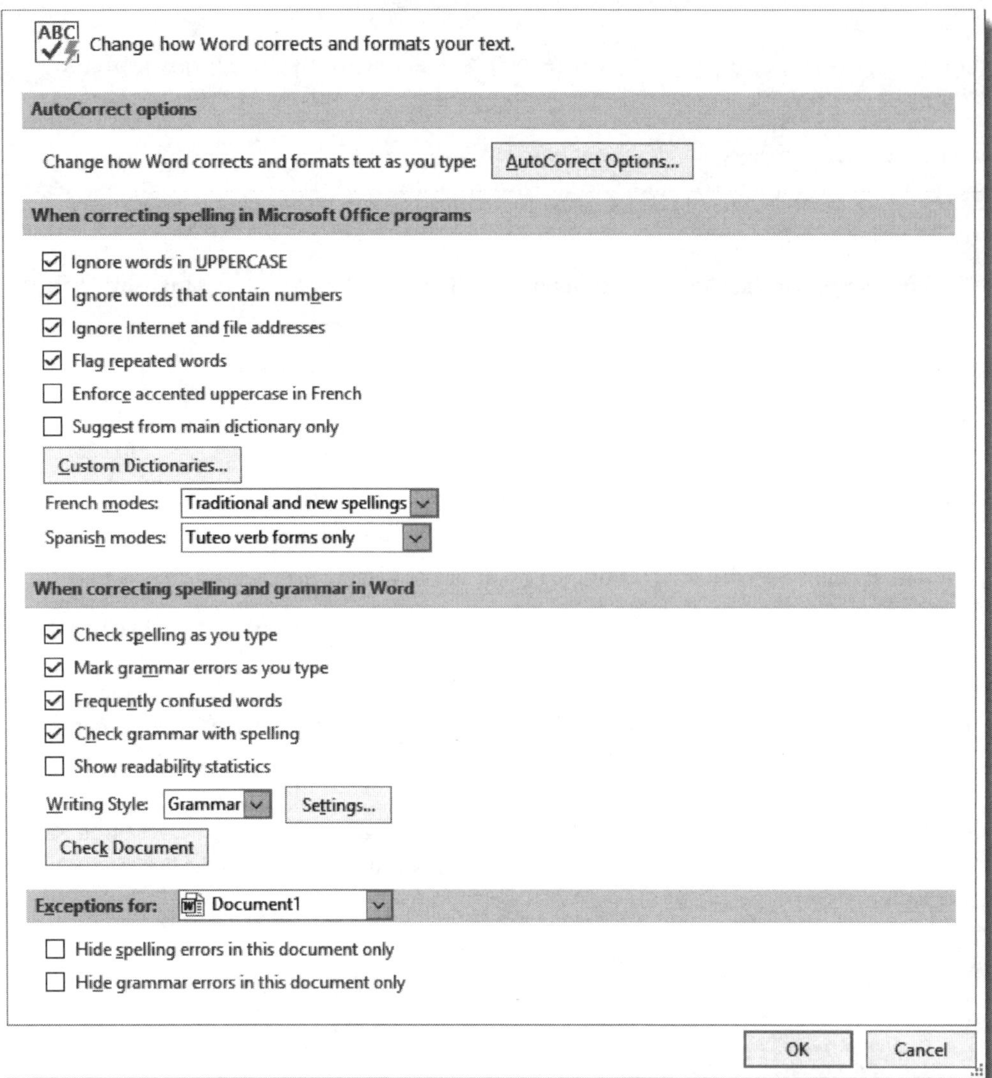

- Most options are controlled simply by a check box or drop-down menu.
- Click **Custom Dictionaries** to manage additional custom dictionaries you want to use, for example, with industry or company-specific terms.
- Click **AutoCorrect Options** to change how AutoCorrect monitors and corrects misspellings as you type.
- Click **Settings** to open the **Grammar Settings** window, with specific grammar and style checking options.
- Click **Recheck Document** to run a new check on the current document. This resets any spelling or grammar alerts you've already chosen to ignore.

Changing save options

You can change how and where Word saves documents by selecting the Save section of the **Word Options** window. These settings can be useful, depending on your company's policies and your computer's configuration.

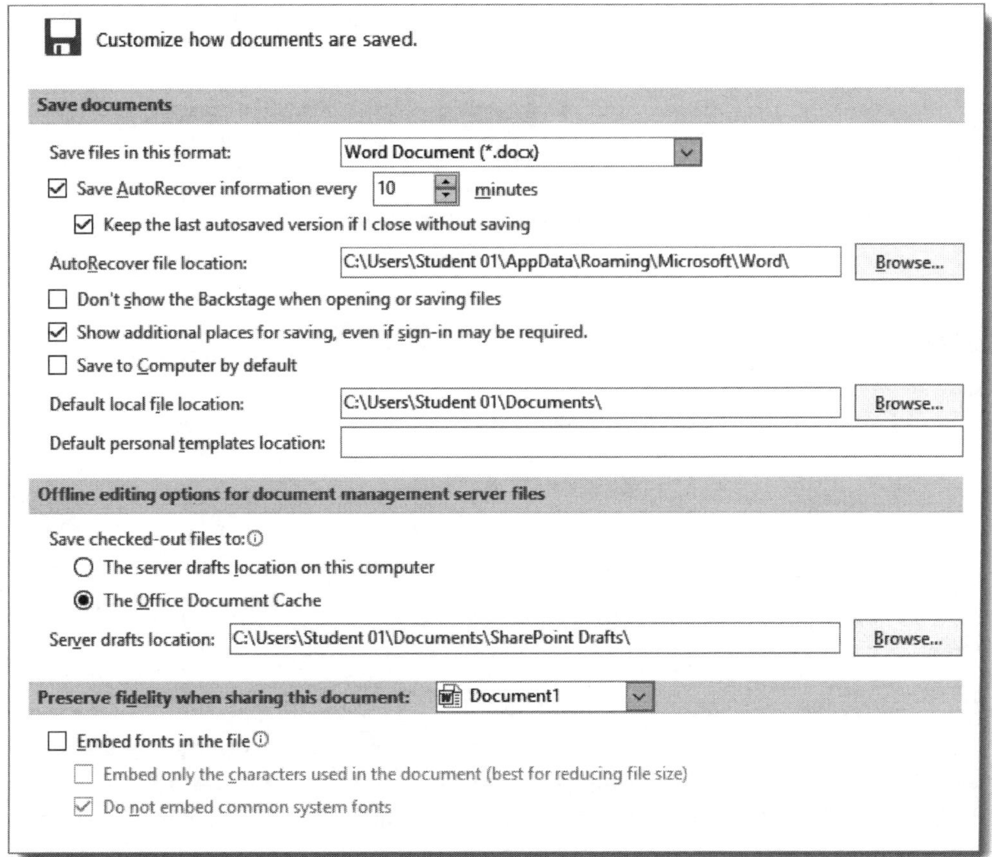

Exam Objective: MOS Word Core 1.5.7

Options for saving documents include:

- File format. By default, Word 2016 saves new files in the .docx format introduced with Word 2007 but updated for this version. However, if you usually create documents using another format, such as Word 97-2003 .doc or OpenDocument, you can change this option and avoid having to set it every time you save a new file.
- Default file location. Normally this is your user Documents folder (My Documents in Windows XP.) You can also set it to any location you have access to, even a network drive.
- AutoRecover options. You can change how often Word saves AutoRecover information, whether it keeps a copy if you close the file without saving, and where AutoRecover information is saved.
- Offline reading options. For use with SharePoint document management systems.
- Font embedding options. For sharing documents with users who may not have all of the same fonts installed.

The Trust Center window

Exam Objective: MOS Word Core 1.4.10

From the Trust Center section of the **Word Options** window, you can click **Trust Center Settings** to open the **Trust Center** window, with additional options for privacy and security in Word.

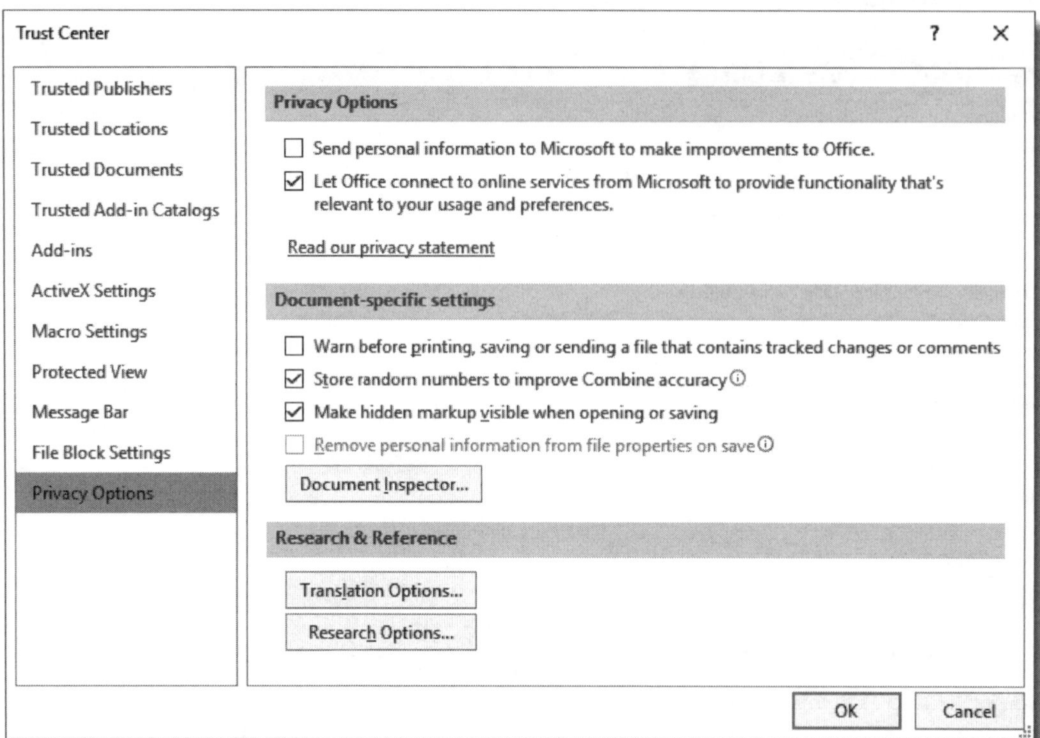

Most of the options in the Trust Center have to do with security settings to apply to open documents. Because Word documents are so common, and because they support powerful features like macros and ActiveX controls, they're also a popular means for distributing malware. To prevent such documents from harming your computer, Word restricts what documents can run risky content, and in some cases opens them in the read-only Protected View.

In general, you shouldn't need to change Trust Center settings, but if you do, use caution. If you make your settings too permissive, you put yourself at risk of malware, and if you make them too restrictive, you might have trouble viewing safe documents.

Exercise: Customizing Word Options

In this exercise, you'll change settings in the **Word Options** window.

Do This	How & Why
1. Open `About Us options`.	In the current data folder. Note that some words not part of Word's default dictionary, such as "Supremo," aren't marked as misspelled. This is because the document was already spell-checked and Word was instructed to ignore them.
2. In Backstage view, click **Options**.	The **Word Options** window opens, showing the General section.

Do This	How & Why
3. Under "Personalize your copy of Microsoft Office," enter your name and initials.	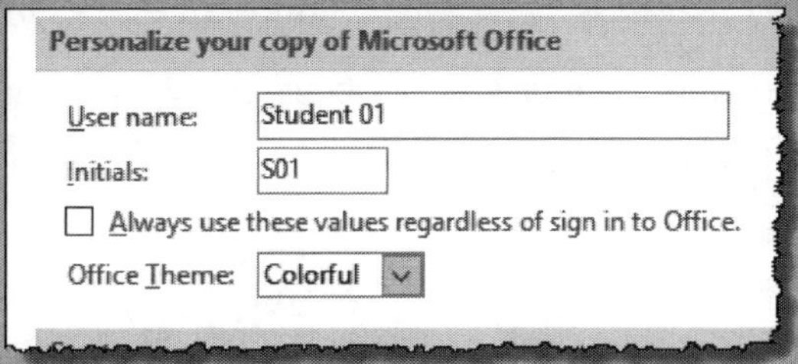 Personalize your copy of Microsoft Office User name: Student 01 Initials: S01 Always use these values regardless of sign in to Office. Office Theme: Colorful
4. Change Word's proofing options.	
a) In the left column, click **Proofing**.	The Proofing options are displayed on the right.
b) Clear **Ignore words that contain numbers**.	Normally, Word assumes a word like "Step12" is intentionally written that way, but now it's flagged as a misspelling.
c) Click **Recheck Document**.	A window appears, asking if you really want to reset the spelling and grammar checker.
d) Click **Yes**.	You can't see the results yet, but you will by the end of the activity.
5. Change Word's AutoRecover settings.	
a) In the left column, click **Save**.	
b) Set "Save AutoRecover information every" to **5** minutes.	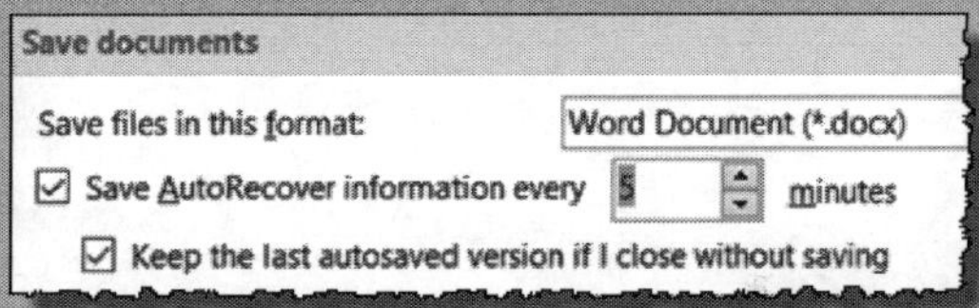 Save documents Save files in this format: Word Document (*.docx) Save AutoRecover information every 5 minutes Keep the last autosaved version if I close without saving Type it, or use the spin buttons.
6. As time permits, examine other parts of the **Word Options** window.	Think about which available options might make your work thus far in Word easier or harder.
7. Click **OK**.	
8. Click **Spelling & Grammar**.	On the Review tab. Words such as "Supremo" are now caught by the spell checker. 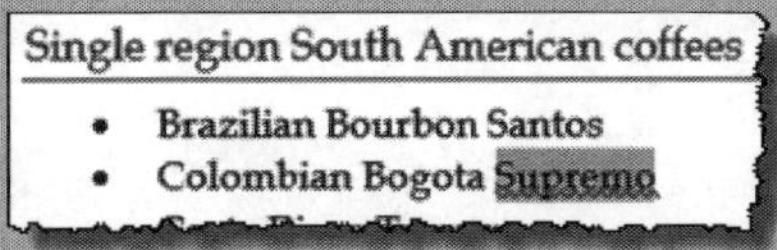 Single region South American coffees • Brazilian Bourbon Santos • Colombian Bogota Supremo Because you reset the spell-checking options, the previously ignored words are marked again.

Assessment: Configuring Word options

1. You probably shouldn't use stricter security settings than the Trust Center defaults. True or false?
   - True
   - False
2. What features can you control in the Proofing section of the Word Options window? Choose all that apply.
   - Additional editing languages
   - AutoCorrect
   - AutoRecover
   - Custom dictionaries
   - Macro settings
3. Changes you make in the Word Options window might affect other Microsoft Office applications such as Excel and PowerPoint. True or false?
   - True
   - False

Module B: Working with templates

If you're like most Word users, you'll create documents using templates installed with Word, downloaded from Office.com, or provided by your company. If those options aren't enough, templates are still just a kind of Word document, so you can modify them or create new ones to suit your needs.

You will learn:

- About the Template Organizer
- How to attach a new template to an existing document
- How to create templates
- How to modify existing templates

The Templates and Add-ins window

Exam Objective: MOS Word Core 1.1.1, 1.1.4

You can manage your templates from the **Templates and Add-ins** window. To access it, you're first going to need to either display the Developer tab on the ribbon, or select **Templates** from the Manage list in the Add-ins section of the **Word Options** window.

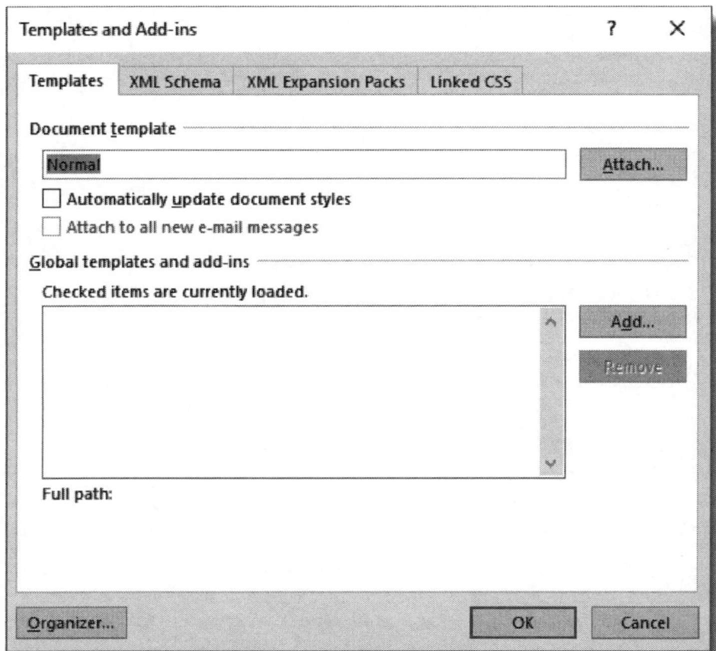

The window has two sections: one for adding a document template to the current document, and one for managing global templates. Although they're both called templates and use the same file extensions, they do very different things, so it's important to distinguish the two.

- *Document templates* contain document content, styles, macros, and other content such as custom toolbars or ribbon tabs. They are stored in the Office Templates folder. Document templates are what most people mean when they discuss templates, and are the sort of templates you'll be working with in this course.

- *Global templates* don't usually contain content or styles. In fact, the styles in a global template aren't generally available for other documents. They hold building blocks, program customizations, and other add-on content. Global templates are located in Word's startup folder or in the Building Blocks folder, and are loaded when you start Word.

Attaching templates

When you create a document from a template, it inherits that template's contents. This could include page content, available styles, macros, or building customizations. The whole new document, effectively, is built from what's in that template.

Exam Objective: MOS Word Core 1.1.4 and Expert 1.1.2

It's different when you attach a new template to an existing document. The existing document, by default, isn't changed at all. If you attach a sales invoice template to a document, the blank invoice form won't be inserted. Unless you specify otherwise, it won't even update the document's styles to match those of the template. Instead, attaching a template makes that template's contents *available* to the document. This is useful when you want to use macros, building blocks, or interface customizations from another template in your documents.

You can attach a template from the **Templates and Add-ins** window.

1. On the Templates tab, click **Attach**.
2. Select a template, and click **Open**.
3. If you want to change the document's styles to match those of the new template, check **Automatically update document styles**.
4. Click **OK**.

The Organizer window

You don't need to attach a new template to get access to its contents. You can also copy styles or macros from one document to another, or manage them within a document, using the **Organizer** window.

Exam Objective: MOS Word Expert 1.1.5

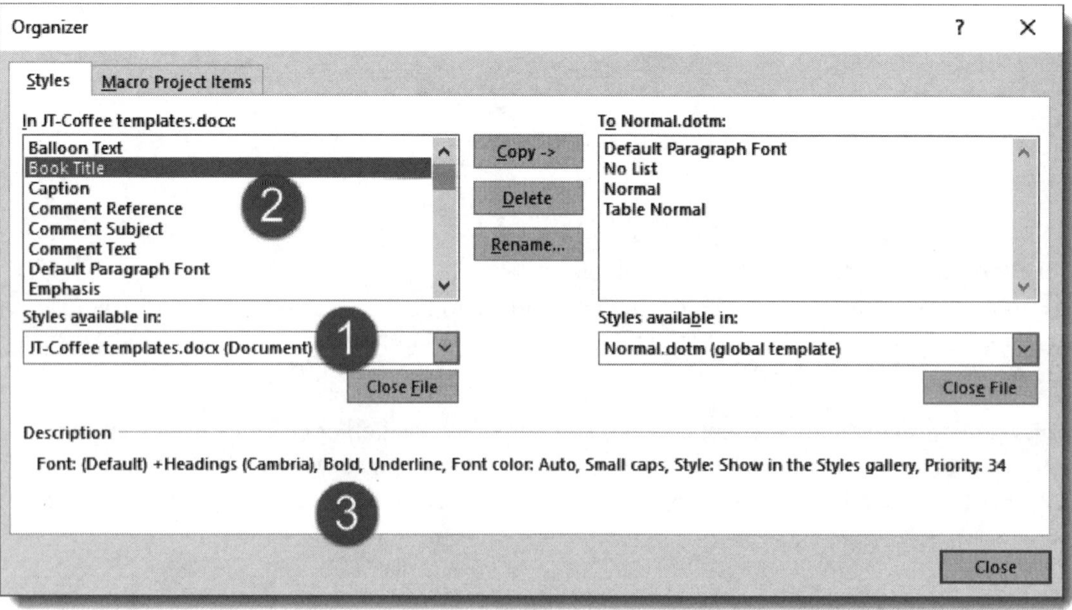

The window has two tabs: Styles, and Macro Project Items. Both have the same interface; only the content shown in each is different. You can access the contents of two documents simultaneously, with each shown as a list on one side of the window.

The "Styles available in" list shows a currently open file as well as its type (document or template). By default, it displays the currently open document on the left, and the default `Normal.dotm` template on the right.

The *Styles list* shows styles that are part of the selected file.

The *Description* area shows properties for the currently selected style.

Managing styles with the Organizer

In the Organizer, you can copy, delete, or rename styles from any template or other document.

Exam Objective: MOS Word Expert 1.1.4, 1.1.5, 1.1.6

1. In the **Templates and Add-ins** window, click **Organizer**.
2. Select the files you want to access:
   - From either "Styles available in" list, you can choose between open files and templates.
   - If you want to access a different file, click **Close File** on either side, then **Open File** to find the one you want.
3. On either side, select a style you want to manage.
   - Click **Delete** to delete a custom style. You can't delete built-in styles, such as Heading 1.
   - Click **Rename** to rename a style. You can't entirely rename a built-in style; instead, Word gives it a *style alias*, separated from the original name by a comma.
   - Click **Copy** to copy a style to the other file.
4. When you're done making changes, click **Close**.

   You're asked to save changes to any files you've changed.

Exercise: Attaching a template

you'll attach a template to an existing document and use the Organizer to import additional styles.

Do This	How & Why
1. In Windows Explorer, double-click `Product list.dotx`.	This file's a template, so you're actually creating a new document based on it. It contains some placeholder text and custom styles.
2. Close the file without saving.	
3. Display the Developer tab.	This makes it easier to access the **Templates and Add-ins** window.
a) Right-click the ribbon, and click **Customize the Ribbon**.	The **Word Options** window opens.
b) On the right list, check **Developer**.	
c) Click **OK**.	The Developer tab is now displayed on the ribbon.
4. Attach the Product list template to the `JT-Coffee2` document.	
a) Open `JT-Coffee2`.	This file has a product list, but you'd rather use the styles from the Product list. You could copy this text into a new document based on that template, but instead, you'll attach the template to this document.
b) Save the document as `JT-Coffee templates`.	
c) On the Developer tab, click **Document Template**.	In the Templates group. The **Templates and Add-ins** window opens.
d) Click **Attach**.	The **Attach Template** window opens. It's showing the `Templates` folder.
e) Select **Product List**, and click **Open**.	You'll have to navigate to the current module data folder.
f) Check **Automatically update document styles**.	If you don't check this, it doesn't actually apply the styles from the template.
g) Click **OK**.	The styles from the template are applied to the document.

Do This	How & Why
5. Import custom styles from the Fancy formatted list document.	You have some custom styles in another version of this document, and you'd like to import them into this one.
a) Open the **Templates and Add-ins** window.	Click **Document Template**.
b) Click **Organizer**.	The **Organizer** window opens. It currently displays styles in `JT-Coffee templates` and `Normal.dotm`.
c) On the right side of the window, click **Close File**.	To close Normal.dotm.
d) Click **Open file**.	
e) Navigate to the current data folder.	Because only templates are currently displayed, you don't see the file you need.
f) Click **All Word Templates**, and select **All Word Documents**.	Now you can see the other Word documents in the folder.
g) Select **Fancy Formatted list**, then click **Open**.	The right side now shows that document's styles.
h) On the right side, click **Product description**	You'll have to scroll down. In Fancy formatted list.docx Normal Product description Product name Quote Strong
i) Press **Ctrl**, and click **Product name**.	You can select and copy multiple styles at once.
j) Click **Copy**.	Styles · Macro Proje To JT-Coffee templates Placeholder Text Product description Product name You have to scroll down, but the styles are now in `JT-Coffee templates`.
k) Click **Close**.	The new styles aren't actually used anywhere in the document yet.
6. Apply the **Product description** style to each product description paragraph in the document.	Use the **Styles** window.
7. Save and close `JT-Coffee templates`.	An example follows.

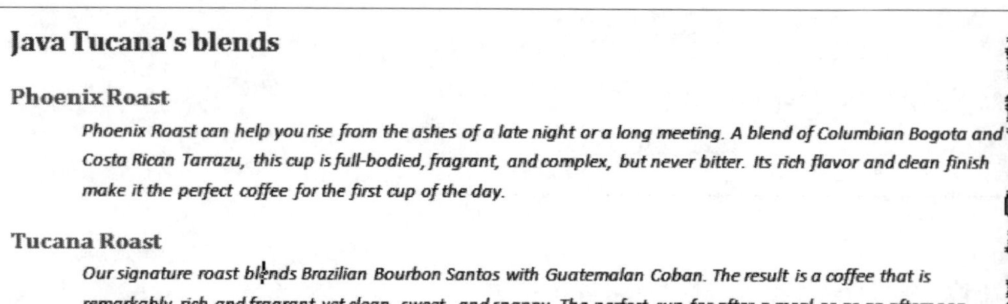

About custom templates

The Organizer isn't the only way to modify templates. You can also create your own, or modify an existing one to suit your needs, editing it as freely as you would any other Word document.

Exam Objective: MOS Word Expert 1.1.1, 4.2.3

Templates you create or download are stored in the default templates folder. Its location depends on your Windows version: in Windows 10, it's `C:\Users\[username]\Documents\Custom Office Templates\`. To view all templates in this folder, click **Personal** in the New section of Backstage view. This displays the Personal Templates list.

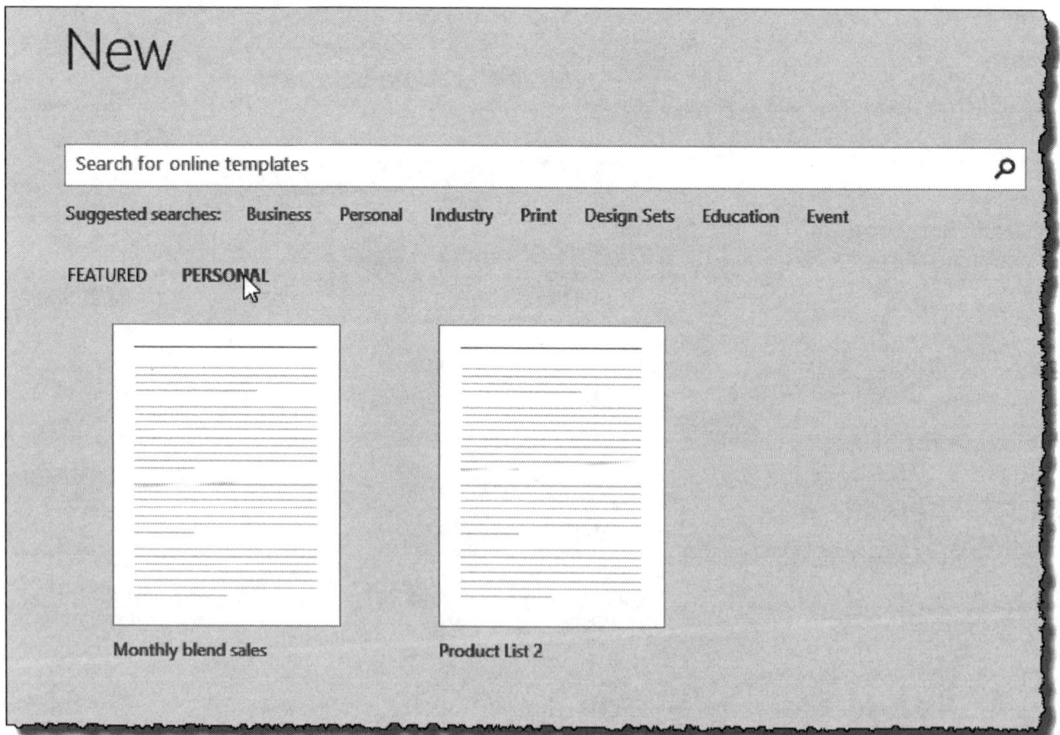

Creating templates

Exam Objective: MOS Word Expert 1.1.1, 4.2.3

You can create a new template by saving any open document as a template.

1. Add any content to the document you want to appear in the template.
   You can start with a blank document, or open an existing document or template and modify it.
2. Open the **Save As** window.
   Click **Save As** in Backstage view, or press **F12**. To browse for a destination folder.
3. From the Save as Type list, choose a template type.
   - If the template doesn't contain any macros, choose **Word Template (*.dotx)**.
   - If the template contains macros, choose **Word Macro-Enabled Template (*.dotm)**.
   - If the template needs to be compatible with Word 2003 or earlier, choose **Word 97-2003 Template (*.dot)**.
4. Choose a file location.
   If you want to save to the Custom Office Templates folder, you can navigate easily to it in the upper part of the **Save As** window.

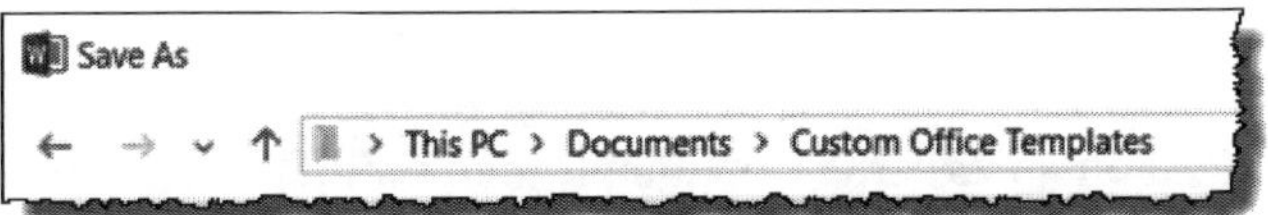

Modifying templates

Modifying a template can seem challenging. If you just open the template as a new document or by double-clicking it in Windows Explorer, Word actually creates a new document based on the template. Because the template is opened with the document, if you try to save over the original template, you'll receive an error message.

You can always save the template under a new name, delete the original, and rename the new one, but that's a lot of work. Instead, it's easiest to open the original template as a template, rather than as a document. Then you can save it normally. There are multiple ways you can make sure you're opening a template itself, and not just using it to create a new document.

Exam Objective: MOS Word Expert 1.1.1

- In Backstage view, be sure to use the **Open** window, not the **New** window.
- You can also open a template you've recently edited by looking in the Recent Documents list. Templates are easily recognized by their icon or their ".dotx" filename extension.

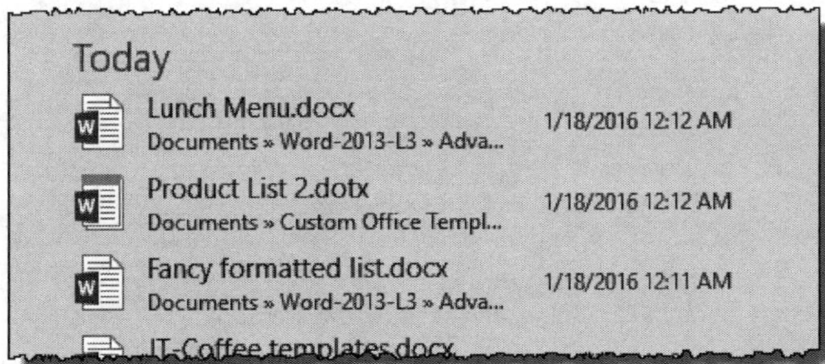

- In Windows Explorer, you can open a template itself by right-clicking it, then clicking **Open**.

Troubleshooting Normal.dotm

One of the most important templates you use is the Normal template, Normal.dotm. It's the template used for creating new blank documents, and it specifies Word's default styles. It also contains many customizations you make to Word settings. Unfortunately, if the template is corrupted or modified improperly, this can cause a wide variety of problems with Word.

If you suspect problems in Normal.dotm, you can always just delete it: if the file does not exist, Word creates a new copy on startup, using the default settings. The drawback of doing so is that it deletes any modifications you've made to the template yourself, so to be safe, you might want to rename or copy the original, in case you want it back later.

1. Close Word.
2. In Windows Explorer, navigate to the Templates folder.
   In `C:\Users\<username>\AppData\Roaming\Microsoft\Templates`.
3. Delete Normal.dotm.
   - Optionally, rename it or move it to another folder.
4. Start Word.

Exercise: Creating a template

In this exercise, you'll create a new template based on an existing document, then modify it.

Do This	How & Why
1. Open `2014 blend sales`.	It shows a table with sales figures. You'll use it to make a blank monthly sales table.
2. Remove the sales figures from the table.	
a) Edit the first cell to read `Monthly Sales`.	
b) Select the cells with sales data.	Don't select the Regional Total row or Product total column.
c) Press **Delete**.	To clear the contents of the cell. The totals data aren't updated immediately, but don't worry about that yet.
3. Save the file as a template.	The Custom Office Templates folder automatically opens as the destination.

Do This	How & Why
a) In Backstage view, click **Save As > Computer > Browse**.	Or press **F12**. The **Save As** window opens.
b) From the "Save as type" list, select **Word Template (*.dotx)**.	File name: 2015 blend sales.dotx Save as type: Word Template (*.dotx)
4. Name and save the file, and close the template.	
a) In the File name field, type `Monthly blend sales`.	
b) Click **Save**.	
c) Close the template.	
5. Create a new document that's based on the `Monthly blend sales` template.	
a) In Backstage view, click **New > Personal**.	To view the available list of custom templates.
b) Click **Monthly blend sales**.	The new document opens, with a name like `Document[XX]`. It contains the blank table, but isn't perfect: it still has the old totals, and you want to add a title above the table.
c) Close the document without saving.	
6. Modify the template.	
a) In Backstage view, click **Open**.	If you were to click New, you'd only be opening a new *document* based on the template.
b) Navigate to the Custom Office Templates folder, and double-click **Monthly blend sales**.	It opens as "Monthly blend sales.dotx," so you're editing the template itself.
c) Select the entire table.	Outside the upper-left corner, click the Select Table button that becomes visible. You want to keep the formulas in the totals rows but update them to match the blank table.
d) Press **F9**.	All the total cells now read "0."
e) Above the table, type `Blend sales for [Month]`.	
f) Format the paragraph in the **Title** style.	
g) Save and close the template.	

Do This	How & Why
7. Create a new document based on the Monthly blend sales template.	Click **New > Personal**, and click **Monthly blend sales**. The document now reflects your changes.
8. Close the document without saving.	

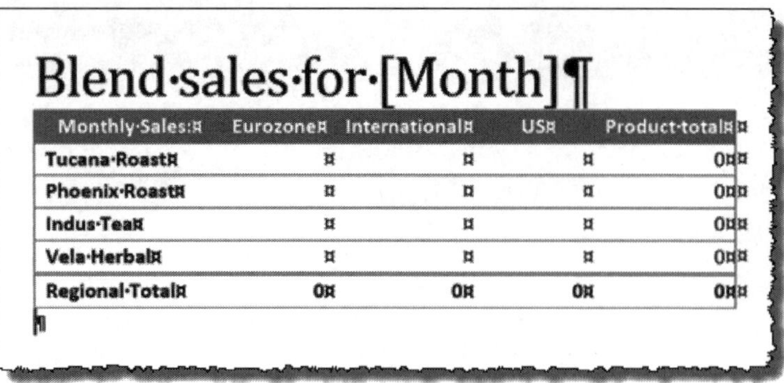
Blend·sales·for·[Month]¶

Monthly·Sales:	Eurozone	International	US	Product·total
Tucana·Roast				0
Phoenix·Roast				0
Indus·Tea				0
Vela·Herbal				0
Regional·Total	0	0	0	0

Assessment: Working with templates

1. When you attach a new template to a document, it doesn't necessarily change the document's appearance. True or false?
    - True
    - False
2. What can you do from the Organizer window? Choose all that apply.
    - Copy a style between templates.
    - Copy building blocks between templates.
    - Delete a custom style.
    - Delete a template.
3. The easiest way to modify a template is to create a new document based on it, then save it as a template using the same name. True or false?
    - True
    - False

Module C: Tracking and reviewing changes

When you make a lot of revisions to a document, especially one you're collaborating on with others, it can be hard to keep track of versions, and even harder to easily discuss or review changes made. You can use comments and tracking to do these things right inside a Word document, and even combine changes and comments made by multiple users to address them all at once.

You will learn how to:

- Track document changes
- Change markup display settings
- Review changes and comments
- Combine or compare different versions of a document

Document tracking

If you want to keep track of changes made to a document, or give yourself or another user a chance to review them before making them permanent, you can use Word's Track Changes feature. Commands for tracking changes are on the Review tab, in the Tracking group.

The Tracking group, with Track Changes enabled

When tracking is enabled, any change made to the document is recorded, and the original content as well as the changes are preserved. If multiple users make changes to the same document, each user's changes are marked in a different color. Word can even distinguish between content moved using cut and paste commands, and content moved simply by typing or deleting it. By default, new text is underlined, while deleted text is struck through. Tracked changes formatted in this way, as well as document comments, are collectively called *markup*.

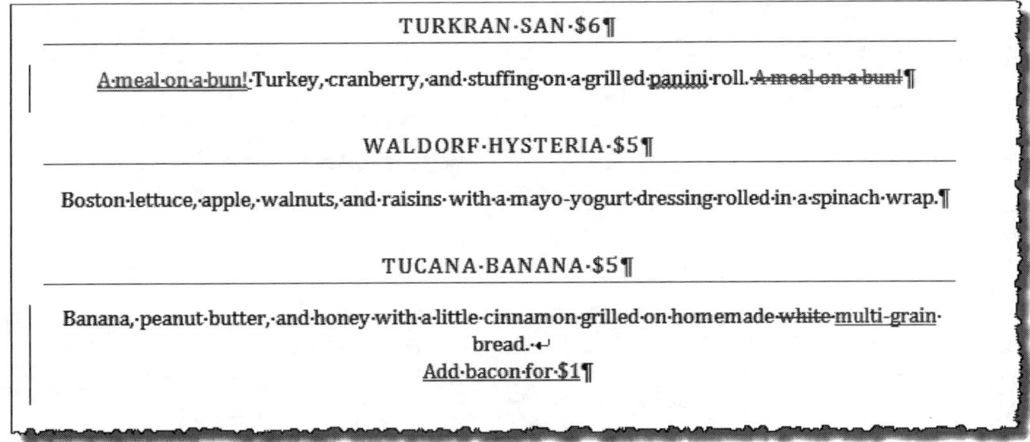

TURKRAN·SAN·$6¶

A·meal·on·a·bun!·Turkey,·cranberry,·and·stuffing·on·a·grilled·panini·roll.·~~A·meal·on·a·bun!~~¶

WALDORF·HYSTERIA·$5¶

Boston·lettuce,·apple,·walnuts,·and·raisins·with·a·mayo-yogurt·dressing·rolled·in·a·spinach·wrap.¶

TUCANA·BANANA·$5¶

Banana,·peanut·butter,·and·honey·with·a·little·cinnamon·grilled·on·homemade·~~white~~·multi-grain·bread.·↵
Add·bacon·for·$1¶

Tracking changes

Exam Objective: MOS Word Expert 1.3.1, 1.3.4, 1.3.5

You can track changes only when tracking is enabled, but even when you disable it again, the markup remains in your document until you accept or reject it.

- To turn tracking on or off, click **Track Changes**, or press **Ctrl+Shift+E**.
- To discourage others from turning tracking off, click **Track Changes > Lock Tracking**.

  You can optionally add a password.

- All changes you make will display your Office user name. To change it, go to the General section of the **Word Options** window.

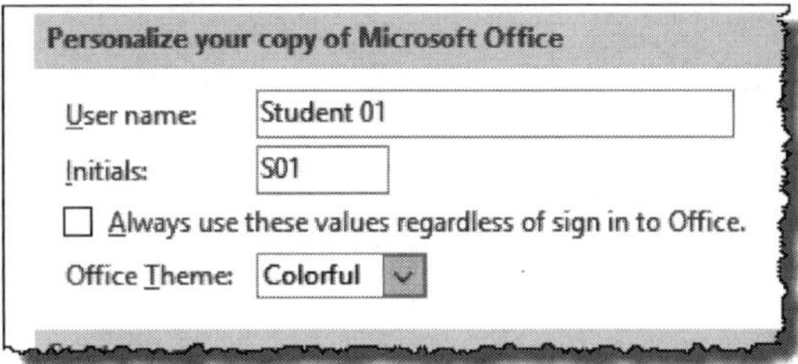

Exercise: Using document tracking

In this exercise, you'll track changes to a draft document for later review.

Do This	How & Why
1. Open `Lunch Menu`, and save it as `Lunch Menu comments`.	
2. On the Review tab, click **Track Changes**.	To turn tracking on.
3. If necessary, in the Display for Review list, select **All Markup**.	
4. Make changes to the document.	You'll be comparing your changes with a coworker's later, so they need to be tracked.
a) In the first menu item, select the word "role."	You'll correct this misspelling first.

Do This	How & Why
b) Type `roll`.	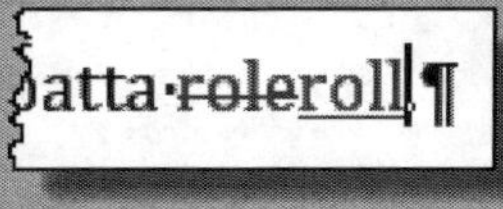 The original word is struck through and the new one is underlined.
c) At the end of the Tucana Banana description, on a new line, type `Add bacon for $1`.	After placing the cursor, press **Enter**, then type the words.
d) Format the soup bowl item using the **Heading 3** style.	 When you change formatting, the markup appears as a balloon in the margin, like a comment.
5. Move a menu item.	Moved content is displayed with different markup than changed content.
a) Select the entire Turkran San item and description.	Drag in the left margin to select both paragraphs. 
b) Press **Ctrl+X**.	To cut the text. It appears just like a deletion, red with a strikethrough.
c) Place the insertion point just in front of Surf and Surf.	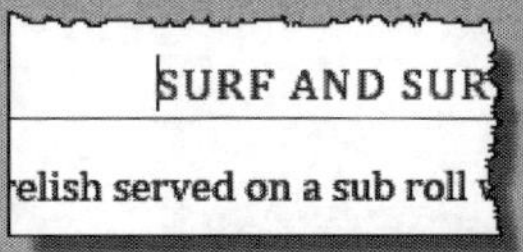
d) Press **Ctrl+V**.	Now the old location is green with a double strikethrough, and the new location is green with a double underline. 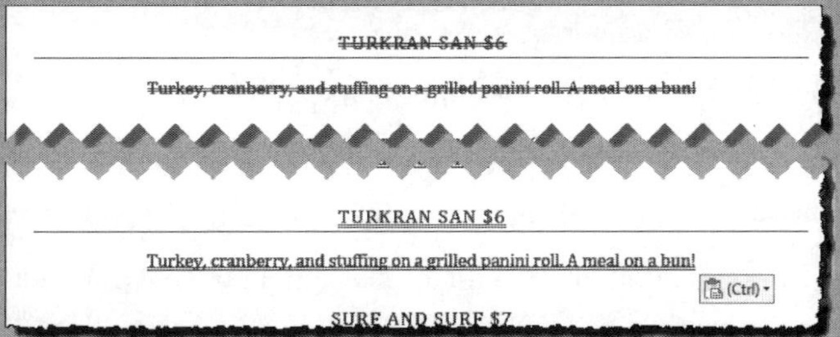
6. Turn off tracking.	Click **Track Changes**. Further changes won't be tracked, but the existing markup is still there.
7. Save the document.	Leave it open.

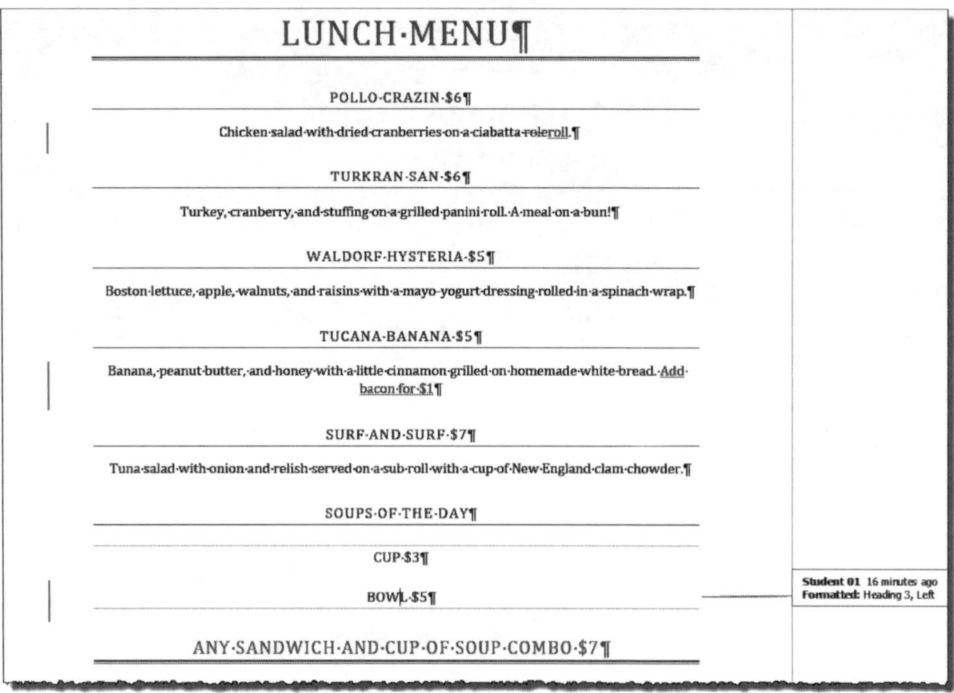

Viewing markup

When tracking is enabled, Word automatically records all changes you make. However, you can easily change how tracked changes are actually displayed in the document.

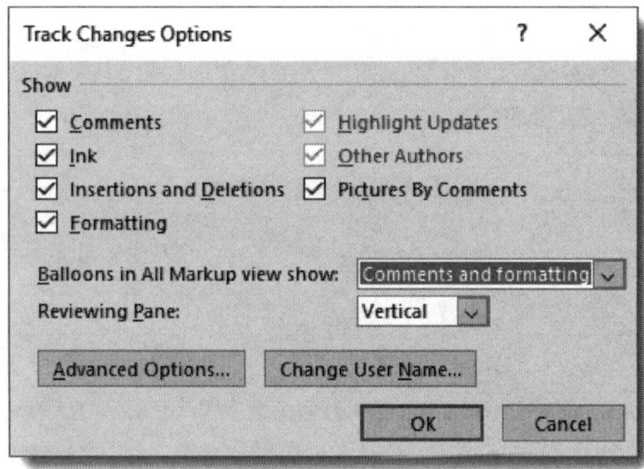

- To view the document without markup, use the Display for Review list.
  - To see the original document without markup, click **Original**.
  - To see the final document without markup, click **No Markup**.
  - To see the document with all markup, choose **All Markup**.
  - To see partial markup with less clutter, choose **Simple Markup**.

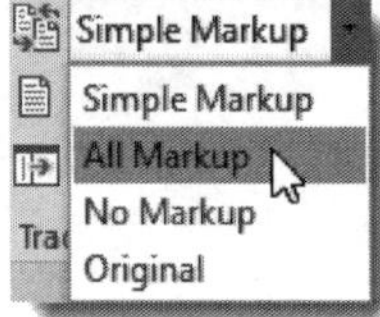

- To show or hide individual markup elements, open the Show Markup menu and check or clear elements.

- Click **Show Markup > Balloons** to choose whether to display changes inline or in balloons alongside the main document.
- If the document has changes by multiple users, click **Show Markup > Specific people** to show or hide changes by specific people.

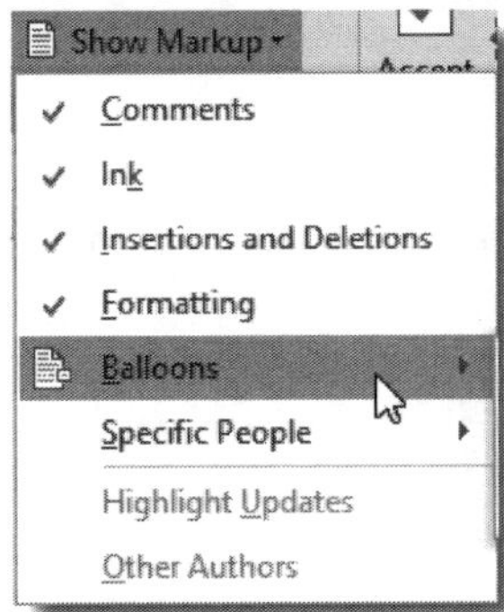

- To view a summary of markup in a separate pane instead of the document body, click **Reviewing Pane** and choose either horizontal or vertical format.
- To open the Track Changes Options window with all display options, click the **Change Tracking Options** launcher in the Tracking group.

Changing advanced tracking options

Word tracks insertions, deletions, and moves as separate types of changes, formatting each distinctly so you know which is which. If you want to change how they are displayed, or even not to track certain types of change, you can use the **Advanced Track Changes Options** window. To do so, click **Advanced Options** in the **Track Changes Options** window.

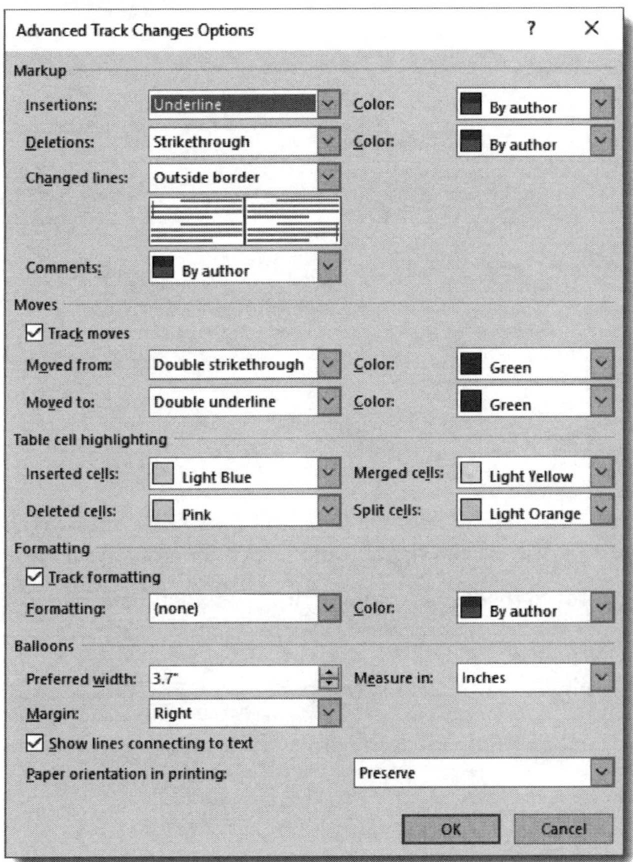

- By default, most changes are color-coded according to the author responsible. use the Color list for a type of change to set a single color regardless of author.
- You can separately change the formatting and color of inserted, deleted, and moved text.
- You can separately change the color of inserted, deleted, merged, and split table cells.
- Use the **Changed lines** list to choose how altered lines in the text are marked.
- Use the Balloons section to change balloon size and locations.
- To change how documents with visible tracked changes display, use the Paper orientation in printing list.
  - Choose **Preserve** to print in the document's normal orientation.
  - Choose **Force Landscape** to print in landscape format whenever tracked changes are visible. This leaves more space for balloons.
- To stop tracking moves, clear **Track moves**.
- To stop tracking formatting changes, clear **Track Formatting**.

Using the Revisions pane

Whether markup is fully displayed in the document or not, you can review all tracked changes in the Revisions pane.

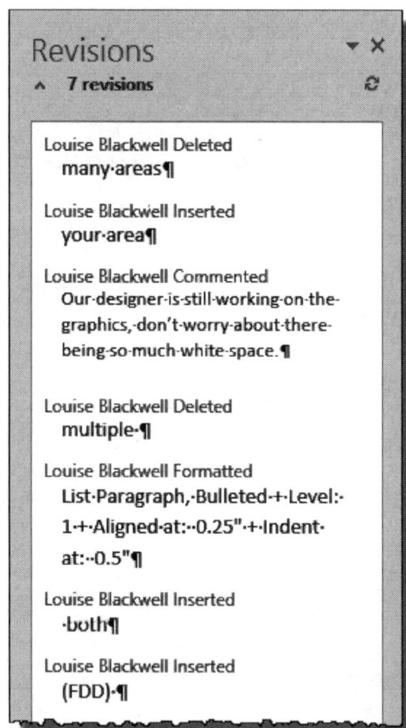

- Click **Reviewing Pane > Reviewing Pane Vertical** to display the pane to the left of the document.
- Click **Reviewing Pane > Reviewing Pane Horizontal** to display the pane below the document.
- To alter a revision further, edit it directly in the Revisions pane.
- To navigate to any change in the document, double-click it in the Revisions pane.
- To display a tally of each type of change made to the document, click the downward-pointing arrow below "Revisions."

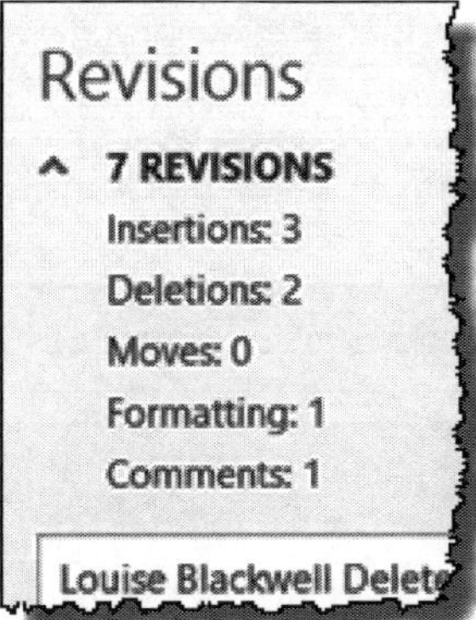

Exercise: Viewing markup

`Lunch menu comments` should still be open. You'll change how markup is displayed in a document.

Do This	How & Why
1. Explore the Revisions pane.	
a) In the Tracking group, click **Reviewing Pane.**	The Revisions pane opens, listing all the changes you made in the previous exercise.
b) In the Revisions pane, click	To view the summary of tracked changes.
c) Scroll to the bottom of the document.	
d) Double-click the first change in the Revisions pane.	Where you deleted "role". The document scrolls up to display the change you selected.
2. View the document's markup options.	
a) Open the Display for Review list.	In the Tracking group.
b) Click **No Markup**.	The markup and original text are hidden, so it looks like you edited the document without even tracking changes. They're still visible in the Revisions pane, however.

Do This	How & Why
c) From the Display for Review list, click **Original**.	To display the document without changes.
d) From the Display for Review list, click **Simple Markup**.	Now the details of the changes aren't shown, only the bars to the left indicating what lines of the document have been changed.
e) Click any of the red bars on the left.	All markup is displayed again.
3. Change what markup is displayed.	
a) Click **Show Markup > Insertions and Deletions**.	All insertions, deletions, and moved content are replaced with their end results. There's no indication changes were even made, even in the Revisions pane.
b) Click **Show Markup > Balloons > Show All Revisions Inline**.	The balloon marking the formatting change you made vanishes. It's still marked on the left of the page and in the Revisions pane.
c) In the Tracking group, click .	The **Change Tracking Options** window opens. It collects the options you've been using into one place.
d) Check **Insertions and Deletions**.	The changes aren't shown immediately this way.
e) From the Balloons in All Markup View show list, choose **Comments and Formatting**.	
4. Change advanced tracking options.	This document is going to be edited by multiple people, so you want to make sure moved content is color-coded by author.
a) Click **Advanced Options**.	The **Advanced Track Changes Options** window opens.
b) From the Changed lines list, choose **Right Border**.	In the Markup section.

Do This	How & Why
c) In the Moves section, change both Color boxes to **By Author**.	It's at the top of the list. Moves Track moves Moved from: Double strikethrough Color: By author Moved to: Double underline Color: By author Table cell highlighting
d) Click **OK** twice.	To close both options windows. The changes you've made are reflected in the document's markup.
5. Close the **Revisions** pane.	Click **Reviewing Pane**.
6. Save and close the document.	Leave Word open.

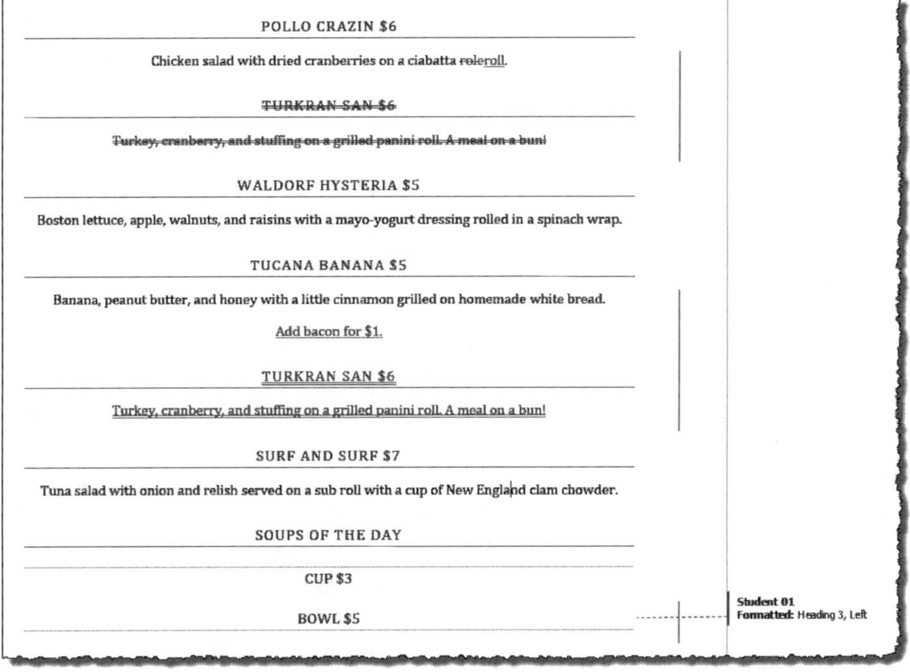

POLLO CRAZIN $6

Chicken salad with dried cranberries on a ciabatta ~~role~~roll.

~~TURKRAN SAN $6~~

~~Turkey, cranberry, and stuffing on a grilled panini roll. A meal on a bun!~~

WALDORF HYSTERIA $5

Boston lettuce, apple, walnuts, and raisins with a mayo-yogurt dressing rolled in a spinach wrap.

TUCANA BANANA $5

Banana, peanut butter, and honey with a little cinnamon grilled on homemade white bread.

Add bacon for $1.

TURKRAN SAN $6

Turkey, cranberry, and stuffing on a grilled panini roll. A meal on a bun!

SURF AND SURF $7

Tuna salad with onion and relish served on a sub roll with a cup of New England clam chowder.

SOUPS OF THE DAY

CUP $3

BOWL $5

Student 01
Formatted: Heading 3, Left

Reviewing changes

As useful as tracked changes are for a document in progress, once you're ready to finalize it, you want to review the changes, deciding which you want to accept or reject. You can find these commands in the Changes group.

Exam Objective: MOS Word Expert 1.3.2

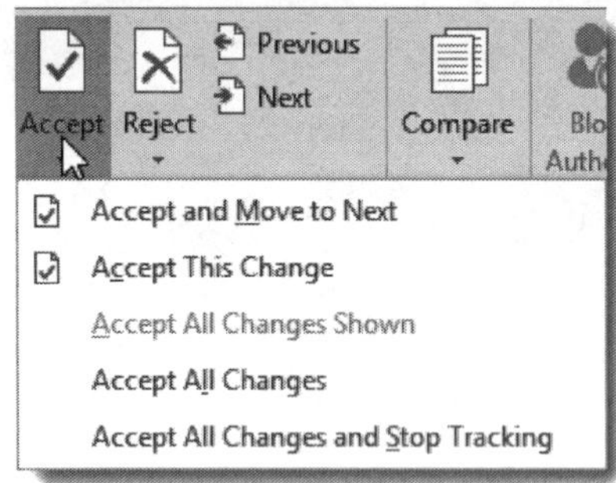

- To navigate through changes in the document, click **Next** or **Previous**.
- To accept a change, click **Accept**.
- To reject a change, click **Reject**.
- To automatically move to the next change, open the **Accept** or **Reject** menu, and select the **Move to Next** option.
- To accept all changes in the document at once, click **Accept** > **Accept All Changes**.
- To reject all changes, click **Reject** > **Reject All Changes**.

Document comparison

Tracking changes over multiple document versions can be difficult, especially when multiple editors are involved. In an ideal situation, all users work with the same document and track all their changes, and you can simply use the Changes commands to finalize it. If this isn't the case, you can use the Compare or Combine commands to merge multiple different revisions into a single document, and then review changes all at once.

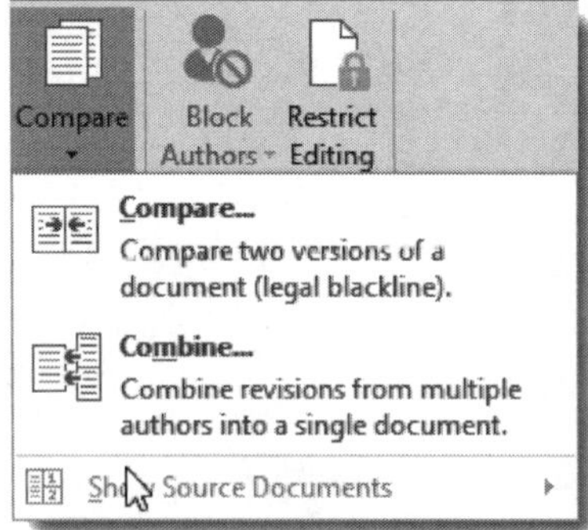

Both commands are very similar, but which you want to use depends on your situation.

- The **Combine** command is best for when you have multiple versions of the document, each with its own comments and tracked changes. Combining brings all the changes into one consolidated document.

- The **Compare** command is best for when you have documents without tracked changes. Word looks at the content differences between the two documents, and marks them as changes for you to accept or reject.

Comparing or combining documents

Exam Objective: MOS Word Expert 1.3.4

Once you decide whether to compare or combine documents, the steps for both are virtually the same, as are the available options in the **Compare Documents** or **Combine Documents** window.

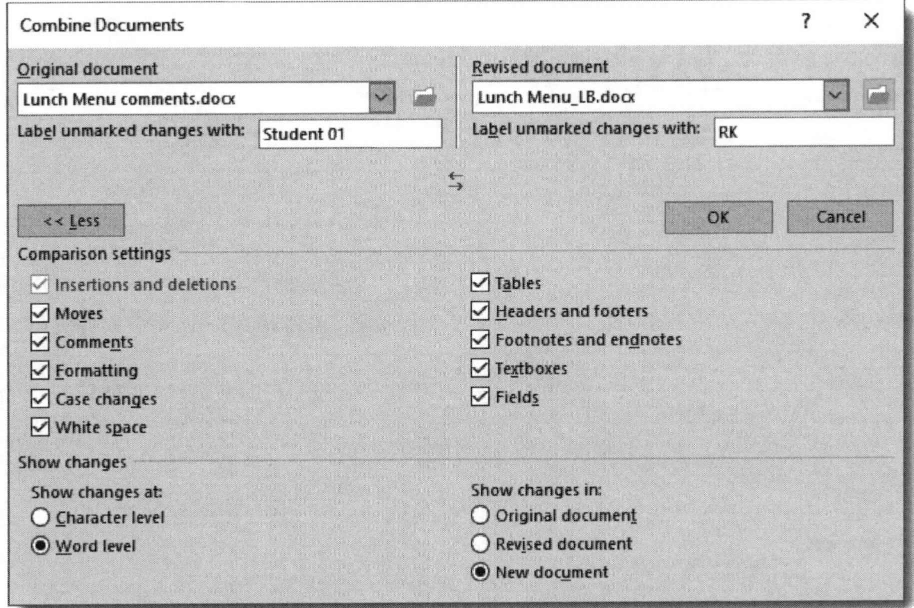

1. Click **Compare > Compare Documents** or **Compare > Combine Documents**.
2. Choose the original document. This is treated as the original document for the sake of changes in the consolidated one.
    - You can select from a list of recent documents or browse for one.
    - If you're comparing documents, this should be the oldest revision.
    - Choose a user name for unmarked changes in the document. By default, this is the document's last editor.
3. Choose the revised document, in the same way you did the original.
4. If you need to view additional options, click **More**.
    - Under Comparison settings, check or clear the types of changes you want to compare between the documents. By default, all are selected.
    - Under Show changes, choose how they appear. By default, they're displayed on the word level, and open in a new consolidated document that doesn't affect either source document.
5. Click **OK**.

If you have more than two versions of a document to compare or combine, you can repeat the process to add another into the combined document.

Working with combined documents

Exam Objective: MOS Word Expert 1.3.4

Once you compare or combine documents, Word opens the consolidated document in the center of the window, with the source documents and Reviewing Pane open as separate panes.

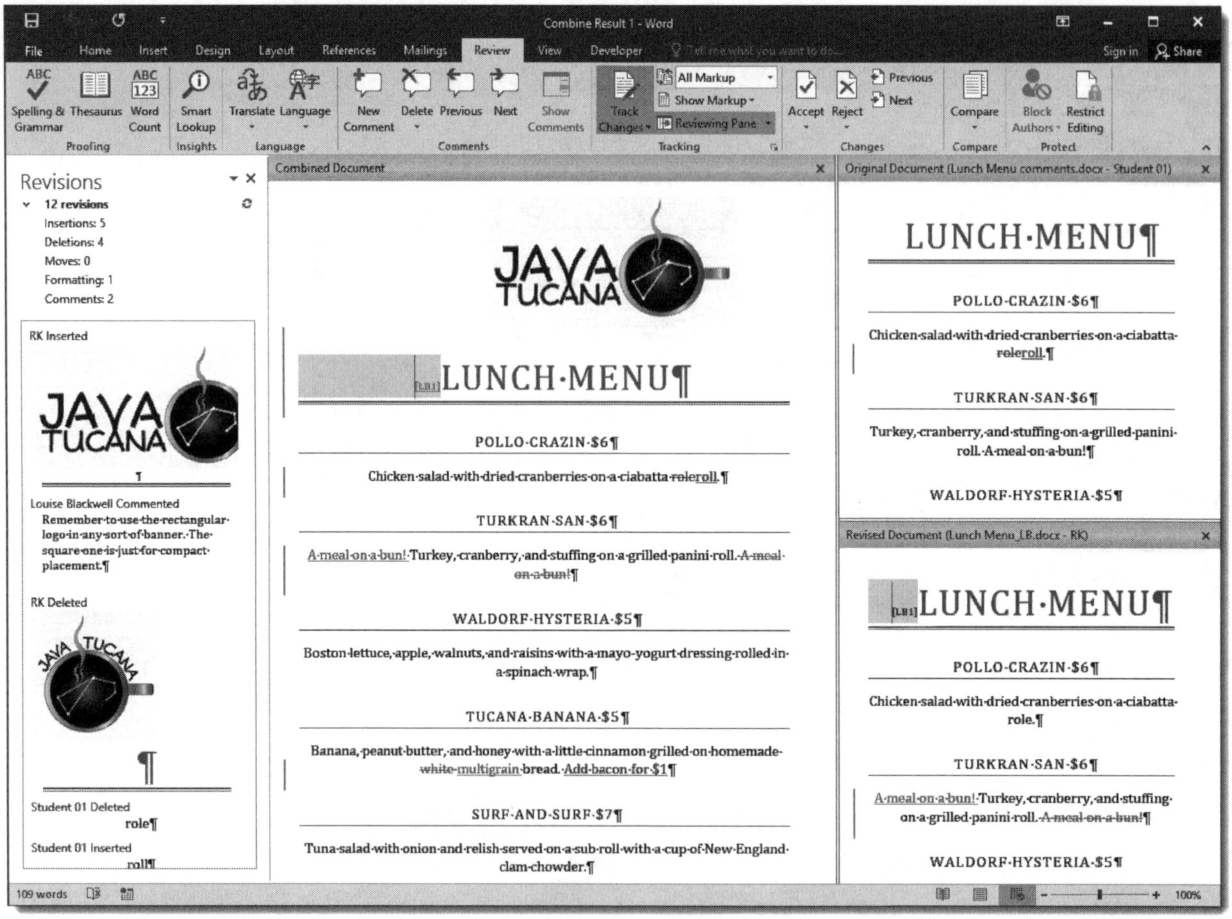

- Scrolling through any of the displayed documents automatically scrolls the others to match.
- If you've created a new document, you need to save it.
- To review changes, use the Changes group, just as you would normally.
- To review comments, use the Comments group.
- To hide or display the source documents, click **Compare > Show Source Documents**.

Exercise: Reviewing a combined document

To complete this exercise, you need to have completed the previous exercise, **Using document tracking**. You'll combine your tracked document with another created by a coworker, and then review changes in the combined document.

Do This	How & Why
1. Close any open documents.	
2. Combine `Lunch Menu comments` with `Lunch Menu_LB`.	A coworker of yours made her own revisions to the same document. You'll put the changes into a single document and review them all at once.
a) On the Review tab, click **Compare > Combine**.	The **Combine Documents** window opens.
b) From the Original document list choose `Lunch Menu comments`.	If it's not displayed in the list, click to browse for the file.
c) In the Revised document list, browse for **Lunch Menu_LB**.	Each document should have a different name for unmarked changes.
d) Click **More**.	To view additional options. You don't need to change any of these this time.
e) Click **OK**.	The new document is open in the center pane, with the source documents on the right and the Reviewing Pane on the left.
3. Observe the changes in each pane.	Each source document displays changes made in that document, while the combined document shows both. The Revisions pane provides a summarized list. All changes are color-coded according to the user who made them. Additionally, Louise Blackwell added comments to her version of the document.
4. Review changes in the document.	
a) In the Changes group, click **Next**.	To highlight the first change. Louise replaced the logo at the top of the menu with a different version.
b) Click **Accept > Accept and Move to Next**.	It's not very visible in the main document, but the accepted change is removed from the Revisions pane. The next change is a comment from Louise, explaining the logo change.
c) In the Comments group, click **Delete**.	You no longer need the comment.

Do This	How & Why
d) Move to the next change.	 When you replace content, Word views it as two separate changes, an addition and a deletion. In this case, the original logo is hidden behind the new one, but it's still there.
e) Click **Accept > Accept and Move to Next**.	Usually, you should accept or reject both halves of a replacement, or you might get unexpected results. The next change is the misspelling you corrected.
f) Accept both parts of the change.	Click **Accept > Accept and Move to Next** twice. You and Louise both moved some text. This becomes a little more complicated, since the two changes conflict with each other.
g) Click **Reject > Reject and Move to Next**.	The **Tracked Move Conflict Dialog** window appears, notifying you of the conflict. 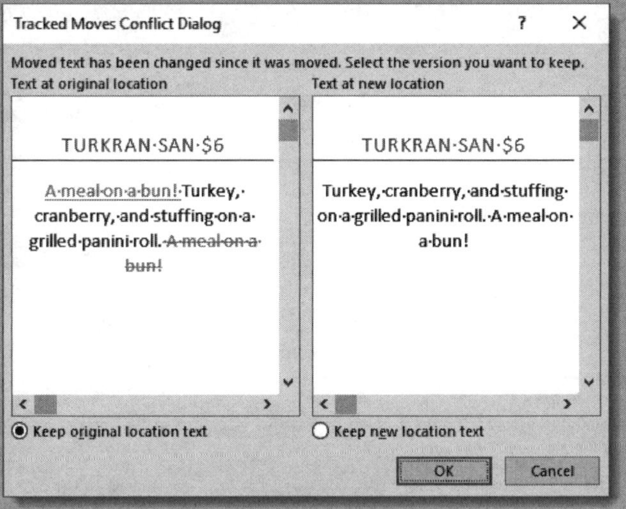
h) Click **Keep new location text**.	It might seem a little counter-intuitive, but it refers to keeping the text that you moved (which had been otherwise unchanged), without the changes that Louise applied.
i) Click **OK**.	The whole entry's location and text reverts to the original document's.
j) Click **Accept > Accept All Changes**.	To accept all the remaining changes in the document. All that's left is one comment from Louise about document colors. You'll leave it there for now.

Do This	How & Why
5. Save the combined document as `Lunch Menu combined`, and close it.	With the Combined Document pane selected, click **Save**.

Assessment: Tracking and reviewing changes

1. When multiple users have made tracked changes in a document, they are __________.
   - All identical
   - Displayed in different colors
   - Displayed in separate panes
   - Formatted differently
2. Two people have made their own revisions to a document, but neither has tracked changes. How can you best consolidate both sets of changes into a new document?
   - Combine the documents.
   - Compare the documents.
   - Compare each document with the original version, then combine the results of each comparison.
   - None of the above: without tracked changes, you have to reconcile them manually.
3. Even when you hide certain types of markup using the Show Markup options, they'll still be visible in the Revisions pane. True or false?
   - True
   - False
4. By default, a double-strikethrough indicates that text has been ________. Choose the best answer.
   - Commented upon
   - Deleted
   - Moved
   - Reformatted

Summary: Advanced document management

You learned how to:

- Configure Word options, including proofing, saving, and security
- Create, modify, organize, and attach templates
- Track changes to a document, review them, and combine or compare different versions of the same document

Synthesis: Advanced document management

1. Look through the **Word Options** window to see what changes might help you in your use of Word so far.
   In particular, examine AutoCorrect and grammar options that might be useful, or not useful, for your writing style and workplace environment.
2. Open `Franchise information draft.docx`, and save it as `Franchise information edited.docx`.
3. While tracking changes, look over and edit the document. When you're done, save and close it.
   Look for misspellings and awkward phrasings, and consider formatting changes.
4. Combine `Franchise information edited.docx` with `Franchise information_LB.docx`. Review all changes, and save the document as `Franchise information combined.docx`.
   When prompted, keep your formatting changes.
5. Download a job application template from Office.com, and customize it to suit a local Java Tucana branch. Save it as a new template.
   Hint: You can use `Logo.png` and an address of your choice.

Chapter 14: Using references

You will learn how to:

- Create bookmarks and cross-references
- Index documents
- Cite external sources

Module A: Internal references

Word allows you to create references inside a document, both to mark text you might want to find later and to refer to other parts of the same document. This can be helpful when you're working with long documents, whether in Word or in print.

You will learn how to:

- Create bookmarks
- Create cross-references

About bookmarks

Bookmarks are a way to mark a location or selection in a document, so that you can navigate to it or refer to it later. This can be helpful for finding your way through large documents. Unlike a table of contents, bookmarks are also suitable for marking content for editing reasons, such as a section you need to revise or expand. Once you've created a bookmark, you can also refer to it in index entries, or create *cross-references* within the document to link to it.

Exam Objective: MOS Word Core 1.2.3

You can create or manage bookmarks from the **Bookmark** window.

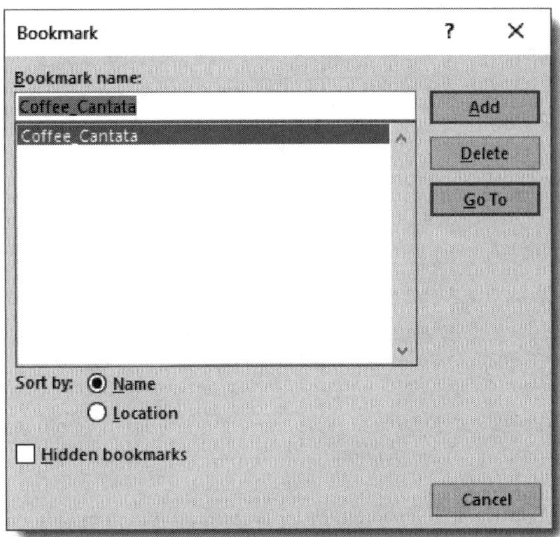

Word also automatically creates its own bookmarks, called *hidden bookmarks*, based on content and formatting in the document. Hidden bookmarks are created by internal Word processes: for example, when you insert a table of contents, Word creates bookmarks for each entry in the table. Usually, hidden bookmarks aren't important to users, and they're not displayed in the **Bookmark** window unless you check **Hidden bookmarks**.

Creating bookmarks

Exam Objective: MOS Word Core 1.2.3

You can create a bookmark from a location in a document, or from a selection.

1. Click a location, or select part of the document.
2. On the Insert tab, click **Bookmark**.
3. Type a name in the Bookmark name field.
   - The first character of the name must be a letter.
   - All other characters may be numbers or letters.
   - The name can't contain spaces, but you can use underscores instead.
   - To replace an existing bookmark, click its name instead of typing one.
4. Click **Add**.

Managing bookmarks

Once you've created bookmarks, you can use or remove them from the **Bookmarks** window.

Exam Objective: MOS Word Core 1.2.4

1. Click **Bookmark** on the Insert tab.
2. Select the bookmark you want to use.
   - Click **Go To** to navigate to the bookmark.
   - Click **Delete** to remove the bookmark (but not the text to which it refers).

   In large documents with many bookmarks, you can use the **Sort by** buttons to order them by either name or location.

Changing bookmarks

You can move or copy bookmarks, or change their content. If you don't know where a document's bookmarks are or don't understand how editing can change them, you might experience undesired results. Bookmarks are normally hidden—even when you display formatting—but you can make them visible by checking **Show bookmarks** in the Advanced section of the **Word Options** window.

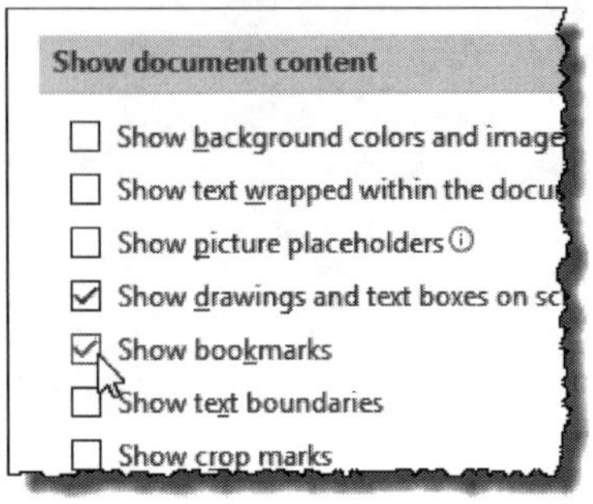

Visible bookmarks appear as brackets around selected text. Bookmarks that point to locations rather than selections appear as I-beams.

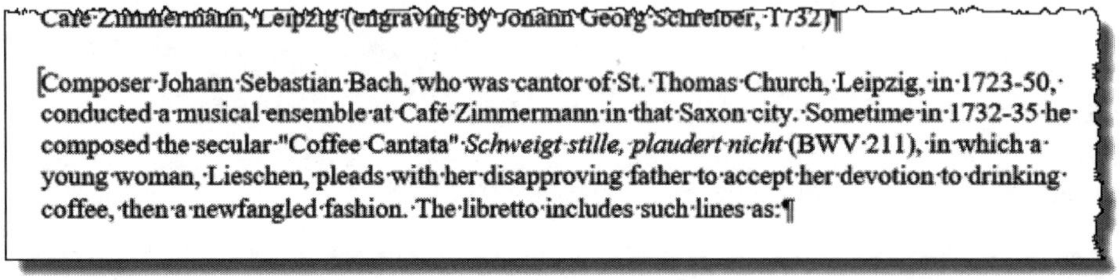

- It's often simplest just to remove and recreate a bookmark, rather than attempting to edit it.
- You can add content to a bookmark by inserting it within the bookmark's brackets. Any content added outside the brackets isn't part of the bookmark.
- Cutting and pasting a bookmark and its entire contents moves the bookmark itself to the new location, even if it's in another document.
- If you copy or cut a bookmark with all its contents, then paste it within the same document, only its content is copied. The bookmark itself remains where it was.
- If you copy an entire bookmark, then paste it into another document, the bookmark and its contents now exist in both documents.
- Only the whole bookmark can be moved or copied. If you delete, copy, or move only part of a bookmark's contents, only the contents are affected; the bookmark's placeholder remains.

Exercise: Using bookmarks

Do This	How & Why
1. Open `History of coffee`, and save it as `History of coffee bookmarked`.	
2. Create a bookmark.	
a) Navigate to the bottom of page 7.	It shows an excerpt from the "Coffee Cantata." You'll bookmark that and its descriptive text.
b) Select the libretto and the preceding paragraph.	
The text continues onto the next page, so don't miss that.	
c) On the Insert tab, click **Bookmark**.	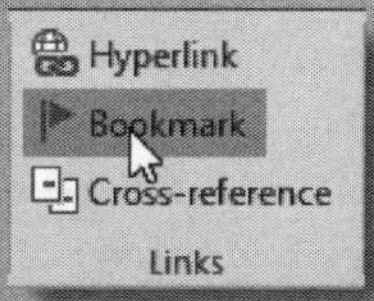 The **Bookmark** window opens.
d) In the Bookmark Name field, type `Coffee_Cantata`.	Remember that bookmark names can't contain spaces. 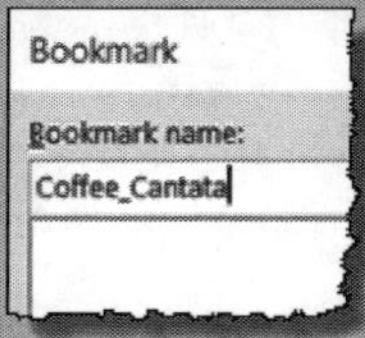
e) Click **Add**.	To create the bookmark and close the window.
3. Create additional bookmarks.	
a) Select the last three paragraphs of page 2.	Starting with "There are several legendary accounts" and ending with "likely to be apocryphal."
b) Click **Bookmark**.	The window opens.
c) Name the bookmark `Legendary_origins`.	Type it and click **Add**.

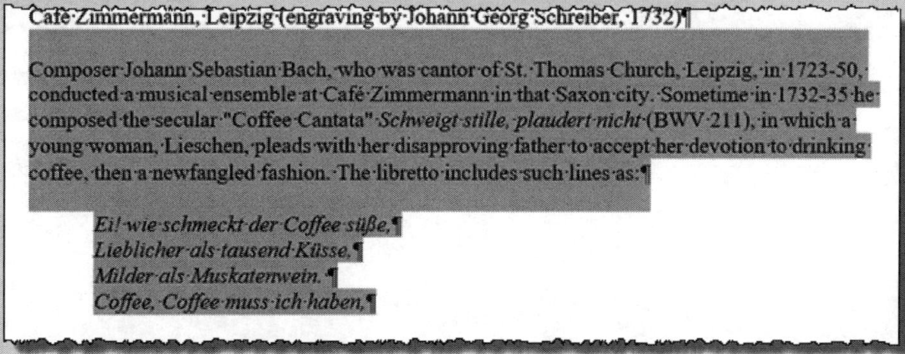

Do This	How & Why
d) Bookmark the "Women's petition against coffee" quote on page 6, with a name of your choosing.	It's the last paragraph before the France header.
4. Navigate to the bookmarks you've created.	
a) Place the insertion point at the top of the document.	
b) Click **Bookmark.**	The **Bookmark** window opens. The bookmark you created is now in the list.
c) Click **Coffee_Cantata**.	
d) Click **Go To**.	Word navigates to and selects the full text of the bookmark.
e) Navigate to each of the other bookmarks.	Select the bookmark, then click **Go To**. To move to each.
f) In the Sort by list, click **Location**.	The displayed order changes to reflect the bookmarks' order in the document.
5. Click **Close**.	To close the **Bookmark** window.
6. Save the document.	Leave it open for the next exercise.

About cross-references

One practical use of bookmarks is for creating cross-references. A *cross-reference* is text in a document that refers to another location in the document. For example, a cross-reference might say "on page 3." Because it's a field, the cross-reference updates whenever the referenced text moves. Additionally, you can make the cross-reference a hyperlink, so that in Word you can hold down **Ctrl** and click the link to navigate to the referenced content.

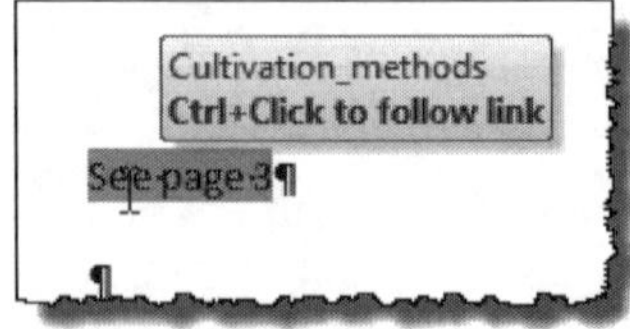

Cross-references have some advantages over hyperlinks. Not only can a cross-reference automatically update to reflect changes in the target's name or location, but unlike an ordinary hyperlink it looks like ordinary text when the document is printed. The chief disadvantage of cross-references is that they can only link inside the same document, not to other files or network locations.

Cross-references aren't specific to bookmarks. You can also create cross-references to headings, footnotes, endnotes, figures, equations, tables, and numbered items. Nor does a cross-reference have to only name the location; it can duplicate the entire text of a caption or bookmark.

Inserting cross-references

You can insert a cross-reference at the insertion point using the **Cross-reference** window.

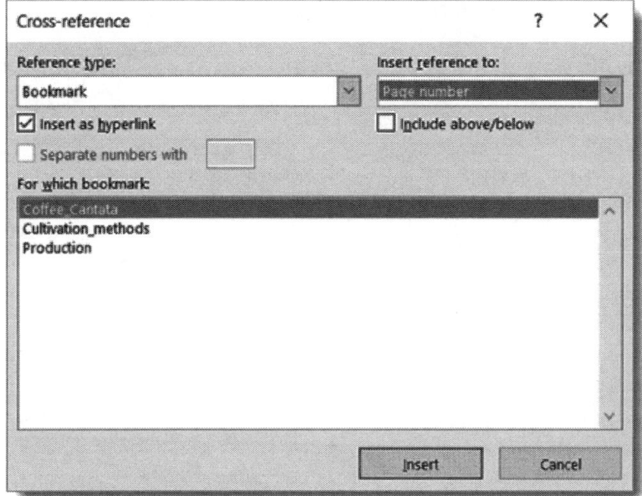

1. On either the Insert tab or the References tab, click **Cross-reference**.

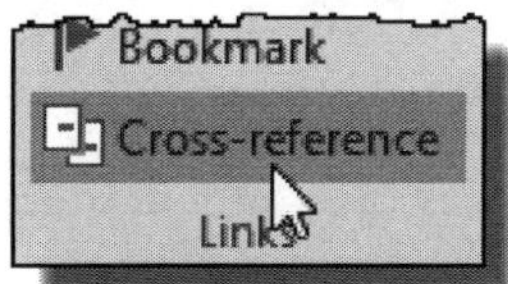

2. Choose an option from the Reference type list.
3. Choose a reference from the list below.
4. Choose how you want the reference to appear on the page.
   - Choose a reference appearance from the "Insert reference to" list.
   - Check **Include above/below** to make the reference specify whether it's pointing above or below in the document.
   - Clear **Insert as hyperlink** if you don't want the reference to be a hyperlink.

   The available options depend on what reference type you're using.
5. Click **Insert**.

   The **Cross-references** window remains open until you click **Close**.

Creating hyperlinks to bookmarks

When you insert a hyperlink, you can choose a bookmark as a destination. Unlike a cross-reference, the displayed text is static, and won't update automatically to reflect changes in the target.

- To insert a hyperlink to a bookmark in the current document, click **Place in this Document**, and scroll to the end of the list.

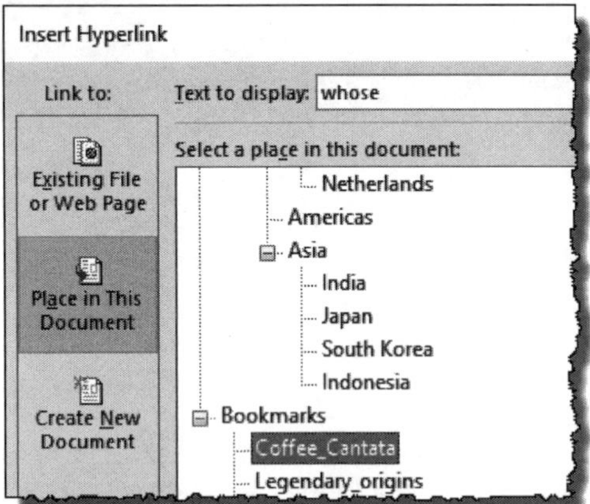

- To insert a hyperlink to a bookmark in the other document, navigate to that document and click **Bookmark**. Then navigate to the bookmark you want in the **Select Place in Document** window.

Exercise: Using cross-references

To complete this exercise, you need to have completed the previous exercise, **Creating a bookmark**. `History of coffee bookmarked` is still open.

In this exercise, you'll add cross-references to a document.

Do This	How & Why
1. Create a cross-reference.	You'll start by making a cross-reference to an earlier heading.
a) Navigate to page 3.	
b) In the second paragraph under the images, place the insertion point after the first sentence.	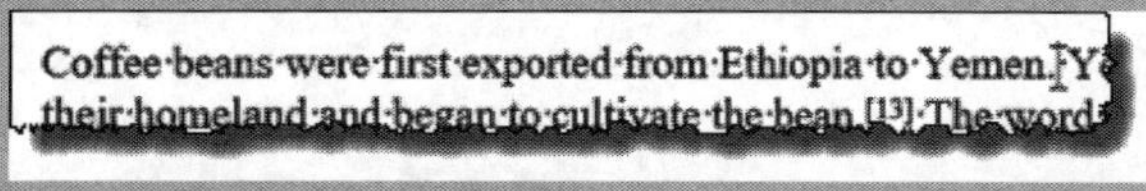
c) On the Insert tab, click **Cross-reference**.	The **Cross-reference** window opens, and the document text scrolls to the location of the insertion point. You can create a bookmark to the text you want, but there's already a heading in the right place, so you can use that.
d) From the Reference type list, choose **Heading**.	The list below now shows the headings in the document.
e) In the "For which heading" list, click **First use**.	You'll have a link to an earlier discussion of coffee's Ethiopian origins.
f) From the "Insert reference to" list, choose **Page number**.	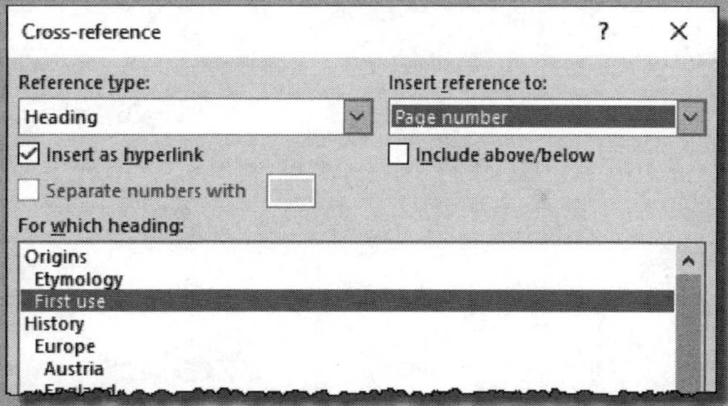
g) Click **Insert**.	 In this format, the cross reference is just the number itself, so you need to enter an explanation.
2. Edit the text to make the cross-reference clearer.	You could edit the field itself, but that would revert it when it's updated. So you'll just type outside the field.
a) Before the page number, type `(See page`	Include spaces both before and after the text.
b) After the page number, type `.)`	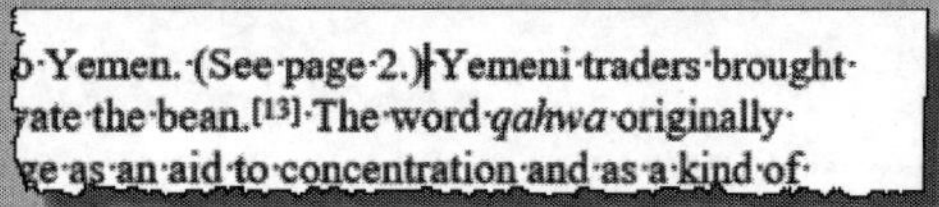

Do This	How & Why
3. Hold down **Ctrl** and click the cross-reference.	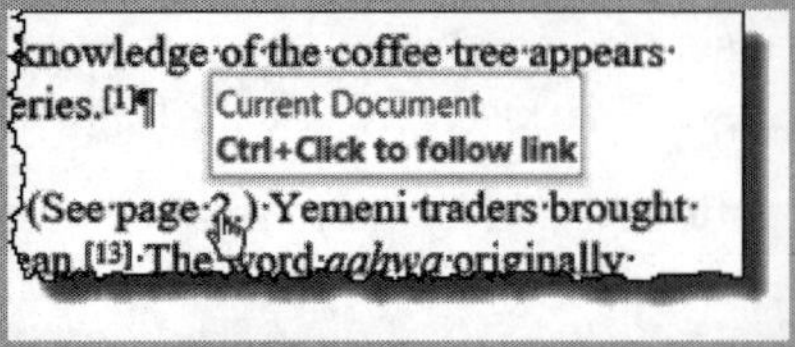 To navigate to the First use heading.
4. Create a cross-reference to one of the bookmarks you created.	
a) On page 1, click right after the image caption, then press **Enter** twice.	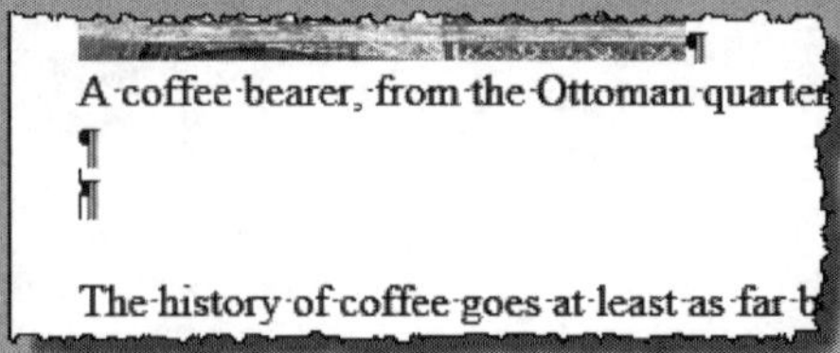
b) In the Reference type list of the **Cross-Reference** window, select **Bookmark**.	
c) Clear **Insert as Hyperlink**.	This time won't actually make the cross-reference a link.
d) Verify that **Bookmark text** is selected in the Insert reference to field.	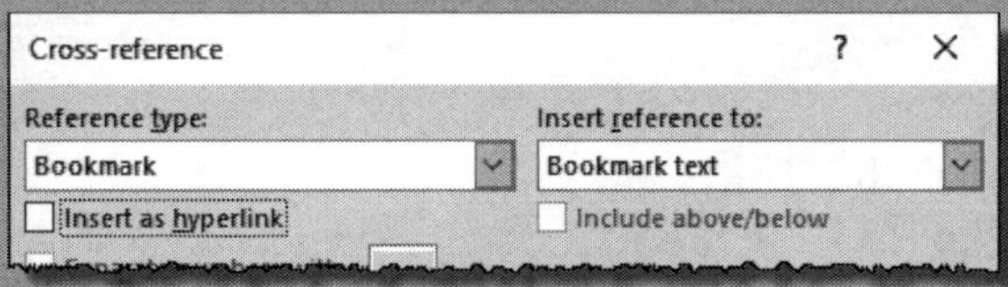
e) From the bookmarks list, choose **Coffee_Cantata** and click **Insert**.	The entire content of the bookmark is duplicated at the insertion point.
5. Close the **Cross-reference** window.	Click **Close**.
6. Display bookmark locations.	
a) In Backstage View, click **Options**.	The **Word Options** window opens.
b) In the Show document content section of the Advanced page, check **Show bookmarks**.	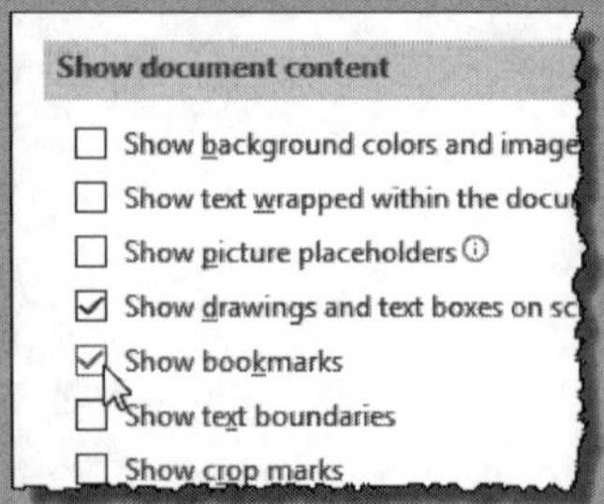
c) Click **OK**.	To close the **Word Options** window. The bookmark text you just inserted doesn't look any different, though it is a field if you click on it.
d) Go to the bottom of page 8.	Bookmark brackets surround the Coffee_Cantata bookmark you made earlier.

Do This	How & Why
7. Modify the Coffee_Cantata bookmark.	You don't really want the bookmark at the start of the document to display the paragraph describing the libretto, only the quote itself. You'll alter the bookmark instead.
a) Select the first paragraph of the bookmark.	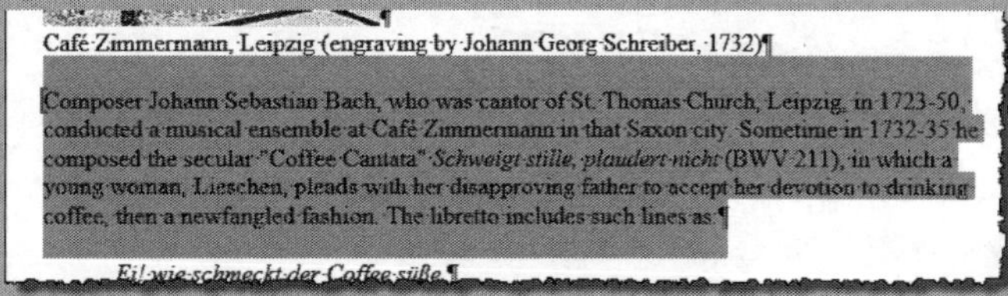
b) Cut the selected text.	The bookmark bracket now begins at the start of the quote.
c) Press **Left** and then press **Enter**.	To insert a new paragraph after the image caption.
d) Press **Ctrl+V**.	To paste the cut paragraph.
e) Press **Delete**.	To delete the blank paragraph. The description of the libretto is no longer inside the bookmark. 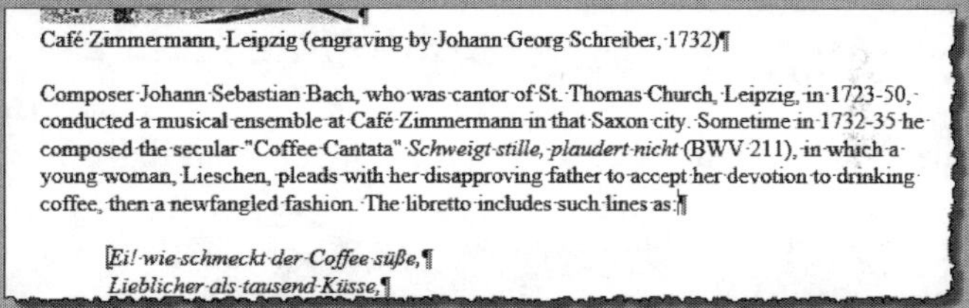
f) Return to the top of the document.	The paragraph still is displayed in the bookmark you inserted.
g) Right-click anywhere in the bookmark field and click **Update Field**.	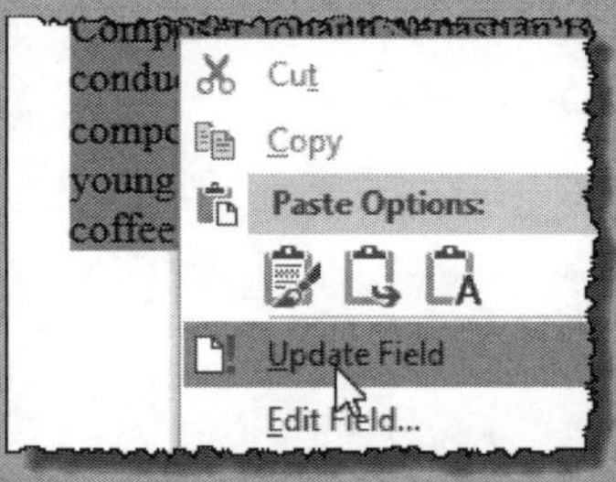 The bookmark now only displays the libretto quote itself.
8. Save and close the document.	

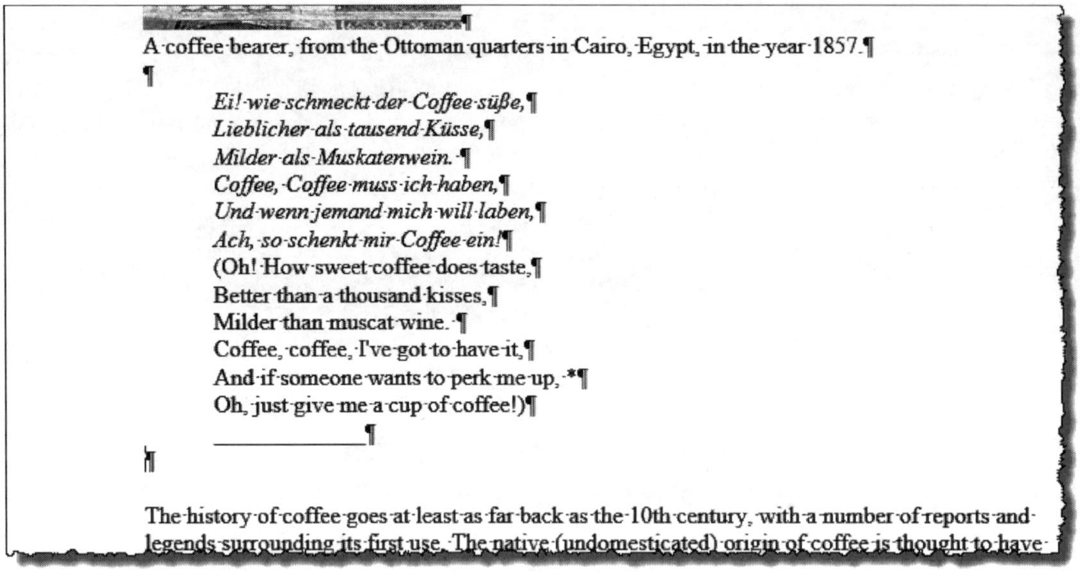

A coffee bearer, from the Ottoman quarters in Cairo, Egypt, in the year 1857.¶
¶
Ei! wie schmeckt der Coffee süße,¶
Lieblicher als tausend Küsse,¶
Milder als Muskatenwein. ¶
Coffee, Coffee muss ich haben,¶
Und wenn jemand mich will laben,¶
Ach, so schenkt mir Coffee ein!¶
(Oh! How sweet coffee does taste,¶
Better than a thousand kisses,¶
Milder than muscat wine. ¶
Coffee, coffee, I've got to have it,¶
And if someone wants to perk me up, *¶
Oh, just give me a cup of coffee!)¶
____________¶
¶

The history of coffee goes at least as far back as the 10th century, with a number of reports and legends surrounding its first use. The native (undomesticated) origin of coffee is thought to have

Assessment: Internal references

1. What is true about bookmark names? Choose all that apply.
   - They cannot contain spaces.
   - They cannot contain underscores.
   - They may begin with a letter or a number.
   - They must begin with a letter.
   - They must begin with a number.
2. When you move the full contents of a bookmark, the bookmark itself also moves. True or false?
   - True
   - False
3. Cross-references are useful, even if you're planning to print the document. True or false?
   - True
   - False.
4. Unlike an ordinary hyperlink, a cross-reference _________. Choose all that apply.
   - Appears as normal text when printed
   - Automatically updates its text whenever fields are updated
   - Can point to a bookmark
   - Can point to an external document

Module B: Indexing

When you create long documents or books, especially for printing, you might want to create an index. Word can automatically generate an index using index entries you create in the document text.

You will learn how to:

- Mark index entries
- Create indices
- Modify indices

About index entries

When you create a table of contents, Word can recognize what should be in it just by the text you've already formatted as headings. An index isn't as simple, as there's no pre-existing formatting that tells Word what's important enough to be included. This means you need to create *index entries*, markers in the document text to denote key terms or concepts.

> Other accounts attribute the discovery of coffee to Sheik Abou'l Hasan Schadheli's disciple, Omar. According to the ancient chronicle (preserved in the Abd-Al-Kadir manuscript), Omar, who was known for his ability to cure the sick through prayer, was once exiled from Mocha{ XE "Coffee varieties:Mocha" } to a desert cave near Ousab. Starving, Omar chewed berries from nearby shrubbery, but found them to be bitter. He tried roasting the beans to improve the flavor,

Index Entry (XE) fields are part of the document's hidden formatting, which you can hide or display by clicking **Show/Hide**. At the minimum, the field contains a *main entry*, the general term that appears in the index itself. Optionally, you can add a *subentry*, a more specific term that appears beneath the main entry. You can also create a *cross-reference*, which points to another term in the index.

An index entry can be for a word, a phrase, or a symbol. You can even create index entries for longer topics spanning multiple pages by first defining them as bookmarks.

Commands for creating indices and index entries are on the References tab, in the Index group.

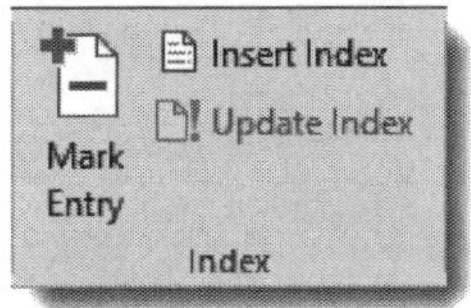

Marking index entries

You can make an index entry in the **Mark Index Entry** window.

Exam Objective: MOS Word Expert 3.1.3

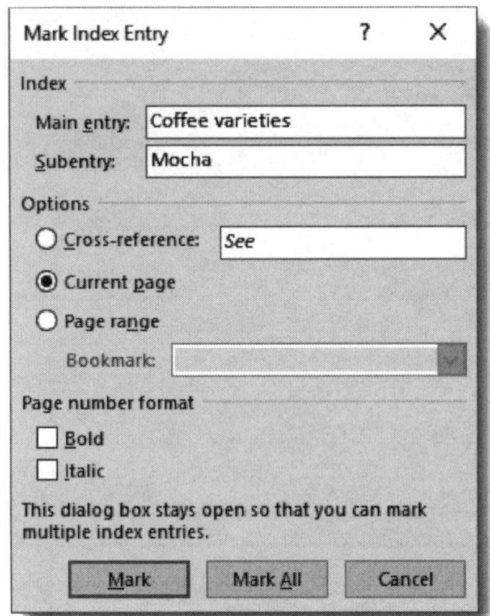

1. Select any text in the document.
2. In the Index group, click **Mark Entry**.
3. Set the entry name.
   - By default, "Main entry" is the text you selected. You can edit it to whatever you like.
   - "Subentry" is optional, but can also be whatever you like.
   - You can add a third-level entry by typing **:** after the subentry, followed by the third-level entry.

   Note: Index entries are case-sensitive; for example, if you use "fast," "Fast," and "FAST" in separate entries, they appear on three different lines of the finished index. They're also sensitive to spaces, so don't insert extra spaces before or after the entry—this includes the colons used to separate entry levels.
4. Set additional options.
   - By default, the entry appears at the current page.
   - To create a cross-referenced entry, click **Cross-reference**, and type the other entry to which you want to point.
   - To point to a page range you've defined as a bookmark, click **Page range**, and select the bookmark from the list.
   - Check **Bold** or **Italic** to format the page number for the entry.
5. Mark the entry.
   - Click **Mark** to create an index entry on just the selected text.
   - Click **Mark All** to create an index entry for each recurrence of the selected text in the document. This can save time and trouble but might result in unhelpful entries.

The **Mark Index Entry** window doesn't close after you create an entry. Instead, it stays open so you can keep making new entries. Once you've made one entry, you need only to select new text in the document, then click the window again. When you're done making entries, click **Close**.

Creating indices

Once you've created entries, you can tell Word to compile them into an index. Although it's common to put the index at the end of a document, you can insert it anywhere you like. Simply place the insertion point, and click **Insert Index** to open the **Index** window. Note index entries and formatting marks can change pagination when they're displayed. Don't forget to hide formatting before you generate the index.

Exam Objective: MOS Word Expert 3.1.1, 3.1.2, 3.1.3, 3.1.4

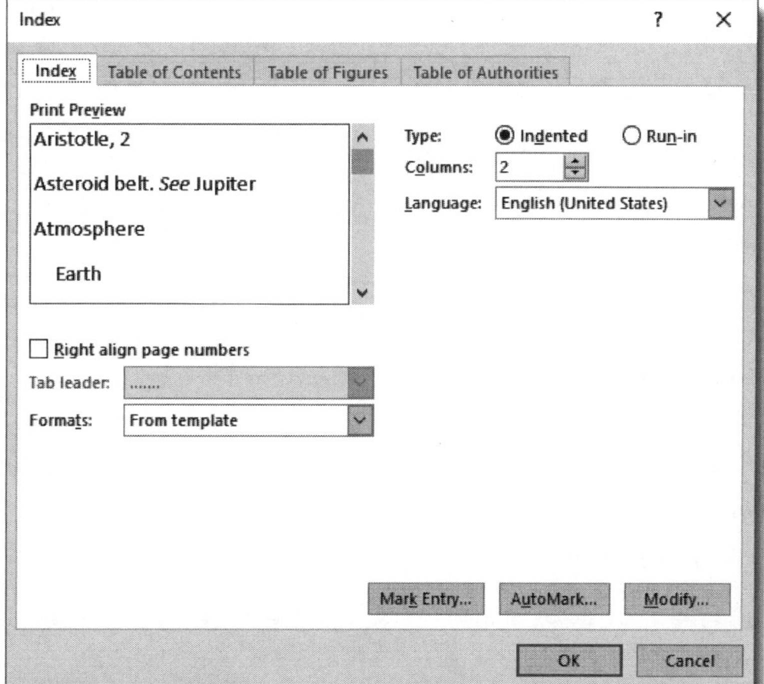

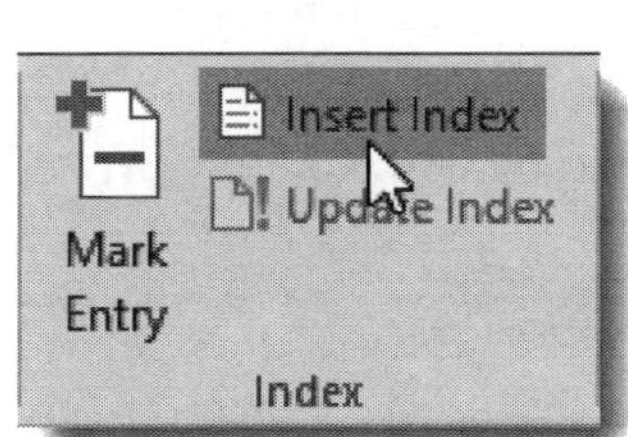

The Index window might not seem very intuitive at first. The way commands work together doesn't really match up with how they're grouped in the window, and some options are available only if you've made a particular choice elsewhere in the window. Fortunately, you can always look to the Print Preview pane to see how your current settings will appear in an index with sample data.

- To change the overall formatting of the index, use the Formats list.
- If you use the default "From template" format, you can click **Modify** to modify the text style of index entries. There are paragraph styles defined for up to nine index levels.
- To change how subentries are displayed, use the Type buttons.
  - Click **Indented** to display each subentry on its own line, indented below a main entry. This is the default setting, and generally produces neater results.
  - Click **Run-in** to display all subentries immediately after the main entry, separated by semicolons. This can be harder to read, but it's useful if you need to save space in a long index.
- If you're using an Indented index, you can check **Right align page numbers** and select a tab leader from the list, such as a dotted or dashed line. Otherwise, page numbers immediately follow the entry.
- By default, the index is generated in two-column format; however, you can select from one to four columns.
- If you have more than one language installed, you can use the Language list to select which of them Word uses for alphabetization rules.
- Click **Mark Entry** to close the **Index** window and open the **Mark Index Entry** window.
- Click **AutoMark** to generate automatic index entries based on a list of terms in an external file.

Once you're satisfied with your settings, click **OK** to insert the index.

Modifying indices

You can change an existing index, either to correct problems or to reflect changes made to the rest of the document.

 **Exam Objective:** MOS Word Expert 3.1.2

- To change an index entry, edit the field's contents manually, or delete the entry and create a new one.
- To manually add a subentry, or further levels, separate each level with a colon. Don't use any spaces before or after the colon.
- To manually add a cross-reference, type `\t "<cross-reference text>"` after the entry, inside the field.

```
{XE "Chairs:wicker" \t "See Furniture"}
```

- To format the page entry as bold or italic, type `\b` or `\i` in front of the index term.

```
{XE \b "Chairs:wicker"}
```

- To update index entries and page numbers, place the insertion point anywhere in the index and click **Update Index**.
- You can change the index's formatting in either of two ways:
  - Delete the index, and insert a new one.
  - Right-click the index, and click **Edit Field**, then **Index**. You can then change settings in the **Index** window.
- You can manually edit the index itself, but remember that any manual changes you make are lost if you update the index later.

Troubleshooting index problems

If you're lucky, your index will be accurate and look good on the first try. If you're not, you're going to have to go back and make changes. There are a number of common problems you might encounter, but most of them come down to either an outdated index or incorrect entries. Remember that the index doesn't update automatically, so when you make changes to the document they won't be reflected in the index until you update it.

- If page numbers are still incorrect after an update, make sure that you're not showing hidden formatting. These marks, including XE fields, can change the pagination of the whole document.
- If entries that should be identical aren't combining properly into one term, that means there's some difference between the entry fields.
  - Verify that both entries are in the same case.
  - Check mismatching entries for extra spaces. There shouldn't be any extra spaces in the entry text, even before or after delimiters such as colons, semicolons, or quotation marks.
  - Check for formatting differences between the two entries.
  - If you want to be certain multiple entries are identical, copy and paste one entry to all the others.
- If the index isn't sorted properly, or its letter headings are incorrect, there are multiple possible causes.
  - Verify that the index is generated in the correct language. Different languages use different orders for alphabetization.

- Tracked changes can interfere with index sorting. If this is the problem, you might not be able to generate an accurate index until you've reviewed all changes.
- If an entry you've created doesn't appear in the index, even after an update, there might be a syntax error in the update. This is especially likely if you've manually typed or modified the entry. Try deleting the entry and creating a new one.
- Page ranges can have a number of problems.
  - When a term has multiple entries on consecutive pages, it appears as a list, rather than as a range. For example, "25, 26, 27" instead of "25-27." If you want to have an index entry for a whole section of text, define it as a bookmark, and then create a single entry for the bookmark.
  - Even when you've created a bookmark, it can be unreliable. Avoid using special characters when naming it, and be aware that when you edit the contents of a bookmarked range, doing so might affect the index. You might need to delete and recreate the bookmark to fix the index entry.
- If your cross-references aren't formatted properly, you'll have to format them in their respective entries. They're ordinary text, so you can use normal formatting controls, but you can't apply named styles.

Exercise: Creating an index

In this exercise, you'll mark index entries and subentries in a long document, then use them to assemble an index.

Do This	How & Why
1. Open `History of coffee`, and save it as `History of coffee indexed`.	This document is 11 pages long, with multiple sections, so you've decided to add an index.
2. Display formatting, if necessary.	Click **Show/Hide** on the Home tab, or press **Ctrl+*.**
3. Create an index entry.	You'll start by marking some index entries for Arabica, the most popular species of coffee.
a) On page 2, select the word "arabica."	
b) On the References tab, click **Mark Entry**.	The **Mark Index Entry** window opens; "arabica" is already in the Main entry field.
c) Click **Mark**.	The index entry appears in the text. The **Mark Index Entry** window remains open.
4. Manually edit the new entry.	The entry you just created, like the word you initially selected, is in italics. You just want it to appear as normal text in the index, so you'll have to fix it.

Do This	How & Why
a) In the index entry, select "arabica."	Don't close the **Mark Index Entry** window. 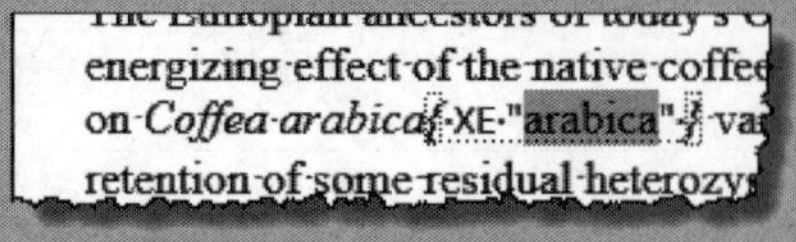
b) Remove the italics from the text.	Use the Font controls, or press **Ctrl+I**.
5. Mark additional instances of "arabica."	This time, you'll be careful of the formatting when you make the entry.
a) Select the next instance of "arabica."	It's on page 8, in the second paragraph under "Netherlands."
b) Click the **Mark Index Entry** window.	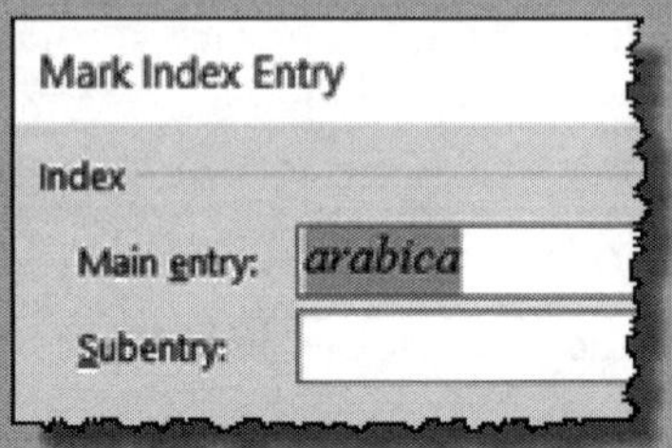 The text you've selected automatically appears as the main entry.
c) Select the main entry text, and press **Ctrl+I**.	To remove the italics from the text.
d) Click **Mark**.	This time, the index entry is normal text.
e) Mark the next instance of the word.	In the second paragraph under "Americas." Select it, then click **Mark**.
f) Mark the first instance of the word on page 10.	It's capitalized, so you'll need to edit the entry.
6. Insert index entries for "coffeehouses," with subentries by location.	The document variously uses "coffee house" and "coffeehouse" in singular and plural form. You'll use one standardized index term.
a) Select the first instance of "coffee houses."	In the last paragraph on page 3.
b) In the **Mark Index Entry** window, edit the Main Entry and Subentry fields as shown.	An entry or subentry can be a phrase or symbol rather than a single word.

Do This	How & Why
c) Click **Mark**.	
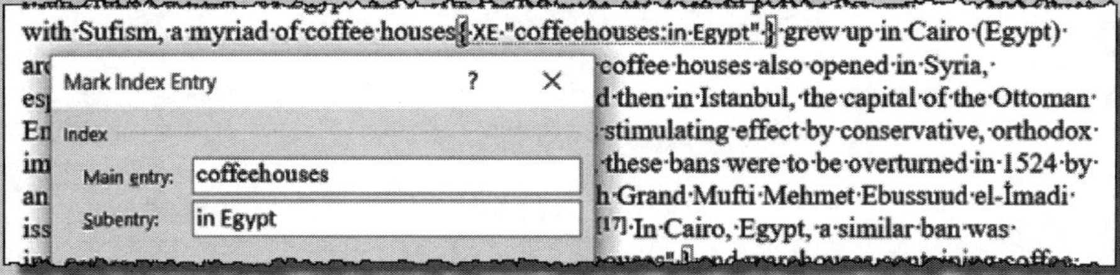	
d) On the next line, create an entry for coffeehouses in Syria.	Select the term, then type `coffeehouses` after Main entry and `in Syria` after Subentry.
e) Create an entry for coffeehouses in Austria.	Near the top of page 5.
7. Insert an index.	Space isn't really a concern, so you'll place the index on its own page with clear formatting.
a) At the end of the document, insert a next-page section break.	On the Page Layout tab, click **Break > Next Page**.
b) Type `Index` and format it as **Heading 1**.	
c) Press **Enter**.	To create a new paragraph. You'll place the index here.
d) Hide formatting marks.	Press **Ctrl+***. To make sure the page numbers are accurate when you print.
e) On the References tab, click **Insert Index**.	The **Index** window opens. A preview of the default format is displayed in the upper left.
f) From the Formats list, choose **Formal**.	This style includes headings for each letter, and right-aligned page numbers with dotted lines for a tab leader.
g) Observe the other settings.	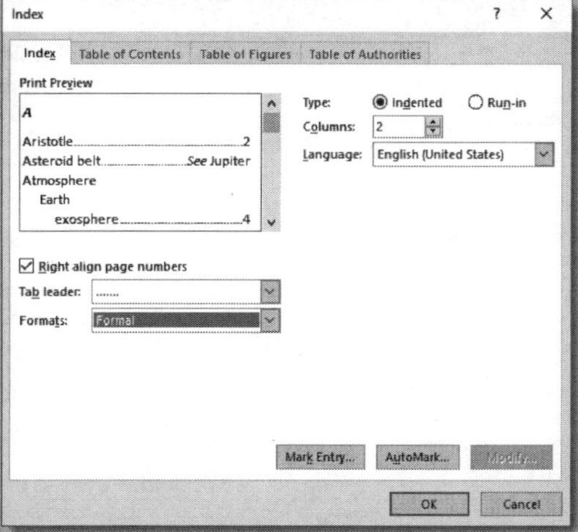 You'll keep the default Type, Columns, and Language settings.

Do This	How & Why
h) Click **OK**.	

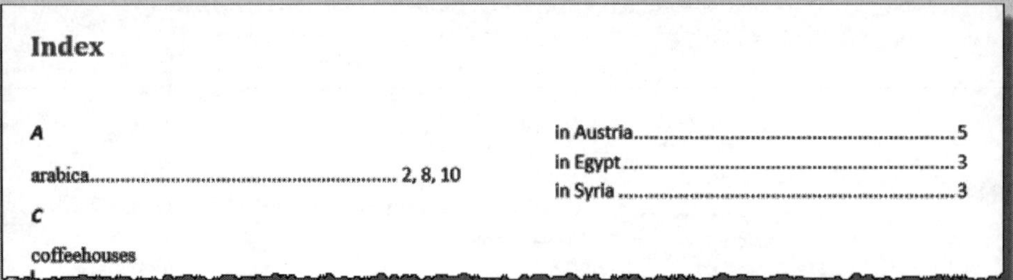

The "coffeehouses" entry and its subentries are split across two columns. This might sort out as you add more entries, but if it doesn't in the final version, you might need to make adjustments.

Do This	How & Why
8. At the bottom of page 8, create an index entry for the first instance of "Bourbon."	It's a proper name, so capitalize it, but make sure it's not in italics.
9. Update the index.	Your newest entry isn't reflected just yet.
a) Click inside the index.	
b) Hide formatting again.	When you create a new entry, it is automatically displayed.
c) In the Index group, click **Update Index**.	The index is updated to include the new entry.
10. Close the **Mark Index Entry** window.	
11. Save and close the file.	

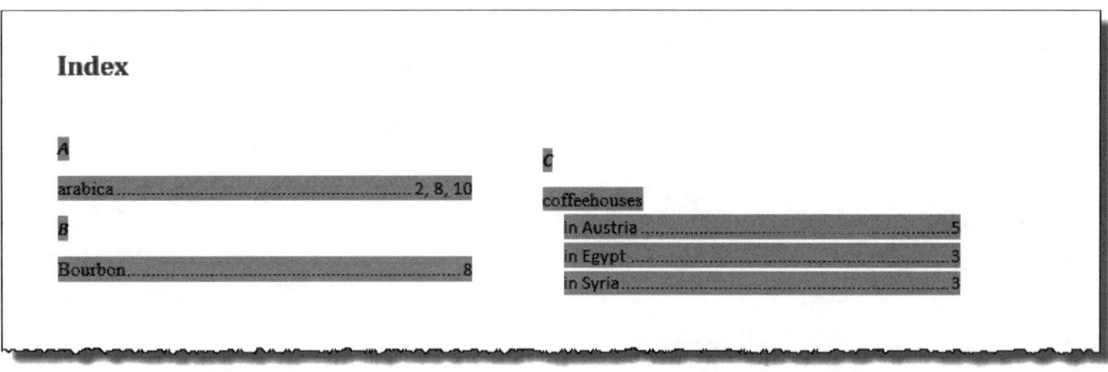

Assessment: Indexing

1. Word can only create two index levels. True or false?
   - True
   - False
2. What index type might you use if you have a lot of subentries but space is limited? Choose the best response.
   - Cross-referenced
   - Indented
   - Right-aligned
   - Run-in
3. You shouldn't copy and paste or manually edit index entries, as doing so can interfere with how the XE field code works. True or false?
   - True
   - False

Module C: Citing external sources

In informal documents, external references are simple: you can insert a hyperlink to a web page or file, or refer to the title of a book or other document. By contrast, academic or professional documents can have formal standards for citing your sources of information. Word allows you to create *citations* that refer to these external sources, and later to compile them into a central *bibliography* for the document.

You will learn how to:

- Create and manage sources
- Add citations
- Compile a bibliography
- Create a table of authorities in a legal document

About citations

When you make a formal document, whether it's a school paper or a professional publication, you need to cite external works you used for research. There's nothing to prevent you from just manually adding citations or compiling a bibliography at the end of your document, but Word provides automated tools to make the whole process easier and more accurate. Word can store a list of all your sources, format citations in your preferred style, and assemble a bibliography. You can even insert placeholders for sources, then come back and fill them in later.

A citation field in a document.

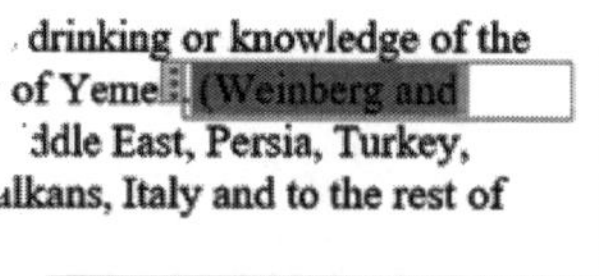

Whether you start out using placeholders or not, citations are only useful if you eventually create sources representing books, journals, websites, patents, or other publications they refer to. Once you've added a source to Word's master list, you can cite it from any document you create, and add it to a bibliography.

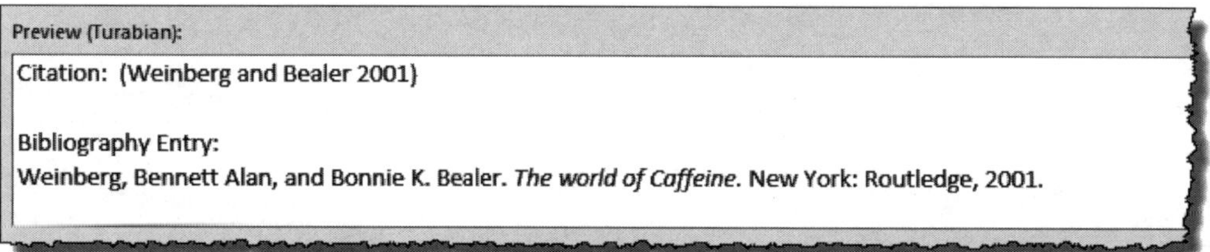

Commands for adding citations and bibliographies, as well as managing your sources, are located on the References tab, in the Citations & Bibliography group.

Citation styles

You can choose from a variety of citation styles to use in your documents. Each style is a standard created by a different organization: which you should adhere to depends on your field and your audience. Word includes a number of these styles by default: if you need a different one, it can be downloaded from a third-party vendor. You can choose the style for your document from the Style list in the Citations & Bibliography group.

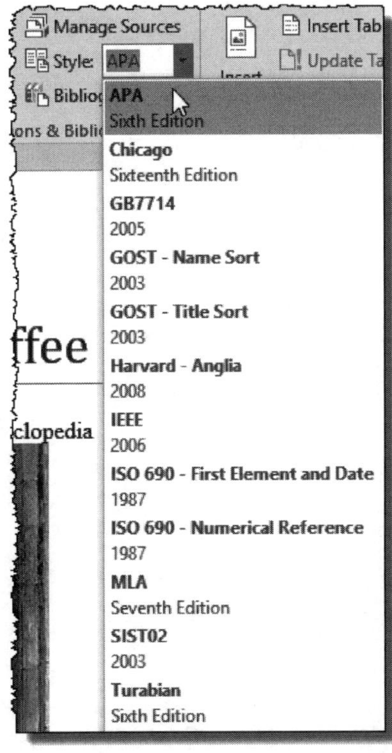

APA	Created by the American Psychological Association, but common in other academic disciplines.
Chicago	Created by the University of Chicago. A popular US style, especially in the social sciences.
GB7714	Created by the Standardization Administration of China, and used in Chinese documents.
GOST	Created by the former USSR government, now maintained by the Euro-Asian Council for Standardization, Metrology and Certification (EASC). Typically used in the Commonwealth of Independent States.
Harvard - Anglia	Created by the University Library at Anglia Ruskin University. A popular UK academic style.
ISO 690	Created by the International Organization for Standardization, and commonly used in Europe. Covers all sorts of published material including text, images, audio recordings, and electronic documents.
MLA	Created by the Modern Language Association of America. Commonly used in English and the humanities.
SIST-02	Created by the Japan Science and Technology Agency, and intended primarily for Japanese scientific journals.
Turabian	Created by Kate Turabian. A simplified version of Chicago style, designed for students writing research papers.

When you change the style in a document, all existing citations are reformatted to that standard, but because each style has its own set of fields, it's best to decide on a style before you start defining any sources.

Inserting citations

You can insert citations to defined sources, or placeholders for sources that you can define later. You can also define sources as part of creating a citation.

Exam Objective: MOS Word Core 4.1.5, 4.1.6

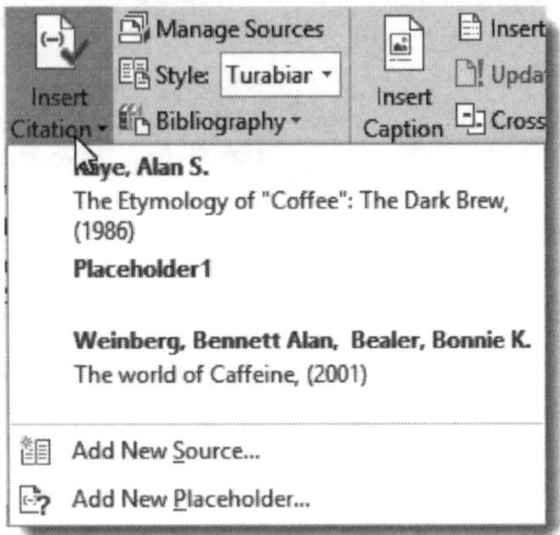

1. Place the insertion point where you want the citation.
2. Click **Insert Citation** and choose an option.
   - If you're citing a source you've already defined, you can choose it from the list.
   - If you want to cite a new source, click **Add New Source** to open the **Create Source** window.
   - If you want to place your citation but define the source later, click **Add New Placeholder**. You're then asked to name the placeholder in the **Placeholder Name** window.

Creating sources

When you add a new source, the **Create Source** window opens, with fields relevant to your current style. You can choose the type of source and specify relevant information, then click **OK** when you're done. The fields you need to enter depend on the type of source and the style you're choosing. Word can give you recommendations, but for formal documents it's important that you understand the requirements of your chosen style as well.

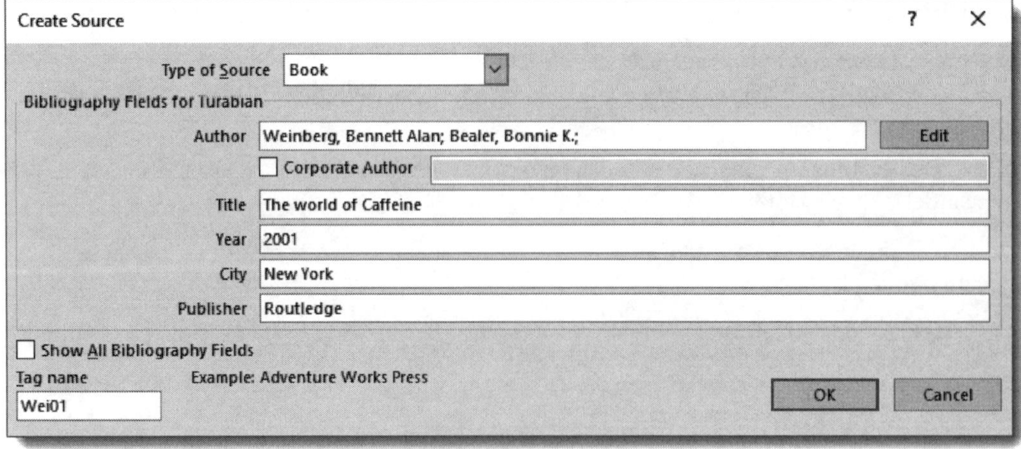

- Select the type of source you're citing from the Type of Source list. This changes the other available fields in the window.
- Check **Show All Bibliography Fields** to display hidden fields.
- Multiple authors can be separated by semicolons. Word attempts to automatically recognize first and last names, but you can click **Edit** to specify this directly.
- Every source has a unique *tag name*, or field identifier. It's automatically generated by Word, but you can manually edit it. The tag name is case-sensitive.
- Some source types may have seemingly overlapping fields, for example both Author and Book Author in the "Book Section" source. In this case, Author would be the author of the particular section or chapter being cited, and Book Author the author of the overall book.

Note: If you want to use an entire book as a source and cite different parts of it in separate citations, don't use the Book Section type. Instead, just reference the whole book as a source and specify pages by editing the individual citation.

Editing citations and sources

You can edit a citation or the source it refers to by activating the citation field, then clicking the **Citation Options** button to its right. A menu opens.

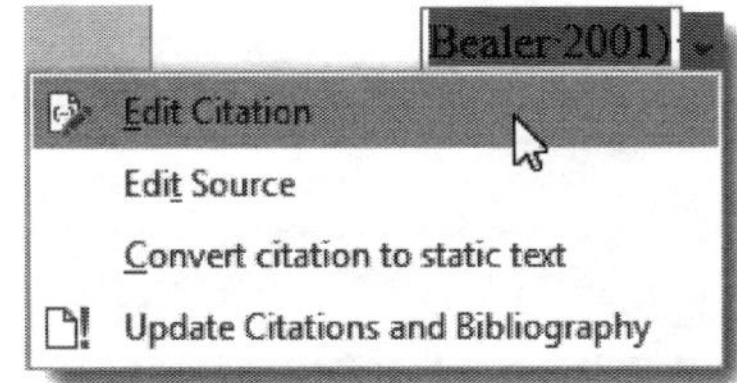

- Click **Edit Citation** to refer to specific pages of a source, or to control just what elements of the citation are shown.

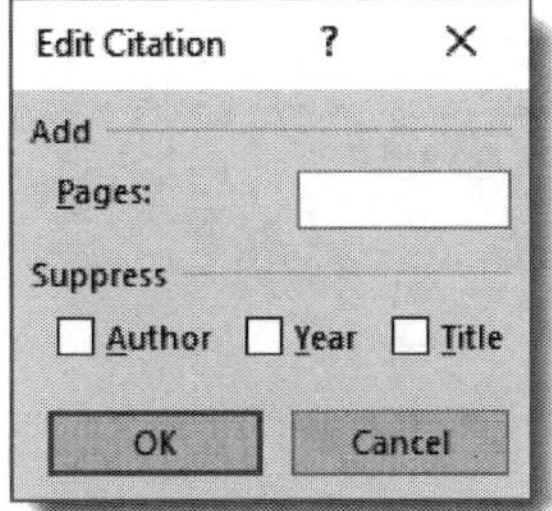

- Click **Edit Source** to edit the source itself. The **Edit Source** window is almost exactly like the **Create Source** window.
- Click **Convert citation to static text** to remove the field code.
- Click **Update Citations and Bibliography** to update all citation and bibliography fields in the document.

Managing sources

The **Source Manager** window contains not only a list of all sources cited in the current document, but a master list of all sources you've entered on your computer. You can use it to import sources you've used previously, or from an XML file. To access the Source Manager, click **Manage Sources**.

Exam Objective: MOS Word Expert 3.2.5

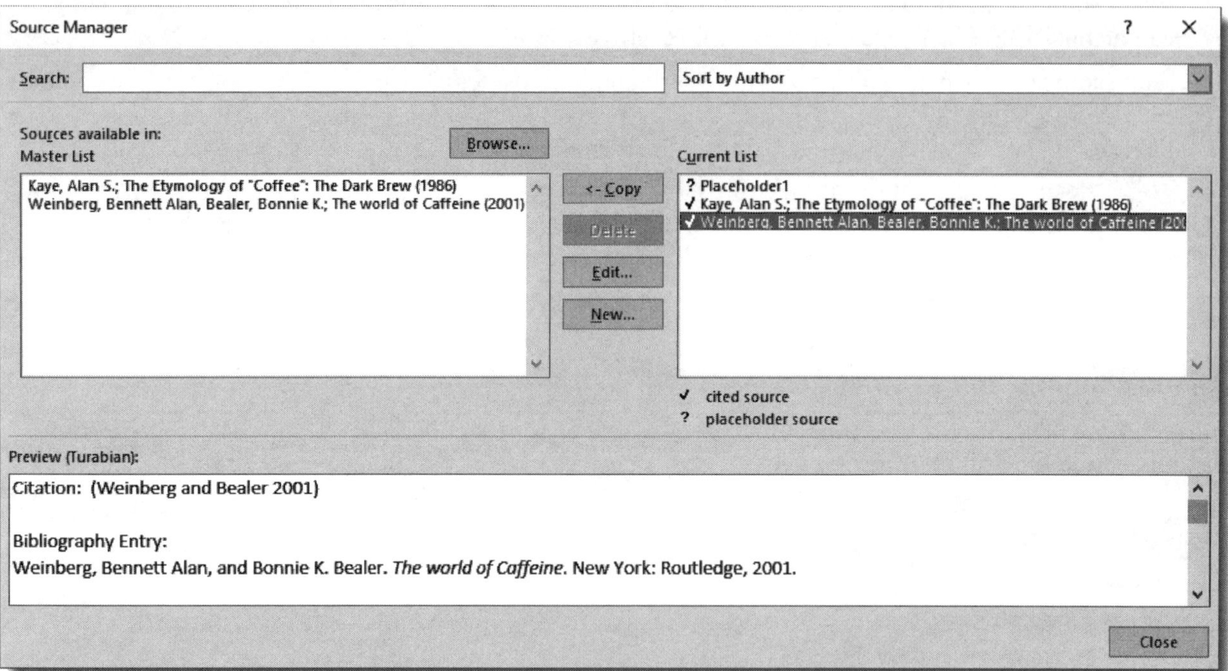

- Use the Search by and Sort fields to find the sources you want from a long list.
- You can select a source in either the Master List or Current List by clicking it.
  - Click **Copy** to copy the source to the other list.
  - Click **Edit** to edit the source in the active list.
  - Click **Delete** to delete the source from the active list. You can't delete a source from the Current List if it has a citation in the document: you need to delete all its citations first.
  - Click **New** to create a new source in the active list.
- Use the Preview pane to review how the selected source appears as both a citation and a bibliography entry in the current style.
- To open an XML bibliography file, click **Browse**. You can use this to import master lists from another computer.

Exercise: Creating citations and sources

Do This	How & Why
1. Open `History of coffee`, and save it as `History of coffee referenced`.	This document is adapted from a Wikipedia page and still has its citation markings. You'll remove them and replace them with a Word bibliography.
2. In the Citations & Bibliography group, select **Turabian Sixth Edition** from the Style list.	It's a common and simple style, so you'll use it for this document. 
3. Insert a citation for a new source.	
a) Delete the first citation marking on page 1.	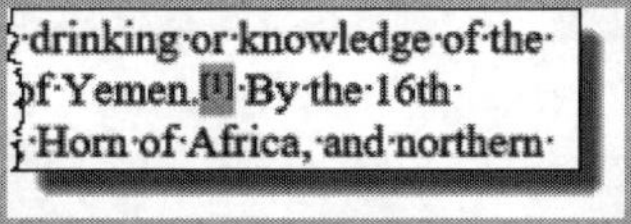 You do have the original article's list of sources handy, so you'll enter them in Word.
b) In the Citations & Bibliography group, click **Insert Citation > Add New Source**.	The **Create Source** window opens. In the Type of source list, **Book** is selected.
c) In the Title field, type `The World of Caffeine`.	
d) In the Author field, type `Bennett Alan Weinberg; Bonnie K. Bealer`.	Because this book has two authors, you can separate their names by a semicolon.
e) Next to the Author field, click **Edit**.	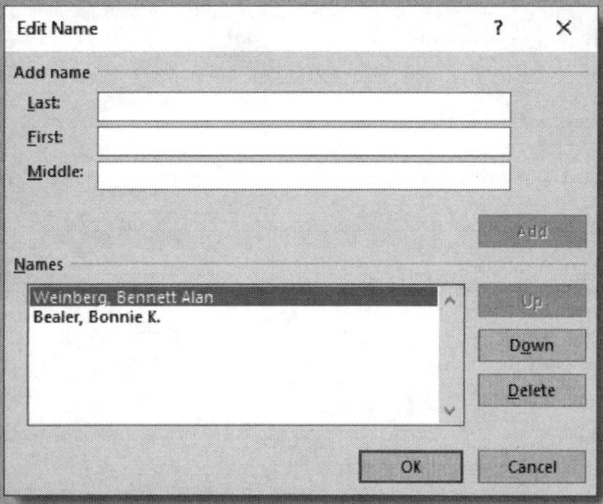 The **Edit Name** window opens. Word has recognized them as separate names, and even placed them last name first. If it hadn't have done so, you could fix them here.
f) Click **OK**.	To return to the **Create Source** window.

Do This	How & Why
g) Complete the source information as shown:	The tag name is automatically generated by Word. You don't need to edit it.
h) Click **OK**.	The citation field spans two lines, but that's okay for now. **Note:** Depending on whether you selected the space before the next sentence, you might need to insert a space after the citation.
4. Add a page reference to the citation.	The reference you have is specifically to pages 3-4 of the book.
a) Click the citation.	To select the field. A frame appears around it.
b) Click **Citation Options > Edit Citation**.	Citation Options is the button to the right of the field frame. The **Edit Citation** window opens.
c) In the Pages field, type `3-4`.	
d) Click **OK**.	The citation now includes page numbers.
5. Create a placeholder reference.	

Do This	How & Why
a) At the end of the paragraph, select and delete "[2]."	You'll get the information for this one later.
b) Click **Insert Citation > Add New Placeholder**.	The **Placeholder Name** window opens, with the default name "Placeholder 1" selected. You'll keep that.
c) Click **OK**.	
6. Insert a reference to a journal article.	Each type of source has its own relevant fields.
a) Select and delete placeholder [6].	It's at the end of the first paragraph on page 2, just above the "First use" heading.
b) Place the insertion point at that same location, if necessary, and add a new source.	Click **Insert Citation > Add New Source**.
c) From the Type of source list, choose **Journal Article**.	The fields in the **Create Source** window change to show those used by journal articles.
d) Fill out the fields as follows.	Notice that in a journal entry, pages are a recommended field.
e) Click **OK**.	To insert the entry. The citation here doesn't mention the pages cited, but they'll appear in the bibliography.
7. Add citations to an existing source.	*The World of Caffeine* is cited other times in the document, so you can just insert new citations without defining it again.
a) Select and delete the first [1] under the First use heading.	Wikipedia uses the same number for every citation to the same source, so you know it's one you've defined already. It's near the top of the first paragraph.
b) Click **Insert Citation**.	The sources you've defined are in the gallery now, including the placeholder.

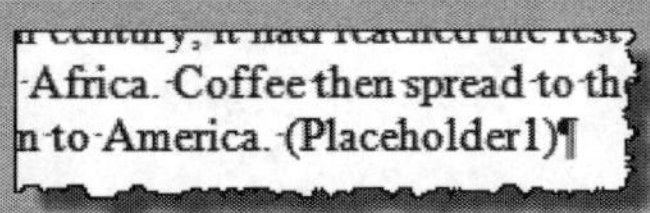

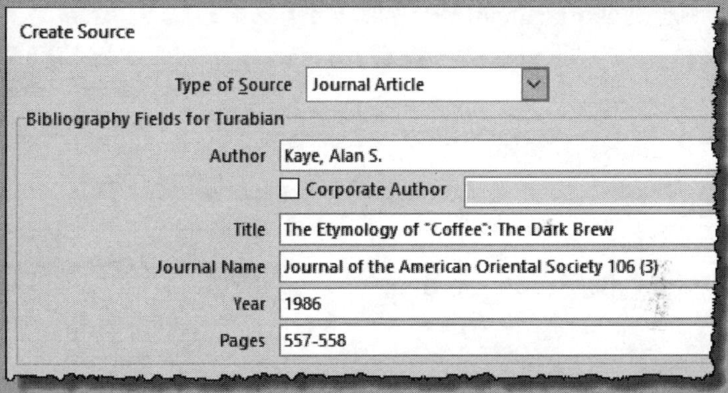

Do This	How & Why
c) Click *The World of Caffeine* in the gallery.	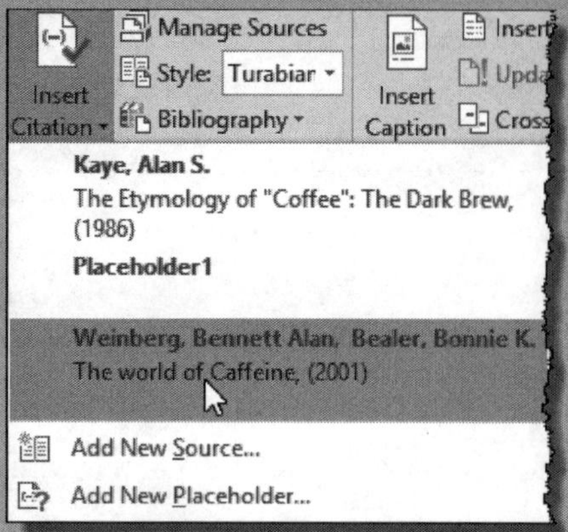 To insert a new citation to the existing source.
d) Insert citations for every other reference to *The World of Caffeine*.	There are three more in the First Use section, and one at the beginning of History. You can search for "[1]" if you don't see them.
8. Examine your sources.	
a) Click **Manage Sources**.	To open the **Manage Sources** window.
b) Examine the Master List and Current List.	The Current List contains the sources you just defined, as well as the placeholder. The two defined sources have also been copied to the Master List so you can import them into future documents.
c) Click each source in the Master List pane.	The details for each source appear in the Preview pane.
d) Click **Sort by Author**.	You can sort by author, tag, title, or year. If you had a lot more sources saved this would be pretty useful.
e) Click **Browse**.	The master list is stored in sources.xml, in the Bibliography folder.
f) Click **Cancel**.	
g) Click **Close**.	To close the window.

Do This	How & Why
9. Save the document.	
10. Manage the sources list in a new document.	
a) Open a new blank document.	Press **Ctrl+N**.
b) Click **Insert Citation**.	The list is blank.
c) Click **Manage Sources**.	The two sources you've defined are in the Master List pane, but the Current List pane is empty.
d) Select the first source on the left and click **Copy**.	The journal article is copied to the Current List pane. 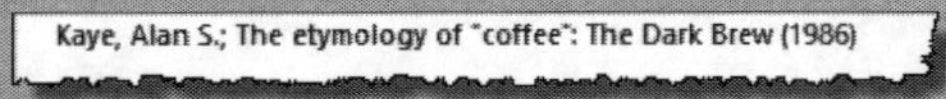 Kaye, Alan S.; The etymology of "coffee": The Dark Brew (1986)
e) Click **Close**.	To close the **Manage Sources** window.
11. Click **Insert Citation**.	The source you copied to the new document appears, but the whole master list does not. 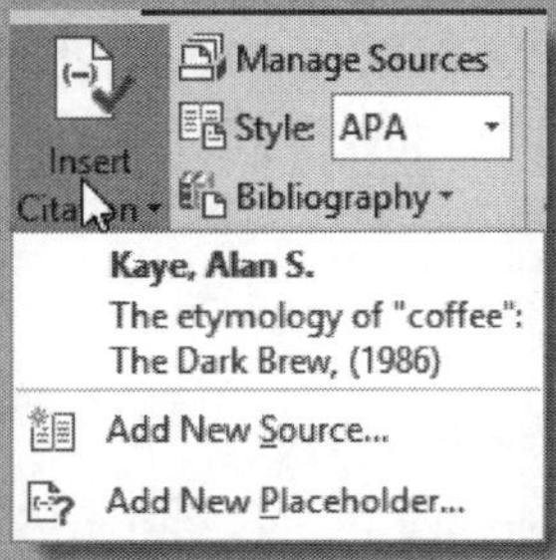 Manage Sources / Style: APA / Insert Citation / Bibliography / Kaye, Alan S. The etymology of "coffee": The Dark Brew, (1986) / Add New Source... / Add New Placeholder...
12. Close the blank document without saving.	Leave History of coffee referenced open.

Inserting a bibliography

Once you've made some citations, you can generate a bibliography. Like an index, it's traditionally placed at the end of a document, but you can place it wherever you'd like.

Exam Objective: MOS Word Core 4.1.1 and Expert 4.1.7

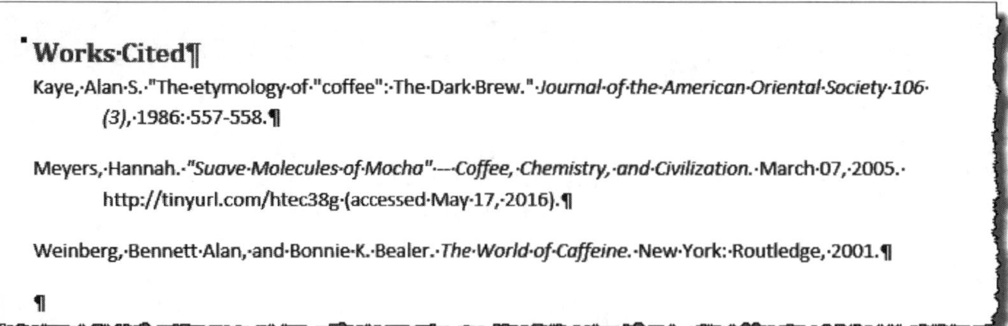

1. Place the insertion point.
2. Click **Bibliography**, and select an option.
   - Select a predefined style from the gallery by clicking it.
   - To insert a simple bibliography you can customize later, click **Insert Bibliography**.
3. If you customize a format, you can click **Bibliography > Save Selection to Bibliography Gallery** to open the **Create New Building Block** window.

Updating bibliographies

An inserted bibliography is a field just like a citation. You can select it to change its format or update it in the same way.

A bibliography field selected to show its options menu.

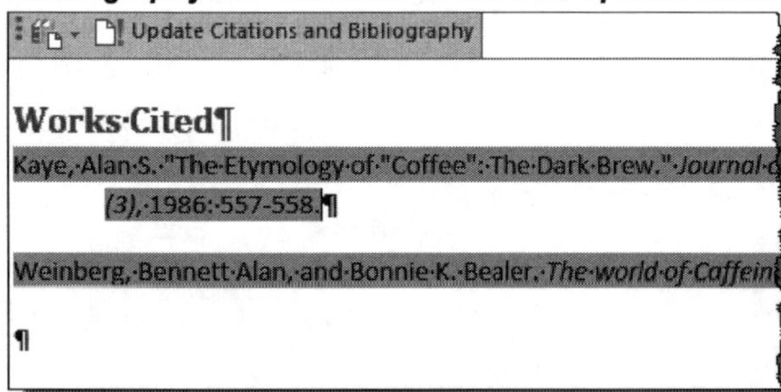

- To update a bibliography, select it and click **Update Citations and Bibliography**.
  You can also click **Update Citations and Bibliography** from the menu of any citation.
- To change the entire bibliography to a different format, click and select the format you want.
- To convert a bibliography to static text, click **> Convert bibliography to static text**.
  After converting to static text, you won't be able to automatically update it, but you can manually edit it however you like.

Tables of Authorities

Exam Objective: MOS Word Expert 3.2.4

A more specific form of reference Word supports is the Table of Authorities format, which is used only in legal documents. A *Table of Authorities*, instead of published works, lists citations of legal cases, statutes, regulations, or other rules. As with other types of references, you can mark individual citations in the document, and then generate the Table of Authorities to compile them in indexed format.

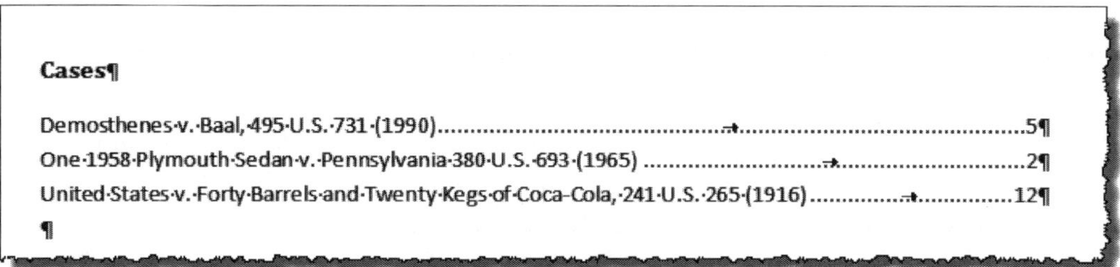

Cases¶

Demosthenes·v.·Baal,·495·U.S.·731·(1990).......................................5¶
One·1958·Plymouth·Sedan·v.·Pennsylvania·380·U.S.·693·(1965)..........................2¶
United·States·v.·Forty·Barrels·and·Twenty·Kegs·of·Coca-Cola,·241·U.S.·265·(1916)..............12¶
¶

It's important not to confuse legal citations with bibliographic citations: they use different formats, they are stored separately, and the former is much more specialized in purpose. If you work in the legal industry, Tables of Authorities are likely to be very useful to you. Otherwise, you can safely ignore them.

Marking legal citations

When you're creating a Table of Authorities, you first need to mark citations using the **Mark Citation** window. The process is similar to marking index entries, but with important differences.

Exam Objective: MOS Word Expert 3.2.4, 3.2.5

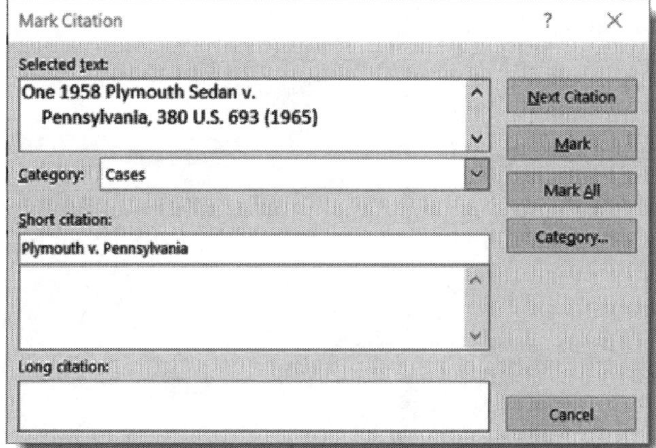

1. Select a reference, such as a case name.
2. Click **Mark Citation** in the Table of Authorities group, or press **Alt+Shift+I**.
3. In the **Mark Citation** window, edit the Selected text field, if necessary.

   The appearance of this field determines how it appears in the Table of Authorities later. If you're making a new citation, it is automatically entered in the Long citation field when you mark it.
4. Choose a category from the Category list.
   - You can select options such as **Cases**, **Statutes**, or **Regulations**. The Table of Authorities sorts citations by category.
   - If you need to edit or add categories, click **Category**.
5. Edit the Short citation field.

The Short citation field is how Word identifies the entries in the Table of Authorities, as opposed to how they appear in the table itself. Feel free to abbreviate this, or use the style for subsequent references to the same citation.

6. Click **Mark** to mark the citation.
   - Click **Mark All** to mark all citations matching the selected text or short citation.
   - Click **Next Citation** to find the next citation matching the selected text or short citation.
7. Continue marking citations.
   - As with creating an index entry, you can select other text in the document, and simply click the **Mark Entry** window again.
   - If you're marking a new reference to a citation you've already made, click it in the Short citation list.
   - When you're done marking citations, click **Close**.

Inserting Tables of Authorities

You can insert a single Table of Authorities for your document, or you can insert it for a single category at a time. If you've inserted an index, the process is similar.

Exam Objective: MOS Word Expert 3.2.4, 3.2.5

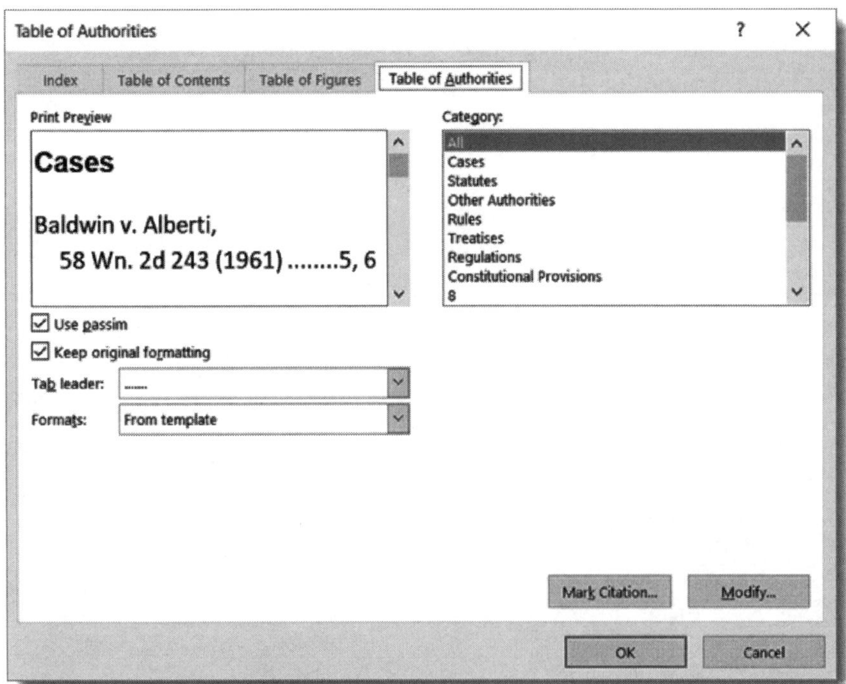

1. Place the insertion point.
2. On the References tab, click **Insert Table of Authorities**.
3. Select the category to insert, or click **All** to insert all citations sorted by category.
4. Set additional options.
   - Clear **Use passim** if you don't want Word to use "passim" instead of page numbers for entries with several citations.
   - Clear **Use original formatting** if you want all entries to match Word's Table of Authorities style instead of the formatting used for the citations you made.

- Use the Tab Header and Formats list to change the formatting.
- Click **Modify** to change the Table of Authorities or TOA Heading styles.
- Preview your settings in the Print Preview pane.

5. Click **OK** to insert the finished Table of Authorities.
6. Align the table as necessary using Paragraph group controls on the Home tab, or tab stops on the ruler.

If you make further changes after inserting a Table of Authorities, in the Table of Authorities group, click **Update Table**.

Exercise: Creating a bibliography

In this exercise, you'll cite external sources for a document, then compile them into a bibliography.

Do This	How & Why
1. Insert a bibliography.	
a) Insert a new section at the end of the document.	On the Page Layout tab, click **Breaks > Next Page**.
b) On the Reference tab, click **Bibliography > Works Cited**.	To insert a bibliography using an existing building block. It doesn't include the placeholder reference you created, only the sources you defined.
2. Create a source for the placeholder reference.	The placeholder was to a web-based source whose location had changed. You'll fill it out now that you have the proper details.
a) On the References tab, click **Manage Sources**.	
b) In the Current List pane, click **Placeholder 1**.	The preview shows there's no source defined. Citation: (Placeholder1) Bibliography Entry: **There are no sources in the current document.**
c) Click **Edit**.	The **Edit Source** window opens. It's just like the **Create Source** window.
d) From the Type of Source list, choose **Web site**	Since web sites are easily changed, a web site citation not only needs to show when the page was created, but also when you accessed it.

Do This	How & Why
e) Fill out the fields as shown.	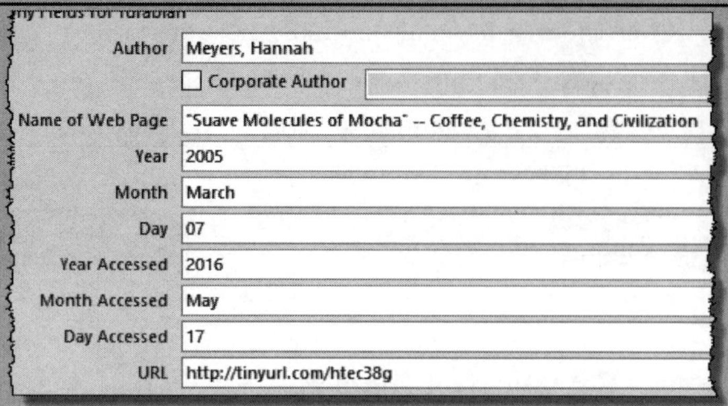 Author: Meyers, Hannah; Corporate Author (unchecked); Name of Web Page: "Suave Molecules of Mocha" -- Coffee, Chemistry, and Civilization; Year: 2005; Month: March; Day: 07; Year Accessed: 2016; Month Accessed: May; Day Accessed: 17; URL: http://tinyurl.com/htec38g
f) Edit the tag name to read `Smm1`.	You don't want it to remain "Placeholder1".
g) Click **OK**.	The new source is listed and cited.
3. Click **Copy**.	To copy the new source into the master list.
4. Click **Close**.	The Manage Sources list closes, but the new source isn't in the bibliography.
5. Update the bibliography.	
a) Click the Works Cited list.	A box with buttons surrounds it.
b) Click **Update Citations and Bibliography**.	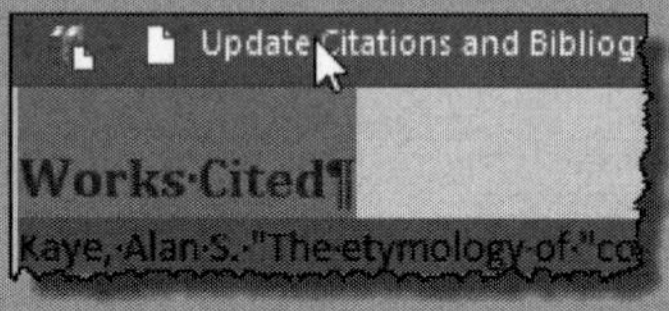 Update Citations and Bibliog… / Works·Cited¶ / Kaye,·Alan·S.·"The·etymology·of·"co… The web site is added to the list.
c) Click away from the Works Cited list to deselect it.	
6. Scroll up to page 1.	The placeholder citation now shows the added source. 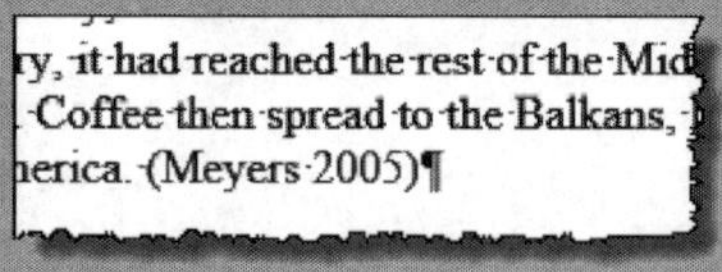 …y,·it·had·reached·the·rest·of·the·Mid… ·Coffee·then·spread·to·the·Balkans,… …erica.·(Meyers·2005)¶
7. Save and close the file.	

Works·Cited¶

Kaye,·Alan·S.·"The·etymology·of·"coffee":·The·Dark·Brew."·*Journal·of·the·American·Oriental·Society·106·(3)*,·1986:·557-558.¶

Meyers,·Hannah.·*"Suave·Molecules·of·Mocha"·—·Coffee,·Chemistry,·and·Civilization.*·March·07,·2005.·http://tinyurl.com/htec38g·(accessed·May·17,·2016).¶

Weinberg,·Bennett·Alan,·and·Bonnie·K.·Bealer.·*The·World·of·Caffeine.*·New·York:·Routledge,·2001.¶

¶

Assessment: Citing external sources

1. The citation style you should use depends largely on your subject matter and chosen audience. True or false?
   - True
   - False
2. Which of the following statements are true about sources?
   - Each source must have a unique tag name.
   - Each source must have a unique title.
   - Every source you define is stored in a master list on your computer.
   - Multiple authors must be entered one at a time in a separate window.
   - The field names you're prompted to enter depend on the type of source.
3. How can you keep a customized bibliography format? Choose the best response.
   - Download it from Office.com
   - Save it as a building block
   - Save it as a document template
   - You can't, but must manually edit it for each document.
4. A Table of Authorities is typically found only in what kind of document? Choose the best reply.
   - Educational
   - Humanities
   - Legal
   - Scientific

Summary: Using references

You should now know how to:

- Use bookmarks to mark important points in a long document, and refer to bookmarks or other document locations using cross-references
- Mark index entries, use them to compile an index, and troubleshoot indexing problems
- Cite external sources, then assemble them into a bibliography or Table of Authorities

Synthesis: Using references

To complete this exercise, you should have completed the other exercises in the chapter. If you haven't, you'll just have additional work to do.

In this exercise, you'll practice adding references to a document.

1. Open `History of coffee indexed`, and save it as `History of coffee synthesis`.
2. Create bookmarks for important sections in the text.
3. Create new index references for key terms in the text. Include references to the bookmarks you created, and use cross-references, as applicable.
4. Update the index to reflect your new references. Correct any errors that appear.
5. Add citations to the document. Begin by importing the sources you've already created from the master list.

   You can find a full list of sources for the article in the `Article references` document. You don't need to add all of them, and some might not contain all fields, but you can get a feel for adding various kinds of sources.
6. Insert a bibliography before the index.

Chapter 15: Creating mailings

You will learn how to:

- Create or import recipient lists for mailings and labels
- Create a form letter using a mail merge
- Create envelopes and labels

Module A: Recipient lists

When you want to create a mailing to multiple recipients, you don't need to make a separate copy and address a separate envelope to each of them. Instead, you can use Word's Mail Merge feature to create envelopes or mailing labels, create personalized form letters, or even generate email messages for an entire list of people. Before you can do any of these, you must first either create or import a recipient list, with all the information you need for each recipient.

You will learn how to:

- Create and customize a recipient list
- Import a recipient list from an external data source
- Import a recipient list from your Outlook contacts

About merge fields

To appear different to each recipient, a mail merge uses a type of field called a *merge field*. In the master document, each merge field is a placeholder for a value from the recipient list, such as a name, a street address, or any other information associated with a particular recipient. Once you've composed the master and complete the mail merge, Word creates a separate copy for each recipient, each with that recipient's information.

A mail merge being composed

Hello «FirstName»,

Java Tucana's tenth anniversary is coming up, and we're celebrating by introducing a whole new line of premium coffees and teas from all over the world. Since we never would have made it here without loyal customers like «Company», we'd like to offer you an exclusive sample pack along with your next order.

The same mail merge as seen by a recipient

Hello Dan,

Java Tucana's tenth anniversary is coming up, and we're celebrating by introducing a whole new line of premium coffees and teas from all over the world. Since we never would have made it here without loyal customers like Agio Legal Services, we'd like to offer you an exclusive sample pack along with your next order.

By default, a recipient list contains a list of *records*, one for each recipient. Each record contains all the fields you might need to contact that person: first and last name, title and company name, full mailing address, home and work phone numbers, and email address. You can add additional fields if you need them. For example, the owner of a pet-grooming business could include a field with the names of customers' pets and include them in a mailing.

You can create a recipient list from scratch by typing it into Word, but if you already have the information in another form such as a table or database, you can import it instead. You can even create a recipient list from your Outlook contacts. The commands to create a recipient list are found on the Mailings tab, in the **Select Recipients** menu.

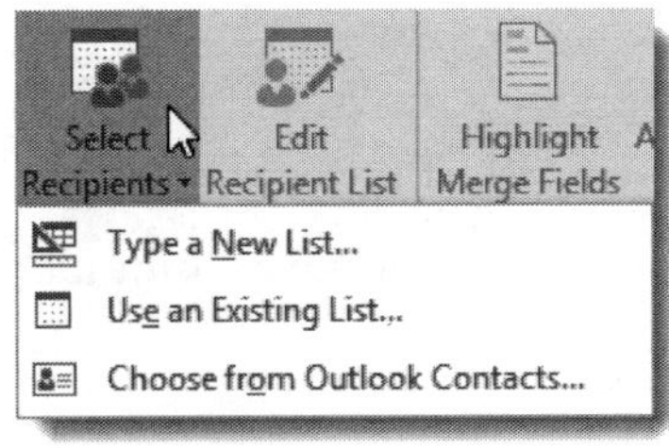

Creating recipient lists

If you need to enter a recipient list from scratch, you can use the **New Address List** window.

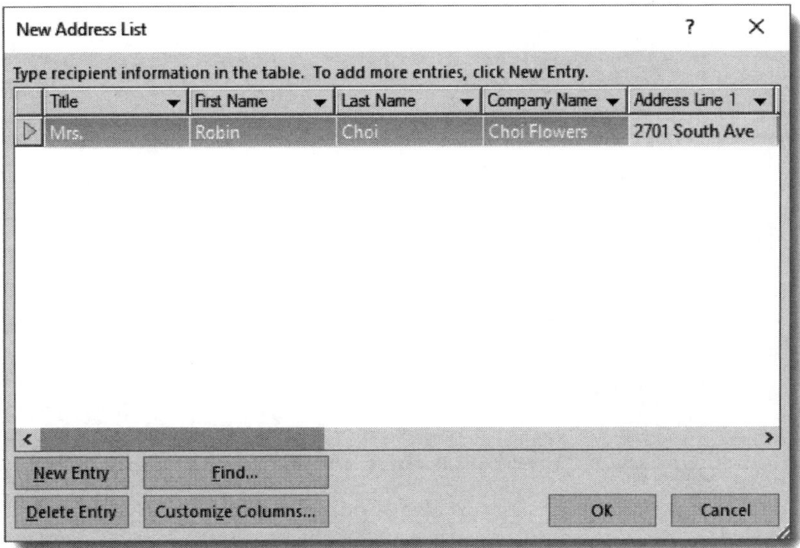

Exam Objective: MOS Word Expert 3.3.6

1. On the Mailings tab, click **Select Recipients > Type a New List**.
2. In the **New Address List** window, enter the first recipient's information.
    - To move to the next field, press **Tab**.
    - To move to a previous field, press **Shift+Tab**.
    - You need to fill in every field you plan to use in the mail merge, but you can leave others blank.
3. Continue adding new recipients.
    - To add a new recipient, click **New Entry**, or press **Tab** at the last field of the current entry.
    - To delete a recipient, select it and click **Delete Entry**.
4. Click **OK**.

Customizing address list columns

Exam Objective: MOS Word Expert 3.3.1, 3.3.2

When you're creating a new recipient list, you can add or change columns by clicking **Customize Columns**. This opens the **Customize Address List** window.

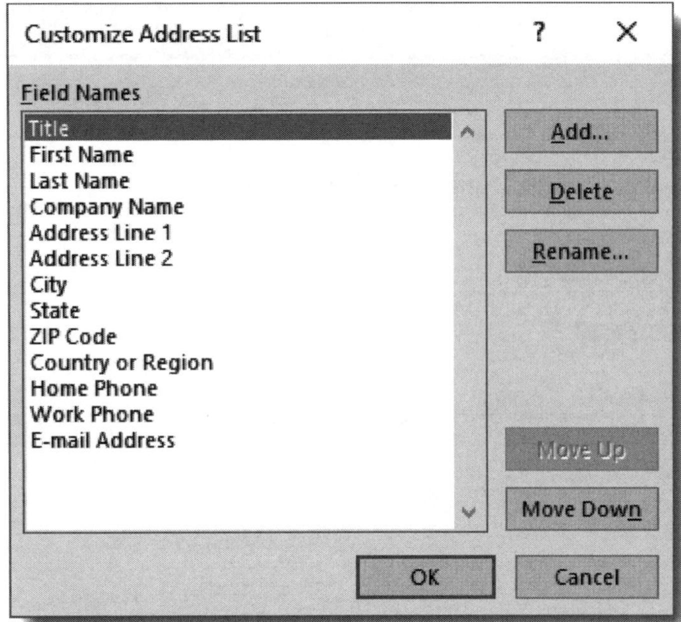

- To change the column order, select a field, and click **Move Up** or **Move Down**.
- To add a new field, click **Add** and type its name.
- To rename an existing field, select it and click **Rename**.
- To delete a field, select it and click **Delete**.
- Click **OK** to save your changes and close the window.

Importing recipient lists

As you can imagine, typing a new recipient list can be very time-consuming, so if you already have the data in a file, you're better off importing it. Word allows you to import recipient lists in many formats. The most common are Excel workbooks, Access databases, Outlook contact folders, or text files in tab-delineated or comma-delimited format. You can also use SQL database connections, tables in Word documents, or a variety of other sources. Before you import an external list, make sure it has all the fields you're going to need for your purposes, such as all mailing address fields for labels, or valid email addresses for an email message.

Exam Objective: MOS Word Expert 3.3.6

The Select Table window shown when opening an Excel workbook.

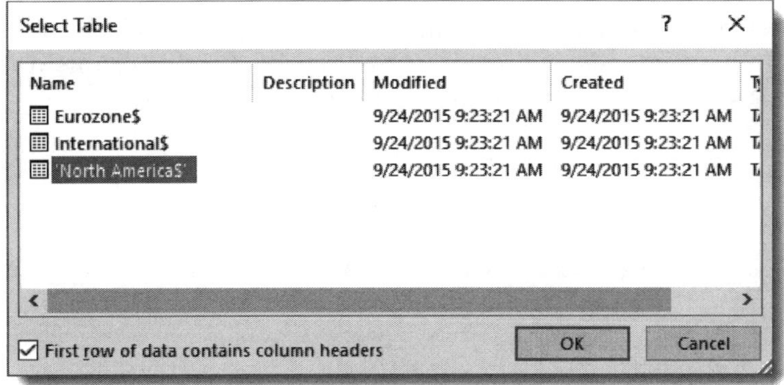

1. Choose a data source.
   - To import from a file, click **Select Recipients > Use an Existing List**. Navigate to the file, then click **OK**.
   - To import from an existing database connection, click **Select Recipients > Use an Existing List**, and navigate to the `Documents\My Data Sources` folder.
   - To import from a new database connection, click **Select Recipients > Use an Existing List**, then click **New Data Source**.
2. If prompted, specify where to look within the data source.
   - If you're opening a file with multiple tables or worksheets, select an entry in the **Select Table** window, then click **OK**.

     Note: If Word isn't sure how to read the chosen file, you may have to answer additional questions.
   - If you're importing contacts from Outlook, select a contacts folder in the **Select Contacts** window, then click **OK**.
   - If you're creating a new database connection, follow the steps in the **Data Creation Wizard**.

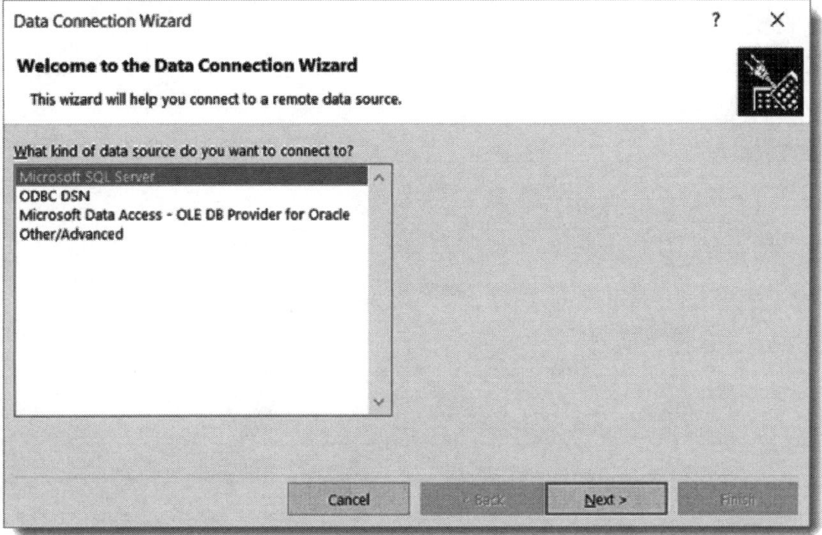

Editing recipient lists

In an ideal situation, your data source is properly formatted, up to date, and contains only the recipients you want. In practice, you're probably going to have to make some adjustments. To do so, click **Edit Recipient List** to open the **Mail Merge Recipients** window, which has controls to sort, filter, and edit the list.

Exam Objective: MOS Word Expert 3.3.3, 3.3.4, 3.3.7

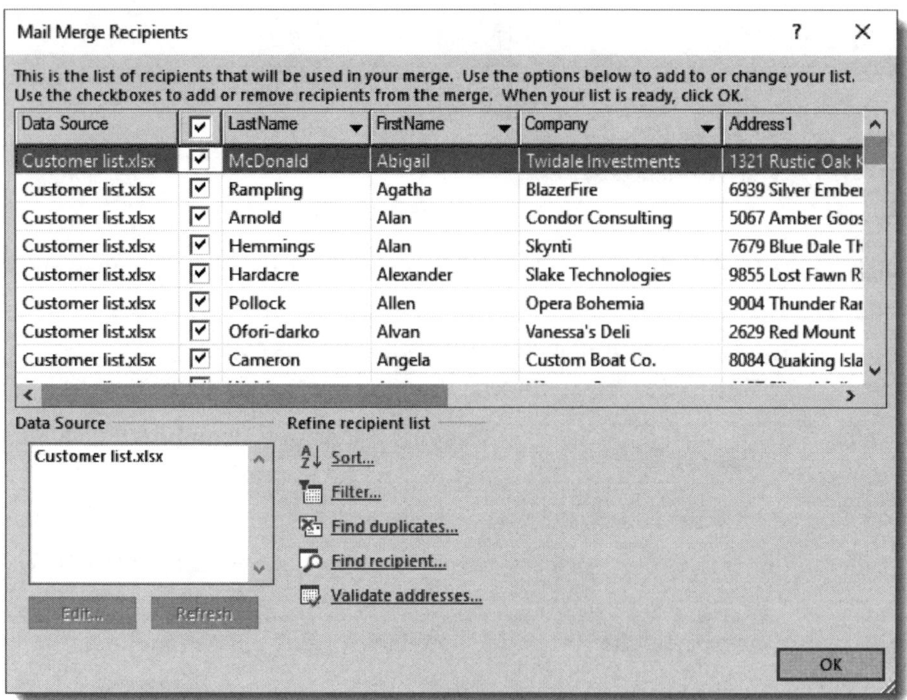

- To add or remove recipients from the merge, use the check boxes.
- To sort by a field, click its column header.
- For more advanced sorting options, click the arrow next to a column header, or click **Sort** under "Refine recipient list."

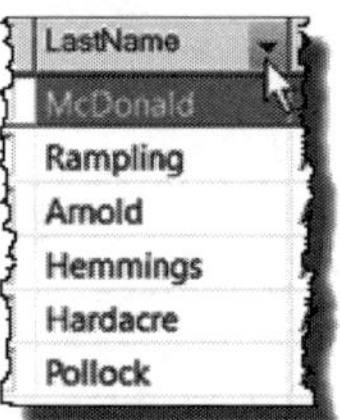

- To filter the list, click **Filter**, and select filtering terms.

  The **Filter and Sort** window opens.

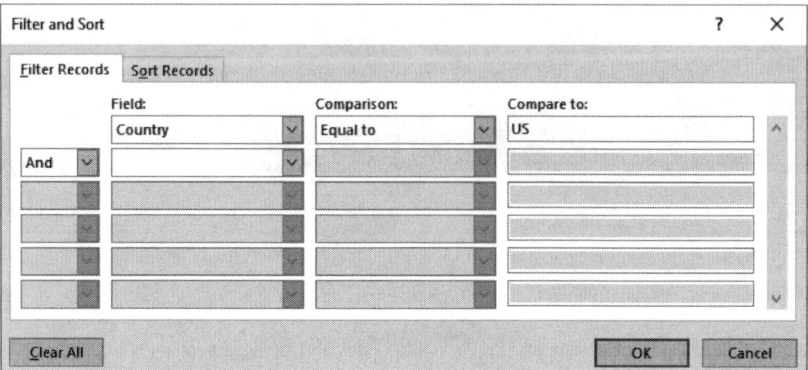

- To look for duplicate entries, click **Find Duplicates**.
- You can't edit entries directly. Instead, select a data source from the Data Source list, and click **Edit**.

  This opens the **Edit Data Source** window, which behaves almost exactly like the **New Address List** window.
- If you have an address validation add-in for Office, click **Validate Addresses** to use it.
- When you've finished making changes, click **OK**.

Exercise: Defining a recipient list

In this exercise, you're creating a recipient list for a mailing to your corporate customers. You'll manually enter a recipient using Word, then import additional recipients from an Excel workbook.

Do This	How & Why
1. Open `Form letter`.	This has the beginnings of a form letter, but to make it a mail merge, you need to define recipients.
2. Start a new recipient list.	
a) Click **Select Recipient > Type a New List**.	The **New Address List** window opens.
b) Click **Customize Columns**.	The **Customize Address List** window opens. You'll remove the fields you're not going to use.
c) With **Title** selected, click **Delete**.	You're asked to confirm your deletion.
d) Click **Yes**.	
e) Select **E-Mail Address**.	
f) Delete the field.	Click **Delete**, then **Yes**.
g) Click **OK**.	The fields you deleted are no longer in the list.
3. Enter a recipient's information.	
a) In the first row of the First Name column, type `Robin`.	
b) Press **Tab**.	To move to the Last Name field.
c) Type `Choi`, then press **Tab**.	To move to the Company Name field.
d) Click **Delete Entry**.	You just found out you have the full list of names in an Excel workbook, so you'll import them instead.
e) Click `Yes`.	To confirm the deletion.
f) Click **OK**.	You're prompted to save the list in your `Data Sources` folder. There's no point in saving a blank list, so you should have simply pressed **Cancel**.

Do This	How & Why
g) Click **Cancel** twice.	To discard the current list.
4. Import a recipient list.	
a) Click **Select Recipients > Use an Existing List**.	The **Select Data Source** window opens. It's like a normal **Open** window but includes a New Source button near the bottom.
b) Navigate to the current module folder.	You have an Excel workbook with a list of all your corporate customers.
c) Select **Customer List** and click **Open**.	The **Select Table** window opens, showing the worksheets in the Customer List workbook.
d) Click **North America**.	The first row of the worksheet does contain column headers, so you'll leave the box checked.
e) Click **OK**.	To close the window and import the list. Notice that a number of new commands on the Mailings tab are now active.
5. Check the recipient list for duplicates.	You want to send only one letter to each company.
a) Click **Edit Recipient List**.	The **Mail Merge Recipients** window opens with the list you've just imported.
b) Scroll through the list.	There aren't any blank fields, and everything seems to be the right sort of information. You'll check for less obvious errors next.
c) Under Refine recipient list, click **Find duplicates**.	The **Find Duplicates** window opens. No duplicates were found.

Do This	How & Why
d) Click **OK**.	You realize that two contacts defined at the same company wouldn't appear as duplicates. You'll try something else. To close the window.
e) Sort the list by the Company column.	Company Sort Ascending Sort Descending (All) (Blanks) (Nonblanks) (Advanced...) Click the arrow in the column heading, then click **Sort Ascending**.
f) Scroll through the list, looking for duplicate company names.	The list has two contacts defined for Eatenbread Digital Productions at the same address.

g) Clear Zita Guttorp's entry.

Data Source	☑	LastName	FirstName	Company	Address1
Customer list.xlsx	☑	Cisowski	Phaedra	Eatenbread Digital Pro...	4435 V St. NW
Customer list.xlsx	☐	Guttorp	Zita	Eatenbread Digital Pro...	4435 V St. NW
Customer list.xlsx	☑	Lambert	Leah	Flashdog, Inc.	7617 Foggy Islanc
Customer list.xlsx	☑	Lee	Melanie	Flying Brace Systems	6363 Pleasant Coı
Customer list.xlsx	☑	Trulli	Calli	Gleeson Associates	1927 Hazy Quay

Phaedra Cizowski is your current contact there, but Zita's was apparently never removed from the list.

Do This	How & Why
6. Check the list for foreign addresses.	You want to mail the letter only to customers in the US and Canada, so you need to make sure no other addresses are in the list.
a) Click **Filter**.	The **Filter and Sort** window opens.
b) From the Field list, choose **Country**.	You want to filter the list to include only addresses with "US" or "CA" in the Country field.
c) In the "Compare to" field, type `US`.	The Comparison field is already "Equal to," which is what you want.
d) In the first box of the second row, select **Or**.	Or
e) Set the second field to look for Canadian addresses.	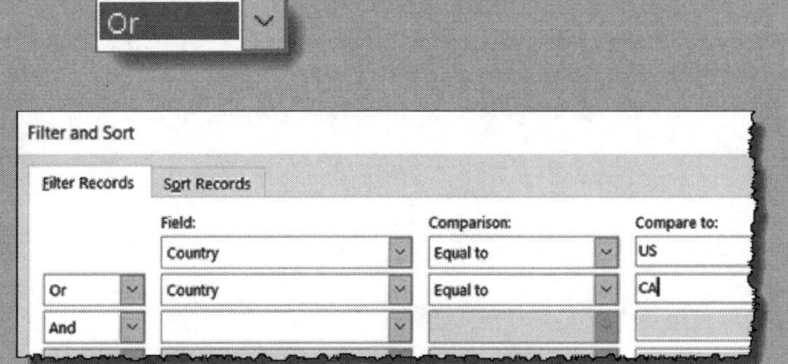

Do This	How & Why
f) Click **OK**.	To apply the filter. You can't directly see if any addresses are hidden, but they won't be included in the merge.
g) Click **OK**.	To close the **Mail Merge Recipients** window.
7. Save the document as `Special offer letter`.	If you're continuing with the Form letters module, you don't need to close it.

Assessment: Recipient lists

1. A recipients list doesn't allow custom fields, but there are generic fields you can use however you like. True or false?
   - True
   - False
2. You can import a recipient list from a text file. True or false?
   - True
   - False
3. After customizing an imported address list, you find a misspelled street name. How can you most easily correct it? Choose the best answer.
   - Click Validate addresses in the Mail Merge Recipients window.
   - Edit the data source in its original application, then repeat the import process.
   - Edit the field directly in the Mail Merge Recipients window.
   - Open the data source from within the Mail Merge Recipients window, and edit the field there.

Module B: Performing mail merges

Once you have a recipients list, you're ready to actually compose your mail merge by inserting merge fields into a document. You can then preview results, look for errors, and finally execute the merge.

You will learn how to:

- Insert merge fields
- Use rules
- Preview merge results
- Finalize a mail merge

The mail merge process

There are several steps to the mail merge process. You can perform them manually one at a time, using commands on the Mailings tab, or you can use the Mail Merge Wizard to walk you through them, but the process is the same either way. Whichever method you use in practice depends on your tastes, but once you know how to use the manual process, you'll understand how to use the wizard as well.

The Mailings tab

The Mail Merge Wizard pane.

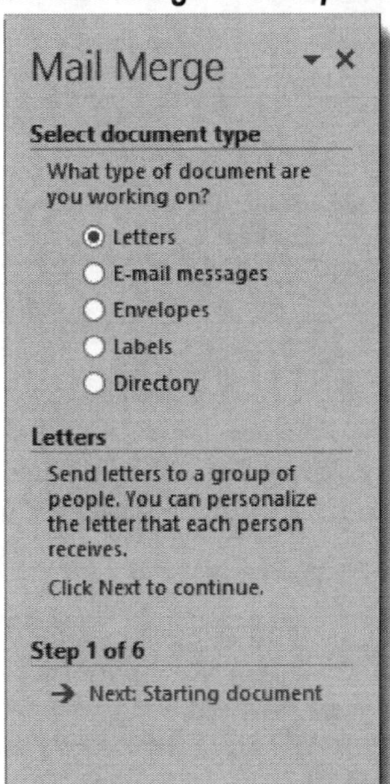

Beginning mail merges

You can begin a mail merge from a blank document, a document created from a template, or an existing document. If you're performing the mail merge manually, you should open the sort of document you want before you begin the process. If you're using the wizard, you can start the wizard first and open a template or document later. Either way, you begin by clicking **Start Mail Merge** and selecting a menu option.

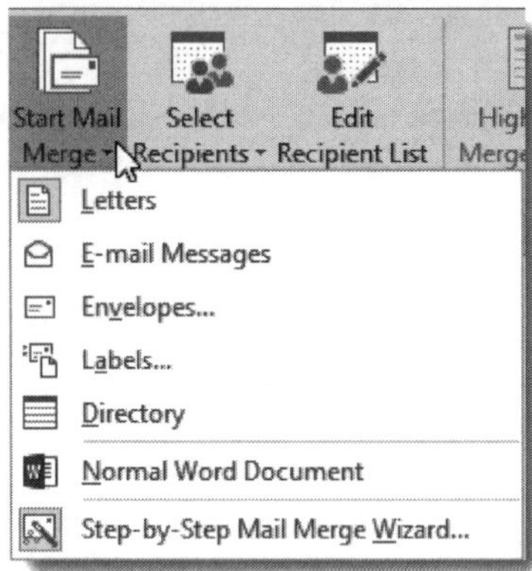

- Click **Letters** to create a form letter to print or distribute in Word format.
- Click **E-mail Messages** to create a mass email to send using Outlook.
- Click **Envelopes** to create a set of mailing envelopes addressed to the recipient list. Each will have your return address.
- Click **Labels** to create a set of mailing labels addressed to the recipients list.
- Click **Directory** to create a catalog or directory, such as a membership list.
- Click **Normal Word Document** to remove all merge data, such as recipient lists, and revert the document to a normal Word document.
- Click **Step by Step Mail Merge Wizard** to open the Mail Merge wizard pane. You can still work manually with the pane open.

If you choose **Envelopes** or **Labels**, you're prompted for formatting options. Regardless of which menu option you choose, if you haven't defined a recipients list, you need to do so before inserting merge fields.

Inserting merge fields

Exam Objective: MOS Word Core 3.3.7 and Expert 2.1.6

Once you have a document type and recipients list, you can compose the mail merge much as you would any document of its type. You can also insert fields from the Write & Insert Fields group.

- To quickly insert a field, click the lower half of the **Insert Merge Field** button to open a menu with a list of fields in your recipients list.
- Alternatively, click the upper half of the **Insert Merge Field** button to open the **Insert Merge Field** window. It has the same fields, but you can use it to insert multiple fields in sequence.

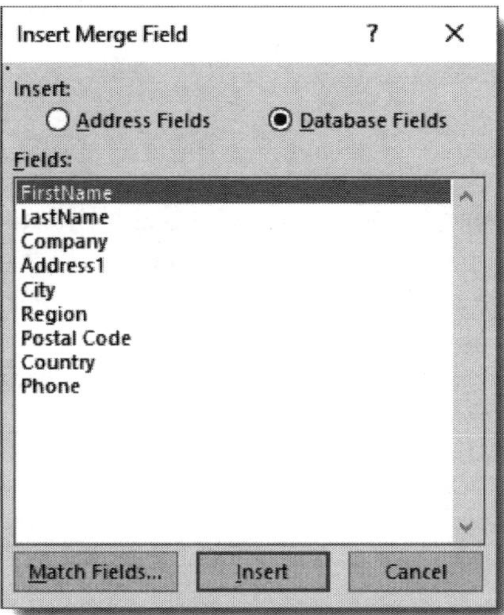

- Click **Address Block** to insert an entire mailing address at once, rather than having to insert one field at a time.

  The **Insert Address Block** window has additional options for included fields and formatting, as well as a preview of the result.

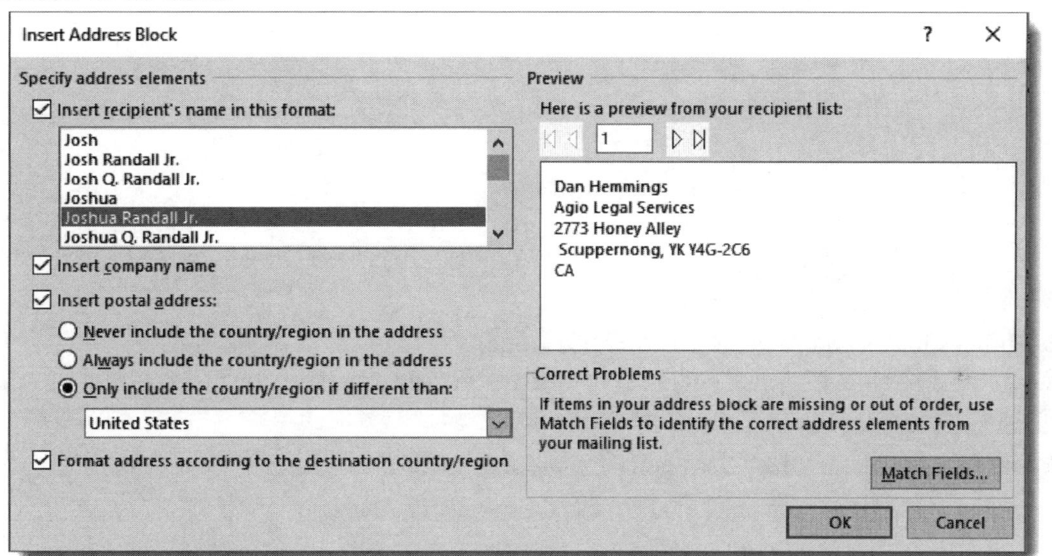

- Click **Greeting Line** to insert a greeting line for a letter, using a format of your choice.

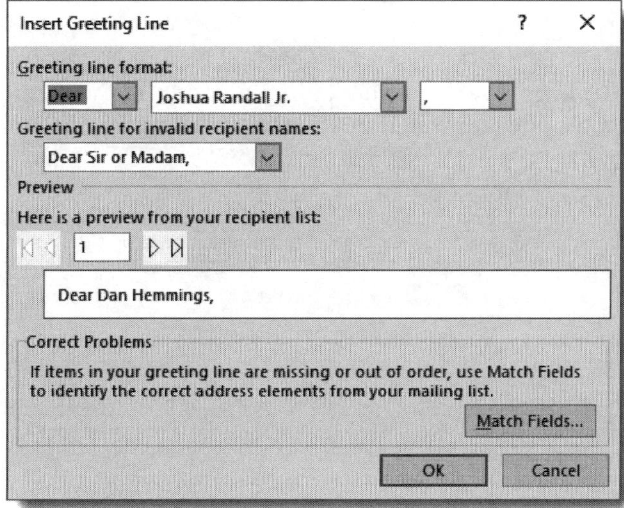

Matching fields

Exam Objective: MOS Word Expert 3.3.3, 3.3.4

As you preview results in address blocks or greeting lines, you might notice some fields not appearing as they should, or not appearing at all. If this happens, it's possible that your data source used different field names than Word does, and when you imported the recipient list Word didn't identify the fields correctly. You can fix this from the **Match Fields** window.

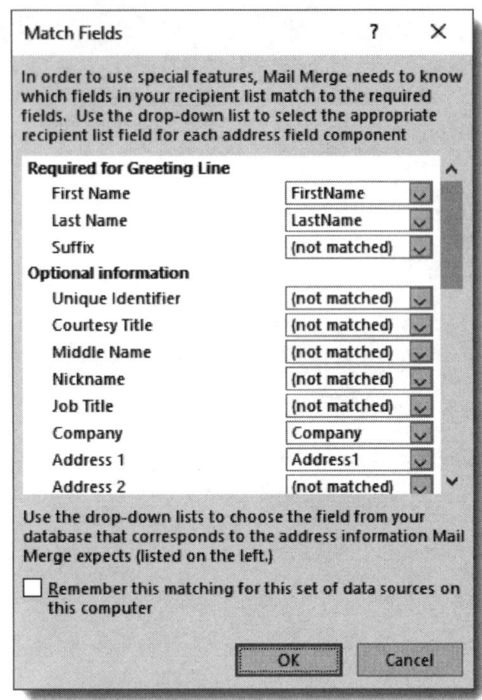

1. Click **Match Fields** in the Write & Insert Fields group.

   You can instead click **Match Fields** in either the **Insert Address Block** or **Insert Greeting Line** windows.

2. Look for the name of a field that isn't behaving properly.
3. Click the list next to the field name, and choose the correct database field.
4. After correcting all problem fields, click **OK**.

Inserting merge rules

In addition to inserting merge fields, you can use *merge rules* to further tailor the results of the merge, depending on the current record. For example, you could add conditional text to the document according to the contents of a field, or even skip recipients entirely if their fields don't match. You can insert one of these fields by clicking **Rules** in the Write & Insert Fields group.

Exam Objective: MOS Word Expert 3.3.2, 3.3.3

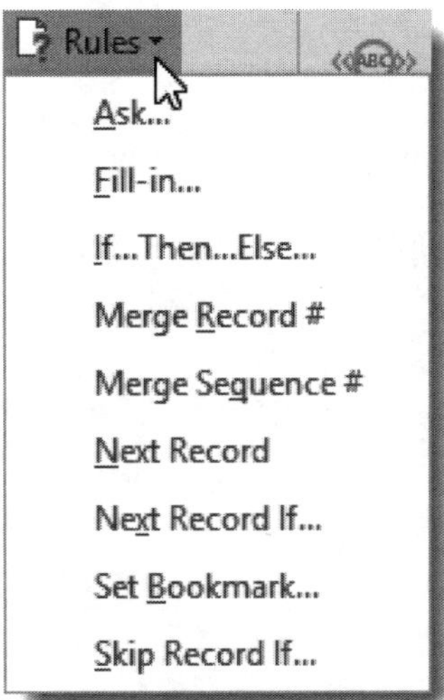

Some of these rules are rather specialized, but the "Next Record If" and "If...Then...Else" rules are powerful ways to tailor your results, especially if you have the right data in your recipients list.

- Click **Next Record If** to insert a field that skips any record that meets a certain set of criteria, effectively filtering your recipient list when you create the merge. Examples of filters include:
  - All recipients from a specific state
  - All recipients whose Company field is blank
  - All recipients whose Total Orders field is less than 10

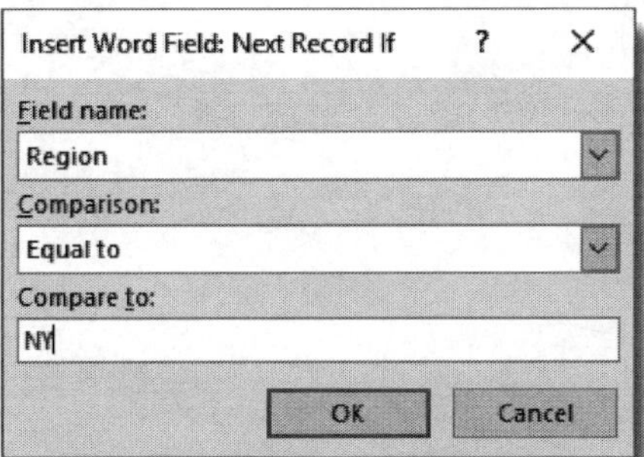

- Click **If...Then...Else** to conditionally include text that depends on fields in the current record. You can even specify alternate text to include if the record doesn't meet the condition. Possible examples include:
  - A custom offer for customers in a specific country
  - A "his" or "her" choice, depending on the recipient's gender
  - Alternate "thank you" statements for donors who have given more or less than $1000 to your charity

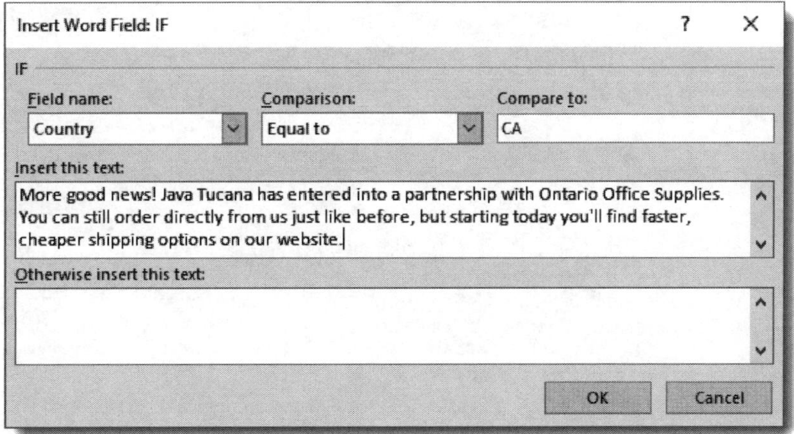

Exercise: Composing a mail merge

To complete this activity, you should have completed the **Defining a recipient list** exercise in the Recipient Lists module, and `Special offer letter` should be open with a recipient list inserted. Otherwise, abbreviated instructions are included in this activity. You'll insert merge fields into a document.

Do This	How & Why
1. If you have not defined a recipient list, do so now.	If you have done so, skip to step 2.
a) Open `Form letter`, and save it as `Special offer letter`.	
b) Import the North America worksheet from `Customer list`.	Click **Select Recipients > Use Existing List**, then select the `Customer list` workbook.
c) Sort the customer list by company.	Click **Edit Recipient List**, then click the arrow at the top of the Company column. Finally, click **Sort Ascending**.
d) Clear the check box next to Zita Guttorp's entry, then click **OK**.	Zita works for Eatenbread Digital Productions.
2. Insert an address block at the top of the document.	
a) Place the insertion point at the top of the document.	
b) In the Write & Insert Fields group, click **Address Block**.	To open the **Insert Address Block** window.
c) Examine the window.	On the left, you can choose how to format the address block. You'll keep most of these options. On the right is a preview of the first record.
d) Under "Insert postal address," click **Always include the country/region in the address**.	Because the current preview is in Canada, it doesn't change, but you notice the province isn't displaying properly.
e) Under Correct Problems, click **Match Fields**.	The **Match Fields** window opens. It lists how each Mail Merge field maps to fields in your data source. The State field is not matched.

Do This	How & Why
f) From the State list, choose **Region**.	If necessary.
g) Click **OK**.	Now the province displays properly in the preview pane, but the postal address setting reverted to the default.
h) Under Insert Postal Address, click **Always include the country/region in the address**.	Now it will show the country for all entries.
i) Click **OK**.	For now, it appears as a single line.
3. On the next line, insert a greeting line.	Click **Greeting Line**, review the format, and click **OK**.
4. Insert a merge field in the letter body.	You'll replace "your company" with the Company field.
a) Select "your company" in the first paragraph.	
b) Press **Delete**.	
c) Click **Insert Merge Field > Company**.	Make sure to click the lower half of the button to open the menu.
5. Insert a merge rule.	The second paragraph references something that only applies to Canadian customers. You'll turn it into a merge rule.
a) Select the entire second paragraph, and press **Ctrl+X**.	You'll cut it to the clipboard first.
b) Press **Enter**.	To insert a new paragraph.
c) Place the insertion point in the new, blank paragraph.	
d) Click **Rules > If...Then...Else**	The **Insert World Field: IF** window opens.
e) From the Field Name list, select **Country**.	
f) In the "Compare to" field, type `CA`.	

Do This	How & Why
g) Paste the cut text into the "Insert this text" field.	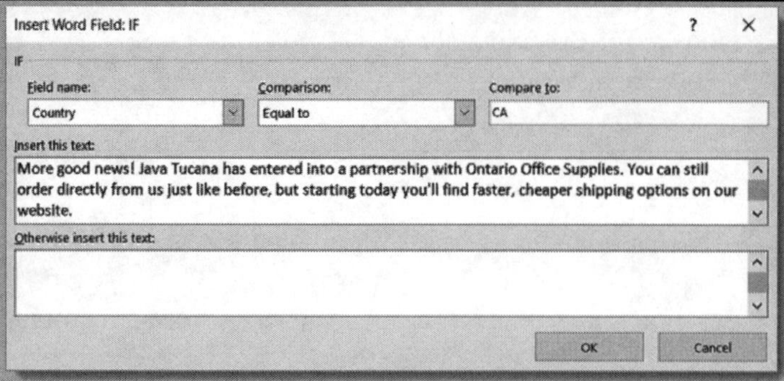 Insert Word Field: IF IF Field name: Country Comparison: Equal to Compare to: CA Insert this text: More good news! Java Tucana has entered into a partnership with Ontario Office Supplies. You can still order directly from us just like before, but starting today you'll find faster, cheaper shipping options on our website. Otherwise insert this text: OK Cancel
h) Click **OK**.	To insert the field. IF fields don't show a placeholder like ordinary merge fields; they preview automatically. Because the first record is Canadian, it does display.
6. Replace "Chris Marshall" in the closing with your own name.	
7. Save the document.	You'll leave it open for the next exercise.

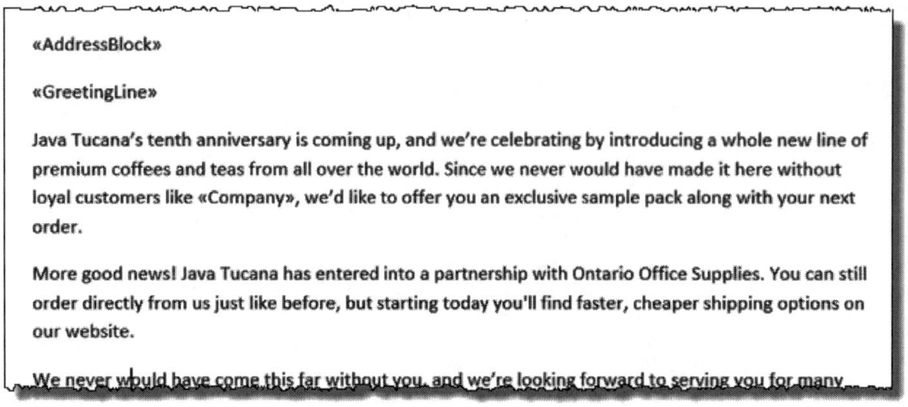

«AddressBlock»

«GreetingLine»

Java Tucana's tenth anniversary is coming up, and we're celebrating by introducing a whole new line of premium coffees and teas from all over the world. Since we never would have made it here without loyal customers like «Company», we'd like to offer you an exclusive sample pack along with your next order.

More good news! Java Tucana has entered into a partnership with Ontario Office Supplies. You can still order directly from us just like before, but starting today you'll find faster, cheaper shipping options on our website.

We never would have come this far without you, and we're looking forward to serving you for many

Previewing results

Once you've composed your document, you can click **Preview Results** to see how each record will appear in the final output. The Go to Field box in the Preview Results group shows the number of the current record.

Exam Objective: MOS Word Expert 3.3.8

You can navigate between records whether or not you're previewing results, but if you're not, you usually won't see any difference.

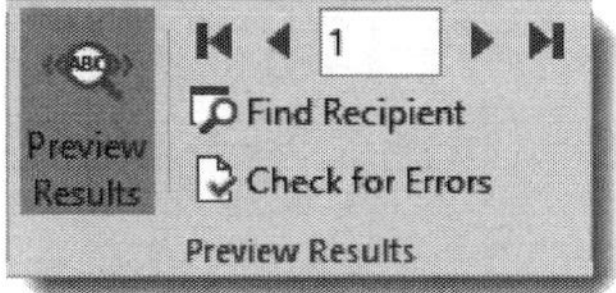

- Use the navigation buttons to move between documents.
  - **First Record**
  - **Previous Record**
  - **Next Record**
  - **Last Record**
- To navigate to a specific record number, type it in the Go to Record box and press **Enter**.
- To find a recipient by name or other field contents, click **Find Recipient**.
- Click **Highlight Fields** to show or hide field highlighting.
- If...Then...Else rules apply to the current record, whether or not you have **Preview Results** selected.
- Click **Check for Errors** to specify how you'd like Word to handle any errors when you complete the merge.
  - Click **Simulate the merge** to check for errors without actually finalizing anything. Otherwise, the merge isn't checked for errors until you actually perform it.
  - By default, Word pauses and reports any error that occurs.
  - You can also have the merge complete automatically and report errors in a new document.

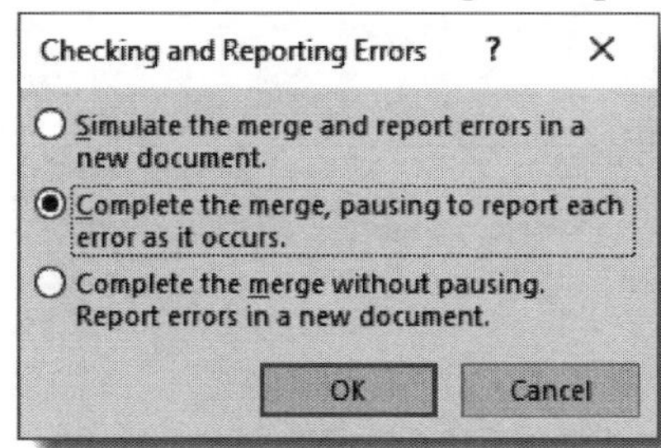

Editing fields

When you insert the wrong merge field or make some other simple error, it might be easiest just to delete and insert it again. If you want to make other changes, you can edit the field. For most fields, you do so in the **Field** window.

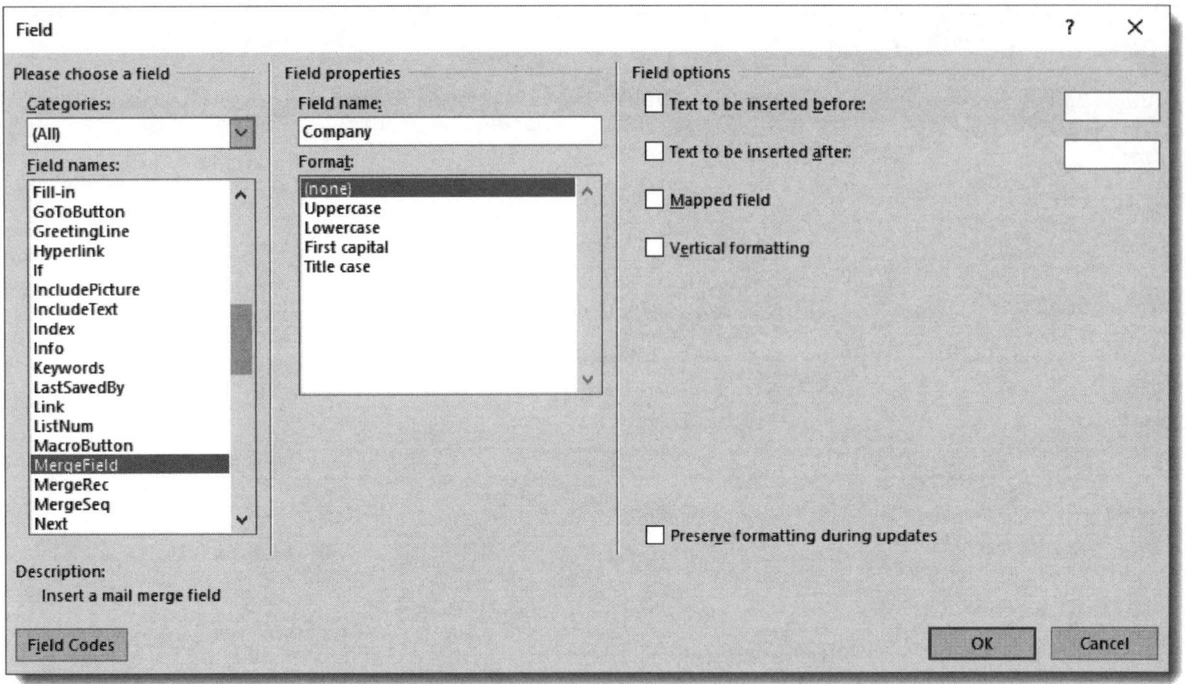

The **Field** window isn't just for merge fields; in fact, you can use it for any sort of field. The exact options available depend on the field type.

Exam Objective: MOS Word Expert 3.3.3, 3.3.4

1. Right-click the field, and click the command to edit it.
    - For an Address Block field, click **Edit Address Block**. The **Modify Address Block** window opens, with the same options you saw while inserting it.
    - For a Greeting Line field, click **Edit Greeting Line**. The **Modify Greeting Line** window opens.
    - For other fields, click **Edit Field**. The **Field** window opens.
2. In the **Field** window, choose an entry from the Field names list.
    - If you're not changing the type of field, you don't need to change this setting.
    - Use the Categories list to narrow your options.
    - All merge fields are in the Merge Field category. Simple merge fields use the MergeField type.
3. In the Field properties section, make formatting choices.
    - Depending on the field, this might include text fields, lists, or buttons.
    - For a merge field, type the database field name in the "Field name" field, and choose a formatting option from the list below.
4. In the Field Options section, choose additional settings.
    - This section does not appear for all field types.
    - Check **Preserve formatting during updates** to keep formatting changes from being lost when you update fields.
5. Click **OK**.

Finalizing merges

Once you're confident with the results of the preview, you can finish the merge. You can either output the results of the merge to a Word document for further editing, to a printer, or to Outlook email messages.

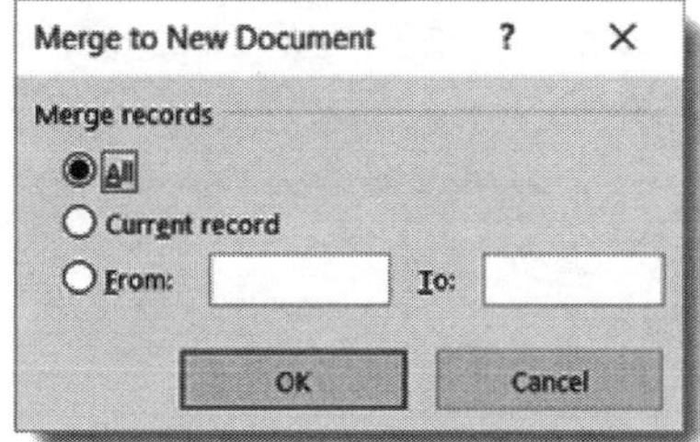

1. Choose the merge type.
   - To merge to a Word document, click **Finish & Merge** > **Edit Individual Documents**.
   - To directly print a mail merge, click **Finish & Merge** > **Print Documents**.
   - To send the merge via email, click **Finish & Merge** > **Send Email Messages**.
2. Set merge options.
   - When merging to a new document or a printer, you can choose to print all records, the current record, or a numbered range of records.
   - When merging to email you have the same options, but in addition, you must specify a subject, and choose a merge field to use for recipient addresses.

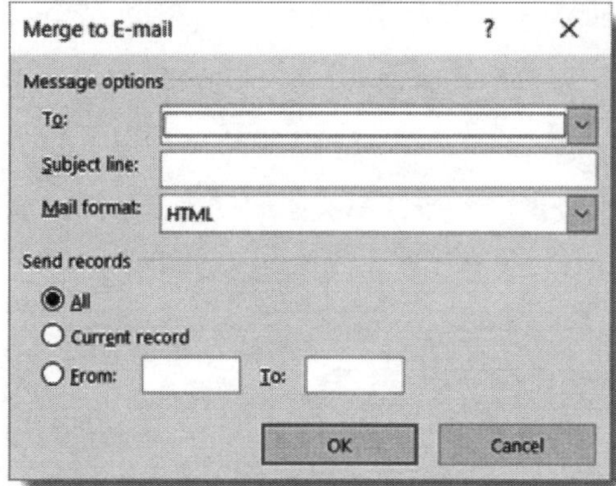

3. Click **OK**.
   - If you merge to a new document, Word generates a single document, with each record separated by a Next Page section break.
   - If you merge to a printer, it is sent as a single print job.
   - If you merge to email, each record is sent by Outlook as a separate message addressed only to that recipient.

Exercise: Completing a mail merge

To complete this activity, you'll need to have completed the **Composing a mail merge** exercise. `Special offer letter` is still open. You'll review and complete the mail merge you just composed.

Do This	How & Why
1. In the Write & Insert Fields group, click **Highlight Merge Fields**.	Gray highlighting appears on the AddressBlock, GreetingLine, and Company merge fields. The IF field isn't highlighted.
2. Click **Preview Results**.	The actual information for the first record appears.
3. Select the first four lines of the address field.	Don't select the country field. It should remain a lighter shade of gray than those selected.
4. On the Home tab, click , and then click **Remove Space After Paragraph**.	The address block is now more tightly spaced, but still separated from the greeting line.
5. Preview some other records.	
a) In the Preview Results field, click .	To preview the next record. This is a US address, so the IF field does not appear in the letter.
b) Click .	To return to the first record.
c) Click .	To move to record 61.
d) Click .	To return to the first record.
e) In the Go To Record field, type a number from 1 to 61, and then press **Enter**.	To navigate to that record.
6. Finalize the merge.	
a) Click **Finish & Merge > Edit Individual Documents**.	The **Merge to New Document** window opens. By default, all records are selected.
b) Click **OK**.	A new document opens.
c) On the first page, click the address block.	Because the document is finalized, it's no longer a field.

Do This	How & Why
d) Scroll through the document.	There are 60 pages, each with a different record **Note:** There were 61 records in the data source, but you chose not to include one in the earlier exercise.
7. Save the document as `Merged form letter`.	
8. Save and close `Special offer letter`.	

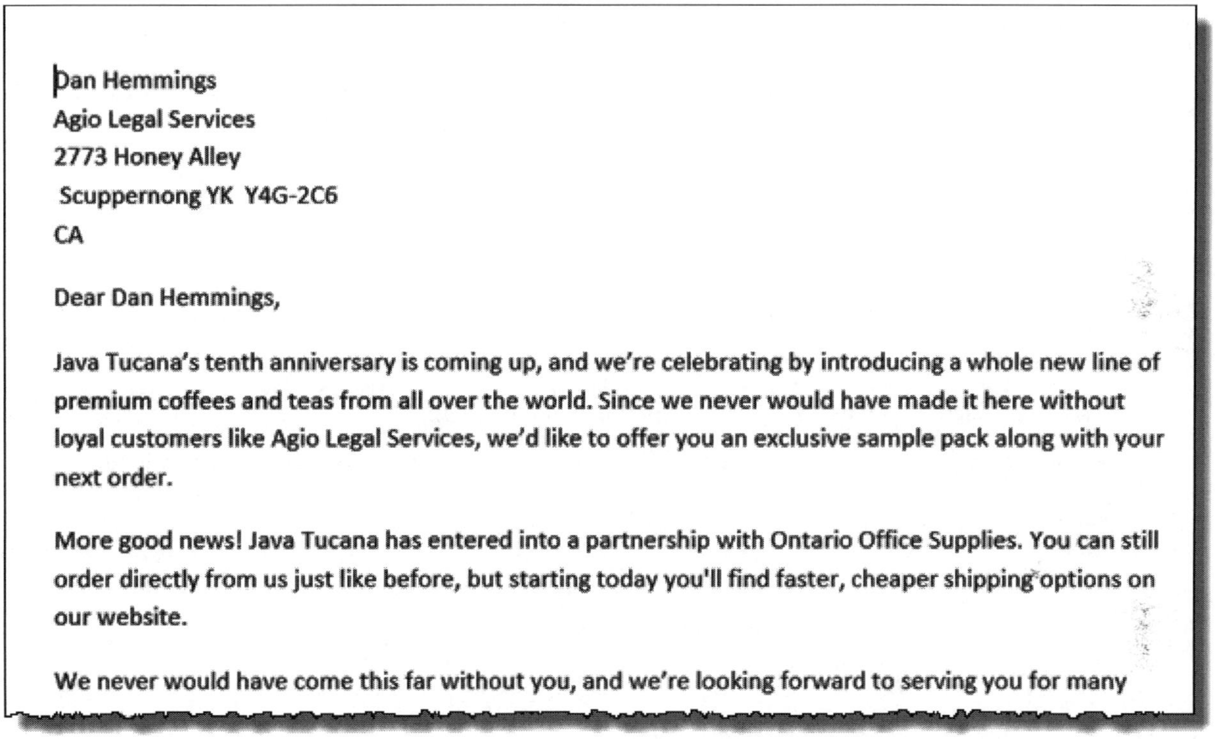

Dan Hemmings
Agio Legal Services
2773 Honey Alley
Scuppernong YK Y4G-2C6
CA

Dear Dan Hemmings,

Java Tucana's tenth anniversary is coming up, and we're celebrating by introducing a whole new line of premium coffees and teas from all over the world. Since we never would have made it here without loyal customers like Agio Legal Services, we'd like to offer you an exclusive sample pack along with your next order.

More good news! Java Tucana has entered into a partnership with Ontario Office Supplies. You can still order directly from us just like before, but starting today you'll find faster, cheaper shipping options on our website.

We never would have come this far without you, and we're looking forward to serving you for many

Assessment: Performing mail merges

1. The Mail Merge Wizard is a very different process than manually performing a mail merge. True or false?
    - True
    - False
2. What would you use to skip a record that matched certain criteria? Choose the best response.
    - A merge field
    - A merge filter
    - A merge match
    - A merge rule
3. The process for editing a merge field can be used on other types of fields as well. True or false?
    - True
    - False
4. What happens when you finalize a merge and choose a document output? Choose the best response.
    - Word creates each record as a separate document in the same folder as the original document.
    - Word creates a single new document with each record in its own section.
    - Word inserts each record as a new section in the existing document.
    - Word preserves the merge fields, and only finalizes the records once you print the document.

Module C: Envelopes and labels

Word allows you to print envelopes and shipping labels in a wide variety of standard sizes, assuming your printer's feed mechanism is compatible with them. You can manually enter addresses to print individual envelopes, single labels, or sheets of labels. You can also use a mail merge to print envelopes or labels addressed to an entire mailing list.

You will learn how to:

- Print envelopes
- Print labels
- Address envelopes or labels using a mail merge

Envelope and label printing

Unlike most Word documents, there's not much point in making an envelope or sheet of labels unless you're going to print it out, and there's more to it than just making sure your printer works and has paper. First, you need to know what size your envelopes or labels are so that you can format them properly. Word supports a wide variety of envelopes in both US and international standard sizes, and popular label sizes from a variety of manufacturers. If you're not sure which you need, it should be listed on the envelope or label packaging.

Some of the available sizes for printing envelopes.

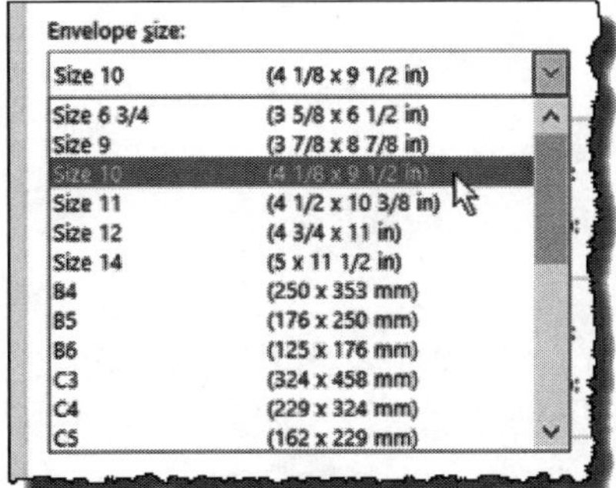

The second challenge is your printer itself. Not all printers are designed to easily manage varied envelope sizes and thicknesses, and the twists and turns in paper feeding can make self-stick labels peel off and get stuck inside a printer mechanism. Most desktop printers can handle envelopes or labels if you manually feed them, but before you print them, consult the printer's documentation regarding envelopes and labels.

Printing individual envelopes

You can print an individual envelope from the Envelopes tab of the **Envelopes and Labels** window. You can also insert an envelope page into an open document for later printing.

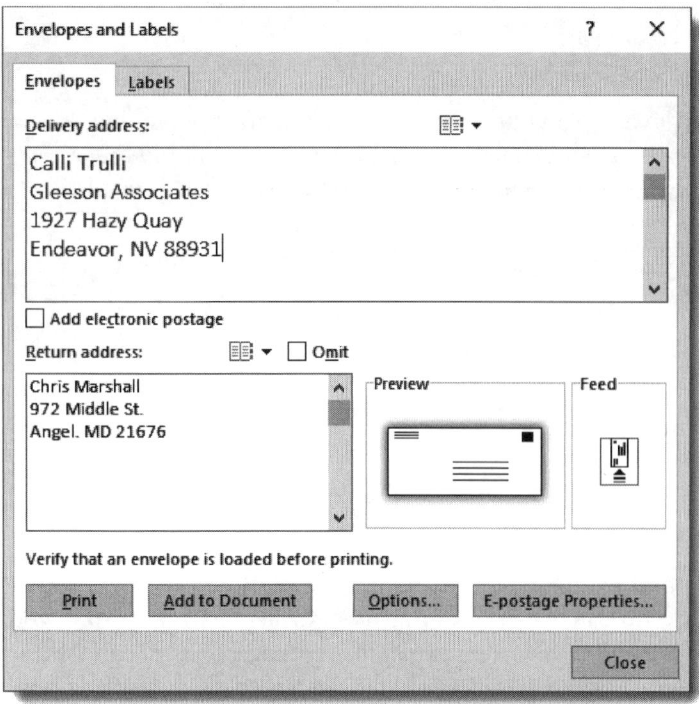

1. With any document open, on the Mailings tab, in the Create group, click **Envelopes**.
2. In the delivery address field, type the recipient's address.
   - If you use Outlook contacts to track mailing addresses, you can click to choose one from your address book.
   - If you have an E-postage add-in installed, check **Add electronic postage** to include it.
3. In the Return address field, enter the return address for the envelope.
   - By default, this is the mailing address stored in the Advanced section of the **Word Options** window. The first time you enter a mailing address, you're asked to save it as the default.
   - As with the delivery address, you can choose one from your address book.
   - If you don't want to include a return address, check **Omit**.
4. To change envelope size, printing format, or printer feed options, click **Options**.
   - The Preview and Feed sections show your current formatting and feeding options.
   - To change the address font, right-click the selected text, and click **Font**.
5. Finalize the envelope.
   - To directly print the envelope, click **Print**.
   - To insert the envelope before the first page of the open document, click **Add to Document**.

Setting envelope options

Clicking **Options** in the **Envelopes and Labels** window opens the **Envelope Options** window, which contains formatting and printing options.

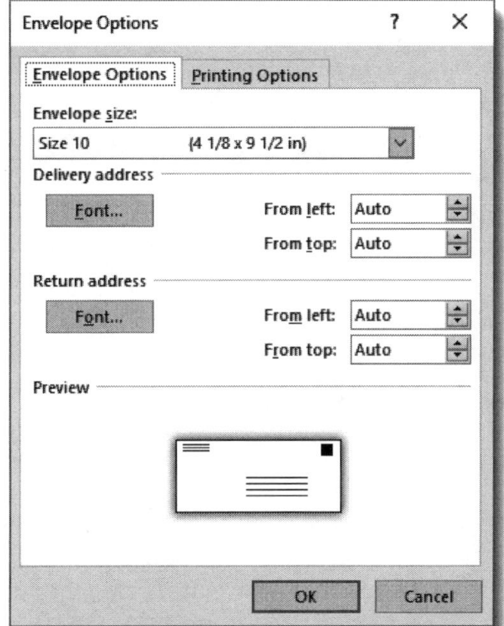

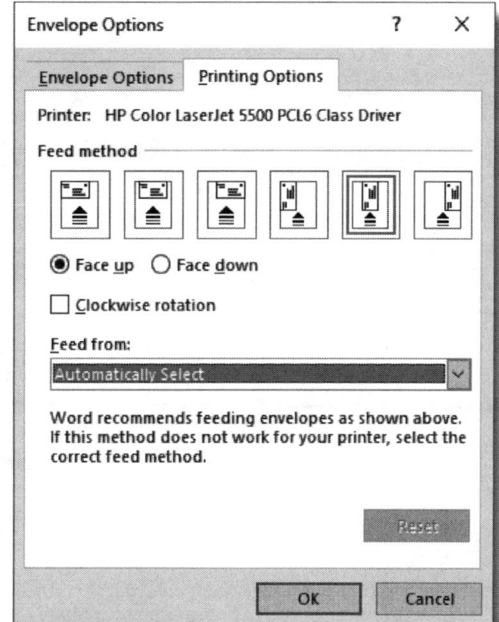

- On the Envelope Options tab, set the envelope format.
  - Choose a size from the Envelope size list.
  - To change delivery or return address font formatting, click the corresponding **Font** button.
  - Reposition either address label by entering **From Left** and **From Top** values.
- The Printing Options tab displays options for your currently selected printer.
  - Choose a tray from the Feed From list.
  - In the Feed method section, click the thumbnail corresponding to how you will physically insert the envelope into the printer.

Printing individual labels

Without using a mail merge, you can either print individual labels on a sheet or an entire page of identical labels. You can also use the same process to create a full-page table, sized to your label format, and edit the labels individually.

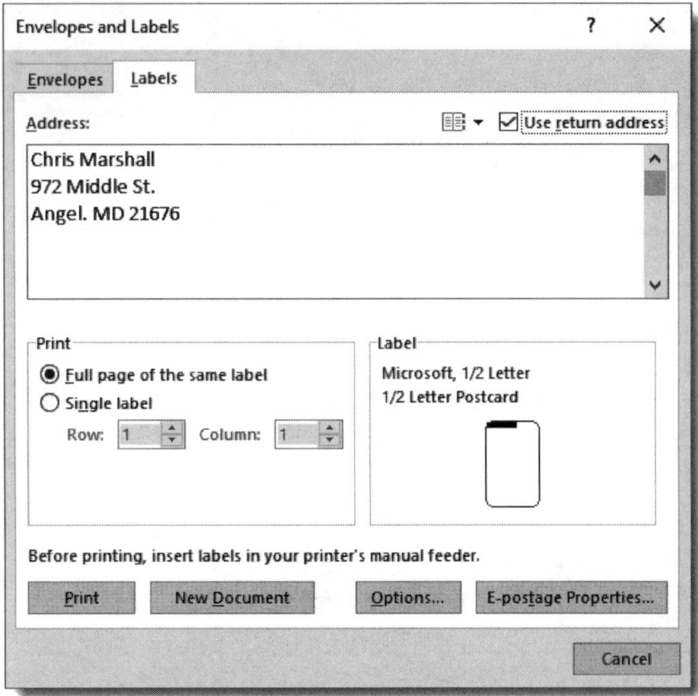

1. With any document open, click **Labels** on the Mailings tab.
2. Enter the label contents in the Address field.
   - Click to insert an address from your Outlook address book.
   - Check **Use return address** to print your default return address.
   - To format the label, right-click selected text, and click **Font**.
   - If you want to manually edit multiple labels, you can leave this blank for now.
3. To choose a label format, click **Options**.

   You can choose from commercial label formats, define a custom format, and choose printer feed settings in the **Label Options** window.

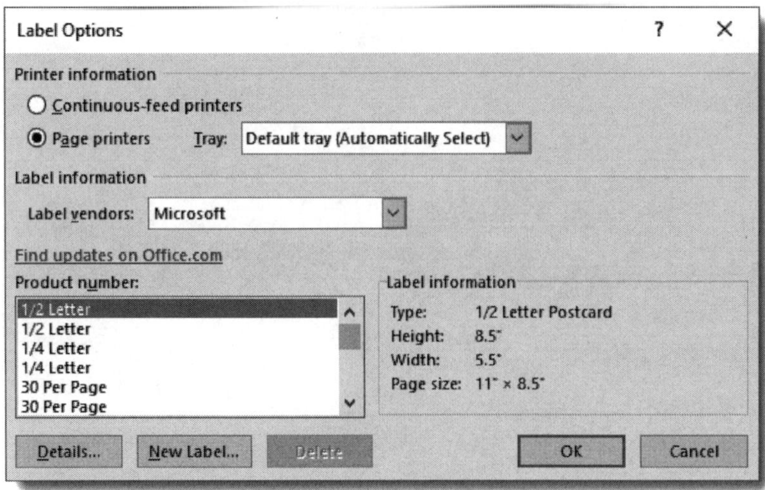

4. Choose whether to print a whole page of the same label, or a single label on a sheet.
   To print a single label, choose the row and column to print on the page.
5. Finalize the labels.
   - Click **Print** to send the labels directly to your default printer.
   - Click **New Document** to generate a full-page table in a new document according to your chosen settings.

Exercise: Printing an envelope

In this exercise, you'll create a single envelope for printing.

Do This	How & Why
1. Create a blank document.	
2. On the Mailings tab, click **Envelopes**.	The **Envelopes and Labels** window opens, with the Envelopes tab active.
3. In the Delivery address field, enter a mailing address, as shown.	
4. Type your mailing address in the Return address field.	
5. Set envelope and printing options.	
a) Click **Options**.	To open the **Envelope Options** window.
b) On the Envelope Options tab, open the **Envelope size** list.	You can choose from a variety of standard sizes, or define your own.
c) Click **US Legal**.	The Preview changes to reflect the larger envelope format.
d) Select **Size 10**.	You'll switch back to a typical envelope size.

Do This	How & Why
e) Click the Printing Options tab.	To view the feed method and paper source. The available options depend on your installed printer.
f) Click **OK**.	To return to the **Envelopes and Labels** window.
6. Click **Add to Document**.	A window appears, asking if you want to save the new return address as your default.
7. Click **Yes**.	The envelope is inserted as its own page at the start of the document.
8. If necessary, display formatting symbols.	The Show/Hide button, on the Home tab.
9. Save the document as `Mailing envelope`, and close it.	

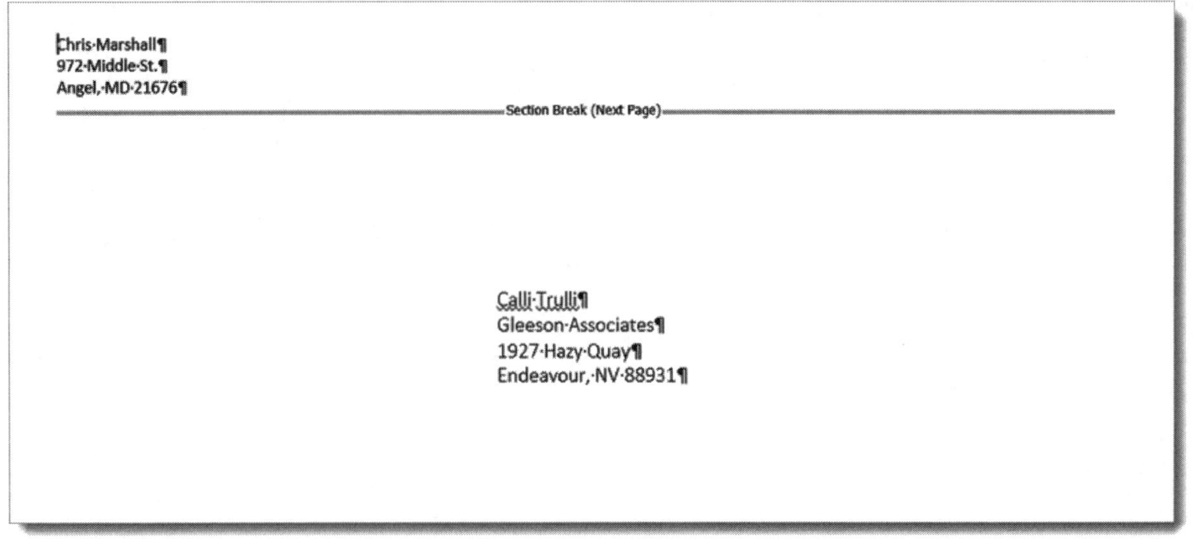

Envelope and label merges

Once you know how to create a mail merge as well as individual envelopes and labels, it's easy to create envelopes or labels for an entire mailing list. You just need to choose envelopes or labels as your merge type, and use the AddressBlock field for generating addresses. You can filter your data source and use merge rules, as you would for any other merge, and specify formatting and printing options, as you would for individual envelopes and labels.

You can use label merges for purposes other than merely mailing. For instance, you could label inventory drawers using a mail merge and a parts list.

Creating envelope merges

An envelope merge uses the same merge fields as a form letter, but using an envelope's formatting settings.

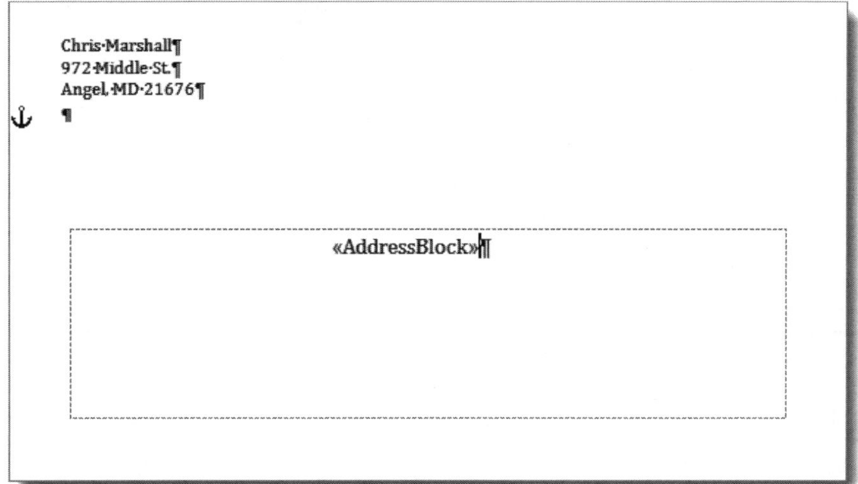

1. Click **Start Mail Merge** > **Envelopes**.
2. Choose settings in the **Envelope Options** window, then click **OK**.
3. Click **Select Recipients** to create or import a data source.
4. Edit the envelope.
   - Insert an AddressBlock field or other merge fields using the Write & Insert Fields group.
   - Use merge rules to filter records or insert conditional text.
   - If you don't want to use the default return address, you can edit it or even insert fields there.
5. Preview and finish the merge.

Creating label merges

Creating label merges is a little different from creating other merge types, because more than one label is printed on a page. Instead of a section break between records, label merges use a Next Record field to separate records, one for each label after the first.

Additionally, every merge field must be included in every label on the page, or all records might not print. You can manually do this, but it's easier to have word automatically update the whole page.

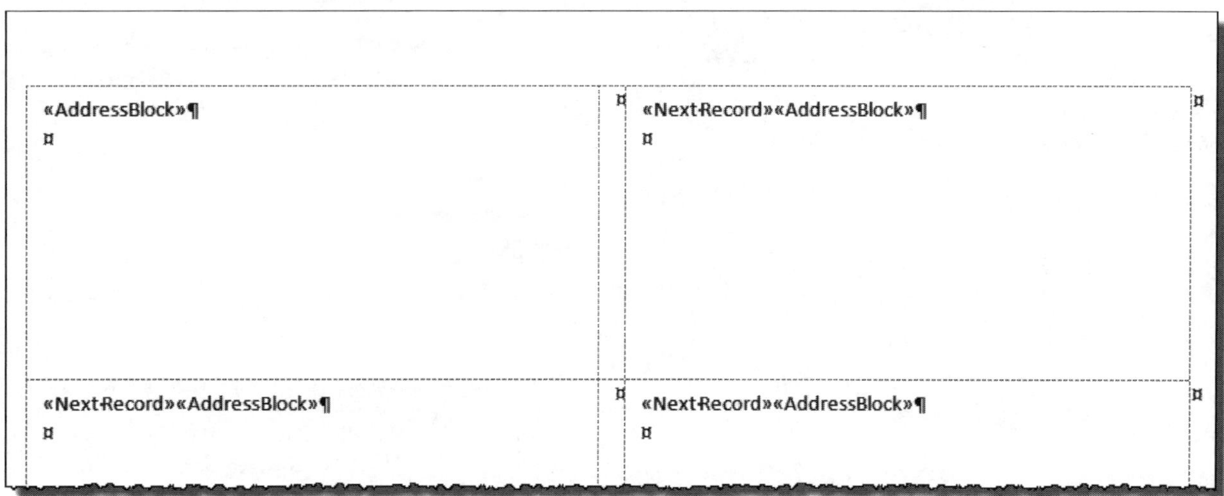

1. Click **Start Mail Merge > Labels**.
2. Choose label and printer settings in the **Label Options** window, and click **OK**.
3. Click **Select Recipients** to create or import a data source.
4. Edit the first label on the page.

   You can insert and format ordinary text, merge fields, and rules just as you would in an ordinary document.
5. Click **Update Labels** in the Write & Insert Fields group to copy the contents of the first label to the rest of the page.

   Word also automatically inserts a Next Record field on each subsequent label.
6. Preview and finish the merge as usual.

Exercise: Creating a label merge

In this exercise, you'll create mailing labels for a customer list.

Do This	How & Why
1. Start a label merge.	
a) Create a new blank document.	
b) On the Mailings tab, click **Start Mail Merge > Labels**.	The **Label Options** window opens.
c) From the Label Vendors list, choose **Avery US Letter**.	Verify that **Page Printers** is selected above.
d) In the product number list, click **5160 Easy Peel Address Labels**.	This is a common US label size.
e) Click **OK**.	To create a blank sheet of labels with ten rows of three columns.
2. Import the North America worksheet from `Customer list`.	Click **Select Recipients > Use Existing List**, then select the `Customer list` workbook. Word automatically inserts a Next Record field into each cell after the first.
3. Insert an AddressBlock field in the first cell of the table.	You'll need to click **Match Fields** and match the State field in the address block to the Region code in the data source.
4. Click **Preview Results**.	There are two problems. First, the whole address doesn't fit on the label. Second, only the first label on the page has an address in it. You'll fix both of them.

Do This	How & Why
5. Remove the spacing after each paragraph in the address block.	Select the text. Then on the Home tab, click [icon] then click **Remove Space Before Paragraph**.
6. In the Write & Insert Fields group, click **Update Labels**.	The merge field and formatting are copied to all the other cells.
7. Finalize the merge.	
a) Click **Finish & Merge > Merge to Individual Documents**.	The **Merge to New Document** window opens.
a) Click **OK**.	All 61 records are inserted into a new document. The last page has only one record.
8. Save the new document as `Customer labels`, and close it.	
9. Close the original document without saving.	

Assessment: Envelopes and labels

1. In general, you need a specialized printer to output envelopes or labels in Word. True or false?
    - True
    - False
2. It's a good idea to define yourself as an Outlook contact, so you can easily insert yourself in the Return address field of envelopes. True or false?
    - True
    - False
3. When you create a page of labels, what does Word use to separate individual labels? Choose the best answer.
    - Section breaks
    - Tab stops
    - Table cells
    - Text boxes
4. When you create a label merge, how does Word separate each record? Choose the best answer.
    - An AddressBlock field
    - A Next Record field
    - A section break
    - A table cell

Summary: Creating mailings

You should now know how to:

- Create a recipients list in Word, or from an external data source such as a worksheet or database
- Create a form letter or email using merge fields
- Print individual envelopes or labels
- Use a mail merge to generate envelopes or labels for a mailing list

Synthesis: Creating mailings

In this exercise, you'll create merged mailings to a customer list.

1. Compose a form letter addressed to all US customers listed in the `Customer list` Excel workbook. Include a greeting line of your choice, and merge fields and rules within the letter text.
2. Create mailing envelopes for the same customer list. Use an envelope format of your choice.

Chapter 16: Macros and forms

You will learn how to:

- Run and use macros
- Create forms

Module A: Macros

As you use Word more often and for more complicated tasks, you might find yourself repeating the same steps over and over. You can save time by creating a macro that automatically performs those steps at the click of a button or press of a keystroke combination.

You will learn:

- About macros and macro security
- How to record macros
- How to run macros
- How to edit macros

About macros

You might have heard of macros in the context of power users doing complex and complicated tasks, or as part of a puzzling troubleshooting session. They can sound pretty intimidating. To some extent, this is true: macros are powerful tools used by experienced users, and they do require additional awareness of Word security settings. But it's easy to learn the basics and use macros to automate even your common tasks.

At its heart, a *macro* is a series of tasks you could do manually but is performed automatically by Word. You can record a macro one step at a time in Word, or compose it in the *Visual Basic for Applications* (VBA) editor included with Office. You can store it in a document or in a global template, and run it using a button or keystroke combination. You can even configure a macro to run whenever you open a document.

Commands related to macros are located on the Developer tab of the ribbon, in the Code group. The Developer tab isn't displayed by default, so you need to customize the ribbon to display it before you can record or manage macros. Otherwise, you can run only existing macros linked to buttons or keystrokes.

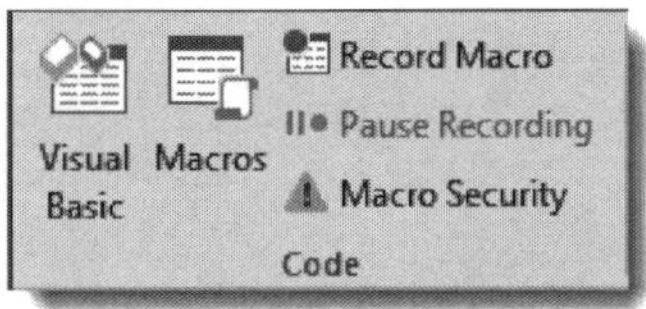

Macro security

Exam Objective: MOS Word Core 1.4.10

Macros are essentially small programs that run within Word or other Office applications. Like other programs, they can pose a security risk. When earlier versions of Office first introduced powerful macro capabilities, *macro viruses* became a real threat. In 1999, for example, the "Melissa virus" infected as many as 20% of the world's computers. Melissa was a Word virus: when you opened the document it would automatically run and mail itself to the first 50 people in your Outlook contacts. Because it spread so rapidly and generated so many messages, the virus bogged down email servers worldwide. Melissa didn't damage files or user data directly, but other macro viruses did.

The reason macro viruses of the 1990s did so much damage was because older Office versions weren't designed with security in mind. These viruses still exist, but Word 2016 has features designed to prevent macros from running without your knowledge or approval. Familiarity with these features is important not just to protect yourself from malicious viruses, but to make sure you can easily run the macros you want to use.

The first line of security is in file types. Ordinary Word 2010 documents have a .docx extension, and templates have a .dotx extension. Neither of these file types can contain macros. You can save macros only in macro-enabled documents (.docm) and macro-enabled templates. This way, you know which files might contain macros before you open them. The .doc and .dot files used by Word 2003 (and earlier) can also contain macros: it's best not to save documents in these formats without good reason, but you should also be aware that when you receive them from someone else, they might pose a security risk.

Even if you don't have file extensions displayed on your computer, you can still see the file type in the Open window or Windows Explorer. Additionally, macro-enabled documents and templates have a different icon with a blue symbol.

Truly amazing but ordinary Word document.docx	2015-09-25 15:12	Microsoft Word Document
Truly amazing but ordinary Word template.dotx	2015-09-25 15:15	Microsoft Word Template
Truly amazing macro-laden Word document.docm	2015-09-25 15:23	Microsoft Word Macro-Enabled Document
Truly amazing macro-laden Word template.dotm	2015-09-25 15:17	Microsoft Word Macro-Enabled Template

The second line of defense is Word's security settings. By default, even when the file type allows macros in a document, Word will run them only if the document is in a trusted folder, or if you've designated it as a trusted document. Otherwise, Word displays a security warning above the document window.

Recording macros

The easiest way to create a macro, especially when you don't know VBA code, is to manually record it step by step. You can choose the macro's name and options from the **Record Macro** window.

Exam Objective: MOS Word Core 1.4.8, 1.4.9

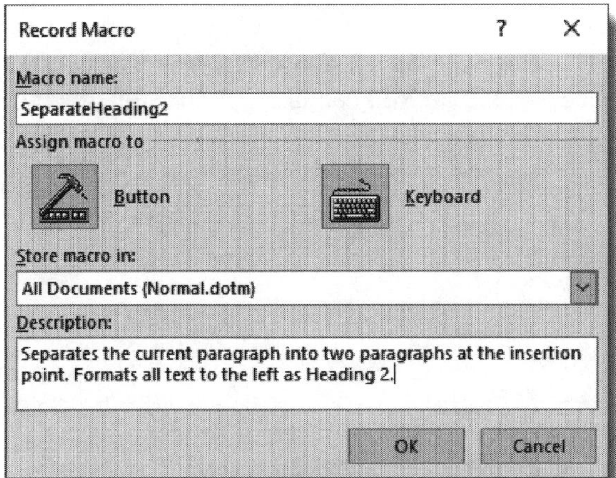

Optionally, you can assign a macro to a button on the Quick Access toolbar or ribbon, or to a keyboard shortcut. Either way, all available macros are listed among available commands in the **Word Options** window, and you can assign either a button or keyboard shortcut later.

Note: You can use most, but not all, Word commands when recording a macro. In particular, you can't use the mouse to place the insertion point or select text in the document. Instead, you must either record using the keyboard to navigate and select text, or design a macro that applies to text you've already selected.

1. On the Developer tab, in the Code group, click **Record Macro**.
   The Record Macro button is now replaced by the Stop Recording button.

2. Set options in the **Record Macro** window.
   - The macro name may include letters, numbers, and underscores, but not spaces.
   - By default, the macro is stored in the default template, `Normal.dotm`. You can also store it in the currently open document, if its file type allows macros.
   - In the Description field, describe the macro in terms that help you or other users remember its function and purpose.
3. Accept the macro settings.
   - To assign a button to the macro, click **Button** to open the **Word Options** window.
   - To assign a keyboard shortcut to the macro, click **Keyboard** to open the **Customize Keyboard** window.
   - To begin recording without assigning either, click **OK**.

   When Word is recording, the mouse pointer shows a cassette-tape icon.

4. Record the macro by manually performing its commands in Word.
   If you need to perform any commands you don't want to include in the macro, click **Pause Recording**. When you're done, click **Resume Recorder**.
5. When you're finished recording, click **Stop Recording**.

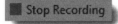

Assigning macros to buttons

If you choose to assign a macro to a button when you create it, you're automatically sent to the Quick Access Toolbar section of the **Word Options** window. If you want to assign a button later, you can do it in much the same way you would for any other command on the Quick Access toolbar. You can also use the same method to add it to a custom ribbon tab.

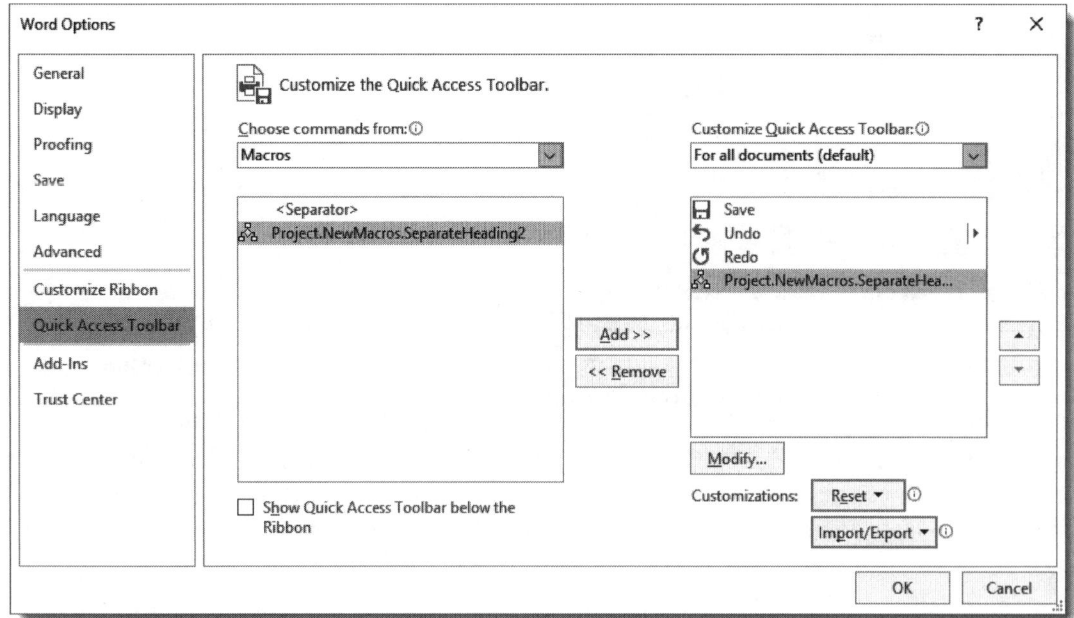

1. If you've already created the macro, open the **Word Options** window, and click **Quick Access Toolbar**.

2. From the "Choose Commands from" list, choose **Macros**.
   If you're creating a new macro, you'll begin here.
3. Select the macro in the left column.
4. Click **Add**.
5. Optionally, click **Modify**, then select a name and icon for the macro.
6. Click **OK**.

Assigning macros to keyboard shortcuts

Just like assigning a macro to a button, it's easiest to assign a macro to a keyboard shortcut when you create it. You can still do so later by opening the same **Customize Keyboard** window.

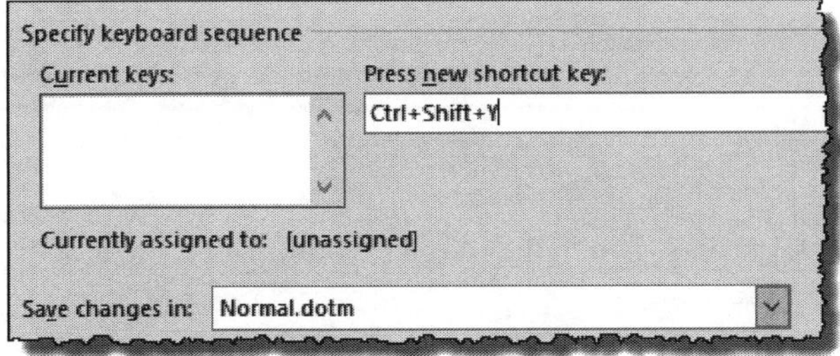

Exam Objective: MOS Word Core 1.4.9

1. If you've already created the macro, open the **Word Options** window, and click **Customize Ribbon**.
2. At the bottom of the window, click **Customize**.
3. In the Categories section of the **Customize Keyboard** window, choose **Macros**.
   If you're creating the macro now, you'll begin here.
4. Select the macro in the right column.
5. Click in the "Press new shortcut key" field, then press a key combination.

   Note: When you enter a shortcut, a "Currently assigned to" field appears. If it's already in use, try a different combination.
6. When you've decided on a shortcut, click **Assign**.
   - To remove a shortcut that's already assigned, click it in the Current keys list, then click **Remove**.
   - To change where the keyboard shortcut is saved, choose a location from the "Save changes in" list.
7. When you're finished, click **Close**.

Running macros

You can run a macro multiple ways, or even record one that automatically runs at a predetermined time, such as when you start Word or open a document. For example, you can create a macro that automatically sets a document to a certain zoom level when you open it. If a macro acts according to an insertion point or text selection, be sure to do so before running the macro.

- Click an assigned macro button on the ribbon or Quick Access toolbar.
- Press an assigned keyboard shortcut.
- In the Code group, click **Macros** to open the **Macros** window. Then select the macro you want, and click **Run**.

- To make a macro run automatically, you need to give it a special name, depending on when you want it to run.
  - `AutoExec` runs when you start Word.
  - `AutoExit` runs when you close Word.
  - `AutoOpen` runs when you open a document.
  - `AutoClose` runs when you close a document.
  - `AutoNew` runs when you create a new document.

Note: An Auto macro can run only if it's stored in the right location, and you can have only one of each AutoMacro in a given location. AutoOpen and AutoClose are stored in the document that runs them. AutoNew must be in the template used to create the new document. AutoExec and AutoExit must be in the default template, meaning you can have only one for all Word documents.

Exercise: Creating a macro

To access the Code group, you'll need to display the Developer tab. You can do so by customizing the ribbon. It also will be helpful to show formatting marks.

In this exercise, you'll record a macro, assign it to a keyboard shortcut, and run it.

Do This	How & Why
1. In the current module folder, open `Coffee varieties`.	Every product name in the document is manually formatted and in the same paragraph as the description. You want them formatted as headings on their own lines, and you'll record a macro to make your job easier.
2. In the first product listing, place the insertion point immediately to the left of the word "Brazil."	Brazilian Bourbon Santos: Brazil Santos. Always a good choice, this Right after the space.
3. Start a new macro.	
a) On the Developer tab, in the code group, click **Record Macro**.	Record Macro Pause Recording The **Record Macro** window opens.
b) In the Macro name field, type `SeparateHeading2`.	The name can't contain spaces.
c) In the Description field, type `Places text left of insertion point in new paragraph, and applies Heading 2 style`.	This text is to remind you or coworkers of what the macro does.
d) From the "Store macro in" list, select **Coffee varieties**.	Store macro in: Coffee varieties.docx (document)

Do This	How & Why
e) You'll store the macro in the document.	
f) Click **Keyboard**.	The **Customize Keyboard** window opens. The macro is already selected.
4. Assign a keyboard shortcut.	
a) In the "Press new shortcut key" field, press **Ctrl+Alt+S**.	The keyboard shortcut is already assigned to another command, so you'll use something else.
b) Press **Delete**, then press **Ctrl+Shift+Y**.	This combination shows as unassigned, so you'll keep it. Specify keyboard sequence / Current keys: / Press new shortcut key: Ctrl+Shift+Y / Currently assigned to: [unassigned]
c) Click **Assign**.	The shortcut is added to the Current Keys field.
d) Click **Close**.	The mouse pointer shows the Recording icon, and the Record Macro button on the ribbon is replaced with Stop Recording.
5. Record the macro.	You'll go through the process of formatting one product name the way you want it.
a) Press **Enter**.	To insert a paragraph break between the product name and description.
b) Press the left arrow key.	To return to the previous paragraph. You'll remove the space and colon next.
c) Press **Backspace** twice.	
d) Press **Shift+Home**.	To select the rest of the line. Because you're recording a macro, you can't select text with the mouse.
e) On the Home tab, click **Heading 2** in the Styles gallery.	You can still use the mouse to click commands. The Heading 2 style is applied to the Brazilian Bourbon Santos product name.
f) On the Developer tab, click **Stop Recording**.	To finish the macro.
6. Run the macro on the next product.	

Do This	How & Why
a) Place the insertion point before the second product description.	Immediately to the left of the word "Rich."
b) Press **Ctrl+Shift+Y**.	The macro inserts a new paragraph, deletes the space and colon, and reformats the product name, just as you did manually.
7. Save the document.	
a) On the Quick Access toolbar, click **Save**.	Word warns you that the current document format doesn't allow you to save macros.
b) Click **No**.	The **Save As** window opens.
c) In the File name field, type `Coffee varieties macro`.	
d) From the Save as type list, select **Word Macro-Enabled Document (*.docm)**.	
e) Save and overwrite the file.	This time the document is saved successfully.
f) Close the document.	
8. Start a macro in a new document.	You'll create a macro that draws and formats a table.
a) Open a new blank document.	Press **Ctrl+N**.
b) Start recording a new macro stored in the current document.	Click **Record Macro** on the Developer tab, then select the current document from the Store macro in list.
c) Name the macro `CoffeeTable`.	

Do This	How & Why
d) Describe the macro as `Creates a table to list coffee varieties by roast and body`.	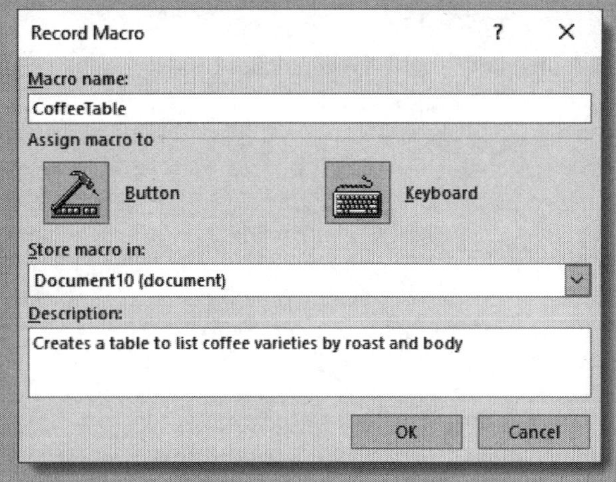
e) Click **OK**.	To start recording the macro.
9. Record the new macro.	
a) Insert a 4x4 table.	
b) Press **Tab**.	 **Note:** Remember that when you're recording a macro, you can only navigate with the keyboard, not the mouse. To move to the second cell.
c) In the second cell of the top row, type `Light-bodied`.	You'll fill out the row and column headers.
d) In the next two cells, type `Medium-bodied` and `Full-bodied`.	Navigate using the Tab or arrow keys.

e) In the left column, type `Light roast`, `Medium roast`, and `Dark roast` in rows 2-4.

¤	Light-bodied¤	Medium-bodied¤	Full-bodied¤
Light·roast¤	¤	¤	¤
Medium·roast¤	¤	¤	¤
Dark·roast¤	¤	¤	¤

Do This	How & Why
f) On the Table Tools | Design tab, choose table style Grid Table 5 Dark - Accent 5.	
g) On the Developer tab, click **Stop Recording**.	
10. Assign the CoffeeTable macro to a button.	
a) Right-click the ribbon and click **Customize Quick Access Toolbar**.	The **Word Options** window opens.
b) From the Choose commands from list, select **Macros**.	The macro you just created is listed.
c) Click **Project.NewMacros.CoffeeTable**, then click **Add**.	It's added to the right column.
d) Click **OK**.	A new button for the macro appears on the Quick Access Toolbar.
11. Test the new macro and button.	
a) Create a new paragraph in the document window.	
b) In the Quick Access toolbar, click the macro button.	An identical table is created at the insertion point.
12. Save the new document as `Table macro.docm`.	Don't forget to select **Word macro-enabled document** from the Save as type list.
13. Close the document.	

Managing macros

To manage your macros, in the code group, click **Macros**.

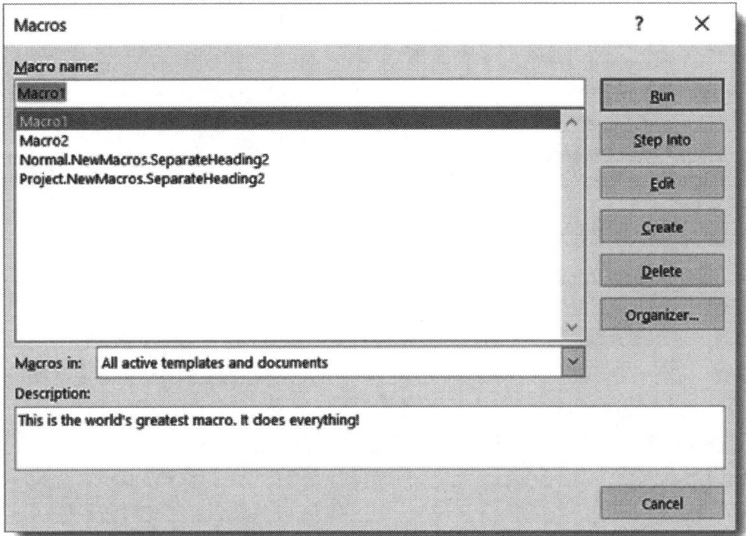

- To view or edit a macro's description, select it.
- To filter which macros are displayed, select an open document or template from the "Macros in" list.
- To run a macro, select it, and click **Run**.
- To edit a macro, click **Edit**.
- To test a macro a step at a time, click **Step Into**, then press **F8** to continue step by step through it.
- To delete a macro, select it, and click **Delete**.
- To create a new macro in the VBA editor, type a name, and click **Create**.
- To copy macros between templates and documents, click **Organizer**.

Using the macro Organizer

When you click **Organizer** in the Macros window, the **Organizer** window opens. It has commands to copy, delete, and rename macro modules.

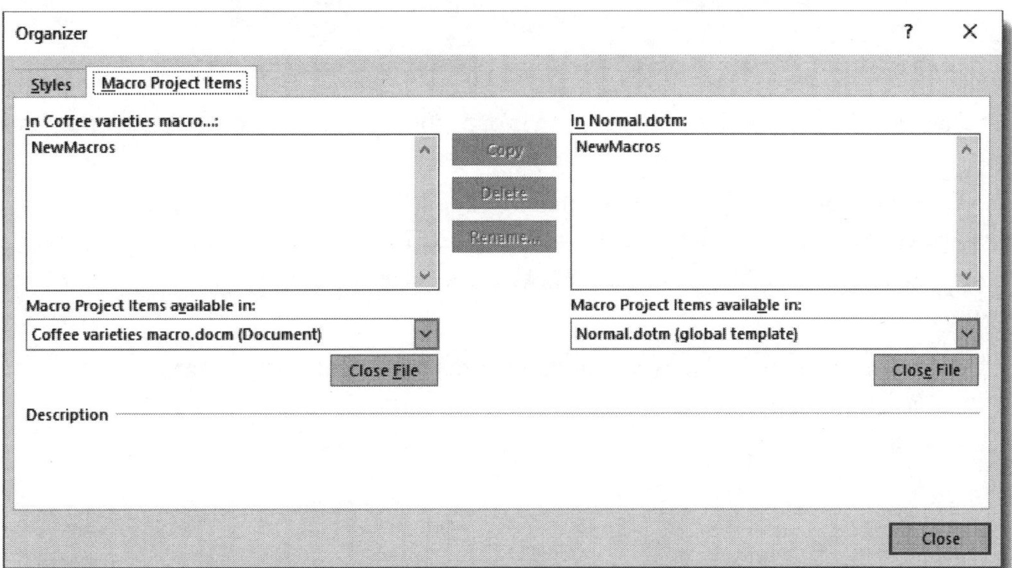

If you've used the Organizer to manage styles, you'll find the interface very familiar. On each side is an open file: by default, one is the current document, and one is the default template. Above the file name is a list of the modules in that file.

- To close one file, click **Close File** on its respective side.
- To open a new file, click **Open File**.
- To copy a module from one file to the other, select it, and click **Copy**.
- To delete a module in one file, select it, and click **Delete**.
- To rename a module, select it, and click **Rename**.
- When you're finished making changes, click **Close**.

Managing macro security

You should always keep security in mind when opening macro-enabled files. By default, when you open a macro-enabled document that isn't a trusted file or in a trusted location, you see a security warning and no macros can run. You can bypass this to enable macros in the document, but always be careful not to enable macros in a document you don't trust.

Exam Objective: MOS Word Core 1.4.10

- To trust an individual document, click **Enable Content** in the Security Warning bar.
- For some files, such as those on network drives, or file types that might be blocked, you need to click **OK** or **Open in Help Window** in a separate **Security Warning** window.

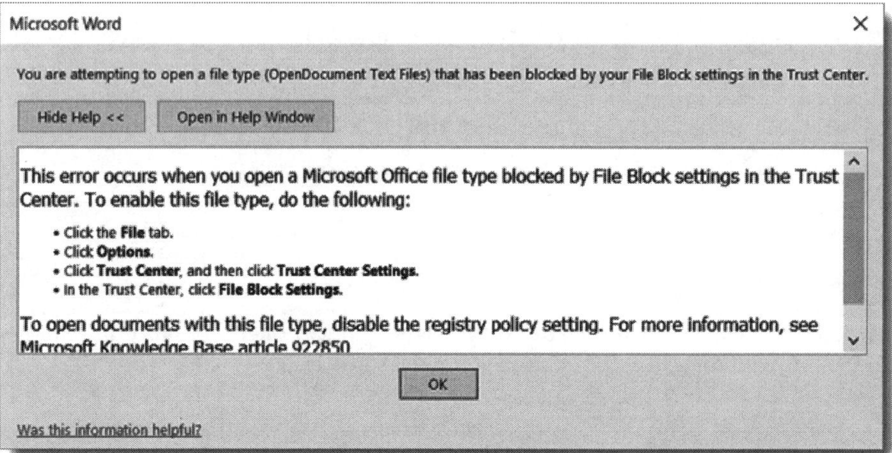

- To make broader changes to Word's settings, in the Code group, click **Macro Security** to open the **Trust Center** window.
  - Click **Macro Settings** to change basic security settings for running macros. Too loose a setting renders you vulnerable to macro viruses; too strict a setting can keep you from running the macros you want.
  - Click **Trusted Locations** to add or change trusted folders for opening files. This can be dangerous, so don't do so lightly.
  - Click **Trusted Documents** to change how Word handles trusted documents, or to clear the current list of trusted documents.

- Click **File Block Settings** to change how Word handles file types, including those created in earlier Word versions.

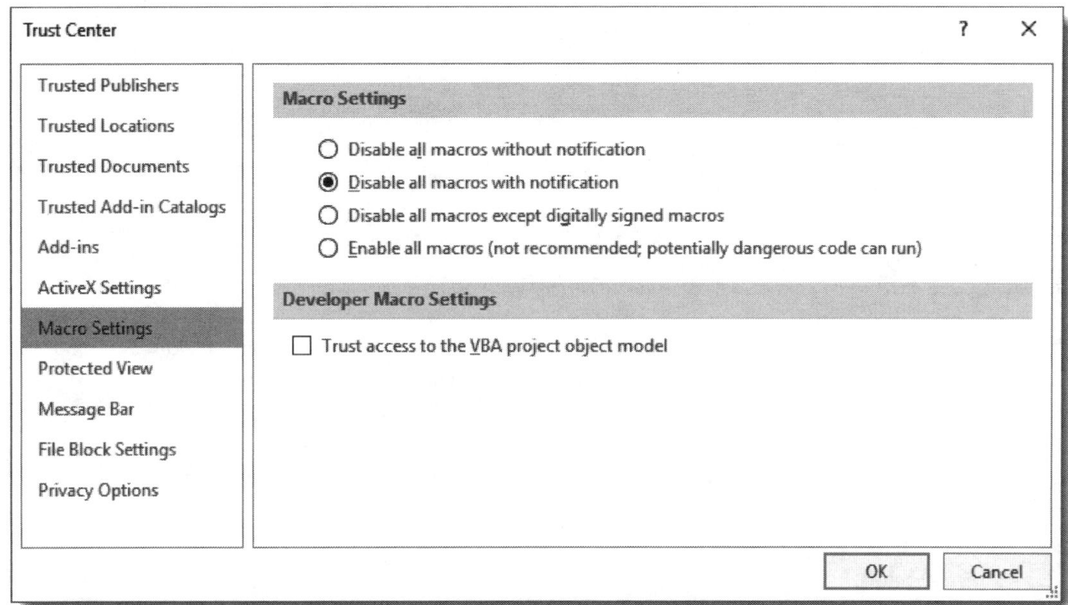

Exercise: Organizing macros

Do This	How & Why
1. Open `Coffee varieties macro`.	If a security warning bar appears at the top of the document window, click **Enable Content** to trust the file and enable macros. If the **Restrict Editing** pane opens, click to close it.
2. View macro security settings.	
a) On the Developer tab, in the Code group, click **Macro Security**.	To open the Macro Settings section of the Trust Center. Word is set to disable macros with notification.
b) In the left column, click **Trusted Locations**.	Word currently trusts locations of the Templates and Startup folders. This lets you easily run macros in a template you've saved.
c) Click **Trusted Documents**.	Here, you can change settings for trusted documents, for example, to clear the current document from the trusted documents list.
d) Click **Cancel**.	
3. Open the Macro Organizer.	You want to copy a macro from another document.
a) On the Developer tab, click **Macros**.	The **Macros** window opens. Only SeparateHeading2 macro is available.

Do This	How & Why
b) Click **Organizer**.	The Organizer window opens. On one side it shows the macro modules in `Coffee varieties macro.docm`, and on the other side it shows the macro modules in the `Normal.dotm` global template.
c) Under `Normal.dotm`, click **Close File**.	You need to open another file.
d) Click **Open File**.	By default, it opens to the Templates folder.
e) Navigate to the current chapter folder.	It should be in the Documents folder. You won't see any files there, but only since the browser is only showing template files.
f) From the file type list, choose **All Word Documents**.	To display the documents in the folder.
g) Click **Table Macro**, then click **Open**.	Now you can organize macros in both of the documents you created them in. 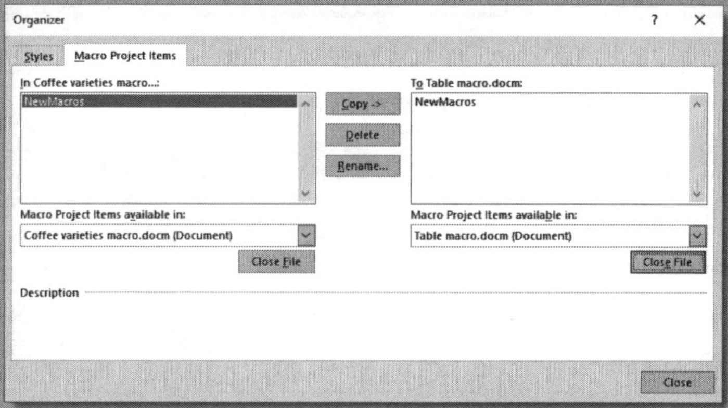
4. Organize your macros.	You want to copy the CoffeeTable macro into Coffee varieties macro.
a) On the right side, click **NewMacros**.	You can only copy whole modules, rather than individual macros.
b) Click **Copy**.	An error message appears, since there's already a NewMacros module in the other file. 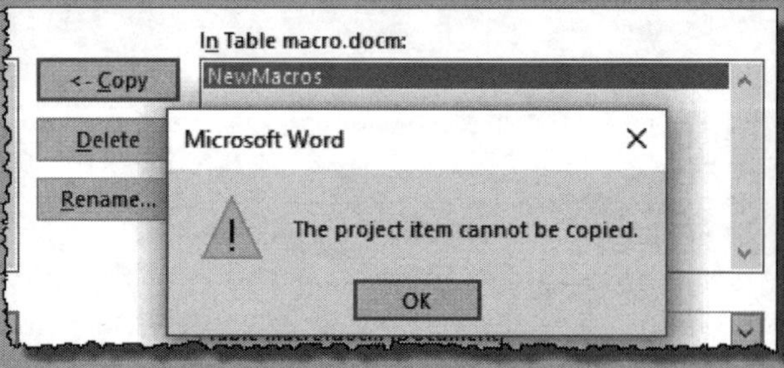
c) Click **OK**.	To close the error window.
d) Click **Rename**.	The **Rename** window opens.

Do This	How & Why
e) Type **TableMacro** and click **OK**.	In Table macro.docm: TableMacro
f) Click **Copy**.	This time the module is copied to `Copy varieties macro`. Styles Macro Project Items To Coffee varieties macro...: NewMacros TableMacro
g) Click **Close**.	You're asked whether to save your changes to Table macro as well.
h) Click **Save**.	The window closes.
5. Test the copied macro.	
a) Place the insertion point at the end of the document.	Create a new blank paragraph if necessary.
b) Click **Macros**.	Both macros now appear in the current document. Macro name: CoffeeTable CoffeeTable SeparateHeading2
c) Click **CoffeeTable**, then click **Run**.	To run the macro and create the table. It's a different color this time, but only because this document has different theme colors.
6. Save `Coffee varieties macro`.	Leave it open for the next exercise.

VBA code

Excel macros are actually programs written in Visual Basic for Application (VBA). VBA code lives in *modules*, and a particular macro is stored in a *procedure* within a module.

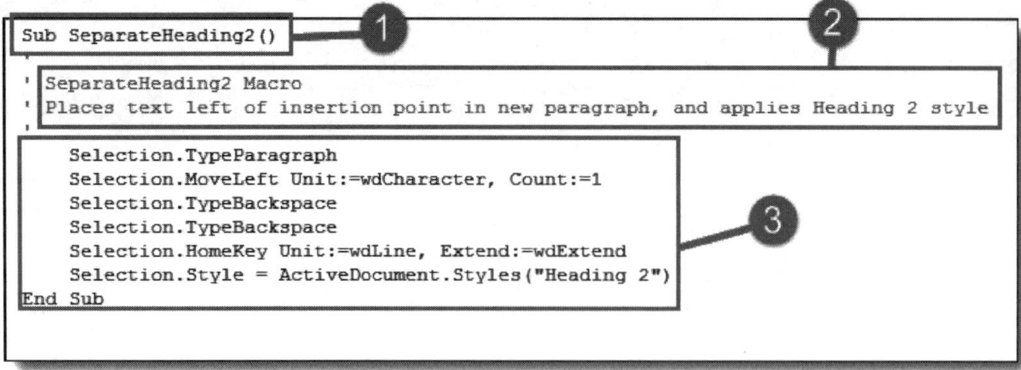

The *procedure name* identifies the procedure (or macro name).

Comments in green explain what the code does but have no effect when the program runs.

Statements are the individual programming commands in the procedure (or macro).

Editing macros

As you learned earlier, you can create macros by recording them in Word or by coding them in VBA. Either way, Word stores the macro as a VBA program. So, when you edit or step into a macro, Word opens the **Visual Basic Editor** in a separate window, displaying the macro.

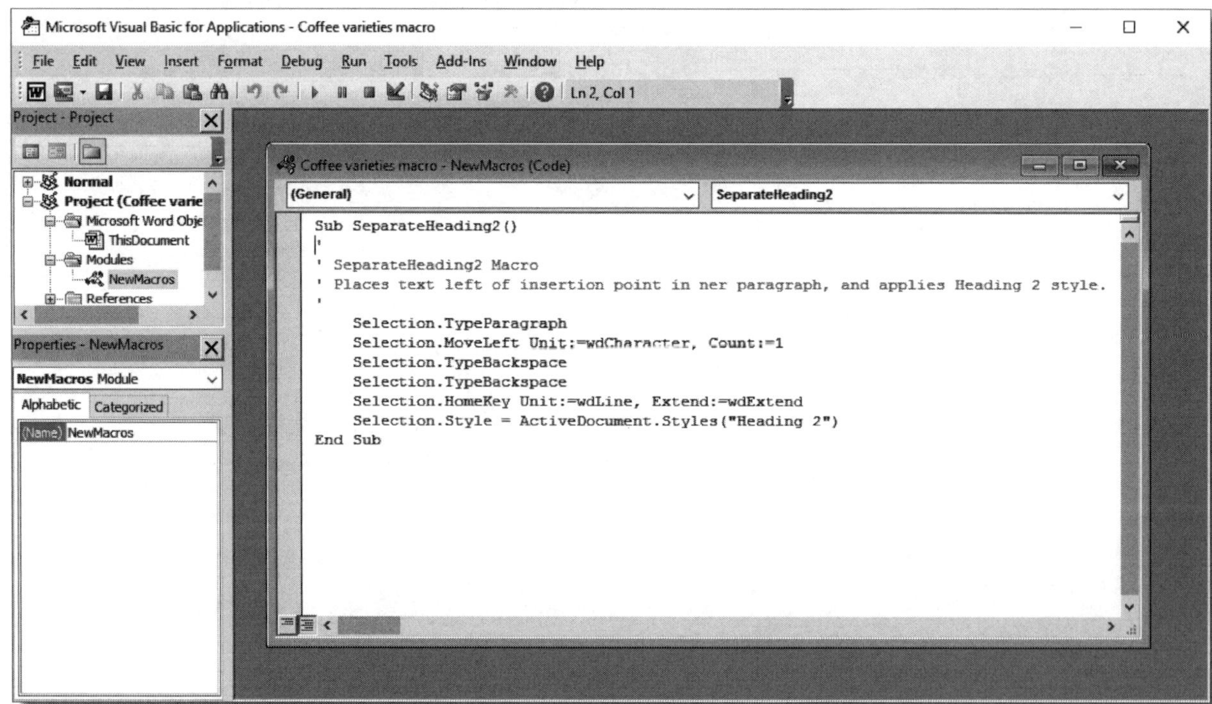

Programming in Visual Basic is beyond the scope of this course, but if you find yourself using macros regularly, you might want to learn the basics. Even a little coding knowledge can make it easy to make simple tweaks without having to record the macro all over again.

1. In the **Macros** window, click **Edit**.
2. Edit the macro.
   - VBA stores individual macros inside *modules*. The open window in the editor represents a module.
   - Each macro within a module begins with a `Sub` statement containing the macro name, and ends with an `End Sub` statement.
   - Each line within the macro represents a step in it. The purpose of some is easy to guess just by reading them, but others will mean little to VBA novices.
   - VBA code is very syntax-sensitive. Improper spacing, case, or punctuation can change a macro's functions or render it invalid.
3. Click **File > Close and Return to Microsoft Word**, or press **Alt+Q**.

Exercise: Editing a macro

To complete this exercise, you need to have completed the **Creating a macro** exercise. `Coffee variety macros` is closed. You'll view VBA code and make changes to a macro.

Do This	How & Why
1. View VBA code for the SeparateHeading2 macro.	You actually want the macro to format text as Heading 3, but you don't want to record it again, so you'll see how complicated the code looks instead.
a) Click **Macros**.	To open the **Macro** window. You can manage macros in any active document or template here.
b) Under Macro name, select the **SeparateHeading2** macro.	
c) Click **Edit**.	The **Visual Basic Editor** opens, with the macro open in a window.
d) Look at the code.	If you didn't perform the last exercise exactly as described, the code might look slightly different. Keywords are blue, comments are green, and the rest of the code is black. Each step corresponds to an action in the macro: adding a new paragraph, deleting text, applying styles, etc.
2. Edit the macro.	You can make the change you need without any serious coding knowledge.

Do This	How & Why
a) Edit the `Selection.Style` line as shown.	Because "Heading 2" is a named style, you can edit it to "Heading 3."
b) Edit the macro's name in the first line to read `SeparateHeading3`.	You could just change the code and it would work, but you want the macro's name and description to remain accurate.
c) In the green comment text, and in the line below it, change both instances of "2" to `3`. These lines aren't executed but are used to describe what the code does.	
d) Click **File > Close and Return to Microsoft Word**.	You can instead press **Alt+Q**. To close the editor window.
3. Test the edited macro.	
a) Place the insertion point after the Costa Rican Tarrazu product name.	Right before the word "One."
b) Press **Ctrl+Shift+Y**.	When you renamed the macro, the keyboard shortcut referring to the original name stopped working. Nothing happens. You can assign it a new keyboard shortcut, but just to test it, you can run it from the **Macros** window.
c) Click **Macros**. Under Macro name, select **SeparateHeading3**.	The macro's name has been changed to SeparateHeading3, but the description still mentions Heading 2.
d) Fix the heading name in the Description field.	You can edit macro descriptions from the **Macros** window.
e) Click **Run**.	To close the **Macros** window and run the macro. The product name is formatted as Heading 3 this time.
4. View the Table macro.	You'll open this one from inside the VBA editor.

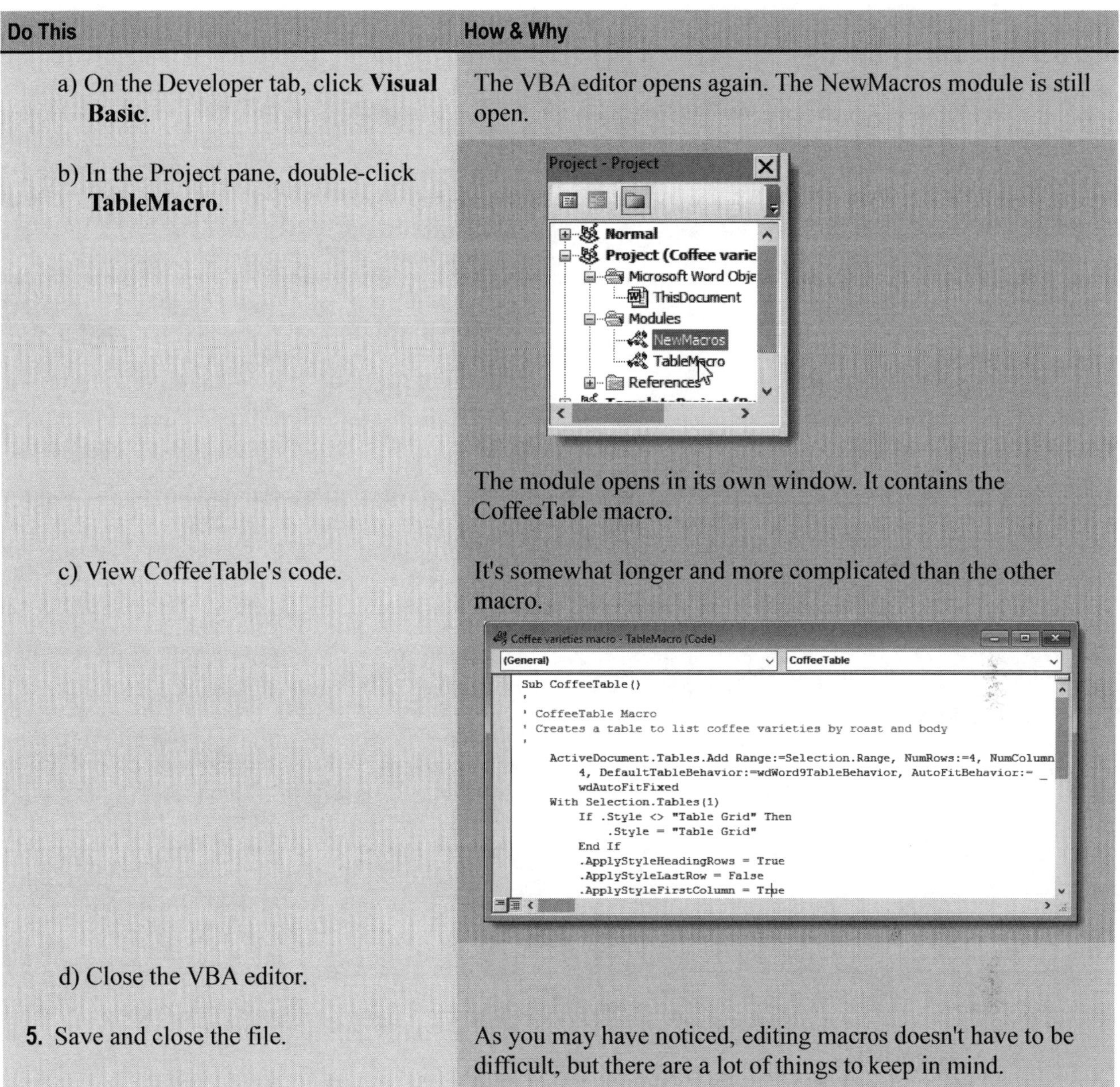

Do This	How & Why
a) On the Developer tab, click **Visual Basic**.	The VBA editor opens again. The NewMacros module is still open.
b) In the Project pane, double-click **TableMacro**.	The module opens in its own window. It contains the CoffeeTable macro.
c) View CoffeeTable's code.	It's somewhat longer and more complicated than the other macro.
d) Close the VBA editor.	
5. Save and close the file.	As you may have noticed, editing macros doesn't have to be difficult, but there are a lot of things to keep in mind.

The SeparateHeading3 macro at the end of the exercise.

Coffee varieties macro - NewMacros (Code)

(General) | SeparateHeading3

```
Sub SeparateHeading3()
'
' SeparateHeading3 Macro
' Places text left of insertion point in ner paragraph, and applies Heading 3 style.
'
    Selection.TypeParagraph
    Selection.MoveLeft Unit:=wdCharacter, Count:=1
    Selection.TypeBackspace
    Selection.TypeBackspace
    Selection.HomeKey Unit:=wdLine, Extend:=wdExtend
    Selection.Style = ActiveDocument.Styles("Heading 3")
End Sub
```

Assessment: Macros

1. Regardless of how you create a macro, Word stores it as a VBA program. True or false?
   - True
   - False
2. Which window lets you move macros from one document to another?
   - Macro
   - Organizer
   - Recorder
   - Visual Basic Editor
3. What do you need to do to make a macro run whenever you start Word? Choose all that apply.
   - Configure the Trust Center to allow all macros
   - Name it AutoExec
   - Name it AutoOpen
   - Store it in the default template
   - Store it in AutoExec.dot

Module B: Forms

By now, you should have the skill to easily create a printed form that recipients can write answers on and return to you. Word also allows you to create electronic forms using special fields. When you distribute an electronic form as a Word document or web page, other users can fill it out and return it with the data in digital form, so that you can use it later.

You will learn how to:

- Add form controls to a document
- Control form permissions
- Distribute forms

Form elements

In general, any form in any application has two necessary elements: data fields and labels. *Data fields* are the areas of the form that hold user input, and *labels* are the existing content that explains what data the user needs to enter. This means that data fields have to be editable by users, but labels do not.

In some applications, data fields and labels are explicitly paired when you create them. In Word, they're not. Labels are regular document text, and you can insert data fields, or *controls*, into the form wherever you like. You can even easily lock it, so that users can enter data but not modify the rest of the document.

Even if you don't lock a document, controls stand out in Word. They're visually distinct, and by default, most include uniformly formatted placeholder text. When you select one, it's surrounded by a frame, including the control's name.

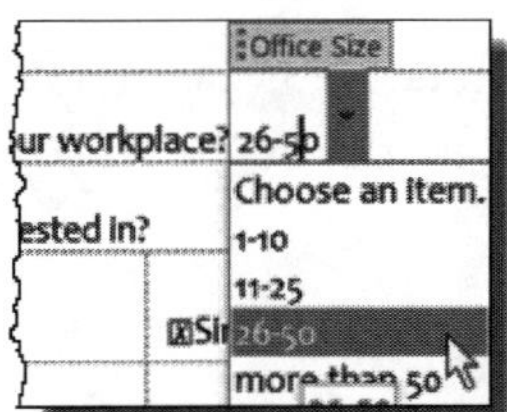

When you're editing a form, you can click **Design Mode** on the Developer tab. It highlights controls more clearly and gives you additional editing options.

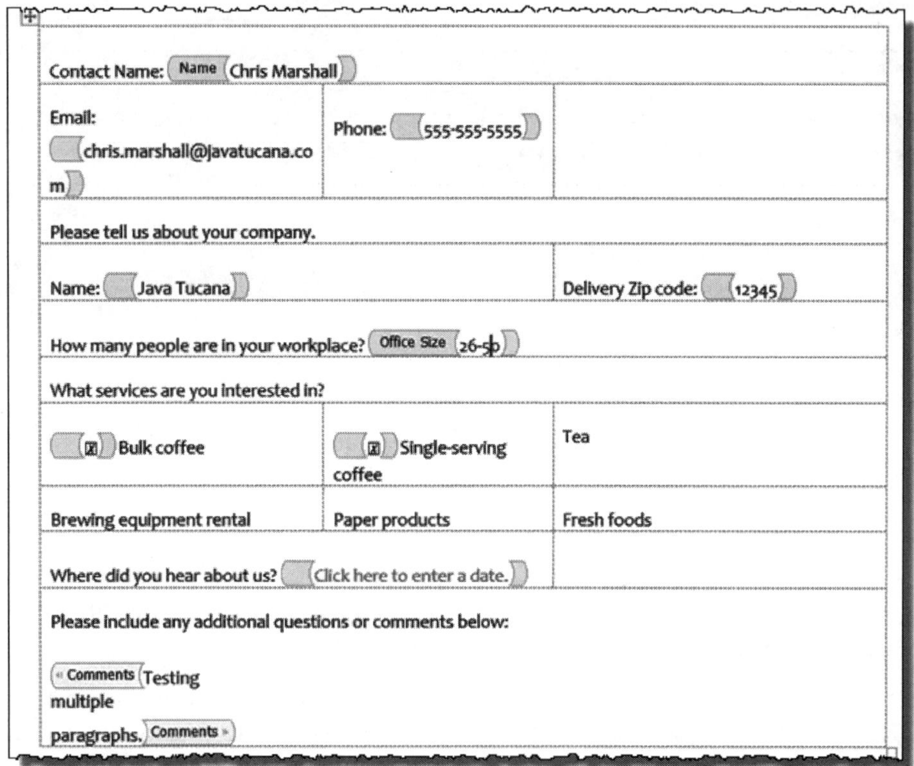

Content controls

Before you can insert controls, you need to display the ribbon's Developer tab. Once you do so, it's as simple as clicking the control you want in the Controls group.

There are a wide variety of controls, both in terms of the type of data they hold, and the way they operate within Word. The newest class of control is the *content control*, introduced in Word 2007. There are eight types of content control, each with different rules for the data that users can enter.

Icon	Name	User can
	Rich Text	Enter text with formatting, tables, or pictures.
	Plain Text	Enter only unformatted text.
	Check Box	Check or clear a binary value.
	Drop-Down List	Choose one of a list of pre-written options.
	Combo Box	Choose one pre-written option, or type in a custom one.

Icon	Name	User can
	Date Picker	Choose a date.
	Picture	Insert a single picture.
	Building Block Gallery	Insert a building block from a specific building block gallery.

Creating forms

Exam Objective: MOS Word Expert 3.3.3

You can insert form controls right within regular document content, so you can either add them as you compose the document, or lay out the document and place the controls last.

- You can add a content control by simply clicking it in the Controls group.
- To delete a content control, select it and press **Delete**.
- Different form controls can take different amounts of space. Especially when you place multiple controls on one line, you might want to use tables or other layout methods to make sure each control is in just the right place.
- Content controls take more space on the page in Design Mode, so turn it off to preview the document as the user will see it.
- Most content controls contain instructional text that appears until the user enters data. You can edit that text in Design Mode.

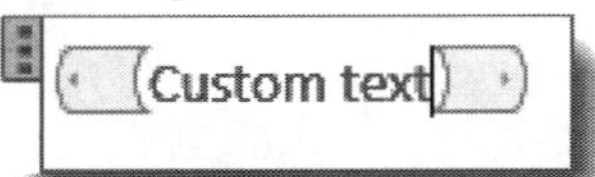

- You can create nested content controls by placing content controls inside a Rich Text control.

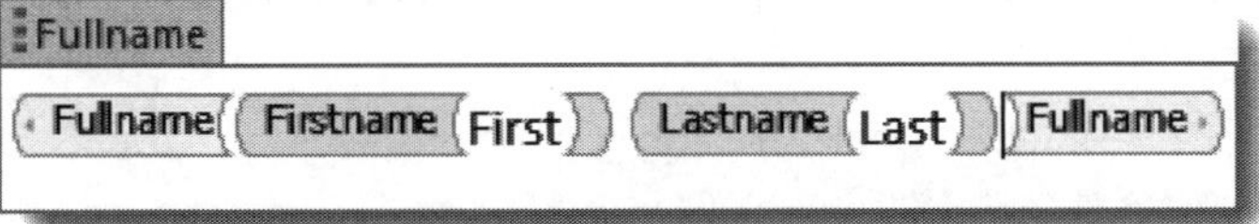

- To edit a control's properties, select it, and in the Controls group, click **Properties**.
- Choose control types according to the data you want to collect.
  - Use plain text controls instead of rich text when user-chosen formatting would not be useful.
  - Use check boxes for independent yes/no answers. Although multiple check boxes might represent a group of related questions, Word sees them all as independent values.
  - Use drop-down lists when you want users to choose from a fixed list of answers, and combo boxes when you also want them to be able to write their own.
- Before the form will actually work, you need to lock it. This allows users to fill in the form, but not to change the fields themselves, or other content that's part of the form.

  a) Select a range in the document, including both the form controls and the content you want to protect.

  b) In the Controls group, click **Group** > **Group**.
- To unlock a form protected with the Group control, select the area, and click **Group** > **Ungroup**.

Setting content control properties

Exam Objective: MOS Word Expert 3.3.4

All content controls share some common properties, but some vary among their control types, which you can set in the **Content Control Properties** window.

The properties for a plain text content control.

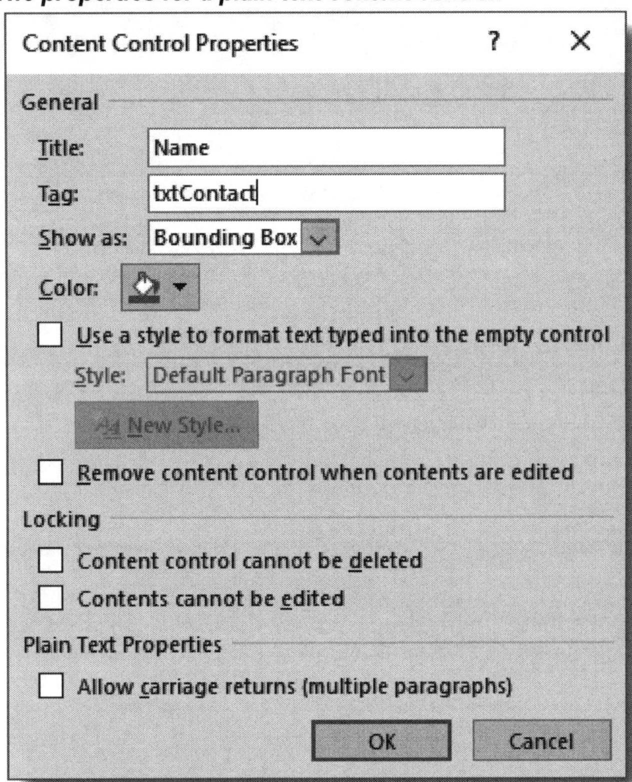

- In the Title field, type a short descriptive name for users to see. It appears in the control frame when users select it.
- In the Tag field, type a unique name for developers to use. It is only visible in Design Mode, and is the identifier VBA code your database associates with that control.

  Note: Tags should be unique, contain no spaces, and be in a standardized format that coders can recognize. Word doesn't enforce this, so you need to be mindful as part of the design process.

- If you want to set a particular style for the field's contents, check **Use a style to format contents**.
- To keep a user from deleting the control—even if the form is not otherwise locked—check **Content control cannot be deleted**. It can still be deleted in Design Mode.
- To keep users from editing the instructional text, check **Contents cannot be edited**. This prevents users from filling out the form.
- Set additional properties according to the control type. For example, you can choose whether to allow multiple paragraphs in a plain text control, or the appearance of check boxes. Some controls, such as lists and date pickers, provide more complex options.

Setting list properties

Exam Objective: MOS Word Expert 3.3.4

When you set properties for a Drop-Down List or Combo Box Control, you also need to define the choice in the list. Each choice has two fields: *Display Name* is what users see in the list; *Value* is what VBA code and your database see. By default, a choice's value is the same as its display name.

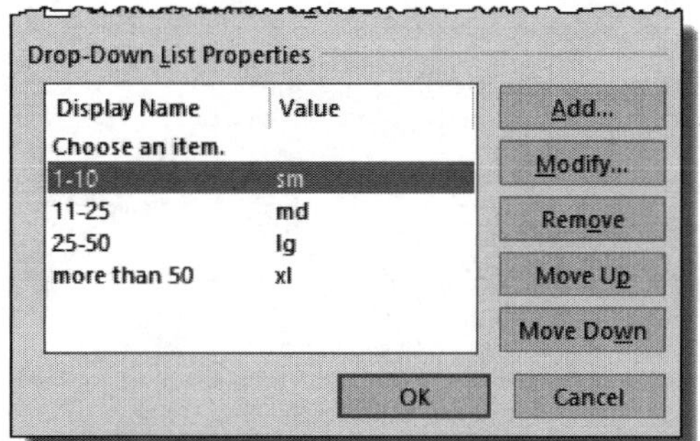

- To create a new choice, click **Add**.
- To change the properties of a selected choice, click **Modify**.
- To remove the selected choice, click **Remove**.
- To change the display order, click **Move Up** or **Move Down**.

Setting date picker properties

When you insert a date picker control, you can set both the date format users see, and the format Word uses to store the data.

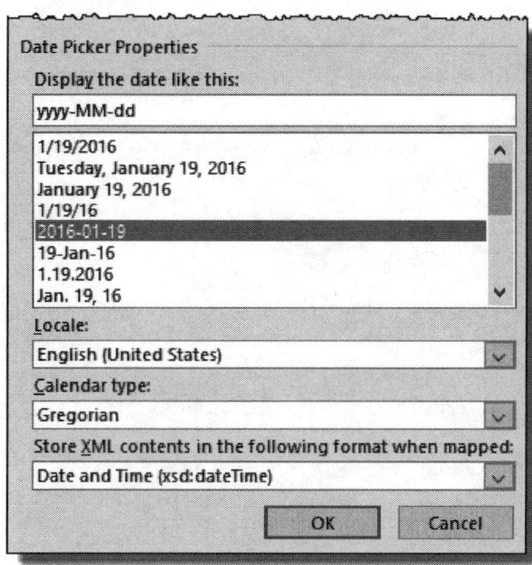

Exam Objective: MOS Word Expert 3.3.4

- From the Display list, choose or type the format you want users to see. You can choose a time, a date, or both.
- From the Store XML contents list, select the format you want Word to store data in. It should match whatever your database uses.
- You can choose a calendar type and locale from your installed options.

Exercise: Creating a form

To complete this exercise, the Developer tab should be displayed. If it isn't already, you can do so from the Customize Ribbon section of Word Options. You'll insert content controls and configure their properties.

Do This	How & Why
1. Open `Office services`, and save it as `Office services form`.	This is a draft document for a digital form. It already has labels, so you'll add content controls.
2. Place a plain-text content control.	Most data you need from your prospective customers will be unformatted text.
a) Insert a space after The Contact Name label.	
b) On the Developer tab, in the Controls group, click .	
	The new content control is inserted, along with default instructional text.
3. Set the control's properties.	
a) In the Controls group, click **Properties**.	The **Content Control Properties** window appears.
b) In the Title field, type `Name`.	The Title will be seen by the user, so it should be simple and descriptive.
c) In the Tag field, type `txtContact`.	Tags are called by code, so they should be unique and follow a clear naming convention.
d) Observe the other options.	You don't need to format the control or allow for multiple paragraphs. You'll lock the form as a whole later.
e) Click **OK**.	The "Name" title appears on the frame.
f) Click **Design Mode**.	
	In Design Mode, brackets enclose the control, showing the txtContact tag.
g) Edit the instructional text to read `Enter your name.`	
	In Design Mode, you can edit instructional text.
4. Insert additional plain-text fields.	

Do This	How & Why
a) Insert a space after "Email:" and click Aa .	Email: Click or tap here to enter text. It doesn't fit in the cell, but you'll check it outside of Design Mode later.
b) Insert plain text controls in the Phone, Name, and Delivery Zip code cells.	You don't need to add properties to these yet.
c) Insert a plain-text control in a new line below "Please include any additional questions or comments below."	You still only need plain text, but here you want to allow multiple paragraphs.
d) Set the new control's Title to `Comments` and its Tag to `txtComments`.	Click **Properties** first.
e) Check **Allow carriage returns (multiple paragraphs)**.	Users can now enter multiple paragraphs of commentary.
f) Click **OK**.	
5. Insert a drop-down list.	You'll let customers pick their office size from a list of values.
a) Insert a space after "How many people are in your workplace?"	
b) Click .	To insert a drop-down list content control.
c) Set the list's Title to `Office Size` and its Tag to `lstSize`.	In the **Content Control Properties** window.
d) Click **Add**.	The **Add Choice** window opens.
e) In the Display name field, type `1-10`.	The Value field is automatically updated to match.
f) In the Value field, select the values and type `sm`.	The display name is visible to users, and the value is sent to the database.
g) Click **OK**.	Drop-Down List Properties Display Name — Value Choose an item. 1-10 — sm The value is inserted.

Do This	How & Why
h) Insert three more choices, as shown.	Click **Add**, and enter the display names and values.
	Display Name / Value Choose an item. 1-10 sm 11-25 md 26-50 lg more than 50 xl
i) Click **OK**.	To close the properties window.
6. Insert checkbox fields.	Users can choose any combination of product types, so you'll make them check boxes.
a) Place a check-box field to the left of "Bulk Coffee."	Place the insertion point, and click .
b) Set the control's tag value to `chkBulk`.	You don't need to give it a title.
c) Insert a check box for "Single-serving coffee."	Use `chkSingle` for a tag.
7. Test the form.	You can't save data without a database and VBA programming, but you can view the form and enter data.
a) Turn off **Design Mode**.	The field brackets vanish. The Delivery Zip code field still doesn't fit in its cell.
b) Drag the cell boundary to the left.	If necessary, display the table's gridlines (click **View Gridlines**, on the Table Tools Layout tab).
	Until it fits on one line.
c) In the Contact Name field, type your name.	Because these are content controls, you don't need to lock the form to fill them out.
d) Continue filling out the form, pressing **Tab** between each control.	Select a value from the drop-down list, and check both boxes. Enter more than one paragraph into the last field.
8. Lock the form.	You need to enter more fields and properties, but you can still test it to make sure it locks properly.
a) Select the entire document.	Press **Ctrl+A**.
b) Click **Group > Group**.	

Do This	How & Why
c) Try editing the document.	You can still fill out fields, but you can't change anything else.
d) Click **Group > Ungroup**.	To unlock the form.
9. Save and close the document.	

Contact Name: Chris Marshall		
Email: chris.marshall@javatucana.com	Phone: 555-555-5555	
Please tell us about your company.		
Name: Java Tucana		Delivery Zip code: 12345
How many people are in your workplace? 26-50		
What services are you interested in?		
☒Bulk coffee	☒Single-serving coffee	Tea
Brewing equipment rental	Paper products	Fresh foods
Where did you hear about us?		
Please include any additional questions or comments below: Testing multiple paragraphs.		

Legacy tools

In addition to content controls, you can also insert the older *legacy tools*. These include *legacy form* controls, used by earlier versions of Word, and ActiveX controls, which were designed for web pages but can be used in documents via macros. Legacy tools don't have all the features and convenience of content controls, but they're compatible with older versions of Word, and you can use them in the .doc format used by Word 2003 (and earlier). Word 2003 users can't use forms with content controls, even if they have the add-on to view .docx files.

There are six icons in the Legacy Forms menu, but only three of them are form fields.

Icon	Name	Function
	Text Form Field	Inserts a text field. The text within the field cannot be formatted, but the field itself can be.
	Check Box Form Field	Inserts a check box field which users can check or clear.
	Drop-Down Form Field	Inserts a field which can hold a list of pre-written options. Users can select a value, but not enter their own.
	Insert Frame	Inserts a static field like a text box, which users cannot edit.
	Form Field Shading	Toggles shading of form fields.
	Reset Form Fields	Clears all fields in the form.

By contrast, ActiveX controls allow you to add a wider variety of controls to a form. Not only can you add combo boxes, option buttons, spin buttons, or command buttons, you can click **Legacy Tools > More Controls** to add any available ActiveX control on your system.

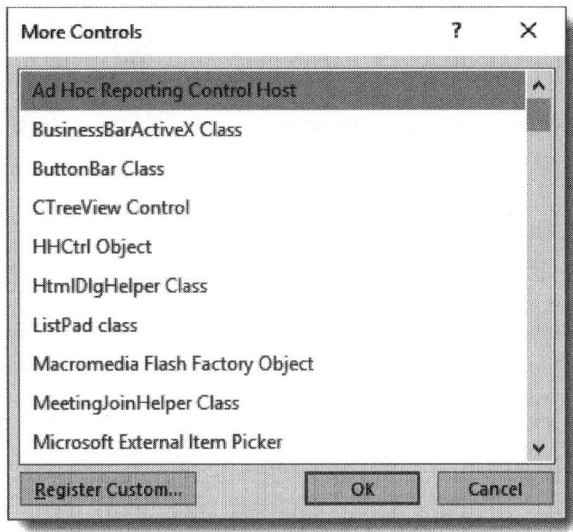

Choosing form types

The most important question about using legacy tools isn't how to place them, but rather when to use them in the first place. There are a wider variety of content controls, they're in many ways easier to configure, and they're much better designed to connect with external XML databases. That said, there are times when you should use legacy fields.

In a given document you should always choose one form type and stick with it, rather than mixing legacy controls and content controls.

- If the document is saved in Word 97-2003 format, or if your users might have Word 2003 or earlier, you must use legacy forms.
- Legacy forms can output field data as a separate text file, instead of linking it to a database using VBA.
- While legacy forms allow fewer control types than content controls, they allow more freedom with some formatting elements:
  - They can be more easily linked with macros.
  - Legacy text controls can limit data length, or automatically format input such as currency values.
  - Legacy form fields can be used to perform calculations.
- Legacy forms are also called *protected forms*, because they function only when you use document protection features to lock the entire form. This prevents spell-checking and inserting pictures from working without special code. Content controls don't have this restriction.
- ActiveX controls allow a lot of flexibility, but they have some significant drawbacks.
  - They are primarily designed for web pages, though they can be used in documents.
  - They rely on VBA and are difficult to use without coding knowledge.
  - ActiveX is only supported by Windows, so ActiveX controls will not work in other operating systems, even OS X versions of Office.

Setting legacy field properties

Much as with content controls, you can access a legacy field's properties by selecting it and clicking **Properties**. Each type has its own properties, and they differ from those of the corresponding content control type.

Exam Objective: MOS Word Expert 3.3.2

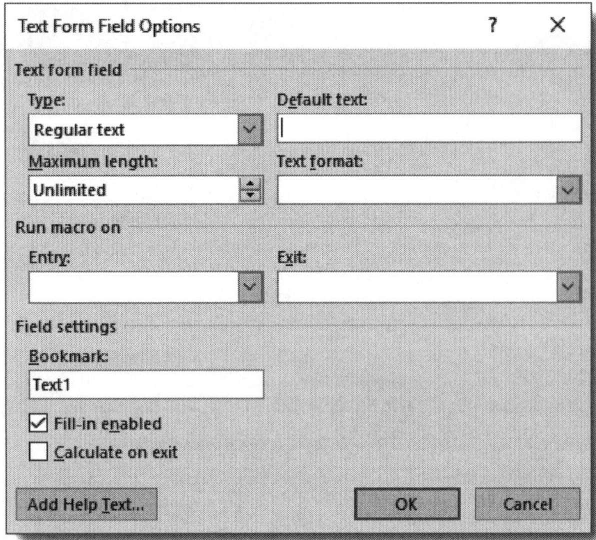

- To run a macro when selecting or deselecting the control, choose it from the Entry or Exit lists.
- Set a unique bookmark for the control in the Bookmark field.
- Text fields have specific options governing the content that users can enter.
  - You can set Type as text, a number, a date, or a calculation.
  - For each type, you can set one corresponding field for default content, and another for formatting.
  - You can set an optional maximum length for user input.
- Check-box fields can be checked or cleared by default.
- Drop-down fields contain multiple items you can edit and rearrange, much like their content control counterparts. Combo boxes are not available.
- Legacy fields don't have instructional text. To add context-sensitive help to a field, click **Add Help Text**.

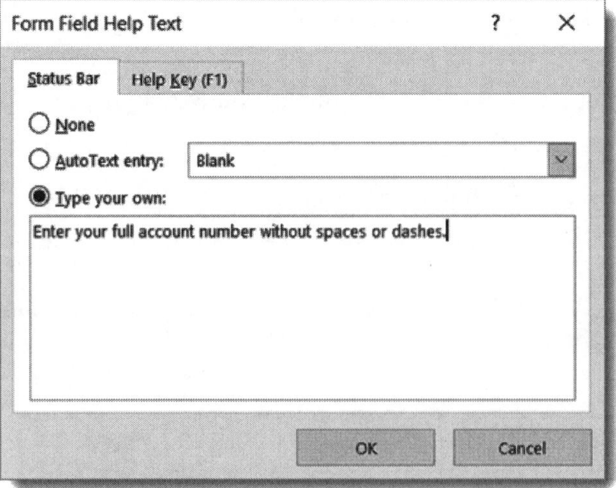

Protecting forms

When you provide users with any form to fill out, you want them to input data into the form controls but not to edit the rest of the document. In fact, legacy forms require you to do this: if the form isn't locked, or protected, users can't enter data into the fields. Unlike content controls, you can't use the Group command; instead, you need to use Word's document protection features.

Exam Objective: MOS Word Expert 1.2.3

- To protect a form with legacy fields, you need to restrict editing for the entire document.
  a) On the Developer tab, click **Restrict Editing**.
     To open the Restrict Editing pane.
  b) Under Editing restrictions, check **Allow only this type of editing in the document**.
  c) Select **Filling in forms** from the list.
  d) Click **Yes, Start Enforcing Protection**.
  e) Optionally, you can enter a password, and then click **OK**.

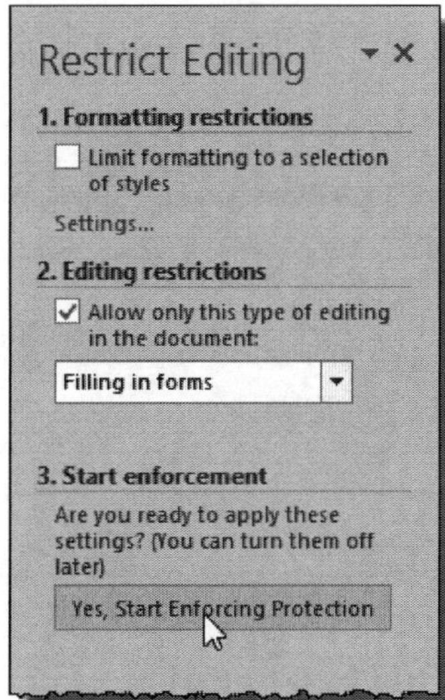

- To unlock a form protected with editing restrictions, click **Restrict Editing**, then **Stop Protection**. Enter the password, if prompted.
- If you're using content controls, you can either restrict editing for the entire document, or use the Group command to lock only part of the document.

Exporting form data

Once users fill out your form, you still need to export the data into a more usable format. Although doing so is beyond the scope of this course, you've already seen the tools used to accomplish it. As you saw when creating a mail merge, you can connect Word documents to external data sources such as Excel workbooks or Open Database Connectivity (ODBC)–compatible databases. Once you've done that, the same VBA code that enables Word macros can also be used to pull data from forms and send it to the database.

Legacy forms allow a simpler method you can use to output data into a separate text file when the document is saved.

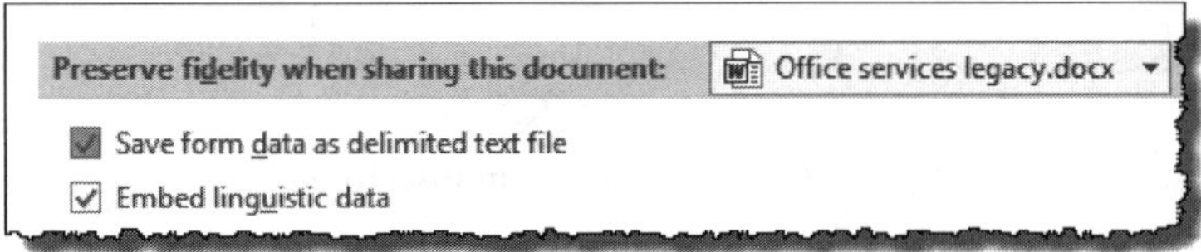

1. Configure the document to export form data.
   a) Open the **Word Options** window.
   b) In the Advanced section, scroll to "Preserve fidelity when sharing this document."
   c) Choose either the current document, or **All New Documents**.
   d) Check **Save form data as delimited text file**.
   e) Click **OK**.
2. When you save the document, Word prompts you to save its form data separately.
   a) When you save the form document, choose a name and location for the accompanying text file.
   b) In the **File Conversion** window, set text encoding options.

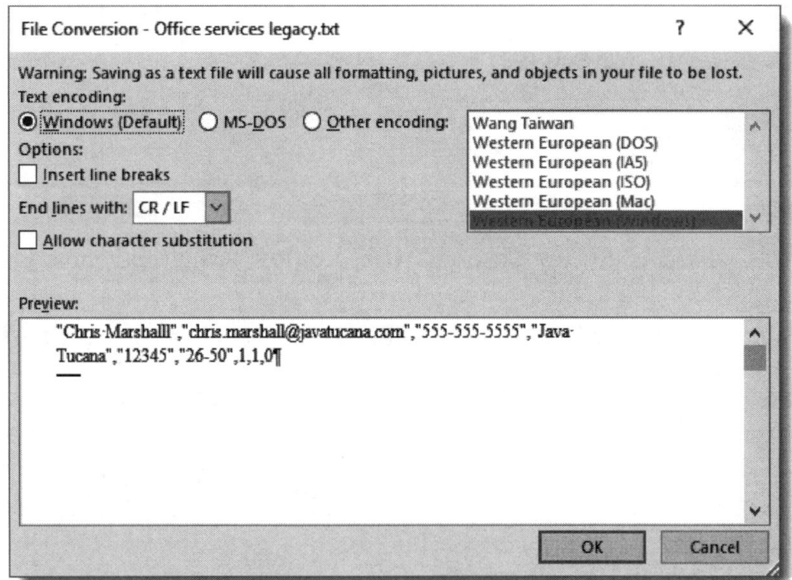

   c) Click **OK**.

Exercise: Creating a legacy form

In this exercise, you'll create a form using legacy controls.

Do This	How & Why
1. Open `Office services`, and save it as `Office services legacy`.	This is a draft document for a digital form. It already has labels, so you'll add content controls.
2. Place a text form field.	Most data you need from your prospective customers will be unformatted text.
a) Insert a space after The Contact Name label.	
b) On the Developer tab, in the Controls group, click > .	The new legacy control is inserted. Unlike a content control, it doesn't show any default instructional text.
3. Set the control's properties.	
a) In the Controls group, click **Properties**.	The **Text form field** window appears.
b) Click the **Type** list.	You can use text fields for text, numbers, dates, times, and calculations.
c) Click away from the list.	You'll keep it as regular text.
d) View the Format list.	You can format the text as uppercase or lowercase. You can also capitalize just the first letter, or the first letter of each word. You'll keep the default.
e) In the Bookmark field, type `txtContact`.	Bookmarks are called by code, so they should be unique and follow a clear naming convention.
f) Click **Add Help Text**.	The **Form Field Help Text** window opens.
g) Type `Enter the full name of your preferred contact.`	
h) Click **OK**.	To close the window.

Do This	How & Why
i) Observe the other options.	You don't need to set a default value or maximum length, and you're not configuring any macros to run.
j) Click **OK**.	To close the options window. The field itself doesn't look any different, but you'll be able to view the help text once you're finished.
4. Insert a zip code field.	Since this form will only be going to US customers, postal codes should always be five-digit numbers.
a) Insert a space after Delivery Zip code, then click > .	
b) Open the **Text Form Field Options** window.	Click **Properties**.
c) Name the field `txtZip`.	In the Tag field.
d) From the Type list, choose **Number**.	The fields on the right change to Default number and Number format.
e) From the Number format list, select **0**.	Now users will only be able to enter simple numeric values.
f) In the Maximum length field, enter `5`.	
g) Set the help text to `Enter a five-digit Zip code`.	Click **Add Help Text**, type it, then click **OK**.
h) Click **OK**.	To close the options window.
5. Insert a drop-down form field.	You'll let customers pick their office size from a list of values.
a) Insert a space after "How many people are in your workplace?"	
b) Click > .	To insert a drop-down list content control.
c) Set the list's bookmark to `lstSize`.	In the **Content Control Properties** window.
d) Click **Add**.	The **Add Choice** window opens.
e) In the Drop-down item field, type `1-10`.	Drop-down legacy fields don't have separate display names and values.

Do This	How & Why
f) Click **Add**.	The item is inserted.
g) Insert three more choices, as shown.	Enter the values then click **Add**.
h) Enter appropriate help text.	Something like `Choose the number of people who will be using our products.`
i) Click **OK**.	To close the properties window. The first value you added, 1-10, is displayed by default.
6. Add check box form fields.	Legacy check boxes work almost exactly like content control check boxes.
a) Insert a legacy check box field after Bulk coffee.	Enter a space then click > .
b) Name the field `chkBulk`.	Click **Properties** first. You don't need to enter help text.
c) Add check boxes for Single serve coffee and Tea.	Name them chkSingle and chkTea.
7. Add additional text fields for email, phone, and company name.	
a) Set Phone as a number field.	
b) In the Number format field, type `###-###-####`.	This will automatically format your entry as a nine-digit phone number with dashes.
c) Choose a unique name for each field.	Try something like txtCompanyName for the name field.
8. Lock the form.	Since this is a legacy form, you'll need to protect the entire document in order to test it.
a) On the Developer tab, click **Restrict Editing**.	The Restrict Editing pane appears.
b) Under Editing restrictions, check **Allow only this type of editing in the document**.	

Do This	How & Why
c) Select **Filling in forms** from the list.	2. Editing restrictions Allow only this type of editing in the document: Filling in forms
d) Click **Yes, Start Enforcing Protection**.	The **Start Enforcing Protection** window opens, asking for a password.
e) Click **OK**.	You don't need a password just to test it.
9. Save the document.	
10. Test the form.	
a) Click inside the Contact name field.	The help text appears in the status bar at the bottom of the window.
b) Type your name and press **Tab**.	To move to the email field.
c) Enter your email address and press **Tab**.	You set Phone as a number field.
d) Type a full phone number, without dashes, and press **Tab**.	The dashes are automatically added.
e) Enter a company name.	
f) In the Delivery Zip code field, type any six digit number.	Since you entered a maximum value, the field accepts the first five digits, but ignores the last.
g) Click **1-10**.	In the drop-down list. A list opens with the values you added.
h) Select any value.	
i) Check all three boxes.	

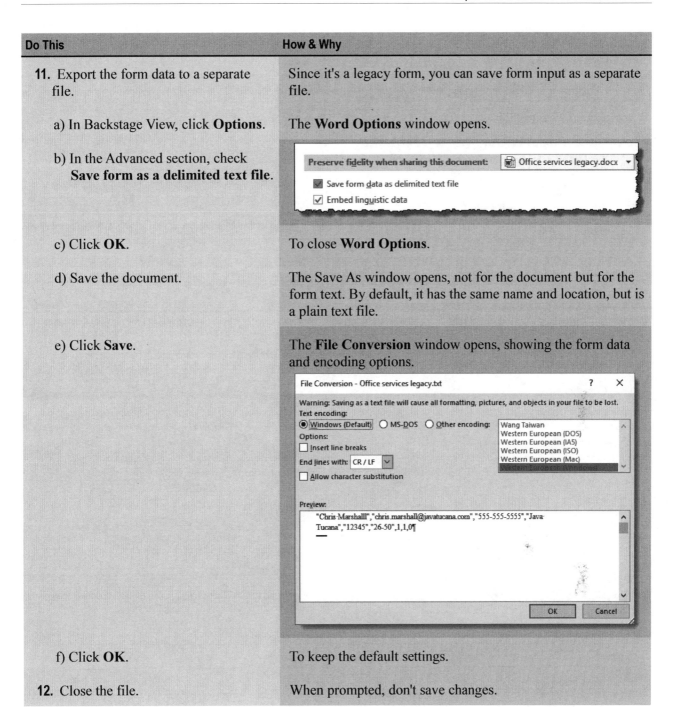

Do This	How & Why
11. Export the form data to a separate file.	Since it's a legacy form, you can save form input as a separate file.
a) In Backstage View, click **Options**.	The **Word Options** window opens.
b) In the Advanced section, check **Save form as a delimited text file**.	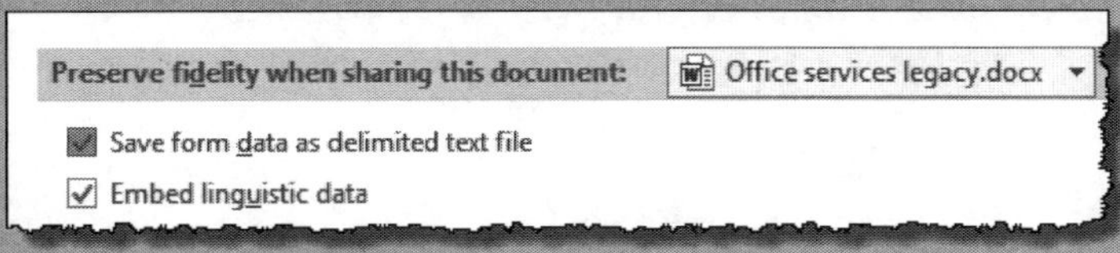
c) Click **OK**.	To close **Word Options**.
d) Save the document.	The Save As window opens, not for the document but for the form text. By default, it has the same name and location, but is a plain text file.
e) Click **Save**.	The **File Conversion** window opens, showing the form data and encoding options. 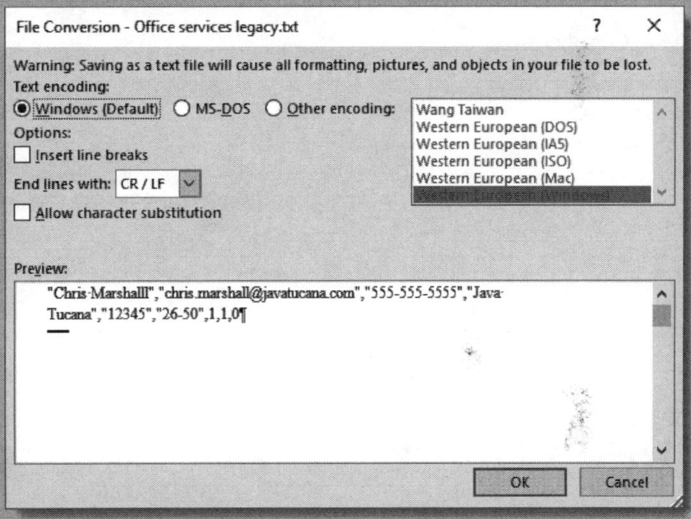
f) Click **OK**.	To keep the default settings.
12. Close the file.	When prompted, don't save changes.

Assessment: Forms

1. Which form controls require document protection to function? Choose the best answer.
   - ActiveX controls
   - Content controls
   - Legacy form fields
   - All of the above.
2. Although they can be selected individually, check-box controls are arranged in groups using tag properties. True or false?
   - True
   - False
3. What kind of control should you use if you want users to either select an existing option or enter a new one? Choose the best answer.
   - Building Block Gallery
   - Combo Box
   - Drop-Down List
   - Rich Text
4. To export content control form data to a database, you need to use VBA code. True or false?
   - True
   - False

Summary: Macros and forms

You should now know how to:

- Record macros in Word, assign them to buttons or keystroke combinations, and copy them between documents and templates
- Create forms using content controls and legacy form fields, choose appropriate form controls, and set their properties

Synthesis: Macros and forms

In this exercise, you'll use macros and forms to prepare documents for potential franchisees.

1. Create a macro in `Franchise information` that removes the bullet from the current paragraph and applies the First word style to its first word. Store the macro in the file itself.
2. Run the macro on each bulleted paragraph in the document.
3. Save the document as a macro-enabled file type.
4. Create a form by inserting controls into `Franchise application`.
   - Use appropriate control types and properties for each field.
   - Java Tucana expects franchisees to have a $500,000 net worth and $100,000 in liquid assets, but has different tiers of investment for those with more.
   - There are opportunities for single-franchise owners, multiple unit owners, and office coffee service distributors.
   - Applicants should be able to answer any or all of the last four questions independently.
5. Lock and test the form.
6. Save the document as `Franchise application form`.

Appendix A: Internationalization and accessibility

You will learn how to:

- Configure language options in Windows, Office, and Word
- Manage document accessibility

Internationalization

The Language section of the Word Options window contains language settings for the Word interface, including those for the keyboard, as well as for editing/proofing features, such as dictionaries and grammar checking. However, before setting language options in Office applications, it's necessary to make sure that Windows is configured to work in the desired language(s) and download any additional language packs that might be required.

You will learn how to:

- Set the Windows display language
- Download and install additional language packs

Configuring Windows language options

Before you set language options in Office applications, it's important to make sure that your Windows operating system has the necessary language(s) installed. From there, you can download any other necessary language pack. Once you do so, that language becomes available for use throughout Office.

Exam Objective: MOS Word Expert 4.3.1

1. Click **Start** > **Settings**.
   To open the **Settings** window.
2. Click **Time & language**.
3. Click **Region & language**.
   In the left pane. Under Languages, the default display language and any other installed languages are displayed.

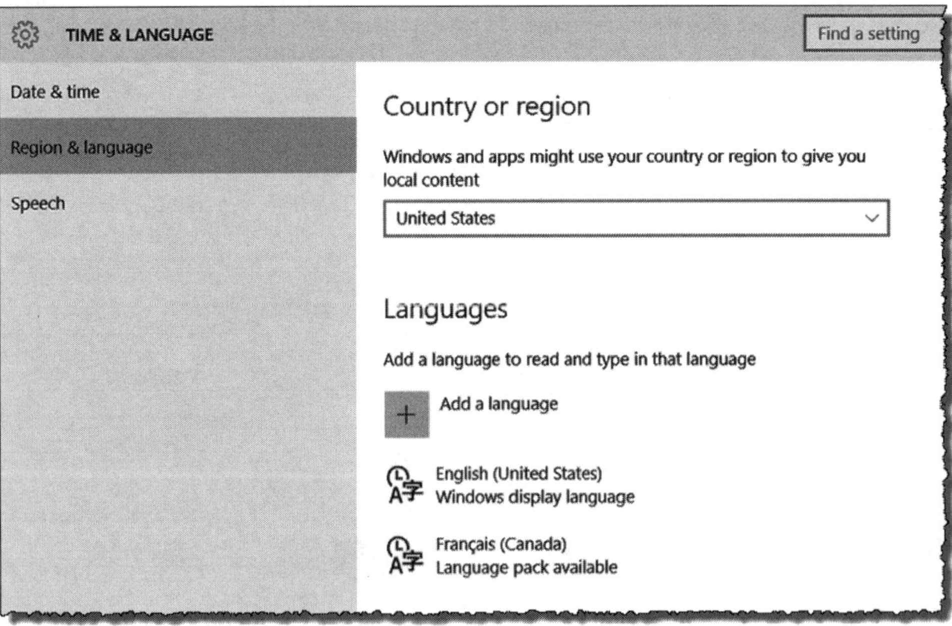

4. Click **Add a language**.
   To add a Windows display language.
5. Scroll through the list of displayed languages, and select the language(s) you want to add.

6. To download and install the language pack for that particular language, click **Language pack available** for that language, then click **Options**.

   To display the download options for that language.

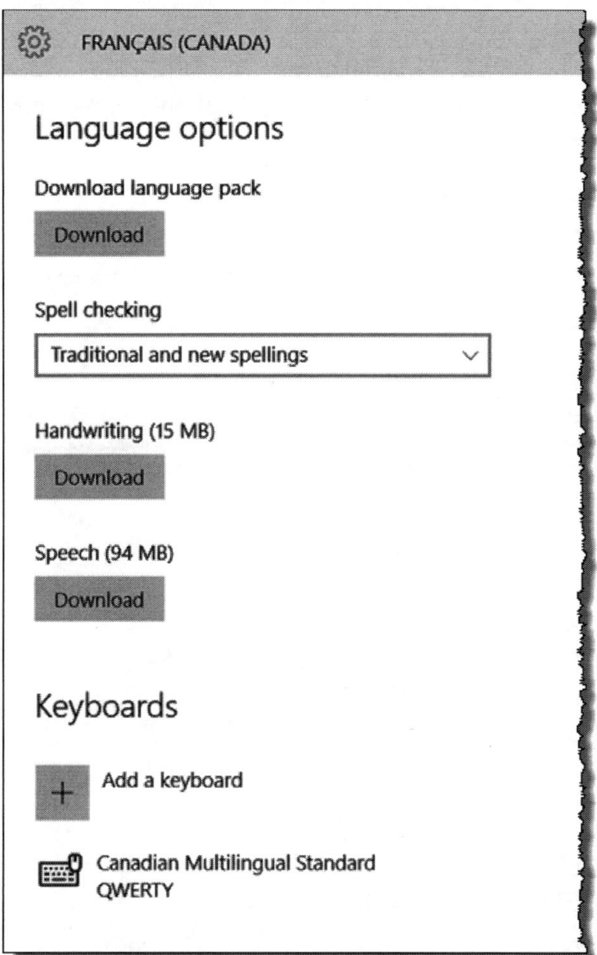

7. Download any or all of a language's components that you wish to make available to Windows and Office. The Settings window displays the download progress.

   Once you install the necessary language pack, click it to set it as the default system language, view its options, or remove it.

Configuring Office language options

Exam Objective: MOS Word Expert 4.3.1, 4.3.5

Once you configure your language options in Windows, they're available to use in Office applications as well. The Language section of the **Word Options** window provides you with access to all the settings you need to display Word's environment in the language(s) you would like.

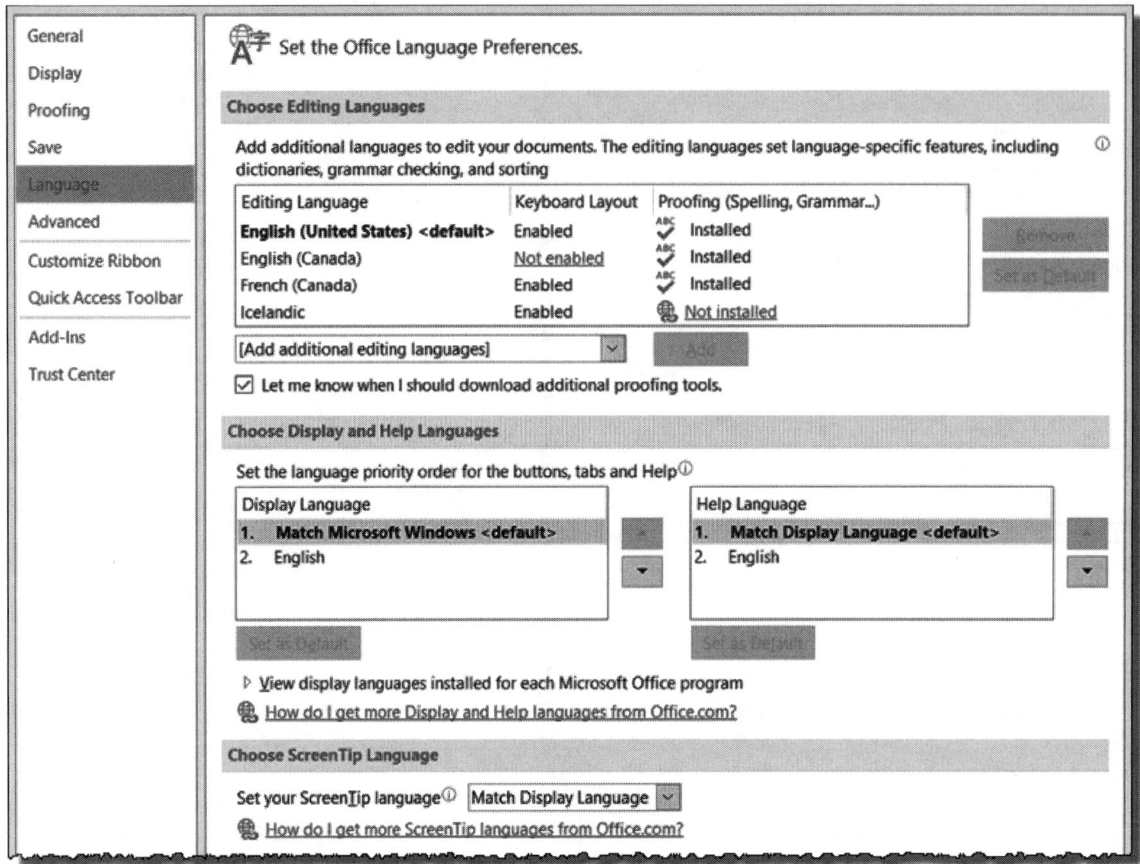

- The *Choose Editing Languages* section is where you select the languages in which you wish to edit, including one that you can specify as the default. You can choose additional languages from the "Add additional editing languages" drop-down list, then click **Add** to install them.
- The *Choose Display and Help Languages* section allows you to do just that. It's important to note that the two languages you choose for these respective features need not be the same. This can be particularly helpful, for example, to users learning a second language: the display language might be set to the one they're learning, while the help language might be their native one, with which they're more comfortable. Note that by default, Display Language is set to match the default Windows language setting. Another useful feature is the ability to set a different display language for each Office application.
- The *Choose ScreenTip Language* section allows you to set the language of the ScreenTips that display when you point to ribbon tools, for example. There, you can allow the ScreenTip language to match the display language (the default setting), or it can be any other installed language. In addition, you can click the link provided to download more ScreenTip languages from Office.com.

Managing accessibility in documents

In today's multimedia world, it's become commonplace to be able to view a single document on a computer, as a printout, as a webpage, on a smartphone, and so on. In addition, it's important to make documents more accessible to those with limited dexterity and movement, vision, and so on, as well as other disabilities. Fortunately, Office applications provide users, particularly those with disabilities, easier access to their many features.

Many of the techniques you've already learned, such as using a clear and easily read/scanned document structure and layout, or customizing the ribbon or the Quick Access toolbar, can help greatly in allowing users better access to documents and tools. But there are a few additional features and settings worth exploring.

You will learn how to:

- Check Word documents for accessibility
- Add alt-text to document elements
- Use keystrokes to navigate the ribbon

Adding alt-text to document elements

Exam Objective: MOS Word Expert 4.3.2, 4.3.3, 4.3.5

Adding alternative text, or *alt-text*, to your documents enables people who have trouble seeing graphic objects to read descriptions of them. A quick way to check your documents for places where features, such as alt-text, might be added is by using the Accessibility Checker.

1. In Backstage view, on the Info pane, click **Check for Issues > Check Accessibility**.
   The Accessibility Checker pane opens.

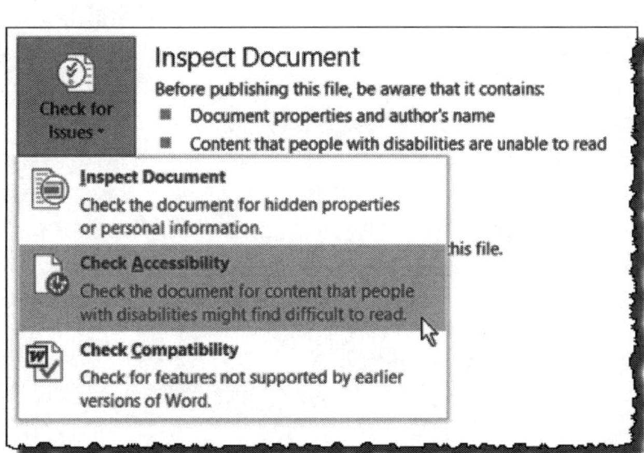

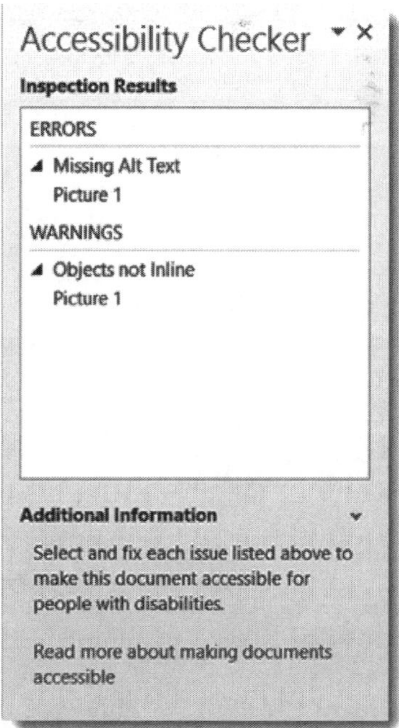

2. In the Errors box, click the object to which you wish to add alt-text.
   Under Missing Alt Text. Under Additional Information, instructions are given for adding alt-text.
3. Right-click the object, and select **Format Picture**.
   The **Format Picture** pane opens.

4. Click **Layout & Properties**.

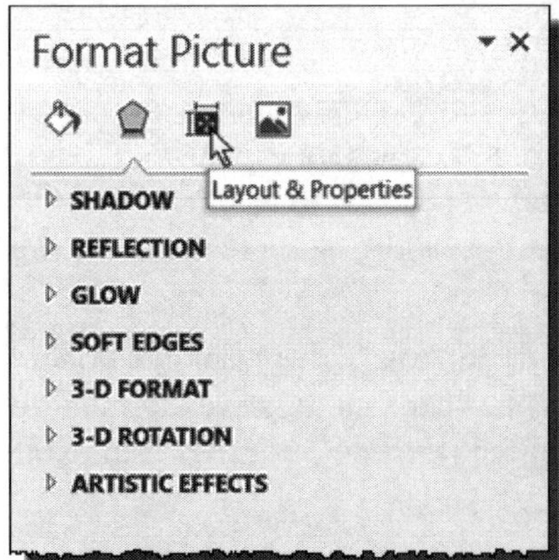

5. Click **ALT TEXT**, then enter a title and description of the object in their respective boxes.

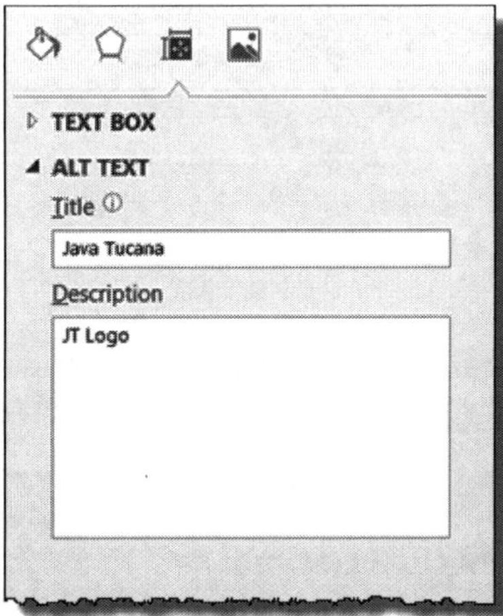

Customizing tools for accessibility

To make Word more accessible, you can customize the arrangement of tools on the ribbon, and use keystrokes to navigate it.

Exam Objective: MOS Word Expert 4.3.3, 4.3.4,4.3.6

1. Open the **Word Options** window, and click **Advanced**.
2. Under Display, check **Show shortcut keys in ScreenTips**, if necessary.
   This setting affects all Office applications.
3. Press the **Alt** (or **F10**) key.
   The ribbon tabs and Quick Access toolbar buttons are labeled with keystroke characters.

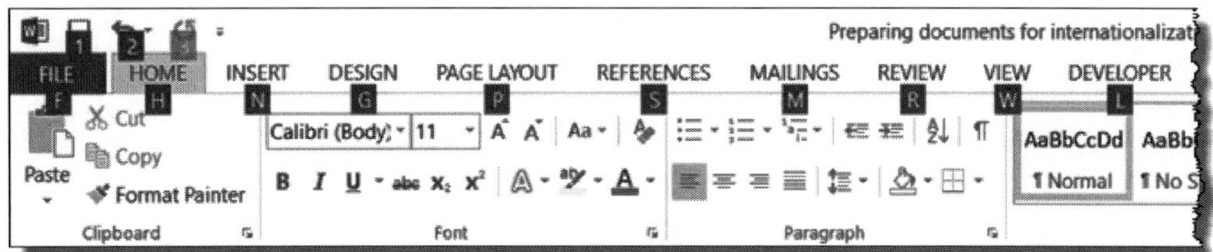

4. Click a displayed tab letter.
   The tab is displayed, and keystroke labels are displayed for each tool or command.

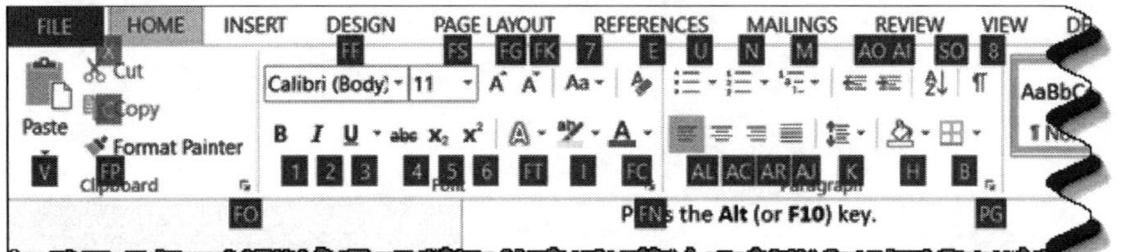

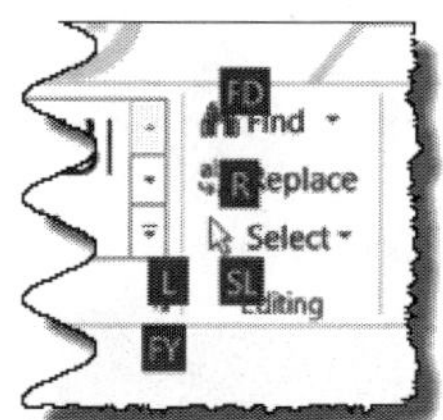

It's also important to remember that individual documents can be tweaked further for increased accessibility, using formatting features such as +Body and +Heading fonts. Always structure your documents with an eye toward making them as readable and easily scanned as possible. Particularly for an international audience, keep sentences relatively short and easily understood, and be sure to highlight and illustrate (where appropriate) important points.

Alphabetical Index